Exploring BeagleBone®

Second Edition

Exploring BeagleBone®

Tools and Techniques for Building with Embedded Linux®

Second Edition

Derek Molloy

WILEY

Exploring BeagleBone®: Tools and Techniques for Building with Embedded Linux®, Second Edition

Published by
John Wiley & Sons, Inc.
10475 Crosspoint Boulevard
Indianapolis, IN 46256
www.wiley.com

Copyright © 2019 by John Wiley & Sons, Inc., Indianapolis, Indiana
Published simultaneously in Canada

ISBN: 978-1-119-53316-0
ISBN: 978-1-119-53315-3 (ebk)
ISBN: 978-1-119-53317-7 (ebk)

Manufactured in the United States of America

C10006638_113018

For general information on our other products and services please contact our Customer Care Department within the United States at (877) 762-2974, outside the United States at (317) 572-3993 or fax (317) 572-4002.

Wiley publishes in a variety of print and electronic formats and by print-on-demand. Some material included with standard print versions of this book may not be included in e-books or in print-on-demand. If this book refers to media such as a CD or DVD that is not included in the version you purchased, you may download this material at http://booksupport.wiley.com. For more information about Wiley products, visit www.wiley.com.

Library of Congress Control Number: 2018962584

To Sally, Daragh, Eoghan, Aidan, and Sarah

About the Author

Dr. Derek Molloy is an associate professor in the Faculty of Engineering and Computing's School of Electronic Engineering at Dublin City University, Ireland. He lectures at undergraduate and postgraduate levels in object-oriented programming with embedded systems, digital and analog electronics, and connected embedded systems. His research contributions have largely been in the fields of computer and machine vision, embedded systems, 3D graphics/visualization, and e-learning.

Derek produces a popular YouTube video series that has introduced millions of people to embedded Linux and digital electronics topics. In 2013, he launched a personal web/blog site that is visited by thousands of people every day and that integrates his YouTube videos with support materials, source code, and user discussion. In 2015, he published the first edition of this book on the BeagleBone platform, *Exploring BeagleBone*, and followed up in June 2016 with *Exploring Raspberry Pi*. Both of these books have received strong acclaim for both their depth of coverage and accessibility.

Derek has received several awards for teaching and learning. He was the winner of the 2012 Irish Learning Technology Association (ILTA) national award for Innovation in Teaching and Learning. The award recognizes his learning-by-doing approach to undergraduate engineering education, which utilizes electronic kits and online video content. In 2012, as a result of fervent nominations from his students and peers, he was also awarded the Dublin City University President's Award for Excellence in Teaching and Learning. This learning-by-doing approach is strongly reflected in his books.

You can learn more about Derek, his work, and his other publications at his personal website, www.derekmolloy.ie.

About the Technical Editor

Marcia K. Wilbur is a technical communicator consulting in the semiconductor field, focusing on industrial IoT (IIoT). Marcia holds degrees in computer science, technical communication, and information technology. As the Copper Linux User Group interim president, she is heavily involved in the East Valley maker community, leading regular Raspberry Pi, BeagleBone, Banana Pi/Pro, and ESP8266 projects, including home automation, gaming consoles, surveillance, network, multimedia and other "pi fun."

In addition to tinkering, she volunteers to aid disaster-stricken areas in getting access to public domain content to enable students to continue learning. For fun, she serves the community as the lead Debian developer for Linux Respin, a backup and distro customization tool.

Credits

Acquisitions Assistant
Devon Lewis

Project Editor
Adaobi Obi Tulton

Technical Editor
Marcia K. Wilbur

Production Editor
Barath Kumar Rajasekaran

Copy Editor
Kim Wimpsett

Production Manager
Katie Wisor

**Content Enablement and
Operations Manager**
Pete Gaughan

Marketing Manager
Christie Hilbrich

Associate Publisher
Jim Minatel

Project Coordinator, Cover
Brent Savage

Proofreader
Debbye Butler

Indexer
Johnna VanHoose Dinse

Cover Designer
Wiley

Cover Image
Courtesy of Derek Molloy

Acknowledgments

Many thanks to everyone at John Wiley & Sons, Inc once again for their exceptional work on this project: to Jim Minatel for encouraging me to take on the revision of this book and for supporting the enhancement of a book that engages in deeper learning; to Devon Lewis for guiding the project forward and for his expert support and help throughout the development of this book; to Adaobi Obi Tulton, the project editor, for driving this project to completion in the most efficient way possible—it was a real pleasure to work with such an accomplished and adept editor for the third time; to Kim Wimpsett, the copy editor, for translating this book into readable U.S. English; to Barath Kumar Rajasekaran, the production editor, for bringing everything together to create a final, polished product. Thanks to the technical editor, Marcia Wilbur, for her careful review and constructive feedback on the technical content in this book. Continued thanks to the technical editors from my previous titles, Tom Betka, Robert Zhu (Microsoft), and Jason Kridner (BeagleBoard.org Foundation), on whose advice this work is based. Thanks also to Cathy Wicks (Texas Instruments) for her advice and support in the development of this book.

Continued thanks to the thousands of people who take the time to comment on my YouTube videos, blog, and website articles. I always appreciate the feedback, advice, and comments—it has really helped in the development of the topics in all of my books.

The School of Electronic Engineering at Dublin City University is a great place to work, largely because of its *esprit de corps* and its commitment to rigorous, innovative, and accessible engineering education. Thanks again to all of my colleagues in the school for supporting, encouraging, and tolerating me in the development of this book. Thanks in particular must go to Noel Murphy and Conor Brennan for sharing the workload of the school executive with me while I was once again absorbed in a book. Thanks again to (my brother) David Molloy for his expert software advice and support. Thanks to Jennifer Bruton, Martin Collier, Pascal Landais, Michele Pringle, Robert Sadleir, Ronan Scaife, and John Whelan for their ongoing expertise, support, and advice on the various titles I have written.

The biggest thank-you must of course go to my own family once again. This revision was written over six months, predominantly at night and on weekends. Thanks to my wife, Sally, and our children, Daragh, Eoghan, Aidan, and Sarah for putting up with me (once again) while I was writing this book. Thank you, Mam, Dad, David, and Catriona for your endless lifelong inspiration, support, and encouragement. Finally, thank you to my extended family for your continued support, understanding, and constancy.

Contents at a Glance

Introduction   xxix

Part I   Beagle Board Basics   1

Chapter 1   The Beagle Hardware Platform   3

Chapter 2   Beagle Software   31

Chapter 3   Exploring Embedded Linux Systems   71

Chapter 4   Interfacing Electronics   139

Chapter 5   Practical Beagle Board Programming   185

Part II   Interfacing, Controlling, and Communicating   245

Chapter 6   Interfacing to the Beagle Board Input/Outputs   247

Chapter 7   Cross-Compilation, Eclipse, and Building Linux   307

Chapter 8   Interfacing to the Beagle Board Buses   341

Chapter 9   Interacting with the Physical Environment   401

Chapter 10   Real-Time Interfacing Using External Slave Processors   455

Part III   Advanced Beagle Board Systems   495

Chapter 11   The Internet of Things   497

Chapter 12   Wireless Communication and Control   555

Chapter 13   Beagle Board with a Rich User Interface   599

Chapter 14   Images, Video, and Audio   643

Chapter 15   Real-Time Interfacing with the PRU-ICSS   673

Chapter 16   Embedded Kernel Programming   717

Index   745

Contents

Introduction		xxix
Part I	**Beagle Board Basics**	1
Chapter 1	**The Beagle Hardware Platform**	3
	Introduction to the Boards	3
	Who Should Use the Beagle Platform	6
	When to Use Beagle Boards	7
	When Should You Not Use the Beagle Boards	7
	BeagleBone Documentation	8
	The Beagle Hardware	10
	BeagleBone Versions	10
	The Beagle Hardware	12
	Beagle Accessories	19
	Highly Recommended Accessories	19
	Headers for the PocketBeagle	20
	Micro-SD Card (for Booting or Flashing eMMCs)	20
	External 5V Power Supply (for Peripherals)	22
	Ethernet Cable (for Wired BBB Network Connection)	22
	HDMI Cable (for Connection to Monitors/Televisions)	22
	USB to Serial UART TTL 3.3 (for Finding Problems)	23
	Optional Accessories	24
	USB Hub (to Connect Several USB Devices to a USB Host)	25
	Micro-HDMI to VGA Adapters (for VGA Video and Sound)	25
	Wi-Fi Adapters (for Wireless Networking)	25
	USB Webcam (for Capturing Images and Streaming Video)	25
	USB Keyboard and Mouse (for General-Purpose Computing)	26
	Capes	26
	How to Destroy Your Board!	27
	Summary	29
	Support	29

Chapter 2	**Beagle Software**	**31**
	Linux on the Beagle Boards	32
	Linux Distributions for Beagle Boards	32
	Create a Linux Micro-SD Card Image	33
	Communicating with the Boards	34
	Installing Drivers	34
	Wired Network Connections	35
	Internet-over-USB (All Boards)	36
	Regular Ethernet (BBB and BeagleBoard Only)	39
	Ethernet Crossover Cable (BBB and BeagleBoard Only)	40
	Communicating with Your Board	42
	Serial Connection over USB	42
	Serial Connection with the USB-to-TTL 3.3 V Cable	43
	Connecting Through Secure Shell	44
	Secure Shell Connections Using PuTTY	45
	Chrome Apps: Secure Shell Client	45
	Transferring Files Using PuTTY/psftp over SSH	46
	Controlling the Beagle Board	48
	Basic Linux Commands	48
	First Steps	49
	Basic File System Commands	50
	Environment Variables	52
	Basic File Editing	53
	What Time Is It?	54
	Package Management	56
	Beagle-Specific Commands	58
	Expand the File System on an SD Card	59
	Update the Kernel	60
	Interacting with the On-Board LEDs	61
	Shutdown	63
	Node.js, Cloud9, and BoneScript	64
	Introduction to Node.js	64
	Introduction to the Cloud9 IDE	66
	Introduction to BoneScript	67
	Summary	69
	Further Reading	69
Chapter 3	**Exploring Embedded Linux Systems**	**71**
	Introducing Embedded Linux	72
	Advantages and Disadvantages of Embedded Linux	73
	Is Linux Open Source and Free?	74
	Booting the Beagle Boards	74
	Bootloaders	74
	Kernel Space and User Space	83
	The systemd System and Service Manager	85
	Managing Linux Systems	90
	The Superuser	90

System Administration   92
  The Linux File System   92
  Links to Files and Directories   94
  Users and Groups   95
  File System Permissions   98
  The Linux Root Directory   102
  Commands for File Systems   103
  The Reliability of SD Card/eMMC File Systems   111
Linux Commands   113
  Output and Input Redirection (>, >>, and <)   113
  Pipes (| and tee)   114
  Filter Commands (from sort to xargs)   115
  echo and cat   117
  diff   118
  tar   119
  md5sum   120
Linux Processes   121
  How to Control Linux Processes   121
  Foreground and Background Processes   122
Other Linux Topics   124
Using Git for Version Control   124
  A Practice-Based Introduction   126
    Cloning a Repository (git clone)   126
    Getting the Status (git status)   128
    Adding to the Staging Area (git add)   128
    Committing to the Local Repository (git commit)   129
    Pushing to the Remote Repository (git push)   129
  Git Branching   130
    Creating a Branch (git branch)   130
    Merging a Branch (git merge)   132
    Deleting a Branch (git branch -d)   132
  Common Git Commands   133
Desktop Virtualization   134
Code for This Book   135
Summary   136
Further Reading   136
Bibliography   137

Chapter 4   Interfacing Electronics   139
Analyzing Your Circuits   140
  Digital Multimeter   140
  Oscilloscopes   141
Basic Circuit Principles   143
  Voltage, Current, Resistance, and Ohm's Law   143
  Voltage Division   145
  Current Division   146

Implementing Circuits on a Breadboard   147
Digital Multimeters and Breadboards   149
Example Circuit: Voltage Regulation   150
Discrete Components   152
Diodes   152
Light-Emitting Diodes   153
Smoothing and Decoupling Capacitors   156
Transistors   158
Transistors as Switches   159
Field Effect Transistors as Switches   162
Optocouplers/Optoisolators   164
Switches and Buttons   166
Hysteresis   168
Logic Gates   169
Floating Inputs   173
Pull-Up and Pull-Down Resistors   173
Open-Collector and Open-Drain Outputs   174
Interconnecting Gates   175
Analog-to-Digital Conversion   177
Sampling Rate   177
Quantization   178
Operational Amplifiers   178
Ideal Operational Amplifiers   178
Negative Feedback and Voltage Follower   181
Positive Feedback   181
Concluding Advice   182
Summary   182
Further Reading   183

Chapter 5   **Practical Beagle Board Programming**   **185**
Introduction   186
Performance of Different Languages   186
Setting the CPU Frequency   190
Scripting Languages   192
Scripting Language Options   192
Bash   193
Lua   196
Perl   197
Python   198
Dynamically Compiled Languages   201
JavaScript and Node.js on the Beagle boards   201
Java on the Beagle Boards   203
C and C++ on the Beagle Boards   207
C and C++ Language Overview   210
Compiling and Linking   211
Writing the Shortest C/C++ Program   213
Static and Dynamic Compilation   215
Variables and Operators in C/C++   215

Pointers in C/C++ 219
C-Style Strings 221
LED Flashing Application in C 223
The C of C++ 224
First Example and Strings in C++ 225
Passing by Value, Pointer, and Reference 226
Flashing the LEDs Using C++ (non-OO) 227
Writing a Multicall Binary 228
Overview of Object-Oriented Programming 229
Classes and Objects 229
Encapsulation 230
Inheritance 231
Object-Oriented LED Flashing Code 233
Interfacing to the Linux OS 236
Glibc and Syscall 237
Improving the Performance of Python 239
Cython 239
Boost.Python 242
Summary 244
Further Reading 244
Bibliography 244

Part II   Interfacing, Controlling, and Communicating   245

Chapter 6   Interfacing to the Beagle Board Input/Outputs   247
General-Purpose Input/Outputs 248
Introduction to GPIO Interfacing 248
GPIO Digital Output 250
GPIO Digital Input 255
GPIO Configuration 257
Internal Pull-Up and Pull-Down Resistors 258
GPIO Pin Configuration Settings 258
Interfacing to Powered DC Circuits 265
C++ Control of GPIOs 267
The Linux Device Tree 271
Flattened Device Tree on the Beagle Boards 272
Modifying a Board Device Tree 276
Boot Configuration Files 278
Analog Inputs and Outputs 280
Analog Inputs 280
Enabling the Analog Inputs 280
Analog Input Application—A Simple Light Meter 282
Analog Outputs (PWM) 285
Output Application—Controlling a Servo Motor 289
BoneScript 290
Digital Read and Write 290
Analog Read 292

	Analog Write (PWM)	293
	GPIO Performance	294
	Advanced GPIO Topics	295
	More C++ Programming	295
	Callback Functions	295
	POSIX Threads	297
	Linux poll (sys/poll.h)	298
	Enhanced GPIO Class	299
	Using GPIOs without Using sudo	302
	Root Permissions with setuid	304
	Summary	306
	Further Reading	306
Chapter 7	**Cross-Compilation, Eclipse, and Building Linux**	**307**
	Setting Up a Cross-Compilation Toolchain	308
	Cross-Compiling Under Debian	309
	Testing the Toolchain	311
	Emulating the armhf Architecture	312
	Cross-Compilation with Third-Party Libraries (Multiarch)	314
	Cross-Compilation Using Eclipse	315
	Installing Eclipse on Desktop Linux	315
	Configuring Eclipse for Cross-Compilation	316
	Remote System Explorer	318
	Integrating GitHub into Eclipse	322
	Remote Debugging	322
	Automatic Documentation (Doxygen)	328
	Adding Doxygen Editor Support in Eclipse	330
	Cross-Building Linux	330
	Downloading the Kernel Source	331
	Building the Linux Kernel	332
	Building a Poky Linux Distribution (Advanced)	335
	Summary	340
Chapter 8	**Interfacing to the Beagle Board Buses**	**341**
	Introduction to Bus Communication	342
	I²C	343
	I²C Hardware	343
	I²C on the Beagle Boards	344
	I²C Devices on the Beagle Boards	345
	An I²C Test Circuit	346
	A Real-Time Clock	346
	The ADXL345 Accelerometer	347
	Wiring the Test Circuit	348
	Using Linux I2C-Tools	348
	i2cdetect	348
	i2cdump	349
	i2cget	353
	i2cset	354

I²C Communication in C   356
Wrapping I²C Devices with C++ Classes   358
SPI   360
SPI Hardware   361
SPI on the Beagle Boards   363
Testing an SPI Bus   363
A First SPI Application (74HC595)   365
Wiring the 74HC595 Circuit   366
SPI Communication Using C   367
Bidirectional SPI Communication in C/C++   370
The ADXL345 SPI Interface   370
Connecting the ADXL345 to the Beagle Boards   372
Wrapping SPI Devices with C++ Classes   373
Three-Wire SPI Communication   375
Multiple SPI Slave Devices   376
UART   377
The Beagle Board UART   378
UART Examples in C   380
Beagle Board Serial Client   381
LED Serial Server   383
UART Applications: GPS   386
CAN Bus   388
Beagle Board CAN Bus   389
SocketCAN   390
A CAN Bus Test Circuit   392
Linux CAN-utils   393
A SocketCAN C Example   394
Logic-Level Translation   396
Summary   398
Further Reading   399

Chapter 9   Interacting with the Physical Environment   401
Interfacing to Actuators   402
DC Motors   403
Driving Small DC Motors (up to 1.5A)   406
Controlling a DC Motor Using sysfs   407
Driving Larger DC Motors (Greater Than 1.5 A)   409
Controlling a DC Motor Using C++   411
Stepper Motors   412
The EasyDriver Stepper Motor Driver   413
A Beagle Board Stepper Motor Driver Circuit   414
Controlling a Stepper Motor Using C++   415
Relays   417
Interfacing to Analog Sensors   418
Protecting the ADC Inputs   420
Diode Clamping   421
Op-Amp Clamping   422

Analog Sensor Signal Conditioning   427
    Scaling Using Voltage Division   427
    Signal Offsetting and Scaling   428
Analog Interfacing Examples   431
    Infrared Distance Sensing   431
    ADXL335 Conditioning Example   436
Interfacing to Local Displays   438
    MAX7219 Display Modules   438
    Character LCD Modules   441
Building C/C++ Libraries   445
    Makefiles   446
    CMake   447
        A Hello World Example   448
        Building a C/C++ Library   449
        Using a Shared (.so) or Static (.a) Library   452
Summary   453
Further Reading   454

Chapter 10   Real-Time Interfacing Using External Slave Processors   455
Real-Time Beagle Board   456
    Real-Time Kernels   456
    Real-Time Hardware Solutions   458
Extended GPIO Availability   458
    The MCP23017 and the I²C Bus   460
        Controlling the GPIO LED Circuit   461
        Reading the GPIO Button State   462
        An Interrupt Configuration Example (Advanced)   463
    The MCP23S17 and the SPI Bus   464
    A C++ Class for the MCP23x17 Devices   465
Adding External UARTs   468
The Arduino   471
    An Arduino Serial Slave   474
        A UART Echo Test Example   475
        UART Command Control of an Arduino   478
    An Arduino I²C Slave   481
        An I²C Test Circuit   481
        I²C Register Echo Example   482
        I²C Temperature Sensor Example   484
        I²C Temperature Sensor with a Warning LED   486
        Arduino Slave Communication Using C/C++   488
        An I²C Ultrasonic Sensor Application   490
Summary   493
Further Reading   493

Part III   Advanced Beagle Board Systems   495

Chapter 11   The Internet of Things   497
The Internet of Things   498
A Beagle Board IoT Sensor   499
The Beagle Board as a Sensor Web Server   501

Installing and Configuring a Web Server 502
Configuring the Apache Web Server 503
Creating Web Pages and Web Scripts 503
PHP on the Beagle Board 506
GNU Cgicc Applications (Advanced) 508
Replacing Bone101 with Apache 511
A C/C++ Web Client 512
Network Communications Primer 513
A C/C++ Web Client 514
Secure Communication Using OpenSSL 516
A Beagle Board as a "Thing" 518
ThingSpeak 518
The Linux Cron Scheduler 521
System crontab 521
User crontab 523
Sending E-mail from the Beagle Board 524
If This Then That 526
IoT Frameworks 528
MQ Telemetry Transport 529
MQTT Server/Broker 531
MQTT Publisher/Subscriber on a Beagle Board 533
The mqtt-spy Debug Tool 534
Writing MQTT Code 535
A Paho MQTT Publisher Example 535
A Paho MQTT Subscriber Example 537
Adafuit IO 539
Configuring the Adafruit IO Account 540
Connecting to Adafruit IO with MQTT 542
An MQTT Node.js Publish Example 543
The C++ Client/Server 545
IoT Device Management 548
Remote Monitoring of a Beagle Board 548
Beagle Board Watchdog Timers 549
Static IP Addresses 551
Power over Ethernet 551
PoE Power Extraction Modules (Advanced Topic) 553
Summary 554

Chapter 12 Wireless Communication and Control 555
Introduction to Wireless Communications 556
Bluetooth Communications 557
Installing a Bluetooth Adapter 558
Checking the LKM 559
Configuring a Bluetooth Adapter 560
Making the Beagle Board Discoverable 561
Android App Development with Bluetooth 563
Wi-Fi Communications 564
Installing a Wi-Fi Adapter 564

The NodeMCU Wi-Fi Slave Processor   568
    Flashing with the Latest Firmware   569
    Connecting the NodeMCU to Wi-Fi   570
    Programming the NodeMCU   571
    The NodeMCU Web Server Interface   574
    JSON   575
    The NodeMCU and MQTT   577
ZigBee Communications   579
    Introduction to XBee Devices   579
        AT versus API Mode   581
    XBee Configuration   582
        XCTU   582
        Configuring an XBee Network Using XCTU   583
    An XBee AT Mode Example   584
        Setting Up the Arduino XBee Device (XBeeA)   584
        Setting Up the PocketBeagle XBee Device (XBeePB)   586
    An XBee API Mode Example   589
        Setting Up the PocketBeagle XBee Device (XBee1)   589
        Setting Up the Stand-Alone XBee Device (XBee2)   589
        XBee API Mode and Node.js   590
        XBee and C/C++   592
Near Field Communication   593
Summary   596

Chapter 13   Beagle Board with a Rich User Interface   599
Rich UI Beagle Board Architectures   600
    Beagle Boards as General-Purpose Computers   601
        Connecting a Bluetooth Input Peripheral   603
    BeagleBone with a LCD Touchscreen Cape   604
    Virtual Network Computing   605
        VNC Using VNC Viewer   605
        VNC with Xming and PuTTY   606
        VNC with a Linux Desktop Computer   607
    Fat-Client Applications   608
Rich UI Application Development   608
    Introduction to GTK+ on the Beagle Boards   609
        The "Hello World" GTK+ Application   609
        The Event-Driven Programming Model   610
        The GTK+ Temperature Application   611
    Introduction to Qt for the Beagle Board   612
        Installing Qt Development Tools   613
        The "Hello World" Qt Application   613
Qt Primer   615
    Qt Concepts   615
        The QObject Class   617
        Signals and Slots   617
    Qt Development Tools   618

A First Qt Creator Example   620
A Qt Temperature Sensor GUI Application   621
Remote UI Application Development   625
   Fat-Client Qt GUI Application   626
   Multithreaded Server Applications   629
   A Multithreaded Temperature Service   632
     Parsing Stream Data   634
   The Fat Client as a Server   635
     Parsing Stream Data with XML   638
     The Beagle Board Client Application   639
Summary   641
Further Reading   641

Chapter 14 Images, Video, and Audio   **643**
Capturing Images and Video   644
   USB Webcams   644
   Video4Linux2 (V4L2)   646
     Image Capture Utility   647
     Video4Linux2 Utilities   648
     Writing Video4Linux2 Programs   650
Streaming Video   652
Image Processing and Computer Vision   654
   Image Processing with OpenCV   654
   Computer Vision with OpenCV   656
   Boost   659
BeagleBone Audio   660
   Core Audio Software Tools   661
   Audio Devices for the Beagle Boards   661
     HDMI and USB Audio Playback Devices   661
     Internet Radio Playback   664
     Recording Audio   664
     Audio Network Streaming   666
     Bluetooth A2DP Audio   666
   Text-to-Speech   669
Summary   670
Further Reading   670

Chapter 15 Real-Time Interfacing with the PRU-ICSS   **673**
The PRU-ICSS   674
   The PRU-ICSS Architecture   674
   The Remote Processor Framework   675
   Important Documents   676
Development Tools for the PRU-ICSS   676
   The PRU Code Generation Tools   677
   The PRU Debugger   677
Using the AM335x PRU-ICSS   679
   Setting Up the Board for Remoteproc   679
   Testing Remoteproc under Linux   680

A First PRU Example   683
  PRU-ICSS Enhanced GPIOs   683
  A First PRU Program   686
    A First PRU Program in C   686
    A First PRU Program in Assembly   688
The PRU-ICSS in Detail   691
  Registers   691
  Local and Global Memory   692
  PRU Assembly Instruction Set   696
PRU-ICSS Applications   698
  PRU-ICSS Performance Tests   698
  Utilizing Regular Linux GPIOs   702
  A PRU PWM Generator   704
  A PRU Sine Wave Generator   708
  An Ultrasonic Sensor Application   709
Summary   714
Further Reading   714

Chapter 16   Embedded Kernel Programming   717
Introduction   718
  Why Write Kernel Modules?   718
  Loadable Kernel Module Basics   719
A First LKM Example   720
  The LKM Makefile   722
  Building the LKM on a Beagle Board   723
  Testing the First LKM Example   724
    Testing the LKM Parameter   726
An Embedded LKM Example   727
  Interrupt Service Routines   729
  Performance   733
Enhanced Button GPIO Driver LKM   733
  The kobject Interface   734
Enhanced LED GPIO Driver LKM   741
  Kernel Threads   742
Conclusions   744
Summary   744

Index   745

Introduction

The Beagle platform continues to amaze! Given the proliferation of smartphones, the idea of holding in one hand a computer that is capable of performing two billion instructions per second is easy to take for granted—but the fact that you can modify the hardware and software of such small yet powerful devices and adapt them to suit your own needs and create your own inventions is nothing short of amazing. Even better, you can purchase a board for as little as $25 in the form of a PocketBeagle.

The Beagle boards on their own are too complex to be used by a general audience; it is the capability of the boards to run Linux that makes the resulting platform accessible, adaptable, and powerful. Together, Linux and embedded systems enable ease of development for devices that can meet future challenges in smart buildings, the Internet of Things (IoT), robotics, smart energy, smart cities, human-computer interaction (HCI), cyber-physical systems, 3D printing, smart manufacturing, interactive art, advanced vehicular systems, and many, many more applications.

The integration of high-level Linux software and low-level electronics represents a paradigm shift in embedded systems development. It is revolutionary that you can build a low-level electronics circuit and then install a Linux web server, using only a few short commands, so that the circuit can be controlled over the internet. You can easily use a Beagle board as a general-purpose Linux computer, but it is vastly more challenging and interesting to get underneath the hood and fully interface it to electronic circuits of your own design—and that is where this book comes in!

This book should have widespread appeal for inventors, makers, students, entrepreneurs, hackers, artists, dreamers—in short, anybody who wants to bring the power of embedded Linux to his or her products, inventions, creations, or projects and truly understand the Beagle platform in detail. This is not a recipe book—with few exceptions, everything demonstrated here is explained at a level that will enable you to design, build, and debug your own extensions of the concepts presented here. Nor is there any grand design project at the end of this book for which you must purchase a prescribed set of components and peripherals to achieve a specific outcome. Rather, this book is about providing you with enough background knowledge and "under-the-hood" technical details to enable and motivate your own explorations.

I strongly believe in learning by doing, so I present examples using low-cost, widely available hardware so that you can follow along. Using these hands-on examples, I describe what each step means in detail so that when you substitute your own hardware components, modules, and peripherals you will be able to adapt the content in this book to suit your needs. As for that grand project or invention—that is left up to you and your imagination!

When writing this book, I had the following aims and objectives:

- To explain embedded Linux and its interaction with electronic circuits—taking you through the topics from mystery to mastery!

- To provide in-depth information and instruction on the Linux, electronics, and programming skills that are required to master a pretty wide and comprehensive variety of topics in this domain.

- To create a collection of practical "Hello World" hardware and software examples on each and every topic in the book, from low-level interfacing, general-purpose input/outputs (GPIOs), analog-to-digital converters (ADCs), buses, and UARTs, to high-level libraries such as OpenCV, Qt, and complex and powerful topics, such as real-time interfacing with the PRU-ICSS, and Linux kernel programming.

- To ensure that each circuit and segment of code is specifically designed to work with a Beagle board. Every circuit and code example in this book was built and tested on the BeagleBone Black wireless and PocketBeagle boards.

- To use the "Hello World" examples to build a library of code that you can use and adapt for your own Beagle projects.

- To make all of the code available on GitHub in an easy-to-use form.

- To support this book with strong digital content, such as the videos on the DerekMolloyDCU YouTube channel, and a custom website, www.exploringbeaglebone.com.

- To ensure that by the end of this book you have everything you need to imagine, create, and build *advanced* Beagle board projects.

I wrote this second edition because of the popularity of the first edition of *Exploring BeagleBone*. The number of pages in this edition is more than 20 percent of the first edition, increased to include the following major additions:

- Full coverage of new Beagle boards, with a particular emphasis on the PocketBeagle and BeagleBone Black wireless boards

- Updated content to account for all recent changes to the Linux kernel and operating system

- Inclusion of electronics interfacing approaches, such as protection of I/O pins using optocouplers, the CAN bus, and many additional interfacing application examples using external I/O circuits

- New work on real-time interfacing using external slave processors, with a particular emphasis on building I²C digital sensors

- A full account of new Internet of Things (IoT) full-stack frameworks, with an emphasis on MQTT and interfacing to Adafruit IO

- Full coverage of building wireless sensor networks using technologies such as Wi-Fi, Bluetooth, NFC, and ZigBee

- A complete rewrite of the PRU-ICSS chapter to account for Texas Instruments' decision to move away from UIO to Linux Remoteproc

- Inclusion of new work on writing Linux loadable kernel modules (LKMs)

Why the BeagleBone and PocketBeagle?

The Beagle boards are powerful single-board computers (SBCs), and while there are other SBCs available on the market, such as the Raspberry Pi and Intel NUC boards, the Beagle platform has one key differentiator—it was built to be interfaced to! For example, the Beagle board's microprocessor package even contains two additional on-chip microcontrollers that can be used for real-time interfacing—an area in which other Linux SBCs have significant difficulty.

Unlike most other SBCs, the Beagle boards are fully open-source hardware. The BeagleBoard.org Foundation provides source schematics, hardware layout, a full bill of materials, and comprehensive technical reference manuals, enabling you to modify the design of the Beagle platform and integrate it into your own product. In fact, you can even fork the hardware design onto Upverter (www.upverter.com) under a Creative Commons Attribution-ShareAlike license (see tiny.cc/beagle001 for the full schematics). This is a useful feature should you decide to take your newest invention to market!

How This Book Is Structured

There is no doubt that some of the topics in this book are quite complex—the Beagle boards are complex devices! However, everything that you need to master the devices is present in the book within three major parts.

- Part I, "Beagle Board Basics"
- Part II, "Interfacing, Controlling, and Communicating"
- Part III, "Advanced Beagle Board Systems"

In the first part in the book, you learn about the hardware and software of the Beagle board platform in Chapters 1 and 2 and subsequently gain more knowledge through these three primer chapters:

- Chapter 3, "Exploring Embedded Linux Systems"
- Chapter 4, "Interfacing Electronics"
- Chapter 5, "Practical Beagle Board Programming"

If you are a Linux expert, electronics wizard, and/or software guru, then feel free to skip the primer chapters; however, for everyone else, you'll find a concise but detailed set of materials to ensure that you gain all the knowledge required to effectively and safely interface to your Beagle boards.

The second part of the book, Chapters 6 to 10, provides detailed information on interfacing to the Beagle board GPIOs, analog inputs, buses (I^2C, SPI, CAN bus), UART devices, USB peripherals, and real-time interfacing to slave processors. You'll learn how you can configure a cross-compilation environment so that you can build large-scale software applications. This part also describes how you can combine hardware and software to provide your board with the ability to interact effectively with its physical environment.

The final part of the book, Chapters 11 to 16, describes how the Beagle board can be used for advanced applications such as Internet of Things (IoT); rich user interfaces; images, video, and audio; real-time interfacing using the PRU-ICSS; and kernel programming. Along the way you will meet many technologies, including TCP/IP, ThingSpeak, Adafruit IO, PoE, Wi-Fi, Bluetooth, Zigbee, RFID, MQTT, cron, Apache, PHP, e-mail, IFTTT, VNC, GTK+, Qt, XML, JSON, multi-threading, client/server programming, V4L2, video streaming, OpenCV, Boost, USB audio, Bluetooth A2DP, text-to-speech, and Remoteproc.

Conventions Used in This Book

This book is filled with source code examples and snippets that you can use to build your own applications. Code and commands are shown as follows:

```
This is what source code looks like.
```

When presenting work performed in a Linux terminal, it is often necessary to display both input and output in a single example. A bold type is used to distinguish the user input from the output. Here's an example:

```
debian@ebb:~$ ping www.exploringbeaglebone.com
PING lb1.reg365.net (195.7.226.20) 56(84) bytes of data.
64 bytes from lb1.reg365.net (195.7.226.20): icmp_req=1 ttl=55 time=25.6 ms
64 bytes from lb1.reg365.net (195.7.226.20): icmp_req=2 ttl=55 time=25.6 ms
...
```

The $ prompt indicates that a regular Linux user is executing a command, and a # prompt indicates that a Linux superuser is executing a command. The ellipsis symbol (…) is used whenever code or output not vital to understanding a topic has been cut. I've edited the output like this to enable you to focus on only the most useful information. You are encouraged to repeat the steps in this book yourself, whereupon you will see the full output. In addition, the full source code for all examples is provided along with the book.

There are some additional styles in the text. Here are some examples:

- New terms and important words appear in *italics* when introduced.
- Keyboard strokes appear like this: Ctrl+C.
- All URLs in the book appear in this font: www.exploringbeaglebone.com.
- A URL-shortening service is used to create aliases for long URLs that are presented in the book. These aliases have the form tiny.cc/beagle102 (e.g., link 2 in Chapter 1). Should the link address change after this book is published, the alias will be updated.

There are several features used in this book to identify when content is of particular importance or when additional information is available.

WARNING   This type of feature contains important information that can help you avoid damaging your Beagle board.

NOTE   This type of feature contains useful additional information, such as links to digital resources and useful tips, which can make it easier to understand the task at hand.

FEATURE TITLE

This type of feature goes into detail about the current topic or a related topic.

What You'll Need

Ideally you should have a Beagle board before you begin reading this book so that you can follow along with the numerous examples in the text. If you do not yet have a board, it would be worth reading Chapter 1 before placing an order. Currently the board is manufactured by both CircuitCo and Embest—the boards from either manufacturer are compatible with the designs and operations in this book. You can purchase one of the boards in the United States from online stores such as Adafruit Industries, Digi-Key, Mouser, SparkFun, and Jameco Electronics. They are available internationally from stores such as Farnell, Radionics, Watterott, and Tigal.

A full list of recommended and optional accessories for the Beagle platform is provided in Chapter 1. In addition, each chapter contains a list of the electronics components and modules required if you want to follow along with the text. The book website provides details about where these components can be acquired.

Errata

I have worked really hard to ensure that this book is error free; however, it is always possible that something was overlooked. A full list of errata is available on each chapter's web page at the companion website. If you find any errors in the text or in the source code examples, I would be grateful if you could send the errors using the companion website so that I can update the web page errata list and the source code examples in the code repository.

Digital Content and Source Code

The primary companion site for this book is www.exploringbeaglebone.com. It contains videos, source code examples, and links to further reading. Each chapter has its own individual web page. In the unlikely event that this website is unavailable, you can find the code at www.wiley.com/go/exploringbeaglebone2e.

All the source code is available through GitHub, which allows you to download the code to your Beagle board with one command. You can also easily view the code online at tiny.cc/beagle002. Downloading the source code to your board is as straightforward as typing the following at the Linux shell prompt:

```
debian@ebb:$ git clone https://github.com/derekmolloy/exploringbb.git
```

If you have never used Git before, don't worry—it is explained in detail in Chapter 3. Now, on with the adventures!

Beagle Board Basics

In This Part

Chapter 1: The Beagle Hardware Platform
Chapter 2: Beagle Software
Chapter 3: Exploring Embedded Linux Systems
Chapter 4: Interfacing Electronics
Chapter 5: Practical Beagle Board Programming

The Beagle Hardware Platform

In this chapter, you are introduced to the BeagleBone platform hardware and its variant boards. The chapter focuses in particular on the BeagleBone and PocketBeagle boards and the various subsystems and physical inputs/outputs of these boards. In addition, the chapter lists accessories that can be helpful in developing your own Beagle-based projects. By the end of this chapter, you should have an appreciation of the power and complexity of this computing platform. You should also be aware of the first steps to take to protect your boards from physical damage.

Introduction to the Boards

Beagle boards are compact, low-cost, open-source Linux computing platforms that can be used to build complex applications that interface high-level software and low-level electronic circuits. These are ideal platforms for prototyping project and product designs that take advantage of the power and freedom of Linux, combined with direct access to input/output pins and buses, allowing you to interface with electronics components, modules, and USB devices. The following are some characteristics of the single-board computing (SBC) boards:

- They are powerful, containing a processor that can perform up to 2 billion instructions per second.
- They are widely available at relatively low-cost, as little as $25–$90 depending on the board chosen.
- They support many standard interfaces for electronics devices.
- They use little power, running at between 1W (idle) and 2.3W (peak).
- They are expandable through the use of daughter boards and USB devices.
- They are strongly supported by a huge community of innovators and enthusiasts.
- They are open-hardware and support open-software tools and applications for commercial and noncommercial applications.

The BeagleBone and PocketBeagle boards run the Linux operating system, which means you can use many open-source software libraries and applications directly with them. Open-source software driver availability also enables you to interface devices such as USB cameras, keyboards and Wi-Fi adapters with your project, without having to source proprietary alternatives. Therefore, you have access to comprehensive libraries of code that have been built by a talented open-source community; however, it is important to remember that the code typically comes without any type of warranty or guarantee. If there are problems, then you have to rely on the good nature of the community to resolve them. Of course, you could also fix the problems yourself and make the solutions publicly available.

> **NOTE** The BeagleBone and PocketBeagle boards are quite different in physical appearance, as displayed in Figure 1-1, but they are similar devices under the hood. To illustrate this, both boards are typically booted with the same Linux image on a micro-SD card. The Linux image will automatically detect and configure the differing hardware during the boot sequence depending on the board it is booting.

The BeagleBoard.org Foundation is a U.S. nonprofit corporation that aims to provide embedded systems education in open-source hardware and software. Over the last ten years, the Foundation has developed high-quality boards that are renowned in the open-source community for their detailed documentation, for their extensive support, and for providing a strong bridge between idea prototyping and commercial product design.

The platform boards are formed by the integration of a high-performance microprocessor on a printed circuit board (PCB) and an extensive software ecosystem. The physical PCB is not a complete product; rather, it is a prototype reference design that you can use to build a complete product. It is an open-hardware platform, meaning you can download and use the Beagle-Bone or PocketBeagle hardware schematics and layouts directly within your own product design. In fact, despite the impressive capability of these boards, they do not fully expose all the features and interfaces of the Texas Instruments Sitara AM335x System on Chip (SoC).

Recent BeagleBone and PocketBeagle boards utilize an Octavo Systems System-in-Package (SiP), which incorporates the Sitara AM335x processor along with DDR memory, power management functionality, and all required passive components into a single ball-grid array (BGA) package, as displayed in Figure 1-1. This SiP design approach vastly simplifies the circuit layout of boards that are based on the AM335x processor platform and has allowed for the small form-factor of the PocketBeagle. You should keep this approach in mind should you decide to commercialize your designs, as it could accelerate the time-to-market of the final product by many months.

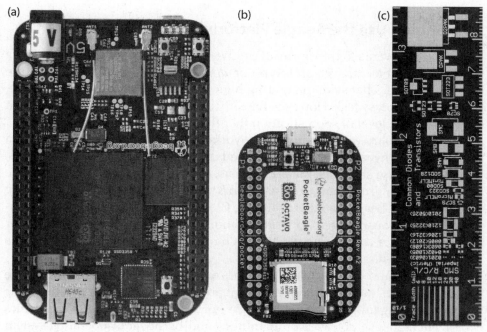

Figure 1-1: (a) BeagleBone Black Wireless, (b) PocketBeagle, and (c) an Adafruit PCB Ruler for relative scale

One impressive feature of the Beagle platform is that board functionality can be extended with daughter boards, called *capes*, which connect to the expansion headers (the two black 2 × 23 connector rows in Figure 1-1(a), or the unpopulated 2 × 18 rows in Figure 1-1(b)). You can design your own capes and attach them securely to your board using these headers. In addition, many capes are available for purchase that can be used to expand the functionality of your board. Some examples of these are described later in this chapter.

The first five BeagleBone PCBs were designed by Gerald Coley, a co-founder of the BeagleBoard.org Foundation who is now the president of Embedded Product Design (www.emprodesign.net). Over the past few years, the boards and several of its capes have been manufactured by CircuitCo (www.circuitco.com), Element14 (www.element14.com), and its subsidiary Embest (www.embest-tech.com). Therefore, when you purchase a Beagle board, you are not purchasing it from the BeagleBoard.org Foundation; rather, the foundation is the focal point for a community of developers and users.

> **NOTE**   CircuitCo has provided a short video of the BeagleBone Black manufacturing process at tiny.cc/beagle101— it highlights the complexity of the device and the work that goes into its manufacture.

Who Should Use the Beagle Platform

Anybody who wants to transform an engineering concept into a real interactive electronics product, project, prototype, or work of art should consider using the Beagle platform. That said, integrating high-level software and low-level electronics is not an easy task. However, the difficulty involved in an implementation depends on the level of sophistication that the project demands.

The BeagleBoard.org community is working hard to ensure their platform is accessible by everyone who is interested in integrating it into their projects, whether they are students, makers, artists, or hobbyists. Tools and software development environments, such as Jason Kridner's BoneScript Node.js library (a co-founder of BeagleBoard.org) and the Cloud9 integrated development environment (IDE), enable users to write and build code directly in a web browser that is capable of controlling electronics hardware. The BoneScript library is introduced in Chapter 2.

For more advanced users, with electronics or computing knowledge, the Beagle platform enables additional development and customization to meet specific project needs. Again, such customization is not trivial: You may be an electronics expert, but high-level software programming and/or the Linux operating system might cause you difficulty. Or, you may be a programming guru but you have never wired an LED! This book aims to cater to all types of users, providing each type of reader with enough Linux, electronics, and software exposure to ensure that you can be productive, regardless of your previous experience level.

When to Use Beagle Boards

The Beagle boards are perfectly placed for the integration of high-level software and low-level electronics in any type of project. Whether you are planning to build an automated home management system, robot, smart display, sensor network, vending machine, or internet-connected work of interactive art, the boards have the processing power to do whatever you can imagine of an embedded device.

The major advantage over more traditional embedded systems, such as the Arduino, PIC, and AVR microcontrollers, is apparent when you leverage the Linux OS for your projects. For example, if you built a home automation system using the BeagleBone and you then decided that you wanted to make certain information available on the internet, you could simply install a web server. You could then use server-side scripting or your favorite programming language to interface with your home automation system to capture and share the information. Alternatively, your project might require secure remote access. In that case, you could install a secure shell (SSH) server simply by using the Linux command `sudo apt install sshd` (these commands are covered in Chapter 2). This could potentially save you weeks of development work. In addition, you have the comfort of knowing that the same software is running securely on millions of machines around the world. Linux also provides you with device driver support for many USB peripherals and adapters, making it possible for you to connect cameras, Wi-Fi adapters, and other low-cost consumer peripherals directly to your platform, without the need for complex and/or expensive software driver development. If you are connecting an embedded system to the internet or to a display (e.g., a touchscreen or monitor), you should consider a Linux SBC such as the Beagle boards before any other option.

When Should You Not Use the Beagle Boards

The Linux OS was not designed for real-time or predictable processing. As a result, there are significant challenges in using this OS for deterministic processing tasks such as sampling a sensor precisely every one-millionth of a second. Therefore, in its default state, the Beagle boards are not an ideal platform for real-time systems applications. Sophisticated real-time versions of Linux are available, but they are currently targeted at experienced Linux developers. However, unlike many other Linux SBCs, the BeagleBone does have an on-board solution that goes some way toward resolving this interfacing problem. Within the AM335x SoC, there are two on-board microcontrollers, called *programmable real-time units* (PRUs), which can be programmed for real-time interfacing applications. This is an advanced topic that is described in Chapter 15.

There are low-cost dedicated solutions available for real-time sampling and control tasks (such as the TI MSP430 or SimpleLink wired and wireless MCUs) that may be more appropriate for real-time interfacing. It is also important to remember that you can interconnect such real-time microcontrollers to the Beagle boards via electrical buses (e.g., I²C, UART, CAN bus, and Ethernet) and have the Linux SBC act as the central processor for a distributed control system. This is an important concept as part of the Internet of Things (IoT) and is described in detail in Chapters 10, 11, and 12.

The second application type that the Beagle platform will find difficult is that of playing or processing high-definition video. The processing overhead of software decoding and playing encoded video streams is immense and is beyond the capability of the BeagleBone at high-definition video resolutions. The Raspberry Pi (www.raspberrypi.org) board has this capability because its Broadcom BCM2835/7 processors were designed for multimedia applications, and it has a hardware implementation of H.264/MPG-4 decoders and encoders. For applications such as running Kodi home media center (kodi.tv), you are better off purchasing a Raspberry Pi 3 (Model B+). In addition, you should of course purchase my book, *Exploring Raspberry Pi*, from the same Wiley mini-series!

If your intention is to develop an embedded Linux image processing or computer vision platform, then you should consider the Xilinx Zynq platform (tiny.cc/beagle102), as it integrates an ARM-based processor that can run Linux alongside the hardware programmability of an FPGA. This allows the computationally intensive but parallelizable image processing functionality to be offloaded from the Linux kernel to the programmable logic hardware. Boards such as the PYNQ, ZYBO, or Arty Z7 are available, but be aware that they are complex devices.

For interfacing Linux to electronic circuits, it is hard to beat the Beagle boards, as the range of input/outputs, openness of the platform, and quality of documentation available are second to none.

BeagleBone Documentation

This book integrates my experiences in developing for the Beagle platform with supporting background materials on embedded Linux, software development, and general electronics to create an in-depth guide to building with this platform. However, it is simply not possible to cover everything in just one book, so I have avoided restating information that is listed in the key documents and websites described in this section. The first starting point for supporting documentation is always the following:

- **The BeagleBoard.org website:** This provides the main support for this platform, with software guides, community links, and downloads to support your development. An excellent "Getting Started" guide and blog are available at www.beagleboard.org.

A huge amount of documentation is available on the BeagleBone platform, but the most important documents are as follows:

- **Sitara AM335x ARM Cortex-A8 Technical Reference Manual (TRM):**[1] The key component of the Beagle boards are their Texas Instruments SoCs, and this document contains anything you could possibly want to know about the internal workings of the AM335x. It is a complex device, and that is reflected in the length of the AM3358 TRM—5,113 pages! If you need to understand something about the inner workings of the micproprocessor or the device configuration on the BeagleBone or PocketBeagle, it is likely that the answer is contained in this document. I refer to tables in the TRM throughout this book so that ideally you will become familiar with the language contained therein. This document and the datasheet for the SoC are available free from www.ti.com/product/am3358.

- **The PocketBeagle System Reference Manual (SRM):** This is a live wiki document that describes the PocketBeagle hardware. It is maintained by the BeagleBoard community: tiny.cc/beagle103.

- **BeagleBone Black System Reference Manual (SRM):** This is the core document that describes the BeagleBone Black hardware. It is available at tiny.cc/beagle104.

Key websites are also available to support your learning on this platform, with combinations of tutorials, discussion forums, sample code libraries, Linux distributions, and project ideas to stimulate your creative side. Here is a selection of important websites:

- **The website for this book:** www.exploringbeaglebone.com
- **My personal blog site:** www.derekmolloy.ie
- **The eLinux.org Wiki:** www.elinux.org
- **The Linux Foundation:** www.linuxfoundation.org

Getting started with the Beagle platform software is described in Chapter 2. The remainder of this chapter discusses the physical boards, explaining the functionality that is available, summarizing the SRM, and providing some examples of the types of peripherals and capes that you might like to connect to your board.

---

[1] At the time of writing, this is in revision P (March 2017) and has the TI document identification SPRUH73P.

The Beagle Hardware

At its heart, the Beagle boards use the Texas Instruments Sitara AM335x Cortex A8 ARM microprocessor. While the BeagleBone and PocketBeagle are the focus of this book, other boards have been developed by BeagleBoard.org, including BeagleBoard, BeagleBoard XM, and the Arduino Tre (BeagleBoard and Arduino combined on a single board). The BeagleBone and PocketBeagle are discussed in detail in the next section, but here are some summary details on the different boards (in historical order):

- **(2008) BeagleBoard ($125):** The original open-hardware ARM-based development board that had HD video support. It has a 720MHz ARM A8 processor but no on-board Ethernet.

- **(2010) BeagleBoard xM ($149):** Similar to BeagleBoard, except with a 1GHz ARM (AM37x) processor, 512MB memory, four USB ports, and Ethernet support. Despite the low cost of the new BeagleBone boards, the BeagleBoard xM is popular for its C64+TMDSP core for digital signal processing (DSP) applications.

- **(2011) BeagleBone ($89):** Smaller footprint than the BeagleBoard. It has a 720MHz processor and 256MB memory, Ethernet support, low-level input/output (e.g., analog to digital converters), but no on-board video support.

- **(2013) BeagleBone Black ($45–$55):** This board enhances the BeagleBone with a 1GHz processor, 512MB of DDR3 memory, Ethernet, eMMC storage, and HDMI video support.

- **(2014-2018) BeagleBone Green, BeagleBone Enhanced, BeagleBone Black Wireless, BeagleBone Blue Wireless, and PocketBeagle ($25–$90):** Variant boards that are substantially based on the BeagleBone Black platform.

- **(2017) BeagleBoard X15 ($270):** High-performance BeagleBoard based on the Sitara AM5728 that has dual 1.5GHz ARM Corex-A15 processors, with integrated C66x DSPs, ARM Cortex-M4 real-time processors, and PRUs (`tiny.cc/beagle105`).

The BeagleBone and PocketBeagle boards are the focus of this book, mainly because of their feature sets and price points in comparison to the other offerings; however, most of the discussion in this book applies generally to all platforms.

BeagleBone Versions

As previously mentioned, there are several versions of the BeagleBone available, as illustrated in Figure 1-2, in particular the older BeagleBone White, or just BeagleBone; the BeagleBone Black (BBB); and the wireless versions. All boards have a small form factor, fitting neatly inside an Altoids mint tin; in fact, the PocketBeagle fits inside a tiny Altoids Smalls tin.

> **NOTE** Traditionally, Altoids tins have been upcycled by engineers as a low-cost housing for electronics projects. Given the complexity of the BeagleBone boards, it is impressive that the boards fit inside these tins—it also helps to explain the rounded corners on the BeagleBone boards! Holes can be formed in the case to provide access to the board connectors, but of course it is necessary to electrically insulate the aluminum tin before using it to house your board.

To achieve such a small form factor, the components are densely placed on the BeagleBone, and a six-layer PCB is used to achieve interconnects. As an example, the AM335x (ZCZ) processors used on the BeagleBone Black platforms have a ball grid array of 324 pins, with a 0.80mm ball pitch.

(a) (b)

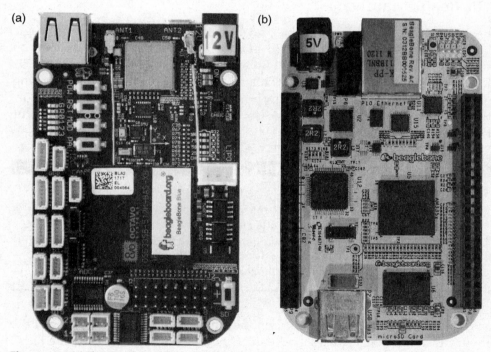

Figure 1-2: (a) The BeagleBone Blue with the Octavo OSD3358 SiP, (b) the original BeagleBone White with the AM335x SoC

Table 1-1 lists the main similarities and differences between the current Beagle boards. The obvious choice factors are the price and network connectivity options.

- The non-wireless BBB has Ethernet connectivity, which can be particularly useful for applications in which the board acts as a network Bridge Router (e.g., for 6LoWPAN applications).

- When wireless networking is required, the BBB Wireless works well in mobile connected embedded applications where video may be required, and the BeagleBone Blue is strong for mobile tasks that interface to motors, for applications such as robotics and automation.

- The PocketBeagle is particularly useful when cost, size, and weight are important considerations for a project. Despite having no on-board wireless connectivity, this can be added and customized for a particular project. For example, you might add one of Wi-Fi, Bluetooth, or 802.15.4-based communications to your project by interfacing modules to the boards USB or UART connections. Interestingly, the bottom side of the PocketBeagle has no components, which means that it can be mounted flush to a carrier printed-circuit board (PCB).

The Beagle Hardware

Figures 1-3, 1-4, and 1-5 detail the core systems of the BBB and PocketBeagle boards. The first set of callouts, 1 to 8, identify and describe the key systems on the BBB. The microprocessor on the BBB is a Texas Instruments Sitara AM335x Cortex A8 ARM Microprocessor.[2] It is a reduced instruction set computing (RISC) processor, so at 1,000MHz the processor executes 2,000 million instructions per second (MIPS). The processor runs at about 1W idle and 2.3W for heavy processing loads.

> **POCKETBEAGLE USB ON-THE-GO**
>
> The PocketBeagle can use USB On-the-Go (OTG) to connect to USB peripherals. USB OTG is often used for devices that switch between the roles of USB client and host. For example, USB OTG connectors are often used to allow cell phones or tablet computers to connect to external USB storage devices. The USB OTG connector allows the PocketBeagle host to connect to a slave device such as a Wi-Fi or Bluetooth adapter. One such adapter is illustrated later in the chapter in Figure 1-8(b).

The next set of callouts, 9 to 19, identifies the various connectors on the BBB, their physical characteristics, and their function. For connector 18, the JTAG connector, there are 20 pre-tinned pads. You need to purchase a connector (such as Samtec FTR-110-03-G-D-06) for this and carefully solder it to the board.

Table 1-2 details the various inputs and outputs that are available on the expansion headers. There are 92 pins on these headers (2×46) on the

---

[2]Early BBB boards used an XAM3359AZCZ100 processor, but more recent boards (from Rev C) use the AM3358BZCZ100 (even within the OSD3358 SiP). The feature set that is exposed to the BBB platform is the same, so the notation AM335x is used.

Table 1-1: A High-Level Comparison of Recent Beagle Boards

MODEL	BEAGLEBONE BLACK	BEAGLEBONE BLACK WIRELESS	POCKETBEAGLE	BEAGLEBONE BLUE	BEAGLEBOARD X15
Approximate price	$55	$70	$25	$90	$270
Processor	1GHz AM335x with two 32-bit PRUs	1GHz AM335x with two 32-bit PRUs	1GHz AM335x with two 32-bit PRUs	1GHz AM335x with two 32-bit PRUs	Two 1.5GHz ARM A15s, C66 DSP Cores, two ARM M4s and four PRUs
Memory	512MB DDR3	512MB DDR3	512MB DDR3	512MB DDR3	2GB DDR3
Storage	On-board 4GB eMMC and micro-SD card slot	On-board 4GB eMMC and micro-SD card slot	micro-SD card slot	On-board 4GB eMMC and micro-SD card slot	On-board 4GB eMMC and micro-SD card slot
Video	On-board HDMI	On-board HDMI	None	None	On-board HDMI (full)
Debugging	JTAG pads	JTAG pads	JTAG pads	JTAG pads	20-pin JTAG header
Interfacing	Two 46-pin female GPIO headers	Two 46-pin female GPIO headers	Two 36-pin unpopulated headers	JST interfaces and 24-pin male header bank	Four 60-pin headers
Wired Ethernet	10/100 Ethernet	None	None	None	Two Gigabit Ethernet
Wireless Network	None; available through USB Wi-Fi adapters	802.11bgn and Bluetooth 4.1 with BLE	None	802.11bgn and Bluetooth 4.1 with BLE	None

Continues

Table 1-1: (*continued*)

MODEL	BEAGLEBONE BLACK	BEAGLEBONE BLACK WIRELESS	POCKETBEAGLE	BEAGLEBONE BLUE	BEAGLEBOARD X15
Supply	5 V USB or DC jack	5 V USB or DC jack	5 V USB and via header pins	12 V DC jack	12 V DC jack (5A)
Application	General-purpose prototyping with video and Ethernet	General-purpose prototyping with video and Wi-Fi/ Bluetooth	Self-contained Linux IoT or interfacing applications	Mobile robotics applications; includes an IMU, barometer, LiPo support, and H-bridges	High-end DSP and real-time interfacing applications, including eSATA and USB3

	Function	BeagleBone	PocketBeagle	Details
①	Processor	AM335x	OSD3358-SM	A powerful Texas Instruments Sitara ARM-A8 processor that is standalone or enclosed in an Octavo Systems System-In-Package (SiP) such as the OSD3358-SM.
		2 x PRUs	2 x PRUs	Programmable Real-time Units (PRUs). Microcontrollers that allow for real-time interfacing.
		Graphics Engine	Graphics Engine	Processor has a 3D graphics engine (Imagination Technologies PowerVR SGX530) that is capable of rendering 20 million polygons per second.
②	Graphics	HDMI Framer	None	The framer converts the LCD interface available on the AM335x processor into a HDMI signal (no HDCP).
③	Memory	512 MB DDR3	512 MB DDR3	The amount of system memory affects performance and the type of applications that can be run.
④	On-board Storage	eMMC (MMC1)	None	A 4GB on-board embedded multi-media card (eMMC), which is an SD card on a chip. The BeagleBone boards can boot without an SD card.
⑤	Power Management	TPS65217C	TPS65217C	Power management IC (PMIC). Sophisticated power management IC that has voltage regulators and is controlled by the main processor. Supports LiPo batteries.
⑥	Ethernet Processor	Ethernet PHY (10/100)	None	BBB can be connected to a network using a LAN8710A physical interface to an RJ45 connector. Not available on the wireless versions.
⑦	LEDs	6 x LEDs	4 x LEDs	Power LED and four user LEDs. The wired BeagleBone has LEDs on the RJ45 Ethernet socket (yellow = 100M link up, green = traffic).
⑧	Buttons	3 x Buttons	1 x Button	Power button. The BeagleBone boards have a reset button and a boot switch button for choosing to boot from the eMMC or the SD card.
	Connectors			
⑨	Video Out	micro-HDMI (HDMI-D)	None	For connecting to monitors and televisions. Supports resolutions up to 1280 x 1024 at 60Hz. It can run 1920 x 1080 but at 24Hz. Has HDMI CEC support.
		Audio out (HDMI-D)	None	HDMI can be broken out to a 3.5mm audio jack using accessories.
⑩	Network	Ethernet (RJ45)	None	10/100 Ethernet via a RJ45 connector. On board Wi-Fi and Bluetooth is available on the BeagleBone Black/Blue Wireless.
⑪	DC Power	5V DC supply (5.5mm) 12V DC supply on Blue	None	For connecting 5V DC mains PSUs to the board. PocketBeagle is usually powered via the USB connector but can be powered by battery or the expansion header.
⑫	SD Card	micro-SD card slot	micro-SD card slot	3.3V micro-SD card slot. The BeagleBone can be booted from this slot, flashed from this slot, or it can be used for additional storage when the board is booted from the eMMC.
⑬	Serial Debug	6 Pin Connector (0.1")	None	(UART0) Used with a serial TTL3V3 cable to connect to the serial console. This functionality is also available via USB on both boards.
⑭	USB	1 x USB 2.0 Client (mini-USB or micro-USB)	1 x USB OTG	(USB0) Connects to your desktop and can power the board.
⑮		1 x USB 2.0 Host (USB-A)		(USB1) You can connect USB peripherals (e.g., Wi-Fi) to the board with this connector.
⑯ ⑰	Expansion Headers	Two 2x23 pin 0.1" female headers	Two 2x18 pin 0.1" unpopulated headers	These headers are multiplexed to provided access to a range of input/output features. Not all functionality is available at the same time. Used to connect capes.
⑱	Other Debug	JTAG	JTAG	Unpopulated JTAG header that can be used to debug a board when used with additional hardware and software.
⑲	Other Power	Battery connectors	via headers	It is possible to solder pins to these points on the BeagleBone or to the headers on the PocketBeagle to power the board. Read the SRM carefully!

Figure 1-3: Table of BeagleBone and PocketBeagle subsystems and connectors

BeagleBone and 72 pins on the PocketBeagle (2 × 36); however, not all are available for general-purpose input/outputs (GPIOs). Several of the connections have a fixed configuration:

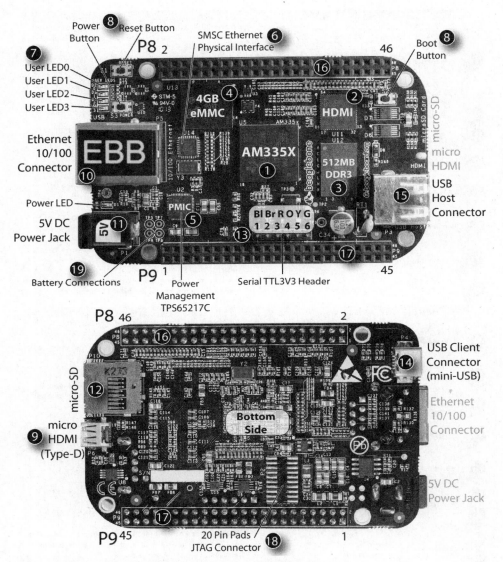

Figure 1-4: The BeagleBone Black (BBB) top and bottom views

- Several pins are connected to ground.
- Pins are required to support the analog inputs (e.g., a 1.8V reference voltage).
- Pins are allocated to 3.3V and 5V voltage supplies.

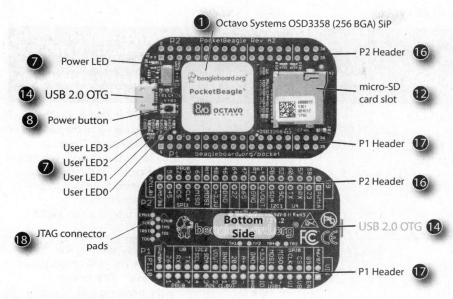

Figure 1-5: The PocketBeagle top and bottom views

The remaining connectors are available to be multiplexed to many different functions, several of which are listed in Table 1-2. The function of each of these input/output types is discussed in Chapter 6 and Chapter 8.

Table 1-2: Functionality Available on the Expansion Headers

EXPANSION HEADERS	BEAGLEBONE P8 AND P9	POCKETBEAGLE P1 AND P2	NOTE: NOT ALL FUNCTIONALITY LISTED HERE IS AVAILABLE SIMULTANEOUSLY. PLEASE SEE CHAPTER 6 FOR DETAILS.
GPIO	65	44	All general-purpose input/outputs are 3.3V tolerant and can only source or sink relatively small currents.
PWM	8	4	Pulse width modulated (PWM) outputs allow you to send a type of variable analog output (0V to 3.3V). PWM can be used to control servo motors or LEDs.

Continues

Table 1-2: (*continued*)

EXPANSION HEADERS	BEAGLEBONE P8 AND P9	POCKETBEAGLE P1 AND P2	NOTE: NOT ALL FUNCTIONALITY LISTED HERE IS AVAILABLE SIMULTANEOUSLY. PLEASE SEE CHAPTER 6 FOR DETAILS.
Analog Input	7	8	12-bit 1.8V analog inputs that are always available on the headers (not multiplexed). These can be used for reading sensor values, but be careful as they are only 1.8V tolerant. Note that six are 1.8V tolerant on the PocketBeagle, but two are 3.3V tolerant.
Power Supply	5V, 3.3V	5V, 3.3V	5V and 3.3V supplies are available. The ADC circuitry also provides a 1.8V reference voltage, but this should not be used as a general supply.
Timers	4	4	Can be used to generate external clocks for interfacing to devices.
I2C	2	2	I2C is a digital bus that allows you to connect several modules to each of these two-wire buses at the same time. There are two public buses and one additional private bus.
UART	4	3	Used for serial communication between two devices. UART0 is the Serial Debug connector on the BeagleBone.
CAN	2	2	CAN Bus is used for Controller Area Networks (CAN), often on industrial processes or vehicles to communicate between various networked systems. There is a CAN cape available for the BeagleBone.
SPI	2	2	Serial Peripheral Interface (SPI) provides a synchronous serial data link over short distances. It uses a master/slave configuration and requires four wires for communication.

EXPANSION HEADERS	BEAGLEBONE P8 AND P9	POCKETBEAGLE P1 AND P2	NOTE: NOT ALL FUNCTIONALITY LISTED HERE IS AVAILABLE SIMULTANEOUSLY. PLEASE SEE CHAPTER 6 FOR DETAILS.
GPMC	1	1	General-purpose memory controller (GPMC) is used to connect to external memory devices like FPGAs or ASICs. This fast bus conflicts with the eMMC on the BeagleBone.
MMC	2	2	Interface buses that are used to connect the micro-SD card and the eMMC to the processor.
LCD	1	1	Useful for LCD screens (e.g., LCD capes). This interface conflicts with the HDMI Framer on the BeagleBone.
McASP	2	2	General-purpose audio serial port—multichannel audio serial port (McASP), connected to the HDMI framer on the BeagleBone.

Beagle Accessories

Most boards (except the PocketBeagle) are packaged with a USB 2.0 cable (either a mini-USB plug or micro-USB-to-USB-A plug), which is used to connect the BeagleBone (via the USB client connector) to a desktop computer. The boards do not come with a micro-SD card, and you will need one for the PocketBeagle in particular. The BeagleBone boots out of the box without the need for a card, as the Linux installation is already present on the board's eMMC.

The boards can be connected to a display using an HDMI cable (except on the BeagleBone Blue and the PocketBeagle), but most of the examples in this book assume the boards are used in headless mode—that is, not connected directly to a display; rather, the board is used as a networked device that interfaces to electronic circuits, USB modules, and wireless sensors.

Highly Recommended Accessories

The following accessories are recommended for purchase along with your board. If you are planning to carry out development work, then you should probably have most of them.

Headers for the PocketBeagle

If you plan on interfacing the PocketBeagle to electronic circuits, then the first thing you need to do is add male or female header pins to the P1/P2 expansion headers, as these are unpopulated. Depending on your application you can use two 2 × 18 female (2.54mm/0.1" spacing) headers or break-away male strip headers (2.54mm/0.1" spacing) that can be cut to 2 × 18 size, as illustrated in Figure 1-6(a). These can be mounted on the top side or bottom side of the PocketBeagle; however, the headers do not fit well against the OSD3358 module when mounted on the top side. The bottom side also has a useful pin identifier key, as illustrated in Figure 1-5. Surprisingly, the dimensions of the OSD3358 module also means that the component side of the board sits flat on a work surface. Therefore, my preference is to mount the pins on the bottom side, as illustrated in Figure 1-6(b).

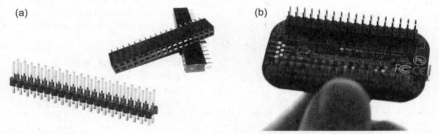

Figure 1-6: (a) Female and male header connectors; (b) the PocketBeagle with male headers soldered to the bottom of the board

In my experience, female headers are safer to use than male headers, as it is easy to accidentally short across two male header pins when these are stacked in a 2 × 18 array. And, you can connect to female headers simply with strands of wire.

> **NOTE** When soldering the male or female headers to the PocketBeagle, begin with the pins that are closest to the OSD3358 module. While slightly more expensive, four 1 × 18 headers make the soldering process more straightforward. Use a breadboard to help keep the header pins aligned and vertical.

Micro-SD Card (for Booting or Flashing eMMCs)

A micro-SD card enables you to boot any board or write a new Linux image to a board that has an eMMC. If you have a BeagleBone, then the card can be important if you accidently damage the Linux file system during your experimentation, as the micro-SD card will enable you to restore your system using a "flasher" configuration. Ideally, you should have two dedicated SD cards, one for a boot image and one for a flasher configuration. Be careful not to mix them up!

Purchase a genuine, branded micro-SD card of at least 4GB capacity. Ideally you should use an 8–64GB micro-SD card with wear-levelling functionality. Larger micro-SD cards also work, but these may be cost prohibitive—alternative approaches to increasing the storage capacity include the use of USB storage devices.

You may also require a micro-SD-to-SD adapter so that it can be used in your computer's card reader. Many micro-SD cards are bundled with the adapter, which is a cheaper option than purchasing them separately. The micro-SD card should be of Class 10 or greater, as the faster read/write speed will save you time in writing images in particular. A blank micro-SD card can also be used for additional file system storage (discussed in Chapter 3), so the greater the card capacity, the better.

ADDING A SECOND USB PORT TO THE POCKETBEAGLE

The PocketBeagle has a single USB port, which makes it difficult to power the board, connect to it over serial USB, and configure it to use a Wi-Fi adapter simultaneously. You can easily add a second USB port to the PocketBeagle for as little as $0.20 using the adapter boards that are illustrated in Figure 1-7(a), which can be wired to the PocketBeagle as illustrated in Figure 1-7(b) and Figure 1-7(c). The PocketBeagle pins used in these figures are configured to act as a USB port by default, but you may need to reboot the board for the port to be enabled. You can check that your USB device is detected using the lsusb command. For example, when a USB memory key is plugged into a USB A module, it will result in an output such as the following:

```
debian@ebb:~$ lsusb
Bus 002 Device 002: ID 13fe:4100 Kingston Tech Company Inc. Flash drive
Bus 002 Device 001: ID 1d6b:0002 Linux Foundation 2.0 root hub
Bus 001 Device 001: ID 1d6b:0002 Linux Foundation 2.0 root hub
```

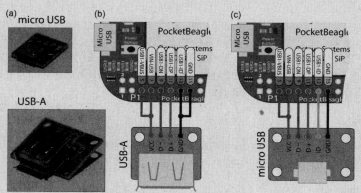

Figure 1-7: Adding low-cost USB socket adapters to the PocketBeagle to add a second USB device, (a) a micro USB and USB-A module; (b) a USB-A wiring configuration; (c) a micro USB wiring configuration

External 5V Power Supply (for Peripherals)

You can power the boards directly using the USB connection from your desktop/ laptop computer to the USB client connector on the boards. For getting started, that is perfectly fine; however, once you begin to connect accessories such as Wi-Fi adapters, USB cameras, or on-board displays, it is possible that the power available over USB will not be sufficient for your configuration.

You can purchase a 5V DC regulated switching power supply that plugs directly into a mains socket. It should have a minimum DC output current of 1A. However, you should aim for a 2A current supply (2A × 5V=10W), if possible.

The BeagleBone Blue requires a 12V DC power supply with an output current of 3A. The 5V barrel connector (5.5mm diameter) from the supplies should be center positive in all cases.

Ethernet Cable (for Wired BBB Network Connection)

The Beagle boards can use a special networking mode, called internet-over-USB, to create a virtual network between the board and your desktop; however, if you are connecting the BBB to your home network, then you can use a Cat5 network patch cable to connect your BBB to the network using its RJ45 10/100 Ethernet connector. If you are planning to use more than one BBB simultaneously and network stability is important to your application, you could invest in a low-cost multi-port switch, which can be placed close to your desktop computer.

HDMI Cable (for Connection to Monitors/Televisions)

Several Beagle boards have a HDMI framer and connector that can be easily connected to a monitor or television that has an HDMI or DVI connector. The BBB has a micro-HDMI socket (HDMI-D), so be careful to match that to your monitor/television type (usually HDMI-A or DVI-D). The cable you are likely to need is a "HDMI-Micro-D Plug to HDMI-A Male Plug." A 1.8m (6ft.) cable should cost no more than $10. Be careful with your purchase—an HDMI-C (mini-HDMI) connector will *not* fit the BBB.

Alternatively, you can purchase a low-cost ($3) micro-HDMI (HDMI-D) plug to regular HDMI (HDMI-A) socket adapters or micro-HDMI (HDMI-D) plug to DVI-D socket adapter cables. These enable you to use regular-size HDMI-A or to connect to DVI-D devices, respectively (see Figure 1-8(a)).

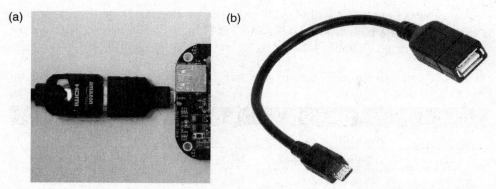

Figure 1-8: (a) BBB connected to micro-HDMI-to-HDMI adapter and then to a low-cost HDMI-A-to-DVI-D cable; (b) a USB OTG connector with the PocketBeagle

USB to Serial UART TTL 3.3 (for Finding Problems)

The USB-to-serial UART TTL serial cable is one accessory that is really useful when there are problems with the Linux installation on your board. It can provide you with a console interface to the board, without the need for connection to an external display and keyboard.

Please ensure that you purchase the *3.3V level* version and ideally purchase a version with six one-way 0.1" female headers pre-attached so that it can be used with the BeagleBone or the PocketBeagle. This cable contains a chipset and requires that you install drivers on your desktop computer, creating a new COM port. The FTDI TTL-232R-3V3 cable, as displayed in Figure 1-9(a), works well and provides a stable connection (about $20). See tiny.cc/beagle106 for the datasheet and the "VCP" link to the software drivers for this adapter cable. Cheaper alternatives are available ($0.60), such as CH340G chipset devices as illustrated in Figure 1-9(c), but be careful that you set the voltage selector to be 3.3V.

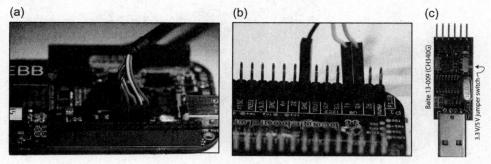

Figure 1-9: (a) The USB-to-TTL 3.3V serial cable; (b) its connection to the BBB (connection colors are black, brown, red, orange, yellow, and green); and (c) a low-cost USB-to-TTL connector

The cable connects to a serial UART on the BeagleBone or PocketBeagle boards. With your Beagle board powered using a regular USB 5V supply, connect the cable as described in Table 1-3, and as illustrated in Figure 1-9(b).

Table 1-3: Serial Debug Connections from the FTDI Cable to the BeagleBone or the PocketBeagle Board

FUNCTION	FTDI CABLE	BEAGLEBONE	POCKETBEAGLE
Ground	Black GND wire	Pin 1 J1 Header GND	GND P1 Header
TX→RX	Orange transmit wire	Pin 4 J1 Header RXD	U0 RX P1 Header
RX←TX	Yellow receive wire	Pin 5 J1 Header TXD	U0 TX P1 Header

Please note that the expansion headers are described in detail in Chapter 6. If you are planning to flash your own images to the BeagleBone or if you have a board that is not booting, I recommend you purchase one of these cables. The use of this cable is discussed in Chapter 2 and Chapter 3.

> **WARNING** The Beagle boards are 3.3V tolerant (and 1.8V in the case of some pins) but also have a 5V supply available on header pins. The easiest way to destroy your board is to accidentally connect these pins to a circuit that requires 3.3V logic levels or to accidentally short these pins with other pins on the GPIO header. Please be especially careful when working with the 5V pins.

Optional Accessories

The following sections describe optional accessories that you may need, depending on the applications that you are developing (see Figure 1-10).

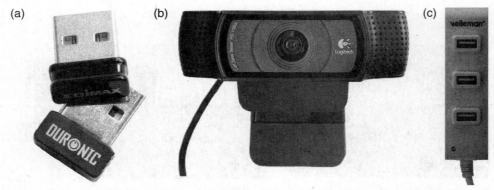

Figure 1-10: (a) USB Wi-Fi adapters; (b) the Logitech C920 camera; (c) a Velleman USB hub (bus powered)

USB Hub (to Connect Several USB Devices to a USB Host)

If you are planning to connect more than one USB device to your board at the same time, then you will need a USB hub. USB hubs are either bus powered or externally powered. Externally powered hubs are more expensive; however, if you are powering several power-hungry adapters (Wi-Fi in particular), then you may need a powered hub. Ensure that you plug the USB hub into the Beagle board host connector *before* powering on the Beagle board. I have tried different brands of USB hub and these have all worked without difficulty.

Micro-HDMI to VGA Adapters (for VGA Video and Sound)

Several low-cost micro-HDMI-to-VGA adapters are for sale (e.g., on Amazon or eBay) for converting the HDMI output to a VGA output. As well as providing for VGA video output, many of these connectors provide a separate 3.5mm audio line out, which can be used if you want to play audio using your BeagleBone, without requiring a television, high-end amplifier, or monitor. There are also USB audio adapters available that can provide high-quality playback and recording functionality. These adapters and their usage are described in Chapter 14.

Wi-Fi Adapters (for Wireless Networking)

The BeagleBone Wireless boards have on-board Wi-Fi, but for the BBB and PocketBeagle you can use a USB Wi-Fi adapter. Many different adapters are available, such as those in Figure 1-10(a); however, not all adapters will work under Linux. The Linux distribution and the chipset inside the adapter will determine the likelihood of success. You can find a list of adapters that are confirmed as working at `tiny.cc/beagle107`. However, please be aware that manufacturers can change chipsets within the same product and that buying an adapter from the list does not guarantee that it will work. You are more likely to succeed if you can confirm the chipset in the adapter you are planning to purchase, and evaluate that against the list. Wi-Fi configuration and applications are discussed in detail in Chapter 12, which tests a range of different low-cost adapters that are widely available.

USB Webcam (for Capturing Images and Streaming Video)

Attaching a USB webcam can be a low-cost method of integrating image and video capture into your projects. In addition, utilizing Linux libraries such as Video 4 Linux and Open Source Computer Vision (OpenCV) enables you to build "seeing" applications.

In Chapter 14, different webcams are examined, but the text focuses on the use of the Logitech C920 webcam in particular for video streaming applications (see Figure 1-10(b)). This is a relatively pricey webcam (at about $70), but it is capable of streaming full HD video directly when using the Beagle boards, as it has H.264/MPG-4 hardware encoding built into the camera. This greatly reduces the workload for the board, allowing the processor to be available for other tasks. As with Wi-Fi adapters, it would be useful to confirm that a webcam works under Linux before you purchase it for that specific purpose. We'll look at several camera types in Chapter 14.

USB Keyboard and Mouse (for General-Purpose Computing)

It is possible to connect a USB keyboard and mouse separately to a USB hub or to use a 2.4GHz wireless keyboard and mouse combination. Small wireless handheld combinations are available, such as the iPazzPort Wireless Mini, Rii i8, and eSynic mini, all of which include a handheld keyboard with integrated touchpad. A USB Bluetooth adapter is also useful for connecting peripherals to the board.

Capes

Capes are daughter boards that can be attached to the P8/P9 expansion headers on the BeagleBone boards or the P1/P2 expansion headers on the PocketBeagle. These are called *capes* (as in Superman's cape) because of the shape of the boards as these wrap around the RJ45 Ethernet connector on the BBB. You can connect up to four capes at any one time when the capes are compatible with each other.

Some capes use a significant number of pins. For example, you will look at the LCD4 cape in Chapter 13. The LCD4 cape uses the P8 header pins 27 through 46 and some of the analog inputs for its buttons and resistive touch interface. If you are using the eMMC for booting the BBB, then few pins remain for GPIO use. In addition, the LCD cape does not carry forward the pin headers. Figure 1-11 shows two views of this cape when connected to the BBB, running the standard Debian Linux distribution. Similar issues arise with other capes.

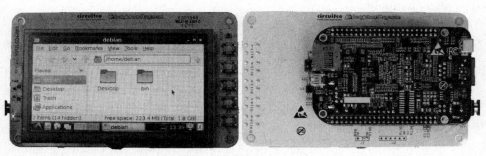

Figure 1-11: The LCD4 cape (top and bottom view)

More than 100 capes are currently available for the BeagleBone and Pocket-Beagle boards; you can find a full list at www.beagleboard.org/cape. Here is a selection of some example capes that you might find useful in your projects:

- The LCD capes are available in different sizes: 7" (800×480), 4" (480×272), and 3" (320×240), with the 4" version captured in Figure 1-11. These have resistive touch screens, meaning you use a stylus (or fingernail) to interact with the screens. This is different than the capacitive touch screens on recent phones/tablets. The Manga Screen 2 is a HDMI-compatible multi-touch LCD screen alternative that is available in a 4.8" (720p) or 5.9" (1080p) version. See tiny.cc/beagle108.

- The Adafruit Proto cape, as illustrated in Figure 1-12(a), is a low-cost (~$10) bare cape, which you can use to transfer your breadboard design to a more solid platform. Several other breadboard and prototyping capes are available for the BeagleBone and PocketBeagle boards. One particularly notable cape is the BaconBits cape (tiny.cc/beagle110), which adds seven-segment displays, an accelerometer, LEDs, POTs, buttons, and a USB-to-serial bridge to the PocketBeagle.

- The Replicape ($179) is an impressive open-source 3D printer cape that has five stepper motor drivers, including micro-stepping support. See www.thing-printer.com for more information.

(a) 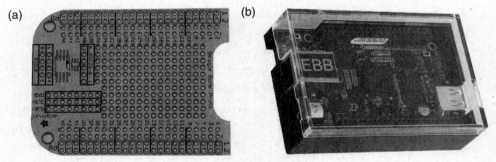 (b)

Figure 1-12: (a) The Proto cape; (b) a suitable enclosure case

You have to be careful about compatibility when interconnecting capes. There is a compatibility table covering the more common capes at tiny.cc/beagle109. The preceding list is just a small selection. Many more capes are available, and it is likely that additional capes will be developed over time.

How to Destroy Your Board!

The Beagle boards are complex and delicate devices that are easily damaged if you do not show due care. If you are moving up from boards like the Arduino to the Beagle platform, then you must be especially careful when connecting circuits that you built for that platform. Unlike the Arduino Uno, the microprocessor on the boards cannot be replaced—if you damage the SoC or SiP, you will need to buy a new board!

Here are some things that you should *never* do:

- Do not shut the board down by pulling out the power jack/USB power. Correctly shut the board down by using a software shutdown (e.g., by pressing the power button once) or by holding the power button for about eight seconds for a "hard" power down. This enables the power management IC (PMIC) to shut down the board correctly. If you need to remove power by disconnecting the power supply, hold the reset button while doing so to lower system power usage.

- Do not place a powered board on metal surfaces (e.g., aluminum-finish computers) or on worktops with stray/cut-off wire segments, resistors, etc. If you short the pins (or the solder points) on the expansion headers, you can easily destroy your board. You can buy a case from suppliers such as Adafruit (see Figure 1-12(b)). Alternatively, you can attach small rubber feet to the board.

- Do not connect circuits that source/sink other than very low currents from/to the expansion headers. The maximum current that you can source from many of these header pins is 4-6mA and the maximum current you can sink is 8mA. The power rail and ground pins can source and sink larger currents. The Arduino allows currents of 40mA on each input/output. This issue is covered in Chapter 4 and Chapter 6.

- The GPIO pins are 3.3V tolerant (most of the ADCs are 1.8V tolerant). Do not connect a circuit that is powered at 5V or you will destroy the board. This is discussed in Chapter 4, Chapter 6, and Chapter 8.

- Do not connect circuits that apply power to the expansion header while the board is not powered on. Make sure that all self-powered interfacing circuits are gated by the 3.3V supply line or through the use of optocouplers. This is covered in Chapter 6.

Here are two steps that you should *always* follow:

- Carefully check the pin numbers you are using. There is a large number of pins in each header, and it is easy to plug into header connector 17 instead of 15. For connections in the middle of the headers, I always count twice—up from the left and down from the right.

- Read the SRM for your board in detail before connecting complex circuits of your own design.

If your board is dead and it *is* your fault, then I'm afraid that after you perform all the checks at www.beagleboard.org/support, you will have to purchase a new board. If it *is not* your fault, then see the BBB/PocketBeagle SRM manual and www.beagleboard.org/support website to return a defective board for repair by requesting a return merchandise authorization (RMA) number.

Summary

After completing this chapter, you should be able to do the following:

- Describe the capability of the Beagle boards and their suitability for different project types
- Source the important documents that will assist you in working with the Beagle platform
- Describe the major hardware systems and subsystems on the different boards
- Identify important peripherals and accessories that you can buy to enhance the capability of your board
- Have an appreciation of the power and complexity of the Beagle boards as physical computing devices
- Be aware of the first steps to take in protecting your boards from physical damage

Support

The key sources of additional support documentation were listed earlier in this chapter. If you are having difficulty with the Beagle platform and the issues are not described in the documentation, then you should use these two resources:

- The BeagleBoard Google Group, which is available at groups.google.com/d/forum/beagleboard. Please read the frequently asked questions (FAQs) and search the current questions before posting a new question.
- There is a live chat available at www.beagleboard.org/chat or directly on the Beagle IRC channel (by joining #beagle on irc.freenode.net) using a free IRC client such as X-Chat for Linux, HexChat for Windows, or Colloquy for macOS.

Please remember that the people in this group and IRC channel are community members who volunteer their time to respond to questions.

Beagle Software

In this chapter, you are introduced to the Linux operating system and software tools that can be used with the Beagle boards. This chapter aims to ensure that you can connect to your board and control it. By the end of this chapter, you should be able to "blink" a system LED having followed a step-by-step guide that demonstrates how you can use Linux shell commands in a Linux terminal window. In this chapter, you are also introduced to a library of software functions, called BoneScript, which can be used with Node.js and the Cloud9 integrated development environment to build code that flashes the same system LED.

EQUIPMENT REQUIRED FOR THIS CHAPTER:

- Any Beagle board
- USB cable (typically USB A male to mini- or micro-USB A male)
- Micro-SD card (4GB or greater; Class 10+)
- Network infrastructure and cabling (optional)

Further details on this chapter are available here:
www.exploringbeaglebone.com/chapter2/.

Linux on the Beagle Boards

A *Linux distribution* is a publicly available version of Linux that is packaged with a set of software programs and tools. There are many different Linux distributions, which are typically focused on different applications. For example, high-end server owners might install Red Hat Enterprise, CentOS, Debian, or OpenSUSE; desktop users might install Ubuntu, Debian, Fedora, or Linux Mint. The list is endless, but at the core of all distributions is a common Linux kernel, which was conceived and created by Linus Torvalds in 1991.

In deciding on a Linux distribution to use for your embedded system platform, it is sensible to choose one with these attributes:

- The distribution is stable and well supported.
- There is a good package manager.
- The distribution is lean and suited to a low storage footprint for embedded devices.
- There is good community support for your particular device.
- There is device driver support for any peripherals you want to attach.

Linux Distributions for Beagle Boards

There are many different distributions of Linux for embedded system platforms, including expensive proprietary versions for real-time programming. At their heart, they all use the mainline Linux kernel, but each distribution contains different tools and configurations that result in quite different user experiences. The main open-source distributions used by the community on the Beagle boards include Debian, Ångström, Ubuntu, and Arch Linux.

Debian (a contraction of "Debbie and Ian") is a community-driven Linux distribution that has an emphasis on open-source development. There is no commercial organization involved in the development of Debian; in fact, there is a formal social contract (`tiny.cc/beagle201`) that states that Debian will remain entirely free (as in software freedom). The Debian distribution is used for many of the practical steps in this book; in fact, it is recommended as the distribution of choice for the Beagle boards, and it is currently distributed with new BeagleBone boards. In addition, Debian is used throughout this book as the distribution for the Linux desktop computer, as it provides excellent support for cross-platform development through Debian Cross-Toolchains (see `wiki .debian.org/CrossToolchains`). Currently, there are different versions of Debian available for download from the BeagleBoard.org website.

- *Debian Stretch LXQt*, which has the Lightweight Qt Desktop (LXQt) environment installed. This version should be used if you are attaching the board to a monitor or an LCD panel.

- *Debian Stretch IoT,* which is a headless image that has a much smaller footprint on the micro-SD card and (of greater consequence) the eMMC of a BeagleBone.

Ångström is a stable and lean Linux distribution that is widely used on embedded systems. The team of developers behind Ångström is experienced in customizing Linux distributions for embedded devices such as set-top boxes, mobile devices, and networking devices. Impressively, Ångström can scale down to devices with only megabytes of flash storage. Ångström makes extensive use of *BusyBox,* a multicall binary (a single executable that can do the job of many) used to create a compact version of command-line utilities that are found on Linux systems. Many of my YouTube videos use Ångström, as it was the primary distribution for the BeagleBone for quite some time.

Ubuntu is closely related to Debian; in fact, it is described on the Ubuntu website (www.ubuntu.com) as follows: "Debian is the rock upon which Ubuntu is built." Ubuntu is one of the most popular desktop Linux distributions, mainly because of its focus on making Linux more accessible to new users. It is easy to install and has excellent desktop driver support, and there are binary distributions available for the Beagle boards.

Arch Linux is a lightweight and flexible Linux distribution that aims to "keep it simple," targeting competent Linux users in particular by giving them complete control and responsibility over the system configuration. There are prebuilt versions of the Arch Linux distribution available for the Beagle boards; however, compared to the other distributions, it currently has less support for new Linux users (see www.archlinux.org).

> **NOTE**   Don't be too worried that you might damage the Linux file system when you are practicing with the Beagle boards. In the worst case, you might have to write a new Linux image to the micro-SD card or to the eMMC. It takes about 20–45 minutes to write the image to the board. There is a guide to writing a new image to the BeagleBone eMMC on the chapter web page at www.exploringbeaglebone.com/chapter2/.

Create a Linux Micro-SD Card Image

The easiest way to set up an SD card so that it can be used to boot the PocketBeagle or other Beagle boards is to download a Linux distribution image file (.img file in a compressed .xz wrapper) from beagleboard.org/latest-images and write it to an SD card using an image writer utility such as Etcher (etcher.io). Etcher is particularly useful because it can use the compressed image file directly. The application is available for Windows, Mac, and Linux host machines.

> **WARNING** All previous content on the micro-SD card is lost after performing this action. Please double-check that you are writing the downloaded image to the correct device on your desktop machine when using the Etcher tool.

Communicating with the Boards

When you are ready to try your Beagle board, the first thing you should do is connect it to your desktop computer using a USB lead. After you apply power, the board will connect to the desktop in USB client mode. Once it's connected and discovered, your file manager, such as Windows Explorer, will display the contents of the board's FAT partition, as shown in Figure 2-1. The BeagleBoard.org team has put together a really excellent HTML guide on getting started with your board. You should double-click the START.htm file to display the guide, which is illustrated in Figure 2-1, within a web browser.

Figure 2-1: The START.htm guide to setting up your board (running under Windows 10)

> **NOTE** Earlier versions of Linux on the Beagle boards had important boot files, such as MLO, u-boot.img, and uEnv.txt, on the FAT partition shown in Figure 2-1. In recent images, these files have moved to the /boot/ directory on the Linux partition and to a hidden partition, which means they cannot be edited directly from Windows.

Installing Drivers

Follow the steps in the guide displayed in Figure 2-1. With the latest Beagle board Linux images you should no longer have to install drivers for your operating system. If you have an older image and need to install drivers, browse to the

`Drivers` folder and install the correct version. Once the board is fully booted, several new devices should be available on your desktop computer. For example, you will now have the following devices:

- Access to the FAT partition of the board (like a USB memory key).
- Serial access to the board using a new *Gadget Serial* driver COM port.
- A *Linux USB Ethernet/RNDIS Gadget* (for internet-over-USB). RNDIS stands for Remote Network Driver Interface Specification.

These new devices can be used to connect to the board. As you progress through the guide while the board is attached to your PC, the guide will highlight active connections, as illustrated in Figure 2-2. Similar steps for Linux and Mac desktop computers are available in the startup guide.

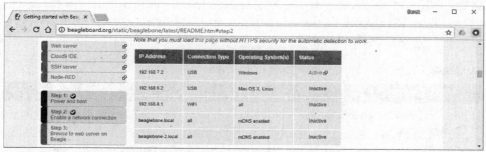

Figure 2-2: The `START.htm` guide will highlight active connections

Wired Network Connections

There are three main ways to connect to and communicate with the board over a wired network, each with its own advantages and disadvantages. The first way is to use *internet-over-USB*, which creates a "private" virtual LAN using a single USB cable. This approach works for all Beagle boards, but the following approaches require a board that has an Ethernet adapter. The second way is to use *regular Ethernet*, and the third is to use an *Ethernet crossover cable*. Connecting to the board over a network can be a stumbling block for beginners. It is usually straightforward if you are working at home with control of your own network; however, complex networks, such as those in universities, can have multiple subnets for wired and wireless communication. In such complex networks, routing restrictions may make it difficult, if not impossible, to connect to the board over regular Ethernet.

NOTE Several boards have on-board Wi-Fi capabilities, but you may need to connect to the board over an internet-over-USB or serial connection to configure Wi-Fi for connection to your network. The default Wi-Fi address is 192.168.8.1, as listed in Figure 2-2.

To modify the configuration files for a Wi-Fi adapter, you can use the USB-to-TTL cable that is described in the next section. Once you have a wired connection to the board, jump to Chapter 12 on configuring Wi-Fi, before continuing from this point.

Alternatively, you could mount the micro-SD card for the target board under a desktop Linux OS (or another booted BeagleBone) and modify the configuration files directly.

Internet-over-USB (All Boards)

The standard BeagleBoard.org Linux distributions provide support for internet-over-USB using the Linux USB Ethernet/RNDIS Gadget device. For new users and for users within complex network infrastructures, this is probably the best way to get started with your board. For this setup you need only the board, a USB cable, and access to a desktop computer, ideally with administrator access levels. Table 2-1 describes the advantages and disadvantages of internet-over-USB for connecting to a board.

Table 2-1: Advantages and Disadvantages of Internet-over-USB

ADVANTAGES	DISADVANTAGES
Provides a stable network setup for beginners.	Without significant effort, you are limited to a single board per desktop.
When you do not have access to, or control of, network infrastructure hardware, you can still connect the board to the internet.	Network sharing configuration can be difficult, especially on Macintosh desktop computers. Additional configuration must also be performed on the board's Linux OS.
Power is supplied by your desktop machine over USB.	Your desktop machine must be running to transfer data to/from the internet.

NOTE By default, with internet-over-USB, the board has the fixed IP address 192.168.7.2 under Windows and 192.168.6.2 under macOS and Linux. From the perspective of the Beagle board, the desktop machine has the fixed address 192.168.7.1 under Windows and 192.168.6.1 under macOS and Linux.

For example, if you fully installed the board drivers under Windows, you should now have a new network connection (click Start, type **view network status and tasks**, and select "Change adapter settings"). Figure 2-3 shows a typical Network Connections window under Windows. In this case, "Ethernet 3" is the Linux USB Ethernet/RNDIS Gadget device. The desktop computer remains connected to your regular LAN (via Ethernet 2 in my case), which provides access to the internet and to a new private LAN that contains only the desktop computer (e.g., 192.168.7.1) and your board (e.g., 192.168.7.2). You can open a web browser and connect to the board's web server by typing **192.168.7.2** (or **192.168.6.2** on a Mac/Linux machine) in the address bar, as illustrated in Figure 2-3.

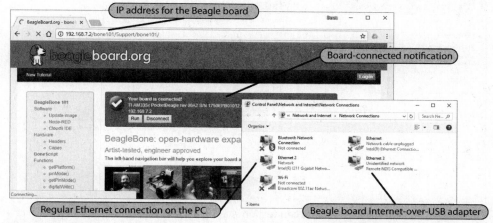

Figure 2-3: Windows network connections with Internet-over-USB connection and a web browser connection

At this point, you can connect to the board's web server using a web browser so you have a fully functional private network; however, you may also want the board to have full direct access to the internet so that you can download files and update Linux software directly on the board. To do this, you need to share your main network adapter so that traffic from the board can be routed through your desktop machine to the internet. For example, under Windows, use the following steps:

1. Choose your desktop/laptop network adapter that provides you with internet access. Right-click it and choose Properties.

2. In the dialog that appears, as shown on the left side of Figure 2-4, click the Sharing tab at the top and enable the option "Allow other network users...."

3. In the drop-down list, choose your private LAN (e.g., referring to Figure 2-4, this is "Ethernet 3" in my case). Click OK.

4. Right-click the private LAN (e.g., Ethernet 3) and select Properties.

5. Double-click Internet Protocol Version 4. In this dialog, select "Obtain an IP address automatically" and enable "Obtain DNS server address automatically" (see Figure 2-4 on the right side).

6. Click OK and then Close to save the configurations.

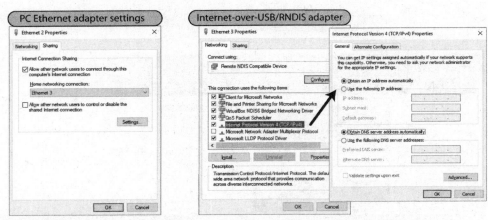

Figure 2-4: Configuring the network connection sharing properties under Windows

The steps are similar under macOS using Apple Menu ⇨ System Preferences ⇨ Sharing. If all goes well, you will not have noticed any difference at this point, and you should be able to reload the web page that is shown in Figure 2-3. It can take about one minute for the network configuration to finalize. Please note that the impact of the last two steps can be appreciated only when you open a terminal connection to the board.

> **WARNING** If you are planning to jump ahead, there is one more step to complete before your board will be able to "see" the internet. This change, which has to be made directly on the board, is covered later in this chapter in the section titled "What Time Is It?" Please note it may be necessary to unshare and reshare the internet connection if you are having internet connectivity problems, which may arise if the shared connection is used over a number of days.

NETWORK SHARING FOR LINUX DESKTOP USERS

The settings for a Linux desktop to enable network sharing are as follows:

1. With the internet-over-USB device attached, type `ifconfig` or `ip addr` in a terminal, which results in a display of the attached network interfaces.

2. Find your main adapter (e.g., `eth0`) and internet-over-USB adapter (e.g., `eth1`).

3. Use the `iptables` **program to configure the Linux kernel firewall rules.**

```
molloyd@debian:~$ sudo iptables --table nat --append POSTROUTING
--out-interface
eth0 -j MASQUERADE
molloyd@debian:~$ sudo iptables --append FORWARD --in-interface eth1 -j
ACCEPT
```

4. **Then, use the following command to turn on IP forwarding:**

```
molloyd@debian:~$ sudo sh -c "echo 1 > /proc/sys/net/ipv4/ip_forward"
```

Regular Ethernet (BBB and BeagleBoard Only)

By "regular" Ethernet, I mean connecting the board to a network in the same way you would connect your desktop computer using a wired connection. For the home user and power user of the BeagleBone Black (BBB), regular Ethernet is probably the best solution for networking and connecting to the board. Table 2-2 lists the advantages and disadvantages of using this type of connection. The main issue is the complexity of the network—if you understand your network configuration and have access to the router settings, then this is by far the best configuration. If your network router is distant from your desktop computer, you can use a small network switch, which can be purchased for as little as $10–$20. Alternatively, you could purchase a wireless access point with an integrated multiport router for $25–$35 so that you can integrate BeagleBone Black Wireless (BBBW) boards.

Table 2-2: Regular Ethernet Advantages and Disadvantages

ADVANTAGES	DISADVANTAGES
You have full control over IP address settings and dynamic/static IP settings.	You might need administrative control or knowledge of the network infrastructure.
You can connect and interconnect many BBBs to a single network (including wireless devices).	The BBB needs a source of power (which can be a mains-powered adapter).
The BBB can connect to the internet without a desktop computer being powered on.	The setup is more complex for beginners if the network structure is complex.

The first challenge with this configuration is finding your BBB on the network. By default, the board is configured to request a *Dynamic Host Configuration Protocol* (DHCP) IP address. In a home network environment, this service is usually provided by a DHCP server that is running on the integrated modem-firewall-router-LAN (or some similar configuration) that connects the home to an internet service provider (ISP).

DHCP servers issue IP addresses dynamically from a pool of addresses for a fixed time interval, called the *lease time*, which is specified in your DHCP configuration. When this lease expires, your board is allocated a different IP address the next time it connects to your network. This can be frustrating, as you may have to search for your board on the network again. It is possible to set the IP address of your board to be *static* so that it is fixed at the same address each time the board connects. Wireless connections and static IP connections are discussed in Chapter 12.

There are a few different ways to find your board's dynamic IP address.

- Use a web browser to access your home router (often address 192.168.1.1, 192.168.0.1, or 10.0.0.1). Log in and look under a menu such as Status for DHCP Table. You should see an entry that details the allocated IP address, the physical MAC address, and the lease time remaining for a device with hostname `beaglebone`. Here's an example:

```
Leased Table
IP Address        MAC Address Client    Host Name    Register Information
192.168.1.116     c8:a0:30:c0:6b:48     beaglebone   Remains 23:59:51
```

- Use a port-scanning tool like `nmap` under Linux or the *Zenmap* GUI version that is available for Windows (see `tiny.cc/beagle202`). The command `nmap -T4 -F 192.168.1.*` will scan for devices on a subnet. You are searching for an entry that typically has five open ports (e.g., 22 for SSH, 53 for DNS, 80 for the BeagleBoard.org web guide, 3000 for the Cloud 9 IDE, and 8080 for an Apache web server). It should also identify itself with Texas Instruments.

- You could use a serial-over-USB connection to connect to the board and type **ifconfig** to find the IP address. The address is the `inet addr` value associated with the `eth0` adapter. This is discussed shortly.

Once you have the IP address, you can test that it is valid by entering it in the address bar of your web browser (it's `192.168.1.116` in the previous example). Your browser should display the same page shown in Figure 2-3.

Ethernet Crossover Cable (BBB and BeagleBoard Only)

An Ethernet crossover cable is a cable that has been modified to enable two Ethernet devices to be connected directly together, without the need for an Ethernet switch. It can be purchased as a cable or as a plug-in adapter. Table 2-3 describes the advantages and disadvantages of this connection type.

Table 2-3: Crossover Cable Network Advantages and Disadvantages

ADVANTAGES	DISADVANTAGES
When you do not have access to network infrastructure hardware, you can still connect to the BBB.	If your desktop machine has only one network adapter, then you will lose access to the internet. It is best used with a device that has multiple adapters.
BBB may have internet access if the desktop has two network adapters.	BBB still needs a source of power (can be a mains-powered adapter).
Provides a reasonably stable network setup.	Replicates the functionality of internet-over-USB, so try that approach first.

Most modern desktop machines have an automatic crossover detection function (Auto-MDIX) that enables a regular Ethernet cable to be used. The network interface on the Beagle boards also supports Auto-MDIX; therefore, this connection type can be used when you do not have access to network infrastructure. If you have two network adapters on your desktop machine (e.g., a laptop with a wired and wireless network adapter), then you can easily share the connection to the internet with your BBB by bridging both adapters. For example, these are the steps that you must take under the Windows OS:

1. Plug one end of a regular (or crossover) Ethernet cable into the BBB and the other end into a laptop Ethernet socket.

2. Power on the BBB by attaching a USB power supply.

3. You can then bridge the two network connections—under Windows click Start, type **view network status** and tasks, select "Change adapter settings," select the two network adapters (wired and wireless) at the same time, right-click, and choose Bridge Connections. After some time, the two connections should appear with the status "Enabled, Bridged," and a network bridge should appear.

4. Reboot the BBB. Once the board has rebooted, it should obtain an IP address directly from the DHCP server of your network.

You can then communicate with the BBB directly from anywhere on your network (including the PC/laptop itself) using the steps described in the next section. This connection type is particularly useful inside complex network infrastructures such as those in universities, as the laptop can connect to the BBB using the address that it is assigned. The BBB can also continue to connect to the internet.

Communicating with Your Board

Once you have networked the board, the next thing you will want to do is communicate with it. You can connect to the Beagle board using either a serial connection over USB, USB-to-TTL, or a network connection, such as that just discussed. The network connection should be your main focus, as that type of connection provides your board with full internet access. The serial connection is generally used as a fallback connection when problems arise with the network connection. As such, you may skip the next section, but the information is here as a reference for when problems arise.

> **NOTE**   The default login details for Debian are username debian with the password *temppwd*. Under Ubuntu use ubuntu/temppwd. Ångström and Arch Linux have username root and no password (just press Enter).

Serial Connection over USB

If you installed the device drivers for the Beagle board in the previous section, the *Gadget Serial device* will allow you to connect to the board directly using a terminal emulator program. Serial connections are particularly useful when the board is close to your desktop computer and connected via the USB cable. It is often a fallback communications method when something goes wrong with the network configuration or software services on the board.

To connect to the board via the serial connection, you need a terminal program. Several third-party applications are available for Windows, such as RealTerm (realterm.sourceforge.io) and PuTTY (www.putty.org). PuTTY is also used in the next section. Most distributions of desktop Linux include a terminal program (try Ctrl+Alt+T or use Alt+F2 and type **gnome-terminal** under Debian). A terminal emulator is included by default under macOS (e.g., type **screen/dev/tty.usbmodemfa133 115200**).

To connect to the Beagle board over the USB serial connection, you need to know some information.

- **COM port number:** You can find this by opening the Windows Device Manager and searching under the Ports section. Figure 2-5 captures an example Device Manager, where the Gadget Serial device is listed as COM3. This will be different on different machines.

- **Speed of the connection:** By default you need to enter **115,200** baud to connect to the board.

- **Other information you may need for other terminal applications:** Data bits = 8; Stop bits = 1; Parity = none; and, Flow control = XON/XOFF.

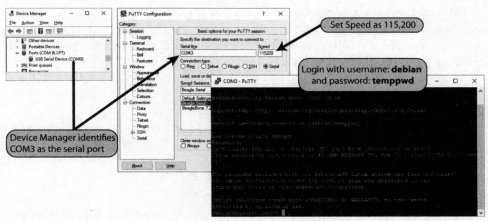

Figure 2-5: Windows Device Manager and opening a PuTTY serial connection to the board

Save the configuration with a session name so that it is available each time you want to connect. Click Open, and it is important that you *press Enter when the window appears*. When connecting to Debian, you should see the following output:

```
Debian GNU/Linux 9 beaglebone ttyGS0

BeagleBoard.org Debian Image 2018-03-05
Support/FAQ: http://elinux.org/Beagleboard:BeagleBoneBlack_Debian
default username:password is [debian:temppwd]
beaglebone login: debian
Password: temppwd
debian@beaglebone:~$
```

This allows you to log in with username `debian` and password `temppwd`.

On a Linux desktop computer, you can install the `screen` program and connect to the serial-over-USB device with these commands:

```
molloyd@debian:~$ sudo apt-get install screen
molloyd@debian:~$ screen /dev/ttyUSB0/ 115200
```

Serial Connection with the USB-to-TTL 3.3 V Cable

For this serial connection type, you need the specialized cable (or the cheaper alternative in Figure 1-9(c)) that is described in Chapter 1. Find the COM port from Windows Device Manager that is associated with a device called USB Serial Port. Plug in the cable to the six-pin connector beside the P9 header (black lead to the white dot/J1), as illustrated in Figure 1-9(a), or to the PocketBeagle expansion header as illustrated in Figure 1-9(b).

You can then open a serial connection using PuTTY (115,200 baud), and you will see the same login prompt as earlier. However, when you reboot the board, you will also see the full console output as the board boots, which begins with the following (in the case of the PocketBeagle):

```
U-Boot SPL 2018.01-00002-ge9ff418fb8 (Feb 20 2018 - 20:14:57)
Trying to boot from MMC1
U-Boot 2018.01-00002-ge9ff418fb8 (Feb 20 2018 - 20:14:57 -0600),
Build: jenkins-github_Bootloader-Builder-38
CPU  : AM335X-GP rev 2.1
I2C:   ready
DRAM:  512 MiB
...
Model: BeagleBoard.org PocketBeagle
...
```

This is the ultimate fallback connection, as it allows you to see what is happening during the boot process, which is described in the next chapter.

Connecting Through Secure Shell

Secure Shell (SSH) is a useful network protocol for secure encrypted communication between network devices. You can use an SSH terminal client to connect to the SSH server that is running on port 22 of your board, which allows you to do the following:

▪ Log in remotely to the board and execute commands

▪ Transfer files to and from the board using the *SSH File Transfer Protocol* (SFTP)

▪ Forward X11 connections, which allows you to perform virtual network computing (covered in Chapter 13)

By default, the BeagleBone Linux distributions run an SSH server (*sshd* on Debian and *Dropbear* on Ångström) that is bound to port 22. There are a few advantages in having an SSH server available as the default method by which you log in remotely to your board. In particular, you can open port 22 of the board to the internet using the port forwarding functionality of your router. Please ensure that you set a password on the root user account before doing this. You can then remotely log in to your board from anywhere in the world if you know its IP address. A service called *dynamic DNS* that is supported on most routers allows your router to register its latest address with an online service. The online service then maps a domain name of your choice to the latest IP address that your ISP has given you. The dynamic DNS service usually has an annual cost, for which it will provide you with an address of the form MyBeagle.servicename.com.

Secure Shell Connections Using PuTTY

PuTTY (www.putty.org) was mentioned earlier as a way of connecting to your board using serial-over-USB. PuTTY is a free, open-source terminal emulator, serial console, and SSH client that you can also use to connect to the board over the network. PuTTY has a few useful features.

- It supports serial and SSH connections.
- It installs an application called *psftp* that enables you to transfer files to and from the Beagle board over the network from your desktop computer.
- It supports SSH X11 forwarding, which is required in Chapter 13.

Figure 2-6 captures the PuTTY Configuration settings. Choose SSH as the connection type, enter the IP address for your board (192.168.7.2 or 192.168.6.2 if you are using internet-over-USB), use port 22 (the default), and then save the session with a useful name for future use. Click Open and log in using your username and password. You may get a security alert that warns about man-in-the-middle attacks, which may be a concern on insecure networks. Accept the fingerprint and continue. macOS and Linux users can run the Terminal application with similar settings (e.g., ssh -X root@192.168.6.2).

Figure 2-6: PuTTY SSH configuration settings on a Windows PC beside an open SSH terminal connection

You will see the basic Linux commands that can be issued later in this chapter, but first it is necessary to examine how you can transfer files to and from the board.

Chrome Apps: Secure Shell Client

The Chrome web browser has support for Chrome extensions—applications that behave like locally installed (or native) applications but are written in HTML5, JavaScript, and CSS. Many of these applications use Google's Native Client

(NaCl, or Salt!), which is a sandbox for running compiled C/C++ applications directly in the web browser, regardless of the OS. The benefit of NaCl is that applications can achieve near-native performance levels, as they can contain code that uses low-level instructions.

There is a useful Chrome extension called *Secure Shell Extension* available. Open a new tab on the Chrome browser and click the Apps icon. Go to the Chrome Web Store and search the store for *Secure Shell*. Once it is installed, it will appear as the Secure Shell App when you click the Apps icon again. When you start up the Secure Shell App, you will have to set the connection settings as in Figure 2-6, and the application will appear as in Figure 2-7.

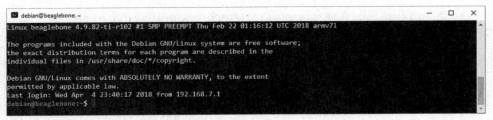

Figure 2-7: The Secure Shell Chrome extension

> **NOTE**   There is an additional terminal emulator available on the Beagle boards by default. Later in this chapter you will be introduced to the Cloud9 IDE, which also provides a web-based SSH client. You can see this in Figure 2-11 on the bottom-right side of the figure.

Transferring Files Using PuTTY/psftp over SSH

The PuTTY installation also includes File Transfer Protocol (ftp) support that enables you to transfer files to and from your board over your network connection. You can start up the *psftp* (PuTTY secure file transfer protocol) application by typing `psftp` in the Windows Start command text field.

At the `psftp>` prompt, you can connect to the board by typing `open debian@192.168.7.2` (e.g., the board address for internet-over-USB on a Windows PC). Your desktop machine is now referred to as the *local* machine, and the Beagle board is referred to as the *remote* machine. When you issue a command, you are typically issuing it on the remote machine. After connecting, you are placed in the home directory of the user account you used. Therefore, under the Debian distribution, if you connect as the user `debian`, you are placed in the `/home/Debian/` directory.

To transfer a single file `c:\temp\test.txt` from the local desktop computer to the Beagle board, you can use the following steps:

```
psftp: no hostname specified; use "open host.name" to connect
psftp> open debian@192.168.7.2
Using username "debian".
Remote working directory is /home/debian
psftp> lcd c:\temp
New local directory is c:\temp
psftp> mkdir test
mkdir /home/debian/test: OK
psftp> put test.txt
local:test.txt => remote:/home/debian/test.txt
psftp> dir test.*
Listing directory /home/debian
-rw-r--r--    1 debian    debian             0 Apr  5 00:46 test.txt
```

Commands that are prefixed with an `l` refer to commands issued for the local machine, e.g., `lcd` (local change directory) or `lpwd` (local print working directory). To transfer a single file, the `put` command is issued, which transfers the file from the local machine to the remote machine. The `get` command can be used to transfer a file in reverse. To "put" or "get" multiple files, you can use the `mput` or `mget` command. Use `help` if you have forgotten a command.

There are free GUI-based SFTP applications available for Windows, such as WinSCP, which is displayed in Figure 2-8. It can be downloaded for free from `winscp.net`. Alternatives include FileZilla (`filezilla-project.org`) and Cyberduck (`cyberduck.io`) for Windows and Mac.

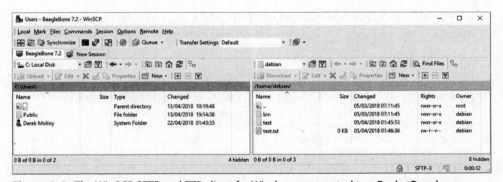

Figure 2-8: The WinSCP SFTP and FTP client for Windows connected to a PocketBeagle

If you are using a Linux client machine, you can use the command `sftp` instead of `psftp`. Almost everything else remains the same. The SFTP client application is also installed on the BeagleBoard.org Linux distribution by default, so you can reverse the order of communication, that is, having the board act as the client and another machine as the server.

Here are some useful hints and tips with the psftp/sftp commands:

- mget -r * will perform a recursive get of a directory. This is useful if you want to transfer a folder that has several subfolders. The -r option can also be used on the get, put, and mput commands.

- dir *.txt will apply a filter to display only the .txt files in the current directory.

- mv can be used to move a file/directory on the remote machine to a new location on the remote machine.

- reget can be used to resume a download that was interrupted. The partially downloaded file must exist on the local machine.

Controlling the Beagle Board

At this point you should be able to communicate with your board using an SSH client application, so this section investigates the commands that you can issue for your first interactions with this Linux SBC.

Basic Linux Commands

When you first connect to the board with SSH, you are prompted to log in. Under Debian, you can log in with username debian and password temppwd.

```
login as: debian
debian@192.168.7.2's password: temppwd
Linux beaglebone 4.9.82-ti-r102 #1 SMP PREEMPT Thu Feb 22 01:16:12 UTC
2018 armv7l The programs included with the Debian GNU/Linux system are
free software; the exact distribution terms for each program are
described in the individual files in /usr/share/doc/*/copyright.
Debian GNU/Linux comes with ABSOLUTELY NO WARRANTY, to the extent
permitted by applicable law.
Last login: Thu Apr  5 00:08:01 2018 from 192.168.7.1
debian@beaglebone:~$
```

You are now connected to the board, and the Linux terminal is ready for your command. The $ prompt means you are logged in as a regular user account (superusers have a # prompt). For a new Linux user, this step can be quite daunting, as it is not clear what arsenal of commands is at your disposal. This section provides you with sufficient Linux skills to get by. It is written as a reference with examples so that you can come back to it when you need help. Some of the commands used are described in more detail in Chapter 3.

First Steps

The first thing you might do is determine which version of Linux you are running. This can be useful when you are asking a question on a forum.

```
debian@beaglebone:~$ uname -a
Linux beaglebone 4.9.82-ti-r102 #1 SMP PREEMPT Thu Feb 22 01:16:12 UTC
2018 armv7l GNU/Linux
debian@beaglebone:~$ cat /etc/dogtag
BeagleBoard.org Debian Image 2018-03-05
```

In this case, Linux 4.9.82 is being used, which was built for the ARMv7 architecture on the date that is listed and packaged for the BeagleBoard.org image on the date that is listed in the "dog tag."

The Linux kernel version is described by numbers in the form $X.Y.Z$. The X number changes only rarely (version 3.0 was released in 2011 and 4.0 in 2015). The Y value changes several times per year (4.8 was released in October 2016 and 4.9[1] in December 2016). The Z value changes regularly.

Next, you could use the passwd command to set a nondefault debian user account password.

```
debian@beaglebone:~$ passwd
Changing password for debian.
(current) UNIX password: temppwd
Enter new UNIX password: newpasswd
Retype new UNIX password: newpasswd
passwd: password updated successfully
```

Table 2-4 lists other useful first-step commands.

Table 2-4: Useful First Commands in Linux

COMMAND	DESCRIPTION
more /etc/issue	Returns the Linux distribution you are using.
ps -p $$	Returns the shell you are currently using (e.g., bash).
whoami	Returns who you are currently logged in as (e.g., debian).
uptime	Returns how long the system has been running.
top	Lists all the processes and programs executing. Press Ctrl+C to close the view.

---

[1]Interestingly, release 4.9 included explicit support for the Raspberry Pi Zero, the BeagleBoard-X15 rev B1, and additional ARM-based processors. It also came with significant networking and file system improvements.

Basic File System Commands

This section describes the basic commands that you will need to move around on, and manipulate, a Linux file system. When using Debian and Ubuntu user accounts, you often must prefix the word sudo at the start of certain commands. That is because sudo is a program that allows users to run programs with the security privileges of the superuser. User accounts are discussed in the next chapter. For the moment, the basic file system commands that you need are listed in Table 2-5.

Table 2-5: Basic File System Commands

NAME	COMMAND	OPTIONS AND FURTHER INFORMATION	EXAMPLE(S)
List files	ls	-a shows all (including hidden files).	ls -al
		-l displays long format.	
		-R gives a recursive listing.	
		-r gives a reverse listing.	
		-t sorts last modified.	
		-S sorts by file size.	
		-h gives human-readable file sizes.	
Current directory	pwd	Print the working directory.	pwd -P
		-P prints the physical location.	
Change directory	cd	Change directory.	cd /home/debian
		cd and then Enter or cd ~/ takes you to the home directory.	cd /
		cd / takes you to the file system root.	
		cd .. takes you up a level.	
Make a directory	mkdir	Make a directory.	mkdir test
Delete a file or directory	rm	Delete a file.	rm bad.txt
		-r recursive delete (use for directories).	rm -r test
		-d remove empty directories.	
Copy a file or directory	cp	-r recursive copy.	cp a.txt b.txt
		-u copy only if the source is newer than the destination or the destination is missing.	cp -r test testa
		-v verbose copy (i.e., show output).	

NAME	COMMAND	OPTIONS AND FURTHER INFORMATION	EXAMPLE(S)
Move a file or directory	`mv`	-i prompts before overwrite.	`mv a.txt c.txt`
		No -r for directory. Moving to the same directory performs a renaming.	`mv test testb`
Create an empty file	`touch`	Create an empty file or update the modification date of an existing file.	`touch d.txt`
View content of a file	`more`	View the contents of a file. Use the Spacebar for the next page.	`more d.txt`
Get the calendar	`cal`	Display a text-based calendar.	`cal 01 2019`

That covers the basics, but there is so much more! The next chapter describes file ownership, permissions, searching, I/O redirection, and more. The aim of this section is to get you up and running. Table 2-6 describes a few shortcuts that make life easier when working with most Linux shells.

Table 2-6: Some Time-Saving Terminal Keyboard Shortcuts

SHORTCUT	DESCRIPTION
Up arrow (repeat)	Gives you the last command you typed and then the previous commands on repeated presses.
Tab key	Autocompletes the file name, the directory name, or even the executable command name. For example, to change to the Linux /tmp directory, you can type **cd /t** and then press Tab, which will autocomplete the command to **cd /tmp/**. If there are many options, press the Tab key again to see all the options as a list.
Ctrl+A	Brings you back to the start of the line you are typing.
Ctrl+E	Brings you to the end of the line you are typing.
Ctrl+U	Clears to the start of the line. Pressing Ctrl+E and then Ctrl+U clears the line.
Ctrl+L	Clears the screen.
Ctrl+C	Kills whatever process is currently running.
Ctrl+Z	Puts the current process into the background. Typing **bg** then leaves it running in the background, and **fg** then brings it back to the foreground. This is discussed in the "Linux Processes" section in the next chapter.

Here is an example that uses several of the commands in Table 2-5 to create a directory called `test` in which an empty text file `hello.txt` is created. The entire `test` directory is then copied to the `/tmp` directory, which is off the Linux root directory.

```
debian@beaglebone:~$ cd ~/
debian@beaglebone:~$ pwd
/home/debian
debian@beaglebone:~$ mkdir test
debian@beaglebone:~$ cd test
debian@beaglebone:~/test$ touch hello.txt
debian@beaglebone:~/test$ ls
hello.txt
debian@beaglebone:~/test$ cd ..
debian@beaglebone:~$ cp -r test /tmp
debian@beaglebone:~$ cd /tmp/test/
debian@beaglebone:/tmp/test$ ls -l
total 0
-rw-r--r-- 1 debian debian 0 Apr  5 00:50 hello.txt
```

WARNING   Linux assumes you know what you are doing! It will gladly allow you to do a recursive deletion of your root directory when you are logged in as root (I won't list the command). *Think before you type when logged in as root!*

NOTE   Sometimes it is possible to recover files that are lost through accidental deletion if you use the `extundelete` command immediately after the deletion. Read the command manual page carefully and then use steps such as the following:

```
molloyd@beaglebone:~/ $ sudo apt-get install extundelete
molloyd@beaglebone:~/ $ mkdir ~/undelete
molloyd@beaglebone:~/ $ cd ~/undelete/
molloyd@beaglebone:~/undelete$ sudo extundelete --restore-all
--restore-directory . /dev/mmcblk0p2
```

Environment Variables

Environment variables are named values that describe the configuration of your Linux environment, such as the location of the executable files or your default editor. To get an idea of the environment variables that are set on your board, issue an `env` call, which provides you with a list of the environment variables on your account. Here, `env` is called on the Debian IoT image:

```
debian@beaglebone:~$ env
...
USER=debian
PWD=/home/debian
```

```
HOME=/home/debian
SSH_CLIENT=192.168.7.1 6233 22
SSH_TTY=/dev/pts/0
PATH=/home/debian/bin:/usr/local/sbin:/usr/local/bin:/usr/sbin:/usr/bin:
/sbin:/bin:/usr/local/games:/usr/games
...
```

You can view and modify environment variables according to the following example, which adds the `temp` user directory to the `PATH` environment variable:

```
debian@beaglebone:~$ echo $PATH
/home/debian/bin:/usr/local/sbin:/usr/local/bin:/usr/sbin:/usr/bin
:/sbin:/bin:/usr/local/games:/usr/games
debian@beaglebone:~$ export PATH=$PATH:~/temp
debian@beaglebone:~$ echo $PATH
/home/debian/bin:/usr/local/sbin:/usr/local/bin:/usr/sbin:/usr/bin
:/sbin:/bin:/usr/local/games:/usr/games:/home/debian/temp
```

This change will be lost on reboot. Permanently setting environment variables requires modifications to your .profile file when using the sh, ksh, or bash shell; and to your .login file when using the csh or tcsh shell. To do this, you need to be able to perform file editing in a Linux terminal window.

Basic File Editing

A variety of editors are available, but perhaps one of the easiest to use for new users is also one of the most powerful—the *GNU nano editor*. You can start up the editor by typing **nano** followed by the name of an existing or new filename; for example, typing **nano hello.txt** will display the view captured in Figure 2-9 (after the text has been entered!). Typing **nano -c hello.txt** will also display line numbers, which is useful when debugging program code. You can move freely around the file in the window using the arrow keys and edit or write text at the cursor location. You can see some of the nano shortcut keys listed on the bottom bar of the editor window, but there are many more, some of which are presented in Table 2-7.

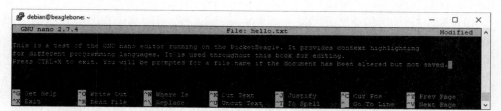

Figure 2-9: The GNU nano editor being used to edit an example file in a PuTTY Linux terminal window

Table 2-7: Nano Shortcut Keys—A Quick Reference

KEYS	COMMAND	KEYS	COMMAND
Ctrl+G	Help	Ctrl+Y	Previous page
Ctrl+C	Cancel	Ctrl+_ or Ctrl+/	Go to line number
Ctrl+X	Exit (prompts save)	Alt+/	Go to end of file
Ctrl+L	Enable long line wrapping	Ctrl+6	Start marking text (then move with arrows to highlight)
Ctrl+O	Save	Ctrl+K or Alt+6	Cut marked text
Arrows	Move around	Ctrl+U	Paste text
Ctrl+A	Go to start of line	Ctrl+R	Insert content of another file (prompts for location of file)
Ctrl+E	Go to end of line	Ctrl+W	Search for a string
Ctrl+Spacebar	Next word	Alt+W	Find next
Alt+Spacebar	Previous word	Ctrl+D	Delete character under cursor
Ctrl+V	Next page	Ctrl+K	Delete entire line

NOTE   Ctrl+K appears to delete the entire line, but it actually removes the line to a buffer, which can be pasted using Ctrl+U. This is a quick way of repeating multiple lines. Also, Mac users may have to set the "meta" key in the Terminal application to get the Alt functionality. Select Terminal ⇨ Preferences ⇨ Settings ⇨ Keyboard, or Terminal ⇨ Preferences ⇨ Profiles ⇨ Keyboard, and choose Use Option as Meta key.

What Time Is It?

A simple question like this causes more difficulty than you can imagine. If you type `date` at the shell prompt, you may get the following:

```
debian@beaglebone:~$ date
Thu Apr  5 01:06:59 UTC 2018
```

which is months out-of-date in this case, even where the board is connected to the desktop PC using an internet-over-USB connection. However, it is likely that the date and time are correct if you are connected via "regular" Ethernet.

If it is wrong, why did the BeagleBoard.org team not set the clock time on your board? The answer is that they could not. Unlike a desktop PC, there is no battery backup on the board to ensure that the BIOS/UEFI settings are retained—in fact, there is no BIOS or UEFI! That topic is examined in detail in the next chapter, but for the moment you need a way to set the time, and for that you can use the Network Time Protocol (NTP). The NTP is a networking protocol for synchronizing clocks between computers. If your board has the correct time, that is only because it is obtaining it from your network. On recent Debian images this is performed by a `systemd` special unit.

```
root@beaglebone:~# systemctl status time-sync.target
• time-sync.target - System Time Synchronized
  Loaded: loaded (/lib/systemd/system/time-sync.target; static;
  vendor preset: enabled)
  Active: active since Sun 2018-04-22 23:51:53 IST; 19min ago
```

If the time is incorrect, it is most likely the case that you do not have internet access. Please see the following feature, "Internet-over-USB Network Settings."

INTERNET-OVER-USB NETWORK SETTINGS

If you are using internet-over-USB, then the call to `ntpdate` likely failed, as you need to direct the IP traffic from your Beagle board through your desktop machine. You must first set up network connection sharing as detailed earlier in the "Internet-over-USB" section. Then, type the following in a Beagle board SSH terminal (please use 192.168.6.1 if you are using a Mac or Linux machine):

```
debian@beaglebone:~$ ping 8.8.8.8
connect: Network is unreachable
debian@beaglebone:~$ sudo -i
root@beaglebone:~# route add default gw 192.168.7.1
root@beaglebone:~# ping 8.8.8.8
PING 8.8.8.8 (8.8.8.8) 56(84) bytes of data.
64 bytes from 8.8.8.8: icmp_seq=1 ttl=57 time=9.87 ms
64 bytes from 8.8.8.8: icmp_seq=2 ttl=57 time=9.08 ms
```

This change means that all traffic is being routed through your desktop computer to the internet. If this step fails, you should check your PC's internet-over-USB sharing settings (perhaps disable and re-enable sharing). You should now be able to resolve domain names too under Debian. Here's an example:

```
root@beaglebone:~# ping www.google.com
ping: www.google.com: Temporary failure in name resolution
root@beaglebone:~# echo "nameserver 8.8.8.8" >> /etc/resolv.conf
root@beaglebone:~# ping www.google.com
PING www.google.com (209.85.203.103) 56(84) bytes of data.
64 bytes from dh-in-f103.1e100.net (209.85.203.103): ... time=11.5 ms
```

As listed here, if the preceding step fails, then you may need to update your `nameserver` settings. If you are still having difficulties, check whether your virus protection software on your host PC is preventing ping calls and network connection sharing. All the settings described earlier are lost on reboot, as you cannot add them to your `.profile` file as you need superuser permissions to call the route command.

> You can use a script such as the `internetOverUSB` script that is in the `/chp02` directory of the GitHub repository. It must be executed using the `sudo` command. This approach is useful if you are switching between "regular" Ethernet and internet-over-USB.
>
> If you notice that this configuration stops working after some time, try unsharing the network connection on the PC and then sharing it again.

Once the time is correct, use the following command, which provides a text-based user interface that allows you to choose your location. The board is now set for Irish standard time (IST) in this example.

```
debian@beaglebone:~$ sudo dpkg-reconfigure tzdata
Current default time zone: 'Europe/Dublin'
Local time is now:      Mon Apr 23 00:06:21 IST 2018.
Universal Time is now:  Sun Apr 22 23:06:21 UTC 2018.
```

Package Management

At the beginning of this chapter, a good package manager is listed as a key feature of a suitable Linux distribution. A *package manager* is a set of software tools that automate the process of installing, configuring, upgrading, and removing software packages from the Linux operating system. Different Linux distributions use different package managers: Ångström uses *OPKG*, Ubuntu and Debian use *APT* (Advanced Packaging Tool) over *DPKG* (Debian Package Management System), and Arch Linux uses *Pacman*. Each has its own usage syntax, but their operation is largely similar. For example, the first row in Table 2-8 lists the command for installing a package using different managers. The table also lists other package management commands that can be used.

Table 2-8: Common Package Management Commands (Using nano as an Example Package)

COMMAND	ÅNGSTRÖM	DEBIAN/UBUNTU
Install a package.	`opkg install nano`	`sudo apt install nano`
Update the package index.	`opkg update`	`sudo apt update`
Upgrade the packages on your system.	`opkg upgrade`	`sudo apt upgrade`[2]
Is nano installed?	`opkg list-installed |grep nano`	`dpkg-query -l |grep nano`
Is a package containing the string nano available?	`opkg list|grep nano`	`apt search nano`

---

[2] It is not recommended that you do this on an eMMC. It can take quite some time to run (often several hours), and serious issues can arise if the board runs out of space on the eMMC during the upgrade.

COMMAND	ÅNGSTRÖM	DEBIAN/UBUNTU
Get more information about a package.	`opkg info nano`	`apt show nano`
		`apt policy nano`
Get help.	`opkg`	`apt help`
Download a package to the current directory.	`opkg download nano`	`apt download nano`
Remove a package.	`opkg remove nano`	`sudo apt remove nano`
Clean up old packages.	Nontrivial. Search for *opkg-clean script*.	`sudo apt autoremove`
		`sudo apt clean`

You should update the package lists at regular intervals (the `sudo` password is your Debian account password) using the `apt update` command. A call to `apt update` downloads the package lists from the internet locations identified in the file `/etc/apt/sources.list`. This does not install new versions of the software; rather, it updates the lists of packages and their interdependencies.

```
debian@beaglebone:~$ sudo apt update
[sudo] password for debian:
Ign:1 http://deb.debian.org/debian stretch InRelease
...
Get:14 http://repos.rcn-ee.com/debian stretch/main armhf Packages [516 kB]
Fetched 10.7 MB in 11s (896 kB/s)
Reading package lists... Done
Building dependency tree
Reading state information... Done
75 packages can be upgraded. Run 'apt list --upgradable' to see them.
debian@beaglebone:~$ sudo apt list --upgradable
Listing... Done
apache2/stable 2.4.25-3+deb9u4 armhf [upgradable from: 2.4.25-3+deb9u3]
...
```

Once this is complete, you can automatically download and install the latest versions of the available software using the `apt upgrade` command. Clearly, you should always perform an `apt update` command before an `apt upgrade`. Please be aware that some of these steps (upgrade in particular) can take quite some time to complete—perhaps even several hours, depending on the currency of your image and the speed of your network connection.

NOTE   Over recent years, the `apt` binary command slowly integrated the features of the `apt-get` and `apt-cache` commands into a single command. Older Linux distributions may require that you use the `apt-get` and `apt-cache` commands.

Wavemon is a useful tool that you can use in configuring Wi-Fi connections (see Chapter 12). If you execute the command, you will see that the package is not installed.

```
debian@beaglebone:~$ wavemon
-bash: wavemon: command not found
```

The platform-specific (Debian in this case) package manager can be used to install the package, once you determine the package name.

```
debian@beaglebone:~$ apt search wavemon
Sorting... Done ... Full Text Search... Done
wavemon/stable 0.8.1-1 armhf
   Wireless Device Monitoring Application
debian@beaglebone:~$ sudo apt install wavemon
Reading package lists... Done
...
Setting up wavemon (0.8.1-1) ...
```

The wavemon command now executes, but unfortunately it will not do anything until you configure a wireless adapter (see Chapter 12).

```
debian@beaglebone:~$ wavemon
wavemon: no supported wireless interfaces found! Check manpage for help.
```

> **NOTE** Sometimes package installations fail, perhaps because another required package is missing. There are *force options* available with the package commands to override checks (e.g., `--force-yes` with the `apt` command). Try to avoid force options if possible, as having to use them is symptomatic of a different problem. Typing `sudo apt autoremove` can be useful when packages fail to install.

Beagle-Specific Commands

There are Beagle-specific tools available for configuring your board that have been developed by the BeagleBoard.org community. These tools simplify some tasks that would otherwise be quite difficult. They are located in the `/opt /scripts/tools` directory and are described in this section. Before you use the tools, check that you have the latest versions.

```
debian@beaglebone:~$ cd /opt/scripts/tools/
debian@beaglebone:/opt/scripts/tools$ git pull || true
Already up-to-date.
debian@beaglebone:/opt/scripts/tools$ ls
```

```
beaglebone-black-eMMC-flasher.sh   grow_partition.sh        update_kernel.sh
developers                         init-eMMC-flasher.sh     version.sh
dtc                                non-mmc-rootfs           wm
eMMC                               readme.txt
graphics                           software
```

Expand the File System on an SD Card

If you have installed a BeagleBoard.org Linux image on a micro-SD card of greater than 4GB capacity, then you should expand the file system to use the full card capacity. In this example, a 32GB micro-SD card is used in a PocketBeagle, and the Debian IoT image size is 4GB. Using the lsblk tool (see Chapter 3), you can see that most of the SD card is unavailable for use, with the df tool indicating that the Linux partition is 54 percent full.

```
debian@beaglebone:~$ lsblk
NAME          MAJ:MIN RM  SIZE RO TYPE MOUNTPOINT
mmcblk0       179:0    0 29.8G  0 disk
└─mmcblk0p1   179:1    0  3.3G  0 part /
debian@beaglebone:~$ df -k
Filesystem        1K-blocks      Used Available Use% Mounted on
udev                 219844         0    219844   0% /dev
tmpfs                 49624      4972     44652  11% /run
/dev/mmcblk0p1      3357264   1684596   1482412  54% /
...
```

You can use the grow partition tool as follows:

```
debian@beaglebone:/opt/scripts/tools$ sudo ./grow_partition.sh
Media: [/dev/mmcblk0]
sfdisk: 2.26.x or greater
Disk /dev/mmcblk0: 29.8 GiB, 32010928128 bytes, 62521344 sectors
...
debian@beaglebone:/opt/scripts/tools$ sudo reboot
```

After reboot, it is clear that the micro-SD card is fully available for use by using the lsblk tool. Now that the full SD card is available, it is safe to call the apt upgrade command.

```
debian@beaglebone:~$ lsblk
NAME          MAJ:MIN RM  SIZE RO TYPE MOUNTPOINT
mmcblk0       179:0    0 29.8G  0 disk
└─mmcblk0p1   179:1    0 29.8G  0 part /
debian@beaglebone:~$ sudo apt upgrade
debian@beaglebone:~$ df -k
Filesystem        1K-blocks      Used Available Use% Mounted on
udev                 219332         0    219332   0% /dev
tmpfs                 49520      5012     44508  11% /run
/dev/mmcblk0p1     30707172   1953168  27455072   7% /
```

Update the Kernel

You can also update to the latest kernel release that is made available by BeagleBoard.org using the update kernel tool as follows:

```
debian@beaglebone:~$ uname -a
Linux beaglebone 4.9.82-ti-r102 #1 SMP PREEMPT Thu Feb 22 01:16:12 UTC 2018
armv7l GNU/Linux
debian@beaglebone:~$ cd /opt/scripts/tools/
debian@beaglebone:/opt/scripts/tools$ sudo ./update_kernel.sh
...
Kernel version options:
---------------------------
LTS44: --lts-4_4
LTS49: --lts-4_9
LTS414: --lts-4_14
STABLE: --stable
TESTING: --testing
info:you are running:[4.9.82-ti-r102],latest is:[4.9.88-ti-r111] updating...
debian@beaglebone:~$ sudo reboot
debian@beaglebone:~$ uname -a
Linux beaglebone 4.9.88-ti-r111 #1 SMP PREEMPT Sun Apr 22 2018 armv7l GNU/
Linux
```

After rebooting the board, you can see that the revision has been updated (from 102 to 111 in this case). You can also use this tool to select a specific kernel from the options displayed earlier. Here's an example:

```
/opt/scripts/tools$ sudo ./update_kernel.sh --ti-rt-channel --lts-4_14
/opt/scripts/tools$ sudo reboot
debian@beaglebone:~$ uname -a
Linux beaglebone 4.14.35-ti-rt-r44 #1 SMP PREEMPT RT Sun Apr 22 06:04:23
```

CREATING A BEAGLEBONE FLASHER IMAGE

To update the Linux image on a BeagleBone eMMC, you need to convert a regular image into a flasher image. You do this by editing the /boot/uEnv.txt file to remove the # in front of the following line:

```
debian@beaglebone:/boot$ more uEnv.txt | grep flasher
#cmdline=init=/opt/scripts/tools/eMMC/init-eMMC-flasher-v3.sh
```

Once the file is saved, reboot the board by pressing the Reset button and then hold the Boot button until the four LEDs light up. The LEDs will then light in a bouncing pattern as the image is being written to the eMMC, which takes about ten minutes. All four LEDs will turn off when this process is complete. Finally, remove the micro-SD card and press the Power button.

Interacting with the On-Board LEDs

In this section, you are going to examine how you can change the behavior of the Beagle board on-board user LEDs—the four blue LEDs that are grouped together on the boards. Each LED can provide information about the board's state.

- USR0 flashes in a heartbeat sequence, indicating the board is alive.
- USR1 flashes during micro-SD card activity.
- USR2 flashes depending on the level of CPU activity.
- USR3 flashes during eMMC activity (set to do nothing by default on the PocketBeagle).

You can change the behavior of these LEDs to suit your own needs, but you will temporarily lose this useful activity information.

Sysfs is a virtual file system that is available under recent Linux kernels. It provides you with access to devices and drivers that would otherwise be accessible only within a restricted kernel space. This topic is discussed in detail in Chapter 6; however, at this point, it would be useful to briefly explore the mechanics of how sysfs can be used to alter the behavior of the user LEDs.

Using your SSH client, you can connect to the board and browse to the directory /sys/class/leds/. The output is as follows:

```
debian@beaglebone:~$ cd /sys/class/leds
debian@beaglebone:/sys/class/leds$ ls
beaglebone:green:usr0  beaglebone:green:usr2
beaglebone:green:usr1  beaglebone:green:usr3
```

NOTE   Sysfs directory locations can vary somewhat under different versions of the Linux kernel. Please check the web page associated with this chapter if the preceding directory is not present on your Linux kernel.

You can see the four (green!) LED sysfs mappings—usr0, usr1, usr2, and usr3. You can change the directory to alter the properties of one of these LEDs—for example, usr3 (use the Tab key to reduce typing).

```
debian@beaglebone:/sys/class/leds$ cd beaglebone\:green\:usr3
debian@beaglebone:/sys/class/leds/beaglebone:green:usr3$ ls
brightness  device  max_brightness  power  subsystem  trigger  uevent
```

Here you see various different file entries that give you further information and access to settings. Please note that this section uses some commands that are explained in detail in the next chapter.

You can determine the current status of an LED by typing the following:

```
/sys/class/leds/beaglebone:green:usr3$ cat trigger
[none] rc-feedback rfkill-any kbd-scrolllock kbd-numlock kbd-capslock
kbd-kanalock kbd-shiftlock kbd-altgrlock kbd-ctrllock kbd-altlock
kbd-shiftllock kbd-shiftrlock kbd-ctrlllock kbd-ctrlrlock usb-gadget
usb-host mmc0 timer oneshot disk-activity ide-disk mtd nand-disk
heartbeat backlight gpio default-on panic
```

where you can see that the USR3 LED is not currently configured for any particular function (i.e., [none]). If it happens to be configured on your board, you can set it to none, as follows:

```
/sys/class/leds/beaglebone:green:usr3$ echo none > trigger
```

You can turn the USR3 LED fully on or off using this:

```
/sys/class/leds/beaglebone:green:usr3$ echo 1 > brightness
/sys/class/leds/beaglebone:green:usr3$ echo 0 > brightness
```

You can even set the LED to flash at a time interval of your choosing. If you watch carefully, you will notice the dynamic nature of sysfs. If you perform an ls command at this point, the directory will appear as follows but will shortly change:

```
/sys/class/leds/beaglebone:green:usr3$ ls
brightness device max_brightness power subsystem trigger uevent
```

To make the LED flash, you need to set the trigger to timer mode by typing **echo timer > trigger**. You will see the USR3 LED flash at a one-second interval. Notice that there are new delay_on and delay_off file entries in the beaglebone:green:usr3 directory, as follows:

```
/sys/class/leds/beaglebone:green:usr3$ echo timer > trigger
/sys/class/leds/beaglebone:green:usr3$ ls
brightness delay_on max_brightness subsystem uevent
delay_off device power trigger
```

The LED flash timer makes use of these new delay_on time and delay_off time file entries. You can find out more information about these values by using the concatenate (catenate) command. Here's an example:

```
/sys/class/leds/beaglebone:green:usr3$ cat delay_on
500
```

This reports the time delay in milliseconds. To make the USR3 LED flash at 10Hz (i.e., on for 50ms and off for 50ms), you can use the following:

```
debian@beaglebone:/sys/class/leds/beaglebone:green:usr3$ sudo -i
root@beaglebone:~# cd /sys/class/leds/beaglebone\:green\:usr3
```

```
root@beaglebone:/sys/class/leds/beaglebone:green:usr3# echo 50 > delay_on
root@beaglebone:/sys/class/leds/beaglebone:green:usr3# echo 50 > delay_off
```

You need to use the root account to perform the preceding operation because the `delay_on` and `delay_off` entries are owned by `root`.

```
root@beaglebone:/sys/class/leds/beaglebone:green:usr3# ls -l delay*
-rw-r--r-- 1 root root 4096 Apr 24 02:08 delay_off
-rw-r--r-- 1 root root 4096 Apr 24 02:07 delay_on
```

Typing **echo none > trigger** returns the LED to its default state on the PocketBeagle, which results in the `delay_on` and `delay_off` file entries disappearing.

Shutdown

> **WARNING**   Physically disconnecting the power without allowing the kernel to unmount the eMMC or the SD card can cause corruption of your file system. The power management chip also needs to be informed of a shutdown.

One final issue to discuss in this section is the correct shutdown procedure for your board, as improper shutdown can potentially corrupt the ext4 file system and/or lead to increased boot times because of file system checks. Here are some important points on shutting down, rebooting, and starting your board:

- Typing **sudo shutdown -h now** shuts down the board correctly. You can delay this by five minutes by typing **sudo shutdown -h +5**.
- Typing **sudo reboot** will reset and reboot the board correctly.
- You can press the Power button (see Figure 1-4 and Figure 1-5) once to "soft" (as in software) shut down the board correctly.
- Holding the Power button for approximately eight seconds performs a hard system power down. This should be avoided unless the board is frozen and will not do a soft shutdown.
- Press the Power button to start the board. Try to avoid physically disconnecting and reconnecting the power jack or USB lead.

If your project design is enclosed and you need an external soft power down, it is possible to wire an external button to a GPIO input on the expansion header and write a shell script that runs on startup to poll the GPIO for an input. If that input occurs, then `/sbin/shutdown -h now` can be called directly.

Node.js, Cloud9, and BoneScript

The BeagleBoard.org Linux distribution comes complete with a set of technologies that you can use to quickly get started with developing software and hardware applications on the boards. These are called Node.js, Cloud9, and BoneScript—*Node.js* is a programming language, *Cloud9* is an online software integrated development environment (IDE) in which you can write Node.js code, and *BoneScript* is a library of code for Node.js that allows you to interact with Beagle board hardware.

Introduction to Node.js

Node.js is a platform for building network applications that uses the same JavaScript engine as the Google Chrome web browser. JavaScript is the programming language that is often used to create interactive interfaces within web pages. Simply put, Node.js is JavaScript on the server side. Its runtime environment and library of code enables you to run JavaScript code applications, without a browser, directly at the Linux shell prompt.

Node.js uses an event-driven, nonblocking input/output model. Event-driven programming is commonplace in user-interface programming. It essentially means that the program's flow of execution is driven by user actions or messages that are transferred from other threads or processes. Interestingly, the fact that it uses nonblocking I/O means that it is suitable for interfacing to the input/output pins on your board, safely sharing resources with other applications. As with all new languages, you should start with a "Hello World!" example. Listing 2-1 sends the string "Hello World!" to the standard output, which is typically a Linux terminal.

Listing 2-1: /chp02/HelloWorld.js

```
console.log("Hello World!");
```

Open an SSH connection to the board, create a directory to contain the HelloWorld.js file, and then enter the code from 1 using nano.

```
debian@beaglebone:~$ cd ~/
debian@beaglebone:~$ mkdir nodeTest
debian@beaglebone:~$ cd nodeTest/
debian@beaglebone:~/nodeTest$ nano HelloWorld.js
```

To execute this code, type **node HelloWorld.js** in the directory containing the JavaScript file. You should see the following output:

```
debian@beaglebone:~/nodeTest$ ls
HelloWorld.js
debian@beaglebone:~/nodeTest$ node HelloWorld.js
Hello World!
```

which should give you an idea of how you can write Node.js programs for the board. The call to the `node` command works because the Node.js runtime environment is preinstalled on the BeagleBoard.org Linux image.

Listing 2-2 provides a more complex Node.js example. It creates a web server that runs on the board at port 5050 and serves a simple "Hello World!" message. Write the program code in the same /nodeTest directory.

Listing 2-2: /chp02/SimpleWebServer.js

```
// A Simple Example Node.js Webserver Running on Port 5050
var http = require('http');  // require the http module
var server = http.createServer(
    function(req,res) {
        res.writeHead(200, {'Content-Type': 'text/plain'});
        res.end('Hello from the Beagle board!\n');
    });
server.listen(5050);
console.log('Beagle Web Server running at http://192.168.7.2:5050/');
```

The example code in Listing 2-2 begins by requiring the Node.js `http` module. It then calls the `http.createServer()` method, which returns an `http.Server` object. The `server.listen()` method is called on the `http.Server` object, where it causes the server to accept connections on a defined port number (i.e., 5050). This method is asynchronous, meaning it does not have to finish before the `console.log()` method is called on the next line. In fact, unless you kill the process on the board, the `server.listen()` method will listen forever. When a connection is made to port 5050, the server will call the listening function, `function(req,res)`, to which is passed a copy of the HTTP request and response references. In this case, the function responds with a short plaintext message.

To execute this program, you type **node SimpleWebServer.js** in the directory containing the source code file, and you should get the following:

```
debian@beaglebone:~/nodeTest$ ls
HelloWorld.js  SimpleWebServer.js
debian@beaglebone:~/nodeTest$ node SimpleWebServer.js
Beagle Web Server running at http://192.168.7.2:5050/
```

where the output indicates that the server is running and listening on port 5050. You can then open a web browser and connect to this simple Node.js web server, where you will see the output, as shown in Figure 2-10. You can use Ctrl+C to kill the web server in the SSH window.

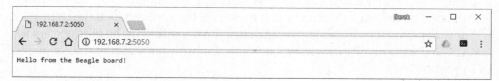

Figure 2-10: Connecting to the Node.js web server

Introduction to the Cloud9 IDE

Wouldn't it be great if there were a way to integrate the development of Node.js code with the execution environment? That is where the Cloud9 IDE is useful. The Cloud9 integrated development environment (IDE) is an impressive web-based coding platform that supports many different programming languages, including JavaScript and Node.js. It enables you to write, run, and debug code directly within your web browser without installing any operating-system-specific tools or applications. If that is not impressive enough, the Cloud9 service has a low enough overhead to run directly on a Beagle board, and it comes preinstalled on the BeagleBoard.org Linux images.

To use the Cloud9 IDE, open Google Chrome or Firefox and connect to your board's address on port 3000. For example, open 192.168.7.2:3000 using the address bar, as shown in Figure 2-11. When you first open Cloud9, it provides an excellent introduction to the user interface and controls.

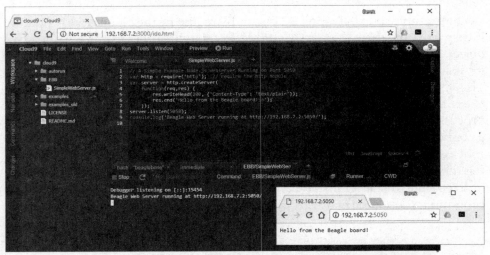

Figure 2-11: The Cloud9 IDE running on the PocketBeagle, executing the SimpleWeb Server.js example

Rather than having to write the code on your desktop machine and transfer it to your board, the Cloud9 interface can save files directly on your board's Linux file system and can even execute them too. In Figure 2-11, a new .js file is created, which contains the code in Listing 2-2. *You must save the file using File ⇨ Save.* You can click the Run button to execute the application. If the Debugger window appears, click Resume. You can click the hyperlink in the output console, and the application output will be visible in the browser window that appears, as in Figure 2-11.

Remember that this `SimpleWebServer.js` program is running on the Beagle board itself. In fact, if you SSH into the board (or use the Cloud9 `bash` terminal window) and execute the following command (described in Chapter 3), you can see that the application process is running, as follows:

```
debian@beaglebone:~# ps aux|grep SimpleWebServer
debian 2157 0.3 2.2 ... node ... "/var/lib/cloud9/EBB/SimpleWebServer.js" ...
```

Clicking the Stop button in the Cloud9 IDE will kill this process.

> **NOTE**   The Cloud9 `bash` **terminal window is a great alternative to PuTTY or the Chrome SSH app for opening an SSH session. The** `bash` **terminal is automatically logged in as user** `debian`. **Be careful of this fact if you are on an insecure network or are opening port 3000 on the board to the internet.**

Introduction to BoneScript

BoneScript is a library of Beagle-specific functionality that has been written for Node.js by BeagleBoard.org cofounder Jason Kridner. The BoneScript library provides the type of input/output functionality that would be familiar to Arduino users but with the advantage that it sits on top of the network capabilities of Node.js running on the Beagle platform. There are detailed descriptions of BoneScript and its functionality at `beagleboard.org/support/bonescript`.

You can use BoneScript to build a simple application to change the state of one of the system LEDs. The code in Listing 2-3 flashes the on-board USR3 LED, once every second, by utilizing the BoneScript library.

Listing 2-3: /chp02/BlinkLED3.js

```
var b = require('bonescript'); // using BoneScript
var LED3Pin = "USR3";          // USR3 is D5 on the Beagle board

b.pinMode(LED3Pin, b.OUTPUT);  // set up LED3Pin as an output
var isOn = false;              // isOn will be a Boolean flag
setInterval(toggleLED, 500);   // each half second call toggleLED()

function toggleLED(){
    isOn = !isOn;                      // invert the isOn state on each call
    if (isOn) b.digitalWrite(LED3Pin, 1);  // light the LED
    else b.digitalWrite(LED3Pin, 0);       // turn off the LED
    console.log('LED On is: ' + isOn);     // output the state
}
```

This program requires the `bonescript` module, which is now referred to in the code as `b`—for example, by using `b.someMethod()`. Therefore, `b.pinMode()` uses the string literal `"USR3"` to identify the pin that is to be set to output mode. A temporary Boolean value `isOn` is used to retain the state of the LED in the code. The Node.js asynchronous global function `setInterval()` is set up to call the `toggleLED()` callback function every 500ms. Each time the `toggleLED()` function is called, the `isOn` Boolean variable is inverted using the NOT operator (i.e., `!true=false` and `!false=true`). You set the LED pin to high if the value of `isOn` is true and to low if its value is false, and the state is outputted to the console.

This program can be executed directly within the Cloud9 IDE. However, it is important to remember that you can still run programs that include the BoneScript library calls directly at the Linux terminal prompt. Therefore, for example, executing the `BlinkLED3.js` code from the Cloud9 location on the Beagle board (as illustrated in Figure 2-12) will also work perfectly, flashing the USR3 LED once per second.

```
debian@beaglebone:/var/lib/cloud9/EBB$ ls
BlinkLED3.js  SimpleWebServer.js
debian@beaglebone:/var/lib/cloud9/EBB$ node BlinkLED3.js
LED On is: true
LED On is: false
LED On is: true
LED On is: false ...
```

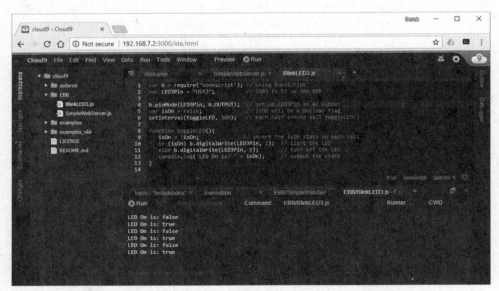

Figure 2-12: The Cloud9 IDE running on the PocketBeagle, executing the BoneScript BlinkLED3.js example

BoneScript is useful for the rapid prototyping of systems, particularly when those systems involve electronics that are to be connected to the internet. However, it is not ideal for high-performance large-scale applications—alternative languages and approaches are described throughout this book for such applications.

Summary

After completing this chapter, you should be able to do the following:

- Communicate with your Beagle board from your desktop computer using network connections such as internet-over-USB and regular Ethernet
- Communicate with your board using fallback serial connections such as serial-over-USB or by using a custom USB-to-TTL 3.3V cable
- Interact with and control the board using simple Linux commands
- Perform basic file editing using a Linux terminal
- Manage Linux packages and set the system time
- Use Linux sysfs to affect the state of board hardware
- Safely shut down and reboot your board
- Use Node.js, Cloud9, and BoneScript to write basic applications and code that interact with your board's hardware

Further Reading

There are many links to websites and documents provided throughout this chapter. The following additional links provide further information on the topics covered:

- The chapter web page includes a video on getting started with internet-over-USB and burning a new image to the SD card: www.exploringbeagle-bone.com/chapter2/
- Node.js API documentation: nodejs.org/api/
- BoneScript library guide: beagleboard.org/support/bonescript

Exploring Embedded Linux Systems

This chapter exposes you to the core concepts, commands, and tools required to effectively manage the Beagle-based embedded Linux system. The first part of the chapter is descriptive; it explains the basics of embedded Linux and the Linux boot process. After that, you learn step-by-step how to manage Linux systems. For this exercise, you are strongly encouraged to open a terminal connection to your board and follow along. Next, the chapter describes the Git source code management system. This topic is an important one because the source code examples in this book are distributed via GitHub. Desktop virtualization is also described; it is useful for cross-platform development in later chapters. The chapter finishes by describing how you can download the source code examples for this book.

EQUIPMENT REQUIRED FOR THIS CHAPTER:

- Any Beagle board with a terminal connection, preferably running Debian

Further details on this chapter are available at www.exploringbeaglebone .com/chapter3/.

Introducing Embedded Linux

First things first: even though the term *embedded Linux* is used in this chapter's title, there is no such thing as embedded Linux! There is no special version of the Linux kernel for embedded systems; it is just the mainline Linux kernel running on an embedded system. That said, the term *embedded Linux* has broad and common use; therefore, it is used here instead of "Linux on an embedded system," which is the more accurate phrasing.

The word *embedded* in the term *embedded Linux* is used to convey the presence of an *embedded system,* a concept that can be loosely explained as some type of computing hardware with integrated software that was designed to be used for a specific application. This concept is in contrast to the personal computer (PC), which is a general-purpose computing device designed to be used for many applications, such as web browsing, word processing, and game play. The line is blurring between embedded systems and general-purpose computing devices. For example, the BeagleBone Black (BBB) or BeagleBoard can be both, and many users will deploy them solely as a capable general-purpose computing device. However, embedded systems have some distinctive characteristics.

- They tend to have specific and dedicated applications.
- They often have limited processing power, memory availability, and storage capabilities.
- They are generally part of a larger system that may be linked to external sensors or actuators.
- They often have a role for which reliability is critical (e.g., controls in cars, airplanes, and medical equipment).
- They often work in real time, where their outputs are directly related to present inputs (e.g., control systems).
- In recent times, connectedness has become a core feature of embedded systems, allowing these to be the building blocks of the Internet of Things (IoT).

Embedded systems are present everywhere in everyday life. Examples include vending machines, household appliances, phones/smartphones, manufacturing/assembly lines, TVs, games consoles, cars (e.g., power steering and reversing sensors), network switches, routers, wireless access points, sound systems, medical monitoring equipment, printers, building access controls, parking meters, smart energy/water meters, watches, building tools, digital cameras, monitors, tablets, e-readers, anything robotic, smart card payment/access systems, and more.

The huge proliferation of embedded Linux devices is thanks in part to the rapid evolution of smartphone technology, which has helped drive down the unit price of ARM-based processors. ARM Holdings PLC is a UK company that licenses the intellectual property of its ARM processors to Texas Instruments (the manufacturer of the processors on the Beagle boards) for up-front fees and a small royalty fee, which is based on the sale price of the processor.

Advantages and Disadvantages of Embedded Linux

There are many embedded platform types, each with its own advantages and disadvantages. There are low-cost embedded platforms, with volume prices of less than $1, such as the Microchip AVR or PIC or Texas Instruments MSP43x processors, and there are high-cost specialized platforms that can cost more than $150, such as multicore digital signal processors (DSPs). These platforms are typically programmed in C and/or assembly language, requiring that you have knowledge of the underlying systems architecture before you can develop useful applications. Embedded Linux offers an alternative to these platforms, in that significant knowledge of the underlying architecture is not required to start building applications. However, if you want to interface with electronic modules or components, some such knowledge is required.

Here are some of the reasons why embedded Linux has seen such growth:

- Linux is an efficient and scalable operating system (OS), running on everything from low-cost consumer-oriented devices to expensive large-scale servers. It has evolved over many years, from when computers were much less powerful than today, but it has retained many of the efficiencies.

- A huge number of open source programs and tools have already been developed that can be readily deployed in an embedded application. If you need a web server for your embedded application, you can install the same one that you might use on a Linux server.

- There is excellent open-source support for many different peripherals and devices, from network adapters to displays.

- It is open source and does not require a fee for its use.

- The kernel and application code is running worldwide on so many devices that bugs are infrequent and are detected quickly.

One downside of embedded Linux is that it is not ideal for real-time applications because of the OS overhead. Therefore, for high-precision, fast-response applications, such as analog signal processing, embedded Linux may not be the perfect solution. However, even in real-time applications, it is often used as the "central intelligence" and control interface for a networked array of dedicated real-time sensors (see Chapter 10). In addition, there are constant developments underway in *real-time operating systems* (RTOS) Linux that aim to use Linux in a preemptive way, interrupting the OS whenever required to maintain a real-time process.

Is Linux Open Source and Free?

Linux is released under the *GNU* General Public License (GPL), which grants users the freedom to use and modify its code in any way; so, *free* generally refers to "freedom" rather than to "without cost." In fact, some of the most expensive Linux distributions are those for embedded architectures. You can find a quick guide to the GPLv3 at www.gnu.org that lists the four freedoms that every user should have (Smith, 2013).

The freedom to use the software for any purpose

The freedom to change the software to suit your needs

The freedom to share the software with your friends and neighbors

And, the freedom to share the changes you make

Even if you are using a distribution that you downloaded "for free," it can cost you significant effort to tailor libraries and device drivers to suit the particular components and modules that you want to use in your product development.

Booting the Beagle Boards

The first thing you should see when you boot a desktop computer is the *Unified Extensible Firmware Interface* (UEFI), which provides legacy support for Basic Input/Output System (BIOS) services. The boot screen displays system information and invites you to press a key to alter these settings. UEFI tests the hardware components, such as the memory, and then loads the OS, typically from the solid-state drive (SSD)/hard drive. Therefore, when a desktop computer is powered on, the UEFI/BIOS performs the following steps:

1. Takes control of the computer's processor
2. Initializes and tests the hardware components
3. Loads the OS off the SSD/hard drive

The UEFI/BIOS provides an abstraction layer for the OS to interact with the display and other input/output peripherals, such as the mouse/keyboard and storage devices. Its settings are stored in NAND flash and battery-backed memory—you can see a small coin battery on the PC motherboard that supports the real-time system clock.

Bootloaders

Like most embedded Linux devices, the Beagle boards do not have a UEFI/BIOS or battery-backed memory by default (a battery-backed real-time clock is added to a board in Chapter 8). Instead, it uses a combination of *bootloaders*.

Bootloaders are typically small programs that perform the critical function of linking the specific hardware of your board to the Linux OS. Bootloaders perform the following:

- Initialize the controllers (memory, graphics, I/O)
- Prepare and allocate the system memory for the OS
- Locate the OS and provide the facility for loading it
- Load the OS and pass control to it

The Beagle boards use an open source Linux bootloader, called *Das U-Boot* ("The" Universal Bootloader). It is custom built for each Beagle board using detailed knowledge of the hardware description, which is provided in board-specific software patches.

The /boot directory contains the Linux kernel and the other files required to boot the board. For example, on the PocketBeagle (with two different kernel versions), you will see the directory listing, as shown here:

```
debian@beaglebone:/boot$ ls -l
-rw-r--r-- 1 root root   159786 Apr 22 07:17 config-4.14.35-ti-rt-r44
-rw-r--r-- 1 root root   163837 Apr 22 11:44 config-4.9.88-ti-rt-r111
drwxr-xr-x 6 root root     4096 Apr 25 01:14 dtbs
-rw-r--r-- 1 root root  4468991 Apr 24 01:01 initrd.img-4.14.35-ti-rt-r44
-rw-r--r-- 1 root root  6523044 Apr 25 01:34 initrd.img-4.9.88-ti-rt-r111
-rw-r--r-- 1 root root      492 Mar  5 13:11 SOC.sh
-rw-r--r-- 1 root root  3634267 Apr 22 07:17 System.map-4.14.35-ti-rt-r44
-rw-r--r-- 1 root root  3939313 Apr 22 11:44 System.map-4.9.88-ti-rt-r111
drwxr-xr-x 2 root root     4096 Mar  5 07:14 uboot
-rw-r--r-- 1 root root     1882 Apr 25 01:26 uEnv.txt
-rwxr-xr-x 1 root root 10379776 Apr 22 07:17 vmlinuz-4.14.35-ti-rt-r44
-rwxr-xr-x 1 root root 10070592 Apr 22 11:44 vmlinuz-4.9.88-ti-rt-r111
```

These files have the following functions:

- The Linux kernel is in the compressed vmlinuz* files.
- The initial RAM disk (file system in memory) is in the initrd* files, which creates a temporary root file system (called an *early user space*) that is used to identify hardware and load the kernel modules that are required to boot the "real" file system.
- The uEnv.txt file sets the boot parameters for your board. You can edit this file to set custom boot properties (e.g., set up a flasher image as described in Chapter 2).

- The System.map* files provide a debug mapping from kernel-specific build codes to human-readable symbols so that any crash dump files can be analyzed. This file is not required for boot.

- The config* files list the options that were chosen when the kernel was built. It is human readable and not required for boot. You can type **more** **/boot/config-4.xxx** to see the build configuration.

- SOC.sh is a script that contains bootloader information that is required when the bootloader is to be upgraded. It is human readable and not required for boot.

- The /boot/dtbs/ directory contains subdirectories with the device tree binaries that are required to boot a board. Each subdirectory provides binaries for a specific kernel build.

> **WARNING**   Do not edit uEnv.txt using Microsoft WordPad, as the file requires Unix newline support. If you must edit uEnv.txt in Windows, install Notepad++ or a similar tool. Please be aware that changing uEnv.txt can prevent your board from booting, so edits should be performed only when you are sure that they are necessary.

Figure 3-1 illustrates the boot process on the Beagle boards, where each boot-loader stage is loaded and invoked by the preceding stage bootloader. The *primary program loader* in the AM335x executes when the reset vector is invoked. It loads the *first stage bootloader* (aka the *second stage program loader*) file called MLO from the eMMC/SD card. This loader initializes clocks and memory and loads the second stage bootloader u-boot.img from the eMMC/SD card. The MLO (~92 KB) and u-boot.img (~420 KB) files exists in a raw area of the SD card that precedes the Linux ext4 partition.[1] For example, when you call lsblk, you see that the ext4 partition begins at sector 8,192 (4,194,304 bytes), as shown here:

```
debian@beaglebone:/boot$ sudo fdisk -l
Disk /dev/mmcblk0: 29.8 GiB, 32010928128 bytes, 62521344 sectors
Units: sectors of 1 * 512 = 512 bytes
Sector size (logical/physical): 512 bytes / 512 bytes
I/O size (minimum/optimal): 512 bytes / 512 bytes
Disklabel type: dos
Disk identifier: 0xaf2e67c6
Device          Boot Start      End Sectors  Size Id Type
/dev/mmcblk0p1 *      8192 62521343 62513152 29.8G 83 Linux
```

which gives sufficient space for storing these files.

---

[1]In earlier Linux images for the BeagleBone, the first and second stage bootloaders were stored on a FAT partition on the eMMC/SD card. The MLO and u-boot.img files were visible in the getting started directory that appears when you connect the Beagle board to your desktop machine.

This file system design has the advantage of making accidental deletion of these critical files unlikely. Importantly, the u-boot.img and MLO files were built using a patched version of the standard U-Boot distribution that was built with full knowledge of the hardware description of the Beagle boards. The second-stage bootloader (U-Boot) performs additional initialization and then loads and passes control to the Linux kernel, which it finds in the /boot/ directory of the ext4 partition.

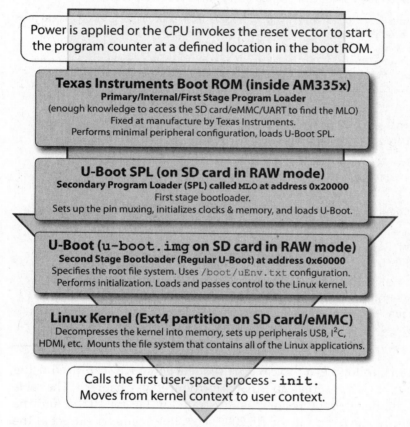

Figure 3-1: The full boot sequence on the Beagle boards

BUILDING A BOOTLOADER FOR THE BEAGLE BOARDS

Building a Beagle board–specific bootloader is an advanced topic that is best per-formed using a cross-compiler toolchain installed on your desktop computer. That topic is examined in Chapter 7; however, the key steps are as follows:

1. The Linux bootloader that is used on the Beagle boards is called Das U-Boot, and its source code is downloaded from git.denx.de/pub/u-boot/. Use a web browser to find the latest version.

2. The source code for U-Boot is modified using patches that have been written specifically for the Beagle boards. Browse at rcn-ee.com/repos/git/u-boot-patches/ to find a version number that is consistent with the U-Boot version in step 1.

3. The Beagle board–specific bootloader is then compiled to a binary file.

4. A uEnv.txt boot configuration text file is written that can be used to pass parameters to the Linux kernel.

   For example, to build U-Boot on the BBB using version 2018.03, use this:

```
debian@ebb:~$ wget ftp://ftp.denx.de/pub/u-boot/u-boot-2018.03.tar.bz2
debian@ebb:~$ tar -xjf u-boot-2018.03.tar.bz2
debian@ebb:~$ cd u-boot-2018.03/
debian@ebb:~/u-boot-2018.03$ wget https://rcn-ee.com/repos/git/u-bo →
ot-patches/v2018.03/0001-am335x_evm-uEnv.txt-bootz-n-fixes.patch
debian@ebb:~/u-boot-2018.03$ patch -p1 < 0001-am335x_evm-uEnv.txt-bo →
otz-n-fixes.patch
```

You should not receive any errors when the patches are applied if you have used consistent versions. Then build U-Boot on the board.

```
debian@ebb:~/u-boot-2018.03$ make am335x_boneblack_config
# configuration written to .config
debian@ebb:~/u-boot-2018.03$ make
```

This takes about 12 minutes to build on the BBB, resulting in the following files:

```
debian@ ebb:~/u-boot-2018.03$ ls -l MLO u-boot.img
-rw-r--r-- 1 debian debian  92252 May  6 12:41 MLO
-rw-r--r-- 1 debian debian 420352 May  6 12:38 u-boot.img
```

The MLO, u-boot.img, and uEnv.txt files are vital to your board booting. The uEnv.txt file sets the boot parameters for your board and can be created using a text editor. By default, it contains information such as the cape options, HDMI options, and so on.

The output that follows is a typical boot sequence that was captured using the USB to UART TTL 3V3 serial cable that is introduced in Chapter 1. The cable was attached the BeagleBone header, as illustrated in Figure 1-11(a), and the data was captured at a baud rate of 115,200. The following is an extract of the console output as a BBB is booting. It displays important system information, such as memory mappings.

```
U-Boot SPL 2018.01-00002-ge9ff418fb8 (Feb 20 2018 - 20:14:57)
Trying to boot from MMC2

U-Boot 2018.01-00002-ge9ff418fb8 (Feb 20 2018 - 20:14:57 -0600),
Build: jenkins-github_Bootloader-Builder-38
```

```
CPU  : AM335X-GP rev 2.1
I2C:   ready
DRAM:  512 MiB
Reset Source: Power-on reset has occurred.
MMC:   OMAP SD/MMC: 0, OMAP SD/MMC: 1
Using default environment

Board: BeagleBone Black
<ethaddr> not set. Validating first E-fuse MAC
BeagleBone Black:
BeagleBone: cape eeprom: i2c_probe: 0x54:
BeagleBone: cape eeprom: i2c_probe: 0x55:
BeagleBone: cape eeprom: i2c_probe: 0x56:
BeagleBone: cape eeprom: i2c_probe: 0x57:
Net:   eth0: MII MODE
cpsw, usb_ether
Press SPACE to abort autoboot in 2 seconds
board_name=[A335BNLT] ...
board_rev=[00C0] ...
Card did not respond to voltage select!
mmc_init: -95, time 13
gpio: pin 56 (gpio 56) value is 0
gpio: pin 55 (gpio 55) value is 0
gpio: pin 54 (gpio 54) value is 0
gpio: pin 53 (gpio 53) value is 1
Card did not respond to voltage select!
mmc_init: -95, time 13
switch to partitions #0, OK
mmc1(part 0) is current device
Scanning mmc 1:1...
gpio: pin 56 (gpio 56) value is 0
gpio: pin 55 (gpio 55) value is 0
gpio: pin 54 (gpio 54) value is 0
gpio: pin 53 (gpio 53) value is 1
switch to partitions #0, OK
mmc1(part 0) is current device
gpio: pin 54 (gpio 54) value is 1
Checking for: /uEnv.txt ...
Checking for: /boot.scr ...
Checking for: /boot/boot.scr ...
Checking for: /boot/uEnv.txt ...
gpio: pin 55 (gpio 55) value is 1
1879 bytes read in 22 ms (83 KiB/s)
Loaded environment from /boot/uEnv.txt
Checking if uname_r is set in /boot/uEnv.txt...
gpio: pin 56 (gpio 56) value is 1
Running uname_boot ...
loading /boot/vmlinuz-4.9.82-ti-r102 ...
9970640 bytes read in 655 ms (14.5 MiB/s)
uboot_overlays: [uboot_base_dtb=am335x-boneblack-uboot.dtb] ...
```

```
uboot_overlays: Switching too: dtb=am335x-boneblack-uboot.dtb ...
loading /boot/dtbs/4.9.82-ti-r102/am335x-boneblack-uboot.dtb ...
61622 bytes read in 56 ms (1 MiB/s)
uboot_overlays: [fdt_buffer=0x60000] ...
uboot_overlays: loading /lib/firmware/BB-BONE-eMMC1-01-00A0.dtbo ...
1440 bytes read in 605 ms (2 KiB/s)
uboot_overlays: loading /lib/firmware/BB-HDMI-TDA998x-00A0.dtbo ...
5127 bytes read in 80 ms (62.5 KiB/s)
uboot_overlays: loading /lib/firmware/BB-ADC-00A0.dtbo ...
711 bytes read in 397 ms (1000 Bytes/s)
uboot_overlays: loading /lib/firmware/univ-bbb-EVA-00A0.dtbo ...
62008 bytes read in 470 ms (127.9 KiB/s)
loading /boot/initrd.img-4.9.82-ti-r102 ...
6510886 bytes read in 435 ms (14.3 MiB/s)
debug: [console=ttyO0,115200n8 bone_capemgr.uboot_capemgr_enabled=1
root=/dev/mmcblk1p1 ro rootfstype=ext4 rootwait coherent_pool=1M
net.ifnames=0 quiet] ...
debug: [bootz 0x82000000 0x88080000:635926 88000000] ...
## Flattened Device Tree blob at 88000000
   Booting using the fdt blob at 0x88000000
   Loading Ramdisk to 8f9ca000, end 8ffff926 ... OK
   reserving fdt memory region: addr=88000000 size=7e000
   Loading Device Tree to 8f949000, end 8f9c9fff ... OK

Starting kernel ...
[    0.001915] clocksource_probe: no matching clocksources found
[    1.459462] wkup_m3_ipc 44e11324.wkup_m3_ipc: could not get rproc handle
[    1.751983] omap_voltage_late_init: Voltage driver support not added
[    1.759505] PM: Cannot get wkup_m3_ipc handle
rootfs: clean, 82338/239520 files, 481317/957440 blocks

Debian GNU/Linux 9 beaglebone ttyS0
BeagleBoard.org Debian Image 2018-03-05
Support/FAQ: http://elinux.org/Beagleboard:BeagleBoneBlack_Debian
default username:password is [debian:temppwd]
beaglebone login:
```

You can see that the initial hardware state is set, but most entries will seem quite mysterious for the moment. These are some important points to note (as highlighted in the preceding output segment):

- The U-Boot SPL first-stage bootloader is loaded first.

- The U-Boot second-stage bootloader is loaded next, and a full hardware description is then available.

- The GPIOs are checked to determine whether to boot from the eMMC or the SD card (e.g., check whether the Boot button is pressed).

- The configuration file /boot/uEnv.txt is loaded and parsed.

- The Linux kernel version is loaded (e.g., `4.9.82-ti-r102`).
- U-Boot loads the U-Boot overlays to configure hardware (e.g., HDMI, analog-to-digital converters).
- The kernel begins executing.

THE BEAGLE FAT PARTITION

Older Linux images for the BBB have a FAT partition on the boot eMMC or SD card that stores the Linux kernel and the bootloaders. This partition is visible as a USB storage device when the BBB is plugged into your desktop computer. For newer images, this USB storage device is still visible, but you will see that there is no FAT partition on the eMMC/SD card. This is because a virtual FAT image file (`.img`) is used instead, which can be found using the symbolic links in the `/var/local/` directory. Here's an example:

```
debian@ebb:/var/local$ ls
bbg_usb_mass_storage.img  bbgw_usb_mass_storage.img  bb_usb_mass_storage.img
```

You can look inside an image file using the `fdisk` tool as follows:

```
root@ebb:~# fdisk -lu /var/local/bb_usb_mass_storage.img
Disk /var/local/bb_usb_mass_storage.img: 18 MiB, 18874368 bytes, 36864 sectors
Units: sectors of 1 * 512 = 512 bytes
Sector size (logical/physical): 512 bytes / 512 bytes
I/O size (minimum/optimal): 512 bytes / 512 bytes
Disklabel type: dos
Disk identifier: 0xf3b130b0
Device                               Boot Start   End Sectors Size Id Type
/var/local/bb_usb_mass_storage.img1 2048 36863   34816   17M   e W95
FAT16(LBA)
```

Using such information, you can mount this image file on your Beagle board as follows. The following offset is calculated using the start sector shown previously, which is multiplied by the number of bytes per sector (as shown previously), giving 2,048 sectors × 512 bytes = 1,048,576 bytes. This value is used in the following `mount` command:

```
root@ebb:~# mkdir /mnt/fat
root@ebb:~# mount -o loop,offset=1048576 -t vfat →
  /var/local/bb_usb_mass_storage.img /mnt/fat
root@ebb:~# cd /mnt/fat
root@ebb:/mnt/fat# ls
App         autorun.inf  Docs       Drivers  LICENSE.txt  README.htm
README.md   scripts      START.htm
```

```
root@ebb:~$ lsblk
NAME          MAJ:MIN RM   SIZE RO TYPE MOUNTPOINT
loop0             7:0   0   17M  0 loop /mnt/fat
mmcblk0         179:0   0 29.8G  0 disk
└─mmcblk0p1     179:1   0 29.8G  0 part /
```

The primary configuration file for the Beagle boards is /boot/uEnv.txt. You can manually edit this file (e.g., sudo nano /boot/uEnv.txt) to enable/disable hardware, to provide Linux command-line arguments, and to use the eMMC flasher script by commenting and uncommenting lines. For example, here is a cut-down configuration file:

```
debian@ebb:/boot$ more uEnv.txt
#Docs: http://elinux.org/Beagleboard:U-boot_partitioning_layout_2.0
###Master Enable
enable_uboot_overlays=1

###Custom Cape
#dtb_overlay=/lib/firmware/<file8>.dtbo
###
###Disable auto loading of virtual capes (emmc/video/wireless/adc)
#disable_uboot_overlay_emmc=1
#disable_uboot_overlay_video=1
#disable_uboot_overlay_audio=1
#disable_uboot_overlay_wireless=1
#disable_uboot_overlay_adc=1

###Cape Universal Enable
enable_uboot_cape_universal=1

cmdline=coherent_pool=1M net.ifnames=0 quiet

##enable Generic eMMC Flasher:
##make sure, these tools are installed: dosfstools rsync
#cmdline=init=/opt/scripts/tools/eMMC/init-eMMC-flasher-v3.sh
```

Remove the comment in front of the last line in the file to call a script that overwrites the BeagleBone eMMC with the Linux image that is on the SD card.

Das U-Boot uses a board configuration file called a *device tree* (also called a *device tree binary*) containing the board-specific information that the kernel requires to boot the board. This file contains all the information needed to describe the memory size, clock speeds, on-board devices, and so on. This device tree binary (DTB), or the *binary*, is created from a DTS (the source) file using the *device tree compiler* (dtc). This topic is described in detail in Chapter 6, when examining how to interface to the Beagle board GPIOs.

```
debian@ebb:/boot/dtbs/4.9.82-ti-r102$ ls -l *.dtb
...
-rw-r--r-- 1 root root  64035 Feb 22 01:26 am335x-boneblack.dtb
```

```
-rw-r--r-- 1 root root  66633 Feb 22 01:26 am335x-boneblack-wireless.dtb
-rw-r--r-- 1 root root 137415 Feb 22 01:26 am335x-boneblue.dtb
-rw-r--r-- 1 root root  61710 Feb 22 01:26 am335x-bonegreen.dtb
...
-rw-r--r-- 1 root root 132769 Feb 22 01:26 am335x-pocketbeagle.dtb
...
```

The DTS has the same syntax as the following extract, which details the four user LED pins and one of the two I²C buses on the BBB:

```
am33xx_pinmux: pinmux@44e10800 {
   pinctrl-names = "default";
   pinctrl-0 = <&userled_pins>;

   userled_pins: pinmux_userled_pins {
     pinctrl-single,pins = <
         0x54 0x07        /* gpmc_a5.gpio1_21, OUTPUT        | MODE7 */
         0x58 0x17        /* gpmc_a6.gpio1_22, OUTPUT_PULLUP | MODE7 */
         0x5c 0x07        /* gpmc_a7.gpio1_23, OUTPUT        | MODE7 */
         0x60 0x17        /* gpmc_a8.gpio1_24, OUTPUT_PULLUP | MODE7 */
     >;
   };
   i2c0_pins: pinmux_i2c0_pins {
     pinctrl-single,pins = <
         0x188 0x70       /* i2c0_sda, SLEWCTRL_SLOW | INPUT_PULLUP */
         0x18c 0x70       /* i2c0_scl, SLEWCTRL_SLOW | INPUT_PULLUP */
     >;
   }; ...
};
```

The full description for the device tree source for Linux 4.*x.x* is available with the source code distribution of this book in the Chapter 3 directory. You will see how to download this code at the end of the chapter. This tree structure is discussed in detail in Chapter 6, when custom circuits are interfaced to the Beagle boards.

Kernel Space and User Space

The Linux kernel runs in an area of system memory called the *kernel space*, and regular user applications run in an area of system memory called *user space*. A hard boundary between these two spaces prevents user applications from accessing memory and resources required by the Linux kernel. This helps prevent the Linux kernel from crashing because of badly written user code; because it prevents applications that belong to one user from interfering with applications and resources that belong to another user, it also provides a degree of security.

The Linux kernel "owns" and has full access to all the physical memory and resources on the Beagle boards. Therefore, you have to be careful that only the most stable and trusted code is permitted to run in kernel space. You can see the architectures and interfaces illustrated in Figure 3-2, where user applications use the GNU C Library (glibc) to make calls to the kernel's system call interface. The kernel services are then made available to the user space in a controlled way through the use of system calls.

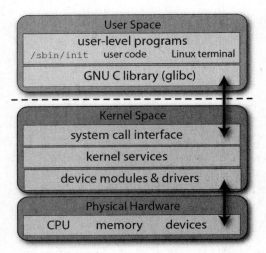

Figure 3-2: The Linux user space and kernel space architectures

A *kernel module* is an object file that contains binary code, which can be loaded and unloaded from the kernel on demand. In many cases, the kernel can even load and unload modules while it is executing, without needing to reboot the board. For example, if you plug a USB Wi-Fi adapter into your board, it is possible for the kernel to use a loadable kernel module (LKM) to utilize the adapter. Without this modular capability, the Linux kernel would be extremely large, as it would have to support every driver that would ever be needed on any Beagle board. You would also have to rebuild the kernel every time you wanted to add new hardware. One downside of LKMs is that driver files have to be maintained for each device. (Interaction with LKMs is described throughout the book, and you will see how you can write your own LKMs in Chapter 16.)

As described in Figure 3-1, the bootloader stages pass control to the kernel after it has been decompressed into memory. The kernel then mounts the root file system. The kernel's last step in the boot process is to call systemd init (/sbin/init on the Beagle boards with the Debian Stretch image), which is the first user-space process that is started and the next topic that is discussed.

READING MEMORY VALUES DIRECTLY (ADVANCED)

On some ARM devices you can configure the MAC address dynamically; however, page 5,067 (26.1.9.4) of the *AM335x ARM Technical Reference Manual* (TRM) states that the "Device uses EFUSE registers mac_id0_lo and mac_id0_hi in the control module for the Ethernet MAC address of the device" (Texas Instruments, 2017). These values are stored in AM335x ROM and cannot be changed. The mac_id0_lo is at offset 630h from 0x44e10000 (see pg. 1,486), and mac_id0_hi is at offset 634h (see pg. 1,487). You can see these memory addresses using a small program called devmem2 that can be downloaded, built, and run as follows:

```
debian@ebb:~$ cd ~/
debian@ebb:~$ wget http://www.lartmaker.nl/lartware/port/devmem2.c
debian@ebb:~$ gcc devmem2.c -o devmem2
debian@ebb:~$ sudo ./devmem2 0x44e10630
Value at address 0x44E10630 (0xb6f2a630): 0xBCDA
debian@ebb:~$ sudo ./devmem2 0x44e10634
Value at address 0x44E10634 (0xb6efd634): 0xE6164A54
debian@ebb:~$ ifconfig eth0
eth0: flags=-28669<UP,BROADCAST,MULTICAST,DYNAMIC>  mtu 1500
       ether 54:4a:16:e6:da:bc  ...
```

The IP address matches the memory values, but in reverse order. Your BeagleBone needs to be connected to the internet for these steps to work correctly.

The systemd System and Service Manager

A *system and service manager* starts and stops services (e.g., web servers, Secure Shell [SSH] server) depending on the current state of the board (e.g., starting up, shutting down). The *systemd* system and service manager is a recent and somewhat controversial addition to Linux that aims to replace and remain backward compatible with *System V (SysV) init*. One major drawback of SysV init is that it starts tasks in series, waiting for one task to complete before beginning the next, which can lead to lengthy boot times. The systemd system is enabled by default in Debian 9 (Stretch). It starts up system services in parallel, helping to keep boot times short, particularly on multicore processors such as the BeagleBoard X15. In fact, you can display the boot time using the following (you may be able to log in some time before the user-space processes have completed):

```
debian@beaglebone:~$ systemctl --version
systemd 232 +PAM +AUDIT +SELINUX +IMA +APPARMOR +SMACK +SYSVINIT
+UTMP +LIBCRYPTSETUP +GCRYPT +GNUTLS +ACL +XZ +LZ4 +SECCOMP +BLKID
+ELFUTILS +KMOD +IDN
debian@beaglebone:~$ systemd-analyze time
Startup finished in 15.638s (kernel) + 45.405s (userspace) = 1min 1.044s
```

As well as being a system and service manager, systemd consists of a software bundle for login management, journal logging, device management, time synchronization, and more. Critics of systemd claim that its development project has suffered from "mission creep" and that it has taken on development work that is outside of its core mission. To some extent, this change in mission has resulted in systemd becoming core to the future of Linux itself, possibly even removing choice from users; however, it is clear that systemd is being widely adopted by many Linux distributions and here to stay.

You can use the `systemctl` command to inspect and control the state of systemd. If called with no arguments, it provides a full list of the services that are running on your board (there can be 100+ services running on a typical board). Use the Spacebar to page, and use Q to quit.

```
debian@beaglebone:~$ systemctl
UNIT                             LOAD   ACTIVE SUB     DESCRIPTION
-.mount                          loaded active mounted Root Mount
apache2.service                  loaded active running The Apache HTTP Server
bonescript-autorun.service       loaded active running Bonescript autorun
connman.service                  loaded active running Connection service
cron.service                     loaded active running Regular background ...
getty@tty1.service               loaded active running Getty on tty1
serial-getty@ttyGS0.service      loaded active running Serial Getty on ttyGS0
serial-getty@ttyS0.service       loaded active running Serial Getty on ttyS0
ssh.service                      loaded active running OpenBSD Secure Shell
...
```

systemd uses *service files*, which have a `.service` extension to configure how the different services should behave on startup, shutdown, reload, and so on; see the `/lib/systemd/system` directory.

The Apache service runs by default upon installation. The systemd system can be used to manage such services on your board. For example, you can identify the exact service name and get its status using the following steps:

```
debian@beaglebone:~$ systemctl list-units -t service | grep apache
apache2.service     loaded active running The Apache HTTP Server
debian@beaglebone:~$ systemctl status apache2.service
 • apache2.service - The Apache HTTP Server
   Loaded: loaded (/lib/systemd/system/apache2.service; enabled; ...
   Active: active (running) since Wed 2018-05-02 16:04:32 IST; 1h 41min ago
  Process: 1029 ExecStart=/usr/sbin/apachectl start
 Main PID: 1117 (apache2)
    Tasks: 55 (limit: 4915)
   CGroup: /system.slice/apache2.service
           └─1117 /usr/sbin/apache2 -k start
           └─1120 /usr/sbin/apache2 -k start
           └─1122 /usr/sbin/apache2 -k start
May 02 16:04:28 beaglebone systemd[1]: Starting The Apache HTTP Server...
May 02 16:04:32 beaglebone systemd[1]: Started The Apache HTTP Server.
```

At this point you can connect to the board on port 8080 using your web browser to verify that the Apache server is running as a service on the board, as illustrated in Figure 3-3.

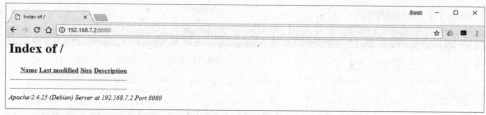

Figure 3-3: The Apache Server running on the Beagle board

You can stop the `apache2` service using the `systemctl` command, whereupon the browser will issue a "connection refused" message.

```
debian@beaglebone:~$ sudo systemctl stop apache2
[sudo] password for debian:
debian@beaglebone:~$ systemctl status apache2
● apache2.service - The Apache HTTP Server
   Loaded: loaded (/lib/systemd/system/apache2.service; enabled; ...
   Active: inactive (dead) since Wed 2018-05-02 17:51:12 IST; 17s ago
  Process: 1969 ExecStop=/usr/sbin/apachectl stop
  Process: 1029 ExecStart=/usr/sbin/apachectl start
 Main PID: 1117 (code=exited, status=0/SUCCESS)
```

The service can then be restarted as follows:

```
debian@beaglebone:~$ sudo systemctl start apache2
```

Table 3-1 provides a summary of systemd commands, using the `apache2` service as a syntax example. Many of these commands require elevation to superuser permissions by use of the `sudo` tool, as described in the next section.

Table 3-1: Common systemd Commands

COMMAND	DESCRIPTION
`systemctl`	List all running services.
`systemctl start apache2`	Start a service. Does not persist after reboot.
`systemctl stop apache2`	Stop a service. Does not persist after reboot.
`systemctl status apache2`	Display the service status.
`systemctl enable apache2`	Enable a service to start on boot.
`systemctl disable apache2`	Disable a service from starting on boot.
`systemctl is-enabled apache2`	Display if a system service starts on boot.

Continues

Table 3-1 (*continued*)

COMMAND	DESCRIPTION
`systemctl restart apache2`	Restart a service (stop and then start).
`systemctl condrestart apache2`	Restart a service only if it is running.
`systemctl reload apache2`	Reload configuration files for a service without halting it.
`journalctl -f`	Follow the systemd log file. Press Ctrl+C to quit.
`sudo hostnamectl --static set-hostname ebb`	Change the hostname.
`hostname`	Display the hostname.
`timedatectl`	Display the time and time zone information.
`systemd-analyze time`	Display the boot time.

The *runlevel* describes the current state of your board and can be used to control which processes or services are started by the `init` system. Under SysV, there are different runlevels, identified as 0 (halt), 1 (single-user mode), 2 through 5 (multiuser modes), 6 (reboot), and S (startup). When the `init` process begins, the runlevel starts at N (none). It then enters runlevel S to initialize the system in single-user mode and finally enters one of the multiuser runlevels (2 through 5). To determine the current runlevel, type the following:

```
debian@beaglebone:~$ who -r
         run-level 5  2018-05-02 16:05
```

In this case, the board is running at runlevel 5. You can change the runlevel by typing **init** followed by the level number. For example, you can reboot your board by typing the following:

```
debian@beaglebone:~$ sudo hostnamectl --static set-hostname ebb
debian@beaglebone:~$ hostname
ebb
```

Also, edit the `/etc/hosts` file to have an entry for `ebb`, or you will receive "unable to resolve host" messages when you use the `sudo` command.

```
debian@beaglebone:~$ more /etc/hosts
127.0.0.1       localhost
127.0.1.1       beaglebone.localdomain  beaglebone   ebb
...
debian@beaglebone:~$ sudo init 6
```

> **NOTE** From this point in the book, the commands described here are used to change the shell prompt to `debian@ebb` (as in "Exploring BeagleBone") instead of `debian@beaglebone` to make the code listings less verbose.

As demonstrated, systemd retains some backward compatibility with the SysV runlevels and their numbers, as the previous SysV commands work correctly under systemd. However, the use of runlevels in systemd is considered to be a dated practice. Instead, systemd uses named *target units*, some of which are listed in Table 3-2, which includes an indicative alignment with SysV runlevels. You can identify the current default target on the board.

```
debian@ebb:~$ systemctl get-default
graphical.target
```

Table 3-2: systemd Targets Aligned with SysV Runlevels

TARGET NAMES	SYSV	DESCRIPTION AND EXAMPLE USE
`poweroff.target`	0	Halt the system: shutdown state for all services
`rescue.target`	1,S	Single-user mode: for administrative functions such as checking the file system
`multi-user.target`	2-4	Regular multiuser modes with no windowing display
`graphical.target`	5	Regular multiuser mode with windowing display
`reboot.target`	6	Reboot the system: reboot state for all services
`emergency.target`	—	Emergency shell only on the main console

This indicates that the current configuration is for the board to have a headful windowing display. You can also see the list of units that the target loads using the following:

```
debian@ebb:~$ systemctl list-units --type=target
UNIT                  LOAD   ACTIVE SUB    DESCRIPTION
basic.target          loaded active active Basic System
cryptsetup.target     loaded active active Encrypted Volumes
getty.target          loaded active active Login Prompts
graphical.target      loaded active active Graphical Interface
local-fs-pre.target   loaded active active Local File Systems (Pre)
local-fs.target       loaded active active Local File Systems
multi-user.target     loaded active active Multi-User System
...
```

If you are using your board as a network-attached device that does not have a display attached (i.e., headless), it is wasteful of CPU/memory resources to have the windowing services running.[2] You can switch to a headless target using the following call, whereupon the LXQt windowing interface will no longer be present, and the `graphical.target` entry will no longer appear in the list of units.

```
debian@ebb:~$ sudo systemctl isolate multi-user.target
debian@ebb:~$ who -r
         run-level 3  2018-05-02 16:18       last=5
```

And, you can re-enable the headful graphical display using the following:

```
debian@ebb:~$ sudo systemctl isolate graphical.target
debian@ebb:~$ who -r
         run-level 5  2018-05-02 16:20       last=3
```

Finally, to set up the board so that it uses a different default runlevel on boot (e.g., for a headless display), you can use the following:

```
debian@ebb:~$ sudo systemctl set-default multi-user.target
Created symlink /etc/systemd/system/default.target →
/lib/systemd/system/multi-user.target.
debian@ebb:~$ systemctl get-default
multi-user.target
```

After reboot, the windowing services (if they are present) do not start, and the notional equivalent SysV runlevel is displayed as runlevel 3.

Managing Linux Systems

In this section, you examine the Linux file system in more detail, building on the commands and tools described in Chapter 2, to ensure that you have full administrative control of your board.

The Superuser

On Linux systems, the system administrator account has the highest level of security access to all commands and files. Typically, this account is referred to as the *root account* or *superuser*. Under Debian, this user account has the username `root`, but it is typically disabled by default; however, you can enable it by typing

---

[2]The Beagle Debian IoT image does not have LXQt windowing services installed by default, but they can be added at any point using the package manager.

`sudo passwd root` from a shell that is logged in with the debian user account (username: `debian`, password: `temppwd`).

```
debian@ebb:~$ sudo passwd root
Enter new UNIX password: myrootpassword
Retype new UNIX password: myrootpassword
passwd: password updated successfully
```

NOTE The naming of the user account as root is related to the fact that it is the only user account with permission to alter the top-level root directory (/). For more information, see `www.linfo.org/root.htm`.

It is recommended when performing general operations on a Linux system that you try to avoid being logged in as the superuser; however, it is important to also remember that when using an embedded Linux system you are typically not running a server with thousands of user accounts! In many applications, a single root user account, with a nondefault password, is likely sufficient. However, using a nonsuperuser account for your development work could protect you from yourself—for example, from accidentally deleting the file system. The debian user account in Debian has been carefully configured to simplify the interaction with hardware, enabling it to be used for the majority of tasks that are described in this book. However, it is important to understand how this custom user account is configured and how it works so well.

Under many Linux distributions, including Debian, a special tool called `sudo` (*superuser do*) is used whenever you want to perform system administration commands. Typically, the tool prompts you for the administrator password and then authorizes you to perform administrator operations for a short time period, also warning you that "with great power comes great responsibility." The debian user account in Debian has been configured so that it requires you to enter a password for superuser elevation.

The next section discusses user accounts management, but if you create a new user account and want to enable it to use the `sudo` tool, the account name must be added to the *sudoers file*, /etc/sudoers, by using the `visudo` tool (type **visudo** while logged in as root, or type **sudo visudo** if logged in as debian). The last lines of the /etc/sudoers file provide the configuration for the debian user account (lines are commented out using the # symbol). It does this by setting the properties for a group, called sudo, of which the user debian is a member:

```
debian@ebb:~$ sudo more /etc/sudoers
# User privilege specification
root      ALL=(ALL:ALL) ALL
# Allow members of group sudo to execute any command
%sudo     ALL=(ALL:ALL) ALL   ...
```

In this configuration, any user in the sudo group is granted privileges on all (first ALL) hostnames to execute commands as any user (second ALL) and to execute all commands (third ALL). The sudo tool works well; however, it can make the redirection of the output of a command more complex, which is apparent later in this chapter. You can add a user to the sudo group as follows:

```
debian@ebb:~$ sudo adduser debian sudo
Adding user 'debian' to group 'sudo' ...
Adding user debian to group sudo
Done.
```

There is another command in Linux that enables you to run a shell with a substitute user: su. Typing **su -** (same as su - root) opens a new shell with full superuser access, and it can be used as follows, after you have enabled root login:

```
debian@ebb:~$ su -
Password: mySuperSecretPassword
root@ebb:~# whoami
root
root@ebb:~# exit
logout
debian@ebb:~$ whoami
debian
```

Instead of doing this, you can create an interactive shell (-i) through the sudo command, as shown here:

```
debian@ebb:~$ sudo -i
root@ebb:~# whoami
root
```

which means that the login-specific resources (e.g., .profile) are read by the shell. The # prompt indicates that you are logged in to the superuser account. To re-disable root login to the board, you can type **sudo passwd -l root**.

System Administration

The *Linux file system* is a hierarchy of directories used to organize files on a Linux system. This section examines the ownership of files, the use of symbolic links, and the concept of file system permissions.

The Linux File System

Linux uses data structures, called *inodes*, to represent file system objects such as files and directories. When a Linux *ext*ended file system (e.g., ext3/ext4) is created on a physical disk, an *inode table* is created. This table links to an inode data structure for each file and directory on that physical disk. The inode data structure for each file and directory stores information such as permission attributes, pointers to raw physical disk block locations, time stamps, and link counts. You can see this with an example by performing a listing `ls -ail` of the root directory, where `-i` causes `ls` to display the inode indexes. You will see the following for the `/tmp` directory entry:

```
debian@ebb:~$ cd /
debian@ebb:/$ ls -ail | grep tmp
41337 drwxrwxrwt  10 root root  4096 May  2 18:17 tmp
```

Therefore, `41337` is the `/tmp` directory's *inode index*. If you enter the `/tmp` directory by using **cd**, create a temporary file (`a.txt`), and perform `ls -ail`, you will see that the current (.) directory has the same inode index.

```
debian@ebb:/$ cd tmp
debian@ebb:/tmp$ touch a.txt
debian@ebb:/tmp$ ls -ail
total 40
41337 drwxrwxrwt 10 root   root   4096 May  2 18:36 .
    2 drwxr-xr-x 21 root   root   4096 Apr 23 01:47 ..
 1893 -rw-r--r--  1 debian debian    0 May  2 18:36 a.txt
```

You can also see that the root directory (..) has the inode index of 2 and that a text file (`a.txt`) also has an inode index, 1893. Therefore, you cannot `cd` directly to an inode index because the inode index might not refer to a directory.

Figure 3-4 illustrates the Linux directory listing and file permissions that relate to working with files under Linux. The first letter indicates the file type—for example, whether the listing is a (d) directory, (1) link, or (-) regular file. There are also some more obscure file types: (c) character special, (b) block special, (p) fifo, and (s) socket. Directories and regular files do not need further explanation, but links need special attention, as described next.

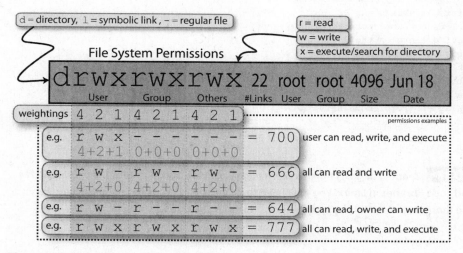

Figure 3-4: Linux directory listing and file permissions

Links to Files and Directories

There are two types of links in Linux: *soft links* and *hard links*. A soft link (or *symbolic link*) is a file that refers to the location of another file or directory. Hard links, conversely, link directly to the inode index, but they cannot be linked to a directory. You create a link using `ln /path/to/file.txt linkname`. You create a symbolic link by adding `-s` to the call. To illustrate the usage, the following example creates a soft link and a hard link to a file `/tmp/test.txt`:

```
debian@ebb:~$ cd /tmp
debian@ebb:/tmp$ touch test.txt
debian@ebb:/tmp$ ln -s /tmp/test.txt softlink
debian@ebb:/tmp$ ln /tmp/test.txt hardlink
debian@ebb:/tmp$ ls -ail
total 40
 41337 drwxrwxrwt 10 root    root    4096 May  2 18:40 .
     2 drwxr-xr-x 21 root    root    4096 Apr 23 01:47 ..
  2172 -rw-r--r--  2 debian debian     0 May  2 18:40 hardlink
  2268 lrwxrwxrwx  1 debian debian    13 May  2 18:40 softlink -> /tmp/test.txt
  2172 -rw-r--r--  2 debian debian     0 May  2 18:40 test.txt
```

The hard link has the same inode index as the `test.txt` file, and you can also see there is a number 2 in front of the file `test.txt` and `hardlink` entry (after the file permissions). This is the number of hard links that are associated with the file. This is a count value that was incremented by 1 when the hard link, called `hardlink`, was created. If you were to delete the hard link (e.g., using `rm hardlink`), this counter would decrement back to 1. To illustrate the difference between soft links and hard links, some text is added to the `test.txt` file.

```
debian@ebb:/tmp$ echo "testing links on the BB" >> test.txt
debian@ebb:/tmp$ more hardlink
testing links on the BB
debian@ebb:/tmp$ more softlink
testing links on the BB
debian@ebb:/tmp$ mkdir sub
debian@ebb:/tmp$ mv test.txt sub/
debian@ebb:/tmp$ more hardlink
testing links on the BB
debian@ebb:/tmp$ more softlink
more: stat of softlink failed: No such file or directory
```

NOTE Manual pages, known as *man pages*, provide documentation on commands and code libraries in Linux. You may have to install the man command before you can use these pages. Do this by typing `sudo apt install man-db`.

You can see that when the test.txt file is moved to the subdirectory, the soft link breaks, but the hard link still works perfectly. Therefore, symbolic links are not updated when the linked file is moved, but hard links always refer to the source, even if moved or removed. To illustrate the last point, the file test.txt can be removed using the following:

```
debian@ebb:/tmp$ rm sub/test.txt
debian@ebb:/tmp$ more hardlink
testing links on the BB
debian@ebb:/tmp$ ls -ail hardlink
2172 -rw-r--r-- 1 debian debian 24 May  2 18:59 hardlink
```

Yet, the file still exists! And it will not be deleted until you delete the hard link called hardlink, thus decrementing the link count to zero. You can see that the count is currently 1 by examining the hardlink entry. Therefore, if a file has a hard link count of zero and it is not being used by a process, it will be deleted. In effect, the filename itself, test.txt, was just a hard link. Note that you cannot hard link across different file systems, because each file system will have its own inode index table that starts at 1. Therefore, inode 269, which is the inode index of the /tmp directory, is likely describing something quite different on another file system. Type the command **man ln** to see a particularly useful guide on linking.

NOTE   You can type **history** to list all previous commands that you have typed. You can also press Ctrl+R to get an interactive search of your history to find a recently used command. Pressing Enter activates the command, and pressing Tab places it on your command line so that it can be modified.

Users and Groups

Linux is a multiuser OS, which uses the following three distinct classes to manage access permissions:

- **User:** You can create different user accounts on your board. This is useful if you want to limit access to processes and areas of the file system. The root user account is the superuser for Debian and has access to every file; so, for example, it may not be safe to run a public web server from this account or the debian user account if the server supports local scripting.

- **Group:** User accounts may be flagged as belonging to one or more groups, whereby each group has different levels of access to different resources (e.g., gpios, I^{2}C buses).

- **Others:** This includes all users of the system besides the file's owner, or a member of the group listed in the permissions.

You can create users at the Linux terminal. The full list of groups is available by typing `more /etc/group`. The following example demonstrates how you can create a new user account on the board and modify the properties of that account to suit your needs. You can list the groups that a user belongs to by typing `groups` at the shell prompt.

```
debian@ebb:~$ groups
debian adm kmem dialout cdrom floppy audio dip video plugdev
users systemd-journal i2c bluetooth netdev cloud9ide xenomai
weston-launch tisdk spi admin eqep pwm gpio
```

EXAMPLE: CREATING A NEW USER ACCOUNT ON THE BEAGLE BOARD

This example demonstrates how you can create a user account and then retrospectively change its properties, using the following steps:

1. Creating a new user account called molloyd on the board

2. Adding the account to a new group of your own design

3. Adding the user account to the standard interfacing groups

4. Resetting the password for the new user account

5. Verifying that the account is working correctly

Step 1: Create a user `molloyd` as follows:

```
debian@ebb:~$ sudo adduser molloyd
[sudo] password for debian:
Adding user 'molloyd' ...
Adding new group 'molloyd' (1001) ...
Adding new user 'molloyd' (1001) with group 'molloyd' ...
Creating home directory '/home/molloyd' ...
Copying files from '/etc/skel' ...
Enter new UNIX password: newpassword
Retype new UNIX password: newpassword
passwd: password updated successfully
Changing the user information for molloyd
Enter the new value, or press ENTER for the default
        Full Name []: Derek Molloy
        Room Number []: Home
        Work Phone []: 353 12345678
        Home Phone []: 353 87654321
        Other []: none
Is the information correct? [Y/n] Y
```

Step 2: Add the user to a new group of your design:

```
debian@ebb:~$ sudo groupadd newgroup
debian@ebb:~$ sudo adduser molloyd newgroup
Adding user 'molloyd' to group 'newgroup' ...
```

```
Adding user molloyd to group newgroup
Done.
debian@ebb:~$ groups molloyd
molloyd : molloyd dialout cdrom floppy audio video plugdev
users i2c spi newgroup
```

Step 3: Add the user to the standard user and interface groups:

```
debian@ebb:~$ sudo usermod -a -G debian,adm,kmem,sudo,dip,plugdev,
users,systemdjournal,i2c,bluetooth,netdev,cloud9ide,gpio,pwm,eqep,
admin,spi,tisdk,weston-launch,xenomai molloyd
debian@ebb:~$ groups molloyd
molloyd : molloyd adm kmem dialout cdrom floppy sudo audio dip
video plugdev users systemd-journal i2c bluetooth netdev cloud9ide
gpio pwm eqep admin spi tisdk weston-launch xenomai debian newgroup
```

Step 4: Reset the password, if required:

```
debian@ebb:~$ sudo passwd molloyd
Enter new UNIX password: temppasswd
Retype new UNIX password: temppasswd
passwd: password updated successfully
debian@ebb:~$ sudo chage -d 0 molloyd
```

You can force the password to expire on login by using sudo chage -d 0 molloyd. For security, the encrypted passwords are stored in the restricted file /etc/shadow, not the public readable /etc/passwd file.

Step 5: Test the account by typing su molloyd from the debian user account and/ or log in with a new Linux terminal (using pwd to print the working directory).

```
debian@ebb:~$ su molloyd
Password: supassword
You are required to change your password immediately
Changing password for molloyd.
(current) UNIX password: temppasswd
Enter new UNIX password: secretpassword
Retype new UNIX password: secretpassword
molloyd@ebb:/home/debian$ whoami
molloyd
molloyd@ebb:/home/debian$ pwd
/home/debian
molloyd@ebb:/home/debian$ cd
molloyd@ebb:~$ pwd
/home/molloyd
molloyd@ebb:~$ touch test.txt
molloyd@ebb:~$ ls -l test.txt
-rw-r--r-- 1 molloyd molloyd 0 May  2 19:52 test.txt
molloyd@ebb:~$ more /etc/group | grep newgroup
newgroup:x:1002:molloyd
```

> The user's home directory for each user account is represented as ~ at the shell prompt. You can see that the `test.txt` file is created with the correct user and group ID. Also, note that the `newgroup` group has only one member, `molloyd`. To delete an account, type `sudo deluser --remove-home molloyd`, which removes the user account and its home directory.

To practice with the topics that were introduced earlier in this chapter, the following examples are performed using the molloyd user account. The first example demonstrates how to change the ownership of a file using the *change ownership* `chown` command and to change the group ownership of the file using the *change group* `chgrp` command.

For the `sudo` tool to be invoked correctly in the example, the user molloyd must be present in the sudo group, which is the case for the user `debian` and the user `molloyd` (from the previous example).

Alternatively, you can edit the `sudoers` file, which is achieved by the debian user account executing the `visudo` command. The file can be modified to include a `molloyd` entry, such as the following:

```
debian@ebb:~$ sudo visudo
debian@ebb:~$ sudo tail -n 1 /etc/sudoers
molloyd ALL=(ALL) ALL
```

The molloyd user account can now execute the `sudo` command and must enter their user password to do so.

EXAMPLE: CHANGING THE OWNERSHIP AND GROUP OF A FILE

SSH to the board and log in as the molloyd user. Use superuser access to change a file `test.txt` in the `/tmp` directory that is owned by the user molloyd with the group molloyd, to have owner root and group root.

```
molloyd@ebb:~$ cd /tmp
molloyd@ebb:/tmp$ touch test.txt
molloyd@ebb:/tmp$ ls -l test.txt
-rw-r--r-- 1 molloyd molloyd 0 May  2 20:03 test.txt
molloyd@ebb:/tmp$ sudo chgrp root test.txt
molloyd@ebb:/tmp$ ls -l test.txt
-rw-r--r-- 1 molloyd root 0 May  2 20:03 test.txt
molloyd@ebb:/tmp$ sudo chown root test.txt
molloyd@ebb:/tmp$ ls -l test.txt
-rw-r--r-- 1 root root 0 May  2 20:03 test.txt
```

File System Permissions

The *file system permissions* state what levels of access each of the permissions classes have to a file or directory. The *change mode* command `chmod` enables a user to change the access permissions for file system objects. You can specify the permissions in a relative way. For example, `chmod a+w test.txt` gives all users write access to a file `test.txt` but leaves all other permissions the same. You can also apply the permissions in an absolute way. For example, `chmod a=r test.txt` sets all users to only have read access to the file `test.txt`. The next example demonstrates how to modify the file system permissions of a file using the `chmod` command.

EXAMPLE: USING THE CHMOD COMMAND IN DIFFERENT FORMS

Change a file `test1.txt` in the `/tmp` directory so that users and group members have read and write access but others have only read access. Perform this task in these three ways:

```
molloyd@ebb:/tmp$ touch test1.txt
molloyd@ebb:/tmp$ ls -l test1.txt
-rw-r--r-- 1 molloyd molloyd 0 May  2 20:23 test1.txt
molloyd@ebb:/tmp$ chmod g+w test1.txt
molloyd@ebb:/tmp$ ls -l test1.txt
-rw-rw-r-- 1 molloyd molloyd 0 May  2 20:23 test1.txt
molloyd@ebb:/tmp$ chmod 664 test1.txt
molloyd@ebb:/tmp$ ls -l test1.txt
-rw-rw-r-- 1 molloyd molloyd 0 May  2 20:23 test1.txt
molloyd@ebb:/tmp$ chmod u=rw,g=rw,o=r test1.txt
molloyd@ebb:/tmp$ ls -l test1.txt
-rw-rw-r-- 1 molloyd molloyd 0 May  2 20:23 test1.txt
```

All three calls to `chmod` have the same outcome.

Table 3-3 provides examples of the command structure for `chown` and `chgrp`. It also lists some example commands for working with users, groups, and permissions.

Table 3-3: Commands for Working with Users, Groups, and Permissions

COMMAND	DESCRIPTION
`chown molloyd a.txt`	Change file owner.
`chown molloyd:users a.txt`	Change owner and group at the same time.
`chown - Rh molloyd /tmp/test`	Recursively change ownership of /tmp/test.
	-h affects symbolic links instead of referenced files.
`chgrp users a.txt`	Change group ownership of the file.
`chgrp -Rh users /tmp/test`	Recursively change with same -h as `chown`.

Continues

Table 3-3 (*continued*)

COMMAND	DESCRIPTION
chmod 600 a.txt	Change permissions (as in Figure 3-4) so that the user has read/write access to the file; group or others have no access.
chmod ugo+rw a.txt	Give users, group, and others read/write access to a.txt.
chmod a-w a.txt	Remove write access for all users using a, which describes *all* (the set of users, group, and others).
chmod ugo=rw a.txt	Set the permissions for all to be read/write.
umask umask -S	List the default permissions settings. Using -S displays the umask in a more readable form.
umask 022 umask u=rwx,g=rx,o=rx	Change the default permissions on all newly created files and directories. The two umask commands here are equivalent. If you set this mask value and create a file or directory, it will be drwxr-xr-x for the directory and -rw-r--r-- for the file. You can set a user-specific umask in the account's .login file.
chmod u+s myexe chmod g+s myexe	Set a special bit called the *setuid bit* (set user ID on execute) and *setgid bit* (set group ID on execute), s, that allows a program to be executed as if by another logged-in user but with the permissions of the file's owner or group. For example, you could use this to allow a particular program to execute as if the root user account executed it. If the file is not executable, a capital S appears, instead of a lowercase s.
chmod 6750 myexe chmod u=rwxs,g=rxs,o=myexe	Set the setuid bit in an absolute way. Both examples will give myexe the permissions -rwsr-s---, where both the setuid and setgid bits are set (note the space before myexe). For security reasons, the setuid bit cannot be applied to shell scripts.
stat /tmp/test.txt	Provides useful file system status information for a file or directory, such as its physical device and inode information, last access, and modify/change times.

Here is an example of the last entry in Table 3-3, the `stat` command:

```
molloyd@ebb:/tmp$ stat /tmp/test.txt
  File: /tmp/test.txt
  Size: 0               Blocks: 0      IO Block: 4096    regular empty file
Device: b301h/45825d    Inode: 2305    Links: 1
Access: (0644/-rw-r--r--)  Uid: (0/ root)   Gid: ( 0/ root)
Access: 2018-05-02 20:03:01.164235706 +0100
Modify: 2018-05-02 20:03:01.164235706 +0100
Change: 2018-05-02 20:03:35.020235710 +0100
 Birth: -
```

Note that each file in Linux retains an access, modify, and change time. You can update the access and modify times artificially using `touch -a text.txt` and `touch -m test.txt`, respectively (the change time is affected in both cases). The change time is also affected by system operations such as `chmod`; the modify time is affected by a write to the file; and, the access time is in theory affected by a file read. However, such operational behavior means that reading a file causes a write! This feature of Linux causes significant wear on the BeagleBone eMMC or SD card and results in I/O performance deficiencies. Therefore, the file access time feature is typically disabled on the boot eMMC/SD card using the mount option `noatime` within the `/etc/fstab` configuration file (covered in the next section). Note that there is also a similar `nodiratime` option that can be used to disable access time updates for directories only; however, the `noatime` option disables access time updates for both files and directories. You can see the `noatime` setting being set on the boot partition in `/etc/fstab` as follows:

```
molloyd@ebb:~$ more /etc/fstab | grep mmcblk
/dev/mmcblk0p1  /  ext4  noatime,errors=remount-ro  0  1
```

Just to finish the discussion of Figure 3-4: The example in the figure has 22 hard links to the file. For a directory this represents the number of subdirectories, the parent directory (..) and itself (.). The entry is owned by root, and it is in the root group. The next entry of 4096 is the size required to store the metadata about files contained in that directory (the minimum size is one sector, typically 4,096 bytes).

One final point: if you perform a directory listing `ls -ld` in the root directory, you will see a `t` bit in the permissions of the `/tmp` directory. This is called the *sticky bit*, meaning that write permission is not sufficient to delete files. Therefore, in the `/tmp` directory any user can create files, but no user can delete another user's files.

```
molloyd@ebb:~$ cd /
molloyd@ebb:/$ ls -dhl tmp
drwxrwxrwt 11 root root 4.0K May  2 20:32 tmp
```

The `ls -dhl` command lists (d) directory names (not their contents), with (h) human-readable file sizes, in (l) long format.

The Linux Root Directory

Exploring the Linux file system can be daunting for new Linux users. If you go to the top-level directory using cd / on the board and type **ls**, you will get the top-level directory structure, of the following form:

```
molloyd@ebb:/$ ls
bbb-uEnv.txt  boot  etc  ID.txt  lost+found  mnt   opt  root
sbin          sys   usr  bin     dev         home  lib  media
nfs-uEnv.txt  proc  run  srv     tmp         var
```

What does it all mean? Well, each of these directories has a role, and if you understand the roles, you can start to get an idea of where to search for configuration files or the binary files that you need. Table 3-4 briefly describes the content of each top-level Linux subdirectory.

Table 3-4: The Linux Top-Level Directory

DIRECTORY	DESCRIPTION
bin	Contains the binary executables used by all of the users and is present in the PATH environment variable by default. Another directory, /usr/bin, contains executables that are not core to booting or repairing the system.
boot	Contains the files for booting the board.
dev	Contains the device nodes (linked to device drivers).
etc	Configuration files for the local system.
home	Contains the user's home directories (e.g., /home/debian).
lib	Contains the standard system libraries.
lost+found	After running fsck (file system check and repair) unlinked files display here. The mklost+found command re-creates the lost+found directory if it is deleted.
media	Used for mounting removable media, such as micro-SD cards.
mnt	Used typically for mounting temporary file systems.
opt	A good place for installing third-party (non-core Linux) optional software.
proc	A virtual file representation of processes running on the board. (For example, if you cd /proc and type cat iomem, you can see some memory mapping addresses.)
root	The home directory of root account under Debian Linux distributions. (This is /home/root on several other distributions.)
run	Provides information about the running system since the last boot.

DIRECTORY	DESCRIPTION
sbin	Contains executables for root user (superuser) system management.
srv	Stores data related to FTP, web servers, rsync, etc.
sys	Contains a virtual file system that describes the system.
tmp	Contains temporary files.
usr	Contains programs for all of the users, and many subdirectories such as /usr/include (C/C++ header files), /usr/lib (C/C++ library files), /usr/src (Linux kernel source), /usr/bin (user executables), /usr/local (similar to /usr but for local users), and /usr/share (shared files and media between users).
var	Contains variable files such as system logs.

Commands for File Systems

In addition to commands for working with files and directories on file systems, there are commands for working with the file system itself. The first commands you should examine are df (remember as *d*isk *f*ree) and mount. The df command provides an overview of the file systems on the board. Adding -T lists the file system types.

```
molloyd@ebb:~$ df -T
Filesystem      Type      1K-blocks    Used Available Use% Mounted on
udev            devtmpfs    219200        0    219200   0% /dev
tmpfs           tmpfs        49496     5604     43892  12% /run
/dev/mmcblk0p1  ext4      30707172  2066088  27342152   8% /
tmpfs           tmpfs       247476        0    247476   0% /sys/fs/cgroup
...
```

The df command is useful for determining whether you are running short on disk space; you can see that the root file system (/) is 8% used in this case, with 27.3 GB (of a 32 GB SD card) available for additional software installations. Also listed are several temporary file system (tmpfs) entries that actually refer to virtual file systems, which are mapped to the board's DDR RAM. (The /sys/fs/* entries are discussed in detail in Chapter 8.)

NOTE If you are running out of space on the eMMC or SD card root file system, check the system logs: /var/log. Excessively large log files are symptomatic of system problems, so review them for any issues. When you have resolved issues, you can clear the messages log by typing cat /dev/null > /var/log/messages with root permission (also check kern.log, daemon.log, and syslog). For example, to clear the message log using a user account without deleting the file or resetting its file permissions, use the following:

```
molloyd@ebb:/var/log$ sudo sh -c "cat /dev/null > messages"
```

```
molloyd@ebb:/var/log$ ls -l messages
-rw-r----- 1 root adm 0 May 6 15:49 messages
```

The shell sh -c **call executes the entire command string in quotations with superuser permissions. This is required because in a call to** sudo cat /dev/null > messages **on its own,** sudo **does not perform the output redirection** >; **rather, it is performed as the molloyd user and therefore will fail because of insufficient permissions. This is the redirection issue with** sudo **that is alluded to earlier in the chapter.**

The list block devices command lsblk provides you with a concise tree-structure list of the block devices, such as SD cards, USB memory keys, and USB card readers (if any), that are attached to the board. As shown in the following output, you can see that mmcblk0 (a boot SD card on a BeagleBone) has a single partition, p1, which is attached to the root of the file system: /. The eMMC on the BeagleBone is present as mmcblk1 in this case, even though the board is booted using the SD card:

```
molloyd@ebb:~$ lsblk
NAME           MAJ:MIN RM  SIZE RO TYPE MOUNTPOINT
mmcblk0         179:0    0 29.8G  0 disk
└─mmcblk0p1     179:1    0 29.8G  0 part /
mmcblk1         179:8    0  3.7G  0 disk
└─mmcblk1p1     179:9    0  3.7G  0 part
mmcblk1boot0   179:24    0   1M  1 disk
mmcblk1boot1   179:32    0   1M  1 disk
```

USB ports (or the SD card on a BeagleBone) can be used for additional storage, which is useful if you are capturing video data and there is insufficient capacity on the eMMC/system SD card. You can test the performance of SD cards to ensure that they meet the needs of your applications using the example that follows.

EXAMPLE: TESTING SD CARD/EMMC READ PERFORMANCE

You can test the read performance of your eMMC/SD cards and controllers using the hdparm **program. For example, on the following BeagleBone with an SD card (** mmcblk0 **) and an eMMC (** mmcblk1 **):**

```
molloyd@ebb:~$ sudo apt install hdparm
molloyd@ebb:~$ sudo hdparm -tT /dev/mmcblk0 /dev/mmcblk1
/dev/mmcblk0:
 Timing cached reads:    444 MB in  2.00 seconds = 221.64 MB/sec
 Timing buffered disk reads:  62 MB in  3.08 seconds =  20.14 MB/sec
/dev/mmcblk1:
 Timing cached reads:    456 MB in  2.00 seconds = 228.08 MB/sec
 Timing buffered disk reads:  52 MB in  3.06 seconds =  17.00 MB/sec
```

you can see that the SD card and the eMMC have similar read performance character-istics. You can utilize the dd command to test write performance, but be careful, as incorrect usage will result in data loss.

Using the mount command with no arguments provides you with further information about the file system on the board.

```
.molloyd@ebb:~$ mount
/dev/mmcblk0p1 on / type ext4 (rw,noatime,errors=remount-ro,data=ordered)
sysfs on /sys type sysfs (rw,nosuid,nodev,noexec,relatime)
proc on /proc type proc (rw,nosuid,nodev,noexec,relatime) ...
```

As previously discussed, the file system is organized as a single tree that is rooted at the root: /. Typing cd / brings you to the root point. The mount command can be used to attach a file system on a physical disk to this tree. File systems on separate physical devices can all be attached to named points at arbitrary locations on the single tree. Table 3-5 describes some file system commands that you can use to manage your file system and thereafter follows two examples that demonstrate how to utilize the mount command for impor-tant Linux system administration tasks.

Table 3-5: Useful Commands for File Systems

COMMAND	DESCRIPTION
du -h /opt du -hs /opt/* du -hc *.jpg	Disk usage: Find out how much space a directory tree uses. Options: (-h) human-readable form, (-s) summary, (-c) total. The last command finds the total size of the JPG format files in the current directory.
df -h	Display system disk space in (-h) human-readable form.
lsblk	List block devices.
dd if=test.img of=/dev/sdX	Write the image to the drive. dd converts and copies a file, where if is the input file and of is the output file. Use this command under Linux to write an image to an SD card.
dd if=/dev/sdX of=test.img	Create an image of the drive. This is typically used under desktop Linux with the following form: sudo dd if=./BB*.img of=/dev/sdX where /dev/sdX is the SD card reader/writer device.
cat /proc/partitions	List all registered partitions.
mkfs /dev/sdX	Make a Linux file system. Also mkfs.ext4, mkfs.vfat. This destroys data on the device. Use this command very carefully!

Continues

Table 3-5 (*continued*)

COMMAND	DESCRIPTION
`fdisk -l`	Note that `fdisk` can be used to manage disks, create partitions, delete partitions, etc. `fdisk -l` displays all existing partitions.
`badblocks /dev/mmcblkX`	Check for bad blocks on the SD card. SD cards have wear leveling controller circuitry. If you get errors, get a new card; don't record them using `fsck`. Run this with root permissions and be aware that it takes some time to run.
`mount /media/store`	Mount a partition if it is listed in `/etc/fstab`.
`umount /media/store`	Unmount a partition. You will be informed if a file is open on this partition.

`sudo apt install tree`
 	
`tree ~/`
	Install the `tree` command and use it to display the directory structure of the user account.

EXAMPLE: FIXING PROBLEMS ON AN EMMC USING AN SD CARD

Occasionally, you make a change to a Linux configuration file on the BeagleBone eMMC Linux boot image that prevents the image from booting or causes the failure of network adapters so that you no longer have access to the device. You can use a Linux SD card boot image (mmcblk0) to boot the BBB, whereupon you can mount the "damaged" eMMC (mmcblk1) as follows:

```
molloyd@ebb:~$ lsblk
    NAME           MAJ:MIN RM  SIZE RO TYPE MOUNTPOINT
    mmcblk0        179:0    0 29.8G  0 disk
    └─mmcblk0p1    179:1    0 29.8G  0 part /
    mmcblk1        179:8    0  3.7G  0 disk
    └─mmcblk1p1    179:9    0  3.7G  0 part
    mmcblk1boot0   179:24   0   1M   1 disk
    mmcblk1boot1   179:32   0   1M   1 disk
```

You can create mount points for the ext4 partition of the "damaged" eMMC.

```
molloyd@ebb:~$ sudo mkdir /media/fix_emmc
molloyd@ebb:~$ sudo mount /dev/mmcblk1p1 /media/fix_emmc
```

You can then browse the file systems on the "damaged" eMMC using your BeagleBone and undo any invalid configuration settings.

```
molloyd@ebb:~$ cd /media/fix_emmc/
molloyd@ebb:/media/fix_emmc$ ls
bbb-uEnv.txt  dev    ID.txt      media         opt   run   sys  var
bin           etc    lib         mnt           proc  sbin  tmp
boot          home   lost+found  nfs-uEnv.txt  root  srv   usr
```

As shown earlier, you can edit files on the ext4 partition. After completing your changes, remember to unmount the eMMC before rebooting and ejecting the SD card. You can then safely remove the mount points.

```
molloyd@ebb:/media/fix_emmc$ cd ..
molloyd@ebb:/media$ sudo umount /media/fix_emmc/
molloyd@ebb:/media$ sudo rmdir /media/fix_emmc/
```

EXAMPLE: MOUNTING AN SD CARD AS ADDITIONAL STORAGE ON A BEAGLEBONE

In this example, the following steps are performed on a secondary SD card:

1. Formatting the secondary SD card to have a Linux ext4 file system

2. Mounting the secondary SD card as /media/store

3. Mounting the secondary SD card automatically at boot time

4. Configuring the card for user write access and displaying its capacity

In this example, the card is a 16GB micro-SD card that has been placed in a BeagleBone card reader. Ensure that the card is blank, because *this step will destroy its contents*; skip to step 2 if you want to retain the SD card's contents.

Step 1: Use lsblk to identify the device.

```
molloyd@ebb:~$ lsblk
NAME           MAJ:MIN RM   SIZE RO TYPE MOUNTPOINT
mmcblk0        179:0     0 14.9G  0 disk
└─mmcblk0p1    179:1     0 14.9G  0 part
mmcblk1        179:8     0  3.7G  0 disk
└─mmcblk1p1    179:9     0  3.7G  0 part /
mmcblk1boot0   179:24    0    1M  1 disk
mmcblk1boot1   179:32    0    1M  1 disk
```

The 16GB card appears as block device /mmcblk0 and can be prepared for a file system of choice. (Note that using mmcblk1 or mmcblk1p1 for the next step will destroy the contents of your eMMC.)

Build a file system as follows:

```
molloyd@ebb:~$ sudo mkfs.ext4 /dev/mmcblk0p1
mke2fs 1.43.4 (31-Jan-2017)
/dev/mmcblk0p1 contains a ext4 file system labelled 'rootfs'
        last mounted on / on Thu Nov  3 17:16:43 2016
Proceed anyway? (y,N) y
...
Writing superblocks and filesystem accounting information: done
```

Step 2: A mount point can be created, and the secondary card can be mounted using the mount command (-t indicates the file type; when omitted, mount attempts to autodetect the file type).

```
molloyd@ebb:~$ sudo mkdir /media/store
molloyd@ebb:~$ sudo mount -t ext4 /dev/mmcblk0p1 /media/store
```

```
molloyd@ebb:~$ cd /media/store
molloyd@ebb:/media/store$ ls
lost+found
molloyd@ebb:/media/store$ lsblk
NAME          MAJ:MIN RM  SIZE RO TYPE MOUNTPOINT
mmcblk0       179:0    0 14.9G  0 disk
└─mmcblk0p1   179:1    0 14.9G  0 part /media/store
...
```

Step 3: Configuring this secondary storage device to be mounted automatically at boot time involves adding an entry to the /etc/fstab file. Add an entry to the last line of the file, as follows:

```
molloyd@ebb:~$ sudo nano /etc/fstab
molloyd@ebb:~$ more /etc/fstab
/dev/mmcblk1p1  /  ext4  noatime,errors=remount-ro  0  1
debugfs          /sys/kernel/debug debugfs defaults  0  0
/dev/mmcblk0p1  /media/store      ext4    defaults,nofail,user,auto 0 0
molloyd@ebb:~$ sudo reboot
```

This entry configures the /dev/mmcblk0p1 to be mounted at /media/store, identifies the file system as ext4 format, and sets the following mount options: defaults (use default settings), nofail (mount the device when present but ignore if absent), user (users have permissions to mount the system), and auto (the card is mounted on startup or if the user types mount -a). The 0 0 values are the dump frequency (archive schedule) and pass number (order for file checking at boot) and should both be set to 0 by default. After reboot, you will see that the SD card is mounted correctly at /media/store.

Unfortunately, this approach may not be satisfactory if you have multiple SD cards that you want to mount at different points. An alternative approach is to use the universally unique identifier (UUID) of the SD card itself to configure the mounting instruction. The UUID for this 16GB card is displayed during step 1, but to identify it explicitly at this point, you can use the following:

```
molloyd@ebb:~$ sudo blkid /dev/mmcblk0p1
/dev/mmcblk0p1: UUID="c9e09a37-3478-4309-8904-86f36f7ca69d"
TYPE="ext4" PARTUUID="0736b542-01"
```

In the /etc/fstab file, you can replace the /dev/mmcblk0p1 entry with the UUID as follows (it should all appear on a single line in the file):

```
molloyd@ebb:~$ more /etc/fstab
...
UUID=c9e09a37-3478-4309-8904-86f36f7ca69d  /media/store  ext4  defa →
ults,nofail,user,auto 0 0
```

Again, the BBB boots correctly, regardless of the presence or absence of the micro-SD card. If an alternative micro-SD card is placed in the card reader, it will not be mounted at /media/store, but you can use its UUID to configure an additional entry in /etc/fstab. In addition, you can hot swap SD cards, whereupon they will be automatically mounted at their individually defined mount points. Ensure that you execute `sudo sync` or `sudo umount /dev/mmcblk0p1` before hot swapping any SD cards. For example, to ready the SD card for removal, use `umount`; to remount it without physical removal and reinsertion, use `mount -a`.

```
molloyd@ebb:~$ sudo umount /dev/mmcblk0p1
molloyd@ebb:~$ sudo mount -a
```

Step 4: The preceding steps result in a mount point that has root user write access only. The mount point can be adapted to give permission so that user accounts who are members of the `users` group can write to the card.

```
debian@beaglebone:/media$ ls -l
drwxr-xr-x 21 root root 4096 Mar  5 07:13 store
debian@beaglebone:/media$ sudo chgrp users store
debian@beaglebone:/media$ sudo chmod g+w store
debian@beaglebone:/media$ ls -l
drwxrwxr-x 21 root users 4096 Mar  5 07:13 store
debian@beaglebone:/media$ df -k
...
/dev/mmcblk0p1  15333104 1796104  12862652  13% /media/store
```

The `df` command is used to display the available capacity. Also, the mount point permission changes persist through reboot.

find and whereis

The `find` command is useful for searching a directory structure for a particular file. It is incredibly comprehensive; type **man find** for a full list of options. For example, use the following call to find the C++ header file `iostream` somewhere on the file system (using `sudo` avoids access permission problems):

```
molloyd@ebb:/$ sudo find . -name iostream*
./usr/include/c++/6/iostream
./usr/share/ti/cgt-pru/include/iostream
./usr/share/ti/cgt-pru/lib/src/iostream
./usr/share/ti/cgt-pru/lib/src/iostream.cpp ...
```

Using `-iname` instead of `-name` ignores upper/lowercase letters in the search name.

The following example finds files in `/home/` that were modified in the last 24 hours and prior to the last 24 hours, respectively:

```
molloyd@ebb:~$ echo "Test file" >> new.txt
molloyd@ebb:~$ sudo find /home -mtime -1
/home/molloyd
/home/molloyd/.bash_history
/home/molloyd/new.txt
molloyd@ebb:~$ sudo find /home -mtime +1
```

```
/home/debian
/home/debian/.xsessionrc
/home/debian/.bash_logout     ...
```

Alternatively, you can use access time (-atime), size (-size), owner (-user), group (-group), and permission (-perm).

> **NOTE** Use the grep **command to recursively search a directory for files that contain a specific string using the following format, where** -r **specifies a recursive search,** -n **displays the location line number in an identified file, and** -e **is followed by the search pattern:**
>
> molloyd@ebb:~$ **sudo grep -rn /home -e "Test"**
> /home/molloyd/new.txt:1:Test file
>
> **For more options, use** man grep.

The whereis command is different in that it can be used to search for the binary executable, source code, and manual page for a program.

```
molloyd@ebb:~$ whereis find
find: /usr/bin/find /usr/share/man/man1/find.1.gz /usr/share/info/find.info.
gz
```

In this case, the binary command is in /usr/bin/, and the man page is in /usr/share/man/man1 (stored in gzip form to save space).

more or less

The more command has been used several times already, and you have likely gleaned its use. It enables you to view a large file or output stream, one page at a time. Therefore, to view a long file, you can type **more filename**. For example, the log file /var/log/messages contains kernel output messages. You can view this file page by page by typing **more /var/log/messages**. However, if you want to keep the display concise, use **-5** to set the page length to be five rows.

```
molloyd@ebb:~$ more -5 /var/log/messages
Apr 30 06:25:05 beaglebone liblogging-stdlog:  ...
Apr 30 03:37:41 beaglebone kernel: [    0.000000] Booting Linux ...
Apr 30 03:37:41 beaglebone kernel: [    0.000000] Linux version ...
--More--(0%)
```

You can use the Spacebar to page through the content and the Q key to quit. There is an even more powerful command called less that you can access.

```
molloyd@ebb:~$ less /var/log/messages
```

The `less` command gives you a fully interactive view using the keyboard. There are too many options to list here. For example, you can use the arrow keys to move up and down. Or, you can page down using the Spacebar, search for a string by typing / (e.g., type /usb to find messages related to USB devices), and then press the N key to go to the next match (or Shift+N key to go to the previous match).

Finally, there is a command specifically for displaying the kernel ring buffer that formats the output with colored markup, which can be called simply using the following:

```
molloyd@ebb:~$ dmesg
```

The Reliability of SD Card/eMMC File Systems

One of the most likely points of failure of a single-board computer (SBC) is its SD card, which is more generally known as a multimedia card (MMC) or an embedded MMC (eMMC) when it is built onto the SBC (as is the case for the BeagleBone). NAND-based flash memory, such as that in MMCs, has a large capacity and a low cost, but it is prone to wear, which can result in file system errors.

The high capacity of MMCs is largely because of the development of multi-level cell (MLC) memory. Unlike single-level cell (SLC) memory, more than 1 bit can be stored in a single memory cell. The high voltage levels required in the process of deleting a memory cell disturbs adjacent cells, so NAND flash memory is erased in blocks of 1KB to 4KB. Over time, the process of writing to the NAND flash memory causes electrons to become trapped, reducing the conductivity difference between the set and erased states. (For a discussion on SLC versus MLC for high-reliability applications, see tiny.cc/beagle301.) MLCs use different charge levels and higher voltages to store more states in a single cell. (Commercial MLC products typically offer 4 to 16 states per cell.) Because SLCs store only a single state, they have a reliability advantage (typically 60,000–100,000 erase/write cycles) versus MLC (typically 10,000 cycles). MMCs are perfectly suitable for daily use in applications such as digital photography or security camera recording; 10,000 cycles should last more than 27 years at one entire card write per day.

However, embedded Linux devices constantly write to their MMCs for tasks such as logging system events in /var/log/. If your board writes to a log file 20 times per day, the lifespan of the SD card could be as low as 8 months. These are conservative figures, and thanks to *wear leveling algorithms*, the lifespan may be much longer. Wear leveling is employed by MMCs during data writes to ensure that rewrites are evenly distributed over the entire MMC media, thus avoiding system failure of Linux devices because of concentrated modifications, such as changes to log files.

For your Beagle board, ensure that you purchase a high-quality branded SD card. In addition, the more unused space you have on the SD card, the better, because it further enhances the wear leveling performance. The BeagleBone uses an eMMC storage—essentially an MMC on a chip that has the same order of reliability as SD cards. However, one important advantage of eMMCs is that the board manufacturer has control over the quality and specification of the storage device used. Finally, most consumer SSDs are also MLC based, with the more expensive SLC-based SSDs typically reserved for enterprise-class servers.

For Beagle applications that require extended reliability, a RAM file system (tmpfs) could be used for the /tmp directory, for the /var/cache directory, and for log files (particularly /var/log/apt). You can achieve this by editing the /etc/fstab file to mount the desired directories in memory. For example, if you have processes that require file data to be shared between them for the purpose of data interchange, you could use the /tmp directory as a RAM file system (tmpfs) by editing the /etc/fstab file as follows:

```
molloyd@ebb:/etc$ sudo nano fstab
molloyd@ebb:/etc$ more fstab
/dev/mmcblk0p1   /    ext4  noatime,errors=remount-ro  0   1
debugfs          /sys/kernel/debug  debugfs  defaults  0   0
tempfs           /tmp   tempfs  size=100M  0   0
molloyd@ebb:/etc$ mkdir /tmp/swap
You can then apply these settings using the mount command:
molloyd@ebb:/etc$ sudo mount -a
And then check that the settings have been applied:
molloyd@ebb:/etc$ mount
...
tmpfs on /tmp/swap type tmpfs (rw,relatime,size=102400k)
```

The root directory (/) is mounted by default with the noatime attribute set, which dramatically reduces the number of writes and increases I/O performance (as described earlier in the chapter). You should apply this attribute when possible to all solid-state storage devices (e.g., USB memory keys), but it is not necessary for RAM-based storage.

Remember that any data written to a tmpfs will be lost on reboot. Therefore, if you use a tmpfs for /var/log, any system errors that caused your board to crash will not be visible on reboot. You can test this fact by creating a file in the /tmp/swap/ directory as configured earlier and rebooting.

The actual RAM allocation grows and shrinks depending on the file usage on the tmpfs disk; therefore, you can be reasonably generous with the memory allocation. Here's an example with the 100 MB /tmp/swap/ tmpfs mounted:

```
molloyd@ebb:/tmp/swap$ cat /proc/meminfo | grep MemFree:
MemFree:          213404 kB
molloyd@ebb:/tmp/swap$ fallocate -l 50000000 test.txt
molloyd@ebb:/tmp/swap$ ls -l test.txt
```

```
-rw-r--r-- 1 molloyd molloyd 50000000 May  4 12:30 test.txt
molloyd@ebb:/tmp/swap$ cat /proc/meminfo | grep MemFree:
MemFree:          164548 kB
molloyd@ebb:/tmp/swap$ rm test.txt
molloyd@ebb:/tmp/swap$ cat /proc/meminfo | grep MemFree:
MemFree:          213296 kB
```

It is possible to use a read-only file system to improve the life span of the SD card and the stability of the file system (e.g., SquashFS compressed file system), but this requires significant effort and is not suitable for the type of prototype development that takes place in this book. However, keep it in mind for a final project or product deployment where system stability is crucial.

Linux Commands

When you are working at the Linux terminal and you type commands such as date, the output of these commands is sent to the standard output. As a result, the output is displayed in your terminal window.

Output and Input Redirection (>, >>, and <)

It is possible to redirect the output to a file using redirection symbols > and >>. The >> symbol was used previously in this chapter to add text to temporary files. The > symbol can be used to send the output to a new file. Here's an example:

```
molloyd@ebb:/tmp$ date > a.txt
molloyd@ebb:/tmp$ more a.txt
Fri May  4 12:33:32 IST 2018
molloyd@ebb:/tmp$ date > a.txt
molloyd@ebb:/tmp$ more a.txt
Fri May  4 12:33:45 IST 2018
```

The >> symbol indicates that you want to append to the file. The following example illustrates the use of >> with the new file a.txt:

```
molloyd@ebb:/tmp$ date >> a.txt
molloyd@ebb:/tmp$ more a.txt
Fri May  4 12:33:45 IST 2018
Fri May  4 12:34:23 IST 2018
```

Standard input using the < symbol works in much the same way. The inclusion of -e enables parsing of escape characters, such as the return (\n) characters, which places each animal type on a new line.

```
molloyd@ebb:/tmp$ echo -e "dog\ncat\nyak\ncow" > animals.txt
molloyd@ebb:/tmp$ sort < animals.txt
```

```
cat
cow
dog
yak
```

You can combine input and output redirection operations. Using the same `animals.txt` file, you can perform operations such as the following:

```
molloyd@ebb:/tmp$ sort < animals.txt > sorted.txt
molloyd@ebb:/tmp$ more sorted.txt
cat
cow
dog
yak
```

Pipes (| and tee)

Simply put, *pipes* (|) enable you to connect Linux commands. Just as you redirected the output to a file, you can redirect the output of one command into the input of another command. For example, to list the root directory (from anywhere on the system) and send (or *pipe*) the output into the `sort` command, where it is listed in reverse (-r) order, use the following:

```
molloyd@ebb:~$ ls / | sort -r
var
usr
...
bin
```

You can identify which user installations in the /opt directory occupy the most disk space: `du` gives you the disk used. Passing the argument -d1 means only list the sizes of 1 level below the current directory level, and -h means list the values in human-readable form. You can pipe this output into the `sort` filter command to do a numeric sort in reverse order (largest at the top). Therefore, the command is as follows:

```
molloyd@ebb:~$ du -d1 -h /opt | sort -nr
500K     /opt/backup
198M     /opt
98M      /opt/source
75M      /opt/cloud9
25M      /opt/scripts
```

Another useful tool, `tee`, enables you to both redirect an output to a file and pass it on to the next command in the pipe (e.g., store and view). Using the previous example, if you want to send the unsorted output of du to a file but display a sorted output, you could enter the following:

```
molloyd@ebb:~$ du -d1 -h /opt | tee unsorted.txt | sort -nr
500K    /opt/backup
198M    /opt
98M     /opt/source
75M     /opt/cloud9
25M     /opt/scripts
molloyd@ebb:~$ more unsorted.txt
500K    /opt/backup
25M     /opt/scripts
98M     /opt/source
75M     /opt/cloud9
198M    /opt
```

You can also use tee to write the output to several files simultaneously:

```
molloyd@ebb:~$ du -d1 -h /opt | tee 1.txt 2.txt 3.txt
500K    /opt/backup
...
molloyd@ebb:~$ ls
1.txt   2.txt   3.txt   unsorted.txt
```

Filter Commands (from sort to xargs)

Each of the filtering commands provides a useful function:

- sort: This command has several options: -r sorts in reverse, -f ignores case, -d uses dictionary sorting and ignores punctuation, -n does a numeric sort, -b ignores blank space, -i ignores control characters, -u displays duplicate lines only once, and -m merges multiple inputs into a single output.

- wc (word count): Calculates the number of words, lines, or characters in a stream. Here's an example:

```
molloyd@ebb:/tmp$ more animals.txt
dog
cat
yak
cow
molloyd@ebb:/tmp$ wc < animals.txt
4  4 16
```

This command returns that there are 4 lines, 4 words, and 16 characters (including hidden characters, e.g., carriage returns). You can select the values independently by using line count (-l), word count (-w), and character count (-m), and -c prints out the byte count (which would also be 16 in this case).

- head: This command displays the first lines of the input, which is useful if you have a long file or stream of information and want to examine only the first few lines. By default, it displays the first 10 lines. You can specify the number of lines using the -n option. For example, to get the first two lines of output of the dmesg command (display message or driver message), which displays the message buffer of the kernel, use the following:

```
molloyd@ebb:~$ dmesg | head -n2
[    0.000000] Booting Linux on physical CPU 0x0
[    0.000000] Linux version 4.9.88-ti-rt-r111 ...
```

- tail: This command works like head except that it displays the last lines of a file or stream. Using it in combination with dmesg provides useful output, as shown here:

```
molloyd@ebb:~$ dmesg | tail -n2
[  178.194805] pvrsrvkm: loading out-of-tree module taints kernel.
[  178.556171] [drm] Initialized pvr 1.14.3699939 20110701 on minor 0
```

- grep: This command parses lines using text and regular expressions. You can use this command to filter output with options, including ignore case (-i), stop after five matches (-m 5), silent (-q), will exit with return status of 0 if any matches are found, specify a pattern (-e), print a count of matches (-c), print only the matching text (-o), and list the filename of the file containing the match (-l). For example, the following examines the dmesg output for the first three occurrences of the string usb, using -i to ignore case:

```
molloyd@ebb:~$ dmesg | grep -i -m3 usb
[    0.809529] usbcore: registered new interface driver usbfs
[    0.809622] usbcore: registered new interface driver hub
[    0.809795] usbcore: registered new device driver usb
```

You can combine pipes. For example, you get the same output by using head and displaying only the first two lines of the grep output.

```
molloyd@ebb:~$ dmesg | grep -i -m3 usb | head -n2
[    0.809529] usbcore: registered new interface driver usbfs
[    0.809622] usbcore: registered new interface driver hub
```

- xargs: This command enables you to construct an argument list that you use to call another command or tool. In the following example, a text file args.txt that contains three strings is used to create three new files. The output of cat is piped to xargs, where it passes the three strings as arguments to the touch command, creating three new files: a.txt, b.txt, and c.txt.

```
molloyd@ebb:~$ echo "a.txt b.txt c.txt" > args.txt
molloyd@ebb:~$ cat args.txt | xargs touch
molloyd@ebb:~$ ls
args.txt  a.txt  b.txt  c.txt
```

Other useful filter commands include awk (to program any type of filter), fmt (to format text), uniq (to find unique lines), and sed (to manipulate a stream). These commands are beyond the scope of this text; for example, awk is a full programming language! Table 3-6 describes useful piped commands to give you some ideas of how to use them.

Table 3-6: Useful Pipe Examples

COMMAND	DESCRIPTION
apt list --installed | grep camera	List the installed packages and search for one that contains the search string camera. Each command in this table is entered on a single line.
ls -lt | head	Display the files in the current directory in order of age.
cat urls.txt | xargs wget	Download the files, listed in URLs within a text file urls.txt.
dmesg | grep -c usb	Count the number of times usb is found in the output of dmesg.
find . -name "*.mp3" | grep -vi "effects" > /tmp/playlist.txt	Search your board (e.g., run from/with sudo) for .mp3 files, ignoring any sound effects files, to create a playlist file in /tmp.

echo and cat

The echo command simply echoes a string, output of a command, or a value to the standard output. Here are a few examples:

```
molloyd@ebb:~$ echo 'hello'
hello
molloyd@ebb:~$ echo "Today's date is $(date)"
Today's date is Fri May  4 13:45:36 IST 2018
molloyd@ebb:~$ echo $PATH
/usr/local/bin:/usr/bin:/bin:/usr/local/games:/usr/games
```

In the first case, a simple string is echoed. In the second case, the " " are present as a command is issued within the echo call, and in the final case the PATH environment variable is echoed.

The echo command also enables you to see the exit status of a command using $?. Here's an example:

```
molloyd@ebb:~$ ls
args.txt  a.txt  b.txt  c.txt
molloyd@ebb:~$ echo $?
0
molloyd@ebb:~$ ls /nosuchdirectory
ls: cannot access '/nosuchdirectory': No such file or directory
molloyd@ebb:~$ echo $?
2
```

Clearly, the exit status for ls is 0 for a successful call and 2 for an invalid argument. This can be useful when you are writing scripts and your own programs that return a value from the main() function.

The cat command (concatenation) facilitates you in joining two files together at the command line. The following example uses echo to create two files: a.txt and b.txt; cat concatenates the files to create a new file c.txt. You need to use -e if you want to enable the interpretation of escape characters in the string that is passed to echo.

```
molloyd@ebb:~$ echo "Hello" > a.txt
molloyd@ebb:~$ echo -e "from\nthe\nPocketBeagle" > b.txt
molloyd@ebb:~$ cat a.txt b.txt > c.txt
molloyd@ebb:~$ more c.txt
Hello
from
the
PocketBeagle
```

diff

The diff command facilitates you in finding the differences between two files. It provides basic output.

```
molloyd@ebb:~$ echo -e "dog\ncat\nbird" > list1.txt
molloyd@ebb:~$ echo -e "dog\ncow\nbird" > list2.txt
molloyd@ebb:~$ diff list1.txt list2.txt
2c2
< cat
---
> cow
```

The value 2c2 in the output indicates that line 2 in the first file changed to line 2 in the second file, and the change is that *cat* changed to *cow*. The character *a* means appended, and *d* means deleted. For a side-by-side comparison, you can use the following:

```
molloyd@ebb:~$ diff -y -W30 list1.txt list2.txt
dog                 dog
cat               | cow
bird                bird
```

where -y enables the side-by-side view and -W30 sets the width of the display to 30-character columns.

If you want a more intuitive (but challenging) difference display between two files, you can use the vimdiff command (installed using **sudo apt install vim**), which displays a side-by-side comparison of the files using the vim (Vi IMproved) text editor (type **vimdiff list1.txt list2.txt** and use the VI key sequence: **Escape : q !** twice to quit or **Escape : w q** to save the changes and quit). Vim requires practice to master the key sequences.

tar

The tar command is an archiving utility that enables you to combine files and directories into a single file (like an uncompressed zip file). This file can then be compressed to save space. To archive and compress a directory of files, such as /tmp, use the following:

```
molloyd@ebb:~$ tar cvfz backup.tar.gz /tmp
molloyd@ebb:~$ ls -l backup.tar.gz
-rw-r--r-- 1 molloyd molloyd 416 May  4 13:54 backup.tar.gz
```

where c means new archive, v means verbosely list files, z means compress with gzip, and f means archive name follows. You might also see .tar.gz represented as .tgz. See Table 3-7 for more examples.

Table 3-7: Useful tar Commands

COMMAND	DESCRIPTION
tar cvfz name.tar.gz /tmp	Compress with gzip form.
tar cvfj name.tar.bz2 /tmp	Compress with bzip2 compression (typically a longer delay, but smaller, file). Enter all commands in this table on a single line.
tar cvfJ name.tar.xz /tmp	Compress with xz file format (used in .deb package files).
tar xvf name.tar.*	Decompress compressed file (x indicates extract). It will autodetect the compression type (e.g., gzip, bz2).

Continues

Table 3-7 (*continued*)

COMMAND	DESCRIPTION
`tar xvf name.tar.* /dir/file`	Extract a single file from an archive. Works for a single directory too.
`tar rvf name.tar filename`	Add another file to the archive.
`tar cfz name-$(date +%m%d%y).tar.gz /dir/filename`	Create an archive with the current day's date; useful for scripts and cron job backups. Note that there must be a space between `date` and `+%m%d%y`.

md5sum

The `md5sum` command enables you to check the hash code to verify that the files have not been corrupted maliciously or accidentally in transit. In the following example, the wavemon tool is downloaded as a `.deb` package but not installed. The `md5sum` command can be used to generate the md5 checksum.

```
molloyd@ebb:~$ sudo apt download wavemon
Get:1 http://deb.debian.org/debian stretch/main armhf wavemon armhf
0.8.1-1 [49.3 kB] Fetched 49.3 kB in 0s (247 kB/s)
molloyd@ebb:~$ ls -l *.deb
-rw-r--r-- 1 root root 49286 Jan  2 2017 wavemon_0.8.1-1_armhf.deb
molloyd@ebb:~$ md5sum wavemon_0.8.1-1_armhf.deb
557728e1da32bb7f68b09099755c9ca3  wavemon_0.8.1-1_armhf.deb
```

You can now check this checksum against the official checksum to ensure you have a valid file. Unfortunately, it can be difficult to find the checksums for individual packages online. If wavemon is installed, the checksums are in `/var/lib/dpkg/info/wavemon.md5sums`. You can install a utility under Debian called `debsums` to check the integrity of the file and its constituent parts.

```
molloyd@ebb:~$ sudo apt install debsums wavemon
molloyd@ebb:~$ debsums wavemon_0.8.1-1_armhf.deb
/usr/bin/wavemon                                              OK
...
/usr/share/man/man5/wavemonrc.5.gz                           OK
/usr/share/menu/wavemon                                      OK
```

If you are building your own packages that you want to distribute, it would be useful to also distribute a checksum file against which users can verify their downloaded repository. An alternative to `md5sum` is `sha256sum`, which can be used in the same way.

```
molloyd@ebb:~$ sha256sum wavemon_0.8.1-1_armhf.deb
6536009848b1063e831d7d9aae70f6505e46e8ecc88e161f6bd7034ba11ae1dc
```

Linux Processes

A process is an instance of a program that is running on the OS. You need to be able to manage the processes that are running on your board, understand foreground and background processes, and kill a process that becomes locked.

How to Control Linux Processes

The ps command lists the processes currently running on the board. Typing **ps** shows that the following PocketBeagle is running two user processes, the bash shell with process ID (PID) 1953 and the ps command itself, which is running with PID 1968. The ps PID is different every time you run it because it runs to completion each time.

```
molloyd@ebb:~$ ps
  PID TTY          TIME CMD
 1953 pts/0    00:00:00 bash
 1968 pts/0    00:00:00 ps
```

To see all running processes, use **ps ax**. In the following example, it is filtered to search for the string "apache" to discover information about the apache2 processes that are running on the board:

```
molloyd@ebb:~$ ps ax | grep apache
 1107 ?        Ss     0:00 /usr/sbin/apache2 -k start
 1110 ?        Sl     0:00 /usr/sbin/apache2 -k start
 1111 ?        Sl     0:00 /usr/sbin/apache2 -k start
 1970 pts/0    S+     0:00 grep apache
```

It is clear that three different processes are running for the service, enabling it to handle multiple simultaneous connections. In this example, all threads are currently waiting for an event to complete (s), PID 1107 is the session leader (ss), 1110 and 1111 are its multithreaded clones (s1), and the 1970 grep process is in the foreground group (s+). As described earlier, a call to **systemctl status apache2** provides information about the services running on the PocketBeagle—if you execute the call, you will see that the process PIDs match those displayed by a call to ps.

Foreground and Background Processes

Linux is a multitasking OS that enables you to run processes in the background while using a program that is running in the foreground. This concept is similar to the behavior of a windowing system (e.g., Windows, macOS). For example, the desktop clock continues to update the time while you use a web browser.

The same is true of applications that run in a terminal window. To demonstrate that, here is a small segment of C code to display "Hello World!" every five seconds in a Linux terminal. Exactly how this works is covered in Chapter 5, but for the moment, you can enter the code verbatim into a file called `HelloBeagle.c` using the nano file editor within the molloyd user home directory, as follows:

```
molloyd@ebb:~$ nano HelloBeagle.c
molloyd@ebb:~$ more HelloBeagle.c
#include<unistd.h>
#include<stdio.h>
int main(){
   int x=0;
   do{
      printf("Hello Beagle!\n");
      sleep(5);
   }while(x++<50);
   return 0;
}
```

The program has 50 iterations, displaying a message and sleeping for five seconds on each iteration. After saving the file as `HelloBeagle.c`, it can be compiled to an executable by typing the following (`-o` specifies the executable filename):

```
molloyd@ebb:~$ gcc HelloBeagle.c -o hello
molloyd@ebb:~$ ls -l hello
-rwxr-xr-x 1 molloyd molloyd 8384 May  4 16:26 hello
```

If this works correctly, you will now have the source file and the executable program called `hello` (note that the executable x flag is set). It can then be executed.

```
molloyd@ebb:~$ ./hello
Hello Beagle!
Hello Beagle!
^C
```

It will continue to output this message every five seconds; it can be killed using Ctrl+C. However, if you would like to run this in the background, you have two options.

The first way is that, instead of using Ctrl+C to kill the process, use Ctrl+Z, and then at the prompt type the **bg** (*background*) command.

```
molloyd@ebb:~$ ./hello
Hello Beagle!
```

```
^Z
[1]+  Stopped                    ./hello
molloyd@ebb:~$ bg
[1]+ ./hello &
molloyd@ebb:~$ Hello Beagle!
Hello Beagle!
Hello Beagle!
```

When you press Ctrl+Z, the ^z displays in the output. When **bg** is entered, the process is placed in the background and continues to execute. In fact, you can continue to use the terminal, but it will be frustrating, because "Hello Beagle!" displays every five seconds. You can bring this process back into the foreground using the **fg** command.

```
molloyd@ebb:~$ fg
./hello
Hello Beagle!
^C
molloyd@ebb:~$
```

The application is killed when Ctrl+C is typed (displays as ^c).

The second way to place this application in the background is to execute the application with an **&** symbol after the application name.

```
molloyd@ebb:~$ ./hello &
[1] 1992
molloyd@ebb:~$ Hello Beagle!
Hello Beagle!
Hello Beagle!
```

The process has been placed in the background with PID 1992 in this case. To stop the process, use **ps** with this PID or find the PID using the ps command.

```
molloyd@ebb:~$ ps |grep hello
 1992 pts/0    00:00:00 hello
molloyd@ebb:~$ Hello Beagle!
```

To kill the process, use the **kill** command.

```
molloyd@ebb:~$ kill 1992
[1]+  Terminated              ./hello
```

You can confirm that a process is dead by using ps again. If a process doesn't die, you can use a -9 argument to ensure death! (e.g., kill -9 1992). A separate command, pkill, will kill a process based on its name, so in this case you can kill the process as follows:

```
molloyd@ebb:~$ pkill hello
```

One more command worth mentioning is `watch`, which executes a command at a regular interval and shows the outcome full screen on the terminal. For example, to watch the kernel message log, use the following:

```
molloyd@ebb:~$ watch dmesg
```

You can specify the time interval between each execution using -n followed by the number of seconds. A good way to understand `watch` is to execute it as follows:

```
molloyd@ebb:~$ watch -n 1 ps a
Every 1.0s: ps a          ebb: Fri May  4 16:34:52 2018
  PID TTY        STAT    TIME COMMAND
 1033 tty1       Ss+     0:00 /sbin/agetty --noclear tty1 linux
 ...
 2018 pts/0      S+      0:00 watch -n 1 ps a
 2046 pts/0      S+      0:00 watch -n 1 ps a
 2047 pts/0      S+      0:00 sh -c ps a
 2048 pts/0      R+      0:00 ps a
```

You will see the PID of `ps`, `sh`, and `watch` changing every one (1) second, making it clear that `watch` is actually executing the command (`ps`) by passing it to a new shell using **sh -c**. The reason why `watch` appears twice in the list is that it spawns itself temporarily at the exact moment that it executes `ps a`.

Other Linux Topics

At this point of the book, I have covered the core commands for working with Linux on the Beagle boards; however, there is much more to cover on the topic of managing Linux systems. For example, how do you configure a Wi-Fi adapter? How do you use `cron` to schedule jobs? These topics and many others are detailed as you work through the book. For example, cron jobs are covered in Chapter 11, in the context of the Internet of Things.

Using Git for Version Control

Simply put, *Git* is a system that enables you to track changes to the content of a software project as it develops. Git, designed by Linus Torvalds, is used today for mainline Linux kernel development. Git is an incredibly useful system to understand for two main reasons: you can use Git when developing your own software, and you can gain an appreciation of how to work with Linux kernel source distributions. In developing your own software, Git is particularly useful for backing up your code and redeploying it to multiple Beagle boards.

Git is a distributed version control system (DVCS) for source control management. A *version control system* (VCS) tracks and manages changes to documents of any type. Typically, documents that have been changed are marked with revision numbers and time stamps. It is possible to compare revisions and even revert to older versions of the documents. There are two types of VCSs.

- **Centralized:** These systems, such as Apache Subversion (SVN), work on the basis that there is a single "master" copy of the project. The workflow is straightforward: you pull down changes from a central server, make your changes, and commit them back to the master copy.

- **Distributed:** Using these systems, such as Git and Selenic Mercurial, you do not pull down changes; instead, you clone the entire repository, including its entire history. The clone of the repository is just as complete as the master copy and can even become the master copy if required. Thankfully, by today's standards, text documents and programming source code do not occupy much disk space. Importantly, the DVCS model does not prevent you from having a central master repository that everybody uses; take a look at `git.kernel.org`.

The main advantage of a DVCS over a CVCS is that you can quickly commit and test changes locally, on your own system, without ever having to push them to a master copy; however, changes can be pushed when they reach an appropriate level of quality. The only significant disadvantage is the amount of disk space required to store the project and its entire history, which grows over time.

Git is a DVCS that is focused on programming source control and management. It enables you to create parallel developments that do not affect the original. You can even revert to an older version of one of the source code files or an older version of the entire project. The project, with its associated files and history, is called a *repository*. This capability is particularly useful in large-scale programming projects for which you may go down a development pathway with the project that is ultimately unsuccessful. The facility for parallel development is also important if you have several people working on the same project.

Git is written in C, and although it originated from the need for version control tools in the development of Linux kernel code, it is used by many other open source developments such as Eclipse and Android.

The easiest way to understand Git is to go through the steps of actually using it. Therefore, the next section is structured as a step-by-step guide. If it is not already, Git is easily installed using `sudo apt install git`, so you should be able to follow the steps, directly at the terminal. *GitHub* is used in this book as the remote repository for providing the source code examples. Except for pushing the source code to the server, you can do everything in this guide without a GitHub account. GitHub provides free public repository accounts but charges a fee for private repositories, such as those that would be required for retaining intellectual property rights.

> **NOTE**   If you are planning to write a large software project and do not want to make it publicly available on www.github.com or pay a subscription fee, you can currently host small-scale private repositories at sites such as bitbucket.org and gitlab.com. With some work, you can even set up GitLab on your own server, as there is an open-source version of the platform.

A Practice-Based Introduction

In this guide, I create a repository called *test* on GitHub. Initially, it contains only a README.md file with a short description of the "test" project.

As shown in Figure 3-5, nearly all operations are local operations. A checksum is performed on every file in Git before it is stored. The checksum ensures that Git will be aware if a modification is made outside of Git itself, including file system corruption. Git uses 40-character hash codes for the checksums. This helps Git keep track of changes between the local repository and remote repository, which enables the range of local operations.

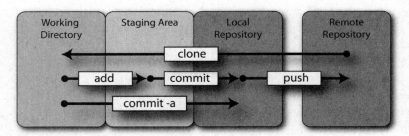

Figure 3-5: The basic Git workflow

Cloning a Repository (git clone)

Cloning a repository means making a copy of all the files in the repository on your local file system, as well as the history of changes to that project. You do this operation only once. To clone the repository, issue the command **git clone** followed by the fully formed repository name:

```
molloyd@ebb:~$ cd ~/
molloyd@ebb:~$ git clone https://github.com/derekmolloy/test.git
Cloning into 'test'...
remote: Counting objects: 20, done.
remote: Total 20 (delta 0), reused 0 (delta 0), pack-reused 20
Unpacking objects: 100% (20/20), done.
```

You now have a full copy of the test repository in the /test/ directory. Your repository is just as complete as the version on the GitHub server; if you were to deploy it over a network, file system, other Git server, or even a different GitHub account, it could assume the role as the main version of this repository. Although there is no need for a central server, it is usually the case, because it enables multiple users to "check in" source code to a known master repository. The repository is created in the /test/ directory, and it currently contains the following:

```
molloyd@ebb:~/test$ ls -al
total 20
drwxr-xr-x 3 molloyd molloyd 4096 May  4 23:18 .
drwxr-xr-x 4 molloyd molloyd 4096 May  4 23:16 ..
drwxr-xr-x 8 molloyd molloyd 4096 May  4 23:16 .git
-rw-r--r-- 1 molloyd molloyd    4 May  4 23:16 .gitignore
-rw-r--r-- 1 molloyd molloyd   59 May  4 23:16 README.md
```

You can see the README.md file that was created when the project was initialized on GitHub; you can use more to view the contents of this file. The directory also contains a hidden .git subdirectory, which contains the following files and directories:

```
molloyd@ebb:~/test$ cd .git
molloyd@ebb:~/test/.git$ ls
branches   config    description  HEAD  hooks   index   info
logs       objects   packed-refs  refs
```

The hidden .git folder contains all the information about the repository, such as commit messages, logs, and the data objects. For example, the remote repository location is maintained in the config file.

```
molloyd@ebb:~/test/.git$ more config | grep url
       url = https://github.com/derekmolloy/test.git
```

The "Further Reading" section at the end of this chapter directs you to an excellent book on Git, which is freely available online, that describes the nature of the .git directory structure in detail. Thankfully, in the following discussion, you do not have to make changes in the .git directory structure because you have Git commands to do that for you.

> **NOTE**   This step-by-step guide uses my test repository; however, you can easily create your own repository on GitHub. After you set up a free account on GitHub, go to the + button and then New repository. Give the repository a name and a description, make it publicly available, choose to initialize it with a README, and then choose "Create repository." You can then follow these instructions using your own account, and as a result you will be able to push back from the Beagle board to your own repository on GitHub.

Getting the Status (git status)

Now that the repository exists, the next step is to add a new text file to the working directory, where it will be in an untracked state. When you call the command git status, you can see a message stating that "untracked files" are present.

```
molloyd@ebb:~/test$ echo "Just some text" > newfile.txt
molloyd@ebb:~/test$ git status
On branch master
Your branch is up-to-date with 'origin/master'.
Untracked files:
  (use "git add <file>..." to include in what will be committed)
        newfile.txt
nothing added to commit but untracked files present (use "git add" to track)
```

The next step is to add any untracked files to the staging area. However, if you did not want to add a set of files, you could also create a .gitignore file to ignore those files. For example, this could be useful if you are building C/C++ projects and you decide that you do not want to add intermediate .o files. Here is an example of creating a .gitignore file in order to ignore C/C++ .o files:

```
molloyd@ebb:~/test$ echo "*.o" > .gitignore
molloyd@ebb:~/test$ more .gitignore
*.o
molloyd@ebb:~/test$ touch testobject.o
molloyd@ebb:~/test$ git status
On branch master
Your branch is up-to-date with 'origin/master'.
Untracked files:
  (use "git add <file>..." to include in what will be committed)
        newfile.txt
nothing added to commit but untracked files present (use "git add" to track)
```

In this case, two files are untracked, but there is no mention of the testobject.o file, as it is being correctly ignored. Note that the .gitignore file is itself part of the repository and so will persist when the repository is cloned, along with its revision history and so on.

Adding to the Staging Area (git add)

The files in the working directory can now be added to the staging area by typing git add .

This command adds all the files in the working directory, with the exception of the ignored files. In this example, two files are added from the working directory to the staging area, and the status of the repository can then be displayed using the following:

```
molloyd@ebb:~/test$ git add .
molloyd@ebb:~/test$ git status
On branch master
Your branch is up-to-date with 'origin/master'.
Changes to be committed:
  (use "git reset HEAD <file>..." to unstage)
      new file:   .gitignore
      new file:   newfile.txt
```

To delete (*remove*) a file from the staging area, use `git rm somefile.ext`.

Committing to the Local Repository (git commit)

After you add files to the staging area, you can commit the changes from the staging area to the local Git repository. First, you may want to add your name and e-mail address variables to identify who is committing the changes.

```
molloyd@ebb:~/test$ git config --global user.name "Derek Molloy"
molloyd@ebb:~/test$ git config --global user.email "derek@myemail.com"
```

These values are set against your Linux user account, so they will persist when you next log in. You can see them by typing `more ~/.gitconfig`.

To permanently commit the file additions to the local Git repository, use the `git commit` command.

```
molloyd@ebb:~/test$ git commit -m "Testing repository for BeagleBone"
[master b2137ee] Testing repository for BeagleBone
 2 files changed, 2 insertions(+)
 create mode 100644 newfile.txt
 create mode 100644 .gitignore
```

The changes are flagged with the username, and a message is also required. If you want to detail the message inline, use -m to set the commit message.

> **NOTE** The shortcut `git commit -a` commits *modified* files directly to the local repository, without requiring a call to `add`. It does not add new files. Refer to Figure 3-5, shown earlier in this chapter.

Pushing to the Remote Repository (git push)

To perform this step, you must have your own GitHub account. The `git push` command pushes any code updates to the remote repository. You must be registered to make changes to the remote repository for the changes to be applied.

In Git 2.0, a new more conservative approach, called *simple*, has been taken to push to remote repositories. It is chosen by default, but a warning message can be squelched, and the push can be performed as follows (replace the user details and repository name with your own account details):

```
molloyd@ebb:~/test$ git config --global push.default simple
molloyd@ebb:~/test$ git push
Username for 'https://github.com': derekmolloy
Password for 'https://derekmolloy@github.com': mySuperSecretPassword
Counting objects: 4, done.
Compressing objects: 100% (2/2), done.
Writing objects: 100% (4/4), 350 bytes | 0 bytes/s, done.
Total 4 (delta 0), reused 0 (delta 0)
To https://github.com/derekmolloy/test.git
   61b6ee4..b2137ee  master -> master
```

After the code has been pushed to the remote repository, you can pull changes back to a local repository on any machine by issuing a `git pull` command from within the local repository directory.

```
molloyd@ebb:~/test$ git pull
Already up-to-date.
```

In this case, everything is already up-to-date.

Git Branching

Git supports the concept of branching, which enables you to work on multiple different versions of the set of files within your project. For example, to develop a new feature in your project (version 2) but maintain the code in the current version (version 1), you could create a new branch (version 2). New features and changes that are made to version 2 will not affect the code in version 1. You can then easily switch between branches.

Creating a Branch (git branch)

Suppose, for example, you want to create a new branch called `mybranch`; you can do so using the command `git branch mybranch`, and then you can switch to that branch using `git checkout mybranch`, as shown here:

```
molloyd@ebb:~/test$ git branch mybranch
molloyd@ebb:~/test$ git checkout mybranch
Switched to branch 'mybranch'
```

Now, to demonstrate how this works, suppose that a temporary file called `testmybranch.txt` is added to the repository. This could be a new code file for your project. You can see that the status of the branch makes it clear that the working directory contains an untracked file.

```
molloyd@ebb:~/test$ touch testmybranch.txt
molloyd@ebb:~/test$ ls
newfile.txt  README.md  testmybranch.txt  testobject.o
molloyd@ebb:~/test$ git status
On branch mybranch
Untracked files:
  (use "git add <file>..." to include in what will be committed)
        testmybranch.txt
nothing added to commit but untracked files present (use "git add" to track)
```

You can then add this new file to the staging area of the branch using the same commands.

```
molloyd@ebb:~/test$ git add .
molloyd@ebb:~/test$ git status
On branch mybranch
Changes to be committed:
  (use "git reset HEAD <file>..." to unstage)
        new file:   testmybranch.txt
```

You can commit this change to the mybranch branch of the local repository. This change will affect the mybranch branch but have no impact on the master branch.

```
molloyd@ebb:~/test$ git commit -m "Test commit to mybranch"
[mybranch 63cae5f] Test commit to mybranch
 1 file changed, 0 insertions(+), 0 deletions(-)
 create mode 100644 testmybranch.txt
molloyd@ebb:~/test$ git status
On branch mybranch
nothing to commit, working tree clean
molloyd@ebb:~/test$ ls
newfile.txt  README.md  testmybranch.txt  testobject.o
```

You can see from the preceding output that the file testmybranch.txt is committed to the local repository and you can see the file in the directory.

If you now switch from the branch mybranch to the master branch using the call **git checkout master**, you will see that something interesting happens when you request the directory listing.

```
molloyd@ebb:~/test$ git checkout master
Switched to branch 'master'
Your branch is up-to-date with 'origin/master'.
molloyd@ebb:~/test$ ls
newfile.txt  README.md  testobject.o
```

Yes, the file `testmybranch.txt` has disappeared from the directory! It still exists, but it is in a blob form inside the `.git/objects/` directory. If you return to the branch and list the directory, you will see the following:

```
molloyd@ebb:~/test$ git checkout mybranch
Switched to branch 'mybranch'
molloyd@ebb:~/test$ ls
newfile.txt  README.md  testmybranch.txt  testobject.o
```

The file now reappears. Therefore, you can see just how well integrated the branching system is. At this point, you can go back to the master branch and make changes to the original code without the changes in the `mybranch` branch having any impact on the master code. Even if you change the code in the same file, it has no effect on the original code in the master branch.

Merging a Branch (git merge)

What if you want to apply the changes that you made in the `mybranch` branch to the master project? You can do this by using `git merge`.

```
molloyd@ebb:~/test$ git checkout master
Switched to branch 'master'
Your branch is up-to-date with 'origin/master'.
molloyd@ebb:~/test$ git merge mybranch
Updating b2137ee..63cae5f
Fast-forward
 testmybranch.txt | 0
 1 file changed, 0 insertions(+), 0 deletions(-)
 create mode 100644 testmybranch.txt
molloyd@ebb:~/test$ git status
On branch master
Your branch is ahead of 'origin/master' by 1 commit.
  (use "git push" to publish your local commits)
nothing to commit, working tree clean
molloyd@ebb:~/test$ ls
newfile.txt  README.md  testmybranch.txt  testobject.o
```

Now the `testmybranch.txt` file is in the master branch, and any changes that were made to other documents in the master have been applied. The local repository is now one commit ahead of the remote repository, and you can use `git push` to update the remote repository.

Deleting a Branch (git branch -d)

If you want to delete a branch, use the `git branch -d mybranch` command.

```
molloyd@ebb:~/test$ git branch -d mybranch
Deleted branch mybranch (was 63cae5f).
```

```
molloyd@ebb:~/test$ ls
newfile.txt  README.md  testmybranch.txt  testobject.o
```

In this case, the file `testmybranch.txt` is still present in the master project—and it should be because the branch was merged with the master project. If the branch had been deleted before the merge was performed, the file would have been lost.

Common Git Commands

Table 3-8 summarizes the main Git commands. At this point, you have seen the core use of Git. If you are developing code directly on the Beagle board, Git can be highly useful because you can easily push your developments to a remote repository. That capability can be useful in backing up your code and redeploying the code to multiple boards.

Table 3-8: Summary of the Main Git Commands

OPERATION	DESCRIPTION	OPERATION	DESCRIPTION
git clone	Clone from the remote repository.	git rm	Delete a file or directory from the staging area.
git init	Create a wholly new repository.	git mv	Move or rename a file or folder in the staging area.
git pull	Merge changes from a master repository.	git log	Display a log of commits. The project history.
git fetch	Find what has changed in a master repository without merging.	git tag	Give a commit a name (e.g., version 2).
git status	Show the project's status.	git merge [name]	Merge the branch.
git add	Add a new file or edit an existing file.	git show	Get details about the current or other commit.
git diff	Show the differences that are to be committed.	git branch [name]	Create a new branch. (Use -d to delete.)
git commit	Commit to the repository.	git checkout [name]	Switch to a different branch.
git push	Push changes from the local repository to a remote repository.		

Desktop Virtualization

The BeagleBone and BeagleBoard are capable general-purpose computing platforms, but if you are planning to build a Linux kernel or perform cross-platform development (see Chapter 7), a PC-based Linux installation is highly recommended. You can use a single/dual-boot Linux PC, or if you are a Windows/Mac native, you should investigate desktop virtualization.

Desktop *virtualization* enables a single desktop computer to run multiple OS instances simultaneously. It uses technology called *hypervisors*, which consist of hardware, firmware, and software elements, to create and run software-emulated machines, known as *virtual machines* (VMs). If you want to run multiple OS instances on a single computer, VMs provide an alternative to creating a multiboot configuration.

In virtualization, there are usually two or more distinct OS instances. The *host* OS is the one that was first installed on the physical machine. The hypervisor software is then used to create a *guest* OS within a VM. Figure 3-6 captures a host Windows desktop computer running a guest Debian 64-bit Linux Stretch VM within a window. The Debian installation has the Cairo-Dock desktop interface installed.

Figure 3-6: VirtualBox running Debian 9.4 as a guest OS on a Windows host machine with an SSH session to the PocketBeagle board

Many virtualization products are available, but most have significant costs and proprietary licenses and are limited in the type of guest and host OSs that they support. Two of the most popular Linux desktop virtualization products are VMware Player and VirtualBox. VMware Player (www.vmware.com/products/

player/) is free for personal use. VirtualBox (www.virtualbox.org) is available under a GNU GPLv2 license (some features are available free under a proprietary license).

Both products use *hosted hypervisors* (Type 2) for virtualization, meaning that they run within a regular OS, enabling you to use both machines simultaneously. VirtualBox is available to run on Windows, macOS, and Linux machines, and it can be used to host guest OSs such as Linux, Windows, and macOS. Currently, VMware Player is not available for macOS host installations; instead, you must purchase a product called VMware Fusion.

Both products are powerful, and it is difficult to distinguish between them; however, VirtualBox is released under a GPL, and it supports a useful feature called *snapshots*. A user interface makes it possible to take a snapshot of the guest OS that can be saved for later use. For example, you could take a snapshot before you make a significant configuration change to your guest OS, enabling you to roll back to that configuration should problems arise. The snapshot stores the VM settings, changes in the contents of the virtual disks, and the memory state of the machine at that point in time. Therefore, when a snapshot is restored, the VM continues running at the same point as when the snapshot was taken.

If you install the VirtualBox Guest Additions, you are able to copy and paste text between your guest and host OSs, share directories, and even resize the window dynamically. This chapter's web page (www.exploringbeaglebone.com/chapter3/) provides advice on installing a Linux guest OS under a Windows host OS.

> **NOTE** All Linux packages and software in this book are built and tested using a Debian 64-bit desktop distribution that is installed within a VirtualBox VM.

Code for This Book

Now that you have your Desktop Linux installation up and running under VirtualBox or you are running a regular Linux desktop installation, you can download all the source code, scripts, and documentation discussed in this book by opening a Linux terminal session/window and typing the following (on the desktop machine and Beagle board):

```
molloyd@ebb:~$ sudo apt install git
molloyd@ebb:~$ git clone https://github.com/derekmolloy/exploringBB.git
Cloning into 'exploringBB' ...
molloyd@ebb:~$ cd exploringBB/
molloyd@ebb:~/exploringBB$ ls
chp02   chp05   chp08   chp10   chp12   chp14   extras    License.txt
chp03   chp06   chp09   chp11   chp13   chp15   library   README.md
```

If you want to download the code from within Windows or macOS, a graphical user interface for working with GitHub repositories is available from `windows.github.com` and `mac.github.com`.

> **NOTE**   If you have your own GitHub account, you can use its web interface to fork this repository to your own account or you can watch the repository for updates and changes. A GitHub account without private repositories is currently free of charge. In addition, students can apply for a free account, through the GitHub Student Developer Pack at `education.github.com`. GitHub was purchased by Microsoft in June 2018, which has undertaken to continue to provide an open platform for developers in all industries, with the programming languages and operating systems of their choice (see `tiny.cc/beagle303`).

Summary

After completing this chapter, you should be able to do the following:

- Describe the basic concept of an embedded Linux system
- Describe how embedded Linux devices, such as the Beagle boards, boot the Linux OS
- Describe important Linux concepts, such as kernel space, user space, and system initialization using systemd
- Perform Linux system administration tasks on the Beagle boards
- Use the Linux file system effectively
- Use a range of Linux commands for file and process management
- Manage your own software development projects using Git
- Install a Linux distribution on your desktop computer host OS using desktop virtualization tools, such as VirtualBox
- Download the source code for this book using Git

Further Reading

The following texts can help you learn more about embedded Linux, Linux administration, Git, and virtualization:

- Christopher Hallinan's *Embedded Linux Primer: A Practical Real-World Approach, Second Edition* (Upper Saddle River, NJ: Prentice Hall, 2011).
- The Debian Policy Manual: www.debian.org/doc/debian-policy/.

- To learn more about Git, start with a call to `man gittutorial`, and then if you need detailed information, see Scott Chacon's excellent reference *Pro Git*, at `www.git-scm.com/book/en/v2`; also available in paperback (New York: Apress Media, 2009).

Bibliography

- Git FAQ. (2013, 3 9). Retrieved 2 22, 2014, from Git Wiki: `https://git.wiki.kernel.org/index.php/GitFaq#Why_the_.27Git.27_name.3F`
- Smith, B. (2013, 7 29). A Quick Guide to GPLv3. Retrieved June 14, 2015, from `www.gnu.org/licenses/quick-guide-gplv3.html`

Interfacing Electronics

This chapter introduces you to the type of practical electronics that you need to work correctly and effectively in interfacing electronic circuits with the Beagle boards. The chapter begins by describing some equipment that can be helpful in developing and debugging electronic circuits. It continues with a practical introductory guide to circuit design and analysis, in which you are encouraged to build the circuits and utilize the equipment that is described at the beginning of the chapter. The chapter continues with a discussion on the typical discrete components that can be interfaced to the general-purpose input/outputs (GPIOs) on the Beagle boards, including diodes, capacitors, transistors, optocouplers, switches, and logic gates. Finally, the important principles of analog-to-digital conversion (ADC) are described, as such knowledge is required to interface to the Beagle board ADCs.

EQUIPMENT REQUIRED FOR THIS CHAPTER:

- Components for this chapter (if following along): The full list is provided at the end of this chapter.
- Digilent Analog Discovery (version 1 or 2) *or* access to a digital multimeter, signal generator, and oscilloscope.

Further details on this chapter are available at `www.exploringbeaglebone .com/chapter4/`.

> **NOTE** One chapter cannot be a substitute for full textbooks on digital and analog electronics; however, there are concepts with which you should be comfortable before connecting electronics to the GPIO interface header on the Beagle boards, as incorrect configurations can easily destroy your board. Later chapters depend heavily on the electronics concepts that are described in this chapter; however, it is not vital that you assimilate all of the content in this chapter before you move on. Importantly, this chapter is here as a reference for electronics concepts mentioned in later chapters.

Analyzing Your Circuits

When developing electronics circuits for the Beagle boards, it is useful to have the following tools so that you can analyze a circuit before you connect it to the board's inputs/outputs to reduce the chance of damaging your board. In particular, it is useful to have access to a digital multimeter and a mixed-signal oscilloscope.

> **NOTE** The tools listed here are for your consideration. Be sure to do your homework and seek independent advice before choosing any such product. None of the products included is the result of any type of product placement agreement or request. All prices are approximate.

Digital Multimeter

A digital multimeter (DMM) is an invaluable tool for measuring the voltage, current, and resistance/continuity of circuits. If you don't already have one, try to purchase one with the following features:

- **Auto power off:** It is easy to waste batteries.
- **Auto range:** It is vital that you can select different measurement ranges. Midprice meters often have automatic range selection functionality that can reduce the time required to take measurements.
- **Continuity testing:** This feature should provide an audible beep unless there is a break in the conductor (or excessive resistance).
- **True RMS readings:** Most low-cost meters use averaging to calculate AC(~) current/voltage. True RMS meters process the readings using a true root mean square (RMS) calculation, which makes it possible to account for distortions in waveforms when taking readings. This feature is useful for analyzing phase controlled equipment, solid-state devices, motorized devices, etc.

- **Other useful options:** These options are not strictly necessary but are helpful: backlit display, a measurement hold, large digit displays, a greater number of significant digits, PC connectivity (ideally optoisolated), temperature probe, and diode testing.
- **Case:** Look for a good-quality rubberized plastic case.

Generally, most of the preceding features are available on midprice DMMs with a good level of accuracy (1 percent or better), high input impedances (>10MΩ), and good measurement ranges. High-end multimeters mainly offer faster measurement speed and greater levels of measurement accuracy; some may also offer features such as measuring capacitance, frequency, temperature using an infrared sensor, humidity, and transistor gain. Some of the best known brands are Fluke, Tenma, Agilent, Extech, and Klein Tools.

Oscilloscopes

Standard DMMs provide you with a versatile tool that enables you to measure average voltage, current, and resistance. Oscilloscopes typically only measure voltage, but they enable you to see how the voltage changes with respect to time. Typically, you can simultaneously view two or more voltage waveforms that are captured within a certain bandwidth and number of analog samples (memory). The bandwidth defines the range of signal frequencies that an oscilloscope can measure accurately (typically to the 3dB point, i.e., the frequency at which a sine wave amplitude is ~30 percent lower than its true amplitude). To achieve accurate results, the number of analog samples needs to be a multiple of the bandwidth (you will see why later in this chapter when the Nyquist rate is discussed); and for modern oscilloscopes, this value is typically four to five times the bandwidth, so a 25MHz oscilloscope should have 100 million samples per second or greater. The bandwidth and number of analog samples have the greatest influence on the cost of an oscilloscope.

Several low-cost two-channel oscilloscopes are available, such as those by Owon PDS5022S 25MHz (~$200), feature-rich Siglent SDS1022DL 25MHz (~$325), Rigol DS1052 50MHz (~$325), and Owon SDS6062 60MHz (~$349). Prices rise considerably as the bandwidth increases, to around $1,500 for a 300MHz scope. Agilent digital storage (DSOX) and mixed-signal (MSOX) series scopes would be considered to be mid/high range and cost $3,000 (100MHz) to $16,000 (1GHz). Mixed-signal scopes also provide you with digital bus analysis tools.

The Digilent Analog Discovery 2 with Waveforms (see Figure 4-1) is used to test all the circuits in this book. The Analog Discovery (and similar Analog Discovery 2) is a USB oscilloscope, waveform generator, digital pattern generator, and logic analyzer for the Windows environment. The recently released Waveforms software now has support for Linux (including ARM) and macOS.

The Analog Discovery 2 is generally available for $279. If you are starting out or refreshing your electronics skills, it is a really great piece of equipment for the price.

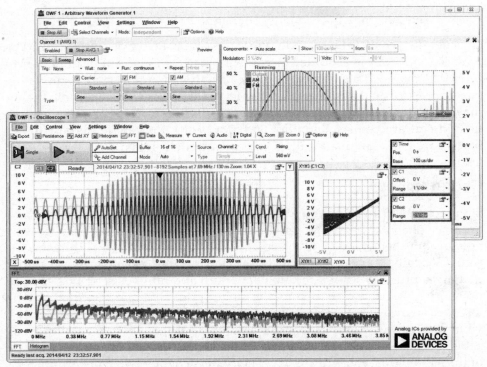

Figure 4-1: The Waveforms application generating a signal and displaying the response from the physical circuit

NOTE   A video I made about the use of the Analog Discovery is available at this chapter's web page: www.exploringbeaglebone.com/chapter4. It demonstrates three different measurement applications of the Analog Discovery: analog analysis of a rectifier diode, using the digital pattern generator and logic analyzer to investigate the behavior of a JK flip-flop, and using the logic analyzer and its I²C interpreter to connect to the BeagleBone Black I²C bus and analyze how it behaves.

The Analog Discovery is used to generate all the oscilloscope plots that are presented in this book, as all examples have been implemented using real circuits. The scope is limited to two channels at 5MHz per channel and 50 million samples per second, for both the waveform generator and the differential oscilloscope. As such, the Analog Discovery is mainly focused on students and learners; however, it can also be useful in deciding upon "must-have" features for your next, more expensive, equipment.

There are alternative mixed-signal USB scopes, such as PicoScopes, which range from $160 to $10,000 (www.picotech.com), and the BitScope DSO, from $150 to $1,000 (www.bitscope.com), which has Linux support. However, based on the feature set that is currently available on USB oscilloscopes, it may be the case that a bench scope with a USB logic analyzer provides the best "bang for your buck."

Basic Circuit Principles

Electronic circuits contain arrangements of components that can be described as being either passive or active. Active components, such as transistors, are those that can adaptively control the flow of current, whereas passive components cannot (e.g., resistors, capacitors, diodes). The challenge in building circuits is designing a suitable arrangement of appropriate components. Fortunately, there are circuit analysis equations to help you.

Voltage, Current, Resistance, and Ohm's Law

The most important equation that you need to understand is Ohm's law. It is simply stated as follows:

$$V = I \times R$$

where:

- Voltage (V), measured in volts (V), is the difference in potential energy that forces electrical current to flow in the circuit. A water analogy is useful when thinking of voltage; many houses have a buffer tank of water in the attic that is connected to the taps in the house. Water flows when a tap is turned on due to the height of the tank and the force of gravity. If the tap were at the same height as the top of the tank of water, no water would flow because there would be no potential energy. Voltage behaves in much the same way; when a voltage on one side of a component, such as a resistor, is greater than on the other side, electrical current can flow across the component.

- Current (I), measured in amps (A), is the flow of electrical charge. To continue the water analogy, current would be the flow of water from the tank (with a high potential) to the tap (with a lower potential). Remember that the tap still has potential and water will flow out of the drain of the sink, unless it is at ground level (GND). To put the level of current in context, when we build circuits to interface with the Beagle board's GPIOs, they usually source or sink only about 5 mA, where a milliamp is one thousandth of an amp.

- Resistance (R), measured in ohms (Ω), discourages the flow of charge. A resistor is a component that reduces the flow of current through the dissipation of power. It does this in a linear fashion, where the power dissipated in watts (W), is given by $P = V \times I$ or, alternatively, by integrating Ohm's law: $P = I^2R = V^2/R$. The power is dissipated in the form of heat, and all resistors have a maximum dissipated power rating. Common metal film or carbon resistors typically dissipate 0.125W to 1W, and the price increases dramatically if this value has to exceed 3W. To finish with the water analogy, resistance is the friction between the water and the pipe, which results in a heating effect and a reduction in the flow of water. This resistance can be increased by increasing the surface area over which the water has to pass, while maintaining the pipe's cross-sectional area (e.g., placing small pipes within the main pipe).

As an example, if you had to buy a resistor that limits the flow of current to 100mA when using a 5V supply, as illustrated in Figure 4-2(a), which resistor should you buy? The voltage dropped across the resistor, V_R, must be 5V, as it is the only component in the circuit. Because $V_R = I_R \times R$, it follows that the resistor should have the value $R = V_R/I_R = 5V/100mA = 50\Omega$, and the power dissipated by this resistor can be calculated using any of the general equations $P = VI = I^2R = V^2/R$ as 0.5W.

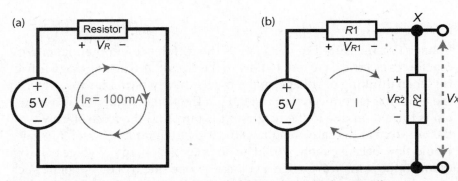

Figure 4-2: (a) Ohm's law circuit example, and (b) a voltage divider example

Buying one through-hole, fixed-value 50Ω metal-film resistor with a 1 percent tolerance (accuracy) costs about $0.10 for a 0.33W resistor and $0.45 for a 1W power rating. You should be careful with the power rating of the resistors you use in your circuits, as underspecified resistors can blow. A 30W resistor will cost $2.50 and can get extremely hot—not all resistors are created equally!

WARNING   Why would it be bad practice to connect a voltage supply's positive terminal to the negative terminal without a resistor? This is called a *short circuit*, and it is the quickest way to damage a sensitive device like the Beagle boards. Connection (hook-up) wire by its nature is a good conductor, and it has a small resistance. A 100M (328ft) roll of 0.6mm (0.023") hook-up wire has a total resistance of about 5Ω; therefore, connecting a 6" length of connection wire between a Beagle board 3.3V supply and its GND terminal would in theory draw 433A ($I = V/R = 3.3V/0.0076Ω$). In practice this will not happen, but the available maximum current would likely damage your board! Also, remember that LEDs do not include a fixed internal resistance, so they behave somewhat like a short circuit when forward biased—LEDs nearly always require current-limiting resistors for this reason!

Voltage Division

If the circuit in Figure 4-2(a) is modified to add another resistor in series, as illustrated in Figure 4-2(b), what will be the impact on the circuit?

- Because one resistor is after the other (they're in series), the total resistance that the current must pass through to circulate in the circuit is the sum of the two values: $R_T = R1 + R2$.

- The supply voltage must drop across the two resistors, so you can say that $V_{supply} = V_{R1} + V_{R2}$. The voltage that drops across each resistor is inversely proportional to the resistor's value. This circuit is called a *voltage divider*.

Suppose you want to calculate on paper the voltage value at point X in Figure 4-2(b) if $R1 = 25Ω$ and $R2 = 75Ω$. The total resistance in the circuit is $R_T = 25 + 75 = 100\,Ω$, and the total voltage drop across the resistors must be 5V; therefore, by using Ohm's law, the current flowing in the circuit is $I = V/R = 5V/100Ω = 50mA$. If the resistance of $R1$ is $25Ω$, then the voltage drop across $V_{R1} = I \times R = 0.05\,A \times 25\,Ω = 1.25\,V$ and the voltage drop across $V_{R2} = I \times R = 0.05\,A \times 75\,Ω = 3.75\,V$. You can see that the sum of these voltages is 5V, thus obeying Kirchoff's voltage law, which states that the sum of the voltage drops in a series circuit equals the total voltage applied.

To answer the question fully, in this circuit, 1.25V is dropped across $R1$ and 3.75V is dropped across $R2$, so what is the voltage at X? To know that, you have to measure X with respect to some other point! If you measured X with respect to the negative terminal of the supply, the voltage drop is V_X in Figure 4-2(b), and it is the same as the voltage drop across $R2$, so it is 3.75V. However, it would be equally as valid to ask the question, "What is the voltage at X with respect to the positive terminal of the supply?" In that case, it would be the negative of the voltage drop across $R1$ (as X is at 3.75V with respect to the negative terminal and the positive terminal is at +5V with respect to the negative terminal); therefore, the voltage at X with respect to the positive terminal of the supply is −1.25V.

To calculate the value of V_X in Figure 4-2(b), the voltage divider rule can be generalized to the following:

$$V_X = V \times \frac{R2}{R1 + R2}$$

You can use this rule to determine a voltage V_X, but unfortunately this configuration is quite limited in practice, because it is likely that the circuit to which you connect this voltage supply, V_X, will itself have a resistance (or load). This will alter the characteristic of your voltage divider circuit, changing the voltage V_X. However, most circuits that follow voltage dividers are usually input circuits that have very high input impedances, and therefore the impact on V_X will be minimal.

Figure 4-3(a) captures a variable resistor, or potentiometer (pot), and an associated circuit where it is used as a stand-alone voltage divider. The resistance between pins 1 and 3 is a fixed value, 10kΩ in the case of the multiturn pot; however, the resistance between pins 3 and the wiper pin (pin 2) varies between 0Ω and 10kΩ. Therefore, if the resistance between pins 2 and 3 is 2kΩ, then the resistance between pins 1 and 2 will be 10kΩ – 2kΩ = 8kΩ. In such a case, the output voltage, V_{out}, will be 1V, and it can be varied between 0V and 5V by turning the small screw on the pot, using a trim tool or screwdriver.

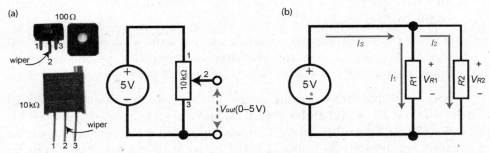

Figure 4-3: (a) Potentiometers and using a variable voltage supply, and (b) a current divider example

Current Division

If the circuit is modified as in Figure 4-3(b) to place the two resistors in parallel, you now have a current divider circuit. Current will follow the path of least resistance, so if $R1 = 100Ω$ and $R2 = 200Ω$, then a greater proportion of the current will travel through $R1$. So, what is this proportion? In this case the voltage drop across $R1$ and $R2$ is 5V in both cases. Therefore, the current I_1 will be $I = V/R = 5V/100Ω = 50mA$, and the current I_2 will be $I = 5V/200Ω = 25mA$. Therefore, twice as much current travels through the 100Ω resistor as the 200Ω resistor. Clearly, current favors the path of least resistance.

Kirchoff's current law states that the sum of currents entering a junction equals the sum of currents exiting that junction. This means that $I_S = I_1 + I_2 = 25mA + 50mA = 75mA$. The current divider rule can be stated generally as follows:

$$I_1 = I \times \left(\frac{R2}{R1+R2} \right), \text{ and } I_2 = I \times \left(\frac{R1}{R1+R2} \right)$$

However, this requires that you know the value of the current I (I_S in this case) that is entering the junction. To calculate I_S directly, you need to calculate the equivalent resistance (R_T) of the two parallel resistors, which is given as follows:

$$\frac{1}{R_T} = \frac{1}{R1} + \frac{1}{R2} \text{ or } R_T = \frac{R1 \times R2}{R1 + R2}$$

This is 66.66Ω in Figure 4-3(b); therefore $I_S = V/R = 5V/66.66\Omega = 75mA$, which is consistent with the initial calculations.

The power delivered by the supply: $P = V \times I = 5V \times 0.075A = 0.375W$. This should be equal to the sum of the power dissipated by $R1 = V^2/R = 5^2/100 = 0.25W$ and $R2 = V^2/R = 5^2/200 = 0.125W$, giving $0.375W$ total, confirming that the law of conservation of energy applies!

Implementing Circuits on a Breadboard

The breadboard is a great platform for prototyping circuits, and it works perfectly with the Beagle boards. Figure 4-4 illustrates a breadboard, describing how you can use the two horizontal power rails for 3.3V and 5V power. The GPIO header on the Beagle boards typically consists of female header pins, which means you can use wire strands to make connections.

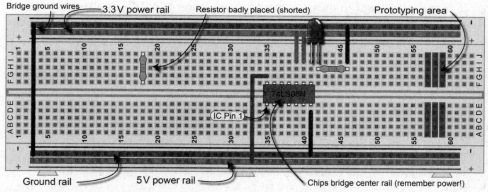

Figure 4-4: The breadboard with a 7408 IC (quad two-input AND gates)

A good-quality breadboard like that in Figure 4-4 (830 tie points) costs about $6 to $10. Giant breadboards (3,220 tie points) are available for about $20. Here are some tips for using breadboards:

▪ Whenever possible, place pin 1 of your ICs on the bottom left so that you can easily debug your circuits. Always line up the pins carefully with the breadboard holes before applying pressure and "clicking" it home. Also, ICs need power!

▪ Leaving a wire disconnected is *not* the same as connecting it to GND (discussed later in this chapter).

- Use a flat-head screwdriver to slowly lever ICs out of the breadboard from both ends to avoid bending the IC's legs.

- Be careful not to bridge resistors and other components by placing two of their pins in the same vertical rail. Also, trim resistor leads before placing them in the board, as long resistor leads can accidentally touch and cause circuit debugging headaches.

- Momentary push buttons typically have four legs that are connected in two pairs; make sure that you orient them correctly (use a DMM continuity test).

- Staples make great bridge connections!

- Some boards have a break in the power rails; bridge this where necessary.

- Breadboards typically have 0.1" spacing (lead pitch) between the tie points, which is 2.54mm metric. Try to buy all components and connectors with that spacing. For ICs, choose the DIP/PDIP (the IC code ends with an N); and for other components, choose the "through-hole" form.

- Use the color of the hook-up wire to mean something—e.g., use red for 5V and black for GND; it can really help when debugging circuits. Solid-core 22AWG wire serves as perfect hook-up wire and is available with many different insulator colors. Pre-formed jumper wire is available, but long wires lead to messy circuits. A selection of hook-up wire in different colors and a good-quality wire-stripping tool enables the neatest and most stable breadboard layouts.

EXAMPLE: MAKING CUSTOM CABLES FOR THE GPIO HEADER

As an alternative to using GPIO expansion boards or pre-crimped jumper wires, you can make custom cables that interface to the PocketBeagle male or female connectors. Custom cables allow for deployable stable connections, custom cable lengths, custom breakout directions, and mixed male/female end connectors. Figure 4-5(a) illustrates a custom-built connector that is attached to a male PocketBeagle header. Figure 4-5(b) illustrates a typical budget-price crimping tool ($20–$35). A video on this topic is available on the chapter web page and at `tiny.cc/beagle401`.

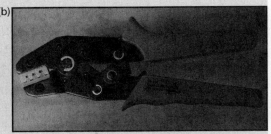

Figure 4-5: (a) The custom-built SPI connector attached to a PocketBeagle, and (b) a low-cost crimping tool

Digital Multimeters and Breadboards

Measuring voltage, current, and resistance is fairly straightforward once you take a few rules into account (with reference to Figure 4-6):

- *DC voltage* (DCV) is measured in parallel with (i.e., across) the component that experiences the voltage drop. The meter should have the black probe in the COM (common) DMM input.

- *DC current* (DCA) is measured in series, so you will have to "break" the connection in your circuit and wire the DMM as if it were a component in series with the conductor in the circuit in which you are measuring current. Use the black probe lead in COM and the red lead in the μAmA input (or equivalent). Do not use the 10A unfused input.

- *Resistance* cannot usually be measured in-circuit, because other resistors or components will act as parallel/series loads in your measurement. Isolate the component and place your DMM red probe in the VΩ input and set the meter to measure Ω. The continuity test can be reasonably effectively used in-circuit, provided that it is de-energized.

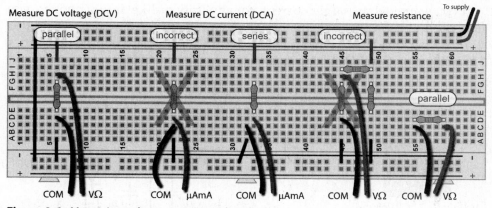

Figure 4-6: Measuring voltage, current, and resistance

If your DMM is refusing to function, you may have blown the internal fuse. Disconnect the DMM probes and open the meter to find the small glass fuse. If you have a second meter, you can perform a continuity test to determine whether it has blown. Replace it with a like value (or PTC)—not a mains fuse!

WARNING   Measuring current directly across a voltage supply (even a 9V battery) with no load is the quickest way to blow the DMM fuse, as most are rated at about 200mA. Check that the probe is in the VΩ input before measuring voltage.

Example Circuit: Voltage Regulation

Now that you have read the principles, a more complex circuit is discussed in this section, and then the components are examined in detail in the following sections. Do not build the circuit in this section; it is intended as an example to introduce the concept of interconnected components.

A voltage regulator is a complex but easy-to-use device that accepts a varied input voltage and outputs a constant voltage almost regardless of the attached load, at a lower level than the input voltage. The voltage regulator maintains the output voltage within a certain tolerance, preventing voltage variations from damaging downstream electronics devices.

The Beagle boards have an advanced Power Management IC (PMIC) that can supply different voltage levels to different devices at different output pins. For example, there is a 5V output, a 3.3V output, and a 1.8V reference for the analog-to-digital converters. You can use the 5V and 3.3V supplies on the board to drive your circuits, but only within certain current supply limits. The BBB can supply up to 1A on the VDD_5V pins on the P9 header (pins 5 and 6) if the BBB is connected to a DC power supply via the 5V jack, and 250mA on the DC_3.3V pins (pins 3 and 4).

If you want to draw larger currents for applications like driving motors, you may need to use voltage regulators like that in Figure 4-7. You can build this directly on a breadboard or you can purchase a "breadboard power supply stick 5V/3.3V" from SparkFun (www.sparkfun.com) for about $15.

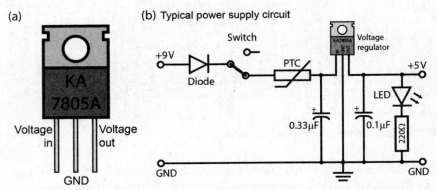

Figure 4-7: (a) The KA7805A/LM7805 voltage regulator, and (b) an example regulator circuit

As shown in Figure 4-7, the pin on the left of the regulator is the voltage supply input. When delivering a current of 500mA, the KA7805/LM7805 voltage regulator will accept an input voltage range of 8V–20V, and will output a voltage (on the right) in the range of 4.8V–5.2V. The middle pin should be connected to the ground rail. The aluminum plate at the back of the voltage regulator is there to dissipate heat. The hole enables you to bolt on a heat sink, allowing for greater output currents, of up to 1A.

The minimum input voltage required is about 8V to drive the KA7805/LM7805 voltage regulator. If your supply voltage is lower than that, then you could use a low-dropout (LDO) voltage regulator, which can require a supply as low as 6V to operate a 5V regulator. The implementation circuit in Figure 4-7 has the following additional components that enable it to deliver a clean and steady 5V, 1A supply:

- The diode ensures that if the supply is erroneously connected with the wrong polarity (e.g., 9V and GND are accidentally swapped), then the circuit is protected from damage. Diodes like the 1N4001 (1A supply) are very low cost, but the downside is that there will be a small forward voltage drop (approximately 1V at 1A) across the diode in advance of the regulator.

- The switch can be used to power the circuit on or off. A slider switch enables the circuit to remain continuously powered.

- The Positive Temperature Coefficient (PTC) resettable fuse is useful for preventing damage from overcurrent faults, such as accidental short circuits or component failure. The PTC enables a holding current to pass with only a small resistance (about 0.25Ω); but once a greater tripping current is exceeded, the resistance increases rapidly, behaving like a circuit breaker. When the power is removed, the PTC will cool (for a few seconds), and it regains its pre-tripped characteristics. In this circuit a 60R110 or equivalent Polyfuse would be appropriate, as it has a holding current of 1.1A and a trip current of 2.2A, at a maximum voltage of 60V DC.

- The $0.33\mu F$ capacitor is on the supply side of the regulator and the $0.1\mu F$ capacitor is on the output side of the regulator. These are the values recommended in the datasheet to remove noise (ripple rejection) from the supply. Capacitors are discussed shortly.

- The LED and appropriate current-limiting resistor provide an indicator light that makes it clear when the supply is powered.

NOTE   There are two main notations to represent current flow: The first is electron current flow, and it is the flow of negative charge. The second is conventional flow notation, and it is precisely the opposite: it is the flow of positive charge, and it is consistent with all semiconductor symbols. This book uses the conventional flow notation to describe current flow direction.

Discrete Components

The previous example circuit used a number of discrete components to build a stand-alone power supply circuit. In this section, the types of components that compose the power supply circuit are discussed in more detail. These components can be applied to many different circuit designs, and it is important to discuss them now, as many of them are used in designing circuits that interface to the Beagle board input/outputs in Chapter 6.

Diodes

Simply put, a diode is a discrete semiconductor component that allows current to pass in one direction but not the other. As the name suggests, a "semi" conductor is neither a conductor nor an insulator. Silicon is a semiconductive material, but it becomes much more interesting when it is doped with an impurity, such as phosphorus. Such a negative (n-type) doping results in a weakly bound electron in the valence band. It can also be positively doped (p-type) to have a hole in the valence band, using impurities such as boron. When you join a small block of p-type and n-type doped silicon together, you get a pn-junction—a diode! The free electrons in the valence band of the n-type silicon flow to the p-type silicon, creating a depletion layer and a voltage potential barrier that must be overcome before current can flow.

When a diode is forward biased, it allows current to flow through it; when it is reverse-biased, no current can flow. A diode is forward-biased when the voltage on the anode (+ve) terminal is greater than the voltage on the cathode (−ve) terminal; however, the biasing must also exceed the depletion layer potential barrier (knee voltage) before current can flow, which is typically between 0.5V and 0.7V for a silicon diode. If the diode is reverse-biased by applying a greater voltage on the cathode than the anode, then almost no current can flow (maybe 1nA or so). However, if the reverse-biased voltage is increasingly raised, then eventually the diode will break down and allow current to flow in the reverse direction. If the current is low, then this will not damage the diode—in fact, a special diode called a Zener diode is designed to operate in this breakdown region, and it can be configured to behave just like a voltage regulator.

The 1N4001 is a low-cost silicon diode that can be used in a simple circuit (see Figure 4-8) to demonstrate the use and behavior of diodes. The 1N4001 has a peak reverse breakdown voltage of 50V. In this circuit, a sine wave is applied that alternates from +5V to −5V, using the waveform generator of the Analog Discovery. When the V_{in} voltage is positive and exceeds the knee voltage, then current will flow, and there will be a voltage drop across the load resistor V_{load}, which is slightly less than V_{in}. There is a small voltage drop across the diode V_d

and you can see from the oscilloscope measurements that this is 0.67V, which is within the expected range for a silicon diode.

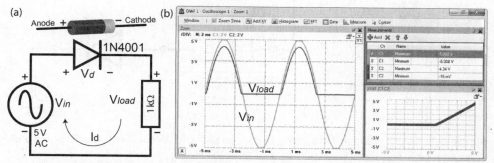

Figure 4-8: Circuit and behavior of a 1N4001 diode with a 5V AC supply and a 1kΩ load resistor

The diode is used in the circuit in Figure 4-7 as a reverse polarity protector. It should be clear from the plot in Figure 4-8 why it is effective, as when V_{in} is negative, the V_{load} is zero. This is because current cannot flow through the diode when it is reverse-biased. If the voltage exceeded the breakdown voltage for the diode, then current would flow; but since that is 50V for the 1N4001, it will not occur in this case. Note that the bottom-right corner of Figure 4-8 shows an XY-plot of output voltage (y-axis) versus input voltage (x-axis). You can see that for negative input voltage the output voltage is 0, but once the knee voltage is reached (0.67V), the output voltage increases linearly with the input voltage. This circuit is called a *half-wave rectifier*. It is possible to connect four diodes in a bridge formation to create a full-wave rectifier.

Light-Emitting Diodes

A light-emitting diode (LED) is a semiconductor-based light source that is often used as a state indication light in all types of devices. Today, high-powered LEDs are being used in car lights, in back lights for televisions, and even in place of filament lights for general-purpose lighting (e.g., home lighting, traffic lights, etc.) mainly because of their longevity and extremely high efficiency in converting electrical power to light output. LEDs provide useful status and debug information about your circuit, often used to indicate whether a state is true or false.

Like diodes, LEDs are polarized. The symbol for an LED is illustrated in Figure 4-9. To cause an LED to light, the diode needs to be forward biased by connecting the anode (+) to a more positive source than the cathode (−). For example, the anode could be connected to +3.3V and the cathode to GND;

however, also remember that the same effect would be achieved by connecting the anode to 0V and the cathode to −3.3V.

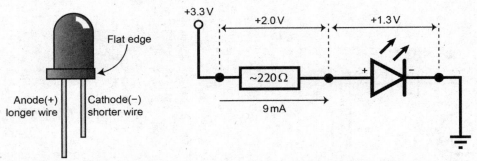

Figure 4-9: An LED example and a circuit to drive an LED with appropriate forward current and voltage levels

Figure 4-9 illustrates an LED that has one leg longer than the other. The longer leg is the anode (+), and the shorter leg is the cathode (−). The plastic LED surround also has a flat edge, which indicates the cathode (−) leg of the LED. This flat edge indication is particularly useful when the LED is in-circuit and the legs have been trimmed.

LEDs have certain operating requirements, defined by a forward voltage and a forward current. Every LED is different, and you need to reference the datasheet of the LED to determine these values. An LED does not have a significant resistance, so if you were to connect the LED directly across your Beagle board's 3.3V supply, the LED would act like a short circuit, and you would drive a large current through the LED, damaging it—but more important, damaging your board! Therefore, to operate an LED within its limits you need a series resistor, called a *current-limiting resistor*. Choose this value carefully to maximize the light output of the LED and to protect the circuit.

> **WARNING**   Do not connect LEDs directly to the GPIOs on the GPIO header without using current-limiting resistors and/or transistor switching, as you will likely damage your board. The maximum current that the Beagle boards can source from a GPIO pin is about 4–6 mA.

Referring to Figure 4-9, if you are supplying the LED from the Beagle board's 3.3V supply and you want to have a forward voltage drop of 1.3V across the LED, you need the difference of 2V to drop across the current-limiting resistor. The LED specifications require you to limit the current to 9mA, so you need to calculate a current-limiting resistor value as follows:

As $V = IR$, then $R = V/I = 2V/0.009A = 222\Omega$

Therefore, a circuit to light an LED would look like that in Figure 4-9. Here a 220Ω resistor is placed in series with the LED. The combination of the 3.3V supply and the resistor drives a current of 9mA through the forward-biased LED; as with this current the resistor has a 2V drop across it, then accordingly the LED has a forward voltage drop of 1.3V across it. Please note that this would be fine if you were connecting to the BBB's DC_3.3V output, but it is *not* fine for use with the BBB's GPIOs, as the maximum current that the BBB can source from a GPIO pin is about 4–6mA. You will see a solution for this shortly, and again in Chapter 6.

It is also worth mentioning that you should not dim LEDs by reducing the voltage across the LED. An LED should be thought of as a current-controlled device, where driving a current through the LED causes the forward voltage drop. Therefore, trying to control an LED with a variable voltage will not work as you might expect. To dim an LED you can use a pulse-width modulated (PWM) signal, essentially rapidly switching the LED on and off. For example, if a rapid PWM signal is applied to the LED that is off for half of the time and on for half of the time, then the LED will appear to be only emitting about half of its regular operating condition light level. Our eyes don't see the individual changes if they are fast enough; they average over the light and dark interval to see a constant, but dimmer illumination.

Figure 4-10 illustrates a PWM square wave signal at different duty cycles. The duty cycle is the percentage of time that the signal is high versus the time that the signal is low. In this example, a high is represented by a voltage of 3.3V and a low by a voltage of 0V. A duty cycle of 0 percent means that the signal is constantly low, and a duty cycle of 100 percent means that the signal is constantly high.

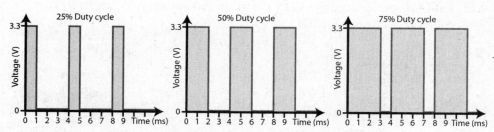

Figure 4-10: Duty cycles of pulse width modulation (PWM) signals

PWM can be used to control the light level of LEDs, but it can also be used to control the speed of DC motors, the position of servo motors, and many more applications. You will see such an example in Chapter 6 when the built-in PWM functionality of the Beagle boards is used.

The period (T) of a repeating signal (a periodic signal) is the time it takes to complete a full cycle. In the example in Figure 4-10, the period of the signal in all three cases is 4ms. The frequency (f) of a periodic signal describes how often a signal goes through a full cycle in a given time period. Therefore, for a signal with a period of 4ms, it will cycle 250 times per second (1/0.004), which is 250 hertz (Hz). We can state that f(Hz) = 1/T(s) or T(s) = 1/f(Hz). Some high-end DMMs measure frequency, but generally you use an oscilloscope to measure frequency. PWM signals need to switch at a frequency to suit the device to be controlled; typically, the frequency is in the kHz range for motor control.

Smoothing and Decoupling Capacitors

A capacitor is a passive electrical component that can be used to store electrical energy between two insulated plates when there is a voltage difference between them. The energy is stored in an electric field between the two plates, with positive charge building on one plate and negative charge building on the other plate. When the voltage difference is removed or reduced, then the capacitor discharges its energy to a connected electrical circuit.

For example, if you modified the diode circuit in Figure 4-8(a) to add a 10μF smoothing capacitor in parallel with the load resistor, the output voltage would appear as shown in Figure 4-11. When the diode is forward biased, there is a potential across the terminals of the capacitor and it quickly charges (while a current also flows through the load resistor in parallel). When the diode is reverse biased, there is no external supply generating a potential across the capacitor/resistor combination, so the potential across the terminals of the capacitor (because of its charge) causes a current to flow through the load resistor, and the capacitor starts to discharge. The impact of this change is that there is now a more stable voltage across the load resistor that varies between 2.758V and 4.222V (the ripple voltage is 1.464V), rather than between 0V and 4.34V.

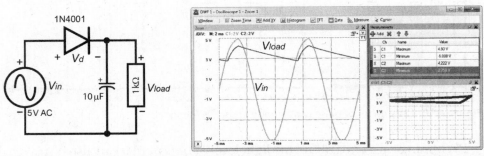

Figure 4-11: Circuit and behavior of a 1N4001 diode with a 5V AC supply, 1kΩ load, and parallel 10μF capacitor

Capacitors use a dielectric material, such as ceramic, glass, paper, or plastic, to insulate the two charged plates. Two common capacitor types are ceramic and electrolytic capacitors. Ceramic capacitors are small and low cost and degrade over time. Electrolytic capacitors can store much larger amounts of energy but also degrade over time. Glass, mica, and tantalum capacitors tend to be more reliable but are considerably more expensive.

Figure 4-12 illustrates a 100nF (0.1µF) ceramic capacitor and a 47µF electrolytic capacitor. Note that the electrolytic capacitor is polarized, with the negative lead marked on the capacitor surface with a band; like the LED, the negative lead is shorter than the positive lead.

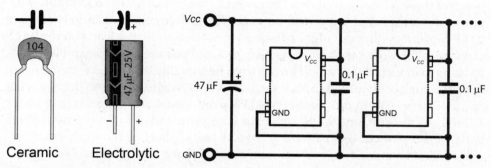

Figure 4-12: Ceramic (nonpolarized) and electrolytic (polarized) capacitors and an example decoupling circuit

The numbering for capacitors is reasonably straightforward; unfortunately, on ceramic capacitors it can be small and hard to read.

- The first number is the first digit of the capacitor value.
- The second number is the second digit of the capacitor value.
- The third number is the number of zeroes, where the capacitor value is in pF (picofarads).
- Additional letters represent the tolerance and voltage rating of the capacitor but can be ignored for the moment.

Therefore, for example:

- 10<u>4</u> = 100<u>000</u>pF = 100nF = 0.1µF
- 10<u>2</u> = 1,0<u>00</u>pF = 1nF
- 47<u>2</u> = 4,7<u>00</u>pF = 4.7nF

The voltage regulator circuit presented earlier (refer to Figure 4-7) used two capacitors to smooth out the ripples in the supply by charging and discharging in opposition to those ripples. Capacitors can also be used for a related function known as *decoupling*.

Coupling is often an undesirable relationship that occurs between two parts of a circuit due to the sharing of power supply connections. This relationship means that if there is a sudden high power demand by one part of the circuit, then the supply voltage will drop slightly, affecting the supply voltages of other parts of the circuit. ICs impart a variable load on the power supply lines—in fact, a load that can change quickly causes a high-frequency voltage variation on the supply lines to other ICs. As the number of ICs in the circuit increases, the problem will be compounded.

Small capacitors, known as *decoupling capacitors*, can act as a store of energy that removes the noise signals that may be present on your supply lines as a result of these IC load variations. An example circuit is illustrated in Figure 4-12, where the larger 47 µF capacitor filters out lower-frequency variations and the 0.1 µF capacitors filter out higher-frequency noise. Ideally the leads on the 0.1 µF capacitors should be as short as possible to avoid producing undesirable effects (relating to inductance) that will limit it from filtering the highest-level frequencies. Even the surface-mounted capacitors used on the Beagle boards to decouple the ball grid array (BGA) pins on the AM335x produce a small inductance of about 1–2 nH. As a result, one 0.1 µF capacitor is recommended for every two power balls, and the traces (board tracks) have to be as "short as humanly possible" (Texas Instruments, 2011). See `tiny.cc/beagle402` for a full guide.

Transistors

Transistors are one of the core ingredients of the AM335x microprocessor, and indeed almost every other electronic system. Simply put, their function can be to amplify a signal or to turn a signal on or off, whichever is required. The Beagle board GPIOs can handle only modest currents, so we need transistors to help us when interfacing them to electronic circuits that require larger currents to operate.

Bipolar junction transistors (BJTs), usually just called *transistors*, are formed by adding another doped layer to a pn-junction diode to form either a p-n-p or an n-p-n transistor. There are other types of transistors, such as field effect transistors (FETs), which are discussed shortly. The name *bipolar* comes from the fact that the current is carried by both electrons and holes. They have three terminals, with the third terminal connected to the middle layer in the sandwich, which is very narrow, as illustrated in Figure 4-13.

Figure 4-13 presents quite an amount of information about transistors, including the naming of the terminals as the base (B), collector (C), and emitter (E). Despite there being two main types of BJT transistor (NPN and PNP), the NPN transistor is the most commonly used. In fact, any transistor examples in this chapter use a single BC547 NPN transistor type.

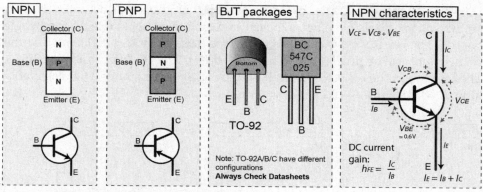

Figure 4-13: Bipolar junction transistors (BJTs)

The BC547 is a 45V, 100mA general-purpose transistor that is commonly available, is low cost, and is provided in a leaded TO-92 package. The identification of the legs in the BC547 is provided in Figure 4-13, but please be aware that this order is not consistent with all transistors—always check the datasheet! The maximum V_{CE} (aka V_{CEO}) is 45V, and the maximum collector current (I_C) is 100mA for the BC547. It has a typical DC current gain (h_{FE}) of between 180 and 520, depending on the group used (e.g., A, B, C). Those characteristics are explained in the next sections.

Transistors as Switches

> **NOTE** For the remainder of this book, FETs rather than BJTs are used in the circuits for switching loads. If you become overwhelmed by the detail in this section, please skip ahead to FETs, which are somewhat easier to apply.

Let's examine the characteristics for the NPN transistor as illustrated in Figure 4-13 (on the rightmost diagram). If the base-emitter junction is forward biased and a small current is entering the base (I_B), the behavior of a transistor is such that a proportional but much larger current ($I_C = h_{FE} \times I_B$) will be allowed to flow into the collector terminal, as h_{FE} will be a value of 180 to 520 for a transistor such as the BC547. Because I_B is much smaller than I_C, you can also assume that I_E is approximately equal to I_C.

Figure 4-14 illustrates the example of a BJT being used as a switch. In part (a) the voltage levels have been chosen to match those available on the Beagle boards. The resistor on the base is chosen to have a value of 2.2kΩ so that the base current will be small ($I = V/R = (3.3\,\text{V} - 0.7\,\text{V})/2200\,\Omega$, which is about 1.2mA). The resistor on the collector is small, so the collector current will be reasonably large ($I = V/R = (5\,\text{V} - \sim 0.2\,\text{V})/100 = 48$ mA).

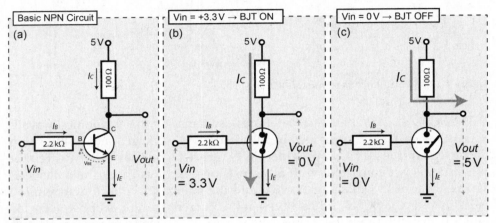

Figure 4-14: The BJT as a switch

Figure 4-14(b) illustrates what happens when an input voltage of 3.3V is applied to the base terminal. The small base current causes the transistor to behave like a closed switch (with a very low resistance) between the collector and the emitter. This means that the voltage drop across the collector-emitter will be almost zero, and all of the voltage is dropped across the 100Ω load resistor, causing a current to flow directly to ground through the emitter. The transistor is saturated because it cannot pass any further current. Because there is almost no voltage drop across the collector-emitter, the output voltage, V_{out}, will be almost 0V.

Figure 4-14(c) illustrates what happens when the input voltage $V_{in} = 0$V is applied to the base terminal and there is no base current. The transistor behaves like an open switch (very large resistance). No current can flow through the collector-emitter junction, as this current is always a multiple of the base current and the base current is zero; therefore, almost all of the voltage is dropped across the collector-emitter. In this case the output, V_{out}, can be up to +5V (though as implied by the illustrated flow of I_C through the output terminal, the exact value of V_{out} depends on the size of I_C, as any current flowing through the 100Ω resistor will cause a voltage drop across it).

Therefore, the switch behaves somewhat like an inverter. If the input voltage is 0V, the output voltage is +5V, and if the input voltage is +3.3V, the output voltage will be 0V. You can see the actual measured values of this circuit in Figure 4-15, when the input voltage of 3.3V is applied to the base terminal. In this case, the Analog Discovery Waveform Generator is used to output a 1kHz square wave, with an amplitude of 1.65V and an offset of +1.65V (forming a 0V to 3.3V square wave signal), so it appears like a 3.3V source turning on and then off, 1,000 times per second. All the measurements in this figure were captured with the input at 3.3V. The base-emitter junction is forward biased, and just like the diode before, this will have a forward voltage of about 0.7V. The actual voltage drop across the base-emitter is 0.83V, so the voltage drop across the base resistor will be 2.440V. The actual base current is 1.1mA ($I = V / R = 2.44 / 2,185\,\Omega$). This current turns on the transistor, placing the transistor in saturation, so the voltage drop across the collector-emitter is very small (measured at 0.2V). Therefore, the collector current is 49.8mA ($I = V / R = (4.93\,\text{V} - 0.2\text{V}) / 96\Omega$ approx.). To choose an appropriate base resistor to place the BJT deep in saturation, use the following practical formula:

$$R_{Base} = \frac{\left(V_B - V_{BE(sat)}\right)}{\left(2 \times \left(I_C \div h_{FE(min)}\right)\right)}$$

For the case of a base supply of 3.3V, with a collector current of 50mA and a minimum gain $h_{FE(min)}$ of 100, $R_{Base} = (3.27 - 0.83) / (2 \times (0.05 / 100)) = 2,440\,\Omega$.

You can find all of these values in the transistor's datasheet. $V_{BE(sat)}$ is typically provided on a plot of V_{BE} versus I_C at room temperature, where we require I_C to be 50mA. The value of $V_{BE(sat)}$ is between 0.6V and 0.95V for the BC547, depending on the collector current and the room temperature. The resistor value is further divided by two to ensure that the transistor is placed deep in the saturation region (maximizing I_C). Therefore, in this case a 2.2kΩ resistor is used, as it is the closest generally available nominal value.

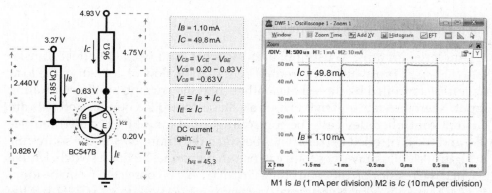

Figure 4-15: Realization of the transistor as a switch (saturation) and confirmation that all relationships hold true[1]

---

[1]You can use the Analog Discovery's differential input feature to "measure" current by placing the probes on either side of a resistor (to measure the voltage across it) and then creating a custom math channel that divides the waveform by the resistor's known resistance value. You then set the units to amps in the channel settings.

Why should you care about this with the Beagle boards? Well, because the boards can only source or sink very small currents from its GPIO pins, you can connect the GPIO pin to the base of a transistor so that a small current entering the base of the transistor can switch on a much larger current, with a much greater voltage range. Remember that in the example in Figure 4-15, a current of 1.1mA is able to switch on a large current of 49.8mA (45 times larger, but still lower than the 100mA limit of the BC547). Using this transistor arrangement with a Beagle board will allow a 5mA current at 3.3V from a GPIO to safely drive a 100mA current at up to 45V by choosing suitable resistor values.

One constraint in using transistors to drive a circuit is that they have a maximum switching frequency. If you increase the frequency of the input signal to the circuit in Figure 4-16 to 500kHz, the output is distorted, though it is still switching from low to high. However, increasing this to 1MHz means that the controlled circuit never switches off.

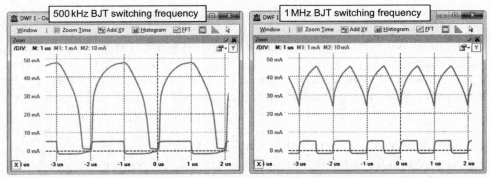

Figure 4-16: Frequency response of the BJT circuit (frequency is 500kHz and 1MHz)

Field Effect Transistors as Switches

A simpler alternative to using BJTs as switches is to use field effect transistors (FETs). FETs are different from BJTs in that the flow of current in the load circuit is controlled by the voltage, rather than the current, on the controlling input. Therefore, it is said that FETs are voltage-controlled devices and BJTs are current-controlled devices. The controlling input for a FET is called the *gate* (G), and the controlled current flows between the drain (D) and the source (S).

Figure 4-17 illustrates how you can use an n-channel FET as a switch. Unlike the BJT, the resistor on the controlling circuit (1MΩ) is connected from the input to GND, meaning that a very small current ($I = V/R$) will flow to GND, but the voltage at the gate will be the same as the V_{in} voltage. A significant advantage of FETs is that almost no current flows into the gate control input. However, the voltage on the gate is what turns on and off the controlled current, I_D, which flows from the drain to the source in this example.

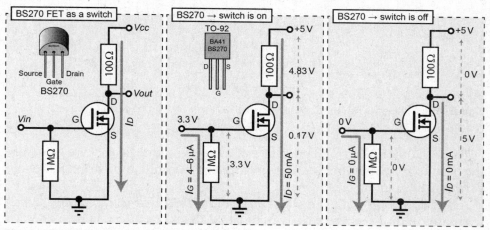

Figure 4-17: The field effect transistor as a switch

When the input voltage is high (3.3V), the drain-source current will flow (I_D = 50mA), so the voltage at the output terminal will be 0.17V, but when the input voltage is low (0V), no drain-source current will flow. Just like the BJT, if you were to measure the voltage at the drain terminal, the output voltage (V_{out}) would be high when the input voltage is low, and the output voltage would be low when the input voltage is high, though again the actual value of the "high" output voltage depends on the current drawn by the succeeding circuit.

The Fairchild Semiconductor BS270 N-Channel Enhancement Mode FET is a low-cost device (~$0.10) in a TO-92 package that is capable of supplying a continuous drain current (I_D) of up to 400mA at a drain-source voltage of up to 60V. However, at a gate voltage (V_G) of 3.3V the BS270 can switch a maximum drain current of approximately 130mA. This makes it ideal for use with the Beagle boards, as the GPIO voltages are in range and the current required to switch on the FET is about 3μA–6μA depending on the gate resistor chosen. One other feature of using a FET as a switch is that it can cope with much higher switching frequencies, as shown in Figure 4-18. Remember that in Figure 4-16 the BJT switching waveform is very distorted at 1MHz. It should be clear from Figure 4-18 that the FET circuit is capable of dealing with much higher switching frequencies than the BJT circuit.

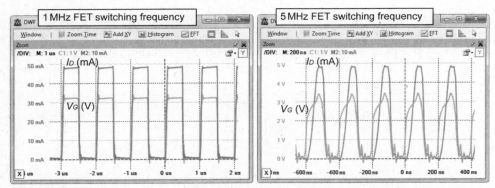

Figure 4-18: Frequency response of the FET circuit as the switching frequency is set at 1 MHz and 5 MHz

The BS270 also has a high-current diode that is used to protect the gate from the type of reverse inductive voltage surges that could arise if the FET were driving a DC motor.

As mentioned, one slight disadvantage of the BS270 is that it can only switch a maximum drain current of approximately 130mA at a gate voltage of 3.3V. However, the high input impedance of the gate means that you can use two (or indeed more) BS270s in parallel to double the maximum current to approximately 260mA at the same gate voltage. Also, the BS270 can be used as a gate driver for Power FETs, which can switch much larger currents.

Optocouplers/Optoisolators

Optocouplers (or optoisolators) are small, low-cost digital switching devices that are used to isolate two electrical circuits from each other. This can be important for your Beagle board circuits if you have a concern that a design problem with a connected circuit could possibly source or sink a large current from/to your board. They are available in low-cost (~$0.15) four-pin DIP form.

An optocoupler uses an LED emitter that is placed close to a photodetector transistor, separated by an insulating film within a silicone dome. When a current (I_f) flows through the LED emitter legs, the light that falls on the photodetector transistor from the LED allows a separate current (I_c) to flow through the collector-emitter legs of the photo detector transistor (see Figure 4-19). When the LED emitter is off, no light falls on the photo detector transistor, and there will be almost no collector emitter current (I_c). There is no electrical connection between one side of the package and the other, as the signal is transmitted only by light, providing electrical isolation for up to $5,300V_{RMS}$ for an optocoupler such as the SFH617A. You can even use PWM with optocouplers, as it is a binary on/off signal.

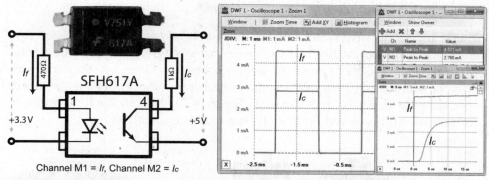

Channel M1 = I_f, Channel M2 = I_c

Figure 4-19: Optocoupler (617A) circuit with the captured input and output characteristics

Figure 4-19 illustrates an example optocoupler circuit and the resulting oscilloscope traces for the resistor and voltage values chosen. These values were chosen to be consistent with those that you might use with the Beagle boards. The resistor value of 470Ω was chosen to allow the 3.3V output to drive a forward current I_f of about 4.5mA through the LED emitter. From Figure 4 in the datasheet,[2] this results in a forward voltage of about 1.15V across the diode); $R = V/I = (3.3V - 1.15V)/0.0045$ A $= 478Ω$. Therefore, the circuit was built using the closest nominal value of 470Ω.

The oscilloscope is displaying current by using the differential inputs of the Analog Discovery to measure the voltage across the known resistor values and using two mathematical channels to divide by the resistance values. In Figure 4-19 you can see that I_f is 4.571mA and that I_c is 2.766mA. The proportionality of the difference is the current transfer ratio (CTR), and it varies according to the level of I_f and the operating temperature. Therefore, the current transfer at 4.571mA is 60.5 percent ($100 \times I_c / I_f$), which is consistent with the datasheet. The rise time and fall time are also consistent with the values in the datasheet of t_r = 4.6µs and t_f = 15µs. These values limit the switching frequency. Also, if it is important to your circuit that you achieve a high CTR, there are optocouplers with built-in Darlington transistor configurations that result in CTRs of up to 2,000 percent (e.g., the 6N138 or HCPL2730). Finally, there are high-linearity analog optocouplers available (e.g., the HCNR200 from Avago) that can be used to optically isolate analog signals.

NOTE   In Chapter 6, example circuits are provided for how to use an optocoupler to protect the Beagle board GPIOs from both an independently powered output circuit (Figure 6-11) and an independently powered input circuit (Figure 6-12).

[2]Vishay Semiconductors. (2013, January 14). SFH617A Datasheet. Retrieved April 13, 2014, from Vishay Semiconductors: www.vishay.com/docs/83740/sfh617a.pdf

Switches and Buttons

Other components with which you are likely to need to work with are switches and buttons. They come in many different forms: toggle, push button, selector, proximity, joystick, reed, pressure, temperature, etc. However, they all work under the same binary principles of either interrupting the flow of current (open) or enabling the flow of current (closed). Figure 4-20 illustrates several different common switch types and outlines their general connectivity.

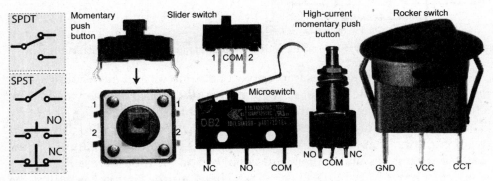

Figure 4-20: Various switches and configurations

Momentary push button switches (SPST—single pole, single throw) like the one illustrated in Figure 4-20 are either normally open (NO) or normally closed (NC). NO means you have to activate the switch to allow current to flow, whereas NC means that when you activate the button, current does not flow. For the particular push button illustrated, both pins 1 and both pins 2 are always connected, and for the duration of time you press the button, all four pins are connected together. Looking at slider switches (SPDT—single pole, double throw), the common connection (COM) is connected to either 1 or 2 depending on the slider position. In the case of microswitches and the high-current push button, the COM pin is connected to NC if the switch is pressed and is connected to NO if the switch is depressed. Finally, the rocker switch illustrated often has an LED that lights when the switch is closed, connecting the power (VCC) leg to the circuit (CCT) leg.

All of these switch types suffer from mechanical switch bounce, which can be extremely problematic when interfacing to microprocessors like the Beagle boards. Switches are mechanical devices and when they are pressed, the force of contact causes the switch to repeatedly bounce from the contact on impact. It only bounces for a small duration (typically milliseconds), but the duration is sufficient for the switch to apply a sequence of inputs to a microprocessor.

Figure 4-21(a) illustrates the problem in action using the rising/falling-edge trigger condition of the Analog Discovery oscilloscope. A momentary push button is placed in a simple series circuit with a 10kΩ resistor, and the voltage is measured across the resistor. When the switch hits the contact, the output is suddenly high, but the switch then bounces back from the contact, and the voltage falls down again. After about 2ms–3ms (or longer), it has almost fully settled. Unfortunately, this small bounce can lead to false inputs to a digital circuit. For example, if the threshold were 3V, this may be read in as 101010101, rather than a more correct value of 000001111.

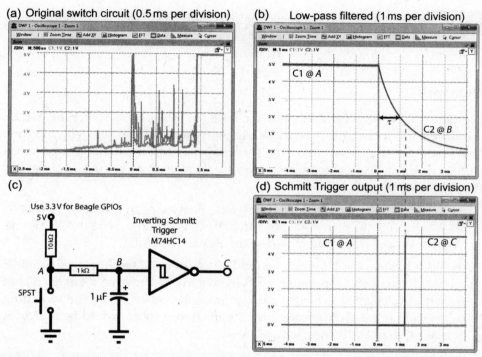

Figure 4-21: (a) Switch bouncing with no components other than the switch and 10kΩ resistor; (b) low-pass filtered output at point *B*; (c) a Schmitt trigger circuit; and, (d) output of the Schmitt trigger circuit at point *C*, versus the input at point *A*

There are a number of ways to deal with switch bounce in microprocessor interfacing:

- A low-pass filter can be added in the form of a resistor-capacitor circuit, as illustrated in Figure 4-21(c) using a 1µF capacitor. Unfortunately, this leads to delay in the input. If you examine the time base, it takes about 2ms before the input reaches 1V. Also, bounce conditions can delay this further. These values are chosen using the RC time constant $\tau = R \times C$, so $\tau(s) = 1{,}000\Omega \times 10^{-6}\,F = 1$ ms, which is the time taken to charge a capacitor to ~63.2% or discharge it to ~36.8%. This value is marked on Figure 4-21(b) at approximately 1.9V.

- Software may be written so that after a rising edge occurs, it delays a few milliseconds and then reads the "real" state.
- For slider switches (SPDT), an SR-latch can be used.
- For momentary push button switches (SPSTs), a Schmitt trigger (74HC14N), which is discussed in the next section, can be used with an RC low-pass filter as in Figure 4-21(c).

NOTE   There are videos on debouncing SPDT and SPST switches on the web page associated with this chapter: www.exploringbeaglebone.com/chapter4.

Hysteresis

Hysteresis is designed into electronic circuits to avoid rapid switching, which would wear out circuits. A Schmitt trigger exhibits hysteresis, which means that its output is dependent on the present input and the history of previous inputs. This can be explained with an example of an oven baking a cake at 350 degrees Fahrenheit.

- **Without hysteresis:** The element would heat the oven to 350°F. Once 350°F is achieved, the element would switch off. It would cool below 350°F, and the element would switch on again. Rapid switching!
- **With hysteresis:** The circuit would be designed to heat the oven to 360°F, and at that point the element would switch off. The oven would cool, but it is not designed to switch back on until it reaches 340°F. The switching would not be rapid, protecting the oven, but there would be a greater variation in the baking temperature.

With an oven that is designed to have hysteresis, is the element *on* or *off* at 350°F? That depends on the history of inputs—it is *on* if the oven is heating; it is *off* if the oven is cooling.

The Schmitt trigger in Figure 4-21(c) exhibits the same type of behavior. The V_{T+} for the M74HC14 Schmitt trigger is 2.9V, and the V_{T-} is 0.93V when running at a 5V input, which means a rising input voltage has to reach 2.9V before the output changes high, and a falling input voltage has to drop to 0.93V before the output changes low. Any bounce in the signal within this range is simply ignored. The low-pass filter reduces the possibility of high-frequency bounces. The response is presented in Figure 4-21(d). Note that the time base is 1ms per division, illustrating how "clean" the output signal is. The configuration uses a pull-up resistor, the need for which is discussed shortly.

Logic Gates

Boolean algebra functions have only two possible outcomes, either true or false, which makes them ideal for developing a framework to describe electronic circuits that are either on or off (high or low). Logic gates perform these Boolean algebra functions and operations, forming the basis of the functionality inside modern microprocessors, such as the AM335x. Boolean values are not the same as binary numbers. (Binary numbers are a base 2 representation of whole and fractional numbers, whereas Boolean refers to a data type that has only two possible values, either true or false.)

It is often the case that you will need to interface to different types of logic gates and systems using the Beagle board GPIOs to perform an operation such as gating an input or sending data to a shift register. Logic gates fall into two main categories:

- **Combinational logic:** The current output is dependent on the current inputs only (e.g., AND, OR, decoders, multiplexers, etc.).

- **Sequential logic:** The current output is dependent on the current inputs and previous inputs. They can be said to have different states, and what happens with a given input depends on what state they are in (e.g., latches, flip-flops, memory, counters, etc.).

BINARY NUMBERS

Simply put, binary numbers are a system for representing numbers (whole or fractional) within a device whereby the *only* symbols available are 1s and 0s. That is a strong *only*, as when you are implementing binary circuits, you don't have a minus sign or a decimal point (binary point to be precise). Like decimal numbers, you use a place-weighted system to represent numbers of the following form:

$$1001_2 = \left(1 \times 2^3\right) + \left(0 \times 2^2\right) + \left(0 \times 2^1\right) + \left(1 \times 2^0\right) = 8 + 0 + 0 + 1 = 9_{10}$$

If you have only four bits to represent your numbers, you can represent only $2^4 = 16$ possible decimal numbers in the range 0 to 15. You can add and subtract numbers, just as you can in decimal, but you tend to add the negative value of the right side of the operation, instead of building subtraction circuits. Therefore, to perform 9 − 5, you would typically perform 9 + (−5). To represent negative numbers, the two's complement form is used. Essentially, this involves inverting the symbols in the binary representation of the positive number and adding 1, so −5 would be +5 (0101), inverted to (1010) + 1 = 1011_2. Importantly, you need to know that this number is in two's complement form; otherwise, it could be mistaken for 11_{10}. Therefore, to perform 9 − 5 on a 4-bit computer, perform 9 + −5 = 1001 + (1011) = 10100.

> The four-bit computer ignores the fifth bit (otherwise it would be a 5-bit computer!), so the answer is 0100, which is 4_{10}. See the video at the chapter web page: www. exploringbeaglebone/chapter4.
>
> To multiply by 2, you simply shift the binary digits left (inserting a 0 on the right-most position), e.g., $4_{10} = 0100_2$. Shift all the digits left, bringing in a 0 on the right side, giving $1000_2 = 8_{10}$. Divide by 2 by shifting to the right.
>
> Finally, understanding binary makes the following infamous joke funny: "There are 10 types of people, those who understand binary and those who don't!"—well, almost funny!

Combinational logic circuits will provide the same output for the same set of inputs, regardless of the order in which the inputs are applied. Figure 4-22 illustrates the core combinational logic gates with their logic symbols, truth tables, and IC numbers. The truth table provides the output that you will get from the gate on applying the listed inputs.

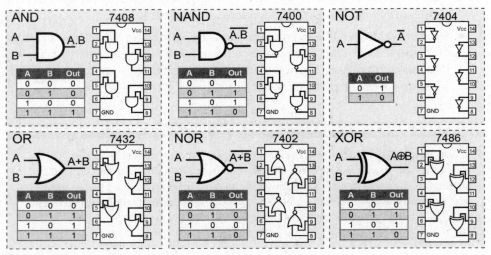

Figure 4-22: General logic gates

NOTE You can find a video on wiring an AND gate at the web page associated with this chapter: www.exploringbeaglebone.com/chapter4.

ICs have a number that describes their manufacturer, function, logic family, and package type. For example, the MM74HC08N in Figure 4-23(a) has a manufacturer code of MM (Fairchild Semiconductor), is a 7408 (quad two-input AND gates), is of the HC (CMOS) logic family, and is in an N (plastic dual in-line package) form.

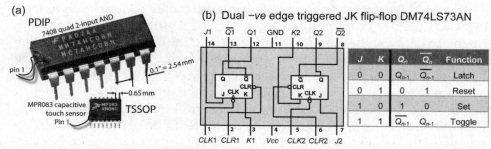

Figure 4-23: (a) IC package examples (to scale), and (b) the JK flip-flop

ICs are available in different package types. Figure 4-23(a) shows to scale a PDIP (plastic dual in-line package) and a small outline package TSSOP (thin shrink small outline package). There are many types: surface mount, flat package, small outline package, chip-scale package, and ball grid array (BGA). You have to be careful when ordering ICs that you have the capability to use them. DIP/PDIP ICs have perfect forms for prototyping on breadboards as they have a 0.1" leg spacing. There are adapter boards available for converting small outline packages to 0.1" leg spacing. Unfortunately, BGA ICs, such as the AM335x SoC and the OSD3358 SiP, require sophisticated equipment for soldering.

The family of currently available ICs is usually transistor-transistor logic (TTL) (with Low-power Schottky (LS)) or some form of complementary metal-oxide-semiconductor (CMOS). Table 4-1 compares these two families of 7408 ICs using their respective datasheets. The *propagation delay* is the longest delay between an input changing value and the output changing value for all possible inputs to a logic gate. This delay limits the logic gate's speed of operation.

Table 4-1: Comparison of Two Commercially Available TTL and CMOS ICs for a 7408 Quadruple Two-input AND gates IC

CHARACTERISTIC	SN74LS08N	SN74HC08N
Family	Texas TTL PDIP Low-power Schottky (LS)	Texas CMOS PDIP High-speed CMOS (HC)
V_{CC} supply voltage	4.5V to 5.5V (5V typical)	2V to 6V
V_{IH} high-level input voltage	min 2V	V_{CC} at 5V min = 3.5V
V_{IL} low-level input voltage	max 0.8V	V_{CC} at 5V max = 1.5V
Time propagation delay (T_{PD})	Typical 12ns($\uparrow$) 17.5ns($\downarrow$)	Typical 8ns ($\uparrow\downarrow$)
Power (at 5V)	5mW (max)	0.1mW (max)

Figure 4-24 illustrates the acceptable input and output voltage levels for both TTL and CMOS logic gates when V_{DD} = 5V. The noise margin is the absolute difference between the output voltage levels and the input voltage levels. This noise margin ensures that if the output of one logic gate is connected to the input of a second logic gate, that noise will not affect the input state. The CMOS logic family input logic levels are dependent on the supply voltage, V_{DD}, where the high-level threshold is 0.7 × V_{DD}, and the low-level threshold is 0.3 × V_{DD}. It should be clear from Figure 4-24 that there are differences in behavior. For example, if the input voltage were 2.5V, then the TTL gate would perceive a logic high level, but the CMOS gate (at 5V) would perceive an undefined level. Also, the output of a CMOS gate, with V_{DD} = 3.3V, would provide sufficient output voltage to trigger a logic high input on a TTL gate, but would not on a CMOS gate with V_{DD} = 5.0V.

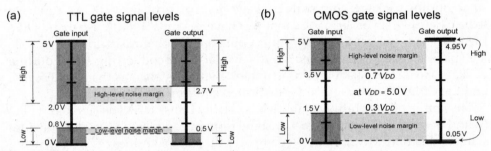

Figure 4-24: Gate signal levels on the input and output of logic gates (a) TTL, and (b) CMOS at 5V

High-Speed CMOS (HC) can support a wide range of voltage levels, including the Beagle board's 3.3V input/outputs. The GND label is commonly used to indicate the ground supply voltage, where V_{EE} is often used for BJT-based devices and V_{SS} for FET-based devices. Traditionally, V_{CC} was used as the label for the positive supply voltage on BJT-based devices and V_{DD} for FET-based devices; however, it is now common to see V_{CC} being used for both.

Figure 4-23(b) illustrates a sequential logic circuit, called a *JK flip-flop*. JK flip-flops are core building blocks in circuits such as counters. These differ from combinational logic circuits in that the current state is dependent on the current inputs and the previous state. You can see from the truth table that if $J = 0$ and $K = 0$ for the input, then the value of the output Q_n will be the output value that it was at the previous time step (it behaves like a one-bit memory). A time step is defined by the clock input (CLK), which is a square wave synchronizing signal. The same type of timing signal is present on the Beagle boards—it is the clock frequency, and a 1GHz clock goes through up to 1,000,000,000 square wave cycles per second!

NOTE   The web page associated with this chapter has a video that explains JK flip-flops in detail, and a video on building a 555 timer circuit, which can be used as a low-frequency clock signal for testing logic circuits.

Floating Inputs

One common mistake when working with digital logic circuits is to leave unused logic gate inputs "floating," or disconnected. The family of the chip has a large impact on the outcome of this mistake. With the TTL logic families these inputs will "float" high and can be reasonably expected to be seen as logic-high inputs. With TTL ICs it is good practice to "tie" (i.e., connect) the inputs to ground or the supply voltage, so that there is absolutely no doubt about the logic level being asserted on the input at all times.

With CMOS circuits the inputs are very sensitive to the high voltages that can result from static electricity and electrical noise and should also never be left floating. Figure 4-25 gives the likely output of an AND gate that is wired as shown in the figure. The correct outcome is displayed in the "Required (A.B)" column.

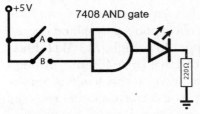

7408 AND gate			74LS08	74HC08
Switch A	Switch B	Required (A.B)	TTL Output	CMOS Output
Closed	Closed	On	On	On
Closed	Open	Off	On	~Off
Open	Closed	Off	On	~Off
Open	Open	Off	On	~Off

Figure 4-25: An AND gate with the inputs accidentally left floating when the switches are open

Unused CMOS inputs that are left floating (between V_{DD} and GND) can gradually charge up because of leakage current and, depending on the IC design, could provide false inputs or waste power by causing a DC current to flow (from V_{DD} to GND). To solve this problem you can use pull-up or pull-down resistors, depending on the desired input state (these are ordinary resistors with suitable values—it's their role that is "pull up" or "pull down"), which are described in the next section.

Pull-Up and Pull-Down Resistors

To avoid floating inputs, you can use pull-up or pull-down resistors as illustrated in Figure 4-26. Pull-down resistors are used if you want to guarantee that the inputs to the gate are low when the switches are open, and pull-up resistors are used if you want to guarantee that the inputs are high when the switches are open.

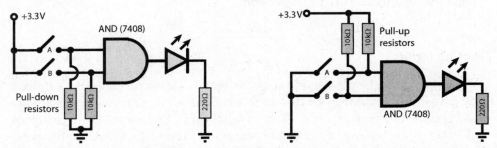

Figure 4-26: Pull-down and pull-up resistors, used to ensure that the switches do not create floating inputs

The resistors are important because when the switch is closed, the switch would form a short circuit to ground if they were omitted and replaced by lengths of wire. The size of the pull-down/up resistors is also important; their value has to be low enough to solidly pull the input low/high when the switches are open but high enough to prevent too much current flowing when the switches are closed. Ideal logic gates have infinite impedance and any resistor value (short of infinite) would suffice. However, real logic gates leak current, and you have to overcome this leakage. To minimize power consumption, you should choose the maximum value that actually pulls the input low/high. A 3.3kΩ–10kΩ resistor will usually work perfectly, but 3.3V will drive 1mA–0.33mA through them respectively and dissipate 3.3mW–1mW of power respectively when the switch is closed. For power-sensitive applications you could test larger resistors of 50kΩ or greater.

The Beagle boards have weak internal pull-up and pull-down resistors that can be used for this purpose. This is discussed in Chapter 6. One other issue is that inputs will have some stray capacitance to ground. Adding a resistor to the input creates an RC low-pass filter on the input signal that can delay input signals. That is not important for manually pressed buttons, as the delay will be on the order of 0.1μs for the preceding example, but it could affect the speed of digital communication bus lines.

Open-Collector and Open-Drain Outputs

To this point in the chapter, all of the ICs have a regular output, where it is driven close to GND or the supply voltage of the IC (V_{CC}). If you are connecting to another IC or component that uses the same voltage level, then that should be fine. However, if the first IC had a supply voltage of 3.3V and you needed to drive the output into an IC that had a supply voltage of 5V, then you may need to perform level shifting.

Many ICs are available in a form with open-collector outputs, which are particularly useful for interfacing between different logic families and for level shifting. This is because the output is not at a specific voltage level, but rather attached to the base input of an NPN transistor that is inside the IC. The output of the IC is the "open" collector of the transistor, and the emitter of the transistor is tied to the IC's GND. It is possible to use a FET (74HC03) instead of a BJT (74LS01) inside the IC, and while the concept is the same, it is called an *open-drain output*. Figure 4-27 illustrates this concept and provides an example circuit using a 74HC03 (quad, two-input NAND gates with open-drain outputs) to drive a 5V circuit. The advantage of the open-drain configuration is that CMOS ICs support the 3.3V level available on the Beagle board's GPIOs. Essentially, the drain resistor that is used in Figure 4-17 is placed outside the IC package, as illustrated in Figure 4-27, and it has a value of 10kΩ in this case.

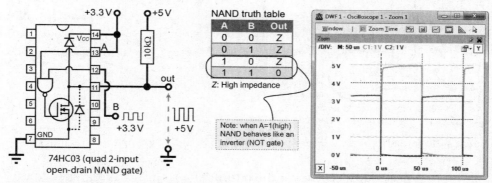

Figure 4-27: Open-drain level-shifting example

Interestingly, a NAND gate with one input tied high (or the two inputs tied together) behaves like a NOT gate. In fact, NAND or NOR gates, each on its own, can replicate the functionality of any of the logic gates, and for that reason they are called *universal gates*.

Open-collector outputs are often used to connect multiple devices to a bus. You will see this in Chapter 8 when the Beagle board's I²C buses are described. When you examine the truth table in the datasheet of an IC, such as the 74HC03, you will see the letter Z used to represent the output (as in Figure 4-27). This means it is a high-impedance output, and the external pull-up resistor can pull the output to the high state.

Interconnecting Gates

To create useful circuits, logic gates are interconnected to other logic gates and components. It is important to understand that there are limits to the interconnect capabilities of gates.

The first limit is the capability of the logic gate to source or sink current. When the output of a gate is logic high, it acts as a current source, providing current for connected logic gates or the LEDs shown in Figure 4-26. If the output of the gate is logic low, the gate acts as a current sink, whereby current flows into the output. Figure 4-28(a) demonstrates this by placing a current-limiting resistor and an LED between V_{CC} and the output of the logic gate, with the LED cathode connected to the logic gate output. When the output of the gate is high, there is no potential difference, and the LED will be off; but when the output is low, a potential difference is created, and current will flow through the LED and be sinked by the output of the logic gate. According to the datasheet of the 74HC08, it has an output current limit (I_O) of ±25mA, meaning that it can source or sink 25mA. Exceeding these values will damage the IC.

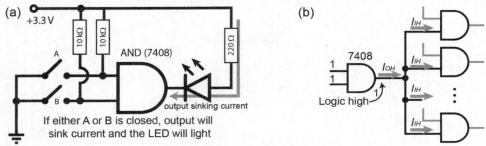

Figure 4-28: (a) Sinking current on the output, and (b) TTL fan-out example

It is often necessary to connect the output of a single (driving) gate to the input of several other gates. Each of the connected gates will draw a current, thus limiting the total number of connected gates. The fan-out is the number of gates that are connected to the output of the driving gate. As illustrated in Figure 4-28(b), for TTL the maximum fan-out depends on the output (I_O) and input current (I_I) requirement values when the state is low (= $I_{OL(max)}/I_{IL(max)}$) and the state is high (= $I_{OH(max)}/I_{IH(max)}$). Choose the lower value, which is commonly 10 or greater. The fan-in of an IC is the number of inputs that it has. For the 7408 they are two-input AND gates, so they have a fan-in of 2.

CMOS gate inputs have extremely large resistance and draw almost no current, allowing for large fan-out capability (>50); however, each input adds a small capacitance ($C_L \approx 3$–10pF) that must be charged and discharged by the output of the previous stage. The greater the fan-out, the greater the capacitive load on the driving gate, which lengthens the propagation delay. For example, the 74HC08 has a propagation delay (t_{pd}) of about 11ns and an input capacitance (C_I) of 3.5pF (assuming for this example that this leads to $t_{pd} = RC = 3.5$ns per connection). If one 78HC08 were driving 10 other similar gates and each added 3.5ns of delay, then the propagation delay would increase to $11 + (10 \times 3.5) = 46$ ns of delay, reducing the maximum operating frequency from 91MHz to 22MHz.

Analog-to-Digital Conversion

The Beagle boards have several analog-to-digital converter (ADC) inputs that can be used to take an analog signal and create a digital representation of this signal. This enables us to connect many different types of sensors, such as distance sensors, temperature sensors, light-level sensors, and so on. However, you have to be careful with these inputs, as they should not source or sink current, because the analog outputs of the sensors are likely to be very sensitive to any additional load in parallel with the output. To solve this problem you need to first look at how operational amplifiers function.

Analog signals are continuous signals that represent the measurement of some physical phenomenon. For example, a microphone is an analog device, generally known as a transducer, which can be used to convert sound waves into an electrical signal that, for example, varies between −5V and +5V depending on the amplitude of the sound wave. Analog signals use a continuous range of values to represent information, but if you want to process that signal using your Beagle board, then you need a discrete digital representation of the signal. This is one that is sampled at discrete instants in time and subsequently quantized to discrete values of voltage, or current. For example, audio signals will vary over time; so to sample a transducer signal to digitally capture human speech (e.g., speech recognition), you need be cognizant of two factors:

- **Sampling rate:** Defines how often you are going to sample the signal. Clearly, if you create a discrete digital sample by sampling the voltage every one second, the speech will be indecipherable.

- **Sampling resolution:** Defines the number of digital representations that you have to represent the voltage at the point in time when the signal is sampled. Clearly, if you had only one bit, you could capture only if the signal were closer to +5V or −5V, and again the speech signal would be indecipherable.

Sampling Rate

Representing a continuous signal perfectly in a discrete form requires an infinite amount of digital data. Fortunately, there are limits to how well human hearing performs, and therefore we can place limits on the amount of data to be discretized. For example, 44.1kHz and 48kHz are common digital audio sampling rates for encoding MP3 files, which means that if you use the former, you will have to store 44,100 samples of your transducer voltage every second. The sample rate is generally determined by the need to preserve a certain frequency content of the signal. For example, humans (particularly children) can hear audio signals at frequencies from about 20Hz up to about 20kHz.

Nyquist's sampling theorem states that the sampling frequency must be at least twice the highest frequency component present in the signal. Therefore, if you want to sample audio signals, you need to use a sampling rate of at least twice 20kHz, which is 40kHz, which helps explain the magnitude of the sampling rates used in encoding MP3 audio files (typically 44,100 samples per second—that is, 44.1kS/s).

Quantization

The Beagle boards have several 12-bit ADC inputs that work in the range of 0–1.8V, which means that there are $2^{12} = 4,096$ possible discrete representations (numbers) for this sampling resolution. If the voltage is exactly 0V, we can use the decimal number 0 to represent it. If the voltage is exactly 1.8V, we can use the number 4,095 to represent it. So, what voltage does the decimal number 1 represent? It is $(1 \times 1.8)/4096 = 0.000439453125$ V. Therefore, each decimal number between 0 and 4,095 (4,096 values) represents a step of about 0.44mV.

The preceding audio sampling example also illustrates one of the challenges you face with the Beagle board configurations. If the sensor outputs a voltage of −5 to +5V, or more commonly 0V to +5V, you need to alter that range to be between 0 and 1.8V to be compatible with the ADC. In Chapter 6, you'll look at how you can solve this problem. A second and more complex problem is that we must not source or sink current from/to the Beagle board's ADC circuitry, and to solve that we need to introduce a powerful concept that predates the digital computer, called the *operational amplifier*.

Operational Amplifiers

Operational amplifiers (op-amps) are composed from many BJTs or FETs within the one IC (e.g., the LM741). They can be used to create several useful circuits, one of which you will need in Chapter 9 to correctly interface to analog sensors.

Ideal Operational Amplifiers

Figure 4-29(a) illustrates an ideal op-amp, placed in a basic circuit with no feedback (aka open-loop). The op-amp has two inputs, a noninverting input (+) and an *inverting* input (−), and it produces an output that is proportional to the difference between them, i.e., $V_{out} = G(V_1 - V_2)$, where V_1 and V_2 are the voltage levels on these two inputs, respectively. Some of the characteristics of an ideal op-amp include the following:

- An infinite open-loop gain, G
- An infinite input impedance
- A zero output impedance

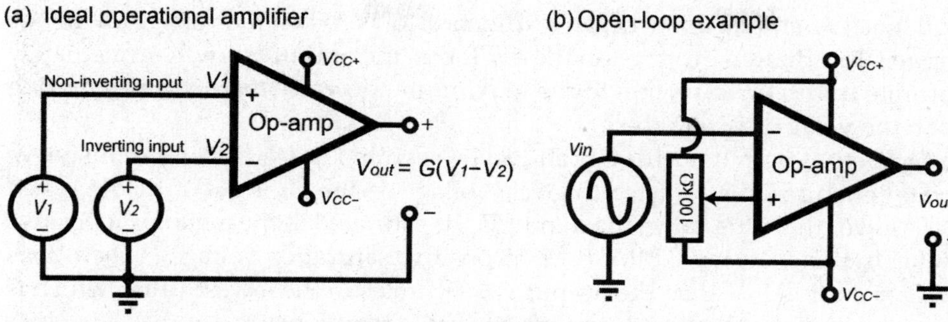

(a) Ideal operational amplifier

(b) Open-loop example

Figure 4-29: (a) The ideal op-amp, and (b) an open-loop comparator example

No real-world op-amp has an infinite open-loop gain, but voltage gains of 200,000 to 30,000,000 are commonplace. Such a gain can be treated as infinite, which means in theory that even a small difference between the inputs would lead to a completely impractical output. For example, a difference of 1V between V_1 and V_2 would lead to a voltage output of at least 200,000V! If that were really the case, I would now be issuing health warnings on the use of op-amps! The output voltage is of course limited by the supply voltage (V_{CC+} and V_{CC-} in Figure 4-29(a)). Therefore, if you supply $V_{CC+} = +5V$ and $V_{CC-} = 0V$ (GND) to an op-amp using a Beagle board, the maximum real-world output would be in the range of 0V to 5V approximately, depending on the exact op-amp used. Likewise, a real-world op-amp does not have infinite input impedance, but it is in the range of 250kΩ to 2MΩ. The term *impedance* is used instead of *resistance*, as the input may be an AC rather than just a DC supply. Likewise, a zero output impedance is not possible, but it will likely be <100Ω.

The LM358 Dual Operational Amplifier is used for the following circuit configurations (www.ti.com/product/lm358). It is an eight-pin IC in a PDIP that contains two op-amps that have a typical open-loop differential voltage gain of 100dB, which is 100,000 in voltage gain (*voltage gain in dB* = 20 × *log* (V_{out}/V_{in})). One advantage of this IC is that it has a wide supply range, in the range of 3V to 32V, meaning you can use the Beagle board's 3.3V or 5V power rails. The LM358 can typically source up to 30mA or sink up to 20mA on the output.

The behavior of an open-loop op-amp is best explained with an example, which is illustrated in Figure 4-29(b). Note that in this case the input is connected to the inverting input of the op-amp (−*ve*), rather than the noninverting input (+*ve*), which means that V_{out} will be positive when V_{in} is lower than the reference voltage. The circuit was built using the LM358, with a supply of $V_{CC+} = 5V$ and $V_{CC-} = 0V$ (GND). A 100kΩ potentiometer was used to allow the voltage on the +*ve* input to be varied. This is the voltage that we are effectively comparing the input voltage with, so this circuit is called a *comparator*. When the voltage on the −*ve* input is greater than the +*ve* input, by even a small amount, the output will quickly saturate in the negative direction to 0V. When the voltage on the $-ve$ input is less than the voltage on the $+ve$ input, the output V_{out} will immediately saturate in the $+ve$ direction to the maximum allowable by this configuration with the value of V_{CC} applied.

The actual output of this circuit can be seen in Figure 4-30(a). In this view, the potentiometer is adjusted to give a voltage on the V+ input of 1.116V. When V− is lower than this value, the output V_{out} is saturated to the maximum positive value. In this case, it is 3.816V (LM358 positive saturation voltage). When V− is greater than 1.116V, then the output V_{out} saturates to the lowest value, which is almost zero (−2mV). Note the inversion that is taking place.

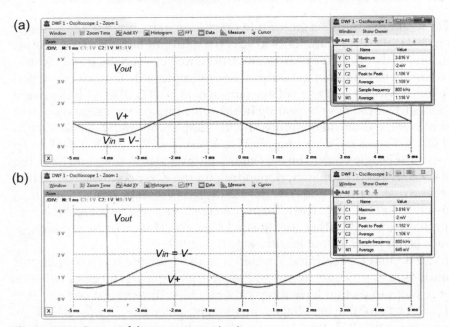

Figure 4-30: Output of the comparator circuit

If everything remains exactly the same but the potentiometer is adjusted to give a different value for V+, in this case 0.645V, the output will be as shown in Figure 4-30(b), where the duty cycle of the output V_{out} will be different. This comparator circuit could also be used to detect low voltage conditions—for example, lighting a warning LED if a battery's voltage output fell below a certain value. The circuit example used in 4-29(b) could be used to generate a PWM signal with a controllable duty cycle, according to the controlling voltage V+.

The large open-loop gain means that op-amps are generally used with feedback, which is directed to the negative or positive op-amp input. This feedback opens up an enormous range of other applications for the op-amp.

Negative Feedback and Voltage Follower

Negative feedback is formed when you connect the output of an op-amp (V_{out}) back to the inverting input ($V-$). When you apply a voltage (V_{in}) to the noninverting input ($V+$) and increase it slowly, as V_{in} increases, then so would the difference between $V+$ and $V-$; however, the output voltage also increases according to $G(V_1 - V_2)$, and this feeds back into the $V-$ input, causing the output voltage V_{out} to be reduced. Essentially, the op-amp attempts to keep the voltage on the inverting ($V-$) input the same as the noninverting ($V+$) input by adjusting the output. The impact of this action is that the value of V_{out} is stabilized to be the same as the V_{in} voltage on $V+$; the higher the gain of the op-amp, the closer this difference will be to zero.

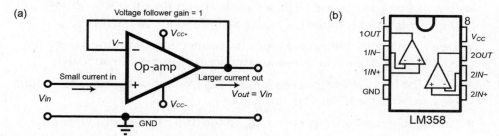

Figure 4-31: The voltage follower op-amp circuit

That action on its own is not very useful to us except that the current required to set the voltage on the input is small, and the op-amp can control much larger currents on the output side. Because the negative feedback keeps the output voltage the same as the input voltage, the configuration as a whole has a gain of 1. This configuration is known as a *voltage follower*, or *unity-gain buffer*, and is illustrated in Figure 4-31. This configuration is important, as it is used in Chapter 6 to protect the ADC circuitry in the Beagle boards, and it is also used to ensure that the ADC reference voltage is not modified by connecting it to a circuit.

Positive Feedback

Negative feedback is the most common type of feedback used with op-amps because of its stabilizing impact. An op-amp in a positive feedback configuration is one in which the output is returned to the positive noninverting input of the op-amp. In such a case the feedback signal supports the input signal. For example, positive feedback can be used to add hysteresis to the open-loop op-amp comparator circuit, by connecting V_{out} to $V+$ through a positive feedback resistor. This can be used to reduce the comparator's response to noise on the input signal.

Concluding Advice

There is a lot of material covered in this chapter. So to finish, here is some general advice for working with electrical components and the Beagle boards:

- Never leave inputs floating. Use pull-up/pull-down resistors on all switches. Check whether unused IC pins need to be tied high/low.
- Ensure that all of the GNDs in your circuit are connected.
- Remember to power your chips with the correct voltage level.
- Don't assume that a new diode, FET, BJT, or logic gate has the same pin layout as the previous component that you used.
- Just like programming, build a simple circuit first, test it, and then add the next layer of complexity. Never assume something works!
- Don't leave wire joints and croc clip connections hanging where they could touch off each other—the same for resistors on breadboards.
- Use a flat-head screwdriver to remove ICs from breadboards, as it is very easy to bend the IC legs beyond repair.
- CMOS ICs are statically sensitive, so touching them with your fingers may damage them, due to the buildup of static electricity on your body. Touch the back of a computer or some grounding metal object before you touch the ICs.
- Don't assume that components have exact or consistent values—in particular, transistor gains and resistor ranges.

Summary

After completing this chapter, you should be able to do the following:

- Describe the basic principles of electrical circuit operation, build circuits on breadboards, and measure voltage and current values
- Use discrete components such as diodes, LEDs, transistors, and capacitors in your own circuit designs
- Use transistors and FETs as switches to control higher current and voltage signals than would be possible by using the Beagle board outputs on their own
- Interconnect and interface to logic gates, being particularly aware of the issues that arise with "floating" inputs

- Describe the principles of analog-to-digital conversion and design basic operational-amplifier circuits
- Combine all of these skills to build the type of circuits that are important for safely interfacing to the Beagle board GPIOs

Further Reading

Documents and links for further reading have been listed throughout this chapter, but here are some further reference documents:

- T. R. Kuphaldt, "Lessons in Electric Circuits," a free series of textbooks on the subjects of electricity and electronics: www.ibiblio.org/kuphaldt/electricCircuits/.
- All About Circuits: www.allaboutcircuits.com provides excellent applied examples of many types of electronic circuits.
- The Electronics Club: www.electronicsclub.info provides electronics projects for beginners and for reference.
- Neil Storey, *Electronics: A Systems Approach*, 5th ed., New York: Pearson, 2013.

Here is a full list of the components that are used in this chapter:

- Breadboard
- Diodes: 1N4001, general-purpose LED
- Transistors: NPN: BC547, FET: BS270
- Voltage regulator: KA7805/LM7805
- PTC: 60R110
- Button and Switch: General purpose SPST and SPDT
- ICs: 74HC73N, 74HC03N, 74LS08N, 74HC08N, 74HC14, LM358N
- Resistors: 1MΩ, 2.2kΩ, 2x10kΩ, 50kΩ, 100Ω, 50Ω, 1kΩ, 470Ω, 220Ω, 100kΩ POT
- Capacitors: 10µF, 1µF, 0.33µF, 0.1µF
- Optoisolator: SFH617A

Practical Beagle Board Programming

This chapter describes several different programming options for the Beagle boards, including scripted and compiled languages. An LED flashing example is provided in all the languages so that you can investigate each language's structure and syntax. The advantages and disadvantages of each language are discussed along with example uses. The chapter then focuses on the C/C++ programming languages, describing their principles and why object-oriented programming (OOP) is appropriate and necessary for the development of scalable embedded systems applications. Finally, the chapter details how you can interface directly to the Linux kernel using the GNU C library. A single chapter can only scratch the surface on this topic, so this one focuses on physical programming tasks, which are required throughout the remainder of this book.

EQUIPMENT REQUIRED FOR THIS CHAPTER:

- Beagle board with a terminal connection (see Chapter 2)
- Desktop Linux Installation (e.g., Debian in a VM—see Chapter 3)

Introduction

As discussed in Chapter 3, embedded Linux is essentially "Linux on an embedded system." If your favorite programming language is available under Linux, then it is also likely to be available for the Beagle boards. So, is your favorite language suitable for programming your board? That depends on what you intend to do with the board. Are you interfacing to electronics devices/modules? Do you plan to write rich user interfaces? Are you planning to write a device driver for Linux? Is performance important, or are you developing an early pre-prototype? Each of the answers to these questions will impact your decision regarding which language you should use. In this chapter, you are introduced to several different languages, and the advantages and disadvantages of each category of language are outlined. As you read through the chapter, try to avoid focusing on a favorite language, but instead use the correct language for the job at hand.

How does programming on embedded systems compare to programming on desktop computers? Here are some points to consider:

- You should always write the clearest and cleanest code that is as maintainable as possible, just as you would on a desktop PC.
- Don't optimize your code until you are certain that it is complete.
- You typically need to be more aware of how you are consuming resources than when programming on the desktop computer. The size of data types matter, and passing data correctly really matters. You need to be concerned with memory availability, file system size, and data communication availability/bandwidth.
- You often need to learn about the underlying hardware platform. How does it handle the connected hardware? What data buses are available? How do you interface with the operating system and low-level libraries? Are there any real-time constraints?

For the upcoming discussion, it is assumed you are planning to do some type of physical computing—that is, interfacing to the different input or outputs on your board. Therefore, the example that is used to describe the structure and syntax of the different languages is a simple interfacing example. Before looking at the languages themselves, we will begin with a brief performance evaluation of different languages running on the Beagle platform in order to put the following discussions in context.

Performance of Different Languages

Which language is the best on the Beagle platform? Well, that is an incredibly emotive and difficult question to answer. Different languages perform better on different benchmarks and different tasks. In addition, a program written in a particular language can be optimized for that language to the point that it is barely recognizable as the original code. Nor is speed of execution always an important factor; you may be more concerned with memory usage, the portability of the code, or the ability to quickly apply changes.

However, if you are planning to develop high-speed or real-time number-crunching applications, then performance may be a key factor in your choice of programming language. In addition, if you are setting out to learn a new language and you may possibly be developing algorithmically rich programs in the future, then it may be useful to keep performance in mind.

A simple test has been put in place to determine the CPU performance of the languages discussed in this chapter. The test uses the *n*-body benchmark (gravitational interaction of planets in the solar system) code from benchmarks-game.alioth.debian.org. The code uses the same algorithm for all languages, and the board is running in the same state in all cases. The test uses 5 million iterations of the algorithm to ensure that the script used for timing does not need to be highly accurate. All of the programs gave the same correct result, indicating that these all ran correctly and to completion. The test is available in the book's Git repository in the directory chp05/performance/. Note that you must have installed Java and other languages on your board to run all of the tests. Use the following call to execute the test:

```
/chp05/performance$ ./run
Running the Tests:
The C/C++ Code Example
-0.169075164   -0.169083134
It took 34 seconds to run the C/C++ test ...
Finished Running the Benchmarks
```

The results of the tests are displayed in Table 5-1. In the first column, you can see the results for the PocketBeagle, running at its top processor frequency of 1GHz. For this number-crunching application, the general-purpose language, C++, performs the task in 34 seconds. This time has been weighted as one unit. Therefore, Java takes 1.15 times longer to complete the same task, the highly optimized Rust completes the task more quickly than C++, Node.js (for Bone-Script) is 1.24 times longer, Perl takes 26.8 times longer, and Python takes 57 times longer. The processing durations in seconds are provided in parentheses. As you move across the columns, you can see that this performance is relatively consistent, even as the processor frequency is adjusted (discussed in the next section) or a desktop i7 64-bit processor is used.

Table 5-1: Numerical Computation Time for 5,000,000 Iterations of the *n*-Body Algorithm on a BeagleBoard.org Debian Stretch Hard-float Image

VALUE	TYPE	POCKETBEAGLE[1] AT 1 GHZ	POCKETBEAGLE AT 600 MHZ	INTEL 64-BIT I7 DEBIAN PC[2]
C++[3]	Compiled	1.00× (34s)	1.00× (57s)	1.00× (0.641s)
C (gcc)	Compiled	0.95× (32s)	0.96× (55s)	0.97× (0.623s)
Rust[4]	Compiled	0.85× (29s)	0.86× (49s)	0.66× (0.425s)
C++14	Compiled	1.06× (36s)	1.07× (61s)	0.95× (0.608s)
Haskell[5]	Compiled	1.06× (36s)	1.05× (60s)	1.78× (1.141s)
Java[6]	JIT	1.15× (39s)	1.16× (66s)	1.28× (0.818s)
Node.js[7]	JIT	1.24× (42s)	1.30× (74s)	1.67× (1.071s)
Mono C#	JIT	1.50× (51s)	1.53× (87.4s)	2.13× (1.363s)
Cython[8]	Compiled	1.97× (67s)	1.96× (112s)	1.19× (0.765s)
Lua[9]	Interpreted	6.41× (218s)	6.31× (360s)	28.6× (18.304s)
Cython	Compiled	22.0× (751s)	22.1× (1262s)	55.8× (35.742s)
Perl	Interpreted	26.8× (910s)	20.3× (1156s)	59.6× (38.214s)
Ruby[10]	Interpreted	34.2× (1162s)	31.0× (1770s)	46.0× (29.454s)
Python	Interpreted	57.0× (1937s)	58.2× (3318s)	98.3× (63.032s)

---

[1] PocketBeagle A2 running at 1GHz, ARMv7 (4.9.88-ti-rt-r111 #1 SMP PREEMPT RT) ARMv7 Processor rev 2 (v7l) supports: half thumb fastmult vfp edsp thumbee neon vfpv3 tls vfpd32. BogoMIPS value is 597.19.

[2] Windows 10 PC running a 64-bit Debian Stretch VirtualBox VM that was allocated 1 thread (of 12) on an Intel i7-5820K @ 3.3GHz, with the VM allocated 10GB of RAM.

[3] gcc version 6.3.0 20170516 (Debian 6.3.0-18+deb9u1).

[4] Rust is a new concurrent programming language that is highly optimized for performance and is sponsored by the Mozilla Foundation. It is like C++ but allows for safer code. While compilation times are longer than C/C++, run-time performance is impressive. It can be installed on your board with the command `curl https://sh.rustup.rs -sSf | sh` from within a regular user shell. Do not use a superuser shell, as by default the language is installed in the user's directory.

[5] Use `sudo apt install haskell-platform` to install the package. Be aware that it is a large package (approx. 1.1GB).

[6] You can use `sudo apt install oracle-java8-jdk` to install the Oracle JDK. If this does not work, then please see the feature on installing Java.

[7] Node.js (`node -v`) is version 6.14.2, and it supports the ARM NEON accelerator processor. Use `sudo apt install nodejs-dev` to install Node.js if is not on your board.

The second column in Table 5-1 indicates the language type, where *compiled* refers to natively compiled languages, *JIT* refers to just-in-time compiled languages, and *interpreted* refers to code that is executed by interpreters. The distinction in these language types is described in detail throughout this chapter and is not quite as clear-cut as presented in the table.

All of the programs use between 98 percent and 99 percent of the CPU while executing. The relative performance of Java, Node.js, and Mono C# is impressive given that code is compiled dynamically ("just-in-time"), which is discussed later in this chapter. Any dynamic compilation latency is included in the timings, as the test script includes the following Bash script code to calculate the execution duration of each program:

```
Duration="5000000"
echo -e "\nThe C++ Code Example"
T="$(date +%s%N)"
./n-body $Duration
T="$(($(date +%s%N)-T))"
T=$((T/1000000))
echo "It took ${T} milliseconds to run the C++ test"
```

The C++14 code is the version of the C++ programming language that was published in 2014 (needs gcc 5+ for full support). This is discussed again later in this chapter. The program contains optimizations that are specific to this release of C++, and interestingly, while this version performs better on the desktop computer, it slightly underperforms on the PocketBeagle. The Java program uses the +AggressiveOpts flag to enable performance optimization, and it was used because it did not involve modifying the source code.

The results for Python are particularly poor because of the algorithmic nature of the problem. However, the benchmarks (benchmarksgame.alioth.debian.org) indicate that the range will be 9 to 100 times slower than the optimized C++ code for general processing to algorithm-rich code, respectively. If you are comfortable with Python and you would like to improve upon its performance, then you can investigate *Cython*, which is a Python compiler that automatically

---

[8] This Cython test involved modifying the Python source code to optimize it. It is not simply the compilation of raw Python code. The second Cython test represents the simple compilation of raw Python source code. Use sudo apt install cython to install Cython on your board.

[9] Use sudo apt install lua5.3 to install Lua under Debian.

[10] Use sudo apt install ruby to install Ruby under Debian.

removes the dynamic typing capability and enables you to generate C code directly from your Python code. Cython and the extension of Python with C/C++ are discussed at the end of this chapter.

The final column provides the results for the same code running on a desktop computer virtual machine. You can see that the relative performance of the applications is broadly in line, but also note that the C++ program runs 40 times faster on the single i7 thread than it does on the PocketBeagle at 1GHz. I hope that will help you frame your expectations with respect to the type of numerical processing that is possible on a standard Beagle board, particularly when investigating computationally expensive applications such as signal processing and computer vision.

As previously discussed, this is only one numerically oriented benchmark test, but it is somewhat indicative of the type of performance you should expect from each language. There have been many studies on the performance of languages; however, a well-specified analysis by Hundt (2011) has found that in terms of performance, "C++ wins out by a large margin. However, it also required the most extensive tuning efforts, many of which were done at a level of sophistication that would not be available to the average programmer."

Setting the CPU Frequency

In the previous section, the clock frequency of the Beagle board was adjusted dynamically at run time. The BeagleBoard.org Debian image has various *governors* that can be used to profile the performance/power usage ratio. For example, if you were building a battery-powered PocketBeagle application that has low processing requirements, you could reduce the clock frequency to conserve power. You can find out information about the current state of the board by typing the following:

```
debian@ebb:~$ sudo apt install cpufrequtils
debian@ebb:~$ cpufreq-info
...
available cpufreq governors: conservative, ondemand, userspace,
powersave, performance, schedutil
 current policy: frequency should be within 300 MHz and 1000 MHz.
             The governor "performance" may decide which speed to use
             within this range.
 current CPU frequency is 1000 MHz.
 cpufreq stats: 300 MHz:0.00%, 600 MHz:0.00%, 720 MHz:0.00%,
 800 MHz:0.00%, 1000 MHz:100.00%
```

You can see that different governors are available, with the profile names conservative, ondemand, userspace, powersave, performance, and schedutil. To enable one of these governors, type the following:

```
debian@ebb:~$ sudo cpufreq-set -g ondemand
debian@ebb:~$ cpufreq-info
... The governor "ondemand" may decide which speed to use within this range.
debian@ebb:~$ sudo cpufreq-set -f 600MHz
debian@ebb:~$ cpufreq-info
... current CPU frequency is 600 MHz.
```

The ondemand is useful as it dynamically switches the CPU frequency. For example, if the CPU frequency is currently 600MHz and the average CPU usage between governor samplings is above the threshold (called the up_threshold), then the CPU frequency will be automatically increased. You can tweak these and other settings using their sysfs entries. For example, to set the threshold at which the CPU frequency rises to the point at which the CPU load reaches 90 percent of available capacity, use the following:

```
debian@ebb:~$ sudo cpufreq-set -g ondemand
debian@ebb:~$ cd /sys/devices/system/cpu/cpufreq/ondemand/
debian@ebb:/sys/devices/system/cpu/cpufreq/ondemand$ ls
ignore_nice_load  min_sampling_rate  sampling_down_factor  up_threshold
io_is_busy        powersave_bias     sampling_rate
debian@ebb: ... /ondemand$ cat up_threshold
95
debian@ebb: ... /ondemand$ sudo sh -c "echo 90 > up_threshold"
debian@ebb: ... /ondemand$ cat up_threshold
90
```

If these tools are not installed on your board, you must install the cpufrequtils package. On Debian Stretch, the default governor is performance, but you can switch to ondemand by editing the cpufrequtils file in /etc/init.d/ as follows:

```
debian@ebb:~$ cd /etc/init.d
debian@ebb:/etc/init.d$ more cpufrequtils | grep GOVERNOR=
GOVERNOR="performance"
debian@ebb:/etc/init.d$ sudo nano cpufrequtils
debian@ebb:/etc/init.d$ more cpufrequtils | grep GOVERNOR=
GOVERNOR="ondemand"
debian@ebb:/etc/init.d$ sudo reboot
```

Scripting Languages

A scripting language is a computer programming language that is used to specify script files, which are *interpreted* directly by a run-time environment to perform tasks. Many scripting languages are available, such as Bash, Perl, Lua, and Python, and these can be used to automate the execution of tasks on a Beagle board, such as system administration, interaction, and even interfacing to electronic components.

Scripting Language Options

Which scripting language should you choose for a Beagle board? There are many strong opinions, and it is a difficult topic, as Linux users tend to have a favorite scripting language; however, you should choose the scripting language with features that suit the task at hand. Here are some examples:

- **Bash scripting:** A great choice for short scripts that do not require advanced programming structures. Bash scripts are used extensively in this book for small, well-defined tasks, such as the timing code in the previous section. You can use the Linux commands discussed in Chapter 3 in your Bash scripts.

- **Perl:** A great choice for scripts that parse text documents or process streams of data. It enables you to write straightforward scripts and even supports the object-oriented programming (OOP) paradigm, which is discussed later in this chapter.

- **Lua:** Is a fast and lightweight scripting language that can be used for embedded applications because of its small footprint. *Lua* supports the object-oriented programming (OOP) paradigm (using tables and functions) and dynamic typing, which is discussed shortly. Lua has an important role in Chapter 12 for the programming of NodeMCU Wi-Fi modules.

- **Python:** Is great for scripts that need more complex structure and are likely to be built upon or modified in the future. Python supports the OOP paradigm and dynamic typing, which is discussed shortly.

These four scripting languages are available for the Beagle standard Debian image. It would be useful to have some knowledge of all of these scripting languages, as you may find third-party tools or libraries that make your current project straightforward. This section provides a brief overview of each of these languages, including a concise segment of code that performs a similar function in each language. It finishes with a discussion about the advantages and disadvantages of scripting languages in general.

> **NOTE** All of the code that follows in this chapter is available in the associated GitHub repository in the `chp05` directory. If you have not done so already, use the command `git clone https://github.com/derekmolloy/exploringbb.git` in a Linux terminal window to clone this repository.

In Chapter 2 an approach is described for changing the state of the on-board LEDs using Linux shell commands. It is possible to turn an LED on or off, and even make it flash. For example, you can use the following:

```
root@ebb:/sys/class/leds/beaglebone:green:usr3# echo none > trigger
root@ebb:/sys/class/leds/beaglebone:green:usr3# echo 1 > brightness
root@ebb:/sys/class/leds/beaglebone:green:usr3# echo 0 > brightness
```

to turn a user LED on and off. This section examines how it is possible to do the same tasks but in a structured programmatic form.

Bash

Bash scripts are a great choice for short scripts that do not require advanced programming structures, and that is exactly the application to be developed here. The first program leverages the Linux console commands such as `echo` and `cat` to create the concise script in Listing 5-1 that enables you to choose, using command-line arguments, whether you want to turn the USR3 LED on or off or place it in a flashing mode. For example, using this script by calling **`./bashLED on`** would turn the USR3 LED on. It also provides you with the trigger status information.

Listing 5-1: chp05/bashLED/bashLED

```bash
#!/bin/bash
LED3_PATH=/sys/class/leds/beaglebone:green:usr3

function removeTrigger
{
  echo "none" >> "$LED3_PATH/trigger"
}

echo "Starting the LED Bash Script"
if [ $# != 1 ]; then
  echo "There is an incorrect number of arguments. Usage is:"
  echo -e " bashLED Command \n  where command is one of "
  echo -e "   on, off, flash or status  \n e.g. bashLED on "
  exit 2
fi
echo "The LED Command that was passed is: $1"
if [ "$1" == "on" ]; then
```

```
  echo "Turning the LED on"
  removeTrigger
  echo "1" >> "$LED3_PATH/brightness"
elif [ "$1" == "off" ]; then
  echo "Turning the LED off"
  removeTrigger
  echo "0" >> "$LED3_PATH/brightness"
elif [ "$1" == "flash" ]; then
  echo "Flashing the LED"
  removeTrigger
  echo "timer" >> "$LED3_PATH/trigger"
  echo "50" >> "$LED3_PATH/delay_on"
  echo "50" >> "$LED3_PATH/delay_off"
elif [ "$1" == "status" ]; then
  cat "$LED3_PATH/trigger";
fi
echo "End of the LED Bash Script"
```

The script is available in the directory /chp05/bashLED/. If you entered the
script manually using the nano editor, then the file needs to have the executable
flag set before it can be executed (the git repository retains executable flags).
Therefore, to allow all users to execute this script, use the following:

```
/chp05/bashLED$ chmod ugo+x bashLED
```

What is happening within this script? First, all of these command scripts
begin with a *sha-bang* #! followed by the name and location of the interpreter
to be used, so #!/bin/bash in this case. The file is just a regular text file, but the
sha-bang is a *magic-number* code to inform the OS that the file is an executable.
Next, the script defines the path to the LED for which you want to change state
using the variable LED3_PATH. This allows the default value to be easily altered
if you want to use a different user LED or path.

The script contains a function called removeTrigger, mainly to demonstrate
how functions are structured within Bash scripting. This function is called later
in the script. Each if is terminated by a fi. The ; after the if statement terminates
that statement and allows the statement then to be placed on the same line. The
elif keyword means else if, which allows you to have multiple comparisons
within the one if block. The newline character \n terminates statements.

> **NOTE** If you happen to be writing scripts under Windows, do not use Windows
> Notepad/WordPad to enter a Bash script. It will place a carriage return and line feed
> at the end of each line, which will mean that you get an error message such as "bad
> interpreter" on the first line of your scripts when these are executed under Linux. If
> necessary, you can install and use Notepad++ under Windows.

The first `if` statement confirms that the number of arguments passed to the script (`$#`) is not equal to `1`. Remember that the correct way to call this script is of the form **`./bashLED on`**. Therefore, `on` will be the first user argument that is passed (`$1`), and there will be one argument in total. If there are no arguments, then the correct usage will be displayed, and the script will exit with the return code `2`. This value is consistent with Linux system commands, where an exit value of 2 indicates incorrect usage. Success is indicated by a return value of `0`, so any other nonzero return value generally indicates the failure of a script.

If the argument that was passed is `on`, then the code displays a message; calls the `removeTrigger` function; and writes the string `"1"` to the `brightness` file in the LED3 `/sys/` directory. The remaining functions modify the USR3 LED values in the same way as described in Chapter 2. You can execute the script as follows:

```
debian@ebb:~/exploringbb/chp05/bashLED$ ./bashLED
    There are no arguments. Usage is:
    bashLED Command where command is one of
    on, off, flash or status e.g. bashLED on
debian@ebb:~/exploringbb/chp05/bashLED$ ./bashLED status
    The LED Command that was passed is: status
    none ... mmc0 [timer] oneshot disk-activity ...
debian@ebb:~/exploringbb/chp05/bashLED$ ./bashLED on
The LED Command that was passed is: on
Turning the LED on
debian@ebb:~/exploringbb/chp05/bashLED$ sudo ./bashLED flash
debian@ebb:~/exploringbb/chp05/bashLED$ ./bashLED off
```

Notice that the script was prefixed by `sudo` when it was called for the flash function only. This is because the flash function enables the timer state on the LED, which creates two new file entries in the directory called `delay_on` and `delay_off`. Unlike the other entries in this directory, these two new entries are not in the `gpio` group, and therefore the user debian does not have permission to write to them.

```
debian@ebb:/sys/class/leds/beaglebone:green:usr3$ ls -l
-rw-rw-r-- 1 root gpio 4096 May 13 09:16 brightness
-rw-r--r-- 1 root root 4096 May 13 17:42 delay_off
-rw-r--r-- 1 root root 4096 May 13 17:42 delay_on  ...
```

For security reasons, you cannot use the setuid bit on a script to set it to execute as root. If users had write access to this script and its setuid bit was set as root, then they could inject any command that they wanted into the script and would have *de facto* superuser access to the system. For a comprehensive online guide to Bash scripting, please see Mendel Cooper's "Advanced Bash-Scripting Guide" at `www.tldp.org/LDP/abs/html/`.

Lua

Lua is the best performing interpreted language in Table 5-1 by a significant margin. In addition to good performance, Lua has a clean and straightforward syntax that is accessible for beginners. The interpreter for Lua has a small footprint—approximately 131 KB in size (`ls -lh /usr/bin/lua5.3`), which makes it suitable for low-footprint embedded applications. For example, Lua can be used successfully on the ultra-low-cost ($2–$5) ESP Wi-Fi modules that are described in Chapter 12, despite their modest memory allocations. In fact, once a platform has an ANSI C compiler, then the Lua interpreter can be built for it. However, one downside is that the standard library of functions is somewhat limited in comparison to other more general scripting languages, such as Python. You can install the Lua interpreter using **sudo apt install lua5.3**.

Listing 5-2 provides a Lua script that has the same structure as the Bash script, so it is not necessary to discuss it in detail.

Listing 5-2: chp05/luaLED/luaLED.lua

```lua
#!/usr/bin/lua5.3
local LED3_PATH = "/sys/class/leds/beaglebone:green:usr3/"

-- Example function to write a value to the GPIO
function writeLED(directory, filename, value)
   file = io.open(directory..filename, "w") -- append dir and file names
   file:write(value)                        -- write the value to the file
   file:close()
end

print("Starting the Lua LED Program")
if arg[1]==nil then                          -- no argument provided?
   print("This program requires a command")
   print("   usage is: ./luaLED.lua command")
   print("where command is one of on, off, or status")
   do return end
end
if arg[1]=="on" then
   print("Turning the LED on")
   writeLED(LED3_PATH, "trigger", "none")
   os.execute("sleep 0.1")
   writeLED(LED3_PATH, "brightness", "1")
elseif arg[1]=="off" then
   print("Turning the LED off")
   writeLED(LED3_PATH, "trigger", "none")
   os.execute("sleep 0.1")
   writeLED(LED3_PATH, "brightness", "0")
elseif arg[1]=="status" then
   print("Getting the LED status")
```

```
   file = io.open(LED3_PATH.."brightness", "r")
   print(string.format("The LED state is %s.", file:read()))
   file:close()
else
   print("Invalid command!")
end
print("End of the Lua LED Program")
```

You can execute this script in the same manner as the `bashLED` script (e.g., `./luaLED.lua on` or by typing `lua luaLED.lua on` from the `/chp05/luaLED/` directory), and it will result in a comparable output. There are two things to be careful of with Lua in particular: strings are indexed from 1, not 0; and functions can return multiple values, unlike most languages. Lua has a straightforward interface to C/C++, which means that you can execute compiled C/C++ code from within Lua or use Lua as an interpreter module within your C/C++ programs. There is an excellent reference manual at `www.lua.org/manual/` and a six-page summary of Lua at `tiny.cc/beagle501`.

Perl

Perl is a feature-rich scripting language that provides you with access to a huge library of reusable modules and portability to other OSs (including Windows). Perl is best known for its text processing and regular expressions modules. In the late 1990s it was a popular language for server-side scripting for the dynamic generation of web pages. Later it was superseded by technologies such as Java servlets, Java Server Pages (JSP), and PHP. The language has evolved since its birth in the 1980s and now includes support for the OOP paradigm. Perl 5 (v5.24+) is installed by default on the Debian Linux image. Listing 5-3 provides a segment of a Perl example that has the same structure as the Bash script, so it is not necessary to discuss it in detail. Apart from the syntax, little has actually changed in the translation to Perl.

Listing 5-3: chp05/perlLED/perlLED.pl (Segment)

```perl
#!/usr/bin/perl
$LED3_PATH = "/sys/class/leds/beaglebone:green:usr3";
$command = $ARGV[0];

# Perl Write to LED3 function, the filename  $_[0] is the first argument
#   and the value to write is the second argument $_[1]
sub writeLED3{
  open(FILE, ">" . $LED3_PATH . $_[0] )
    or die "Could not open the file, $!";
  print FILE $_[1] ;
  close(FILE);
}
```

```perl
sub removeTrigger{
  writeLED3 ( "/trigger", "none");
}

print "Starting the LED Perl Script\n";
# 0 means that there is exactly one argument
if ( $#ARGV != 0 ){
  print "There are an incorrect number of arguments. Usage is:\n";
  print " bashLED Command, where command is one of\n";
  print "  on, off, flash or status e.g. bashLED on\n";
  exit 2;
}
print "The LED Command that was passed is: " . $command . "\n";
if ( $command eq "on" ){
  print "Turning the LED on\n";
  removeTrigger();
  writeLED3 ("/brightness", "1");
}
...  //full listing available in chp05/perlLED/perlLED.pl
```

A few small points are worth noting in the code. The < or > sign on the filename indicates whether the file is being opened for read or write access, respectively; the arguments are passed as $ARGV[0...n], and the number of arguments is available as the value $#ARGV. A file open, followed by a read or write, and a file close are necessary to write the values to /sys/; and the arguments are passed to the subroutine writeLED3 and these are received as the values $_[0] and $_[1], which is not the most beautiful programming syntax, but it works perfectly well. To execute this code, simply type **sudo ./perlLED.pl on**, as the sha-bang identifies the Perl interpreter. You could also execute it by typing **perl perlLED.pl status**.

For a good resource about getting started with installing and using Perl 5, see the guide "Learning Perl" at learn.perl.org.

Python

Python is a dynamic and strongly typed OOP language that was designed to be easy to learn and understand. *Dynamic typing* means you do not need to associate a type (e.g., integer, character, string) with a variable; rather, the value of the variable "remembers" its own type. Therefore, if you were to create a variable x=5, the variable x would behave as an integer; but if you subsequently assign it using x="test", it would then behave like a string. *Statically typed* languages such as C/C++ or Java would not allow the redefinition of a variable in this way (within the same scope). *Strongly typed* means that the conversion of a variable from one type to another requires an explicit conversion. The advantages of object-oriented programming structures are discussed later in this chapter. Python is installed by default on the BeagleBoard Debian image. The Python example to flash the LED is provided in Listing 5-4.

Listing 5-4: chp05/pythonLED/pythonLED.py

```python
#!/usr/bin/python
import sys
LED3_PATH = "/sys/class/leds/beaglebone:green:usr3"

def writeLED ( filename, value, path=LED3_PATH ):
    "This function writes the passed value to the file in the path"
    fo = open( path + filename,"w")
    fo.write(value)
    fo.close()
    return

def removeTrigger():
    writeLED (filename="/trigger", value="none")
    return

print "Starting the LED Python Script"
if len(sys.argv)!=2:
    print "There are an incorrect number of arguments"
    print "  usage is:  pythonLED.py command"
    print "  where command is one of on, off, flash or status."
    sys.exit(2)
if sys.argv[1]=="on":
    print "Turning the LED on"
    removeTrigger()
    writeLED (filename="/brightness", value="1")
elif sys.argv[1]=="off":
    print "Turning the LED off"
    removeTrigger()
    writeLED (filename="/brightness", value="0")
elif sys.argv[1]=="flash":
    print "Flashing the LED"
    writeLED (filename="/trigger", value="timer")
    writeLED (filename="/delay_on", value="50")
    writeLED (filename="/delay_off", value="50")
elif sys.argv[1]=="status":
    print "Getting the LED trigger status"
    fo = open( LED3_PATH + "/trigger", "r")
    print fo.read()
    fo.close()
else:
    print "Invalid Command!"
print "End of Python Script"
```

The formatting of this code is important—in fact, Python enforces the layout of your code by making indentation a structural element. For example, after the line if len(sys.argv)!=2:, the next few lines are "tabbed" in. If you did not tab in one of the lines—for example, the sys.exit(2) line—then it would not be part of the conditional if statement, and the code would always exit at this point in the program. To execute this example, in the pythonLED directory, enter the following:

```
debian@ebb:~/exploringbb/chp05/pythonLED$ sudo ./pythonLED.py flash
Flashing the LED
debian@ebb:~/exploringbb/chp05/pythonLED$ ./pythonLED.py status
... [timer] oneshot disk-activity ide-disk mtd nand-disk heartbeat ...
```

Python is popular on the Beagle platform for good pedagogical reasons, but as users turn their attention to more advanced applications, it is difficult to justify the performance deficit. This chapter concludes with a discussion on how you can use either Cython or combine Python with C/C++ to dramatically improve the performance of Python. However, the complexity of Cython itself should motivate you to consider using C/C++ directly.

To conclude this discussion of scripting, there are several strong choices for applications on the Beagle platform. Table 5-2 lists some of the key advantages and disadvantages of command scripting, when considered in the context of the compiled languages discussed shortly.

Table 5-2: Advantages and Disadvantages of Command Scripting

ADVANTAGES	DISADVANTAGES
Perfect for automating Linux system administration tasks that require calls to Linux commands.	Performance is poor for complex numerical or algorithmic tasks.
Easy to modify and adapt to changes. Source code is always present and complex toolchains (see Chapter 7) are not required to make modifications. Generally, nano is the only tool that you need.	Generally, relatively poor/slow programming support for data structures, graphical user interfaces, sockets, threads, etc.
Generally, straightforward programming syntax and structure that are reasonably easy to learn when compared to languages like C++ and Java.	Generally, poor support for complex applications involving multiple, user-developed modules or components (Python and Perl do support OOP).
Generally, quick turnaround in coding solutions by occasional programmers.	Code is in the open. Direct access to view your code can be an intellectual property or a security concern.
	Lack of development tools (e.g., refactoring).

Dynamically Compiled Languages

With the interpreted languages just discussed, the source code text file is "executed" by the user passing it to a run-time interpreter, which then translates or executes each line of code. JavaScript and Java have different life cycles and are quite distinct languages.

JavaScript and Node.js on the Beagle boards

As discussed in Chapter 2, in the section "Node.js, Cloud9, and BoneScript," Node.js is JavaScript that is run on the server side. JavaScript is an interpreted language by design; however, thanks to the V8 engine that was developed by Google for its Chrome web browser, Node.js actually compiles JavaScript into native machine instructions as it is loaded by the engine. This is called *just-in-time* (JIT) compilation or *dynamic translation*. As demonstrated at the beginning of this chapter, Node.js's performance for the numerical computation tasks is impressive for an interpreted language because of optimizations for the ARMv7 platform.

Listing 5-5 is the same LED code example written using JavaScript and executed by calling the nodejs executable.

Listing 5-5: chp05/nodejsLED/nodejsLED.js

```
// Ignore the first two arguments (nodejs and the program name)
var myArgs = process.argv.slice(2);
var LED3_PATH = "/sys/class/leds/beaglebone:green:usr3"

function writeLED( filename, value, path ){
  var fs = require('fs');
  try {
  // The next call must be syncronous, otherwise the timer will not work
    fs.writeFileSync(path+filename, value);
  }
  catch (err) {
    console.log("The Write Failed to the File: " + path+filename);
  }
}

function removeTrigger(){
   writeLED("/trigger", "none", LED3_PATH);
}

console.log("Starting the LED Node.js Program");
if (myArgs[0]==null){
   console.log("There is an incorrect number of arguments.");
   console.log(" Usage is: nodejs nodejsLED.js command");
```

```
            console.log("  where command is one of: on, off, flash or status.");
            process.exit(2);    //exits with the error code 2 (incorrect usage)
}
switch (myArgs[0]) {
    case 'on':
        console.log("Turning the LED On");
        removeTrigger();
        writeLED("/brightness", "1", LED3_PATH);
        break;
    case 'off':
        console.log("Turning the LED Off");
        removeTrigger();
        writeLED("/brightness", "0", LED3_PATH);
        break;
    case 'flash':
        console.log("Making the LED Flash");
        writeLED("/trigger", "timer", LED3_PATH);
        writeLED("/delay_on", "50", LED3_PATH);
        writeLED("/delay_off", "50", LED3_PATH);
        break;
    case 'status':
        console.log("Getting the LED Status");
        fs = require('fs');
        fs.readFile(LED3_PATH+"/trigger", 'utf8', function (err, data) {
            if (err) { return console.log(err); }
            console.log(data);
        });
        break;
    default:
        console.log("Invalid Command");
}
console.log("End of Node.js script");
```

The code is available in the /chp05/nodejsLED/ directory, and it can be executed by typing **nodejs nodejsLED.js [option]**. The code has been structured in the same way as the previous examples, and there are not too many syntactical differences; however, there is one major difference between Node.js and other languages: *functions are called asynchronously*. Up to this point, all the languages discussed followed a sequential-execution mode. Therefore, when a function is called, the *program counter* (also known as the *instruction pointer*) enters that function and does not reemerge until the function is complete. Consider, for example, code like this:

```
functionA();
functionB();
```

The functionA() is called, and functionB() will not be called until functionA() is fully complete. This is *not* the case in Node.js! In Node.js, functionA() is called first, and then Node.js continues executing the subsequent code, including entering `functionB()`, while the code in `functionA()` is still being executed. This presents a serious difficulty for the current application, with this segment of code in particular:

```
case 'flash':
        console.log("Making the LED Flash");
        writeLED("/trigger", "timer", LED3_PATH);
        writeLED("/delay_on", "50", LED3_PATH);
        writeLED("/delay_off", "50", LED3_PATH);
        break;
```

The first call to `writeLED()` sets up the `sysfs` file system (as described in Chapter 2) to now contain new `delay_on` and `delay_off` file entries. However, because of the asynchronous nature of the calls, the first `writeLED()` call has not finished setting up the file system before the next two `writeLED()` calls are performed. This means that the `delay_on` and `delay_off` file system entries are not found, and the code to write to them fails. You should test this by changing the call near the top of the program from `fs.writeFileSync(...)` to `fs.writeFile(...)`.

To combat this issue you can *synchronize* (prevent threads from being interrupted) the block of code where the three `writeLED()` functions are called, ensuring that the functions are called sequentially. Alternatively, as shown in this code example, you can use a special version of the Node.js `writeFile()` function called `writeFileSync()` to ensure that the first function call to modify the file system blocks the other `writeFileSync()` calls from taking place.

Node.js allows asynchronous calls because they help ensure that your code is "lively." For example, if you performed a database query, your code may be able to do something else useful while awaiting the result. When the result is available, a *callback function* is executed in order to process the received data. This asynchronous structure is perfect for Internet-attached applications, where posts and requests are being made of websites and web services and it is not clear when a response will be received (if at all). Node.js has an *event loop* that manages all the asynchronous calls, creating threads for each call as required and ensuring that the callback functions are executed when an asynchronous call completes its assigned tasks. Node.js is revisited in Chapter 11 when the Internet of Things is discussed.

Java on the Beagle Boards

Up to this point in the chapter, *interpreted languages* are examined, meaning the source code file (a text file) is executed using an interpreter or dynamic translator at run time. Importantly, the code exists in source code form, right up to the point when it is executed using the interpreter.

With traditional *compiled languages*, the source code (a text file) is translated directly into machine code for a particular platform using a set of tools, which we will call a *compiler* for the moment. The translation happens when the code is being developed; once compiled, the code can be executed without needing any additional run-time tools.

INSTALLING JAVA ON THE BEAGLE BOARDS

It is possible to install Oracle Java to the Beagle boards so that you can build and execute Java code directly on your board. There is an installer present in Debian, but it often fails because of Java version and Oracle website changes. In theory you should be able to just type this:

```
debian@ebb:~$ sudo apt-get install oracle-java8-installer
debian@ebb:~$ java -version
```

If the installer fails, you can perform the steps manually using the `curl` command, which is a command-line tool for transferring data with URLs. Browse to the Oracle Java downloads page for the Java Development Kit (JDK) and look for an "ARM 32 Hard Float ABI" version. At the time of writing, Java 10 was available, but not in binary form for ARM 32. Click the Accept License Agreement item and then right-click the link to get the download URL. Use your download URL in place of mine in the following command:

```
debian@ebb:~$ curl -LOb "oraclelicense=a" http://download.ora →
cle.com/otn-pub/java/jdk/8u171-b11/512cd62ec5174c3487ac17c61a →
aa89e8/jdk-8u171-linux-arm32-vfp-hflt.tar.gz
debian@ebb:~$ ls -l *.gz
-rw-r--r-- 1 debian debian 81757896 May 13 23:58 jdk-8u171-...
debian@ebb:~$ sudo mkdir /opt/java-jdk
debian@ebb:~$ sudo tar -C /opt/java-jdk/ -zxf jdk-8u171*.tar.gz
debian@ebb:~$ sudo update-alternatives --install /usr/bin/java →
java /opt/java-jdk/jdk1.8.0_171/bin/java 1
debian@ebb:~$ sudo update-alternatives --install /usr/bin/javac →
javac /opt/java-jdk/jdk1.8.0_171/bin/javac 1
debian@ebb:~$ java -version
java version "1.8.0_171" ...
debian@ebb:~$ javac -version
javac 1.8.0_171
```

These steps may need to be adapted to account for updates to the Oracle website, but the commands should remain consistent. The update-alternatives command is a symbolic link management tool for Linux that allows you to specify a default Java virtual machine and development kit location.

Java is a hybrid language: you write your Java code in a source file, e.g., example.java, which is a regular text file. The Java compiler (javac) compiles and translates this source code into machine code instructions (called *bytecodes*) for a Java *virtual machine* (VM). Regular compiled code is not portable between hardware architectures, but bytecode files (.class files) can be executed on any platform that has an implementation of the Java VM. Originally, the Java VM interpreted the bytecode files at run time; however, more recently, dynamic translation is employed by the VM to convert the bytecodes into native machine instructions at run time.

The key advantage of this life cycle is that the compiled bytecode is portable between platforms, and because it is compiled to a generic machine instruction code, the dynamic translation to "real" machine code is efficient. The downside of this structure when compared to compiled languages is that the VM adds overhead to the execution of the final executable.

The Java Runtime Environment (JRE), which provides the Java virtual machine (JVM), is not installed on the Beagle Debian image by default because it occupies approximately 177MB when installed.

NOTE Large installations such as Oracle Java might cause you to run out of space on your BeagleBone eMMC. You can find the biggest packages that are installed on your distribution using the command dpkg-query -Wf '${Installed-Size}\ t${Package}\n' | sort -n. You can then remove large unused packages using apt remove.

Listing 5-6 provides a source code example that is also available in the GitHub repository in bytecode form.

Listing 5-6: chp05/javaLED/LEDExample.java (Segment)

```java
package exploringBB;
import java.io.*;

public class LEDExample {
  private static String LED3 = "/sys/class/leds/beaglebone:green:usr3";

  private static void writeLED(String fname, String value, String path){
    try{
      BufferedWriter bw = new BufferedWriter(new FileWriter(path+fname));
      bw.write(value);
      bw.close();
    }
    catch(IOException e){
```

```
        System.err.println("Failed to access Sysfs: " + fname);
     }
  }

  private static void removeTrigger(){
     writeLED("/trigger", "none", LED3);
  }

  public static void main(String[] args) {
     System.out.println("Starting the LED Java Application");
     if(args.length!=1) {
        System.out.println("Incorrect number of arguments."); ...
        System.exit(2);
     }
     if(args[0].equalsIgnoreCase("On")||args[0].equalsIgnoreCase("Off")){
        System.out.println("Turning the LED " + args[0]);
        removeTrigger();
        writeLED("/brightness",args[0].equalsIgnoreCase("On")?"1":"0",LED3);
     }
     ...  // full code available in the repository directory
  }
}
```

The program can be executed using the run script that is in the /chp05/ javaLED/ directory. You can see that the class is placed in the package directory exploringBB.

Early versions of Java suffered from poor computational performance; however, more recent versions take advantage of dynamic translation at run time (just-in-time, or JIT, compilation) and, as demonstrated at the start of this chapter, the performance was less than 15 percent slower (including dynamic translation) than that of the natively compiled C++ code, with only a minor additional memory overhead. Table 5-3 lists some of the advantages and disadvantages of using Java for development on the Beagle platform.

Table 5-3: Advantages and Disadvantages of Java on the Beagle Platform

ADVANTAGES	DISADVANTAGES
Code is portable. Code compiled on the PC can be executed on any Beagle board or another embedded Linux platform.	Sandboxed applications do not have access to system memory, registers, or system calls (except through /proc/) or Java Native Interface (JNI).
There is a vast and extensive library of code available that can be fully integrated in your project.	Executing as root is slightly difficult because of required environment variables.

ADVANTAGES	DISADVANTAGES
Full OOP support.	It is not suitable for scripting.
Can be used for user-interface application development on a Beagle board that is attached to a display.	Computational performance is respectable but slower than optimized C/C++ programs. Slightly heavier on memory.
Strong support for multithreading.	Strictly typed and no unsigned integer types.
Has automatic memory allocation and de-allocation using a garbage collector, removing memory leak concerns.	Royalty payment is required if deployed to a platform that "involves or controls hardware."[11]

To execute a Java application under Debian, where it needs access to the /sys/ directory, you need the application to run with root access. Unfortunately, because you need to pass the bytecode (.class) file to the Java VM, you must call sudo and create a temporary shell of the form sudo sh -c 'java myClass'. The application can be executed using the following:

```
.../chp05/javaLED$ sudo sh -c 'java exploringBB.LEDExample Off'
Starting the LED Java Application
Turning the LED Off
.../chp05/javaLED$ sudo sh -c 'java exploringBB.LEDExample On'
Starting the LED Java Application
Turning the LED On
```

NOTE   Instead of logging out and logging in again to apply profile settings, you can use the source command, which evaluates a file as a Tcl (Tool Command Language) script to reload your .profile settings. Type source ~/.profile.

C and C++ on the Beagle Boards

C++ was developed by Bjarne Stroustrup at Bell Labs (now AT&T Labs) during 1983–1985. It is based on the C language (named in 1972) that was developed at AT&T for UNIX systems in the early 1970s (1969–1973) by Dennis Ritchie. As well as adding an *object-oriented* (OO) framework (originally called "C with

---

[11] Currently, pricing for Oracle Java SE is on a per-core basis. Based on the information at blogs.oracle.com/jtc/java-se-embedded-pricing-explained, you can expect to pay approximately $0.71 per unit for a PocketBeagle or BeagleBone device, and $5.36 per-unit for the dual-core A15-based BeagleBoard X15. Alternatively, there are OpenJDK variants of Java that can be used that do not require a royalty payment but in turn do not receive commercial support.

Classes"), C++ also improves the C language by adding features such as better type checking. It quickly gained widespread usage, which was largely due to its similarity to the C programming language syntax and the fact that it allowed existing C code to be used when possible. C++ is not a pure OO language but rather a hybrid, having the organizational structure of OO languages but retaining the efficiencies of C, such as typed variables and pointers.

Unlike Java, C++ is not "owned" by a single company. In 1998 the International Organization for Standardization (ISO) committee adopted a worldwide uniform language specification that aimed to remove inconsistencies between the various C++ compilers (Stroustrup, 1998). This standardization continues today with C++11 approved by the ISO in 2011 (gcc 4.7+ supports the flag `-std=c++11`), C++14 fully supported by gcc version 5, and many features of C++17 supported in gcc version 6 (with more to come in gcc version 7). At the time of writing, the current version of gcc and exact set of features available can be determined using this:

```
debian@ebb:~/exploringbb/chp05/overview$ g++ -v
...
gcc version 6.3.0 20170516 (Debian 6.3.0-18+deb9u1)
debian@ebb:~/exploringbb/chp05/overview$ more version.cpp
#include <iostream>
int main(int argc, char** argv) {
  std::cout << __cplusplus << std::endl;
  return 0;
}
.../chp05/overview$ g++ version.cpp -o version
.../chp05/overview$ ./version
201402
.../chp05/overview$ g++ -std=c++17 version.cpp -o version
.../chp05/overview$ ./version
201500
```

While it is important to understand the functionality available to you through your version of gcc, many of the newer features of C++ are not vital to developing code on embedded devices.

Why am I covering C and C++ in more detail than other languages in this book?

- First, I believe that if you can understand the workings of C and C++, then you can understand the workings of any language. In fact, most compilers (Java native methods, Java virtual machine, JavaScript) and interpreters (Bash, Lua, Perl, and Python) are written in C.

- At the beginning of this chapter, a significant performance advantage of C/C++ over other many languages was described (yes, it was demonstrated using only one random test!). It is also important to remember that the same code running on the PocketBeagle at 1GHz was approximately 53 times slower than the same code running on only one thread (12 total) of an Intel i7-5820K at 3.3GHz.

■ Chapter 16 explains how to develop Linux loadable kernel modules (LKM), which requires a reasonable grasp of the C programming language. Later in this chapter, code is provided that demonstrates how you can communicate directly with Linux kernel space using the GNU C Library (glibc).

■ Many of the application examples in this book such as streaming network data and image processing use C++ and a comprehensive library of C++ code called Qt.

Table 5-4 lists some advantages and disadvantages of using C/C++ on the Beagle boards. The next section reviews some of the fundamentals of C and C++ programming to ensure that you have the skills necessary for the remaining chapters in this book. It is not possible to cover every aspect of C and C++ programming in just one chapter of one book. The "Further Reading" section at the end of this chapter directs you to recommended texts.

Table 5-4: Advantages and Disadvantages of C/C++ on the Beagle Boards

ADVANTAGES	DISADVANTAGES
You can build code directly on the board or you can cross-compile code. The C/C++ languages are ISO standards, not owned by a single vendor.	Compiled code is not portable. Code compiled for your x86 desktop will not run on the Beagle board's ARM processor.
C++ has full support for procedural programming, OOP, and support for generics through the use of STL (Standard Template Library).	Many consider the languages to be complex to master. There is a tendency to need to know everything before you can do anything.
It gives excellent computational performance, especially if optimized; however, optimization can be difficult and can reduce the portability of your code.	The use of pointers and the low-level control available makes code prone to memory leaks. With careful coding these can be avoided and can lead to efficiencies over dynamic memory management schemes.
Can be used for user-interface application development on the Beagle boards using third-party libraries. Libraries such as Qt and Boost provide extensive additional resources for components, networking, etc.	By default, C and C++ do not support graphical user interfaces, network sockets, etc. Third-party libraries are required.
Offers low-level access to glibc for integrating with the Linux system. Programs can be setuid to root.	Not suitable for scripting (there is a C shell, csh, that does have syntax like C). Not ideal for web development either.
The Linux kernel is written in C and having knowledge of C/C++ can help if you ever need to write device drivers or contribute to Linux kernel development.	C++ attempts to span from low-level to high-level programming tasks, but it can be difficult to write very scalable enterprise or web applications.

The next section provides a revision of the core principles that have been applied to examples on the Beagle boards. It is intended to serve as an overview and a set of reference examples that you can come back to again and again. It also focuses on topics that cause my students difficulties, pointing out common mistakes. Also, please remember that course notes for my Object-Oriented Programming module are publicly available at ee402.eeng.dcu.ie along with further support materials.

C and C++ Language Overview

The following examples can be edited using the nano editor and compiled on the Beagle boards directly using the gcc and g++ compilers, which are installed by default. The code is in the directory chp05/overview/.

The first example you should always write in any new language is "Hello World." Listings 5-7 and 5-8 provide C and C++ code, respectively, for the purpose of a direct comparison of the two languages.

Listing 5-7: chp05/overview/helloworld.c

```c
#include <stdio.h>
int main(int argc, char *argv[]){
   printf("Hello World!\n");
   return 0;
}
```

Listing 5-8: chp05/overview/helloworld.cpp

```cpp
#include<iostream>
int main(int argc, char *argv[]){
   std::cout << "Hello World!" << std::endl;
   return 0;
}
```

The #include call is a preprocessor directive that effectively loads the contents of the stdio.h file (/usr/include/stdio.h) in the C case, and the iostream header (/usr/include/c++/6/iostream) file in the C++ case, and copies and pastes the code in at this exact point in your source code file. These header files contain the function prototypes, enabling the compiler to link to and understand the format of functions such as printf() in stdio.h and streams like cout in iostream. The actual implementation of these functions is in shared library dependencies. The angular brackets (< >) around the include filename means that it is a standard, rather than a user-defined include (which would use double quotes).

The main() function is the starting point of your application code. There can be only one function called main() in your application. The int in front of main() indicates that the program will return a number to the shell prompt. As stated, it is good to use 0 for successful completion, 2 for invalid usage, and any other set of numbers to indicate failure conditions. This value is returned to the shell prompt using the line `return 0` in this case. The `main()` function will return 0 by default. Remember that you can use `echo $?` at the shell prompt to see the last value that was returned.

The *parameters* of the `main()` function are `int argc` and `char *argv[]`. As you saw in the scripting examples, the shell can pass *arguments* to your application, providing the number of arguments (`argc`) and an array of strings (`*argv[]`). In C/C++ the first argument passed is `argv[0]`, and it contains the name and full path used to execute the application.

The C code line `printf("Hello World!\n");` allows you to write to the Linux shell, with the `\n` representing a new line. The `printf()` function provides you with additional formatting instructions for outputting numbers, strings, etc. Note that every statement is terminated by a semicolon.

The C++ code line `std::cout << "Hello World!" << std::endl;` outputs a string just like the `printf()` function. In this case, `cout` represents the output stream, and the function used is actually the `<<`, which is called the *output stream operator*. The syntax is discussed later, but `std::cout` means the output stream in the namespace `std`. The `endl` (end line) representation is the same as `\n`. This may seem more verbose, but you will see why it is useful later in the discussion on C++ classes. These programs can be compiled and executed directly on the Beagle board by typing the following:

```
.../chp05/overview$ gcc helloworld.c -o helloworldc
.../chp05/overview$ ./helloworldc
Hello World!
.../chp05/overview$ g++ helloworld.cpp -o helloworldcpp
.../chp05/overview$ ./helloworldcpp
Hello World!
```

The sizes of the C and C++ executables are different to account for the different header files, output functions, and exact compilers that are used.

```
debian@ebb:~/exploringbb/chp05/overview$ ls -l helloworldc*
-rwxr-xr-x 1 debian debian 8348 May 14 02:48 helloworldc
-rwxr-xr-x 1 debian debian 9152 May 14 02:48 helloworldcpp
```

Compiling and Linking

You just saw how to build a C or C++ application, but there are a few intermediate steps that are not obvious in the preceding example, as the intermediate stage outputs are not retained by default. Figure 5-1 illustrates the full build process from preprocessing right through to linking.

You can perform the steps in Figure 5-1 yourself. Here is an example of the actual steps that were performed using the `Helloworld.cpp` code example. The steps can be performed explicitly as follows, so that you can view the output at each stage:

```
debian@ebb:/tmp$ ls -l helloworld.cpp
-rw-r--r-- 1 debian debian 114 May 14 02:51 helloworld.cpp
debian@ebb:/tmp$ g++ -E helloworld.cpp > processed.cpp
debian@ebb:/tmp$ ls -l processed.cpp
-rw-r--r-- 1 debian debian 641377 May 14 02:51 processed.cpp
debian@ebb:/tmp$ g++ -S processed.cpp -o helloworld.s
debian@ebb:/tmp$ ls -l helloworld.s
-rw-r--r-- 1 debian debian 3161 May 14 02:52 helloworld.s
debian@ebb:/tmp$ g++ -c helloworld.s
debian@ebb:/tmp$ ls
helloworld.cpp    helloworld.o    helloworld.s    processed.cpp
debian@ebb:/tmp$ g++ helloworld.o -o helloworld
debian@ebb:/tmp$ ls -l helloworld
-rwxr-xr-x 1 debian debian 9148 May 14 02:53 helloworld
debian@ebb:/tmp$ ./helloworld
Hello World!
```

You can see the text format output after preprocessing by typing **less pro-cessed.cpp**, where you will see the necessary header files pasted in at the top of your code. At the bottom of the file you will find your code. This file is passed to the C/C++ compiler, which validates the code and generates platform-independent assembler code (`.s`). You can view this code by typing **less helloworld.s**, as illustrated in Figure 5-1.

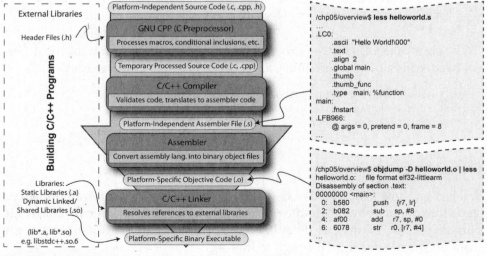

Figure 5-1: Building C/C++ applications on the Beagle boards

This .s text file is then passed to the assembler, which converts the platform-independent instructions into binary instructions for the Beagle board (the .o file). You can see the assembly language code that was generated if you use the objdump (object file dump) tool on your board by typing objdump -D helloworld.o, as illustrated in Figure 5-1.

Object files contain generalized binary assembly code that does not yet provide enough information to be executed on the board. However, after linking the final executable code, helloworld contains the target-specific assembly language code that has been combined with the libraries, statically and dynamically as required—you can use the objdump tool again on the executable, which results in the following output:

```
.../chp05/overview$ objdump -d helloworldcpp | less
helloworldcpp:       file format elf32-littlearm
Disassembly of section .init:
00000668 <_init>:
 668:   e92d4008        push    {r3, lr}
 66c:   eb00002f        bl      730 <call_weak_fn>
 670:   e8bd8008        pop     {r3, pc}
...
```

The first column is the memory address, which steps by 4 bytes (32-bits) between each instruction (i.e., 66c − 668 = 4). The second column is the full 4-byte instruction at that address. The third and fourth columns are the human-readable version of the second column that describes the opcode and operand of the 4-byte instruction. For example, the first instruction at address 668 is a push, which pushes r3, which is one of the ARM processor's sixteen 32-bit registers (labeled r0-r15), followed by lr (the link register, r14) onto the stack.

Understanding ARM instructions is another book in and of itself (see info-center.arm.com). However, it is useful to appreciate that any natively compiled code, whether it uses the OOP paradigm or not, results in low-level machine code, which does not support dynamic typing, OOP, or any such high-level structures. In fact, whether you use an interpreted or compiled language, the code must eventually be converted to machine code so that it can execute on the board's ARM processor.

Writing the Shortest C/C++ Program

Is the HelloWorld example the shortest program that can be written in C or C++? No, Listing 5-9 is the shortest valid C and C++ program.

Listing 5-9: chp05/overview/short.c

```
main(){}
```

This is a fully functional C and C++ program that compiles with no errors and works perfectly, albeit with no output. Therefore, in building a C/C++ program, there is no need for libraries; there is no need to specify a return type for main(), as it defaults to int; the main() function returns 0 by default in C++ and an undefined number in C (see the following echo $? call); and an empty function is a valid function. This program will compile as a C or C++ program as follows:

```
.../chp05/overview$ gcc short.c -o shortc
short.c:1:1: warning: return type defaults to 'int' ...
.../chp05/overview$ g++ short.c -o shortcpp
.../chp05/overview$ ls -l shortc*
-rwxr-xr-x 1 debian debian 8276 May 14 03:10 shortc
-rwxr-xr-x 1 debian debian 8292 May 14 03:10 shortcpp
.../chp05/overview$ ./shortc
.../chp05/overview$ echo $?
0
.../chp05/overview$ ./shortcpp
.../chp05/overview$ echo $?
0
```

This is one of the greatest weaknesses of C and C++. There is an assumption that you know everything about the way the language works before you write anything. In fact, aspects of the preceding example might be used by programmers to demonstrate how clever they are, but they are actually demonstrating poor practice in making their code unreadable by less "expert" programmers. For example, if you rewrite the C++ code in short.cpp to include comments and explicit statements, to create short2.cpp, and then compile both using the -O3 optimization flag, the output will be as follows:

```
.../chp05/overview$ more short.cpp
main(){}
.../chp05/overview$ more short2.cpp
// A really useless program, but a program nevertheless
int main(int argc, char *argv[]){
   return 0;
}
.../chp05/overview$ g++ -O3 short.cpp -o short01
.../chp05/overview$ g++ -O3 short2.cpp -o short02
.../chp05/overview$ ls -l short0*
-rwxr-xr-x 1 debian debian 8292 May 14 03:15 short01
-rwxr-xr-x 1 debian debian 8292 May 14 03:15 short02
```

Note that the executable size is exactly the same! Adding the comment, the explicit return statement, the explicit return type, and explicit arguments has had no impact on the size of the final binary application. However, the benefit is that the actual functionality of the code is much more readily understood by a novice programmer.

Static and Dynamic Compilation

You can build with the flag `-static` to statically link the libraries, rather than the default form of linking dynamically with shared libraries. This means that the compiler and linker effectively place all the library routines required by your code directly within the program executable.

```
.../chp05/overview$ g++ -O3 short.cpp -static -o short_static
.../chp05/overview$ ls -l short_static
-rwxr-xr-x 1 debian debian 448792 May 14 03:19 short_static
```

It is clear that the program executable size has grown significantly from 8KB to 449KB. One advantage of this form is that the program can be executed by ARM systems on which the C++ standard libraries are not installed.

With dynamic linking, it is useful to note that you can discover which shared library dependencies your compiled code is using, by calling `ldd`.

```
.../chp05/overview$ ldd shortcpp
linux-vdso.so.1 (0xbefcd000)
libstdc++.so.6 => /usr/lib/arm-linux-gnueabihf/libstdc++.so.6 (0xb6dcf000)
libm.so.6 => /lib/arm-linux-gnueabihf/libm.so.6 (0xb6d57000)
libgcc_s.so.1 => /lib/arm-linux-gnueabihf/libgcc_s.so.1 (0xb6d2e000)
libc.so.6 => /lib/arm-linux-gnueabihf/libc.so.6 (0xb6c40000)
/lib/ld-linux-armhf.so.3 (0xb6eed000)
```

You can see from this output that the g++ compiler (and glibc) on the Debian image for the Beagle boards has been patched to support the generation of hard floating-point (`gnueabihf`) instructions by default. This allows for faster code execution with floating-point numbers than if it used the soft floating-point ABI (application binary interface) to emulate floating-point support in software (`gnueabi`).

> **NOTE**   The gcc/g++ compilers automatically search certain include and library paths. The include paths are typically `/usr/include/`, `/usr/local/include/`, and `/usr/include/target/` (or `/usr/target/include/`), where `target` in the case of the Beagle boards is typically `arm-linux-gnueabihf`. The library paths are typically `/usr/lib/`, `/usr/local/lib/`, and `/usr/lib/target/` (or `/usr/target/lib/`). Use `g++ -v`, or `c++ -v` for more information, including your target name.

Variables and Operators in C/C++

A *variable* is a data item stored in a block of memory that has been reserved for it. The type of the variable defines the amount of memory reserved and how it should behave (see Figure 5-2). This figure describes the output of the code example `sizeofvariables.c` in Listing 5-10.

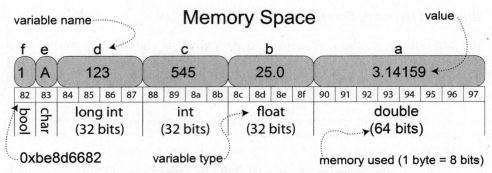

Figure 5-2: Memory allocation for variables running on a 32-bit Beagle board

Listing 5-10 details various variables available in C/C++. When you create a *local variable* c, it is allocated a box/block of memory on the *stack* (predetermined reserved fast memory) depending on its type. In this case, c is an int value; therefore, four bytes (32 bits) of memory are allocated to store the value. Assume that variables in C/C++ are initialized with arbitrary values; therefore, in this case c = 545; replaces that initial random value by placing the number 545 in the box. It does not matter if you store the number 0 or 2,147,483,647 in this box: it will still occupy 32 bits of memory! Please note that there is no guarantee regarding the ordering of local variable memory—it was fortuitously linear in this particular example.

Listing 5-10: chp05/overview/sizeofvariables.c

```
#include<stdio.h>
#include<stdbool.h>       //required for the C bool typedef

int main(){
   double a = 3.14159;
   float b = 25.0;
   int c = 545;            // note: variables are not = 0 by default!
   long int d = 123;
   char e = 'A';
   bool f = true;          // no need for definition in C++
   printf("a val %.4f & size %d bytes (@addr %p).\n", a, sizeof(a),&a);
   printf("b val %4.2f & size %d bytes (@addr %p).\n", b, sizeof(b),&b);
   printf("c val %d (oct %o, hex %x) & " \
          "size %d bytes (@addr %p).\n", c, c, c, sizeof(c), &c);
   printf("d val %d & size %d bytes (@addr %p).\n", d, sizeof(d), &d);
   printf("e val %c & size %d bytes (@addr %p).\n", e, sizeof(e), &e);
   printf("f val %5d & size %d bytes (@addr %p).\n", f, sizeof(f), &f);
}
```

The sizeof(c) operator returns the size of the type of the variable in bytes. In this example, it will return 4 for the size of the int type. The &c call can be read as the *"address of"* c. This provides the address of the first byte that stores the variable c, in this case returning 0xbe8d6688. The %.4f on the first line means display the floating-point number to four decimal places. Executing this program on a PocketBeagle gives the following:

```
/chp05/overview$ ./sizeofvariables
a val 3.1416 & size 8 bytes (@addr 0xbe8d6690).
b val 25.00 & size 4 bytes (@addr 0xbe8d668c).
c val 545 (oct 1041, hex 221) & size 4 bytes (@addr 0xbe8d6688).
d val 123 & size 4 bytes (@addr 0xbe8d6684).
e val A & size 1 bytes (@addr 0xbe8d6683).
f val      1 and size 1 bytes (@addr 0xbe8d6682).
```

The Beagle boards have 32-bit microprocessors, so you are using four bytes to represent the int type. The smallest unit of memory that you can allocate is one byte, so, yes, you are representing a Boolean value with one byte, which could actually store eight unique Boolean values. You can operate directly on variables using operators. The program operators.c in Listing 5-11 contains some points that often cause difficulty in C/C++:

Listing 5-11: chp05/overview/operators.c

```
#include<stdio.h>

int main(){
    int a=1, b=2, c, d, e, g;
    float f=9.9999;
    c = ++a;
    printf("The value of c=%d and a=%d.\n", c, a);
    d = b++;
    printf("The value of d=%d and b=%d.\n", d, b);
    e = (int) f;
    printf("The value of f=%.2f and e=%d.\n", f, e);
    g = 'A';
    printf("The value of g=%d and g=%c.\n", g, g);
    return 0;
}
```

This will give the following output:

```
/chp05/overview$ ./operators
The value of c=2 and a=2.
The value of d=2 and b=3.
The value of f=10.00 and e=9.
The value of g=65 and g=A.
```

On the line c=++a; the value of a is pre-incremented before the equals assignment to c on the left side. Therefore, a was increased to 2 before assigning the value to c, so this line is equivalent to two lines: a=a+1; c=a;. However, on the line d=b++; the value of b is post-incremented and is equivalent to two lines:

d=b; b=b+1;. The value of d is assigned the value of b, which is 2, before the value of b is incremented to 3.

On the line e=(int)f; a C-style cast is being used to convert a floating-point number into an integer value. Effectively, when programmers use a cast, they are notifying the compiler that they are aware that there will be a loss of precision in the conversion of a floating-point number to an int (and that the compiler will introduce conversion code). The fractional part will be truncated, so 9.9999 is converted to e=9, as the .9999 is removed by the truncation. One other point to note is that the printf("%.2f",f) displays the floating-point variable to two decimal places, in contrast, rounding the value.

On the line g='A', g is assigned the ASCII equivalent value of capital A, which is 65. The printf("%d %c",g, g); will display either the int value of g if %d is used or the ASCII character value of g if %c is used.

A const keyword can be used to prevent a variable from being changed. There is also a volatile keyword that is useful for notifying the compiler that a particular variable might be changed outside its control and that the compiler should not apply any type of optimization to that value. This notification is useful on the Beagle board if the variable in question is shared with another process or physical input/output.

It is possible to define your own type in C/C++ using the typedef keyword. For example, if you did not want to include the header file stdbool.h in the sizeofvariables.c previous example, it would be possible to define it in this way instead:

```
typedef char bool;
#define true 1
#define false 0
```

Probably the most common and most misunderstood mistake in C/C++ programming is present in the following:

```
if (x=y){
    // perform a body statement Z
}
```

When will the body statement z be performed? The answer is whenever y is not equal to 0 (the current value of x is irrelevant!). The mistake is placing a single = (assignment) instead of == (comparison) in the if statement. The assignment operator returns the value on the RHS, which will be automatically converted to true if y is not equal to 0. If y is equal to zero, then a false value will be returned. Java does not allow this error, as there is no implicit conversion between 0 and false and 1 and true.

Pointers in C/C++

A pointer is a special type of variable that stores the address of another variable in memory—we say that the pointer is "pointing at" that variable. Listing 5-12 is a code example that demonstrates how you can create a pointer p and make it point at the variable y.

Listing 5-12: chp05/overview/pointers.c

```c
#include<stdio.h>

int main(){
   int y = 1000;
   int *p;
   p = &y;
   printf("The variable has value %d and the address %p.\n", y, &y);
   printf("The pointer stores %p and points at value %d.\n", p, *p);
   printf("The pointer has address %p and size %d.\n", &p, sizeof(p));
   return 0;
}
```

When this code is compiled and executed, it will give the following output:

```
/chp05/overview$ ./pointers
The variable has value 1000 and the address 0xbede26bc.
The pointer stores 0xbede26bc and points at value 1000.
The pointer has address 0xbede26b8 and size 4.
```

So, what is happening in this example? Figure 5-3 illustrates the memory locations and the steps involved. In step 1, the variable y is created and assigned the initial value of 1000. A pointer p is then created with the dereference type of int. In essence, this means that the pointer p is being established to point at int values. In step 2, the statement p = &y; means "let p equal the address of y," which sets the value of p to be the 32-bit address 0xbede26bc. We now say that p is pointing at y. These two steps could have been combined using the call int *p = &y; (i.e., create a pointer p of dereference type int and assign it to the address of y).

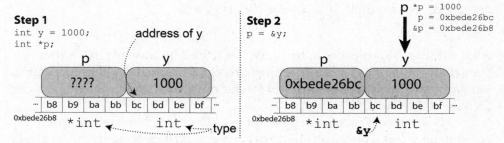

Figure 5-3: Example of pointers in C/C++ on a Beagle board (with 32-bit addressing)

Why does a pointer need a dereference type? For one example, if a pointer needs to move to the next element in an array, then it needs to know whether it should move by four bytes, eight bytes, etc. Also, in C++ you need to be able to know how to deal with the data at the pointer based on its type. Listing 5-13 is another example of working with pointers that explains how a simple error of intention can cause serious problems.

Listing 5-13: chp05/overview/pointers2.c

```c
#include<stdio.h>

int main(){
    int y  = 1000, z;
    int *p = &y;
    printf("The pointer  p has the value %d and address: %p\n", *p, p);
    // Let z = 1000 + 5 and the increment p and y to 1001 -- wrong!!!
    z = *p++ + 5;
    printf("The pointer  p has the value %d and address: %p\n", *p, p);
    printf("The variable z has the value %d\n", z);
    return 0;
}
```

This will give the output as follows:

```
debian@ebb:~/exploringbb/chp05/overview$ ./pointers2
The pointer  p has the value 1000 and address: 0xbeef357c
The pointer  p has the value 1005 and address: 0xbeef3580
The variable z has the value 1005
```

In this example, the pointer p is of dereference type int, and it is set to point at the address of y. At this point in the code the output is as expected, as p has the "value of" 1000 and the "address of" 0xbeef357c. On the next line the intention may have been to increase (post-increment) the value of y by 1 to 1001 and assign z a value of 1005 (i.e., before the post-increment takes place). However, perhaps contrary to your intention, p now has the "value of" 1005 and the "address of" 0xbeef3580.

Why has this occurred? Part of the difficulty of using pointers in C/C++ is understanding the order of operations in C/C++, called the *precedence* of the operations. For example, if you write the statement

```c
int x = 1 + 2 * 3;
```

what will the value of x be? In this case, it will be 7, because in C/C++ the multiplication operator has a higher level of precedence than the addition operator. Similarly, the problem in Listing 5-13 is your possible intention of using *p++ to increment the "value of" p by 1.

In C/C++ the post-increment operator (p++) has precedence over the dereference operator (*p). This means that *p++ actually post-increments the "address of" the pointer p by one int (i.e., 4 bytes), but before that, it is dereferenced (as 1000 in this example) so that it is added to 5 and assigned to z (as visible on the third output line). Most worrying is the second output line, as it is clear that p is now "pointing at" z, which just happens to be at the next address—it could actually refer to an address outside the program's memory allocation. Such errors of intention are difficult to debug without using the debugging tools that are described in Chapter 7. To fix the code to suit your intention, simply use (*p)++, which makes it clear that it is the "value of" p that should be post-incremented by 1, resulting in p having the "value of" 1001 and z having the value 1005. Should this change be applied, the pointer p would not increment its address.

There are approximately 58 operators in C++, with 18 different major precedence levels. Even if you know the precedence table, you should still make it clear for other users what you intend in a statement by using round brackets (()), which have the highest precedence level after the scope resolution (::), increment (++), and decrement (--) operators. Therefore, you should always write the following:

```
int x = 1 + (2 * 3);
```

Finally, on the topic of C pointers, there is also a *void* pointer* that can be declared as void *p;, which effectively states that the pointer p does not have a dereference type and it will need to be assigned at a later stage (see /chp05/ overview/void.c) using the following syntax:

```
int a = 5;
void *p = &a;
printf("p points at address %p and value %d\n", p, *((int *)p));
```

When executed, this code will give an output like the following:

```
The pointer p points at address 0xbea546c8 and value 5
```

Therefore, it is possible to cast a pointer from one dereference type to another, and the *void pointer* can potentially be used to store a pointer of any dereference type. In Chapter 6 void pointers are used to develop an enhanced GPIO interface.

C-Style Strings

The C language has no built-in string type but rather uses an array of the character type, terminated by the null character (\0), to represent a string. There is a standard C library for strings that can be used, as shown in Listing 5-14.

Listing 5-14: chp05/overview/cstrings.c

```
#include<stdio.h>
#include<string.h>
#include<stdlib.h>
```

```
int main(){
    char a[20] = "hello ";
    char b[] = {'w','o','r','l','d','!','\0'};  // the \0 is important

    a[0]='H';                          // set the first character to be H
    char *c = strcat(a,b);             // join/concatenate a and b
    printf("The string c is: %s\n", c);
    printf("The length of c is: %d\n", strlen(c));  // call string length

    // find and replace the w with a W
    char *p = strchr(c,'w');  // returns pointer to first 'w' char
    *p = 'W';
    printf("The string c is now: %s\n", c);

    if (strcmp("cat", "dog")<=0){      // ==0 would be equal
        printf("cat comes before dog (lexiographically)\n");
    }
    //insert "to the" into middle of "Hello World!" string - very messy!
    char *d = " to the";
    char *cd = malloc(strlen(c) + strlen(d));
    memcpy(cd, c, 5);
    memcpy(cd+5, d, strlen(d));
    memcpy(cd+5+strlen(d), c+5, 6);
    printf("The cd string is: %s\n", cd);

    //tokenize cd string using spaces
    p = strtok(cd," ");
    while(p!=NULL){
        printf("Token:%s\n", p);
        p = strtok(NULL, " ");
    }
    return 0;
}
```

The code is explained by the comments within the example. When executed, this code will give the following output:

```
/chp05/overview$ ./cstrings
The string c is: Hello world!
The length of c is: 12
The string c is now: Hello World!
cat comes before dog (lexiographically)
The cd string is: Hello to the World
Token:Hello
Token:to
Token:the
Token:World
```

LED Flashing Application in C

Now that you have covered enough C programming to get by, you can look at how to write the LED flashing application in C. In Listing 5-15 the same structure as the other examples has been retained.

Listing 5-15: chp05/makeLED/makeLED.c

```c
#include<stdio.h>
#include<stdlib.h>
#include<string.h>

#define LED3_PATH "/sys/class/leds/beaglebone:green:usr3"

void writeLED(char filename[], char value[]);  //function prototypes
void removeTrigger();

int main(int argc, char* argv[]){
   if(argc!=2){
        printf("Usage is makeLEDC and one of:\n");
        printf("  on, off, flash or status\n");
        printf(" e.g. makeLED flash\n");
        return 2;
   }
   printf("Starting the makeLED program\n");
   printf("The current LED Path is: " LED3_PATH "\n");

   // select whether command is on, off, flash or status
   if(strcmp(argv[1],"on")==0){
        printf("Turning the LED on\n");
        removeTrigger();
        writeLED("/brightness", "1");
   }
   else if (strcmp(argv[1],"off")==0){
        printf("Turning the LED off\n");
        removeTrigger();
        writeLED("/brightness", "0");
   }
   else if (strcmp(argv[1],"flash")==0){
        printf("Flashing the LED\n");
        writeLED("/trigger", "timer");
        writeLED("/delay_on", "50");
        writeLED("/delay_off", "50");
   }
   else if (strcmp(argv[1],"status")==0){
      FILE* fp;   // see writeLED function below for description
```

```
        char  fullFileName[100];
        char line[80];
        sprintf(fullFileName, LED3_PATH "/trigger");
        fp = fopen(fullFileName, "rt"); //reading text this time
        while (fgets(line, 80, fp) != NULL){
           printf("%s", line);
        }
        fclose(fp);
    }
    else{
        printf("Invalid command!\n");
    }
    printf("Finished the makeLED Program\n");
    return 0;
}

void writeLED(char filename[], char value[]){
    FILE* fp;    // create a file pointer fp
    char  fullFileName[100];  // to store the path and filename
    sprintf(fullFileName, LED3_PATH "%s", filename); // write path/name
    fp = fopen(fullFileName, "w+"); // open file for writing
    fprintf(fp, "%s", value);  // send the value to the file
    fclose(fp);  // close the file using the file pointer
}

void removeTrigger(){
   writeLED("/trigger", "none");
}
```

Build this program by calling the ./build script in the /chp05/makeLED/ directory, and execute it using ./makeLEDC on, ./makeLEDC off, etc.

The only topic that you have not seen before is the use of files in C, but the worked example should provide you with the information you need in the writeLED() function. The FILE pointer fp points to a description of the file that identifies the stream, the read/write position, and its state. The file is opened using the fopen() function that is defined in stdio.h, which returns a FILE pointer. In this case, it is being opened for write/update (w+). The alternatives would be as follows: read (r), write (w), append (a), read/update (r+), and append/update (a+). If you are working with binary files you would append a b to the state—e.g., w+b would open a new binary file for update (write and read). Also, t can be used to explicitly state that the file is in text format.

For a full reference of C functions available in the standard libraries, see www. cplusplus.com/reference/.

The C of C++

As discussed previously, the C++ language was built on the C language, adding support for OOP classes; however, a few other differences are immediately apparent when you start working with general C++ programming. Initially, the biggest change that you will notice is the use of input/output streams and the general use of strings.

First Example and Strings in C++

Listing 5-16 shows the string example, rewritten to use the C++ string library.

Listing 5-16: chp05/overview/cppstrings.cpp

```cpp
#include<iostream>
#include<sstream>      // to tokenize the string
//#include<cstring>    // C++ equivalent of C header if needed
using namespace std;

int main(){
   string a = "hello ";
   char temp[] = {'w','o','r','l','d','!','\0'};   //the \0 is important!
   string b(temp);

   a[0]='H';
   string c = a + b;
   cout << "The string c is: " << c << endl;
   cout << "The length of c is: " << c.length() << endl;

   int loc = c.find_first_of('w');
   c.replace(loc,1,1,'W');
   cout << "The string c is now: " << c << endl;

   if (string("cat")< string("dog")){
      cout << "cat comes before dog (lexiographically)\n";
   }
   c.insert(5," to the");
   cout << "The c string is now: " << c << endl;

   // tokenize string using spaces - could use Boost.Tokenizer
   // or C++11 to improve syntax. Using stringstream this time.
   stringstream ss;
   ss << c;  // put the c string on the stringstream
   string token;
   while(getline(ss, token, ' ')){
      cout << "Token: " << token << endl;
   }
   return 0;
}
```

Build this code by typing **g++ cppstrings.cpp -o cppstrings**. When executed, this code gives the same output as the `cstrings.c` example. Some aspects are more straightforward in C++, but there are some points worth mentioning.

The code uses the `iostream` and `sstream` header files, which are C++ headers. If you want to use a C header file, you need to prepend the name with a *c*; therefore, to use the C `string.h` header file you would use `#include<cstring>`. There is a concept called *namespaces* in C++ that enables a programmer to limit a function or class to a particular scope. In C++ all the standard library functions and classes are limited to the standard namespace. You can explicitly identify that you want to use a class from the `std` namespace by using `std::string`. However, that is quite verbose. The alternative is to use the statement `using namespace std;`, which brings the entire namespace into your code. Do *not* do this in one of your C++ header files, as it will pollute the namespace for anyone who uses your header file.

The code uses `cout`, which is the standard output stream, and the output stream operator (`<<`) to display strings. There is an equivalent standard input stream (`cin`) and the input stream operator (`>>`). The output stream operator "looks to" its right and identifies the type of the data. It will display the data depending on its type, so there is no need for `%s`, `%d`, `%p`, and so on, as you would use in the `printf()` function. The `endl` stream manipulation function inserts a newline character and flushes the stream.

The string objects are manipulated in this example using `+` to append two strings and using `<` or `==` to compare two strings. These operators are essentially functions like `append()` and `strcmp()`. In C++ you can define what these operators do for your own data types (operator overloading).

Passing by Value, Pointer, and Reference

As you have seen with the code samples, functions enable us to write a section of code that can be called several times, from different locations in our code. There are three key ways of passing a value to a function.

- **Pass by value:** This will create a new variable (`val` in the following code example) and will store a copy of the value of the source variable (`a`) in this new variable. Any changes to the variable `val` will not have any impact on the source variable `a`. Pass by value can be used if you want to prevent the original data from being modified; however, a copy of the data has to be made, and if you are passing a large array of data, such as an image, then copying will have a memory and computational cost. An alternative to pass by value is to *pass by constant reference*. In the following example, `a` is also passed as the second argument to the function by constant reference and is received as the value `cr`. The value `cr` can be read in the function, but it cannot be modified.

- **Pass by pointer:** You can pass a pointer to the source data. Any modifications to the value at the pointer (`ptr`) will affect the source data. The call to the function must pass an address (`&b`—address of `b`).

■ **Pass by reference:** In C++ you can pass a value by reference. The function determines whether an argument is to be passed by value or passed by reference, through the use of the ampersand symbol. In the following example, &ref indicates that the value c is to be passed by reference. Any modifications to ref in the function will affect the value of c.

Here is a function with all four examples (passing.cpp):

```cpp
int afunction(int val, const int &cr, int *ptr, int &ref){
   val+=cr;
// cr+=val; // not allowed because it is constant
   *ptr+=10;
   ref+=10;
   return val;
}

int main(){
   int a=100, b=200, c=300;
   int ret;
   ret = afunction(a, a, &b, c);
   cout << "The value of a = " << a << endl;
   cout << "The value of b = " << b << endl;
   cout << "The value of c = " << c << endl;
   cout << "The return value is = " << ret << endl;
   return 0;
}
```

When executed, this code will result in the following output:

```
/chp05/overview$ ./passing
The value of a = 100
The value of b = 210
The value of c = 310
The return value is = 200
```

If you want to pass a value to a function that is to be modified by that function in C++, then you can pass it by pointer or by reference; however, unless you are passing a value that could be NULL or you need to re-assign the pointer in the function (e.g., iterate over an array), then always use pass by reference. Now you are ready to write the LED code in C++!

Flashing the LEDs Using C++ (non-OO)

The C++ LED flashing code is available in makeLED.cpp in the /chp05/makeLED/ directory. As most of the code is similar to the C example, it is not repeated here. However, it is worth displaying the following segment, which is used to open the file using the fstream file stream class. The output stream operator

(<<) in this case sends the string to `fstream`, where the `c_str()` method returns a C++ `string` as a C `string`.

```
void writeLED(string filename, string value){
    fstream fs;
    string path(LED3_PATH);
    fs.open((path + filename).c_str(), fstream::out);
    fs << value;
    fs.close();
}
```

Writing a Multicall Binary

Multicall binaries can be used in Linux to build a single application that does the job of many (e.g., BusyBox in Linux that provides several system tools in a single executable file). There is an example in the `chp05/makeLEDmulti/` directory called `makeLEDmulti.cpp` that uses the first command-line argument to switch the functionality of the application based on the command name that was called. This code has been modified to add a small function:

```
bool endsWith(string const &in, string const &comp){
    return (0==in.compare(in.length()-comp.length(),comp.length(),comp));
}
```

This function checks to see whether the `in` string *ends with* the contents of the `comp` string. This is important because the application could be called using `./flashled` or `./chp05/makeLEDmulti/flashled`, depending on its location. The switching comparison then looks like the following:

```
if(endsWith(cmd,"onled")){
    cout << "Turning the LED on" << endl;
    removeTrigger();
    writeLED("/brightness", "1");
}
```

If you list the files in the directory after calling `./build`, you will see the following files and symbolic links:

```
debian@ebb:~/exploringbb/chp05/makeLEDmulti$ ls -l
-rwxr-xr-x 1 debian debian   542 May 13 00:14 build
lrwxrwxrwx 1 debian debian    12 May 14 04:42 flashled -> makeLEDmulti
lrwxrwxrwx 1 debian debian    12 May 14 04:42 ledstatus -> makeLEDmulti
-rwxr-xr-x 1 debian debian 15344 May 14 04:42 makeLEDmulti
-rw-r--r-- 1 debian debian  2474 May 13 00:14 makeLEDmulti.cpp
lrwxrwxrwx 1 debian debian    12 May 14 04:42 offled -> makeLEDmulti
lrwxrwxrwx 1 debian debian    12 May 14 04:42 onled -> makeLEDmulti
```

Each one of these symbolic links looks like an individual command, even though they link back to the same executable `makeLEDmulti`. The `makeLEDmulti` parses `argv[0]` to determine which symbolic link was used. You can see the impact of that here, where the symbolic links are called:

```
debian@ebb:~/exploringbb/chp05/makeLEDmulti$ ./onled
The current LED Path is: /sys/class/leds/beaglebone:green:usr3
... Turning the LED on ...
debian@ebb:~/exploringbb/chp05/makeLEDmulti$ ./ledstatus
... Current trigger details:
... [none] rc-feedback kbd-scrolllock ...
```

Overview of Object-Oriented Programming

Object-oriented programming is a programming approach that enables organizing software as a collection of objects, which consist of both data and behavior. In contrast to the functional programming examples you have seen to this point, you don't ask the question "What does it do?" first but rather "What is it?" In theory, this means your code is written to allow for future changes to the functionality, without having to redesign the structure of your code. In addition, it should also mean you can decompose your code into modules that can be reused by you and others in future projects.

The following discussion highlights a few core concepts that you need to understand before you can write object-oriented code. The discussion uses pseudocode as the concepts are relevant to all languages that support the OOP paradigm, including C++, Python, Rust, Lua tables, C#, Java, JavaScript, Perl, Ruby, the OOHaskell library, etc.

Classes and Objects

Think about the concept of a television: you do not need to remove the case to use it, as there are controls on the front and on the remote; you can still understand the television, even if it is connected to a games console; it is complete when you purchase it, with well-defined external requirements, such as power supply and signal inputs; and your television should not crash! In many ways that description captures the properties that should be present in a class.

A *class* is a description. It should describe a well-defined interface to your code; represent a clear concept; be complete and well documented; and be robust, with built-in error checking. Class descriptions are built using two building blocks.

- **States (or data):** The state values of the class.
- **Methods (or behavior):** How the class interacts with its data. Method names usually include an action verb (e.g., `setX()`).

For example, here is pseudocode (i.e., not real C++ code) for an illustrative Television class:

```
class Television{
    int channelNumber;
    bool on;
    powerOn() { on = true; }
    powerOff(){ on = false;}
    changeChannel(int x) { channelNumber = x; }
};
```

Therefore, the example Television class has two states and three methods. The benefit of this structure is that you have tightly bound the states and methods together within a class structure. The powerOn() method means nothing outside this class. In fact, you can write a powerOn() method in many different classes without worrying about naming collisions.

An *object* is the realization of the class description—an instance of a class. To continue the analogy, the Television class is the blueprint that describes how you would build a television, and a Television object is the physical realization of those plans into a physical television. In pseudocode this realization might look like this:

```
void main(){
    Television dereksTV();
    Television johnsTV();
    dereksTV.powerOn();
    dereksTV.changeChannel(52);
    johnsTV.powerOn();
    johnsTV.changeChannel(1);
}
```

Therefore, dereksTV and johnsTV are objects of the Television class. Each has its own independent state, so changing the channel on dereksTV has no impact on johnsTV. To call a method, it must be prefixed by the object name on which it is to be called (e.g., johnsTV.powerOn()); calling the changeChannel() method on johnsTV objects does not have any impact on the dereksTV object.

In this book, a class name generally begins with a capital letter, e.g., Television, and an object generally begins with a lowercase letter, e.g., dereksTV. This is consistent with the notation used in many languages, such as Java. Unfortunately, the C++ standard library classes (e.g., string, sstream) do not follow this naming convention.

Encapsulation

Encapsulation is used to hide the mechanics of an object. In the physical television analogy, encapsulation is provided by the box that protects the inner electronic systems. However, you still have the remote control that will have a direct impact on the way the inner workings function.

In OOP, you can decide what workings are to be hidden (e.g., TV electronics) using an *access specifier* keyword called *private* and what is to be part of the *interface* (TV remote control) using the access specifier keyword *public*. It is good practice to always set the states of your class to be private so that you can control how they are modified by public interface methods of your own design. For example, the pseudocode might become the following:

```
class Television{
   private:
      int channelNumber;
      bool on;
      remodulate_tuner();
   public:
      powerOn() { on = true; }
      powerOff(){ on = false;}
      changeChannel(int x) {
         channelNumber = x;
         remodulate_tuner();
      }
};
```

Now the `Television` class has private state data (`on`, `channelNumber`) that is affected only by the public interface methods (`powerOn()`, `powerOff()`, `changeChannel()`) and a private implementation method `remodulate_tuner()` that cannot be called from outside the class.

There are a number of advantages of this approach. First, users of this class (another programmer) need not understand the inner workings of the `Television` class; they just need to understand the public interface. Second, the author of the `Television` class can modify and/or perfect the inner workings of the class without affecting other programmers' code.

Inheritance

Inheritance is a feature of OOP that enables building class descriptions from other class descriptions. Humans do this all the time; for example, if you were asked, "What is a duck?" you might respond with, "It's a bird that swims, and it has a bill instead of a beak." This description is reasonably accurate, but it assumes that the concept of a bird is also understood. Importantly, the description states that the duck has the *additional behavior* of swimming but also that it has the *replacement behavior* of having a bill instead of a beak. You could loosely code this with pseudocode as follows:

```
class Bird{
   public:
      void fly();
      void describe() { cout << "Has a beak and can fly"; }
};
```

```
class Duck: public Bird{    // Duck IS-A Bird
    Bill bill;
  public:
    void swim();
    void describe() { cout << "Has a bill and can fly and swim"; }
};
In this case, you can create an object of the Duck class:
int main(){
    Duck d;         //creates the Duck instance object d
    d.swim();       //specific to the Duck class
    d.fly();        //inherited from the parent Bird class
    d.describe();   //describe() is inherited and overridden in Duck
                    //so, "Has a bill and can fly and swim" would appear
}
```

The example here illustrates why inheritance is so important. You can build code by inheriting from, and adding to, a class description (e.g., swim()) or inheriting from a parent class and replacing a behavior (e.g., describe()) to provide a more specific implementation—this is called *overriding* a method, which is a type of *polymorphism* (multiple forms). Another form of polymorphism is called *overloading*, which means multiple methods can have the same name, in the same class, disambiguated by the compiler by having different parameter types.

You can check that you have an inheritance relationship by the *IS-A* test; for example, a "duck is a bird" is valid, but a "bird is a duck" would be invalid because not all birds are ducks. This contrasts to the *IS-A-PART-OF* relationship; for example, a "bill is a part of a duck." An IS-A-PART-OF relationship indicates that the bill is a member/state of the class. Using this simple check can be useful when the class relationships become complex.

You can also use pointers with objects of a class; for example, to dynamically allocate memory for two Duck objects, you can use the following:

```
int main(){
    Duck *a = new Duck();
    Bird *b = new Duck(); //parent pointer can point to a child object
    b->describe();        //will actually describe a duck (if virtual)
    //b->swim();          //not allowed! Bird does not 'know' swim()
}
```

Interestingly, the Bird pointer b is permitted to point at a Duck object. As the Duck class is a child of a Bird class, all of the methods that the Bird pointer can call are "known" by the Duck object. Therefore, the describe() method can be called. The arrow notation (b->describe()) is simply a neater way of writing (*b).describe(). In this case, the Bird pointer b has the *static type* Bird and the *dynamic type* Duck.

One last point is that an additional access specifier called *protected* can be used through inheritance. If you want to create a method or state in the parent class that you want to be available to the child class but you do not want to make public, then use the protected access specifier.

NOTE   I have notes publicly available at ee402.eeng.dcu.ie on these topics. In particular, Chapters 3 and 4 describe this topic in much greater detail, including material on abstract classes, destructors, multiple inheritance, friend functions, and the standard template library (STL).

Object-Oriented LED Flashing Code

These OOP concepts can now be applied to a real C++ application on the Beagle boards by restructuring the functionally oriented C++ code into a class called LED, which contains states and methods. One difference with the code that is presented in Listing 5-17 is that it allows you to control the four user LEDs using the same OO code. Therefore, using the LED class, four different LED instance objects are created, each controlling one of the board's four physical user LEDs.

Listing 5-17: chp05/makeLEDOOP/makeLEDs.cpp

```cpp
#include<iostream>
#include<fstream>
#include<string>
#include<sstream>
using namespace std;

#define LED_PATH "/sys/class/leds/beaglebone:green:usr"

class LED{
   private:
      string path;
      int number;
      virtual void writeLED(string filename, string value);
      virtual void removeTrigger();
   public:
      LED(int number);
      virtual void turnOn();
      virtual void turnOff();
      virtual void flash(string delayms);
      virtual void outputState();
      virtual ~LED();
};

LED::LED(int number){
   this->number = number;     // set number state to be the number passed
```

```
      // next part is easier with C++11 (see Chp.7) using to_string(number)
      ostringstream s;            // using a stream to contruct the path
      s << LED_PATH << number;   // append LED number to LED_PATH
      path = string(s.str());    // convert back from stream to string
}

void LED::writeLED(string filename, string value){
      ofstream fs;
      fs.open((path + filename).c_str());
      fs << value;
      fs.close();
}

void LED::removeTrigger(){
      writeLED("/trigger", "none");
}

void LED::turnOn(){
      cout << "Turning LED" << number << " on." << endl;
      removeTrigger();
      writeLED("/brightness", "1");
}

void LED::turnOff(){
      cout << "Turning LED" << number << " off." << endl;
      removeTrigger();
      writeLED("/brightness", "0");
}

void LED::flash(string delayms = "50"){
      cout << "Making LED" << number << " flash." << endl;
      writeLED("/trigger", "timer");
      writeLED("/delay_on", delayms);
      writeLED("/delay_off", delayms);
}

void LED::outputState(){
      ifstream fs;
      fs.open( (path + "/trigger").c_str());
      string line;
      while(getline(fs,line)) cout << line << endl;
      fs.close();
}

LED::~LED(){    // A destructor - called when the object is destroyed
      cout << "destroying the LED with path: " << path << endl;
}

int main(int argc, char* argv[]){
      if(argc!=2){
            cout << "Usage is makeLEDs <command>" << endl;
```

```
            cout << "  command is one of: on, off, flash or status" << endl;
            cout << " e.g. makeLEDs flash" << endl;
    }
    cout << "Starting the makeLEDs program" << endl;
    string cmd(argv[1]);

    // Create four LED objects and put them in an array
    LED leds[4] = { LED(0), LED(1), LED(2), LED(3) };

    // Do the same operation on all four LEDs - easily changed!
    for(int i=0; i<=3; i++){
        if(cmd=="on")leds[i].turnOn();
        else if(cmd=="off")leds[i].turnOff();
        else if(cmd=="flash")leds[i].flash("100"); //default is "50"
        else if(cmd=="status")leds[i].outputState();
        else{ cout << "Invalid command!" << endl; }
    }
    cout << "Finished the makeLEDs program" << endl;
    return 0;
}
```

This code can be built and executed by typing the following:

```
/chp05/makeLEDOOP$ ./build
/chp05/makeLEDOOP$ ./makeLEDs status
/chp05/makeLEDOOP$ sudo ./makeLEDs flash
/chp05/makeLEDOOP$ sudo ./makeLEDs off
```

There are scripts in the directory /chp05/ to return the LEDs to their standard state, called restoreLEDsBeagleBone and restoreLEDsPocketBeagle:

```
/chp05$ sudo ./restoreLEDsBeagleBone
/chp05$ sudo ./restoreLEDsPocketBeagle
```

This code is structured as a single class LED with private states for the path and the number, and private implementation methods writeLED() and removeTrigger(). These states and helper methods are not accessible outside the class. The public interface methods are turnOn(), turnOff(), flash(), and outputState(). There are two more public methods.

- The first is a *constructor*, which enables you to initialize the state of the object. It is called by LED led(0) to create the object led of the LED class with number 0. This is similar to the way you assign initial values to an int, e.g., int x = 5;. A constructor must have the same name as the class name (LED in this case), and it cannot return anything, not even void.

- The last is a *destructor* (~LED()). Like a constructor, it must have the same name as the class name and is prefixed by the tilde (~) character. This method is called automatically when the object is being destroyed. You can see this happening when you run the code sample.

The keyword *virtual* is also new. You can think of this keyword as "allowing overriding to take place when an object is dynamically bound." It should always be there (except for the constructor), unless you know that there will definitely be no child class. Removing the `virtual` keyword will result in a slight improvement in the performance of your code.

The syntax `void LED::turnOn(){...}` is simply used to state that the `turnOn()` method is the one associated with the LED class. It is possible to have many classes in the one `.cpp` file, and it would be possible for two classes to have a `turnOn()` method; therefore, the explicit association allows you to inform the compiler of the correct relationship. I have written this code in a single file, as it is the first example. However, you will see in later examples that it is better practice to break your code into *header* files (`.h`) and *implementation* files (`.cpp`).

Ideally the layout of the C++ version of the LED flashing code is clear at this point. The advantage of this OOP version is that you now have a structure that can be built upon when you want to provide additional functionality to interact with the system LEDs. In a later chapter, you will see how you can build similar structures to wrap electronic modules such as accelerometers and temperature sensors and how to use the encapsulation property of OOP to hide some of the more complex calculations from programmers who interface to the code.

Interfacing to the Linux OS

In Chapter 3, the Linux directory structure is discussed, and one of the directories discussed is the `/proc/` directory—the process information virtual file system. It provides you with information about the run-time state of the kernel, and it enables you to send control information to the kernel. In effect, it provides you with a file-based interface from user space to kernel space. There is a Linux kernel guide to the `/proc/` file system at `tiny.cc/beagle502`. For example, if you type the following:

```
debian@ebb:/proc$ cat cpuinfo
processor       : 0
model name      : ARMv7 Processor rev 2 (v7l)
BogoMIPS        : 995.32
Features        : half thumb fastmult vfp edsp thumbee neon vfpv3 tls vfpd32
CPU implementer : 0x41
CPU architecture: 7
CPU variant     : 0x3
CPU part        : 0xc08
CPU revision    : 2       ...
```

it provides you with information on the CPU. Try some of the following: `cat uptime`, `cat interrupts`, `cat version` in the same directory. The example, chp05/proc/readUptime.cpp, provides an example program to read the system uptime and calculate the percentage of system idle time.

Many /proc/ entries can be read by programs that execute with regular user accounts; however, many entries can be written to only by a program with superuser privileges. For example, entries in /proc/sys/kernel/ enable you to configure the parameters of a Linux kernel as it is executing.

You need to be careful with the consistency of the files in /proc/. The Linux kernel provides for *atomic* operations—instructions that execute without interruption. Certain "files" within /proc/ (such as /proc/uptime) are totally atomic and cannot be interrupted while these are being read; however, other files such as /proc/net/tcp are atomic only within each row of the file, meaning that the file will change as it is being read, and therefore simply reading the file may not provide a consistent snapshot.

Glibc and Syscall

The Linux GNU C library, *glibc*, provides an extensive set of wrapper functions for system calls. It includes functionality for handling files, signals, mathematics, processes, users, and much more. See tiny.cc/beagle503 for a full description of the GNU C library.

It is much more straightforward to call a glibc function than it is to parse the equivalent /proc/ entries. Listing 5-18 provides a C++ example that uses the glibc passwd structure to find out information about the current user. It also uses the syscall() function directly to determine the user's ID and to change the access permissions of a file—see the comments in the listing.

Listing 5-18: /exploringbb/chp05/syscall/glibcTest.cpp

```
#include<gnu/libc-version.h>
#include<sys/syscall.h>
#include<sys/types.h>
#include<pwd.h>
#include<cstdlib>
#include<sys/stat.h>
#include<iostream>
#include<signal.h>
#include<unistd.h>
using namespace std;

int main(){
    // Use helper functions to get system information:
    cout << "GNU libc version is: " << gnu_get_libc_version() << endl;

    // Use glibc passwd struct to get user information - no error check!:
    struct passwd *pass = getpwuid(getuid());
```

```
cout << "The current user's login is: " << pass->pw_name << endl;
cout << "-> their full name is: " << pass->pw_gecos << endl;
cout << "-> their user ID is: ". << pass->pw_uid << endl;

// You can use the getenv() function to get environment variables
cout << "The user's shell is: " << getenv("SHELL") << endl;
cout << "The user's path is: "  << getenv("PATH") << endl;

// An example syscall to call a get the user ID -- see sys/syscall.h
int uid = syscall(0xc7);
cout << "Syscall gives their user ID as: " << uid << endl;

// Call chmod directly -- type "man 2 chmod" for more information
int ret = chmod("test.txt", 0666);
// Can use syscall to do the same thing
ret  = syscall(SYS_chmod, "test.txt", 0666);
return 0;
}
```

This code can be tested as follows, where you can see that the file permissions are altered by the program, and the current user's information is displayed:

```
.../chp05/syscall$ touch test.txt
.../chp05/syscall$ chmod 644 test.txt
.../chp05/syscall$ ls -l test.txt
-rw-r--r-- 1 debian debian 0 May 15 03:40 test.txt
.../chp05/syscall$ sudo usermod -c "Exploring BeagleBone" debian
.../chp05/syscall$ g++ glibcTest.cpp -o glibcTest
.../chp05/syscall$ ./glibcTest
GNU libc version is: 2.24
The current user's login is: debian
-> their full name is: Exploring BeagleBone
-> their user ID is: 1000
The user's shell is: /bin/bash
The user's path  is: /home/debian/bin:/usr/local/sbin:/usr/...
Syscall gives their user ID as: 1000
.../chp05/syscall$ ls -l test.txt
-rw-rw-rw- 1 debian debian 0 May 15 03:40 test.txt
```

There are many glibc functions, but the syscall() function requires special attention. It performs a generalized system call using the arguments that you pass to the function. The first argument is a system call number, as defined in /sys/syscall.h—you will need to follow through the header includes files to find the definitions. Alternatively, you can use syscalls.kernelgrok.com to search for definitions (e.g., search for SYS_getuid and you will see that the register eax = 0xc7, as used in Listing 5-18). Clearly, it is better if you use SYS_getuid instead.

Improving the Performance of Python

Despite the popularity of Python, it is clear from Table 5-1 that if you are to use it for certain embedded applications that you may need enhanced performance. This section describes two alternative approaches for addressing the performance issue by investigating Cython, as well as an alternative approach of extending Python with C/C++ code using Boost.Python.

Regardless of the approach taken, the first step is to set up your board so that you build a C/C++ module. You do this by installing the Python development package for the exact version of Python that you are using. Adapt the instructions in this section to use the library versions that you identify using the following steps:

```
debian@ebb:~$ python --version
Python 2.7.13
debian@ebb:~$ python3 --version
Python 3.5.3
debian@ebb:~$ sudo apt install python3-dev
debian@ebb:~$ sudo apt install python-dev
debian@ebb:~$ ls /usr/lib/arm-linux-gnueabihf/libpython*.so
/usr/lib/arm-linux-gnueabihf/libpython2.7.so
/usr/lib/arm-linux-gnueabihf/libpython3.5m.so
```

Cython

Cython is an optimizing compiler for Python and a language that extends Python with C-style functionality. Typically, the Cython compiler uses your Python code to generate efficient C shared libraries, which you can then import into other Python programs. However, to get the maximum benefit from Cython you must adapt your Python code to use Cython-specific syntax. The top-performing Cython entry in Table 5-1 (i.e., at 1.97×) is available at `/performance/cython_opt/nbody.pyx`. If you inspect the code, you will see the use of `cdef` C variable declarations and various variable types (e.g., `double`, `int`), which indicates the removal of dynamic typing from the base Python version (`/performance/n-body.py`).

A concise example is developed here to describe the first steps involved in adapting Python code to create Cython code. The example code proves the relationship $\int_0^\pi \sin(x)dx = 2$ by applying a simple numerical integration approach, as provided in Listing 5-19.

Listing 5-19: /chp05/cython/test.py

```
from math import sin
def integrate_sin(a,b,N):
```

```
dx = (b-a)/N
sum = 0
for i in range(0,N):
    sum += sin(a+i*dx)
return sum*dx
```

The code in Listing 5-19 can be executed directly within the Python interpreter as follows (use `exec(open("test.py").read())` under Python3):

```
debian@ebb:~/exploringbb/chp05/cython$ python
Python 2.7.13 (default, Nov 24 2017, 17:33:09)
>>> from math import pi
>>> execfile('test.py')
>>> integrate_sin(0,pi,1000)
1.9999983550656624
>>> integrate_sin(0,pi,1000000)
1.9999999999984077
```

And, a timer can be introduced to evaluate its performance.

```
>>> import timeit
>>> print(timeit.timeit("integrate_sin(0,3.14159,1000000)",setup  →
="from __main__ import integrate_sin", number=10))
66.1992490292
>>> quit()
```

The `timeit` module allows you to determine the execution duration of a function call. In this example, the PocketBeagle takes 66 seconds to evaluate the function 10 times, with N equal to 1,000,000.

It is possible to get a report on computationally costly dynamic Python behavior within your source code using the following:

```
debian@ebb:~/exploringbb/chp05/cython$ sudo apt install cython
debian@ebb:~/exploringbb/chp05/cython$ cython -a test.py
debian@ebb:~/exploringbb/chp05/cython$ ls -l *.html
-rw-r--r-- 1 debian debian 30610 May 17 01:27 test.html
```

The darker the shade of yellow on a line in the HTML report, the greater the level of dynamic behavior that is taking place on that line.

NOTE   If you have both Python2 and Python3 installed, you may need to install Cython for Python3 as follows (this appears to hang, but leave it run because it can take more than 20 minutes to install):

```
debian@ebb:~$ sudo apt install python3-pip
debian@ebb:~$ sudo pip3 install cython
```

Cython supports static type definitions, which greatly improves the performance of the code. The code can be adapted to `test.pyx` in Listing 5-20 where the types of the variables and return types are explicitly defined.

Listing 5-20: /chp05/cython/test.pyx

```
cdef extern from "math.h":
    double sin(double x)

cpdef double integrate_sin(double a, double b, int N):
    cdef double dx, s
    cdef int i
    dx = (b-a)/N
    sum = 0
    for i in range(0,N):
        sum += sin(a+i*dx)
    return sum*dx
```

An additional configuration file `setup.py` is required, as provided in Listing 5-21, so that Cython can compile the module correctly.

Listing 5-21: /chp05/cython/setup.py

```
from distutils.core import setup
from distutils.extension import Extension
from Cython.Distutils import build_ext

ext_modules = [Extension("test", ["test.pyx"])]
setup(
    name = 'random number sum application',
    cmdclass = {'build_ext' : build_ext },
    ext_modules = ext_modules
)
```

Python can use the `setup.py` configuration file to directly build the `test.pyx` file into C code (`test.c`), which is then compiled and linked to create a shared library (`test.so`). The library code can be executed directly within Python as follows, where the execution duration is 49 seconds—an improvement in performance.

```
.../chp05/cython$ python setup.py build_ext --inplace
running build_ext...
.../chp05/cython$ ls
build  setup.py  test.c  test.html  test.py  test.pyx  test.so
.../chp05/cython$ python
Python 2.7.13 (default, Nov 24 2017, 17:33:09)
>>> import timeit
>>> print(timeit.timeit("test.integrate_sin(0,3.14159,1000000)",  →
setup="import test",number=10))
49.4493851662
```

Cython goes some way to addressing performance concerns that you may have in using Python; however, there is a significant learning curve in adapting Python code for efficiency, which has only been touched upon here. An alternative approach is to write custom C/C++ code modules that add to the capability of Python, rather than using Cython at all.

Boost.Python

An alternative approach is to extend Python with a wrapper that binds C/C++ and Python called *Boost.Python*, which essentially wraps the Python/C API. In addition, it simplifies the syntax and provides support for calls to C++ objects. You can search for the latest release and install Boost.Python on your board using the following steps (~119MB):

```
debian@ebb:~$ apt-cache search libboost-python
libboost-python-dev - Boost.Python Library development files (default
version)
libboost-python1.62-dev - Boost.Python Library development files
libboost-python1.62.0 - Boost.Python Library
debian@ebb:~$ sudo apt install libboost-python1.62-dev
```

A C++ program can be developed as in Listing 5-22 that uses the Boost.Python library and its special BOOST_PYTHON_MODULE(name) macro that declares the Python module initialization functions—essentially replacing the verbose syntax that is present in Listing 5-21.

Listing 5-22: /chp05/boost/ebb.cpp

```cpp
#include<string>
#include<boost/python.hpp>         // .hpp convention for c++ headers
using namespace std;               // just like cpp for source files

namespace exploringbb{             // keep the global namespace clean

    string hello(string name) {    // e.g., returns "Hello Derek!"
       return ("Hello " + name + "!");
    }

    double integrate(double a, double b, int n) {    // same as before
       double sum=0, dx = (b-a)/n;
       for(int i=0; i<n; i++){  sum += sin((a+i)*dx);  }
       return sum*dx;
    }
}

BOOST_PYTHON_MODULE(ebb){          // the module is called ebb
   using namespace boost::python;  // require the boost.python namespace
```

```
    using namespace exploringbb;      // bring in custom namespace
    def("hello", hello);              // make hello() visible to Python
    def("integrate", integrate);      // make integrate() also visible
}
```

The code can be built into a shared library as before. Make sure to include the `boost_python` library in the build options.

```
.../chp05/boost$ g++ -O3 ebb.cpp -fPIC -shared -I/usr/include/ →
python2.7/-lpython2.7 -lboost_python -o ebb.so
.../chp05/boost$ ls -l *.so
-rwxr-xr-x 1 debian debian 30092 May 17 01:56 ebb.so
```

The library can then be used by a Python script, such as that in Listing 5-23.

Listing 5-23: /chp05/boost/test.py

```
#!/usr/bin/python
# A Python program that calls C program code
import ebb

print "Start of the Python program"
print ebb.hello("Derek")
val = ebb.integrate(0, 3.14159, 1000000)
print "The integral result is: ", val
print "End of the Python program"
```

The script in Listing 5-23 can be executed, resulting in the following output:

```
debian@ebb:~/exploringbb/chp05/boost$ ./test.py
Start of the Python program
Hello Derek!
The integral result is:  1.99999999999
End of the Python program
```

The code can be executed directly within Python as follows, where the execution duration is 6.7 seconds—a significant improvement in performance.

```
debian@ebb:~/exploringbb/chp05/boost$ python
>>> import timeit
>>> print(timeit.timeit("ebb.integrate(0, 3.14159, →
1000000)",setup="import ebb",number=10))
6.69945406914
```

Despite its large footprint, Boost.Python is the recommended approach for integrating C/C++ and Python code because of its performance, simplified syntax, and support for C++ classes. See `tiny.cc/beagle504` for further details.

Summary

After completing this chapter, you should be able to

- Describe the multitude of issues that would impact on your choice of programming languages to use in building applications for the Beagle platform
- Write basic scripting language program code on your board that interfaces to the on-board LEDs
- Compare and contrast scripting, hybrid, and compiled programming languages, and their application to the embedded Linux applications
- Write C code examples that interface to the Beagle board's on-board LEDs
- Wrap C code in C++ classes to provide greater program structure
- Write advanced C/C++ code that is capable of interfacing to Linux operating system commands
- Write C/C++ modules that can be called directly from Python

Further Reading

Most of the sections in this chapter contain links to the relevant websites for further reading and reference materials. Here is a list of some books on programming that are relevant to the materials in this chapter:

- *Bad to the Bone: Crafting Electronics Systems with BeagleBone Black*, Steven Barrett and Jason Kridner (Morgan & Claypool, 2015)
- *BeagleBone Cookbook: Software and Hardware Problems and Solutions*, Mark A. Yoder and Jason Kridner (O'Reilly Media, 2015)
- *BeagleBone for Dummies*, Rui Santos and Luís Miguel Costa Perestrelo (Wiley, 2015)

Bibliography

- debian.org. (2013, 12 1). The Computer Language Benchmarks Game. Retrieved 5 17, 2018, from Debian.org: `benchmarksgame.alioth.debian.org`
- Hundt, R. (2011). Loop Recognition in C++/Java/Go/Scala. Proceedings of Scala Days 2011. Mountain View, CA.: `www.scala-lang.org`.
- Stroustrup, B. (1998, 10 14). International standard for the C++ programming language published. Retrieved 5 17, 2018, from www.stroustrup.com: `www.stroustrup.com/iso_pressrelease2.html`

Interfacing, Controlling, and Communicating

In This Part

Chapter 6: Interfacing to the Beagle Board Input/Outputs
Chapter 7: Cross-Compilation, Eclipse, and Building Linux
Chapter 8: Interfacing to the Beagle Board Buses
Chapter 9: Interacting with the Physical Environment
Chapter 10: Real-Time Interfacing Using External Slave Processors

Interfacing to the Beagle Board Input/Outputs

This chapter integrates the Linux, programming, and electronics groundwork from earlier chapters to show you how to build circuits and write programs that interface to Beagle board single-wire inputs and outputs. In this chapter, you will see practical examples that explain how to use a general-purpose input/output (GPIO) to output a binary signal to switch on an LED or to read in a binary input from a push button. Optocoupler circuits are discussed so that you can safely interface to externally powered circuits. Also included are the steps required to read in an analog input and to send out a pulse-width modulated (PWM) output. GPIO interfacing is first performed using sysfs to ensure that you have skills that are transferrable to other embedded Linux devices. Next, BoneScript and memory-mapped approaches are investigated, which are largely specific to the AM335x SoC. Finally, there is a brief discussion on the impact of udev rules and Linux permissions on GPIO interfacing.

EQUIPMENT REQUIRED FOR THIS CHAPTER:

- BeagleBone or PocketBeagle SBC
- General components from Chapter 4 and a generic light-dependent resistor
- Hitec HS-422 Servo Motor (or equivalent)

Further details on this chapter are available at www.exploringbeaglebone.com/chapter6/.

General-Purpose Input/Outputs

At this point in the book, you have seen how to administrate a Linux system, write high-level programming code, and build basic but realistic electronic interfacing circuits. It is now time to bring those different concepts together so that you can build software applications that run on Linux to control, or take input from, electronics circuits of your own design.

Introduction to GPIO Interfacing

It is possible to interface electronic circuits and modules to the Beagle boards in several different ways. Here are some examples:

- **Using the GPIOs on the expansion headers:** This provides you with versatility in terms of the type of circuits that you can connect and is the subject of this chapter.

- **Using the buses (e.g., I²C, SPI, CAN Bus), or UARTs on the expansion headers:** Bus connections enable communications to complex modules such as sensors and displays. This topic is discussed in Chapter 8.

- **Connecting USB modules (e.g., keyboards, Wi-Fi):** If Linux drivers are available, many different electronic device types can be connected to a Beagle board. Examples are provided throughout later chapters.

- **Communicating through Ethernet/Wi-Fi/Bluetooth/ZigBee to electronics modules:** It is possible to build network-attached sensors that communicate to the Beagle boards using network connections. Chapter 11 and Chapter 12 focus on this topic.

The next step in working with a Beagle board is to connect it to circuits using the GPIOs and analog inputs of the expansion headers (as illustrated in Figure 1-5 and Figure 1-6 of Chapter 1). The background material of earlier chapters is important, as this is a surprisingly complex topic that will take some time to get used to, particularly the content on the Linux device tree and pin multiplexing. However, code and example circuits are provided throughout this chapter that you can use to help you build your own circuits.

Figure 6-1 provides you with a first view of the functionality of the inputs and outputs on the BeagleBone's P8 and P9 headers. Many of these pins are *multiplexed*, meaning they have many more functions than what is displayed in the figure. The name listed typically describes the default operation of the pin. An equivalent figure is provided for the PocketBeagle P1 and P2 headers in Figure 6-2.

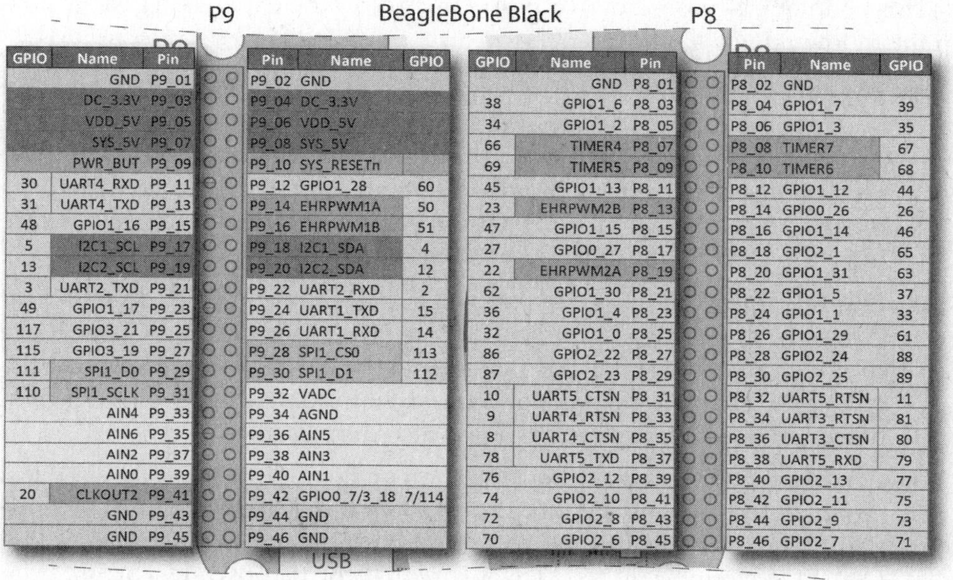

P9 — BeagleBone Black — P8

P9

GPIO	Name	Pin	Pin	Name	GPIO
	GND	P9_01	P9_02	GND	
	DC_3.3V	P9_03	P9_04	DC_3.3V	
	VDD_5V	P9_05	P9_06	VDD_5V	
	SYS_5V	P9_07	P9_08	SYS_5V	
	PWR_BUT	P9_09	P9_10	SYS_RESETn	
30	UART4_RXD	P9_11	P9_12	GPIO1_28	60
31	UART4_TXD	P9_13	P9_14	EHRPWM1A	50
48	GPIO1_16	P9_15	P9_16	EHRPWM1B	51
5	I2C1_SCL	P9_17	P9_18	I2C1_SDA	4
13	I2C2_SCL	P9_19	P9_20	I2C2_SDA	12
3	UART2_TXD	P9_21	P9_22	UART2_RXD	2
49	GPIO1_17	P9_23	P9_24	UART1_TXD	15
117	GPIO3_21	P9_25	P9_26	UART1_RXD	14
115	GPIO3_19	P9_27	P9_28	SPI1_CS0	113
111	SPI1_DO	P9_29	P9_30	SPI1_D1	112
110	SPI1_SCLK	P9_31	P9_32	VADC	
	AIN4	P9_33	P9_34	AGND	
	AIN6	P9_35	P9_36	AIN5	
	AIN2	P9_37	P9_38	AIN3	
	AIN0	P9_39	P9_40	AIN1	
20	CLKOUT2	P9_41	P9_42	GPIO0_7/3_18	7/114
	GND	P9_43	P9_44	GND	
	GND	P9_45	P9_46	GND	

P8

GPIO	Name	Pin	Pin	Name	GPIO
	GND	P8_01	P8_02	GND	
38	GPIO1_6	P8_03	P8_04	GPIO1_7	39
34	GPIO1_2	P8_05	P8_06	GPIO1_3	35
66	TIMER4	P8_07	P8_08	TIMER7	67
69	TIMER5	P8_09	P8_10	TIMER6	68
45	GPIO1_13	P8_11	P8_12	GPIO1_12	44
23	EHRPWM2B	P8_13	P8_14	GPIO0_26	26
47	GPIO1_15	P8_15	P8_16	GPIO1_14	46
27	GPIO0_27	P8_17	P8_18	GPIO2_1	65
22	EHRPWM2A	P8_19	P8_20	GPIO1_31	63
62	GPIO1_30	P8_21	P8_22	GPIO1_5	37
36	GPIO1_4	P8_23	P8_24	GPIO1_1	33
32	GPIO1_0	P8_25	P8_26	GPIO1_29	61
86	GPIO2_22	P8_27	P8_28	GPIO2_24	88
87	GPIO2_23	P8_29	P8_30	GPIO2_25	89
10	UART5_CTSN	P8_31	P8_32	UART5_RTSN	11
9	UART4_RTSN	P8_33	P8_34	UART3_RTSN	81
8	UART4_CTSN	P8_35	P8_36	UART3_CTSN	80
78	UART5_TXD	P8_37	P8_38	UART5_RXD	79
76	GPIO2_12	P8_39	P8_40	GPIO2_13	77
74	GPIO2_10	P8_41	P8_42	GPIO2_11	75
72	GPIO2_8	P8_43	P8_44	GPIO2_9	73
70	GPIO2_6	P8_45	P8_46	GPIO2_7	71

USB

Figure 6-1: The BeagleBone P8/P9 headers with pin names, which describe each pin's default functionality

P1 — PocketBeagle — P2

P1

GPIO	Name	Pin	Pin	Name	GPIO
	VIN	P1.01	P1.02	AIN6/GPIO87	87
109	USB1-DRVVBUS	P1.03	P1.04	PRU1.11	89
	USB1-VBUS	P1.05	P1.06	SPI0-CS	5
	VIN-USB	P1.07	P1.08	SPI0-CLK	2
	USB1-DN	P1.09	P1.10	SPI0-MISO	3
	USB1-DP	P1.11	P1.12	SPI0-MOSI	4
	USB1-ID	P1.13	P1.14	VOUT (3.3V)	
	GND	P1.15	P1.16	GND	
	VREFN	P1.17	P1.18	VREFP	
	AIN0 (1.8V)	P1.19	P1.20	PRU0.16	20
	AIN1 (1.8V)	P1.21	P1.22	GND	
	AIN2 (1.8V)	P1.23	P1.24	VOUT (5V)	
	AIN3 (1.8V)	P1.25	P1.26	I2C2-SDA	12
	AIN4 (1.8V)	P1.27	P1.28	I2C2-SCL	13
117	PRU0.7	P1.29	P1.30	UART0-TX	43
114	PRU0.4	P1.31	P1.32	UART0-RX	42
111	PRU0.1	P1.33	P1.34	GPIO0.26	26
88	PRU1.10	P1.35	P1.36	PWM0A	110

P2

GPIO	Name	Pin	Pin	Name	GPIO
50	PWM1A	P2.01	P2.02	GPIO1.27	59
23	GPIO0.23	P2.03	P2.04	GPIO1.26	58
30	UART4-RX	P2.05	P2.06	GPIO1.25	57
31	UART4-TX	P2.07	P2.08	GPIO1.28	60
15	I2C1-SCL	P2.09	P2.10	GPIO1.20	52
14	I2C1-SDA	P2.11	P2.12	POWER_BTN	
	VOUT (5V)	P2.13	P2.14	VIN-BAT	
	GND	P2.15	P2.16	BAT-TEMP	
65	GPIO2.1	P2.17	P2.18	PRU0.15i	47
27	GPIO0.27	P2.19	P2.20	GPIO2.0	64
	GND	P2.21	P2.22	GPIO1.14	46
	VOUT (3.3V)	P2.23	P2.24	GPIO1.12	44
41	SPI1-MOSI	P2.25	P2.26	NRESET	
40	SPI1-MISO	P2.27	P2.28	PRU0.6	116
7	SPI1-CLK	P2.29	P2.30	PRU0.3	113
19	SPI1-CS	P2.31	P2.32	PRU0.2	112
45	GPIO1.13	P2.33	P2.34	PRU0.5	115
86	AIN5/GPIO86	P2.35	P2.36	AIN7 (1.8V)	

PocketBeagle Rev A2

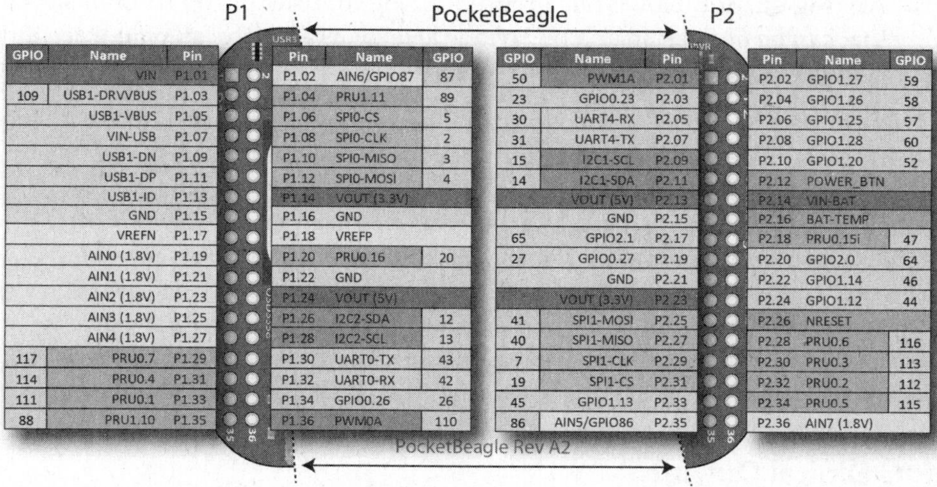

Figure 6-2: The PocketBeagle P1/P2 headers with pin names, which describe each pin's default functionality

NOTE There is a minor error in the silkscreen of the PocketBeagle Rev A2 where P2.24 is incorrectly labeled as GPIO 48, but it is actually GPIO 44, as illustrated in Figure 6-2. This will be corrected in the next board revision.

This chapter discusses how you can interface to the expansion header pins in the following ways:

- **Digital output:** How you can use a GPIO to turn an electrical circuit on or off. The example uses an LED, but the principles hold true for any circuit type; for example, you could even use a relay to turn on/off high-powered devices. A circuit is provided to ensure that you do not draw too much current from a GPIO. A C++ class is developed to make software interfacing straightforward and efficient.

- **Digital input:** How you can read in a digital output from an electrical circuit into a software application running under Linux. Circuits are provided to ensure that this is performed safely for your board. At the end of the chapter, more advanced digital input that allows for efficient detection of an input state change is also discussed.

- **Analog input:** How you can read in an analog output from an electrical circuit in the range of 0 V to 1.8 V (or 3.3 V on selected PocketBeagle pins) using one of the Beagle board's on-board analog-to-digital converters (ADCs). A circuit is provided to ensure that you do not draw current from the reference supply, which would mean that its voltage value could no longer be guaranteed.

- **Analog output:** How you can use PWM to output a proportional signal that can be used as an analog voltage level or as a control signal for certain types of devices, such as servo motors.

This chapter assumes you have read Chapter 4—in particular, switching circuits using FETs and the use of pull-up/down resistors.

> **WARNING**   Please be especially careful when working with the Beagle board headers, as incorrect connections can, and will, destroy your board. Please test all new circuits to ensure that their voltage *and* current levels are within range before connecting them to the headers. Also, please follow the advice on interfacing circuits using FETs, optocouplers, and op-amps, as described in this chapter. Chapter 8 provides additional advice on interfacing to circuits that use different logic voltage levels.

GPIO Digital Output

The example output configuration illustrated in Figure 6-3 uses a GPIO connected to a FET to switch a circuit using the same GPIO on a BeagleBone and a PocketBeagle board. As described in Chapter 4, when a voltage is applied to the gate input of a FET, it will close the virtual drain-source "switch," enabling current to flow from the 5 V supply through the 220 Ω current-limiting resistor and then to GND through a lighting LED. The advantage of this type of circuit is that it can be applied to many on/off digital output applications, as the BS270 FET data sheet indicates that it can drive a constant current of up to 400mA (and a pulsed current of up to 2A) across the drain-source at up to 60V. However, the maximum current is limited in this circuit, not by the FET, because the SYS_5V/VOUT(5V) pin (P9_07/P2.13) can supply a maximum of 250mA. As an alternative on the BeagleBone, the VDD_5V (P9_05 and P9_06) can supply up to 1A, but it is active only if a power supply is plugged into the 5V DC jack.

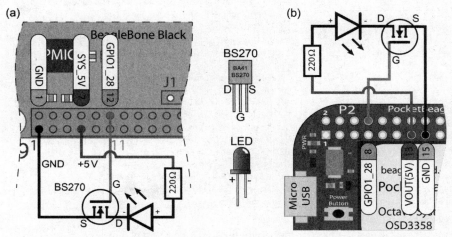

Figure 6-3: A FET-driven LED circuit connected to GPIO 60 on (a) the BeagleBone and (b) the PocketBeagle

Beagle board GPIOs are 3.3V tolerant, and you can only source 4–6 mA and sink about 8mA to each pin. In the example, it is safe to use the 5V supply to drive the LED, as the drain source circuit of the FET is never connected to the gate input. You will also notice that, unlike the example in Chapter 4, there is no resistor on the gate of the FET. It is not necessary in this particular case because an *internal* pull-down resistor is enabled within the BeagleBone or PocketBeagle, by default, on this pin. This is discussed shortly.

> **NOTE**   The BS270 can switch a maximum drain current of approximately 130mA at a gate voltage of 3.3V. The high input impedance of the gate means you can use two BS270s in parallel to double the maximum current to approximately 260mA at the same gate voltage. The BS270 can also be used as a gate driver for Power FETs, which can switch much higher currents.

As described in Figure 6-1 and Figure 6-2, the P9 header pin on the BeagleBone and the P2 on the PocketBeagle have different GPIOs available. GPIO1_28 is available on P9 pin 12 on the BeagleBone and on P2 pin 8 on the PocketBeagle. Once the circuit is built and attached to the Beagle board, you can boot the board and control the LED using a Linux terminal.

THE BEAGLE BOARD CONFIG-PIN TOOL

There is a dash script tool available for the latest BeagleBoard Linux images that allows you to create mappings between header pins and kernel GPIOs at run time. The tool has usage as described in Figure 6-4.

Usage	Description
`config-pin [-a] <pin> <mode>`	Sets the pin to a mode that is valid for the pin. Use `config-pin -l` to list the valid modes. When the pin is set to mode `gpio` there are additional options.
The options for mode `gpio`:	
`in` or `input`	Set the gpio direction to input.
`in+`	Set the gpio direction to input and enable a pull-up resistor on the pin.
`hi-`	Set the gpio direction to input and enable a pull-down resistor on the pin.
`out` or `output`	Set the gpio direction to be an output.
`hi` or `high` or `1`	Set the gpio direction to output and drive the pin high.
`lo` or `low` or `0`	Set the gpio direction to output and drive the pin low.
`config-pin overlay <name>`	Load a named device tree overlay.
`config-pin -l <pin>`	List the valid modes for a pin.
`config-pin -i <pin>`	Show information for a pin.
`config-pin -q <pin>`	Query a pin and report the configuration details.
`config-pin -f [file]`	Read a list of pin configurations from a file.
`config-pin -h`	Display the help text.

use instead of `gpio` (annotation pointing to the in/input, in+, hi-, etc. rows)

Figure 6-4: The `config-pin` tool usage

Figure is based on the help information provided by the `config-pin` script code

Each pin has a default (reset) mode that is defined by the boot configuration of the device tree model. You can alter this mode at run time by specifying the pin and the mode you would like to set. For example, to set p2.08 (i.e., pin 8 on the P2 header) on the PocketBeagle (which is GPIO1_28) to be an input GPIO, you can first query its default state and then change its mux setting to suit your needs:

```
debian@ebb:~$ config-pin -l p2.08
default gpio gpio_pu gpio_pd gpio_input
debian@ebb:~$ config-pin -i p2.08
Pin name: P2_08
Function if no cape loaded: gpio
Function if cape loaded: default gpio gpio_pu gpio_pd gpio_input
Function information: gpio1_28 default gpio1_28 gpio1_28 gpio1_28
                      gpio1_28
Kernel GPIO id: 60
PRU GPIO id: 92
debian@ebb:~$ config-pin -a p2.08 in
debian@ebb:~$ config-pin -q p2.08
P2_08 Mode: gpio Direction: in Value: 0
debian@ebb:~$ cat /sys/class/gpio/gpio60/direction
in
```

The `config-pin` tool is used throughout this chapter and later chapters. If you are interested, its source code is available at `tiny.cc/beagle601`.

The AM335x has four banks (0–3) of 32 GPIOs that are numbered 0 to 31. This means that GPIO1_28 is GPIO 28 of 32 (0–31) on the second GPIO chip of four (0–3). As there are 32 GPIOs on each GPIO chip, the internal GPIO number corresponding to pin GPIO1_28 is calculated as follows: (1×32) + 28 = 60. The total range is GPIO 0 (i.e., GPIO0_0) to GPIO 127 (i.e., GPIO3_31), but as previously discussed, not all AM335x GPIOs are available on the headers of the different Beagle boards.

GPIOs on the BeagleBone P8 header or the PocketBeagle P1 header can also be used, but to keep the figures concise, the P9 header GPIOs on the BeagleBone and P2 header on the PocketBeagle are chosen. To use GPIO 60 as an output, use the following commands at the Linux shell prompt on the PocketBeagle p2.08 (substitute in p9.12 for the BeagleBone):

```
debian@ebb:~$ config-pin -a p2.08 out
debian@ebb:~$ config-pin -q p2.08
P2_08 Mode: gpio Direction: out Value: 0
```

The query result indicates that the pin is now set up as a GPIO in output mode. You can then browse to the relevant GPIO sysfs directory so that you can control the pin directly. The /sys/class/gpio/ directory lists the available GPIOs along with the four GPIO banks (labeled 0, 32, 64, and 96).

```
debian@ebb:~$ cd /sys/class/gpio/
debian@ebb:/sys/class/gpio$ ls
export    gpio117  gpio23  gpio41  gpio50  gpio7    gpiochip96
gpio110   gpio12   gpio26  gpio42  gpio52  gpio86   unexport
gpio111   gpio13   gpio27  gpio43  gpio57  gpio87
gpio112   gpio14   gpio3   gpio44  gpio58  gpio88
gpio113   gpio15   gpio30  gpio45  gpio59  gpio89
gpio114   gpio19   gpio31  gpio46  gpio60  gpiochip0
gpio115   gpio2    gpio4   gpio47  gpio64  gpiochip32
gpio116   gpio20   gpio40  gpio5   gpio65  gpiochip64
```

You can see all the GPIOs that are currently available on the PocketBeagle board. GPIOs that are not available are being utilized for other functions (see Figure 6-2) or have not been physically connected to the headers.

```
debian@ebb:/sys/class/gpio$ cd gpio60
debian@ebb:/sys/class/gpio/gpio60$ ls -l
total 0
-rw-rw-r-- 1 root gpio 4096 Jan  1  2000 active_low
lrwxrwxrwx 1 root gpio    0 May 17 03:25 device -> ...
-rw-rw-r-- 1 root gpio 4096 Jan  1  2000 direction
-rw-rw-r-- 1 root gpio 4096 Jan  1  2000 edge
-rw-rw-r-- 1 root gpio 4096 Jan  1  2000 label
drwxrwxr-x 2 root gpio    0 Jan  1  2000 power
lrwxrwxrwx 1 root gpio    0 May 17 03:25 subsystem -> ...
-rw-rw-r-- 1 root gpio 4096 Jan  1  2000 uevent
```

```
-rw-rw-r-- 1 root gpio 4096 Jan  1  2000 value
debian@ebb:/sys/class/gpio/gpio60$ cat label
P2_08
debian@ebb:/sys/class/gpio/gpio60$ cat direction
out
```

> **NOTE** The input/output direction of a pin can be set using the GPIO sysfs entry or equivalently by using the `config-pin` tool. Here's an example:
>
> **debian@ebb:/sys/class/gpio/gpio60$ cat direction**
> out
> debian@ebb:/sys/class/gpio/gpio60$ **echo in > direction**
> debian@ebb:/sys/class/gpio/gpio60$ **cat direction**
> in
> debian@ebb:/sys/class/gpio/gpio60$ **config-pin -a p2.08 out**
> debian@ebb:/sys/class/gpio/gpio60$ **cat direction**
> out

The GPIO is confirmed as an output, and the value can be changed, which results in the LED connected to GPIO1_28 (as in Figure 6-3) being turned on and off.

```
debian@ebb:/sys/class/gpio/gpio60$ echo 1 > value
debian@ebb:/sys/class/gpio/gpio60$ echo 0 > value
```

To test the performance of this approach, a short script to flash the LED as quickly as possible, using a bash shell script, follows. This does not result in a visible "blink," as the LED is flashing faster than can be visibly observed; however, it can be visualized using an oscilloscope.

```
debian@ebb:~/exploringbb/chp06/flash_script$ more flash.sh
#!/bin/bash
# Short script to toggle a GPIO pin at the highest frequency
#  possible using Bash - by Derek Molloy
echo "out" > /sys/class/gpio/gpio60/direction
COUNTER=0
while [ $COUNTER -lt 100000 ]; do
    echo 0 > /sys/class/gpio/gpio60/value
    echo 1 > /sys/class/gpio/gpio60/value
    let COUNTER=COUNTER+1
done
debian@ebb:~/exploringbb/chp06/flash_script$ ./flash.sh
```

You can see from the oscilloscope trace in Figure 6-5 that the output is cycling every 0.54 ms approximately (although not all cycles are the same length), equating to a frequency of approximately 1.86 kHz, which is not very high for an embedded controller. In addition, the `top` command (executed in another Linux terminal window) indicates that the CPU load for this script is 98 percent.

If you attach a multimeter, you can also see that the current driving the LED is 12 mA, which is large enough to damage a Beagle board if this current were directly sourced from, or sinked to, a GPIO itself.

A C++ class is presented later in this chapter that can be used to control a GPIO, and it achieves higher switching frequencies but with similar CPU loads. If you require a high-frequency periodic switching signal, then PWM, which is discussed later in this chapter, can be used. PWM can achieve frequencies of 1 MHz or higher, without a significant CPU load. If you require a non-periodic output at a high frequency, then you will have to investigate the Programmable Real-Time Units (PRUs) in Chapter 15. However, many applications require the activation of a switched circuit at low frequencies (e.g., controlling motors, smart home control, etc.), and in such cases this configuration is perfectly valid.

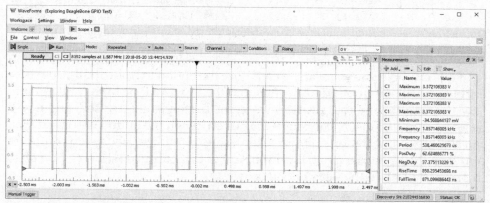

Figure 6-5: Scope output measuring the maximum switching rate for a GPIO controlled with the `flash.sh` script

GPIO Digital Input

The next application uses a GPIO as a *digital input*, which will enable software written on the board to read the state of a push button or any other logic high/low input. This task is first performed using a Linux terminal, and then it is performed using C/C++ code. The LED circuit in Figure 6-3 can be left connected when building this circuit.

The circuit shown in Figure 6-6 uses a normally open push button (SPST) that is connected to the GPIO1_14, which is pin 16 on the BeagleBone P8 header or pin 22 on the PocketBeagle P2 header. You will notice that, having discussed the need for pull-up or pull-down resistors on push button switches in Chapter 4, none are present in this circuit. This is not accidental, as we have control over internal pull-up and pull-down resistors on the Beagle boards using the config-pin tool.

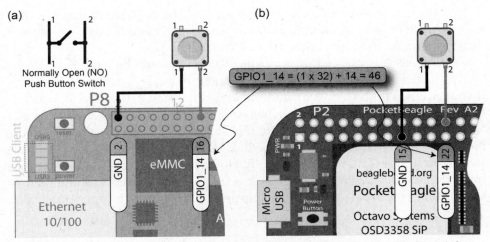

Figure 6-6: A GPIO button input example with an internal pull-up resistor enabled on (a) the BeagleBone and (b) the PocketBeagle

In this example, say you want to configure the button to have a pull-up resistor enabled on the input pin. This means that the input will be high (pulled up to 3.3V through the internal resistor) when the button is not pressed, and it will be low (connected to GND through the button) when the button is pressed. You can set this configuration on the PocketBeagle as follows, where you configure pin 22 on the P2 header as a GPIO input (in) with a pull-up resistor (+) (use p8.16 in place of p2.22 on the BeagleBone board):

```
debian@ebb:~$ config-pin -q p2.22
P2_22 Mode: default Direction: in Value: 0
debian@ebb:~$ config-pin -a p2.22 in+
debian@ebb:~$ config-pin -q p2.22
P2_22 Mode: gpio_pu Direction: in Value: 1
```

The query (-q) output on the last line indicates that the GPIO is an input in pull-up mode (i.e., gpio_pu) and that the present input value is high (1).

You can use sysfs to read the state of the button using a Linux terminal, where GPIO1_14 is GPIO 46 (i.e., $(1 \times 32) + 14$):

```
debian@ebb:~$ cd /sys/class/gpio/gpio46
debian@ebb:/sys/class/gpio/gpio46$ ls -l
-rw-rw-r-- 1 root gpio 4096 Jan  1  2000 active_low
lrwxrwxrwx 1 root gpio    0 May 17 03:25 device -> ...
-rw-rw-r-- 1 root gpio 4096 May 20 17:09 direction
-rw-rw-r-- 1 root gpio 4096 Jan  1  2000 edge
-rw-rw-r-- 1 root gpio 4096 Jan  1  2000 label
drwxrwxr-x 2 root gpio    0 Jan  1  2000 power
```

```
lrwxrwxrwx 1 root gpio    0 May 17 03:25 subsystem -> ...
-rw-rw-r-- 1 root gpio 4096 Jan  1  2000 uevent
-rw-rw-r-- 1 root gpio 4096 Jan  1  2000 value
debian@ebb:/sys/class/gpio/gpio46$ cat direction
in
debian@ebb:/sys/class/gpio/gpio46$ cat value
1
```

And, when the button is pressed, and subsequently released, you'll see this:

```
debian@ebb:/sys/class/gpio/gpio46$ cat value
0
debian@ebb:/sys/class/gpio/gpio46$ cat value
1
```

To reiterate, since there is an internal pull-up resistor enabled on the input, it is "pulled up" to 3.3 V when no input is attached. This means that the button input value is 1 when the button is not pressed. When the button is pressed, the input is grounded and a 0 value is read when it is pressed. Each time you type cat value, you are *polling* the input to check the value. The downside of this approach is that you will not identify a change in the value of the input unless you constantly poll the value state.

Interestingly, if you reconfigure p2.22 to have a pull-down resistor (-) instead of a pull-up resistor using the following:

```
debian@ebb:/sys/class/gpio/gpio46$ config-pin -a p2.22 in-
debian@ebb:/sys/class/gpio/gpio46$ cat value
0
debian@ebb:/sys/class/gpio/gpio46$ cat value
0
```

you will see that the input value is always 0 whether the button is pressed or released. That is because this input is connected via an internal *pull-down* resistor to ground, meaning that the input is connected to ground in either case. It should be clear at this stage that you need to understand the GPIO configuration, including these internal resistors, to use the GPIO pins properly.

GPIO Configuration

The importance of pull-up and pull-down resistors is discussed in some detail in Chapter 4. They ensure that open switches do not allow a GPIO input to float. Such external resistors are typically "strong" pull-up/down resistors in that they "strongly" tie the input to a high/low value using relatively low resistance values (e.g., 5-10 kΩ).

Internal Pull-Up and Pull-Down Resistors

The Beagle boards have "weak" *internal pull-up* and *internal pull-down* resistors that can be configured by setting internal registers in the AM335x SoC. You can physically check whether an internal pull-up or pull-down resistor is enabled on a pin by connecting a 100kΩ resistor between the pin and GND (as shown in Figure 6-7(a), where the shaded area represents functionality that is internal to the AM335x) and then between the pin and the 3.3V supply (as shown in Figure 6-7(b)). If you connect a 100kΩ (the one I used had an actual value of 98.6kΩ) to P8_12 and measure the voltage across it, you will see that the voltage drop is 0V when the resistor is connected to GND, and I measured 2.739V (not 3.3V) when it was connected to the 3.3V rail. This indicates that there is an internal pull-down resistor enabled, and the combination of these resistors is behaving like a voltage divider circuit. You can even estimate the value of the internal pull-down resistor as in Figure 6-7(b).

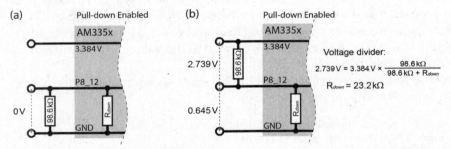

Figure 6-7: Internal BeagleBone pull-down resistor example, with an external resistor connected (a) from the pin to GND, and (b) from the pin to the 3.3V supply

Clearly, P8_12, which is GPIO1_12, has an internal pull-down resistor enabled in this case, but if you perform the same test on P8_26, which is GPIO1_29, you should get a completely different response. When you connect the resistor as shown in Figure 6-7(a), you will get a voltage drop of ~2.624V across the 100kΩ resistor, and almost 0V (~0.162V) when you connect it as in Figure 6-7(b). That is because P8_26 has an internal pull-up resistor enabled by default. Performing the same calculations gives an internal pull-up resistor value of about 28.6kΩ.

You need to factor these resistor values into the behavior of your input/output circuits, and you need to be able to alter the internal resistor configuration in certain circumstances.

GPIO Pin Configuration Settings

As well as configuring pins to have either a pull-up or a pull-down resistor configuration, there are seven different modes for each pin. This is called the *multiplexer mode* (*mmode*) for the pin, and it is set using a three-digit binary number, as described in the first row of Table 6-1. This table is based on information provided in the *AM335x TRM* (GPIOs conf_<module>_<pin> - Table 9-60 of the TRM). Using these bit settings, you can construct a seven-bit value that can be used to configure the exact behavior of a GPIO pin within Linux using device tree overlays, which is discussed shortly.

Table 6-1: GPIO Pin User-Configuration Settings

BIT	AM335X FIELD	DESCRIPTION
0,1,2	mmode	The multiplexer mode: Using the three least-significant bits you can select a mode between 0 and 7, e.g., 000=0, 111=7. This enables each pin to have up to eight different modes.
3	puden	Enable internal pull-up/pull-down resistor: Enable=0, Disable=1.
4	putypesel	Select internal pull-up or pull-down form: Pull-down=0, Pull-up=1.
5	rxactive	Input Active: Receiver disabled=0, Input enabled=1. If this bit is set high, the pin will be an input; otherwise, it will be an output.
6	slewctrl	Slew Control: Fast=0, Slow=1. *Slew rate* provides control over the rise/fall time of an output. You would set this value to slow only if you were using long interconnects, such as on I²C buses.

The mmode is discussed shortly, but when working with GPIOs, the mmode will be 7, and therefore the most common hexadecimal values that are used to configure a GPIO's settings are as follows (bit 6 is the most significant bit [MSB] and is on the LHS):

- 0x27 (0100111) Fast, **Input**, Pull-Down, Enabled and Mux Mode 7
- 0x37 (0110111) Fast, Input, **Pull-Up**, Enabled, Mux Mode 7
- 0x07 (0000111) Fast, Output, Pull-down, **Enabled**, Mux Mode 7
- 0x17 (0010111) Fast, Output, Pull-up, Enabled, **Mux Mode 7**
- 0x2F (0101111) Fast, Input, Pull-down, **Disabled**, Mux Mode 7

These configuration values are useful, as they enable you to set the pins into the exact operational mode that you require. The tables shown in Figures 6-8 and 6-9 provide the most important information required when interfacing to AM335x-based Beagle boards. They have been generated using the SRM, the AM335x TRM, and information that can be gleaned from the Debian Linux distribution. The figures illustrate the mmode options that are available on each of the BeagleBone's P8 and P9 headers and the PocketBeagle's P1 and P2 headers. They are available in PDF form in the GitHub repository (chp06/headers/) so that they can be displayed on your computer in color and printed as required.

BIT MANIPULATION IN C/C++

When performing memory-based manipulation in C/C++, you can use bitwise operations to efficiently manipulate states. It is worth examining a short segment of code to ensure that you are comfortable with these operations. The full example is available at /chp06/bits/bitsTest.cpp. The uint8_t (unsigned 8-bit integer) type and the following display() function are used to create a concise example:

```cpp
string display(uint8_t a) {
   stringstream ss;      // setw() sets width and bitset formats as binary
   ss << setw(3) << (int)a << "(" << bitset<8>(a) << ")";
   return ss.str();
}

int main() {
   uint8_t a = 25, b = 5;     // 8 bits unsigned is in the range 0 to 255
   cout << "A is " << display(a) << " and B is " << display(b) << endl;
   cout << "A & B   (AND) is " << display(a & b) << endl;
   cout << "A | B   (OR)  is " << display(a | b) << endl;
   cout << "  ~A    (NOT) is " << display(~a) << endl;
   cout << "A ^ B   (XOR) is " << display(a ^ b) << endl;
   cout << "A << 1 (LSL) is " << display(a << 1) << endl;
   cout << "B >> 1 (LSR) is " << display(b >> 1) << endl;
   cout << "1 << 8 (LSL) is " << display(1 << 8) << endl; // warning!
   return 0;
}
```

When this code is compiled and executed, it results in the following output:

```
debian@ebb:~/exploringbb/chp06/bits$ g++ bitsTest.cpp -o bits
debian@ebb:~/exploringbb/chp06/bits$ ./bits
A is  25(00011001) and B is   5(00000101)
A & B   (AND) is   1(00000001)
A | B   (OR)  is  29(00011101)
  ~A    (NOT) is 230(11100110)
A ^ B   (XOR) is  28(00011100)
A << 1 (LSL) is  50(00110010)
B >> 1 (LSR) is   2(00000010)
1 << 8 (LSL) is   0(00000000)
```

Please note that 1 shifted left 8 times (1<<8) results in a value of 0 (and a compiler warning!), as overflow has occurred and the 1 has been lost. You can use the limited size of a data type to simplify calculations.

Quite a large amount of information is presented in these two tables, and subsequent chapters in the book will frequently refer to them. For the moment, note a few points that are particularly important:

- Any pin that is highlighted in the $PINS column is already allocated and should not be used unless you disable the functionality that it is allocated to (e.g., the HDMI output or the eMMC). See the Notes column for further details.

- Mode7 is the GPIO mmode.

- As discussed, the GPIO number is calculated by taking the GPIO chip number, multiplying it by 32, and then adding the offset. For example, GPIO1_12 = (1 × 32) + 12 = GPIO 44.

- The $PINS number is *not* the GPIO number. This $PINS number in the table is a software reference for each of the pins, and these values are provided in the second column of the table.

- Highlighted items in the Mode6 and Mode5 columns relate to PRU functionality, discussed in Chapter 15.

The header pins P9_12/P2_08 (used for output) and P8_16/P2_22 (used for input) can be used as an illustration of the information in these tables. These are the pins that were physically tested as described earlier. If you examine Figure 6-8, you will see under P8_12 and P8_26 the following values:

```
Head    $PINS   ADDR/OFFSET   GPIO    Name       Mode7
P9_12    30     0x878/078     60      GPIO1_28   gpio1[28] ...
P8_16    14     0x838/038     46      GPIO1_14   gpio1[14] ...
```

This information is consistent with the output of the show-pins.pl script when executed on the PocketBeagle.

```
debian@ebb:~$ cd /opt/scripts/device/
debian@ebb:/opt/scripts/device$ ls
blue   bone   x15
debian@ebb:/opt/scripts/device$ cd bone
debian@ebb:/opt/scripts/device/bone$ perl show-pins.pl | grep 1.28
P9.12    30 U18 fast rx down 7 gpio 1.28
         ocp/P2_08_pinmux (pinmux_P2_08_default_pin)
debian@ebb:/opt/scripts/device/bone$ perl show-pins.pl | grep 1.14
P8.16    14 V13 fast rx down 7 gpio 1.14
         ocp/P2_22_pinmux (pinmux_P2_22_default_pin)
```

Pin	PB Pin	$PINS	ADDR	GPIO	Name	Mode7	Mode6	Mode5	Mode4	Mode3	Mode2	Mode1	Mode0	CPU	Notes
P8_01			Offset from:		DGND										Ground
P8_02			44e10800		DGND										Ground
P8_03	n/a	6	0x818/018	38	GPIO1_6	gpio1[6]						mmc1_dat6	gpmc_ad6	R9	Allocated emmc2
P8_04	n/a	7	0x81c/01c	39	GPIO1_7	gpio1[7]						mmc1_dat7	gpmc_ad7	T9	Allocated emmc2
P8_05	n/a	2	0x808/008	34	GPIO1_2	gpio1[2]						mmc1_dat2	gpmc_ad2	R8	Allocated emmc2
P8_06	n/a	3	0x80c/00c	35	GPIO1_3	gpio1[3]						mmc1_dat3	gpmc_ad3	T8	Allocated emmc2
P8_07	n/a	36	0x890/090	66	TIMER4	gpio2[2]					timer4		gpmc_advn_ale	R7	
P8_08	n/a	37	0x894/094	67	TIMER7	gpio2[3]					timer7		gpmc_oen_ren	T7	
P8_09	n/a	39	0x89c/09c	69	TIMER5	gpio2[5]					timer5		gpmc_be0n_cle	T6	
P8_10	n/a	38	0x898/098	68	TIMER6	gpio2[4]					timer6		gpmc_wen	U6	
P8_11	P2.33	13	0x834/034	45	GPIO1_13	gpio1[13]	pr1_pru0_pru_r30_15	pr1_mii0_txd1	eQEP2B_in	mmc2_dat1	mmc1_dat5	lcd_data18	gpmc_ad13	R12	
P8_12	P2.24	12	0x830/030	44	GPIO1_12	gpio1[12]	pr1_pru0_pru_r30_14	pr1_mii0_txd2	EQEP2A_IN	MMC2_DAT0	MMC1_DAT4	LCD_DATA19	GPMC_AD12	T12	
P8_13	P2.03	9	0x824/024	23	EHRPWM2B	gpio0[23]	n/a	pr1_mii0_col	ehrpwm2B	mmc2_dat5	mmc1_dat1	lcd_data22	gpmc_ad9	T10	
P8_14	P1.34	10	0x828/028	26	GPIO0_26	gpio0[26]	n/a	pr1_mii0_txen	ehrpwm2_tripzone_in	mmc2_dat6	mmc1_dat2	lcd_data21	gpmc_ad10	T11	
P8_15	P2.18	15	0x83c/03c	47	GPIO1_15	gpio1[15]	pr1_pru0_pru_r31_15	pr1_ecap0_ecap_capin_apwm_o	eQEP2_strobe	mmc2_dat3	mmc1_dat7	lcd_data16	gpmc_ad15	U13	
P8_16	P2.22	14	0x838/038	46	GPIO1_14	gpio1[14]	pr1_pru0_pru_r31_14	pr1_mii0_txd0	eQEP2_index	mmc2_dat2	mmc1_dat6	lcd_data17	gpmc_ad14	V13	
P8_17	P2.19	11	0x82c/02c	27	GPIO0_27	gpio0[27]	n/a	pr1_mii0_txd3	ehrpwm0_synco	mmc2_dat7	mmc1_dat3	lcd_data20	gpmc_ad11	U12	
P8_18	P2.17	35	0x88c/08c	65	GPIO2_1	gpio2[1]	mcasp0_fsr	pr1_mdio_mdclk	pr1_mii1_crs	mmc2_clk	gpmc_wait1	lcd_memory_clk	gpmc_clk_mux0	V12	
P8_19	n/a	8	0x820/020	22	EHRPWM2A	gpio0[22]			ehrpwm2A	mmc2_dat4	mmc1_dat0	lcd_data23	gpmc_ad8	U10	
P8_20	n/a	33	0x884/084	63	GPIO1_31	gpio1[31]	pr1_pru1_pru_r31_13	pr1_pru1_pru_r30_13			mmc1_cmd	gpmc_be1n	gpmc_csn2	V9	Allocated emmc2
P8_21	n/a	32	0x880/080	62	GPIO1_30	gpio1[30]	pr1_pru1_pru_r31_12	pr1_pru1_pru_r30_12			mmc1_clk	gpmc_clk	gpmc_csn1	U9	Allocated emmc2
P8_22	n/a	5	0x814/014	37	GPIO1_5	gpio1[5]						mmc1_dat5	gpmc_ad5	V8	Allocated emmc2
P8_23	n/a	4	0x810/010	36	GPIO1_4	gpio1[4]						mmc1_dat4	gpmc_ad4	U8	Allocated emmc2
P8_24	n/a	1	0x804/004	33	GPIO1_1	gpio1[1]						mmc1_dat1	gpmc_ad1	V7	Allocated emmc2
P8_25	n/a	0	0x800/000	32	GPIO1_0	gpio1[0]						mmc1_dat0	gpmc_ad0	U7	Allocated emmc2
P8_26	n/a	31	0x87c/07c	61	GPIO1_29	gpio1[29]							gpmc_csn0	V6	
P8_27	P2.35	56	0x8e0/0e0	86	GPIO2_22	gpio2[22]	pr1_pru1_pru_r31_8	pr1_pru1_pru_r30_8	pr1_edio_data_out2	pr1_edio_data_in2	gpmc_a1	gpmc_a8	lcd_vsync	U5	Allocated HDMI
P8_28	P1.35	58	0x8e8/0e8	88	GPIO2_24	gpio2[24]	pr1_pru1_pru_r31_10	pr1_pru1_pru_r30_10	pr1_edio_data_out4	pr1_edio_data_in4	pru_mii0_crs	gpmc_a10	lcd_pclk	V5	Allocated HDMI
P8_29	P1.02	57	0x8e4/0e4	87	GPIO2_23	gpio2[23]	pr1_pru1_pru_r31_9	pr1_pru1_pru_r30_9	pr1_edio_data_out3	pr1_edio_data_in3	gpmc_a2	gpmc_a9	lcd_hsync	R5	Allocated HDMI
P8_30	P1.04	59	0x8ec/0ec	89	GPIO2_25	gpio2[25]	pr1_pru1_pru_r31_11	pr1_pru1_pru_r30_11	pr1_edio_data_out5	pr1_edio_data_in5	pr1_mii1_crs	gpmc_a11	lcd_ac_bias_en	R6	Allocated HDMI
P8_31	n/a	54	0x8d8/0d8	10	UART5_CTSN	gpio0[10]	uart5_ctsn		uart5_rxd	mcasp0_axr1	eQEP1_index	gpmc_a18	lcd_data14	V4	Allocated HDMI
P8_32	n/a	55	0x8dc/0dc	11	UART5_RTSN	gpio0[11]	uart5_rtsn		mcasp0_axr3	mcasp0_ahclkx	eQEP1_strobe	gpmc_a19	lcd_data15	T5	Allocated HDMI
P8_33	n/a	53	0x8d4/0d4	9	UART4_RTSN	gpio0[9]	uart4_rtsn		mcasp0_axr3	mcasp0_fsr	eQEP1B_in	gpmc_a17	lcd_data13	V3	Allocated HDMI
P8_34	n/a	51	0x8cc/0cc	81	UART3_RTSN	gpio2[17]	uart3_rtsn		mcasp0_axr2	mcasp0_ahclkr	ehrpwm1B	gpmc_a15	lcd_data11	U4	Allocated HDMI
P8_35	n/a	52	0x8d0/0d0	8	UART4_CTSN	gpio0[8]	uart4_ctsn		mcasp0_axr2	mcasp0_aclkr	eQEP1A_in	gpmc_a16	lcd_data12	V2	Allocated HDMI
P8_36	n/a	50	0x8c8/0c8	80	UART3_CTSN	gpio2[16]	uart3_ctsn			mcasp0_axr0	ehrpwm1A	gpmc_a14	lcd_data10	U3	Allocated HDMI
P8_37	n/a	48	0x8c0/0c0	78	UART5_TXD	gpio2[14]	uart2_ctsn		uart5_txd	mcasp0_aclkx	ehrpwm1_tripzone_in	gpmc_a12	lcd_data8	U1	Allocated HDMI
P8_38	n/a	49	0x8c4/0c4	79	UART5_RXD	gpio2[15]	uart2_rtsn		uart5_rxd	mcasp0_fsx	ehrpwm0_synco	gpmc_a13	lcd_data9	U2	Allocated HDMI
P8_39	n/a	46	0x8b8/0b8	76	GPIO2_12	gpio2[12]	pr1_pru1_pru_r31_6	pr1_pru1_pru_r30_6		eQEP2_index		gpmc_a6	lcd_data6	T3	Allocated HDMI
P8_40	n/a	47	0x8bc/0bc	77	GPIO2_13	gpio2[13]	pr1_pru1_pru_r31_7	pr1_pru1_pru_r30_7	pr1_edio_data_out7	eQEP2_strobe		gpmc_a7	lcd_data7	T4	Allocated HDMI
P8_41	n/a	44	0x8b0/0b0	74	GPIO2_10	gpio2[10]	pr1_pru1_pru_r31_4	pr1_pru1_pru_r30_4		eQEP2A_in		gpmc_a4	lcd_data4	T1	Allocated HDMI
P8_42	n/a	45	0x8b4/0b4	75	GPIO2_11	gpio2[11]	pr1_pru1_pru_r31_5	pr1_pru1_pru_r30_5		eQEP2B_in		gpmc_a5	lcd_data5	T2	Allocated HDMI
P8_43	n/a	42	0x8a8/0a8	72	GPIO2_8	gpio2[8]	pr1_pru1_pru_r31_2	pr1_pru1_pru_r30_2		ehrpwm2_tripzone_in		gpmc_a2	lcd_data2	R3	Allocated HDMI
P8_44	n/a	43	0x8ac/0ac	73	GPIO2_9	gpio2[9]	pr1_pru1_pru_r31_3	pr1_pru1_pru_r30_3		ehrpwm0_synco		gpmc_a3	lcd_data3	R4	Allocated HDMI
P8_45	n/a	40	0x8a0/0a0	70	GPIO2_6	gpio2[6]	pr1_pru1_pru_r31_0	pr1_pru1_pru_r30_0		ehrpwm2A		gpmc_a0	lcd_data0	R1	Allocated HDMI
P8_46	n/a	41	0x8a4/0a4	71	GPIO2_7	gpio2[7]	pr1_pru1_pru_r31_1	pr1_pru1_pru_r30_1		ehrpwm2B		gpmc_a1	lcd_data1	R2	Allocated HDMI
n/a	P2.02			59	GPIO1.27	gpio1[27]	mcasp0_axr1	pr1_mii1_rxer	gpmc_a27	rmii2_rxd0	rgmii2_rd0	gmii2_rxd0	gpmc_a11	V17/T16	
n/a	P2.04			58	GPIO1.26	gpio1[26]	mcasp0_axr0	pr1_mii1_rxdv	gpmc_a26	rmii2_rxd1	rgmii2_rd1	gmii2_rxd1	gpmc_a10	T16/R15	
n/a	P2.06			57	GPIO1.25	gpio1[25]	mcasp0_fsx	pr1_mii_mr1_clk	gpmc_a25	rmii2_crs_dv	rgmii2_rd2	gmii2_rxd2	gpmc_a9	U16/T15	
n/a	P2.10			52	GPIO1.20	gpio1[20]	eQEP1A_in	pr1_mii1_txd0	gpmc_a20	rmii2_txd1	rgmii2_td1	gmii2_txd1	gpmc_a4	R14/R13	
n/a	P2.20			64	GPIO2.0	gpio2[0]	EMU4	pr1_mdio_data	pr1_mii0_crs	mmc2_cmd	rmii2_crs_dv	gpmc_a3	gpmc_csn3	T13/R7	
n/a	P2.25			41	SPI1-MOSI	gpio1[9]	pr1_edc_sync1_out	spi1_cs0	spi1_d1	I2C1_SCL	dcan1_rx	uart4_txd	uart0_rtsn	E17/C13	
n/a	P2.27			40	SPI1-MISO	gpio1[8]	pr1_edc_sync0_out	timer7	spi1_d0	I2C1_SDA	dcan1_tx	uart4_rxd	uart0_ctsn	E18/C12	
n/a	P2.31			19	SPI1-CS	gpio0[19]	EMU2	pr1_pru1_pru_r31_16	spi1_cs1	clkout1	timer4	n/a	xdma_event_intr0	A15/A4	
P8 Header		cat $PINS	ADDR +	GPIO NO.	Name	Mode 7	Mode 6	Mode 5	Mode 4	Mode 3	Mode 2	Mode 1	Mode 0	CPU	

Figure 6-8: The P8 header pins and equivalent PocketBeagle (PB) pins

Pins	PB Pins	$PINS	ADDR	GPIO NO.	Name	Mode7	Mode6	Mode5	Mode4	Mode3	Mode2	Mode1	Mode0	CPU	Notes
P9_01	P1.15		44e10000		GND										Ground
P9_02	P1.16		Off set from		GND										Ground
P9_03	P1.14		44e10800		DC_3.3V										250mA Max Current
P9_04	P1.24				DC_3.3V										250mA Max Current
P9_05					VDD_5V										1A Max Current
P9_06					VDD_5V										1A Max Current
P9_07	P1.01				SYS_5V										250mA Max Current
P9_08					SYS_5V										250mA Max Current
P9_09	P2.12				PWR_BUT										5V Level (pulled up PMIC)
P9_10	P2.28				SYS_RESETn								RESET_OUT	A10	All GPIOs to 4-8mA output
P9_11	P2.05	28	0x870/070	30	UART4_RXD	gpio0[30]	uart4_rxd_mux2		rmii_sdod	rmii2_crs_dv	gpmc_csn4	mii2_crs	gpmc_wait0	T17	and approx. 8mA on input.
P9_12	P2.08	30	0x878/078	60	GPIO1_28	gpio1[28]	mcasp0_aclkr_mux3		mcasp0_sdod	rmii2_dat3	gpmc_dir	mii2_col	gpmc_be1n	U18	
P9_13	P2.07	29	0x874/074	31	UART4_TXD	gpio0[31]			uart4_txd_mux2	rmii2_rxerr	mmc2_sdoc	mii2_rxerr	gpmc_wpn	U17	
P9_14	P2.01	18	0x848/048	50	EHRPWM1A	gpio1[18]	ehrpwm1A_mux1		ehrpwm1A_mux1	gpmc_a18	mmc2_dat1	rgmii2_td3	gpmc_a2	U14	
P9_15	P1.01	16	0x840/040	48	GPIO1_16	gpio1[16]			ehrpwm1B_mux1	gpmc_a16	nla	rgmii2_txen	gpmc_a0	R13	
P9_16	n/a	19	0x84c/04c	51	EHRPWM1B	gpio1[19]	ehrpwm1B_mux1		ehrpwm1B_mux1	gpmc_a19	mmc2_dat2	rgmii2_td2	gpmc_a3	T14	
P9_17	P1.06	5	0x95c/15c	87	I2C1_SCL	gpio0[5]		pr1_ede_data_in1	pr1_uart0_txd	ehrpwm0_synci	I2C1_SCL	spi0_cs1	S	A16	
P9_18	P1.12	86	0x958/158	4	I2C1_SDA	gpio0[4]	pr1_ede_data_out0	pr1_uart0_rxd	ehrpwm0_trizzone	I2C1_SDA	spi0_cs0	spi0_d1	B16	
P9_19	P1.28	95	0x97c/17c	13	I2C2_SCL	gpio0[13]	pr1_ede_latch1_in	pr1_uart0_rts_n	spi1_cs1	I2C2_SCL	dcan0_rx	timer4	uart1_rtsn	D17	Allocated I2C2
P9_20	P1.26	94	0x978/178	12	I2C2_SDA	gpio0[12]	pr1_ede_latch0_in	pr1_uart0_cts_n	spi1_cs0	I2C2_SDA	dcan0_tx	timer6	uart1_ctsn	D18	Allocated I2C2
P9_21	P1.10	85	0x954/154	3	UART2_TXD	gpio0[3]	EMA3_mux1	pr1_ede_latch_in	pr1_uart0_rts_n	ehrpwm0B	I2C2_SDA	spi0_d0	B17	
P9_22	P1.08	84	0x950/150	2	UART2_RXD	gpio0[2]	EMA2_mux1	pr1_uart0_sync0	pr1_uart0_cts_n	ehrpwm0A	I2C2_SCL	spi0_sclk	A17	
P9_23	n/a	17	0x844/044	49	GPIO1_17	gpio1[17]	ehrpwm0_synco		gpmc_a17	rgmii2_rxdv	gpmc_a1	V14	
P9_24	P2.09	97	0x984/184	15	UART1_TXD	gpio0[15]	pr1_pru0_pru_r31_16	pr1_pru0_pru_r30_16	I2C1_SCL	mmc2_sdwr_p	dcan1_rx	mmc2_sdwp	uart1_txd	D15	1.8 ADC Volt. Ref.
P9_25	P2.35	107	0x9ac/1ac	117	GPIO3_21	gpio3[21]	pr1_pru0_pru_r31_7		mcasp0_axr1	eQEP0_strobe	mcasp0_ahclkx	A14	Allocated mcasp0_pins
P9_26	P2.11	14	0x980/180	14	UART1_RXD	gpio0[14]	pr1_pru0_pru_r31_16		I2C1_SDA	dcan1_tx	mmc2_sdwp	uart1_rxd	D16	
P9_27	P2.34	105	0x9a4/1a4	115	GPIO3_19	gpio3[19]	pr1_pru0_pru_r30_5	pr1_pru0_pru_r30_5	mcasp0_fsr	EMA2_mux2	mcasp0_axr3	mcasp0_fsr	C13	Allocated mcasp0_pins
P9_28	P2.30	103	0x99c/19c	113	SPI1_CS0	gpio3[17]	pr1_pru0_pru_r30_3	pr1_pru0_pru_r30_3	eCAP2_in_PWM2_out	spi1_cs0	ehrpw0_synci	mcasp0_ahclkr	C12	Allocated mcasp0_pins
P9_29	P2.33	101	0x994/194	111	SPI1_D0	gpio3[15]	pr1_pru0_pru_r30_1	pr1_pru0_pru_r30_1	mmc1_sdcd_mux1	spi1_d0	ehrpw0_fsx	mcasp0_fsx	B13	Allocated mcasp0_pins
P9_30	P2.32	102	0x998/198	112	SPI1_D1	gpio3[16]	pr1_pru0_pru_r30_2	pr1_pru0_pru_r30_2	mmc2_sdcd_mux1	spi1_d1	ehrpw0_trizzor	mcasp0_axr0	D12	Allocated mcasp0_pins
P9_31	P1.36	100	0x990/190	110	SPI1_SCLK	gpio3[14]	pr1_pru0_pru_r30_0	pr1_pru0_pru_r30_0	mmc0_sdcd_mux1	spi1_sclk	ehrpw0_aclkx	mcasp0_aclkx	A13	Allocated mcasp0_pins
P9_32	P1.18				VADC										1.8V input
P9_33	P1.27				AIN4										Ground for ADC
P9_34					AGND										1.8V input
P9_35	P1.02				AIN6									A8	1.8V input
P9_36	P2.35				AIN5									B8	1.8V input
P9_37	P1.23				AIN2									B7	1.8V input
P9_38	P1.25				AIN3									A7	1.8V input
P9_39	P1.19				AIN0									B6	1.8V input
P9_40	P1.21				AIN1									C7	1.8V input
P9_41A	P1.20	109	0x9b4/1b4	20	CLKOUT2	gpio0[20]	EMA3_mux0	pr1_pru0_pru_r31_16	timer7_mux1	clkout2	tclkin	xdma_event_intr1	D14	Both to P21 of P11
P9_41B	P2.28	116	0x9a8/1a8	116	GPIO3_20	gpio3[20]	pr1_pru0_pru_r31_6		emu3	Mcasp1_axr0		eQEP0_index	mcasp0_axr1	D13	Both to P21 of P11
P9_42A	P2.29	7	0x964/164	7	GPIO0_7	gpio3[18]	xdma_event_intr2	rmii0_sdwp	spi1_sclk		spi1_cs1	uart3_txd	eCAP0_in_PWM0_out	C18	Both to P22 of P11
P9_42B	P1.31	89	0x9a0/1a0	114	GPIO3_18	gpio3[18]	pr1_pru0_pru_r31_14		mmc0_sdwp	mcasp0_axr2	Mcasp0_axr2	eQEP0A_in	Mcasp0_aclkr	B12	Allocated mcasp0_pins
P9_43	P1.22				GND										See Pg.50 of the SRM
P9_44	n/a				GND										Ground
P9_45	n/a				GND										Ground
P9_46	cat				GND										Ground
n/a	P1.03	109			USB1_En	gpio0[13]									F15/M14	
n/a	P1.30	43			UART0-TX	gpio1[11]								spi0_txd	E16/B12	
n/a	P1.32	42			UART0-RX	gpio1[10]								uart0_rxd	E15/A12	
P9	$PINS	ADDR +	GPIO NO.	Name	Mode 7								Mode 1	Mode 0	CPU	Notes

Figure 6-9: The P9 header pins and equivalent PocketBeagle (PB) pins

You can see that the P8_16/P2_22 pin has PINS number 14, physical pad number V13 on the AM335x, fast slew rate, input mode (rx), and a pull-down resistor enabled (down), and it is in GPIO mode 7 (7), which is GPIO1_14. This pin is mapped to pin 16 on the BeagleBone P8 header and pin 22 on the PocketBeagle P2 header.

The fact that the name of the pin is the same as its Mode7 value means that Mode7 is most likely enabled by default. You can test this in Linux as follows (you must use a superuser account):

```
debian@ebb:~$ sudo -i
root@ebb:~# cd /sys/kernel/debug/pinctrl/44e10800.pinmux/
root@ebb:/sys/kernel/debug/pinctrl/44e10800.pinmux# ls
gpio-ranges  pingroups  pinmux-functions  pinmux-pins  pins
root@ebb:/sys/kernel/debug/pinctrl/44e10800.pinmux# cat pins
registered pins: 142
pin   0 (PIN0)   44e10800 00000027 pinctrl-single
...
pin  14 (PIN14)   44e10838 00000027 pinctrl-single
...
```

The pin number is the $PINS value of the pin in question. Therefore, you can see that P8_16 ($PINS value 14) is in mode 0x27, which is an input in Mode7 (gpio1[14]) with a pull-up resistor enabled. Please note that these values will change as you use the config-pin tool.

You can actually query the value at the memory address itself using C code that accesses /dev/mem directly. Because P8_16 ($PINS14) is mapped at the memory address 44e10838 (see the ADDR column in Figure 6-8, or the preceding pins file), you can use the following steps to install Jan-Derk Bakker's devmem2 program (as mentioned in Chapter 3):

```
~$ wget http://www.lartmaker.nl/lartware/port/devmem2.c
~$ gcc devmem2.c -o devmem2
~$ sudo ./devmem2 0x44e10838
/dev/mem opened.
Memory mapped at address 0xb6fc6000.
Value at address 0x44E10838 (0xb6fc6838): 0x27
```

The value 0x27 is expected for $PINS14. You can investigate the source code of devmem2 to see how it can be integrated into your projects.

TI PINMUX TOOL (ADVANCED)

The pinmux is a capable and complex feature of the AM335x platform that allows SBC designers to associate a range of functionality (typically 8 options) with each of the processor pins. This means that some functionality is duplicated on multiple pins for different mux modes. However, depending on the use of different pins, not all options are valid for a particular pin.

You can use the TI PinMux Tool at `dev.ti.com/pinmux` to identify a valid pinmux board configuration. Figure 6-10 illustrates the tool in use. Start a design by choosing the Device as AM335x. You can then choose peripherals that you would like to add to a board design and choose from available pins. This tool is particularly useful should you ever embark on designing your own SBC!

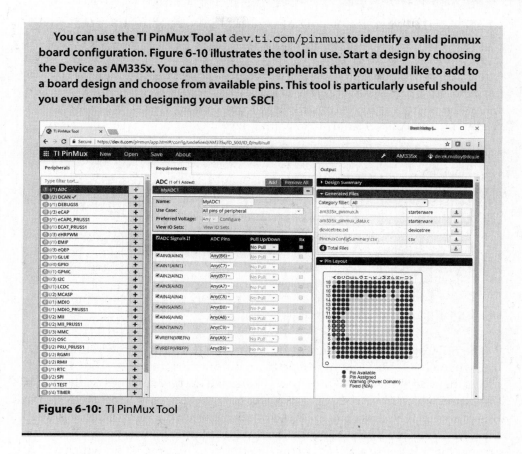

Figure 6-10: TI PinMux Tool

Interfacing to Powered DC Circuits

The Beagle board itself provides the power required for the output and input circuits that are illustrated in Figures 6-3 and 6-6, respectively. The current that can be sourced or sinked by these circuits is limited by the particular board specifications. Therefore, it is often necessary to interface to circuits that are powered by an external supply.

You must be careful when interfacing your board to circuits that have their own power supply (e.g., high-powered LEDs, car alarms, garage openers). For example, you should design the circuit so that it does not attempt to source current from, or sink current to, the GPIOs while the board is powered off. In addition, it would be ideal if you could avoid sharing a GND connection between the circuit and the Beagle board in case that something should go wrong with the circuit or its power supply.

A good solution is to utilize low-cost optocouplers, such as those described in Chapter 4 to design circuits in which there is no electrical connection whatsoever between the Beagle board and the externally powered circuit. Figure 6-11 illustrates an output circuit with an NPN transistor that is placed in a *Darlington pair* arrangement with the optocoupler to switch on or off the externally powered circuit load. A 5V external power supply is used in this example, but a greater DC supply voltage can be used. In addition, the maximum switching current is limited by the transistor characteristics (e.g., of a BC547), not by the optocoupler's output current I_c level.

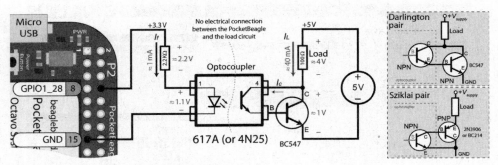

Figure 6-11: The optocoupler output circuit

The 617A optocoupler's current transfer ratio (CTR) of ≈0.5 when I_f = 1mA (i.e., when GPIO1_28 is high) results in an output current of I_c = 0.5mA, which enters the base of the BC547 transistor. This small current switches on the BC547 transistor, which in turn supplies a current of I_L = 40mA to the resistive load in this example. One downside of this configuration is that the voltage supply to the load is reduced by the V_{CE} of the Darlington pair (≈1V). An alternative to this arrangement is to use a *Sziklai pair* as illustrated in Figure 6-11, in which a PNP transistor is connected to the optocoupler output. Both arrangements limit the switching frequency capability of your output circuit (typically to the tens of kilohertz range). Unlike the 617A, the 4N25 exposes the base of the optocoupler receiver. This allows for the placement of additional base emitter resistors to improve the circuit's frequency response.

An optocoupler can also be connected to a GPIO to receive an input from an externally powered DC circuit, as illustrated in Figure 6-12. Importantly, this circuit can be adapted for any DC supply voltage, and it will not sink any current to the GPIO input when the board is powered off. You must choose a resistor value for the input side of the optocoupler to limit the forward current of the diode ($I_{f(max)}$ < 60mA for the 617A/4N25[1]).

GPIO1_14 can be configured to use an internal pull-down resistor by default, so it has a low state when the button is not pressed. The GPIO input circuit in Figure 6-12 sinks approximately 60μA to GPIO1_14 when the button is pressed. Similarly, this is the maximum current that will be sinked by this circuit (when

---

[1]See `tiny.cc/beagle602` and `tiny.cc/beagle603`

I_f and V_f exceed minimal levels for the optocoupler). This circuit can be adapted to handle a varying DC input voltage (within a range) by using a voltage regulator to maintain a value of I_f that is less than $I_{f(max)}$ for the chosen optocoupler.

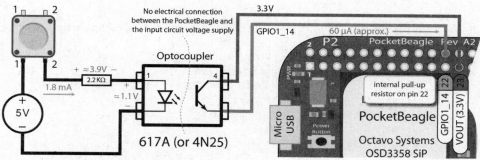

Figure 6-12: The optocoupler input circuit

C++ Control of GPIOs

A C++ class has been written for this book that wraps the GPIO functionality on the Beagle boards to make GPIOs easier to use. Listing 6-1 provides a segment of the class description that lists its basic I/O functionality. The more advanced functionality that has been removed from this code fragment is discussed at the end of this chapter. The implementation of this functionality is similar to the code that was written previously for the Beagle board LEDs. The full code listing is in /chp06/GPIO/GPIO.h and GPIO.cpp.

The C++ code is separated into header (.h) and implementation (.cpp) files, and the process of building applications in this form is called *separate compilation*. Separate compilation makes building large projects more efficient, but it can be difficult to manage all the files. The next chapter introduces the Eclipse integrated development environment (IDE) for cross-compilation, which can make this process seamless.

Listing 6-1: /chp06/GPIO/GPIO.h (Partial Listing)

```
// GPIO Class written by Derek Molloy (www.derekmolloy.ie)
#include<string>
#include<fstream>
using std::string;
using std::ofstream;
#define GPIO_PATH "/sys/class/gpio/"

namespace exploringBB {   //All code is within a namespace

// Enumerations are used to restrict the options
enum GPIO_DIRECTION{ INPUT, OUTPUT };
enum GPIO_VALUE     { LOW=0, HIGH=1 };
enum GPIO_EDGE      { NONE,  RISING, FALLING, BOTH };
```

```
class GPIO {
private:
    int number, debounceTime;
    string name, path;
public:
    GPIO(int number);        //constructor will export the pin
    virtual int getNumber() { return number; }

    // General Input and Output Settings
    virtual int setDirection(GPIO_DIRECTION);
    virtual GPIO_DIRECTION getDirection();
    virtual int setValue(GPIO_VALUE);
    virtual int toggleOutput();
    virtual GPIO_VALUE getValue();
    virtual int setActiveLow(bool isLow=true);   //low=1, high=0
    virtual int setActiveHigh(); //default
    //software debounce input (ms) - default 0
    virtual void setDebounceTime(int time){this->debounceTime = time;}

    // Advanced OUTPUT: Faster write using a stream (~20x)
    virtual int streamOpen();
    virtual int streamWrite(GPIO_VALUE);
    virtual int streamClose();

    // Advanced INPUT: presented at the end of this chapter
    virtual ~GPIO();   //destructor will unexport the pin

private: // Hidden functionality
    int write(string path, string filename, string value);
    int write(string path, string filename, int value);
    string read(string path, string filename);
    ofstream stream;
    ...
};/* End of GPIO class */
} /* namespace exploringBB */
```

You can extend this class through inheritance to add the functionality you require, and you can integrate it into your projects without restrictions on its use. Use of this class is demonstrated in the following short code example in Listing 6-2 that interacts with the LED and button circuits described earlier in this chapter:

Listing 6-2: /chp06/GPIO/simple.cpp

```
#include<iostream>
#include<unistd.h> //for usleep
#include"GPIO.h"
```

```
using namespace exploringBB;
using namespace std;

int main(){
    GPIO outGPIO(60), inGPIO(46);

    // Basic Output - Flash the LED 10 times, once per second
    outGPIO.setDirection(OUTPUT);
    for (int i=0; i<10; i++){
        outGPIO.setValue(HIGH);
        usleep(500000); //micro-second sleep 0.5 seconds
        outGPIO.setValue(LOW);
        usleep(500000);
    }
    // Basic Input example
    inGPIO.setDirection(INPUT);
    cout << "The value of the input is: "<< inGPIO.getValue() << endl;

    // Fast write to GPIO 1 million times
    outGPIO.streamOpen();
    for (int i=0; i<1000000; i++){
        outGPIO.streamWrite(HIGH);
        outGPIO.streamWrite(LOW);
    }
    outGPIO.streamClose();
    return 0;
}
```

You can build and execute this code as follows:

```
.../chp06/GPIO$ g++ simple.cpp GPIO.cpp -o simple -pthread
.../chp06/GPIO$ ./simple
The value of the input is: 0
```

where you need to pass both .cpp files to the compiler, as due to separate compilation the source code is split over multiple files. The -pthread flag is required for class functionality that is described later in this chapter.

This code example flashes the LED 10 times, reads the state of the button, and then flashes the LED 1 million times (in about 25 seconds on a PocketBeagle). To test the performance of this structure, Figure 6-13 captures the signal output of the LED flashing in (a) when the setValue() method is used with no sleep call, and in (b) when the streamWrite() method is used. In (a) it is flashing at about 5.5 kHz, and in (b) it is flashing at about 125 kHz. Unfortunately, the C++ application had to run at 93 percent of CPU usage to generate these outputs, which is not really practical on a multiuser, multiprocess OS such as Linux, and it is certainly not very efficient.

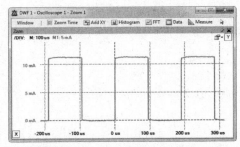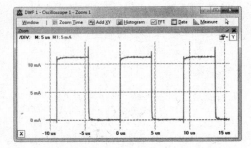

Figure 6-13: The C++ class flashing the LED

PWM is discussed later in this chapter, illustrating how to switch a GPIO using a regular periodic signal, at a fixed frequency, with negligible CPU load. For fast GPIO switching using a nonperiodic signal, the PRU-ICSS (see Chapter 15) would likely be required. An unsafe technique that uses direct access to system memory is also possible; and although it is definitely not recommended, it is explained next because of its value in learning about what is going on "under the hood."

MEMORY-BASED GPIO SWITCHING (ADVANCED)

If the preceding code is not switching fast enough for your applications, mechanisms are available for making a GPIO circuit switch at much higher frequencies, using the information from Chapter 25 in the *AM335x TRM*. However, by doing this you are effectively bypassing the Linux OS, which means that if two processes try to access the same GPIO registers at the same time, then a resource conflict could occur. *These operations are unsafe and could lock up your Linux kernel.* However, a reboot will put everything back in order. Therefore, while it is not recommended for general programming under Linux, an example provides useful insight into how the GPIOs function at the register level and how you can use some of the detail in the *AM335x TRM*.

At the beginning of this section, the devmem2 application is used to read the pin mux settings. You can use the same program to also set values in the AM335x registers. Section 25.4.1 in Chapter 25 of the *AM335x TRM* provides you with the addresses for the bank of GPIOs (from its Table 25-5).

- 13C GPIO_DATAOUT: Used to read the GPIO state
- 190 GPIO_CLEARDATAOUT: Used to set a GPIO low
- 194 GPIO_SETDATAOUT: Used to set a GPIO high

These values are offset from the base GPIO bank address. Because GPIO1_28 is on the GPIO1 bank, you need the base address, which is available in the Peripheral Memory Map table (Table 2-3) of the TRM and has the value 0x4804C000. For reference, GPIO0 is 0x44E07000, GPIO2 is 0x481AC000, and GPIO3 is 0x481AE000. Therefore, you can turn off the LED on P9_12/P2_08 (GPIO1_28) using the following call:

```
debian@ebb:~$ sudo ./devmem2 0x4804c190 w 0x10000000
/dev/mem opened. Memory mapped at address 0xb6f98000.
```

```
Value at address 0x4804C190 (0xb6f98190): 0x10000000
Written 0x10000000; readback 0x0
```

where the value you are writing to the GPIO_CLEARDATAOUT offset (190) from the base of address of GPIO1 (0x4804C000) is the 28th bit—i.e., 1 0000 0000 0000 0000 0000 0000 0000$_2$ converted to hexadecimal = 0x10000000. This will turn the LED off. To turn it on, use the GPIO_SETDATAOUT (194) offset.

```
debian@ebb:~$ sudo ./devmem2 0x4804c194 w 0x10000000
/dev/mem opened. Memory mapped at address 0xb6f29000.
Value at address 0x4804C194 (0xb6f29194): 0x0
Written 0x10000000; readback 0x10000000
```

To read the current state, you can use the GPIO_DATAOUT offset (13C) shown here:

```
debian@ebb:~$ sudo ./devmem2 0x4804c13c
/dev/mem opened. Memory mapped at address 0xb6f29000.
Value at address 0x4804C13C (0xb6f2913c): 0x10000000
```

where 0x10000000 = 0001 0000 0000 0000 0000 0000 0000 0000$_2$. Therefore, the 28th bit from the right (GPIO1_28) is on. Remember that you downloaded the source code for devmem2.c and it can be modified, should you want to perform this type of high-speed, but unsafe, GPIO switching. This topic is examined again in Chapter 15, when the PRU-ICSS is discussed.

The Linux Device Tree

The first introduction to the Linux boot process is in Chapter 3, where it is made clear that Linux running on an embedded device, such as a Beagle board, does not have a BIOS. Rather, to boot and configure the device, it uses files on the SD card or eMMC that describe the machine's hardware. Every type of embedded Linux device has its own unique set of files to describe its platform hardware.

When the original Beagle boards were running older Linux kernels, the specific modifications required to those Linux kernels were applied to the Linux source code directly by using a file called board-am335xevm.c. The popularity of ARM-based microprocessors led to a proliferation of Linux kernel customizations. As a result, Linus Torvalds was unhappy with the amount of code that was being added directly to mainline Linux to describe each and every feature, for each and every ARM device being manufactured (the board-am335xevm.c has more than 4,000 lines of code). Therefore, new ARM boards using the latest Linux kernels use *flattened device tree* (FDT) models instead, a technology that has been used by PowerPC developers for many years.

The device tree was originally designed to be understood by humans in a readable form, which is then converted into an efficient machine-readable format. In 1994 it was formally specified as the *IEEE Standard for Boot (Initialization*

Configuration) Firmware, which provides a standard for boot firmware requirements and practices—see `tiny.cc/beagle604`. It was utilized as early as 1995 in the PowerPC (Apple/Motorola) and by Sun Microsystems as a tree structure to describe hardware. Given the proliferation of ARM devices, it made sense for developers to revisit the device tree, and today more than 1,000 ARM-based boards are now using the device tree model. Until recently the device tree model was implemented only at the Linux kernel boot stage.

The U-Boot second-stage bootloader was introduced in Chapter 3, and an example output is presented that results from a board being booted. In recent years, U-Boot has been developed to support the device tree model so as to avoid hard-coding hardware topology into U-boot. This was achieved by using a trimmed-down version of the Linux driver model that avoids the need for custom C/C++ drivers. Today, U-Boot can store multiple kernel versions along with the device tree in a flattened image tree (FIT) format, which can be signed to allow for secure booting of multiple boot images. This allows multiple boards to be booted with a single image, which is why a single Linux image can boot boards with different hardware configuration, such as the PocketBeagle, a BeagleBone Black Wireless, and so on.

Flattened Device Tree on the Beagle Boards

The flattened device tree is a human-readable data structure that describes the hardware on a particular Beagle board. The FDT is described using device tree source (DTS) files, where a `.dts` file contains a board-level definition and a `.dtsi` file typically contains SoC-level definitions. The `.dtsi` files are typically included into a `.dts` file. Figure 6-14 illustrates the structure of the flattened device tree for the AM335x SoC (more precisely, the more general AM33xx family of SoCs).

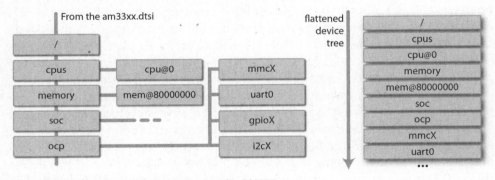

Figure 6-14: The flattened device tree on the AM335x

In the GitHub repository directory that follows, the device tree source files for the Beagle board Linux 4.17.0 kernel are made available so that you can review them:

```
debian@ebb:~/exploringbb/chp06/deviceTree/DTSource4.17.0$ ls
am335x-boneblack-common.dtsi    am335x-bonegreen.dts
am335x-boneblack.dts            am335x-bonegreen-wireless.dts
am335x-boneblack-wireless.dts   am335x-pocketbeagle-common.dtsi
am335x-boneblue.dts             am335x-pocketbeagle.dts
am335x-bone-common.dtsi         am33xx.dtsi
am335x-bone.dts                 am57xx-beagle-x15-common.dtsi
am335x-bonegreen-common.dtsi    am57xx-beagle-x15.dts
```

In particular, examine the beginning of the file, am335x-boneblack.dts (as shown in Listing 6-3), which describes the device tree for the BeagleBone Black. The file is short and largely just lists include files, segments of which are provided in Listing 6-4, Listing 6-5, and Listing 6-6.

Listing 6-3: chp06/deviceTree/DTSource4.17.0/am335x-boneblack.dts

```
/* Copyright (C) 2012 Texas Instruments Incorporated ... */
/dts-v1/;
#include "am33xx.dtsi"
#include "am335x-bone-common.dtsi"
#include "am335x-boneblack-common.dtsi"
/ {
    model = "TI AM335x BeagleBone Black";
    compatible = "ti,am335x-bone-black", "ti,am335x-bone", "ti,am33xx";
};
...
```

Listing 6-4: chp06/deviceTree/DTSource4.17.0/am33xx.dtsi

```
/* Device Tree Source for AM33XX SoC ... */
#include <dt-bindings/gpio/gpio.h>
#include <dt-bindings/pinctrl/am33xx.h>
#include <dt-bindings/clock/am3.h>
/ {
        compatible = "ti,am33xx";
        interrupt-parent = <&intc>;
        chosen { };
         ...
        ocp {
            compatible = "simple-bus";
            #address-cells = <1>;
```

```
        #size-cells = <1>;
        ranges;
        ti,hwmods = "l3_main";
        ....
        gpio0: gpio@44e07000 {
        compatible = "ti,omap4-gpio";
            ti,hwmods = "gpio1";
            gpio-controller;
            interrupt-controller;
            reg = <0x44e07000 0x1000>;
            interrupts = <96>;
        };
        ...
        uart0: serial@44e09000 {
            compatible = "ti,am3352-uart", "ti,omap3-uart";
            ti,hwmods = "uart1";
            clock-frequency = <48000000>;
            reg = <0x44e09000 0x2000>;
            interrupts = <72>;
            status = "disabled";
            dmas = <&edma 26 0>, <&edma 27 0>;
            dma-names = "tx", "rx";
        };
        ...
        epwmss1: epwmss@48302000 {
            compatible = "ti,am33xx-pwmss";
            reg = <0x48302000 0x10>;
            ti,hwmods = "epwmss1";
            #address-cells = <1>;
            #size-cells = <1>;
            status = "disabled";
            ranges = <0x48302100 0x48302100 0x80   /* ECAP */
                      0x48302180 0x48302180 0x80   /* EQEP */
                      0x48302200 0x48302200 0x80>; /* EHRPWM */
            ...
        };
    };
};
```

Listing 6-5: DTSource4.17.0/am335x-bone-common.dtsi

```
/*  Copyright (C) 2012 Texas Instruments Incorporated ... */
/ {
        cpus {
                cpu@0 {
                        cpu0-supply = <&dcdc2_reg>;
                };
        };
```

```
memory@80000000 {
        device_type = "memory";
        reg = <0x80000000 0x10000000>; /* 256 MB */
};

chosen {
        stdout-path = &uart0;
};

leds {
        pinctrl-names = "default";
        pinctrl-0 = <&user_leds_s0>;
        compatible = "gpio-leds";
        led3 {
                label = "beaglebone:green:mmc0";
                gpios = <&gpio1 22 GPIO_ACTIVE_HIGH>;
                linux,default-trigger = "mmc0";
                default-state = "off";
        };
...
```

Listing 6-6: /DTSource4.17.0/am335x-boneblack-common.dtsi

```
#include <dt-bindings/display/tda998x.h>
&mmc1 {
        vmmc-supply = <&vmmcsd_fixed>;
};

&mmc2 {
        vmmc-supply = <&vmmcsd_fixed>;
        pinctrl-names = "default";
        pinctrl-0 = <&emmc_pins>;
        bus-width = <8>;
        status = "okay";
};

&am33xx_pinmux {
        nxp_hdmi_bonelt_pins: nxp_hdmi_bonelt_pins {
            pinctrl-single,pins = <
...
        };
```

These files describe the properties of the CPU, base memory, GPIOs, PWMs, UARTs, user LEDs, and more. There is a full description about what each field in the FDT means at elinux.org/Device_Tree_Usage.

Some of the values should look familiar; for example, the GPIO0 offset is listed as 44e10800, just as described in the "Memory-Based GPIO Switching (Advanced)" feature. You can see that the user led3 is attached to GPIO1_22, and by default it indicates activity on mmc0. Also, please note from Listing 6-4 that uart0 is present at address 44e09000, and one of the PWM outputs (epwmss1) is present at address 48302000, which is important later in this chapter.

These files are compiled into a binary form using a *device tree compiler* (DTC) and are placed on the Linux boot image at /boot/dtbs/, as shown by the following for the PocketBeagle:

```
debian@ebb:/boot/dtbs/4.14.35-ti-rt-r44$ ls -l am335x-pocketbeagle.dtb
-rw-r--r-- 1 root root 124178 Apr 22 07:18 am335x-pocketbeagle.dtb
```

The DTC simply performs a file conversion from DTS (human-readable) to DTB (binary computer-readable) form. This is a straightforward and reversible process, quite different from compilation when using gcc/g++.

The DTB files are used as part of the boot process. To modify the hardware description that is configured on your board, you could modify these DTS files, compile them using the DTC, deploy them to the boot directory, and then reboot your board.

Modifying a Board Device Tree

It is possible to modify the board device tree by taking the device tree source, editing it, and then compiling it using the device tree compiler. It is, however, challenging to ensure that you have the precise versions of the device tree source files for your current build.

```
debian@ebb:~/exploringbb/chp06/deviceTree/DTSource4.17.0$ cp * /tmp
debian@ebb:~/exploringbb/chp06/deviceTree/DTSource4.17.0$ cd /tmp
debian@ebb:/tmp$ ls -l am335x-pocket*
-rw-r--r-- 1 debian debian 64233 May 27 04:25 am335x-pocketbeagle-common.dtsi
-rw-r--r-- 1 debian debian 27474 May 27 04:25 am335x-pocketbeagle.dts
debian@ebb:/tmp$ dtc -version
Version: DTC 1.4.4
```

Robert C. Nelson has provided a much more straightforward method for building the device tree binaries using a dtb-rebuilder script. You can download and use it as follows:

```
debian@ebb:~$ git clone git://github.com/RobertCNelson/dtb-rebuilder.git
debian@ebb:~$ cd dtb-rebuilder/
debian@ebb:~/dtb-rebuilder$ git branch
* 4.4-ti
debian@ebb:~/dtb-rebuilder$ uname -a
Linux ebb 4.9.88-ti-rt-r111 #1 SMP PREEMPT RT ...
debian@ebb:~/dtb-rebuilder$ git checkout 4.9-ti
Branch 4.9-ti set up to track remote branch 4.9-ti from origin.
Switched to a new branch '4.9-ti'
```

where the branch is chosen according to the current board version.

You can then edit the device tree source files (.dts and .dtsi) to make any necessary modifications.

```
debian@ebb:~/dtb-rebuilder$ ls
Bindings COPYING dtc-overlay.sh include Makefile README scripts src
debian@ebb:~/dtb-rebuilder$ cd src/arm/
debian@ebb:~/dtb-rebuilder/src/arm$ ls am335x-pocketbeagle*
am335x-pocketbeagle-common.dtsi  am335x-pocketbeagle-simplegaming.dts
am335x-pocketbeagle.dts
```

In this case, a simple change is made to the PocketBeagle device tree to use a default trigger of "heartbeat" instead of "mmc1" for the USR3 on-board LED.

```
debian@ebb:~/dtb-rebuilder/src/arm$ nano am335x-pocketbeagle-common.dtsi
debian@ebb:~/dtb-rebuilder/src/arm$ more am335x-pocketbeagle-common.dtsi
...
                led@5 {
                        label = "beaglebone:green:usr3";
                        gpios = <&gpio1 24 GPIO_ACTIVE_HIGH>;
                        linux,default-trigger = "heartbeat";
                        default-state = "off";
                };
...
debian@ebb:~/dtb-rebuilder/src/arm$ cd ../../
debian@ebb:~/dtb-rebuilder$ make all
debian@ebb:~/dtb-rebuilder/src/arm$ ls -l am335x-pocketbeagle.dtb
-rw-r--r-- 1 debian debian 132761 May 27 04:52 am335x-pocketbeagle.dtb
```

You can back up the current device tree binary and replace it with this new binary as follows:

```
debian@ebb:/boot/dtbs/4.9.88-ti-rt-r111$ ls -l am335x-pocketbeagle.dtb
-rw-r--r-- 1 root root 132757 Apr 22 11:44 am335x-pocketbeagle.dtb
...$ sudo mv am335x-pocketbeagle.dtb am335x-pocketbeagle.dtb_backup
...$ sudo cp ~/dtb-rebuilder/src/arm/am335x-pocketbeagle.dtb .
...$ ls -l am335x-pocketbeagle.dtb
-rw-r--r-- 1 root root 132761 May 27 04:57 am335x-pocketbeagle.dtb
```

On reboot, both the USR0 and USR3 LEDs now flash with a heartbeat pattern, and you can confirm their state in the usr3 sysfs directory.

```
debian@ebb:~$ cd /sys/class/leds/beaglebone\:green\:usr3
debian@ebb:/sys/class/leds/beaglebone:green:usr3$ ls
brightness device invert max_brightness power subsystem trigger uevent
debian@ebb:/sys/class/leds/beaglebone:green:usr3$ cat trigger
none ... [heartbeat] backlight gpio default-on
```

Boot Configuration Files

Earlier Linux kernel versions on the BeagleBone used a kernel overlay "slots" framework (used throughout the first edition of this book) to allow for the dynamic reconfiguration of hardware, which was necessary when capes were plugged into a Beagle board. The capes identified themselves using identification and version codes that were stored in an on-board EEPROM. The kernel cape manager would use this information to search the /lib/firmware/ directory for the correct overlay. Kernel overlays are currently being phased out by the BeagleBoard.org development team and are being replaced by U-Boot overlays.

Currently, you have control over the configuration of hardware at boot time using the /boot/uEnv.txt configuration file, a segment of which is provided in Listing 6-7.

> **WARNING** Be careful in editing the uEnv.txt file. Editing errors will prevent your board from booting. Should an error arise and your board fail to boot, Chapter 3 describes how you can edit the erroneous file by mounting the associated SD card/ eMMC under a different Linux device.

Currently, this configuration file allows you to

- Revert to the old kernel overlay "slots" model by commenting out the line enable_uboot_overlays=1 with a #. Do that at your own peril!

- Disable on-board devices (e.g., the eMMC, HDMI, on-board Wi-Fi, and the ADCs) by uncommenting the associated line (e.g., disable_uboot_overlay_adc=1).

- Provide support for a custom overlay by specifying it as follows: dtb_overlay=/lib/firmware/<custom>.dtbo. The /lib/firmware/ directory provides a repository of overlays.

- Choose to enable overlays for the PRU-ICSS (rpoc or uio) as described in Chapter 15.

The *Automatic Pin Configuration on Boot* feature in Chapter 15 describes a method for initializing the mode of the header pins at boot time.

Listing 6-7: /boot/uEnv.txt (Segment)

```
#Docs: http://elinux.org/Beagleboard:U-boot_partitioning_layout_2.0
uname_r=4.14.54-ti-rt-r63
#uuid=
#dtb=
```

```
###U-Boot Overlays###
###Documentation: http://elinux.org/Beagleboard:BeagleBoneBlack_Debian
#U-Boot_Overlays
###Master Enable
enable_uboot_overlays=1
###
###Overide capes with eeprom
#uboot_overlay_addr0=/lib/firmware/<file0>.dtbo
...
###
###Additional custom capes
#uboot_overlay_addr4=/lib/firmware/<file4>.dtbo
...
###
###Custom Cape
#dtb_overlay=/lib/firmware/<file8>.dtbo
###
###Disable auto loading of virtual capes (emmc/video/wireless/adc)
#disable_uboot_overlay_emmc=1
#disable_uboot_overlay_video=1
#disable_uboot_overlay_audio=1
#disable_uboot_overlay_wireless=1
#disable_uboot_overlay_adc=1
###
###PRUSS OPTIONS
###pru_rproc (4.4.x-ti kernel)
#uboot_overlay_pru=/lib/firmware/AM335X-PRU-RPROC-4-4-TI-00A0.dtbo
###pru_uio (4.4.x-ti, 4.14.x-ti & mainline/bone kernel)
#uboot_overlay_pru=/lib/firmware/AM335X-PRU-UIO-00A0.dtbo
###
###Cape Universal Enable
enable_uboot_cape_universal=1
###
###Debug: disable uboot autoload of Cape
#disable_uboot_overlay_addr0=1
...
###
###U-Boot fdt tweaks... (60000 = 384KB)
#uboot_fdt_buffer=0x60000
###U-Boot Overlays###
cmdline=coherent_pool=1M net.ifnames=0 quiet

#In the event of edid real failures, uncomment this next line:
#cmdline=coherent_pool=1M net.ifnames=0 quiet video=HDMI-A-1:1024x768
@60e

##enable Generic eMMC Flasher:
##make sure these tools are installed: dosfstools rsync
#cmdline=init=/opt/scripts/tools/eMMC/init-eMMC-flasher-v3.sh
```

Analog Inputs and Outputs

In Chapter 4, the concept of analog-to-digital conversion was introduced, and an operational amplifier voltage-follower circuit was described that can be used to safely read analog inputs. This section describes how you can interface such a circuit to a Beagle board and use Linux sysfs to read values into your software applications.

Analog Inputs

The AM335x has a 12-bit *successive approximation register* (SAR) ADC that is capable of 200,000 samples per second. The input to the SAR is internally selected using an 8:1 analog switch, and the board makes seven of these switched inputs available on the P9/P1 header as ADC inputs. Among other things, the analog inputs can be configured to be used as a four-wire, five-wire, or eight-wire resistive touch screen controller (TSC), and this application is used in Chapter 13. In the current section, the ADC inputs are used as simple one-wire ADC inputs. By default, these inputs are enabled on the board.

> **NOTE**   A *successive approximation* ADC uses an analog voltage comparator to compare the analog input voltage to an estimated digital value that is passed through a digital-to-analog converter (DAC). The result of the analog comparison is used to update the estimated digital value, which is stored in a successive approximation register. The process continues iteratively until all of the bits (12 in the case of a 12-bit ADC) are weighted and compared to the input. Successive approximation ADCs are popular because they provide a good balance of speed, accuracy, and cost; however, the higher the resolution, the slower the ADC performance.

Enabling the Analog Inputs

The analog inputs can be enabled with the use of a virtual cape that is loaded by default. To check that the virtual cape is not disabled (or to disable the cape), verify that the following entry is commented out as follows:

```
debian@ebb:/boot$ more uEnv.txt | grep adc
###Disable auto loading of virtual capes (emmc/video/wireless/adc)
#disable_uboot_overlay_adc=1
```

If the ADCs are enabled, then you can access them directly from sysfs using the /sys/bus/iio/devices/ directory, in which you will find file entries that allow you to read the raw ADC values directly.

```
debian@ebb:~$ cd /sys/bus/iio
debian@ebb:/sys/bus/iio$ ls
```

```
devices  drivers  drivers_autoprobe  drivers_probe  uevent
debian@ebb:/sys/bus/iio$ cd devices/
debian@ebb:/sys/bus/iio/devices$ ls
iio:device0
debian@ebb:/sys/bus/iio/devices$ cd iio\:device0
debian@ebb:/sys/bus/iio/devices/iio:device0$ ls
buffer           in_voltage2_raw  in_voltage6_raw  power
dev              in_voltage3_raw  in_voltage7_raw  scan_elements
in_voltage0_raw  in_voltage4_raw  name             subsystem
in_voltage1_raw  in_voltage5_raw  of_node          uevent
```

If you read the analog input (AIN0), using `cat in_voltage0_raw`, when nothing is connected, the result will be an integer value between 0 and 4,095. The Beagle boards have 12-bit ADCs ($2^{12} = 4,096$), meaning a value between 0 and $2^{12} - 1$ (0 to 4,095) will be returned. You can test this by using the following:

```
debian@ebb:/sys/bus/iio/devices/iio:device0$ cat in_voltage0_raw
3994
debian@ebb:/sys/bus/iio/devices/iio:device0$ cat in_voltage0_raw
3993
```

You can test the full range of an ADC input by connecting the input (P1.19/P9_39 AIN0) to the analog ground/negative pin (P1.17/P9_34 VREFN) and the voltage reference positive pin (P1.18/P9_32 VREFP) on the PocketBeagle/BeagleBone. Performing these connections results in the following outputs:

```
debian@ebb:/sys/bus/iio/devices/iio:device0$ cat in_voltage0_raw
0
debian@ebb:/sys/bus/iio/devices/iio:device0$ cat in_voltage0_raw
4095
```

Next, a simple light-level meter application is built to demonstrate how you can attach sensor circuits to a Beagle board that can be used for sampling and data-logging applications.

3.3 V ADCS ON THE POCKETBEAGLE

There are two 3.3 V ADCs on the PocketBeagle at P1.02 (AIN6) and P2.35 (AIN5). These ADCs are pulled close to 0 V when the pin is left floating, which can be tested as follows:

```
debian@ebb:/sys/bus/iio/devices/iio:device0$ cat in_voltage5_raw
0
debian@ebb:/sys/bus/iio/devices/iio:device0$ cat in_voltage6_raw
1
```

You can test that these are 3.3 V ADCs by connecting the 1.8 V (P1.19 VREFP) voltage to the input and reading the digital input value as follows:

```
debian@ebb:/sys/bus/iio/devices/iio:device0$ cat in_voltage5_raw
2041
```

```
debian@ebb:/sys/bus/iio/devices/iio:device0$ cat in_voltage6_raw
2059
```

The analog values are roughly in the middle of the range. If you tie the pins to a 3.3 V pin (e.g., P1.14), then the output gets close to the maximum of 4,095.

```
debian@ebb:/sys/bus/iio/devices/iio:device0$ cat in_voltage5_raw
3909
debian@ebb:/sys/bus/iio/devices/iio:device0$ cat in_voltage6_raw
3940
```

You can use the 3.3 V pin as a positive reference voltage and GND as a negative reference voltage for these two inputs.

Analog Input Application—A Simple Light Meter

To choose a suitable pairing resistor value R for a *typical light-dependent resistor* (LDR) voltage divider circuit, a good rule of thumb is to use the equation $R = \sqrt{R_{MIN} \times R_{MAX}}$, where R_{MIN} is the measured resistance of the LDR when it is covered (e.g., with your finger) and R_{MAX} is the measured resistance of the LDR when a light source (e.g., phone torch app) is close to its surface. In this example, the resistance of the LDR was 6kΩ when covered and 100Ω when the light source was close. The preceding formula thus gives a value for R of 775Ω, so the combination of a 470Ω and a 330Ω resistor in series provides a suitable value for the potential divider. You could wire the circuit as shown in Figure 6-15, but it is not a recommended configuration.

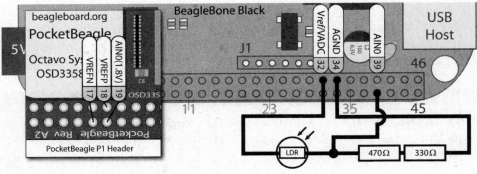

Figure 6-15: ADC LDR circuit (not recommended)

> **NOTE** If you are following this chapter by building the circuits, do not disassemble the LED and button circuits, as they are required later in this chapter.

The problem with the circuit in Figure 6-15 is that it will draw a current from the Vref/VADC(P9_32) pin and act as a variable load. The resistance between *Vref* and AGND varies from 900Ω in the brightest case to 6.8kΩ in the darkest case. In the brightest case, because *Vref* = 1.8V, this means that the current being sourced from *Vref*, $I = 1.8V/900Ω = 2mA$. If you were to wire seven separate circuits like this one, you could end up sourcing up to 14mA from *Vref*, which could damage the board. The AM335x analog front end (AFE) switches between inputs, but the supply voltage will remain powered for all seven circuits. Even if the current is not large enough to damage the board, drawing current from *Vref* will affect the voltage level of the reference voltage itself, which defeats the purpose of having a reference voltage.

To avoid drawing any significant current from the 1.8V *Vref* pin, an op-amp voltage-follower circuit can be used. This op-amp configuration is discussed in Chapter 4. The implementation described in Figure 6-16 uses a LM358P (dual op-amp) IC, where V_{CC} is connected to the SYS_5V rail (DC_3.3V could also have been used) and the positive input (2IN+) to the second op-amp is the BeagleBone 1.8V analog reference voltage *Vref*/VADC(P9_32).

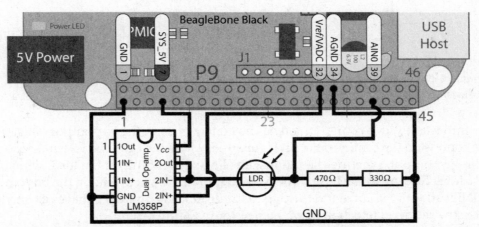

Figure 6-16: ADC LDR circuit using a voltage-follower circuit (recommended)

The raw voltage levels can be read from the ADC using `sysfs`. For the following sample values, the first reading was taken at regular room light levels, the second reading was taken with the LDR surface covered, and the third reading was taken with a light source very close to the sensor.

```
/sys/bus/iio/devices/iio:device0# cat in_voltage0_raw
959
/sys/bus/iio/devices/iio:device0# cat in_voltage0_raw
304
/sys/bus/iio/devices/iio:device0# cat in_voltage0_raw
3651
```

The circuit provides a good range of decimal input values because of the resistor calculation at the start of this section. The current required for input offset and input biasing is typically 2nA and 20nA, respectively, for the LM358, meaning that it will not draw any significant current from the BeagleBone *Vref* pin (P9_32). The actual measured voltage and current values for this circuit are displayed in Figure 6-17, where the "light level" as read from `in_voltage0_raw` was the value 3,466. It should be clear from this figure that there is almost no current being sourced from or sinked to the analog *Vref*, AGND, or AIN0 pins, even though the current flowing through the LDR was about 2mA (as the light level in the room was bright and the LDR resistance was low).

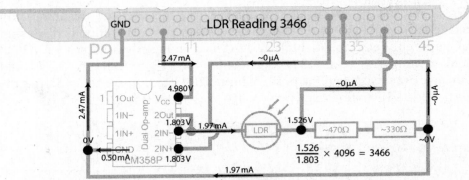

Figure 6-17: Measured voltages and current values with the op-amp in a voltage-follower configuration

Importantly, this configuration has no *loading effect* on the *Vref* output. This is in contrast to the configuration in Figure 6-15, where the LDR and resistors load the *Vref* output, skewing the reference voltage depending on the load, which varies according to the light level. Note that the 1.97mA current on the bottom GND rail was the current returning to the grounding point (it behaves exactly like the return connection from the resistor in Figure 4-2(a)).

Here is a simple C++ application that reads in the LDR value. It is structured so that it reads a single value from any of the AIN pins, by passing the pin number (0–6) to the `readAnalog()` function:

```
~/exploringbb/chp06/ADC# more readLDR.cpp
#include<iostream>
#include<fstream>
#include<string>
#include<sstream>
using namespace std;

#define LDR_PATH "/sys/bus/iio/devices/iio:device0/in_voltage"
```

```
int readAnalog(int number){    // returns the input as an int
    stringstream ss;
    ss << LDR_PATH << number << "_raw";
    fstream fs;
    fs.open(ss.str().c_str(), fstream::in);
    fs >> number;
    fs.close();
    return number;
}

int main(int argc, char* argv[]){
    cout << "Starting the readLDR program" << endl;
    int value = readAnalog(0);
    cout << "The LDR value was " << value << " out of 4095." << endl;
    return 0;
}
~/exploringbb/chp06/ADC# g++ readLDR.cpp -o readLDR
~/exploringbb/chp06/ADC# ./readLDR
Starting the readLDR program
The LDR value was 463 out of 4095.
```

This code works perfectly for reading a sensor occasionally, but it is not good for reading a sensor many times per second.

Analog Outputs (PWM)

The next functionality to be examined is the use of the Beagle board's pulse-width modulation (PWM) outputs to provide low-frequency digital-to-analog conversion (DAC), or for the generation of control signals for motors and certain types of servos. There are eight PWM outputs on the AM335x, three eHRPWM modules (two outputs each), and two eCAP modules. These outputs are described in Figures 6-8 and 6-9, where you can see that the six eHRPWM outputs are each available on two separate pins (e.g., output 2B is available on P8_13 and P8_46). Please see Table 6-2 for the location of the PWMs on the BeagleBone Black (BBB) and PocketBeagle (PB) boards.[2]

See Chapter 15 in the AM335x TRM for full details on the Pulse-Width Modulation Subsystem (PWMSS). The Linux PWM system is described in detail at tiny.cc/beagle605.

To enable a PWM on an output pin, use the config-pin tool and choose the pwm setting. For example, to enable PWM on P1.08 on the PocketBeagle, use the following:

```
debian@ebb:~$ config-pin -a p1.08 pwm
debian@ebb:~$ config-pin -q p1.08
P1_08 Mode: pwm
```

---

[2]Please note that the Linux chip identifier (BBB Chip and PB Chip) can change depending on the device tree configuration of a particular Linux image; however, the memory address mapping to a physical pin on the board will not change.

Table 6-2: The PWMSS on the AM335x and the Connected Pins on the BeagleBone Black (BBB) and the PocketBeagle (PB) Boards

HARDWARE NAME	HARDWARE ADDRESS	BBB CHIP[3]	CHANNEL	BBB PINS	PB CHIP	BP PINS
EHRPWM0	0x48300200	pwmchip0	0A	P9_22/ P9_31	pwmchip0	P1.08/ P1.36
	0x48300260	pwmchip0	0B	P9_21/ P9_29	pwmchip0	P1.10/ P1.33
EHRPWM1	0x48302200	pwmchip2	1A	P9_14/ P8_36	pwmchip2	P2.01
	0x48302260	pwmchip2	1B	P9_16/ P8_34	pwmchip2	n/a
EHRPWM2	0x48304200	pwmchip5	2A	P8_19/ P8_45	pwmchip4	n/a
	0x48304260	pwmchip5	2B	P8_13/ P8_46	pwmchip4	P2.03
ECAP0	0x48300100	pwmchipX	n/a	P9_42	n/a	P2.29
ECAP2	0x48304100	pwmchipX	n/a	P9_28	n/a	P1.32/ P2.30

The PWM pins can then be controlled using the appropriate pwmchip device. Here's an example on the BeagleBone:

```
debian@ebb:/sys/class/pwm$ ls
pwmchip0  pwmchip2  pwmchip3  pwmchip5  pwmchip6
```

Or, here's an example on the PocketBeagle:

```
debian@ebb:/sys/class/pwm$ ls -l
... pwmchip0 -> .../48300000.epwmss/48300200.pwm/pwm/pwmchip0
... pwmchip2 -> .../48302000.epwmss/48302200.pwm/pwm/pwmchip2
... pwmchip4 -> .../48304000.epwmss/48304200.pwm/pwm/pwmchip4
```

You can then control the PWM as follows:

```
debian@ebb:/sys/class/pwm$ cd pwmchip0
debian@ebb:/sys/class/pwm/pwmchip0$ echo 0 > export
debian@ebb:/sys/class/pwm/pwmchip0$ ls
device  export  npwm  power  pwm-0:0  subsystem  uevent  unexport
debian@ebb:/sys/class/pwm/pwmchip0$ cd ..
debian@ebb:/sys/class/pwm$ ls
pwm-0:0  pwmchip0  pwmchip2  pwmchip4
```

---

[3] The pwmchip ordering can change each time a board boots, but a cape universal script at tiny.cc/beagle606 reorders the numbering to provide a consistent structure.

```
debian@ebb:/sys/class/pwm$ cd pwm-0\:0
debian@ebb:/sys/class/pwm/pwm-0:0$ ls -l
-rw-rw-r-- 1 root pwm 4096 Jul 17 05:27 capture
lrwxrwxrwx 1 root pwm    0 Jul 17 05:27 device -> ...
-rw-rw-r-- 1 root pwm 4096 Jul 17 05:27 duty_cycle
-rw-rw-r-- 1 root pwm 4096 Jul 17 05:27 enable
-rw-rw-r-- 1 root pwm 4096 Jul 17 05:27 period
-rw-rw-r-- 1 root pwm 4096 Jul 17 05:27 polarity
drwxrwxr-x 2 root pwm    0 Jul 17 05:27 power
lrwxrwxrwx 1 root pwm    0 Jul 17 05:27 subsystem -> ...
-rw-rw-r-- 1 root pwm 4096 Jul 17 05:27 uevent
```

To set up a PWM signal (EHRPWM0A), the period is supplied in nanoseconds. Therefore, to output a PWM signal that has a period of 4 µs and a 25 percent duty cycle, you set the time period as 1 µs and not the duty cycle percentage.

```
debian@ebb:/sys/class/pwm/pwm-0:0$ sudo sh -c "echo 4000 > period"
debian@ebb:/sys/class/pwm/pwm-0:0$ sudo sh -c "echo 1000 > duty_cycle"
debian@ebb:/sys/class/pwm/pwm-0:0$ cat polarity
normal
debian@ebb:/sys/class/pwm/pwm-0:0$ sudo sh -c "echo 1 > enable"
```

This results in the output in Figure 6-18(a). You can see from the measurements that the period is 4 µs and the frequency is 250 kHz (i.e., 1/4 µs).

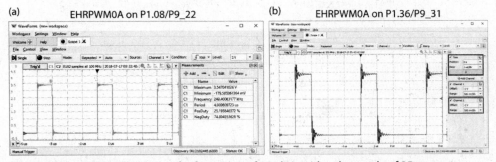

Figure 6-18: EHRPWM0A output for frequency of 250 kHz with a duty cycle of 25 percent

The same EHRPWM0A output is available on P1.36 on the PocketBeagle and can be enabled as follows:

```
debian@ebb:~$ config-pin -q p1.36
P1_36 Mode: default Direction: in Value: 0
debian@ebb:~$ config-pin -a p1.36 pwm
debian@ebb:~$ config-pin -q p1.36
P1_36 Mode: pwm
```

This results in the output in Figure 6-18(b), which overlays both channels exactly.

Now, if you use both P1.08 and P1.10 on a PocketBeagle, which share the same PWM device but different channels (0A and 0B), the following occurs:

```
debian@ebb:~$ config-pin -a p1.10 pwm
debian@ebb:/sys/class/pwm/pwmchip0$ ls
device  npwm    pwm-0:0  subsystem  unexport
export  power   pwm-0:1  uevent
debian@ebb:/sys/class/pwm/pwm-0:1$ ls
capture  duty_cycle  period    power      uevent
device   enable      polarity  subsystem
debian@ebb:/sys/class/pwm/pwm-0:1$ sudo sh -c "echo 4000 > period"
debian@ebb:/sys/class/pwm/pwm-0:1$ sudo sh -c "echo 2000 > duty_cycle"
debian@ebb:/sys/class/pwm/pwm-0:1$ cat polarity
normal
debian@ebb:/sys/class/pwm/pwm-0:1$ sudo sh -c "echo 1 > enable"
```

This results in the output in Figure 6-19(a) where both outputs have the same frequency but different duty cycles (25 percent and 50 percent in this case). Importantly, you cannot change the period when both channels are exported. In fact, to change the frequency of either channel, you must disable one channel beforehand. If you do not disable a channel or if you attempt to set a period duration (in nanoseconds) that is longer than the frequency duration (in nanoseconds), then you will see the following error:

```
debian@ebb:/sys/class/pwm/pwm-0:0$ sudo sh -c "echo 8000 > period"
sh: echo: I/O error
```

(a)   (b)

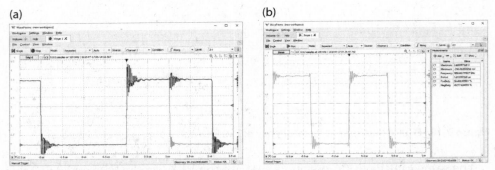

Figure 6-19: (a) Two PWM channels with a 25 percent and 50 percent duty cycle at 250kHz, and (b) PWM at 1MHz with a duty cycle of 50 percent

If you connect a DMM between the PWM pin and GND, the voltage measured with a 5,000 duty period should be 1.657V when the duty period is set as 5,000 and the period is set at 10,000 (that is, the output is 3.314V for half of each cycle and 0V for the other half, and the DMM averages this to 1.657V). Changing the duty cycle period results in the following DMM measurements by default: 0 → 3.314V, 2500 → 2.485 V, 7500 → 0.828 V, and 10,000 → 0.6 mV.

This relationship can be inverted (i.e., 10,000 → 3.314 V) by changing the polarity `echo inversed > polarity`. Setting these values provides you with DAC capability that can be combined with an optocoupler to limit the current drawn from the GPIO pin.

Output Application—Controlling a Servo Motor

Servo motors consist of a DC motor that is attached to a potentiometer and a control circuit. The position of the motor shaft can be controlled by sending a PWM signal to the controller.

The Hitec HS-422 is a low-cost (less than $10), good quality, and widely available servo motor that can be supplied using a 5V supply. It is rated to rotate ±45° from the center. It can rotate in the range ±90°, but the potentiometer does not behave in a linear manner outside of the ±45° range. According to its datasheet, the HS-422 expects a pulse every 20ms that has a duration from 1100μs (to set the position to −45° from the center position) to 1900μs (to set the position to +45° from the center position). The center position can be set by passing a pulse of 1500μs in duration.

Figure 6-20 illustrates the connections and timings for the servo motor that enables it to rotate from −90° using a pulse of 570μs to +90° using a pulse of 2350μs. These values and the center point of 1460μs were manually calibrated and will vary for each individual servo motor.

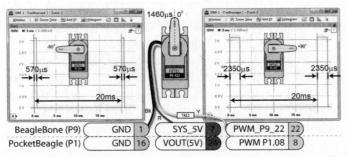

Figure 6-20: Controlling a servo motor using PWM, positioning from −90° to +90° using different pulse widths

The servo motor has three leads: black, red, and yellow. The black lead is connected to GND (P9_01/P1.16), the red lead is connected to a 5V supply (P9_07/P1.24), and the yellow lead is connected via a 1kΩ resistor to the PWM output (`ehrpwm0A`) on P9_22/P1.08. The 1kΩ resistor limits the current sourced from P9_22/P1.08 to about 0.01mA. To manually control a servo motor using `sysfs`, perform the following steps:

```
debian@ebb:/sys/class/pwm/pwmchip0$ echo 0 > export
debian@ebb:/sys/class/pwm/pwmchip0$ cd ..
```

```
debian@ebb:/sys/class/pwm$ ls
pwm-0:0  pwmchip0  pwmchip2  pwmchip4
debian@ebb:/sys/class/pwm$ cd pwm-0\:0
```

The polarity value should be set to `normal` for servo motors so that the duty value represents the duration of a high pulse. If the polarity value is `inversed`, then the signal is inverted, and the `duty_cycle` value would effectively specify the duration of a low pulse, with the signal being high for the remainder of the period. The period is set to 20ms, and the output is enabled.

```
.../sys/class/pwm/pwm-0:0$ sudo sh -c "echo normal > polarity"
.../sys/class/pwm/pwm-0:0$ sudo sh -c "echo 20000000 > period"
.../sys/class/pwm/pwm-0:0$ sudo sh -c "echo 1 > enable"
```

The arm can be rotated to −90°, followed by 0°, and then +90°, with the last step turning off the output, removing the holding torque, and reducing the power consumption of the motor:

```
.../sys/class/pwm/pwm-0:0$ sudo sh -c "echo 570000 > duty_cycle"
.../sys/class/pwm/pwm-0:0$ sudo sh -c "echo 1460000 > duty_cycle"
.../sys/class/pwm/pwm-0:0$ sudo sh -c "echo 2350000 > duty_cycle"
.../sys/class/pwm/pwm-0:0$ sudo sh -c "echo 0 > enable"
```

BoneScript

As initially described in Chapter 2, BoneScript is a JavaScript library for physical computing on the Beagle boards using the Node.js interpreter. The JavaScript language uses asynchronous callback functions, and you can build applications using the Cloud9 IDE or by executing code at the Linux terminal prompt. In this section, the BoneScript library is used for interfacing the Beagle boards to digital and analog input/output circuits, providing you with a quick way to build prototype circuits with the Beagle boards.

Digital Read and Write

Listing 6-8 gives a simple digital read/write example that replicates some of the functionality described in the C/C++ examples when the board is wired, as in Figure 6-3 and Figure 6-6. This program flashes an LED (attached to GPIO 60) five times, while simultaneously reading the button input (attached to GPIO 46) one time.

Listing 6-8: /chp06/bone/simple.js

```
var b      = require('bonescript');
var led    = "P2_08";        // GPIO1_28 (GPIO 60)
var button = "P2_22";        // GPIO1_14 (GPIO 46)
var isOn   = false;          // isOn is a Boolean flag
```

```
console.log('Setting up the inputs and outputs');
b.getPlatform(displayPlatform);
b.pinMode(button, b.INPUT, 7, 'pullup', 'fast');
b.pinMode(led, b.OUTPUT);

console.log('Flashing the LED on GPIO 60');
timer = setInterval(toggleLED, 500); // each 0.5s call toggleLED()
setTimeout(stopTimer, 5000);         // stop after 5 seconds

console.log('Reading the button on GPIO 46');
b.digitalRead(button, display);

console.log('End of the application');

function displayPlatform(platform){
    console.log('Platform name is ' + platform.name);
};

function toggleLED(){
    isOn = !isOn;                    // invert the isOn state on each call
    if (isOn) b.digitalWrite(led, 1);  // light the LED
    else b.digitalWrite(led, 0);       // turn off the LED
};

function stopTimer(){
    clearInterval(timer);
};

function display(x) {
    console.log('Button value = ' + x.value);
};
```

When you execute the code, you will notice a short delay before anything happens. This is caused by the time required to load and initialize Node.js and the BoneScript library. The code example gives the outputs as follows, executed both when the button is pressed and when the button is released:

```
debian@ebb:~/exploringbb/chp06/bone$ node simple.js
Setting up the inputs and outputs
Platform name is TI AM335x PocketBeagle
Flashing the LED on GPIO 60
Reading the button on GPIO 46
End of the application
Button value = 1
debian@ebb:~/exploringbb/chp06/bone$ node simple.js
Setting up the inputs and outputs
Platform name is TI AM335x PocketBeagle
Flashing the LED on GPIO 60
```

```
Reading the button on GPIO 46
End of the application
Button value = 0
```

Analog Read

Listing 6-9 provides an example of reading an ADC input using Node.js and the BoneScript library. This example tests P2.35 on the PocketBeagle, which is a 3.3V input, but any ADC input can be used in its place.

Listing 6-9: /chp06/bone/analogRead.js

```
var b = require('bonescript');
var adc = "P2.35";    // AIN0 P1.19  AIN1 P1.21  AIN2 P1.23
                      // AIN3 P1.25  AIN4 P1.27  AIN5 P2.35 (3.3)
                      // AIN6 P1.02 (3.3V)  AIN7 P2.36
var sampleTime = 1000;
var endTime = 10000;
console.log('Reading AIN on '+adc+' every '+sampleTime+'ms');
timer = setInterval(readAIN, sampleTime);
setTimeout(stopTimer, endTime);

function readAIN() {
    value = b.analogRead(adc);
    console.log('ADC Value = ' + value);
};

function stopTimer(){
  clearInterval(timer);
};
```

This code example reads one of the ADC inputs once per second for 10 seconds and displays the output on the console. When AIN5 is chosen and the input is varied between 3.3 V and GND, the resulting output is as follows:

```
debian@ebb:~/exploringbb/chp06/bone$ node analogRead.js
Reading AIN on P2.35 every 1000ms
ADC Value = 0.9545787545787546
ADC Value = 0.9545787545787546
ADC Value = 0
ADC Value = 0
ADC Value = 0
ADC Value = 0
ADC Value = 0.9543345543345544
ADC Value = 0.9543345543345544
ADC Value = 0.9545787545787546
```

The `analogRead()` function returns the normalized voltage (e.g., where 0.0 = 0 V and 1 .0 = 1.8V for a 1.8V input) that represents the voltage on the ADC input.

Analog Write (PWM)

BoneScript provides support for pulse width modulation (PWM) outputs through its `analogWrite()` function. In Listing 6-10 this function is supplied with the pin number as a string ("P2.01"), the duty cycle value as a normalized float (e.g., 0.75), the modulation frequency in Hz, and a callback function (`display()`) to be called on its completion. It's important to ensure that you have not exported any PWM outputs in sysfs related to the PWMs that are used in your program code, as they can conflict.

Listing 6-10: /chp06/bone/pwm.js

```
var b = require('bonescript');
var pin = "P2_01";
var dutyCycle = 0.75;
var frequency = 10000;

b.pinMode(pin, b.OUTPUT);
b.getPinMode(pin, printPinMux);
b.analogWrite(pin, dutyCycle, frequency, display);

function printPinMux(val){
   console.log('mux = '+val.mux);
   console.log('name = '+val.name);
}

function display(val){
   console.log(val);
}
```

To execute this example, you must do so with root privileges under the current Linux distributions, as the library utilizes the same type of sysfs calls that are described earlier in the chapter.

```
debian@ebb:~/exploringbb/chp06/bone$ sudo nodejs pwm.js
{}
mux = 6
name = EHRPWM1A
```

The output from this code example is visible in Figure 6-21(a), which confirms an output frequency of 10kHz and a duty cycle of 75 percent.

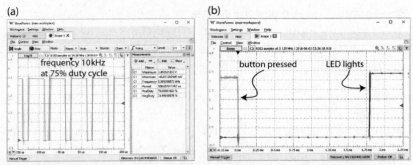

Figure 6-21: BoneScript output for (a) the PWM example, and (b) the button/LED response example

GPIO Performance

The final BoneScript code example in this section, Listing 6-11, is used to evaluate how quickly BoneScript can respond to hardware events. In this example, a button on GPIO 46 is used to trigger a change in the output value of an LED that is attached to GPIO 60. An oscilloscope can then be used to determine the precise time between the button press taking place and the subsequent state change of the LED.

Listing 6-11: /chp06/bone/gpioTest.js

```javascript
var b       = require('bonescript');
var led     = "P2_08";          // GPIO1_28 (GPIO 60)
var button  = "P2_22";          // GPIO1_14 (GPIO 46)
var isOn    = false;            // isOn is a Boolean flag

console.log('Testing the inputs output response');
b.getPlatform(displayPlatform);
b.pinMode(button, b.INPUT, 7, 'pullup', 'fast');
b.pinMode(led, b.OUTPUT);

console.log('Attaching interrupt to GPIO 46');
b.attachInterrupt(button, true, b.CHANGE, buttonPressed);
console.log('End of the application');

function displayPlatform(platform){
   console.log('Platform name is ' + platform.name);
};

function buttonPressed(){
   isOn = !isOn;                 // invert the isOn state on each call
   if (isOn) b.digitalWrite(led, 1);  // light the LED
   else b.digitalWrite(led, 0);       // turn off the LED
};
```

You can execute this code as follows to perform the test:

```
debian@ebb:~/exploringbb/chp06/bone$ node gpioTest.js
Testing the inputs output response
Platform name is TI AM335x PocketBeagle
Attaching interrupt to GPIO 46
End of the application
```

The program stays running until Ctrl+C is pressed in the Linux terminal window. The LED will toggle when the button is pressed and toggle again when the button is released. The scope output in Figure 6-21(b) indicates that the response time is approximately 1.75ms between the time when the button is pressed and the LED lights.

If this level of performance is not sufficient for your particular application, then you might consider implementing the Enhanced GPIO class toward the end of this chapter, which has a response time of 0.3ms for the same circuit configuration.

Advanced GPIO Topics

One serious problem with the GPIO digital input application described earlier is that it requires the `sysfs` file to be repeatedly polled to determine whether a change in its state has occurred. This is processor intensive, or prone to long latency if the frequency of the checks is reduced. This section examines how this problem can be addressed using a significant enhancement of the GPIO C++ class.

More C++ Programming

To understand the first technique, it is necessary to examine some additional programming concepts in C/C++ that are to be used and that can be applied generally to enhance your Beagle board applications. Callback function, POSIX threads, and use of Linux system polling can be used to create a highly efficient GPIO poll that has negligible CPU overhead and fast response times (i.e., less than 0.5ms). The GPIO class that is written for this chapter is enhanced to support this functionality, so an overview of these programming techniques is all that you require.

Callback Functions

Chapter 2 describes the use of callback functions as they are used in Node.js with asynchronous function calls. Essentially, a *callback function* (or *listener function*) is a function that is executed when some type of event occurs. This is vital for asynchronous function calls like those in JavaScript, but it is also useful in C++ applications. For example, in the enhanced GPIO class, this structure is used so that a function can be executed when a physical button is pressed.

Callback functions are typically implemented in C++ using function pointers. *Function pointers* are pointers that store the address of a function. It is possible to pass these pointers to other functions, which can dereference the function pointer and call the function that is passed. This is demonstrated with the code example in Listing 6-12.

Listing 6-12: /chp06/callback/callback.cpp

```cpp
typedef int (*CallbackType)(int);

// some function that receives a callback function
int doSomething(CallbackType callback){
    return callback(10);   //execute callback function, pass 10
}

// the callback function that receives an int value
int callbackFunction(int var){
    cout << "I am the Callback Function! var=" << var << endl;
    return 2*var;
}

int main() {
    cout << "Hello Beagle board" << endl;
    // pass the address of the callbackFunction() to doSomething()
    int y = doSomething(&callbackFunction);
    cout << "Value of y is: " << y << endl;
}
```

Creating a type using typedef simply makes it easier to change the type at a later stage and cleans up the syntax somewhat. The address of the callback-Function() method is passed as a pointer to the doSomething() function. When executed, the output of this code is as follows:

```
Hello Beagle board
I am the Callback Function! var=10
Value of y is: 20
```

This programming structure is quite common in (and underneath) user-interface programming, where functions can be called when a user interacts with display user-interface components such as buttons and menus. It makes sense to apply the same structure to physical push buttons and switches.

POSIX Threads

POSIX threads (*Pthreads*) is a set of C functions, types, and constants that provides everything you need to implement threading within your C/C++ applications on a Beagle board. Adding *threading* to your code allows parts of your code to execute apparently concurrently (the AM335x has a single-core processor), with each thread receiving a "slice" of processing time.

To use Pthreads in your application, you need to include the pthread.h header file and use the -pthread flag when compiling and linking the code using gcc/g++[4]. All the Pthread functions are prefixed with pthread_. Listing 6-13 is an example of using Pthreads on the board to create two parallel counters (the comments describe the structure of the code).

Listing 6-13: /chp06/pthreads/pthreads.cpp

```cpp
#include <iostream>
#include <pthread.h>
#include <unistd.h>
using namespace std;

// Thread function that will execute when the thread is created
//  it passes and receives data by void pointers (See Chapter 5)
void *threadFunction(void *value){
    int *x = (int *)value; // cast the data passed to an int pointer
    while(*x<5){            // while the value of x is less than 5
       usleep(1000);        // sleep for 1ms - encourage main thread
       (*x)++;              // increment the value of x by 1
    }
    return x;               // return the pointer x (as a void*)
}

int main() {               // the main thread
    int x=0, y=0;
    pthread_t thread;       // this is our handle to the pthread
    // create thread, pass reference, addr of the function and data
    if(pthread_create(&thread, NULL, &threadFunction, &x)){
       cout << "Failed to create the thread" << endl;
       return 1;
    }
    // at this point the thread was created successfully
    while(y<5){             // loop and increment y, displaying values
    cout << "The value of x=" << x << " and y=" << y++ << endl;
       usleep(1000);        // encourage the pthread to run
     }
```

---

[4]The Eclipse IDE is used in the next chapter. To use Pthreads in Eclipse, select Project Properties ⇨ C/C++ Build Settings ⇨ GCC C++ Linker ⇨ Miscellaneous ⇨ Linker Flags, and add -pthread.

```
    void* result;              // OPTIONAL: receive data back from pthread
    pthread_join(thread, &result);   // allow the pthread to complete
    int *z = (int *) result;         // cast from void* to int* to get z
    cout << "Final: x=" << x << ", y=" << y << " and z=" << *z << endl;
    return 0;
}
```

Building and executing as follows will result in the following output:

```
~/exploringbb/chp06/pthreads$ g++ -pthread pthreads.cpp -o pthreads
~/exploringbb/chp06/pthreads$ ./pthreads
The value of x=0 and y=0
The value of x=0 and y=1
The value of x=1 and y=2
The value of x=2 and y=3
The value of x=3 and y=4
Final: x=5, y=5 and z=5
```

Run it again, and you may get a different output!

```
The value of x=0 and y=0
The value of x=1 and y=1
The value of x=1 and y=2
The value of x=2 and y=3
The value of x=3 and y=4
Final: x=5, y=5 and z=5
```

The code may result in a slightly different result each time. The usleep() calls have been introduced to encourage the thread manager to switch to the main thread at that point. While the order of the output may change, the final results will always be consistent because of the pthread_join() function call, which blocks execution at this point until the thread has run to completion.

Linux poll (sys/poll.h)

At the beginning of this chapter, code is presented that can be used to detect the state of a button by checking the state of the value file. This is a very processor-intensive operation and not really practical. If you listed the contents of the /sys/class/gpio/ directory, you may have also noticed a file entry called edge that up to now has had no relevance.

```
debian@ebb:/sys/class/gpio$ cd gpio115
debian@ebb:/sys/class/gpio/gpio115$ ls
active_low  device  direction  edge  label  power
subsystem   uevent  value
```

You can use a system function called `poll()` from the `sys/poll.h` header file, which has the following syntax:

```
int poll(struct pollfd *ufds, unsigned int nfds, int timeout);
```

where the first argument specifies a pointer to an array of `pollfd` structures, each of which identifies a file entry to be monitored and the type of event to be monitored (e.g., `EPOLLIN` to read operations, `EPOLLET` edge triggered, and `EPOLLPRI` for urgent data). The next argument, `nfds`, identifies how many elements are in the first argument array. The final argument identifies a timeout in milliseconds. If this value is `-1`, then the kernel will wait forever for the activity identified in the array. This code has been added to the following enhanced `GPIO` class in the `waitForEdge()` methods.

Enhanced GPIO Class

The programming concepts just discussed are complex and may be difficult to understand if it is your first time seeing them; however, these techniques have been used to enhance the GPIO class so that it is faster and more efficient than before. The code in Listing 6-14 integrates the earlier GPIO functionality and the programming concepts that have been just introduced. The public interface methods are also provided.

Listing 6-14: /chp06/GPIO/GPIO.h

```cpp
#define GPIO_PATH "/sys/class/gpio/"
namespace exploringBB {

typedef int (*CallbackType)(int);
enum GPIO_DIRECTION{ INPUT, OUTPUT };
enum GPIO_VALUE{ LOW=0, HIGH=1 };
enum GPIO_EDGE{ NONE, RISING, FALLING, BOTH };

class GPIO {
private:
    int number, debounceTime;
    string name, path;
public:
    GPIO(int number); //constructor will export the pin
    virtual int getNumber() { return number; }

    // General Input and Output Settings
    virtual int setDirection(GPIO_DIRECTION);
    virtual GPIO_DIRECTION getDirection();
    virtual int setValue(GPIO_VALUE);
    virtual int toggleOutput();
    virtual GPIO_VALUE getValue();
    virtual int setActiveLow(bool isLow=true);  //low=1, high=0
```

```
      virtual int setActiveHigh();  //default
      //software debounce input (ms) - default 0
      virtual void setDebounceTime(int time) { this->debounceTime = time; }

      // Advanced OUTPUT: Faster write by keeping the stream alive (~20X)
      virtual int streamOpen();
      virtual int streamWrite(GPIO_VALUE);
      virtual int streamClose();

    virtual int toggleOutput(int time); //threaded invert output every X ms.
    virtual int toggleOutput(int numberOfTimes, int time);
    virtual void changeToggleTime(int time) { this->togglePeriod = time; }
    virtual void toggleCancel() { this->threadRunning = false; }

      // Advanced INPUT: Detect input edges; threaded and non-threaded
      virtual int setEdgeType(GPIO_EDGE);
      virtual GPIO_EDGE getEdgeType();
      virtual int waitForEdge(); // waits until button is pressed
      virtual int waitForEdge(CallbackType callback); // threaded with callback
      virtual void waitForEdgeCancel() { this->threadRunning = false; }

      virtual ~GPIO();   //destructor will unexport the pin
   ...
} /* namespace exploringBB */
```

The tests to evaluate the performance of the class are provided as examples of how to use this class. The test circuit is the combination of the button circuit in Figure 6-6 and the LED circuit in Figure 6-3. Therefore, the button is attached to P8_16/P2.22 (GPIO 46), and the LED is attached to P9_12/P2.08 (GPIO 60). In these tests, the LED will light when the button is pressed.

Listing 6-15 tests the performance of a synchronous poll that forces the program to wait for the button to be pressed before proceeding.

Listing 6-15: /chp06/GPIO/tests/test_syspoll.cpp

```cpp
#include<iostream>
#include<unistd.h>
#include"GPIO.h"
using namespace exploringBB;
using namespace std;

int main(){
   GPIO outGPIO(60), inGPIO(46);
   inGPIO.setDirection(INPUT);      //button is an input
   outGPIO.setDirection(OUTPUT);   //LED is an output
```

```
inGPIO.setEdgeType(FALLING);      //wait for falling edge
outGPIO.streamOpen();             //fast write, ready file
outGPIO.streamWrite(LOW);         //turn the LED off
cout << "Press the button:" << endl;
inGPIO.waitForEdge();             //will wait forever
outGPIO.streamWrite(HIGH);        //button pressed, light LED
outGPIO.streamClose();            //close the output stream
return 0;
}
```

The response time of this code is captured in Figure 6-22(a). This code runs with a ~0% CPU load, as the polling is handled efficiently by the Linux kernel. Using an oscilloscope, the electrical response time is measured between the first rising edge of the button press and the LED turning on. This program responds in 0.3 ms, which is well within physical debounce filter times. Using the debounce filter of the class will not affect this performance, only the delay between repeated button presses. The downside of this code is that the program cannot perform other operations while awaiting the button press.

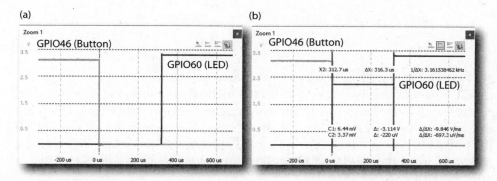

Figure 6-22: Time delay in lighting an LED in response to a button press at ~0 percent CPU usage (a) using sys/poll.h (b) integrating callback functions and Pthreads

The second example, in Listing 6-16, tests the performance of an asynchronous call to the `waitForEdge()` method, which accepts a function pointer and uses Pthreads to free up the program to perform other operations. In this example, the main thread sleeps, but it could be performing other tasks.

Listing 6-16: /chp06/GPIO/tests/test_callback.cpp

```
#include<iostream>
#include<unistd.h> //for usleep
#include"GPIO.h"
using namespace exploringBB;
using namespace std;
```

```
GPIO *outGPIO, *inGPIO;              //global pointers

int activateLED(int var){
    outGPIO->streamWrite(HIGH);      //turn on the LED
    cout << "Button Pressed" << endl;
    return 0;
}

int main(){
    inGPIO = new GPIO(46);           //button
    outGPIO = new GPIO(60);          //LED
    inGPIO->setDirection(INPUT);     //button is an input
    outGPIO->setDirection(OUTPUT);   //LED is an output
    outGPIO->streamOpen();           //fast write to LED
    outGPIO->streamWrite(LOW);       //turn the LED off
    inGPIO->setEdgeType(RISING);     //wait for rising edge
    cout << "You have 10 seconds to press the button:" << endl;
    inGPIO->waitForEdge(&activateLED); //pass the function
    cout << "Listening, but also doing something else..." << endl;
    usleep(10000000);                //allow 10 seconds
    outGPIO->streamWrite(LOW);       //turn off the LED after 10 seconds
    outGPIO->streamClose();          //shutdown
    return 0;
}
```

The significant change in this code is that when the setEdgeType() method is called, a new thread is created within the method, and it immediately returns control so that the main thread can continue to perform operations. The main thread simply sleeps for 10 seconds in this case before turning off the LED. If the button is pressed, the activateLED() function will be called. Whether the button is pressed or not, the LED will be turned off, and the program will exit after the sleep has finished.

The response time of this code is captured in Figure 6-22(b), and it is only marginally slower than the previous code (by ~20µs), which is the cost of the callback function and the Pthreads code. Again, this code has no significant load on the CPU. The full implementation code is available in the GPIO.cpp file, and it can be edited to suit your needs. A more advanced version would use *functors* (function objects) and the C++ Standard Template Library (STL) to remove the requirement for global variables in the callback code.

Using GPIOs without Using sudo

Throughout this chapter, programs and scripts that interface to the input/outputs (e.g., PWM outputs) are sometimes executed using sudo. This can be frustrating, but the alternative of running applications as the superuser is dangerous, in that a coding mistake could damage the file system.

The latest Debian images for the Beagle boards do not require root access to control the GPIOs, allowing them to be owned by a particular user or group, while still protecting the root file system. This is achieved by the use of an advanced feature of Linux called *udev rules* that enables you to customize the behavior of the *udevd* service, which runs on the Debian Linux distribution. This service gives you some userspace control over devices on the boards, such as renaming devices, changing permissions, and executing a script when a device is attached. The first step is to find out information about the `/sys/class/gpio/` directory.

```
debian@ebb:~$ udevadm info --path=/sys/class/gpio --attribute-walk
Udevadm info starts with the device specified by the devpath and then
walks up the chain of parent devices. It prints for every device
found, all possible attributes in the udev rules key format.
A rule to match, can be composed by the attributes of the device
and the attributes from one single parent device.

  looking at device '/class/gpio':
    KERNEL=="gpio"
    SUBSYSTEM=="subsystem"
    DRIVER==""       ...
```

The rules are contained in the `/etc/udev/rules.d/` directory. A new rule can be added as a file using these values, where the file begins with a priority number, where a lower number indicates a higher priority. The current set of rules on the Debian distribution is as follows:

```
debian@ebb:/etc/udev/rules.d$ ls
50-hidraw.rules          81-pwm-noroot.rules       beagle-tester.rules
50-spi.rules             82-gpio-config-pin.rules  tisdk.rules
60-omap-tty.rules        83-eqep-noroot.rules      uio.rules
70-persistent-net.rules  84-gpio-noroot.rules
80-gpio-noroot.rules     85-gpio-noroot.rules
```

The GPIO rule has a mid-to-low-level priority (80) so that it does not interfere with higher-priority device rules. The rule dynamically changes GPIO permissions so that they can be read or written to by users that are in the Linux `gpio` group.

```
debian@ebb:/etc/udev/rules.d$ more 80-gpio-noroot.rules
# /etc/udev/rules.d/80-gpio-noroot.rules
# Corrects sys GPIO permissions on the BB so non-root users in the
# gpio group can manipulate bits
# Change group to gpio
SUBSYSTEM=="gpio", PROGRAM="/bin/sh -c '/bin/chown -R root:gpio →
/sys/devices/platform/ocp/*.gpio'"
# Change permissions to ensure user and group have read/write permissions
```

```
SUBSYSTEM=="gpio", PROGRAM="/bin/sh -c '/bin/chmod -R ug+rw →
/sys/devices/platform/ocp/*.gpio'"
```

Essentially, the rule executes a single line script to change the group of a GPIO device to be `gpio` when it is added. You can edit this rule if for example you want to apply it only for a particular user and test that it works as follows:

```
debian@ebb:/etc/udev/rules.d$ udevadm test --action=add /class/gpio
calling: test
version 232
...
Reading rules file: /etc/udev/rules.d/80-gpio-noroot.rules
...
ACTION=add
DEVPATH=/class/gpio
SUBSYSTEM=subsystem
USEC_INITIALIZED=245064723516
net.ifnames=0
Unload module index
Unloaded link configuration context.
```

For a comprehensive guide on writing udev rules, see `tiny.cc/beagle607`.

Root Permissions with setuid

An alternative to writing udev rules for your application is to use the Linux setuid bit. As described in Chapter 3, this bit allows a program to be executed as if by another logged-in user, but with the permissions of the file's owner or group. To test this functionality, a short program is written in Listing 6-17. This program uses the Linux `geteuid()` function to get the effective user ID of the user executing the binary code. If this function returns the value 0, then the user has full root access rights to the system and can access any input or outputs regardless of their permissions.

Listing 6-17: /chp06/root/root_test.c

```c
#include <stdio.h>
#include <stdlib.h>
#include <fcntl.h>
#include <errno.h>
#include <stdint.h>
#include <unistd.h>

int main(){
    printf("Start of GPIO test program.\n");
```

```
        if(geteuid()!=0) {      // Get effective UID
            printf("You must run this program as root. Exiting.\n");
            return -EPERM;
        }
        printf("Doing something here with root privileges!\n");
        return 0;
    }
```

This program can be built and executed as follows, whereupon the program will fail to get to the section of code that is restricted to the root user.

```
debian@ebb:~/exploringbb/chp06/root$ gcc root_test.c -o root_test
debian@ebb:~/exploringbb/chp06/root$ ./root_test
Start of GPIO test program.
You must run this program as root. Exiting.
```

You could try to change the owner of the program to root (allowing execute permissions for group and others) and execute it as the user debian, but this will fail. Here's an example:

```
debian@ebb:~/exploringbb/chp06/root$ sudo chown root root_test
[sudo] password for debian:
debian@ebb:~/exploringbb/chp06/root$ ls -l root_test
-rwxr-xr-x 1 root debian 8384 Jul 18 02:06 root_test
debian@ebb:~/exploringbb/chp06/root$ ./root_test
Start of GPIO test program.
You must run this program as root. Exiting.
```

Changing the owner to root is insufficient because the program is still executed by the debian user. However, when the setuid bit is set and the file is owned by root, then the program is executed as if by root, regardless of the actual user account that executes it.

```
debian@ebb:~/exploringbb/chp06/root$ sudo chmod u+s root_test
debian@ebb:~/exploringbb/chp06/root$ ls -l root_test
-rwsr-xr-x 1 root debian 8384 Jul 18 02:12 root_test
debian@ebb:~/exploringbb/chp06/root$ ./root_test
Start of GPIO test program.
Doing something here with root privileges!
```

If you rebuild the executable again, then the setuid bit is unset (even if you use sudo on the call to g++). This is for security reasons because otherwise a user could insert malicious source code into the binary executable.

```
debian@ebb:~/exploringbb/chp06/root$ gcc root_test.c -o root_test
debian@ebb:~/exploringbb/chp06/root$ ls -l root_test
-rwxr-xr-x 1 debian debian 8384 Jul 18 02:14 root_test
```

Summary

After completing this chapter, you should be able to do the following:

- Use a Beagle board GPIO to output a binary signal to a digital circuit or read in a binary input from a digital circuit.
- Write shell scripts and C++ code to control a Beagle board GPIO.
- Describe the use of internal pull-up and pull-down resistors.
- Describe the device tree model that is used to configure certain hardware on the Beagle boards and make minor modifications to the model.
- Use a PWM pin to output an analog voltage or as a control signal for motors and certain types of servos.
- Use an analog input to safely read in a value from an analog circuit, using an op-amp to protect the board from damage and/or invalid measurement.
- Write C++ code, which utilizes advanced functionality, to efficiently read in a digital input using a custom GPIO class.
- Use an advanced Linux configuration that allows for user-level control of the sysfs entries.

Further Reading

There are many links to websites and documents provided throughout this chapter. The following additional links provide further information on the topics covered:

- www.exploringbeaglebone.com/chapter6/: All links and videos in the chapter are provided at this site.
- www.exploringbeaglebone.com/API/: Provides the documentation for the classes described in this chapter.

## CHAPTER 7

Cross-Compilation, Eclipse, and Building Linux

To this point in the book, all of the code is built and executed directly on the Beagle boards. However, for larger projects this can be impractical, as you may need to manage many source files within a single project. In addition, compilation times can be slow on the Beagle boards for building large projects. This chapter first describes how you can use your desktop computer to develop applications that can be deployed directly to any Beagle board. The Eclipse integrated development environment (IDE) is then introduced, which allows for advanced development capabilities, such as remote debugging. The chapter finishes by outlining how you can build and deploy a custom Linux kernel.

EQUIPMENT REQUIRED FOR THIS CHAPTER:

- A Linux (ideally Debian 9+) stand-alone or virtual machine (VM) desktop instance (see Chapter 3)
- Any Beagle board for deployment and debugging

Further details on this chapter are available at www.exploringbeaglebone. com/chapter7/.

Setting Up a Cross-Compilation Toolchain

This section describes how you can establish a full-featured cross-compilation environment for building code for the Beagle boards using your desktop computer. A typical C/C++ compiler that is executed on a desktop computer (e.g., Intel x86) will build executable machine code for that platform only. Therefore, a *cross-compiler* is required, as it is capable of creating executable code for the ARM platform directly from your desktop computer, even though it has a different hardware architecture. Linux is generally used on the desktop computer for this task, as cross-compiling code that is written under Windows/macOS to run on an ARM Linux device is a challenging process, particularly when integrating third-party libraries. Therefore, if you are using Windows/macOS you can use the VirtualBox configuration that is described in Chapter 3. In fact, a VirtualBox Debian 64-bit VM is used for all of the desktop work in this book.

The environment and configuration for cross-platform development are ever-evolving processes. While all of the steps in this chapter work at the time of publication, it is likely that some steps in this chapter will change as updates are performed on the Linux kernel, to the toolchain, and to the Eclipse development environment. The primary aim of this chapter is to ensure that you grasp the concepts behind cross-compilation and that you see practical examples of the tools in use.

The first step in cross-compiling Linux applications is the installation of a *Linux toolchain*. A *toolchain* is suitably named, as it is a set of software development tools and libraries (such as gcc, gdb, glibc) that are chained together to enable you to build executable code on one operating system on one type of machine, such as a 64-bit Linux OS on an Intel x86 machine, but to execute them on a different operating system and/or a different architecture, such as a 32-bit Linux OS on an ARM device.

> **NOTE** This chapter assumes that the sudo tool is available on your desktop machine. You must also ensure that your user account is in the sudo group.
>
> ```
> molloyd@desktop:~$ more /etc/hostname
> desktop
> molloyd@desktop:~$ groups
> molloyd cdrom floppy sudo audio dip video plugdev netdev bluetooth
> scanner
> ```
>
> **If not, use a root terminal or console to add the user to the sudo group:**
>
> ```
> root@desktop:~# adduser molloyd sudo
> ```

To begin, you can discover detailed information about your Linux version on your Beagle board by typing the following commands individually or together using `&&`. This information is valuable when deciding which particular toolchain to use.

```
debian@ebb:~$ uname -a && cat /etc/os-release && cat /proc/version
Linux ebb 4.14.44-ti-rt-r51 #1 SMP PREEMPT 2018 armv7l GNU/Linux
PRETTY_NAME="Debian GNU/Linux 9 (stretch)" ...
Linux version 4.14.44-ti-rt-r51 (Debian 6.3.0-18+deb9u1)
#1 SMP PREEMPT Fri Jun 1 08:15:35 UTC 2018
```

Cross-Compiling Under Debian

Traditionally, installing a toolchain was a complex task that involved the integration of many different tools and platform configurations. Thankfully, the latest versions of Debian have strong support for cross-building through the cross-toolchain repository. There are other toolchains available, such as Linaro (`www.linaro.org/downloads/`), but the Debian cross toolchain is a good starting point. You can list the available toolchains as follows:

```
molloyd@desktop:~$ apt-cache search cross-build-essential
crossbuild-essential-arm64 - Info list of cross-build-essential packages
crossbuild-essential-armel - Info list of cross-build-essential packages
crossbuild-essential-armhf - Info list of cross-build-essential packages
crossbuild-essential-mipsel - Info list of cross-build-essential packages
crossbuild-essential-powerpc - Info list of cross-build-essential packages
crossbuild-essential-ppc64el - Info list of cross-build-essential packages
```

You need the ARM hard float (`armhf`) package for building software that is deployed to the Beagle boards.

```
molloyd@desktop:~$ sudo apt install crossbuild-essential-armhf
Setting up gcc-6-arm-linux-gnueabihf (6.3.0-18cross1) ...
Setting up g++-6-arm-linux-gnueabihf (6.3.0-18cross1) ...
Setting up crossbuild-essential-armhf (12.3) ...
```

The installation can be tested by calling the compiler directly.

```
molloyd@desktop:~$ arm-linux-gnueabihf-g++ -v
COLLECT_GCC=arm-linux-gnueabihf-g++ ...
Thread model: posix
gcc version 6.3.0 20170516 (Debian 6.3.0-18)
```

The compiler name is preceded by a triple *X-Y-Z*, where *X* identifies the architecture as `arm`, *Y* identifies the vendor (typically absent for Linux), and *Z* identifies the *application binary interface* (ABI) as `linux-gnueabihf`. The *embedded ABI* (EABI) defines a standardized machine-code-level interface between compiled programs, compiled libraries, and the OS, which aims to ensure that binary code created with one toolchain can be linked with a project that uses a different toolchain or compiler. Therefore, `linux-gnueabihf` can be read as the GNU EABI for Linux that supports hardware-accelerated floating-point operations (i.e., *hard floats*). Hard float operations are much faster than soft float operations as they take advantage of the microprocessor's on-chip *floating-point unit* (FPU), rather than having to perform the calculations using software (i.e., *soft floats*).

DEBOOTSTRAP (ADVANCED)

Debootstrap is a container tool that allows you to install a Debian base system (guest) into a subdirectory of another Linux base system (host). This *change root* approach allows you to change the apparent Linux root directory to another directory on your system. Why would you do this? The most common reason is that you might like to try a new Linux kernel, try new tools, or install a new library on your Linux installation; and you would like to test it first in case it brings down the entire system. You can then install your new libraries and tools in this new (possibly temporary) root directory.

You can instruct your Linux system to change the root temporarily to this new root directory. Once started, you enter `chroot jail` and do not have access to any files outside of the new root directory. You can test all of the new features of your new Linux installation, and when you are finished, you can exit to return to your "real" root, leaving the chroot jail. This structure is useful for developing for the Beagle boards as this new root directory does not need to have the same flavor of Linux or even the same architecture as your main desktop Linux installation.

```
molloyd@desktop:~$ sudo apt install debootstrap systemd-container
molloyd@desktop:~$ sudo debootstrap stretch /var/lib/container/stretch
http://deb.debian.org/debian ...
molloyd@desktop:~$ cd /var/lib/container/stretch
molloyd@desktop:/var/lib/container/stretch$ du
74828.
```

You can configure settings in the container directory before switching to it; for example, provide the container with a hostname.

```
molloyd@desktop:/var/lib/container/stretch$ sudo sh -c "echo EBB_
Stretch →
> etc/debian_chroot"
molloyd@desktop:/var/lib/container/stretch$ more etc/debian_chroot
EBB_Stretch
```

> Providing that you have installed the systemd-container package, you can then run commands in the new namespace container, just as if you were using a change root. The `systemd-nspawn` command is slightly more powerful than the `chroot` command, as it allows you to boot full Linux OSs in a container and provides enhanced virtualization functions.
>
> ```
> molloyd@desktop:~$ sudo systemd-nspawn -D /var/lib/container/stretch
> Spawning container stretch on /var/lib/container/stretch.
> Press ^] three times within 1s to kill container.
> (EBB_Stretch)root@stretch:~# dpkg --add-architecture armhf
> (EBB_Stretch)root@stretch:~# dpkg --print-foreign-architectures
> armhf
> (EBB_Stretch)root@stretch:~# apt install crossbuild-essential-armhf
> ...
> ```
>
> You can follow the remaining steps in this section within such a container. When you want to leave the container, press CTRL+] three times quickly.
>
> ```
> Container stretch exited successfully.
> logout
> ```

Testing the Toolchain

You can test that the toolchain is working correctly by writing a short C++ program, `testcross.cpp`, which can be compiled into binary code using the cross-compiler.

```
molloyd@desktop:~$ nano testcross.cpp
molloyd@desktop:~$ more testcross.cpp
#include<iostream>
using namespace std;
int main(){
    cout << "Testing cross compilation for armhf" << endl;
    return 0;
}
molloyd@desktop:~$ arm-linux-gnueabihf-g++ testcross.cpp -o testcross
molloyd@desktop:~$ ls -l testcross*
-rwxr-xr-x 1 molloyd molloyd 9184 Jun  6 19:05 testcross
-rw-r--r-- 1 molloyd molloyd  125 Jun  6 19:03 testcross.cpp
```

The binary file has an executable flag, but when the binary is invoked, it fails to execute. This is unsurprising, as we are attempting to execute ARM binary instructions on an Intel x86 machine.

```
molloyd@desktop:~$ ./testcross
bash: ./testcross: cannot execute binary file: Exec format error
```

However, the program can be transferred to a Beagle board using sftp as follows:

```
molloyd@desktop:~$ sftp debian@192.168.7.2
debian@192.168.7.2's password:
Connected to 192.168.7.2.
sftp> put testcross
Uploading testcross to /home/debian/testcross
sftp> bye
```

Then SSH to the Beagle board from the desktop machine to confirm that the program works correctly.

```
molloyd@desktop:~$ ssh debian@192.168.7.2
debian@192.168.7.2's password: temppwd
debian@ebb:~$ ls -l testcross
-rwxr-xr-x 1 debian debian 9184 Jun  4 05:59 testcross
debian@ebb:~$ ./testcross
Testing cross compilation for armhf
```

Success! If you see this output, then you are able to build a binary on the desktop machine that can be executed directly on the Beagle board.

Finally, you can use the ldd tool to display the shared library dependencies of the program, which can be useful in debugging dependency problems.

```
debian@ebb:~$ ldd testcross
   linux-vdso.so.1 (0xbef55000)
   libstdc++.so.6 => /usr/lib/arm-linux-gnueabihf/libstdc++.so.6 (0xb6e9b000)
   libm.so.6 => /lib/arm-linux-gnueabihf/libm.so.6 (0xb6e23000)
   libgcc_s.so.1 => /lib/arm-linux-gnueabihf/libgcc_s.so.1 (0xb6dfa000)
   libc.so.6 => /lib/arm-linux-gnueabihf/libc.so.6 (0xb6d0c000)
   /lib/ld-linux-armhf.so.3 (0xb6fb9000)
```

Emulating the armhf Architecture

A package called QEMU can be installed on the desktop machine so that it can emulate the armhf architecture. This is called *user-mode emulation*. QEMU can also perform full *computer-mode emulation*, just like VirtualBox. You can install the QEMU user-mode emulation as follows (please check that you are back on the desktop machine):

```
molloyd@desktop:~$ sudo apt install qemu-user-static
```

You must then notify dpkg that you want to install library packages from multiple architectures on the current machine—in this case for armhf.

```
molloyd@desktop:~$ sudo dpkg --add-architecture armhf
molloyd@desktop:~$ dpkg --print-foreign-architectures
armhf
```

A call to apt update will now list additional packages that are related to this new foreign architecture.

```
molloyd@desktop:~$ sudo apt update
...
Get:7 http://ftp.us.debian.org/debian stretch-updates/main armhf Packages
Get:8 http://ftp.us.debian.org/debian stretch/main armhf Packages
...
All packages are up to date.
```

The armhf instructions can now be emulated on the x86 machine (with a performance cost), and the test program can execute on the desktop machine.

```
molloyd@desktop:~$ arm-linux-gnueabihf-g++ -static testcross.cpp -o testcross
molloyd@desktop:~$ ./testcross
Testing cross compilation for armhf
```

The -static flag indicates that the library code is to be statically built into the executable binary. Errors will otherwise arise, as the appropriate libraries are not present in the correct locations on the x86 machine.

```
molloyd@desktop:~$ arm-linux-gnueabihf-g++ testcross.cpp -o testcross
molloyd@desktop:~$ ./testcross
/lib/ld-linux-armhf.so.3: No such file or directory
```

This error indicates that the ld-linux-armhf.so.3 file is not in the system library directory. A search of the filesystem locates it in the /usr/arm-linux-gnueabihf/lib/ directory.

```
molloyd@desktop:~$ stat /usr/arm-linux-gnueabihf/lib/ld-linux-armhf.so.3
  File: /usr/arm-linux-gnueabihf/lib/ld-linux-armhf.so.3 -> ld-2.24.so
  Size: 10          Blocks: 0          IO Block: 4096    symbolic link
Device: 801h/2049d  Inode: 3673783    Links: 1
Access: (0777/lrwxrwxrwx) Uid: (    0/    root)  Gid: (    0/    root)
Access: 2018-06-06 19:05:59.596392591 -0400
Modify: 2017-05-16 00:01:45.000000000 -0400
Change: 2018-06-06 18:53:51.324392591 -0400
```

One approach to solving this issue is to explicitly call the QEMU tool and specify the library directory, whereupon the program is emulated correctly.

```
molloyd@desktop:~$ qemu-arm-static -L /usr/arm-linux-gnueabihf/ testcross
Testing cross compilation for armhf
```

Cross-Compilation with Third-Party Libraries (Multiarch)

This section is not necessary to cross-compile C/C++ applications; however, it is likely that you will need to add third-party libraries in the future for tasks such as image and numerical processing. Traditionally, this has been a difficult topic, but thanks to recent releases in Debian and Ubuntu, this problem has become much more manageable.

At this point you have a cross-compiler in place, and you should currently be able to cross-compile applications that use the standard C/C++ libraries. However, what if you want to build a C/C++ application that uses a third-party library that contains compiled code? If you install the library on your x86 desktop machine, then that library code will contain native x86 instructions. If you want to use the third-party library and deploy it to your board, then you need to use a library that contains ARM machine code instructions.

Traditionally, developers have used tools like xapt, which converts Debian packages to a cross-platform version on the fly (e.g., xapt -a armhf -m libo-pencv-dev). However, recent releases of Debian (8+) now have strong support for *multiarch*—multi-architecture package installs.

A multiarch-capable package installer can be used to install an armhf library on your desktop machine. The version of dpkg has to be greater than 1.16.2 for multiarch support. Also, if you have not already done so, you should add the armhf target architecture.

```
molloyd@desktop:~$ dpkg --version
Debian 'dpkg' package management program version 1.18.24 (amd64)...
molloyd@desktop:~$ sudo dpkg --add-architecture armhf
molloyd@desktop:~$ dpkg --print-foreign-architectures
armhf
```

Then install a sample third-party library package after performing an update (note the armhf after the package name).

```
molloyd@desktop:~$ sudo apt update
molloyd@desktop:~$ sudo apt install libicu-dev:armhf
Reading package lists... Done ...
The following additional packages will be installed:
  gcc-6-base:armhf icu-devtools libasan3:armhf ...
```

The libicu-dev libraries for utilizing Unicode are installed in the /usr/lib/arm-linux-gnueabihf/ directory. This keeps them separate from the x86 libraries that are stored in the /usr/lib directory, as otherwise they would overwrite your current x86 libraries, which would be problematic.

```
molloyd@desktop:/usr/lib/arm-linux-gnueabihf$ ls libicu*
libicudata.a         libicui18n.so.57.1  libicule.so.57    ...
```

You are done! If necessary, you can configure your C++ build environment to include the `/usr/lib/arm-linux-gnueabihf/` directory. This procedure works well, and it is reasonably straightforward; however, it is relatively new to Linux, and interdependency problems currently arise. See `wiki.debian.org/Multiarch/HOWTO` for more information.

Cross-Compilation Using Eclipse

Eclipse is an integrated development environment (IDE) that enables you to manage your code and integrate cross-compilation tools, debuggers, and other plug-ins to create a sophisticated development platform. It can even be extended to provide full remote debugging support for applications that are physically running on your Beagle board. This is a powerful feature that enables you to debug software applications that are interfacing with the real hardware in your projects but view the debug values within your desktop Eclipse environment.

Eclipse is written in Java and was initially focused on Java software development. However, Eclipse has excellent support for C/C++ development using the C/C++ Development Tooling (CDT) extension.

Installing Eclipse on Desktop Linux

Using a web browser on your Linux desktop or Linux desktop VM running under Windows (see Chapter 3), download the Eclipse installer from `www.eclipse.org`. The version of Eclipse that is used in this guide is Oxygen, which was released in April 2018.

Once you have downloaded Eclipse, decide whether you want to install it for all users or only for the current user by extracting the archive in a suitable location. The Iceweasel, Firefox, or Chromium browser will download the file to the user's `~/Downloads/` directory. Therefore, use the following steps to install Eclipse in a user's account:

```
molloyd@desktop:~$ mkdir temp
molloyd@desktop:~$ cd Downloads/
molloyd@desktop:~/Downloads$ ls eclipse*
eclipse-inst-linux64.tar.gz
molloyd@desktop:~/Downloads$ tar -xvf eclipse* -C ~/temp/
molloyd@desktop:~/Downloads$ cd ~/temp/eclipse-installer/
molloyd@desktop:~/temp/eclipse-installer$ sudo ./eclipse-inst
```

At this point, you should choose the Eclipse IDE for C/C++ Developers option and choose a folder such as `/home/molloyd/eclipse/cpp-oxygen/` as the installation folder. Alternatively, you could run the installer using `sudo` and choose a common directory such as /opt/eclipse/cpp-oxygen/. Execute the Eclipse IDE as follows (as a background process using &):

```
molloyd@desktop:~/eclipse/cpp-oxygen/eclipse$ ./eclipse &
[1] 26682
```

At this point, you can use Eclipse to create C++ applications on the desktop machine that are deployed to the desktop machine. However, since the target platform is your Beagle board, Eclipse must be configured for cross-compilation.

Configuring Eclipse for Cross-Compilation

When Eclipse starts up, you can choose the default workspace directory, and then you will see a brief guide that describes C/C++ development. You can begin configuration by creating a new project using File ⇨ New ⇨ C++ project. As illustrated in Figure 7-1(a), set the project name to **Beagle test**, pick the project type Hello World C++ Project, and set the toolchain to be Cross GCC. Repeatedly click Next until you see the Cross GCC Command dialog, as illustrated in Figure 7-1(b). Enter **arm-linux-gnueabihf-** for the cross-compiler prefix and set its path to /usr/bin. Finally, click Finish.

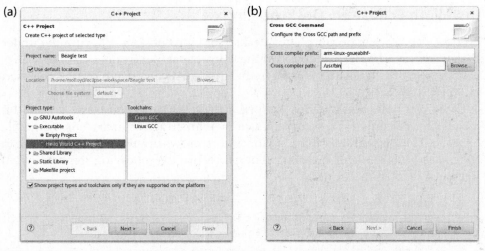

Figure 7-1: Creating a new C++ project in Eclipse: (a) the project settings and (b) the cross-compiler prefix

The Eclipse IDE is now configured for cross-compilation using the cross-compilation toolchain that was set up at the beginning of this chapter. You can choose Project ⇨ Build All and then run on the desktop machine by clicking the green arrow or (Run ⇨ Run). In Figure 7-2 this results in the message !!!Hello World!!! appearing in the Console window. This appears on the desktop computer only if you have installed QEMU, as the executable contains ARM machine code, which is clear from the binary name "Beagle test - [arm/le]" that is highlighted on the top left of Figure 7-2.

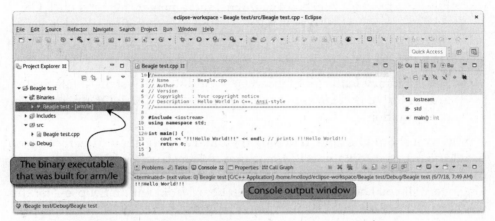

Figure 7-2: The creation and cross-compilation of a C++ project in Eclipse

The preceding steps provide a quick way of configuring the cross-compilation settings within Eclipse Oxygen. Older versions of Eclipse (e.g., Kepler) require you to configure the cross-compiler using the project settings. That option is still available within Eclipse Oxygen—select the project that was just created and then go to Project ⇨ Properties. (If the option is grayed out, it likely means that the project is not selected.) Go to C/C++ Build ⇨ Settings and on the Tool Settings tab you should see the Cross Settings as illustrated in Figure 7-3. Effectively, these settings mean that the arm-linux-gnueabihf-g++ command is used to compile the project code.

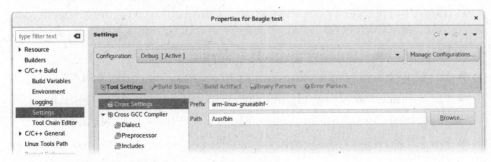

Figure 7-3: Eclipse Oxygen settings for cross-compilation

It should not be necessary to set the C/C++ includes and library settings explicitly as they are included by default by gcc/g++. However, it may be necessary at a later stage, particularly when using third-party libraries. To do this, go to Project ⇨ Properties ⇨ C/C++ General ⇨ Paths and Symbols, and set the following:

- Select Includes ⇨ GNU C (Include directories) ⇨ Add ⇨ File System ⇨ File System, enter **/usr/include/arm-linux-gnueabihf/**, and click OK.

- Select Includes ⇨ GNU C++ (Include directories) ⇨ Add ⇨ File System ⇨ File System, enter **/usr/include/arm-linux-gnueabihf/c++/6/**, and click OK.

- Select Library Paths (not Libraries) ⇨ Add ⇨ File System ⇨ File System and enter **/usr/lib/arm-linux-gnueabihf/**. Click OK to apply the configuration.

Now you should be able to deploy the binary application directly to your Beagle board, as it contains ARM machine code instructions. You can transfer the binary application to your board using sftp, but it would be better in the longer term if you had a direct link to your board from within Eclipse—for this you can use the Remote System Explorer plug-in.

Remote System Explorer

The Remote System Explorer (RSE) plug-in enables you to establish a direct connection between your Eclipse environment and your Beagle board, over a network connection, by using the SSH server on your board. You can install the RSE within Eclipse using Help ⇨ Install New Software. Choose "Oxygen. . ." in the "Work with" section and then choose General Purpose Tools ⇨ Remote System Explorer User Actions. Click Next, follow the steps, and then restart Eclipse.

You should now have RSE functionality within Eclipse. Go to Window ⇨ Show View ⇨ Other ⇨ Remote Systems ⇨ Remote Systems. In the Remote Systems frame that appears, click the Define a Connection to Remote System icon, and in the New Connection dialog, select the following:

- Choose Linux Type and then click Next.
- For Host Name, enter your board's IP address—e.g., **192.168.7.2**.
- For Connection Name, change it to PocketBeagle and then click Next.
- For [Files] Configuration, select ssh.files and then click Next.
- For [Processes] Configuration, select processes.shell.linux and then click Next.
- For [Shells] Configuration, select ssh.shells and then click Finish.

To install the terminal, use Help ⇨ Install New Software. Choose "Oxygen..." in the "Work with" section and then search for *terminal*. Install the TM Terminal View RSE add-in.

You can then right-click the PocketBeagle entry on the Remote Systems tab and choose Open Terminal. You should see the dialog illustrated in Figure 7-4. In this example, the debian user account is used on the PocketBeagle as the account into which the executable code is deployed. Usefully, Eclipse uses a master password system to manage passwords for all of your individual connections.

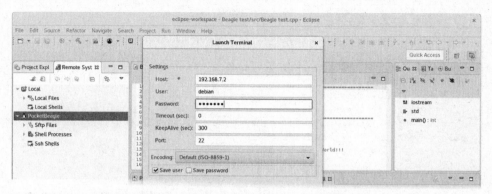

Figure 7-4: Connecting to the Beagle board for the first time using RSE

Once you are connected to the board, you can go to the Project Explorer window, right-click the executable that you just built (Beagle test [arm/le]), and choose Copy. Then go to a directory on the Remote Explorer, such as test-Cross (see Figure 7-5). Right-click it and choose Paste. The file is now on the PocketBeagle and can be executed from the Terminal window—right-click the PocketBeagle entry in the Remote Systems tab and choose Open Terminal. The output of the test program is illustrated in Figure 7-5. It is necessary to set the file to be executable on the first occasion and to rename it to remove the space— don't use spaces in executable filenames! You can break the link between the project name and the build executable name using Project ⇨ Properties ⇨ C/C++ Build ⇨ Settings ⇨ Build Artifact ⇨ Artifact name.

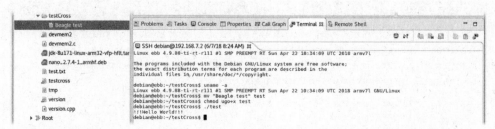

Figure 7-5: The Terminal window, connected to the PocketBeagle and executing the cross-compiled C++ application

One way to automate the process of copying the files from the desktop computer to the Beagle board is by using the secure copy command scp. You can set up your desktop computer so that it does not need to use a password to ssh to the PocketBeagle by using the following steps on the desktop computer (when prompted, you should leave the passphrase blank):

```
molloyd@desktop:~$ ssh-keygen
Generating public/private rsa key pair.
Enter file in which to save the key (/home/molloyd/.ssh/id_rsa):
Enter passphrase (empty for no passphrase):
Enter same passphrase again:
Your identification has been saved in /home/molloyd/.ssh/id_rsa.
...
molloyd@desktop:~$ ssh-copy-id debian@192.168.7.2
...
debian@192.168.7.2's password: temppwd
molloyd@desktop:~$ ssh-add
Identity added: /home/molloyd/.ssh/id_rsa (/home/molloyd/.ssh/id_rsa)
molloyd@desktop:~$ ssh debian@192.168.7.2
Linux ebb 4.9.88-ti-rt-r111 #1 SMP PREEMPT RT 2018 armv7l
...
```

You should now be able to ssh to the PocketBeagle without requiring a password. You can then configure Eclipse under Project ⇨ Properties ⇨ C/C++ Build ⇨ Settings, select the Build Steps tab. In the "Post-build steps" section (not the "Pre-build steps" section) set the Command field to be scp BeagleTest debian@192.168.7.2:/home/debian/testCross/.

You can test this command at the terminal prompt before configuring the Eclipse IDE.

```
molloyd@desktop:~/eclipse-workspace/Beagle test/Debug$ scp BeagleTest →
debian@192.168.7.2:/home/debian/testCross/
BeagleTest                            100%   95KB   2.4MB/s   00:00
debian@ebb:~/testCross$ ls -l
-rwxr-xr-x 1 debian debian 96888 Jun  4 20:39 BeagleTest
```

SECURE COPY (SCP) AND RSYNC

The *secure copy* program, scp, provides a mechanism for transferring files between two hosts using the secure shell (SSH) protocol. For example, to transfer a file test1 .txt from a Linux desktop machine to your board, you can use the following (all commands are executed on the desktop machine):

```
molloyd@desktop:~/test$ echo "Testing SCP" >> test1.txt
molloyd@desktop:~/test$ scp test1.txt debian@192.168.7.2:/tmp
test1.txt                            100%    12     6.9KB/s   00:00
```

To copy a file from the board back to the Linux desktop machine, you can use the following:

```
molloyd@desktop:~/test$ scp debian@192.168.7.2:/tmp/test1.txt test2.txt
test1.txt                        100%   12     6.6KB/s   00:00
molloyd@desktop:~/test$ more test2.txt
Testing SCP
```

Use -v to see full, *verbose* output of the transfer. Using -C will automatically *compress* and decompress the files to speed up the data transfer. Using -r allows for the *recursive* copy of a directory, including all of its files and subdirectories. Using -p will *preserve* the modification times, access times, and modes of the original files. Therefore, to copy the entire desktop test/ directory to the PocketBeagle /tmp/ directory, you could use the following:

```
molloyd@desktop:~$ scp -Cvrp test debian@192.168.7.2:/tmp
...
debug1: compress outgoing: raw data 416, compressed 279, factor 0.67
debug1: compress incoming: raw data 908, compressed 689, factor 0.76
```

Just like scp, the rsync utility can copy files; however, it can also be used to synchronize files and directories across multiple locations, where only the differences are transferred (*delta encoding*). For example, to perform the same operation using rsync, you can use the following:

```
molloyd@desktop:~$ rsync -avze ssh test debian@192.168.7.2:/tmp/test
sending incremental file list
test/
test/test1.txt
test/test2.txt
sent 227 bytes   received 58 bytes   570.00 bytes/sec
total size is 24   speedup is 0.08
```

Using -a requests *archive* mode (like -p for scp), -v requests *verbose* output, -z requests the compression of data (like -C for scp), and -e ssh requests rsync to use the SSH protocol. To test rsync, create an additional file in the test directory and perform the same command again using the following:

```
molloyd@desktop:~$ cd test
molloyd@desktop:~/test$ echo "Testing rsync" >> test3.txt
molloyd@desktop:~/test$ cd ..
molloyd@desktop:~$ rsync -avze ssh test debian@192.168.7.2:/tmp/test
sending incremental file list
test/
test/test3.txt
sent 200 bytes   received 39 bytes   478.00 bytes/sec
total size is 38   speedup is 0.16
```

> Importantly, you can see that only one file has been transferred in this case. The `rsync` utility can delete files after transfer (using `-delete`), which you should use only after performing a dry run (using `-dry-run`).

Integrating GitHub into Eclipse

There is a useful plug-in that can be installed into Eclipse that allows for full GitHub integration, enabling you to link to your own GitHub repositories or to get easy access to the example code and resources for this book. To install it, select Help ➪ Install New Software, and choose "Oxygen..." in the "Work with" section. Then, under the tree item Collaboration, choose "Eclipse GitHub integration with task focused interface."

Once this plug-in is installed, you can select Window ➪ Show View ➪ Other ➪ Git, and there are several options, such as Git Interactive Rebase, Git Reflog, Git Repositories, Git Staging, and Git Tree Compare. If you choose Git Repositories, you then get the option Clone a Git repository and then Clone URI, and you can search for *Derek Molloy*. You should find the repository `derekmolloy/exploringBB`.

If not, you can go back to the Clone URI option and add the repository directly using this: `git://github.com/DerekMolloy/Exploringbb.git` (you can clone all versions of the repository). You will then have full access to the source code in this book directly from within the Eclipse IDE, as captured in Figure 7-6. Because there are so many projects in this repository, the easiest way to use this code is to copy the files that you need into a new project.

Figure 7-6: Eclipse GitHub integration, displaying the `exploringBB` repository

Remote Debugging

Remote debugging is the next step in developing a full-featured, cross-development platform configuration. As you are likely planning to interact with hardware modules that are physically connected to a Beagle board, it would be ideal if you could debug your code live on the board. Remote debugging with Eclipse enables you to control the execution steps and even view debug messages and memory values directly from within Eclipse on your desktop machine.

A short program in Listing 7-1 is used to test that remote debugging is working correctly. This program can be used directly within the /chp07/ repository directory to check that you have local command-line debugging and remote debugging working correctly.

Listing 7-1: /chp07/test.cpp

```
#include<iostream>
using namespace std;
int main(){
    int x = 5;
    x++;
    cout << "The value of x is " << x << endl;
    return 0;
}
```

COMMAND-LINE DEBUGGING

It is possible to use the GNU debugger, gdb, directly at the command line. For example, if you want to debug the code in Listing 7-1 directly on the board, you could perform the following steps (-g ensures that symbolic debugging information is included in the executable):

```
debian@ebb:~/exploringbb/chp07$ sudo apt install gdb
debian@ebb:~/exploringbb/chp07$ g++ -g test.cpp -o test
debian@ebb:~/exploringbb/chp07$ gdb test
GNU gdb (Debian 7.12-6) 7.12.0.20161007-git ...
This GDB was configured as "arm-linux-gnueabihf" ...
(gdb) break main
Breakpoint 1 at 0x85e: file test.cpp, line 4.
(gdb) info break
Num     Type           Disp Enb Address    What
1       breakpoint     keep y   0x0000085e in main() at test.cpp:4
(gdb) run
Starting program: /home/debian/exploringbb/chp07/test
Breakpoint 1, main () at test.cpp:4
4           int x = 5;
(gdb) display x
1: x = 4196633
(gdb) step
5           x++;
1: x = 5
(gdb) step
6           cout << "The value of x is " << x << endl;
1: x = 6
(gdb) continue
Continuing.
```

```
The value of x is 6
[Inferior 1 (process 3495) exited normally]
(gdb) quit
```

The Eclipse IDE executes tools such as gdb **from your chosen toolchain and interprets their outputs, providing a fully integrated interactive display.**

You need the debug server gdbserver to run on the Beagle board for the Eclipse desktop installation to connect to the debugger. Install or update it using the following command:

```
debian@ebb:~$ sudo apt install gdbserver
```

The gdb server executes on the board and is controlled by the Eclipse IDE on the desktop machine. The built executable is still transferred to the board using the RSE configuration described earlier.

The Linux desktop machine requires an ARM-compatible debugger that can connect to the gdb server on the Beagle board. You can install the GNU multi-architecture debugger on the desktop machine as follows:

```
molloyd@desktop:~$ sudo apt install gdb-multiarch
molloyd@desktop:~$ gdb-multiarch --version
GNU gdb (Debian 7.12-6) 7.12.0.20161007-git
```

To complete this configuration, you may need to create a file called .gdbinit in the project folder that defines the remote architecture as arm (it will also allow for additional settings, such as a default breakpoint, etc.).

```
...~/eclipse-workspace/Beagle test$ echo "set architecture arm" >> .gdbinit
...~/eclipse-workspace/Beagle test$ more .gdbinit
set architecture arm
```

Please check that your version of gdb-multiarch is not 7.7.*x*, as there is a known problem in using it to remotely debug ARM code.

COMMAND-LINE REMOTE DEBUGGING

If you are experiencing difficulties with the Eclipse setup, then you can use command-line remote debugging to familiarize yourself with the underlying tools and to test your configuration. The code in Listing 7-1 is once again used for this example. The first step is to execute the gdb server on the board and request that it listens to TCP port (e.g., 12345), as follows:

```
debian@ebb:~/exploringbb/chp07$ gdbserver --multi localhost:12345
Listening on port 12345
```

The use of --multi means that the server has not yet started to debug a target program; therefore, a target must be identified by the desktop machine.

The debugger can then be used to connect to the gdb server from the desktop machine as follows (where `-q test` **requests a quiet mode and for the symbols to be read from the** `test` **binary in the current directory):**

```
molloyd@desktop:~/exploringbb/chp07$ arm-linux-gnueabihf-g++ -g
    test.cpp -o test
molloyd@desktop:~/exploringbb/chp07$ ls -l test
-rwxr-xr-x 1 molloyd molloyd 28680 Jun  7 11:31 test
molloyd@desktop:~/exploringbb/chp07$ gdb-multiarch -q test
Reading symbols from test...done.
(gdb) target extended 192.168.7.2:12345
Remote debugging using 192.168.7.2:12345
Reading /lib/ld-linux-armhf.so.3 from remote target...
0xb6fd7980 in ?? () from target:/lib/ld-linux-armhf.so.3
(gdb) set remote exec-file test
(gdb) break main
Breakpoint 1 at 0x40085e: file test.cpp, line 5.
(gdb) continue
Continuing ...
Breakpoint 1, main () at test.cpp:5
5        int x = 5;
(gdb) display x
1: x = 4196633
(gdb) step
6        x++;
1: x = 5
(gdb) display x
2: x = 5
(gdb) continue
Continuing.
[Inferior 1 (process 3602) exited normally]
```

The final output of the gdb server on the remote board is as follows:

```
debian@ebb:~/exploringbb/chp07$ gdbserver --multi localhost:12345
Listening on port 12345
Remote debugging from host 192.168.7.1
The value of x is 6
Child exited with status 0
```

Just to reiterate, the `test` **program is executed on the Beagle board, but the debugger is controlled on the desktop machine by passing commands over the network.**

Eclipse must be configured so that it can connect to the Beagle board's gdb server. Go to Run ➪ Debug Configurations ➪ Debugger and delete any current debug configurations. Select C/C++ Remote Applications on the left side and right-click it to create a new configuration. In this example, the configuration is called Beagle test Debug, as illustrated in Figure 7-7. The Connection entry can be set to the PocketBeagle connection (as described in the Remote System Explorer section), and you should be able to browse to the remote path (i.e., on the Beagle board) for the C/C++ application, as illustrated.

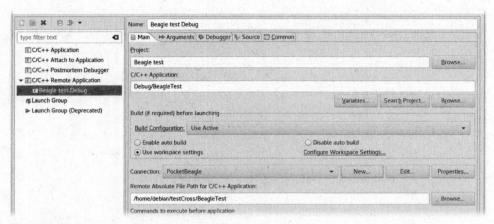

Figure 7-7: Setting the debug configuration

Change the GDB debugger from `gdb` to `gdb-multiarch` or `arm-linux-gnue-abihf-gdb`, as illustrated in Figure 7-8. You should also identify the `.gdbinit` file that was just created. Click the Browse button to the right of "GDB command file" and locate your workspace directory. You may have to right-click the File Explorer window and choose Show Hidden Files to find the hidden file `.gdbinit`. That configuration file can be used to set many more configuration options. For example, it can be used to further configure the remote server and to identify different default breakpoints.

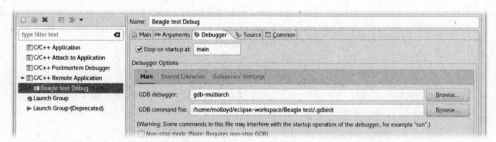

Figure 7-8: Setting up the remote debugger

Any program arguments can be added to the Arguments tab in Figure 7-8. Finally, on the Gdbserver Settings tab (see Figure 7-9), set the executable path and an arbitrary port number for the `gdbserver` command. This allows the desktop computer to remotely invoke the `gdbserver` command on the Beagle board and to connect to it over TCP using its port number.

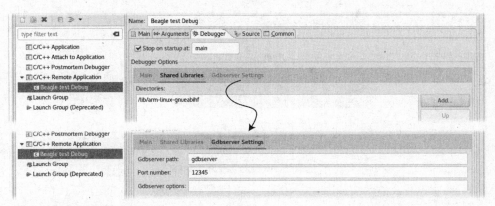

Figure 7-9: Setting the gdbserver port

As illustrated in Figure 7-10, you can enable this debug configuration to be added to the debugger "bug" menu on the main window (see Figure 7-11) by using the Common tab. Finally, you can start debugging by clicking the Debug button in the same dialog window.

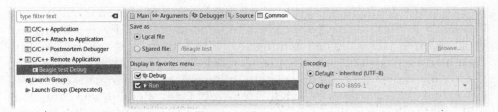

Figure 7-10: Adding to the "bug" menu

When prompted, you should accept the change to a Debug Perspective view, which appears as in Figure 7-11. You can see that the program is currently halted at a breakpoint on line 15 of the program code. The output is displayed in the Console window at the bottom, and the Variables window displays that the current value of x is 6 at this point in the program.

This type of debug view can be invaluable when developing complex applications, especially when the board is connected to electronic circuits and modules. You can use the Step over button to step through each line of your code, watching the variable values, while seeing how the program interacts with physically connected circuits.

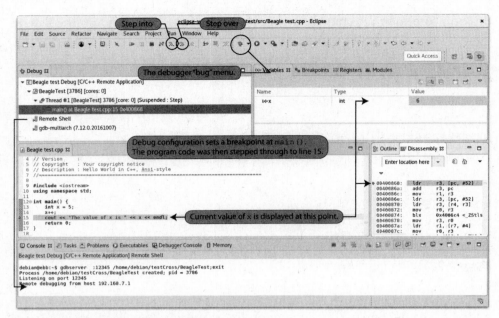

Figure 7-11: The Debug Perspective view

Automatic Documentation (Doxygen)

As your embedded projects grow in capability and complexity, it will become especially important that your code is self-documenting. If you follow good programming practice when naming variables and methods, as discussed in Chapter 5, then you will not have to document every single line of code. Rather, you should write inline documentation comments, using automatic documentation tools like Doxygen or Javadoc, for every class, method, and state. This will enable other programmers to have an immediate understanding of what your code does and how it is structured.

Javadoc is an automatic documentation generator that generates HTML code directly from Java source code. Likewise, *Doxygen* is a tool that can be used for generating documentation from annotated C/C++ source files in HTML, LaTeX, and other formats. Doxygen can also generate documentation for the other programming languages that are discussed in Chapter 5, but the following discussion focuses on how it can be used for C++ documentation and how it can be integrated with the Eclipse IDE. An example output, which documents the C++ GPIO class from Chapter 6, is displayed in Figure 7-12.

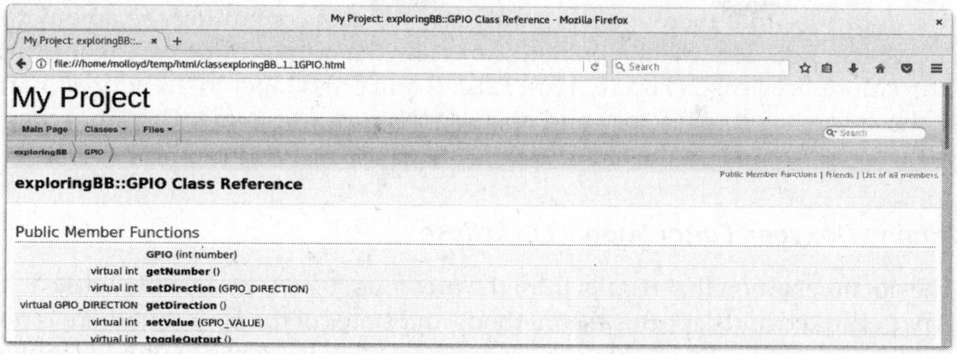

Figure 7-12: Example Doxygen HTML output

First, you need to install Doxygen on the Linux desktop machine using the following command:

```
molloyd@desktop:~$ sudo apt install doxygen
```

Once installed, you can immediately begin generating documentation for your project. For example, copy the GPIO.h and GPIO.cpp files from the chp06/GPIO/ directory into a temporary directory such as ~/temp/ and then build the documentation as follows:

```
molloyd@desktop:~/temp$ ls
GPIO.cpp  GPIO.h
molloyd@desktop:~/temp$ doxygen -g
Configuration file 'Doxyfile' created ...
molloyd@desktop:~/temp$ ls
Doxyfile  GPIO.cpp  GPIO.h
molloyd@desktop:~/temp$ doxygen -w html header.html footer.html stylesheet.css
molloyd@desktop:~/temp$ ls
Doxyfile  footer.html  GPIO.cpp  GPIO.h  header.html  stylesheet.css
```

This automatically generates HTML files that you can customize for your project, adding headers, footers, and style sheets to suit your needs. Next, call the doxygen command on the Doxyfile configuration.

```
molloyd@desktop:~/temp$ doxygen Doxyfile
molloyd@desktop:~/temp$ ls
Doxyfile  footer.html    GPIO.cpp  GPIO.h  header.html  html
latex     stylesheet.css
```

You can see that there are `html` and `latex` folders containing the automatically generated documentation. You can view the output by browsing (e.g., in Chromium/Iceweasel/Firefox, type **file://** and press Enter in the address bar) to the `~/temp/html/` directory and opening the `index.html` file. There is a comprehensive manual on the features of Doxygen at www.doxygen.org.

Adding Doxygen Editor Support in Eclipse

The documentation that results from the previous steps is reasonably limited. It is hyperlinked and captures the methods and states of the class, but there is no deeper description. By integrating Doxygen into Eclipse, you can provide inline commentary that is integrated into your generated documentation output. You do this by enabling Doxygen in the editor. In Eclipse, select Window ⇨ Preferences ⇨ C/C++ ⇨ Editor. In the window at the bottom, under "Workspace default" select Doxygen. Apply the settings, and then in the editor type **/**** followed by the Return key above any method, and the IDE will automatically generate a comment as follows:

```
/**
 * @param number
 */
GPIO::GPIO(int number) {
```

You can then add a description of what the method does, as shown in the following example:

```
/**
 * Constructor for the General Purpose Input/Output (GPIO) class. It
 * will export the GPIO automatically.
 * @param number The GPIO number for the Beagle board pin
 */
GPIO::GPIO(int number) {
```

Cross-Building Linux

The Linux kernel is essentially a large C program that forms the central core of the Linux OS—together with loadable kernel modules (LKMs), it is responsible for managing almost everything that occurs on a Linux-based SBC. The kernel is custom built for each architecture type, which means that there is a different kernel required for the ARMv7 PocketBeagle than the Cortex-A15

BeagleBoard-X15. The custom-built kernel for ARM devices utilizes device tree binary (DTB) files, which provide a standardized description of the device to reduce the amount of custom code required for each device model.

The Debian image contains a full Linux distribution that includes a kernel; however, advanced users may want to replace the kernel with a recent or user-configured kernel. Typically, this involves building the kernel from source code, which can be performed directly on the board, but it can take quite some time. Alternatively, the cross-compilation tools that are described in this chapter can be used, which can greatly reduce compilation time by leveraging the resources of a capable Linux desktop machine.

The following description is written with the assumption that you have installed a cross-compilation toolchain, as described at the beginning of this chapter.

ENABLING SSH ROOT LOGIN WITH DEBIAN STRETCH

To transfer files to certain directories on the Beagle board using `scp` or `rsync`, you may need to enable SSH root login. The first step is to enable root login (as described in Chapter 5) using this:

```
debian@ebb:~$ sudo passwd root
   [sudo] password for debian: ...
```

Then edit the sshd configuration file (`sshd_config`) to permit root login by changing the `PermitRootLogin` value to `yes`. Then restart the service.

```
debian@ebb:/etc/ssh$ sudo nano sshd_config
debian@ebb:/etc/ssh$ more sshd_config | grep RootLogin
PermitRootLogin yes
debian@ebb:/etc/ssh$ sudo systemctl restart sshd
```

Be especially careful not to introduce errors into this configuration file, as any errors may mean that the SSH service will not start up correctly. This would mean you would not be able to access the board via SSH! (You can always reconnect using a serial connection and fix the problem.)

To reverse this configuration, set the `PermitRootLogin` value back to `without-password` and disable root login using `sudo passwd -l root`.

Downloading the Kernel Source

The `BeagleBoard.org` Foundation, through Robert C Nelson, maintains the code that is required to build the kernel for the Beagle boards on a GitHub repository. This reduces the complexity of the build process in comparison to cloning the "vanilla" repository from `www.kernel.org`, as the GitHub repository contains helpful configuration files and scripts. You can clone this repository and build the Linux kernel as follows on a desktop machine:

```
molloyd@desktop:~$ git clone https://github.com/RobertCNelson/bb-kernel.git
Cloning into 'bb-kernel'...
molloyd@desktop:~$ cd bb-kernel/
```

You can select a particular kernel version by listing the available branches and checking out the version you require.

```
molloyd@desktop:~/bb-kernel$ git branch -a
  master
* tmp
  remotes/origin/3.8.13-xenomai
  remotes/origin/HEAD -> origin/master
  remotes/origin/am33x-rt-v4.11
  remotes/origin/am33x-rt-v4.13
  remotes/origin/am33x-rt-v4.14
  remotes/origin/am33x-rt-v4.16
...
  remotes/origin/am33x-v4.9
  remotes/origin/master
molloyd@desktop:~/bb-kernel$ git checkout origin/am33x-rt-v4.14 -b tmp
Branch tmp set up to track remote branch am33x-rt-v4.14 from origin.
Switched to a new branch 'tmp'
```

Building the Linux Kernel

The BeagleBoard.org scripts that are provided make building the kernel straightforward, as they automatically identify missing dependencies and download required toolchains.

```
molloyd@desktop:~/bb-kernel$ ./build_kernel.sh
+ Detected build host [Debian GNU/Linux 9.4 (stretch)] ...
Debian/Ubuntu/Mint: missing dependencies, please install:
sudo apt-get install bc lzma lzop gettext bison flex
* Failed dependency check
molloyd@desktop:~/bb-kernel$ sudo apt-get install bc lzma lzop →
gettext bison flex
```

Once any missing dependencies are installed, the kernel build should be restarted. Shortly thereafter you should be presented with the Kernel Configuration menu, as illustrated in Figure 7-13.

```
molloyd@desktop:~/bb-kernel$ ./build_kernel.sh
+ Detected build host [Debian GNU/Linux 9.4 (stretch)] ...
gcc-linaro-7.2.1-2017.11-x86_64_arm-linux-gnueabihf.tar.xz ...
```

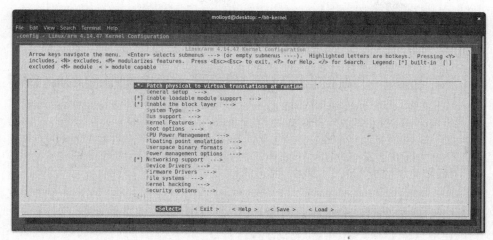

Figure 7-13: The Kernel Configuration menu for Linux 4.14.47

You should browse the configuration menu to see some entries that may be of interest in relation to the Beagle board platform.

- In the Kernel Features menu you can alter the preemption model (see Figure 7-14(a)).

- Under CPU Power Management, you can use the "CPU Frequency scaling" menu to enable/disable the various governors described in Chapter 3. You can also change the default governor from "performance" (currently default) to one of the other governors if you want.

- In the "Floating point emulation" menu, you can see that the configuration includes "Advanced SIMD (NEON) Extension support" for the ARM platform.

- The Device Drivers menu provides options for configuring I²C, SPI, USB devices, and much more.

The configuration is saved in the `.config` file when you exit this tool, and the scripts will continue building the kernel, its associated LKMs, and DTBs. It took approximately 40 minutes to build the kernel on a VM with a single Intel i7 processor core. Please note that you may have to perform a `make clean` between subsequent kernel builds.

The final output kernel files are available in the `deploy/` subdirectory as follows:

```
molloyd@desktop:~/bb-kernel$ cd deploy/
molloyd@desktop:~/bb-kernel/deploy$ ls -sl
total 28164
  420 4.14.47-bone-rt-r14-dtbs.tar.gz
17544 4.14.47-bone-rt-r14-modules.tar.gz
10044 4.14.47-bone-rt-r14.zImage
  156 config-4.14.47-bone-rt-r14
```

These files are consistent in size and role with the kernel files in the `/boot/`, `/boot/dtbs/`, and `/lib/modules/` Beagle board directories that are described in Chapter 3.

THE FULLY PREEMPTIBLE KERNEL (RT) PATCH

The latest BeagleBoard Linux distributions include images that have the PREEMPT_RT patch applied. Typically, the PREEMPT_RT patch is downloaded from `www.kernel.org/pub/linux/kernel/projects/rt/` as a `.gz` file and applied to the exact kernel version that is being built. In Figure 7-14(a), the RT patch has been applied, which results in a new option for a fully preemptible kernel in the `menuconfig` tool.

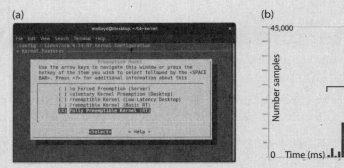

(a) (b)

Figure 7-14: (a) The PREEMPT_RT menuconfig option, (b) the results histogram of the cyclictest with an RT and non-RT kernel

The patched kernel should display a message that includes "RT" when `uname` is called. Figure 7-15(b) illustrates the cyclictest results histogram of the fully preemptible kernel. The results on the PocketBeagle are determined as follows on two different kernels, one with the RT patch applied:

```
debian@ebb:~$ uname -a
Linux ebb 4.9.88-ti-rt-r111 #1 SMP PREEMPT RT ...
Linux ebb 4.14.44-ti-rt-r51 #1 SMP PREEMPT ...
```

Download and build the rt-tests `cyclictest` tool.

```
debian@ebb:~$ git clone git://git.kernel.org/pub/scm/linux/kern →
el/git/clrkwllms/rt-tests.git
debian@ebb:~$ cd rt-tests/
debian@ebb:~/rt-tests$ make all
```

And run the test as follows:

```
debian@ebb:~/rt-tests$ sudo ./cyclictest -t 1 -p 70 -n -i 1000 -l 100000
--smp
policy: fifo: loadavg: 0.03 0.07 0.03 1/198 4089
T: 0 ( 4088) P:70 I:1000 C: 100000 Min: 13  Act: 23  Avg: 26  Max: 106
```

To develop the graph in Figure 7-14(b), the following steps were used (the second step was performed on the RT and non-RT kernels):

```
debian@ebb:~/rt-tests$ sudo apt install gnuplot
debian@ebb:~/rt-tests$ sudo ./cyclictest -h 100 -p 70 -t 1 -q -n -i →
1000 -l 100000 --smp > hist_RT.dat
debian@ebb:~/rt-tests$ echo 'set term png; set terminal pngcairo size →
1600, 1200; set style data histograms; set style fill solid 2 border →
-1; set boxwidth 2.5; set output "plot_compare.png"; set xrange →
[0:50]; plot "hist_RT.dat" using 2 lt rgb "blue", "hist_nonRT.dat" →
using 2 lt rgb "red";' | gnuplot
```

Figure 7-14(b) illustrates that the RT patch (Linux 4.9.88) has lower overall latency than the non-RT patch (Linux 4.14.44) but that the distribution is quite similar, which is not surprising as both kernels had a PREEMPT option set.

Building a Poky Linux Distribution (Advanced)

In the previous section, a new Linux kernel was created so that it could be applied to an existing Debian image distribution. It is also possible to build a custom Linux distribution for the Beagle boards using open-source projects such as *OpenWRT* (www.openwrt.org), *Buildroot* (buildroot.uclibc.org), and the *Yocto Project* (www.yoctoproject.org). These projects aim to create tools, templates, and processes to support you in building custom embedded Linux distributions.

Poky (www.pokylinux.org) is an open-source reference distribution from the Yocto Project that can be used to build customized Linux images for more complex embedded systems, such as the Beagle boards. The Poky platform builder, which is derived from *OpenEmbedded*, can be used to build ready-to-install Linux file system images by automatically downloading and building all of the Linux applications (e.g., SSH servers, gcc, X11 applications) and configuring and installing them within a root file system. The alternative approach to using a build system such as Poky is that you would have to configure each Linux application by hand, matching dependency versions—a difficult task that would have to be repeated for each system type.

Poky uses the *BitBake* build tool to perform tasks such as downloading, compiling, and installing software packages and file system images. The instructions as to which tasks BitBake should perform are contained in metadata *recipe* (.bb) files. There is a full "Poky Handbook" that is co-authored by Richard Purdie of the Linux Foundation at tiny.cc/beagle701.

Here is a short guide that works through the steps that are currently required to build a minimal Linux distribution for the BeagleBone. This is intended as a learning exercise that aims to give you a flavor of what to expect—there are full books written on this topic! Depending on the specification of your PC, these steps can take several hours to complete:

1. Clone the Poky repository (~221 MB) and within this repository clone the TI metadata layer (~12 MB).

```
molloyd@desktop:~$ git clone git://git.yoctoproject.org/poky.git
Cloning into 'poky'...
molloyd@desktop:~$ cd poky
molloyd@desktop:~/poky$ git clone git://git.yoctoproject.org/meta-ti
```

2. Configure the build environment and create the build directory and the files that you can use to configure the build.

```
molloyd@desktop:~/poky$ source oe-init-build-env
You had no conf/local.conf file. This configuration file has
therefore been created for you with some default values...
You can now run 'bitbake <target>'
Common targets are: core-image-minimal ...
molloyd@desktop:~/poky/build$ cd conf
```

Configure the build machine to be the BeagleBone and for the build to include the Dropbear ssh server.

```
molloyd@desktop:~/poky/build/conf$ nano local.conf
molloyd@desktop:~/poky/build/conf$ more local.conf | grep beagle
MACHINE ?= "beaglebone-yocto"
molloyd@desktop:~/poky/build/conf$ more local.conf | grep drop
CORE_IMAGE_EXTRA_INSTALL +="dropbear"
```

3. Add the `meta-ti` recipes directory to the BBLAYERS entry in the bblayers. conf file.

```
molloyd@desktop:~/poky/build/conf$ more bblayers.conf
...
BBLAYERS ?= " \
  /home/molloyd/poky/meta \
  /home/molloyd/poky/meta-poky \
  /home/molloyd/poky/meta-yocto-bsp \
  /home/molloyd/poky/meta-ti \
  "
```

4. Set the cross-compiler variables, and you are ready to build a BeagleBone image. The minimal image is the minimal bootable image, which includes SSH support and so is used here:

```
molloyd@desktop:~/poky$ sudo apt install chrpath diffstat →
  libsdl-dev texinfo
molloyd@desktop:~/poky$ bitbake core-image-minimal
Build Configuration:
BB_VERSION              = "1.39.0"
BUILD_SYS               = "x86_64-linux"
NATIVELSBSTRING         = "debian-9"
TARGET_SYS              = "arm-poky-linux-gnueabi"
MACHINE                 = "beaglebone-yocto"
DISTRO                  = "poky"
DISTRO_VERSION          = "2.5+snapshot-20180609"
TUNE_FEATURES           = "arm armv7a vfp neon ... cortexa8"
TARGET_FPU              = "hard" ...
```

You can make further configuration changes as follows:

```
molloyd@desktop:~/poky/build$ bitbake-layers show-recipes
molloyd@desktop:~/poky/build$ bitbake -c menuconfig busybox
```

You may have to run step 5 several times until you have resolved missing dependencies. At this point, the build should begin—it takes approximately one hour on a VM that has an allocation of six i7 threads. The build results in the following output:

```
...~/poky/build/tmp/deploy/images/beaglebone-yocto$ ls
am335x-boneblack.dtb
am335x-bone.dtb
am335x-bonegreen.dtb
...
MLO
modules-beaglebone-yocto.tgz
u-boot.img
zImage
zImage-am335x-boneblack.dtb
zImage-am335x-bone.dtb
zImage-am335x-bonegreen.dtb
zImage-beaglebone-yocto.bin
```

5. You can create a suitable SD card file system and then write the final image to an SD card. The SD card appears on the Linux VM as sdb. GParted, as illustrated in Figure 7-15, can be used to create a fat32 and ext4 partition to contain the files from step 4.

```
molloyd@desktop:~$ lsblk
NAME    MAJ:MIN RM    SIZE RO TYPE MOUNTPOINT
```

```
...
sdb       8:16   1   59.6G  0 disk
└─sdb1   8:17   1   59.6G  0 part /media/molloyd/disk
molloyd@desktop:~$ sudo apt install gparted
molloyd@desktop:~$ sudo gparted
molloyd@desktop:~$ lsblk
NAME   MAJ:MIN RM   SIZE RO TYPE MOUNTPOINT
...
sdb       8:16   1   59.6G  0 disk
└─sdb1   8:17   1    50M   0 part
└─sdb2   8:18   1   59.6G  0 part
```

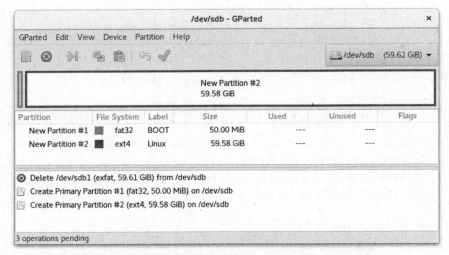

Figure 7-15: The GParted tool being used to create a fat32 and ext4 partition

You can then mount these partitions to temporary locations on the desktop Linux VM and copy the files to appropriate locations.

```
molloyd@desktop:~$ sudo mkdir /mnt/fat
molloyd@desktop:~$ sudo mkdir /mnt/linux
molloyd@desktop:~$ sudo mount /dev/sdb1 /mnt/fat
molloyd@desktop:~$ sudo mount /dev/sdb2 /mnt/linux
...~/poky/build/tmp/deploy/images/beaglebone-yocto$ sudo cp →
 MLO-beaglebone-yocto /mnt/fat/MLO
...~/poky/build/tmp/deploy/images/beaglebone-yocto$ sudo cp →
 u-boot-beaglebone-yocto.img /mnt/fat/u-boot.img
...~/poky/build/tmp/deploy/images/beaglebone-yocto$ sudo tar →
 -xvf core-image-minimal-beaglebone-yocto.tar.bz2 -C /mnt/linux/
```

Finally, you need to create a `uEnv.txt` file on the fat32 partition that configures the kernel, as follows:

```
molloyd@desktop:/mnt/fat$ sudo nano uEnv.txt
molloyd@desktop:/mnt/fat$ more uEnv.txt
loadzimage=load mmc 0:2 ${loadaddr} /boot/zImage
loadfdt=load mmc 0:2 ${fdtaddr} /boot/${fdtfile}
mmcargs=setenv bootargs console=ttyO0,115200n8  root=/dev/
mmcblk0p2 ro
rootfstype= ext4 rootwait fixrtc  ${optargs}
uenvcmd=run loadzimage; run loadfdt; run mmcargs; bootz
${loadaddr} -
${fdtaddr}
molloyd@desktop:~$ sudo umount /dev/sdb1
molloyd@desktop:~$ sudo umount /dev/sdb2
```

Once the board has been booted with the new distribution, you can connect to it using its IP address (see Chapter 2) or via a serial connection and you can log in as root (with no password required).

```
...
Sat Jun  9 11:26:32 UTC 2018
INIT: Entering runlevel: 5
Starting Dropbear SSH server: dropbear.
Starting syslogd/klogd: done
Poky (Yocto Project Reference Distro) 2.5... beaglebone-yocto /dev/ttyO0
beaglebone-yocto login: root
root@beaglebone-yocto:~# uname -a
Linux beaglebone-yocto 4.15.13-yocto-standard #1 PREEMPT ... 2018 armv7l
root@beaglebone-yocto:~# df -h
Filesystem            Size      Used Available Use% Mounted on
/dev/root             58.4G    64.2M     55.3G   0% /
devtmpfs             236.9M        0    236.9M   0% /dev
tmpfs                245.4M    64.0K    245.3M   0% /run
tmpfs                245.4M    44.0K    245.3M   0% /var/volatile
```

The ext4 partition on this minimal image is ~64MB in size, so you do not have access to anything like the same range of tools as within the Debian image. Typically packages are added to the distribution at the build stage, but it is possible to add a package manager such as deb/apt.[1] However, adding typical package management capabilities to your custom build involves pointing /etc/apt/sources.list on the board at your own web server, which contains packages that are custom built for your distribution (e.g., from /poky/build/tmp/deploy/).

At this stage, you can adjust the configuration files, and bitbake will only rebuild packages that are affected by your changes. For example, it is possible

---

[1]Add three line entries for IMAGE_FEATURES += "package-management", +PACKAGE_CLASSES ?= "package_deb", and CORE_IMAGE_EXTRA_INSTALL += "apt" to the local.conf file.

to configure kernel settings using the menuconfig tool (as in Figure 7-13) at this stage and rebuild the SD image within a matter of minutes:

```
molloyd@desktop:~/poky/build$ bitbake virtual/kernel -c menuconfig
molloyd@desktop:~/poky/build$ bitbake virtual/kernel -c compile -f
molloyd@desktop:~/poky/build$ bitbake virtual/kernel
```

One key strength of the Poky build tool is that there is strong community support—please see `pokylinux.org/support/`.

Summary

After completing this chapter, you should be able to

- Install a cross-compilation toolchain under desktop Linux that can be used to build applications for the Beagle boards using your desktop PC.
- Use a package manager to install multi-architecture third-party libraries that may be required for cross-compilation.
- Emulate the ARM architecture on the desktop PC using QEMU.
- Install and configure the Eclipse integrated development environment for cross-compilation to build Linux applications.
- Configure Eclipse for remote deployment of applications, remote debugging, GitHub integration, and automated documentation.
- Build a custom Linux kernel and Poky Linux distribution.

## CHAPTER 8

Interfacing to the Beagle Board Buses

This chapter describes bus communication in detail, explaining and comparing the different bus types that are available on the Beagle boards. It describes how you can configure them for use, and how you can communicate with and control I²C, SPI, and UART devices, using both Linux tools and custom-developed C/C++ code. Practical examples are provided using different low-cost bus devices, such as a real-time clock, an accelerometer, a serial shift register with a seven-segment display, a USB-to-TTL 3.3V cable, and a GPS receiver. Finally, the AM335x DCAN controller is used to send and receive messages to and from a CAN Bus using Linux SocketCAN. After reading this chapter, you should have the skills necessary to begin interfacing almost any type of bus device to the Beagle boards.

EQUIPMENT REQUIRED FOR THIS CHAPTER:

- Any Beagle board
- A real-time clock on a breakout board (e.g., the DS3231)
- ADXL345 accelerometer on an I²C/SPI breakout board
- 74HC595 shift register, seven-segment display, and resistors

- A USB-to-TTL 3.3V cable (see Chapter 1 and Chapter 2)
- A low-cost UART GPS receiver (e.g., the GY-GPS6MV2)
- A low-cost physical-layer CAN Bus module (ideally one with a TI SN65HVD230 CAN controller)

Further details on this equipment and chapter are available at www.exploringbeaglebone.com/chapter8.

Introduction to Bus Communication

In Chapter 6, the use of general-purpose input/outputs (GPIOs) is discussed in detail, which makes it clear how you can connect a Beagle board to stand-alone components. This chapter examines more complex communications that can be performed using the bus interfaces that are available on the Beagle boards. *Bus communication* is a mechanism that enables data to be transferred between the high-level components of an embedded platform, using standardized communications protocols. The three most commonly used embedded system buses are available on the Beagle boards, and they are the subject of this chapter: *Inter-Integrated Circuit* (I²C), *Serial Peripheral Interface* (SPI), and *Controller Area Network* (CAN Bus). In addition, *Universal Asynchronous Receiver/Transmitter* (UART) devices are discussed. These are computer hardware devices that can be configured and used to send and receive serial data. When combined with appropriate driver interfaces, UARTs can implement standard serial communication protocols, such as RS-232, RS-422, or RS-485.

Understanding the behavior and use of bus communication protocols and devices enables the possibility of building advanced Beagle board electronic systems. There are a huge number of complex sensors, actuators, input devices, I/O expanders, and other microcontrollers that conform to these communication protocols, and the Beagle boards are capable of communicating with them all. Several such devices are used in Chapter 9 to interface the boards to the physical environment using sensors and actuators. In addition, Chapter 10 describes how you can use popular microcontrollers to build your own advanced bus devices, which can be interfaced directly to the boards using these buses.

The topics discussed in this chapter are all demonstrated using practical examples with devices that were largely chosen based on their wide availability and low cost. However, the focus of this chapter is on imparting an understanding of the techniques employed in using the board's buses, rather than just describing the specific bus devices used. To this end, the chapter provides generic communications code that you can use to apply the principles described to any device of your choosing.

I²C

Inter-Integrated Circuit (IIC or I²C) is a two-wire bus that was designed by Philips in the 1980s to interface microprocessors or microcontrollers to low-speed peripheral devices. A *master* device, such as a Beagle board, controls the bus, and many addressable *slave* devices can be attached to the same two wires. It has remained popular over the years, mainly because of its relative simplicity and breadth of adoption. It is currently used in smartphones, most microcontrollers, and even environmental management applications in large-scale server farms. Here are some general features of the I²C bus:

- Only two signal lines are required for communication, the *Serial Data* (SDA) line for the bidirectional transmission of data, and the *Serial Clock* (SCL) line, which is used to synchronize the data transfer. Because the bus uses this synchronizing clock signal, the data transfer is said to be *synchronous*. The transmission is said to be *bidirectional* because the same SDA wire can be used for sending and receiving data.

- Each device on the bus can act as a master or a slave. The *master device* is the one that initiates communication, and the *slave device* is the one that responds. Designated slave devices cannot initiate communication with the master device.

- Each slave device attached to the bus is pre-assigned a unique address, which is in either 7-bit or 10-bit form. In the following examples, 7-bit addressing is used, i.e., 0x00 to 0x7F ($2^7 = 128_{10} = 0x80$).

- It has true *multi-master bus facilities*, including collision detection and arbitration if two or more master devices activate at once.

- On-chip noise filtering is built in as standard.

> **NOTE** There is a video on the use of I²C with a BMA180 accelerometer at the chapter web page: www.exploringbeaglebone.com/chapter8. In the video, an application is built using the Qt development environment to capture and graphically display the output of the accelerometer on a desktop computer. That type of application is discussed in Chapter 13.

I²C Hardware

Figure 8-1 illustrates the interconnection of multiple slave devices to the I²C bus. All output connections to the SDA and SCL lines are in open-drain configuration (discussed in Chapter 4), whereby all devices share a common ground connection. This means that devices with different logic families can be inter-mixed on the bus and that a large number of devices can be added to a single bus. In theory, up to 128 devices could be attached to a single bus, but doing so would greatly increase the capacitance of the interconnecting lines. The bus is designed to work over short distances, as long bus lines are prone to electrical interference and *capacitance effects* (e.g., a pair of 22 AWG shielded wires has a capacitance of about 15pF/ft).

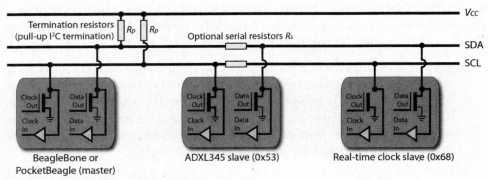

Figure 8-1: The I²C bus configuration

Transmission line capacitance has a huge impact on data transmission rates. In Chapter 4 (see Figure 4-11), when a 10μF capacitor is connected in parallel with a resistive load and an AC voltage supply is applied, the capacitor has a clear smoothing effect on the voltage across the load. This smoothing effect is unwel-come in the transmission of digital data; for example, if a random binary signal (0V–3.3V) switches at a high frequency, then severe smoothing could result in a constant 1.65V signal, which carries no binary information at all. Typically, the longer the bus length and the more I²C devices that are attached to it, the slower the speed of data transmission. There are I²C repeaters available that act as current amplifiers to help solve the problems associated with long lines. Further documentation on the I²C bus is available from NXP directly at `tiny.cc/beagle801`.

I²C on the Beagle Boards

I²C on the Beagle boards supports 7-bit/10-bit addressing, and bus frequencies of up to 400kHz. NXP (formerly Philips) has newer I²C Fast-mode Plus (Fm+) devices that can communicate at up to 1MHz[1], but this capability is not avail-able on the Beagle boards.

---

[1]In 2012 NXP released Ultra Fast-mode (UFm) I²C, which offers a 5MHz mode. However, it is quite different from other I²C modes as it is unidirectional and there is only a single master. It is currently not widely adopted.

The I^{2}C bus requires pull-up resistors (R_p) on both the SDA and SCL lines, as illustrated in Figure 8-1. These are called *termination resistors*, and they usually have a value of between 1kΩ and 10kΩ. Their role is to pull the SDA and SCL lines up to V_{CC} when no I^{2}C device is pulling them down to GND. This pull-up configuration enables multiple master devices to take control of the bus and for the slave device to "stretch" the clock signal (i.e., hold SCL low). *Clock stretching* can be used by the slave device to slow down data transfer until it has finished processing and is ready to transmit. Termination resistors are often also present on the breakout board that is associated with an I^{2}C device. This can be a useful feature, but their equivalent parallel resistance should be factored into your design, particularly if you are using several boards on the same bus. In the I^{2}C demonstration application discussed in this chapter, the PocketBeagle is the master device, and the ADXL345 slave device is on a breakout board that already has 4.7kΩ termination resistors on the board.

The optional *serial resistors* (R_S) shown in Figure 8-1 usually have low values (e.g., 250Ω) and can help protect against overcurrent conditions. The I^{2}C devices are typically attached to the SDA and SCL lines using built-in Schmitt trigger inputs (see Chapter 4) to reduce the impact of signal noise by building in a degree of switching hysteresis.

WARNING   The I^{2}C buses on the Beagle boards are 3.3V tolerant; consequently, you will need logic-level translation circuitry if you want to connect 5V-powered I^{2}C devices to it. That topic is discussed later in this chapter.

I^{2}C Devices on the Beagle Boards

The I^{2}C buses are present by default on the Debian Linux image and are described in Table 8-1. The I^{2}C devices are visible in the /dev/ directory.

```
debian@ebb:/dev$ ls -l i2c*
crw-rw---- 1 root i2c 89, 0 Jun  9 19:24 i2c-0
crw-rw---- 1 root i2c 89, 1 Jun  9 19:25 i2c-1
crw-rw---- 1 root i2c 89, 2 Jun  9 19:25 i2c-2
```

Table 8-1: I^{2}C Buses on the Debian Linux Image on the BeagleBone and PocketBeagle Boards

H/W BUS	S/W DEVICE	SDA PIN	SCL PIN	DESCRIPTION
I2C0	/dev/i2c-0	N/A	N/A	Internal bus for HDMI control
I2C1	/dev/i2c-2	P9_18/P2.11	P9_17/P2.9	General I^{2}C bus
I2C2	/dev/i2c-1	P9_20/P1.26	P9_19/P1.28	General I^{2}C bus

You can see that these devices are owned by the i2c group, and the user debian is a member of that group.

```
debian@ebb:/dev$ whoami
debian
debian@ebb:/dev$ groups
debian ... i2c ... pwm gpio
```

The c file attribute indicates that these are character devices. A character device typically transfers data to and from a user application—they behave like pipes or serial ports, instantly reading or writing the byte data in a character-by-character stream. They provide the framework for many typical drivers, such as those that are required for interfacing to serial communications hardware.

An I²C Test Circuit

Many I²C devices are available that can be connected to the Beagle board, and two different types are described in this section—a real-time clock and an accelerometer. These particular devices have been chosen because they have a low cost, are widely available, are useful, and have high-quality datasheets.

A Real-Time Clock

Unlike a desktop computer, the Beagle boards do not have an onboard battery-backed clock. This means that the clock time is lost on each occasion that the board reboots; however, a network-attached Beagle board can retrieve the current time from the network using the *Network Time Protocol* (NTP). If you are using a board that cannot remain connected to a stable network, then a battery-backed *real-time clock* (RTC) can be a valuable addition.

Devices synchronize time with an RTC only occasionally, so RTCs are typically attached to an I²C bus. If you are purchasing a module, then you should ensure that it is supported by an LKM for your kernel (or by the kernel itself). This allows for full OS integration of the RTC, which is discussed shortly.

```
debian@ebb:~$ uname -a
Linux ebb 4.14.44-ti-rt-r51 #1 SMP PREEMPT ...
debian@ebb:~$ cd /lib/modules/4.14.44-ti-rt-r51/
debian@ebb:/lib/modules/4.14.44-ti-rt-r51$ cd kernel/drivers/rtc/
debian@ebb:/lib/modules/4.14.44-ti-rt-r51/kernel/drivers/rtc$ ls
rtc-bq4802.ko.xz    rtc-ds1742.ko.xz          rtc-msm6242.ko.xz
rtc-cmos.ko.xz      rtc-ds2404.ko.xz          rtc-rp5c01.ko.xz
rtc-ds1286.ko.xz    rtc-hid-sensor-time.ko.xz  ...
```

And there is evidence of additional built-in drivers in:

```
debian@ebb:/sys/bus/i2c/drivers$ ls
...     at24      rtc-ds1307    rtc-max6900    rtc-rx8581    ...
```

The DS3231 has been chosen for this chapter, as it is a high-accuracy RTC that keeps time to ±63 seconds per year (i.e., ±2ppm[2] at 0°C–50°C), and it is widely available in module form at very low cost (even less than $1). The DS3231 is compatible with the DS1307 LKM (`rtc-ds1307.ko`) or built-in kernel code.

The ADXL345 Accelerometer

The Analog Devices ADXL345 is a small, low-cost *accelerometer* that can measure angular position with respect to the direction of the earth's gravitational force. For example, a single-axis accelerometer at rest on the surface of the earth, with the sensitive axis parallel to the earth's gravity, will measure an acceleration of $1g$ (9.81m/s^2) straight upward. While accelerometers provide absolute orientation measurement, they suffer from high-frequency noise, so they are often paired with gyroscopes for accurate measurement of change in orientation (e.g., in game controllers)—a process known as *sensor fusion*. However, accelerometers have excellent characteristics for applications in which low-frequency absolute rotation is to be measured. For simplicity, an accelerometer is used on its own in the following discussions because the main aim is to impart an understanding of the I²C bus.

The ADXL345 can be set to measure values with a fixed 10-bit resolution or using a 13-bit resolution at up to ±16g. The ADXL335 analog accelerometer is utilized in Chapter 9—it provides voltages on its outputs that are proportional to its orientation. Digital accelerometers such as the ADXL345 include analog-to-digital conversion circuitry along with real-time filtering capabilities—they are more complex devices with many configurable options, but it is actually easier to attach them to the board than their analog equivalents. The ADXL345 can be interfaced to the board using an I²C or SPI bus, which makes it an ideal sensor to use in this chapter as an example for both bus types. The chapter web page identifies suppliers from whom you can purchase this particular sensor.

The I²C slave address is determined by the slave device itself. For example, the ADXL345 breakout board has the address 0x53, which is determined at manufacture. Many devices, including the ADXL345, have selection inputs that allow you to alter this value within a defined range.[3] If the device does not have address selection inputs, then you cannot connect two of them to the same bus, as their addresses will conflict. However, there are I²C multiplexers available that would enable you to overcome this problem.

---

[2]Two parts per million evaluates to (31,536,000 seconds per year × ±2) / 1,000,000 = ±63.072 seconds.

[3]The ADXL345's alternative address pin ALT is tied to GND on this particular breakout board, fixing the device at I²C address 0x53, despite the capability of the device itself to be configured for an alternative address.

The data sheet for the ADXL345 is an important document that should be read along with this chapter. It is available at www.analog.com/ADXL345.

Wiring the Test Circuit

Figure 8-2 illustrates a test circuit that can be used to evaluate the function of I²C devices that are attached to the PocketBeagle. In this circuit, an ADXL345 and a DS3231 breakout board are connected to the same I2C1 bus. The ADXL345 has the address 0x53, and the DS3231 has the address 0x68, so there will not be a conflict. The CS input of the ADXL345 breakout board is set high to place the module in I²C mode.

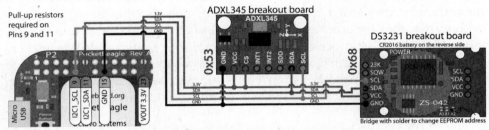

Figure 8-2: Two I²C devices connected to the I2C1 bus on the PocketBeagle board

Even if you do not have these particular sensors, the following discussion is fully representative of the steps required to connect any type of I²C sensor to the Beagle boards. See Table 8-1 for the pins to be used on the BeagleBone boards.

Using Linux I2C-Tools

Linux provides a set of tools, called *i2c-tools*, for interfacing to I²C bus devices; it includes a bus probing tool, a chip dumper, and register-level access helpers. You can install these tools using the following command:

```
debian@ebb:~$ sudo apt install i2c-tools
```

i2cdetect

The first step is to detect that the devices are present on the bus. When the I²C buses are enabled, the i2cdetect command displays this:

```
debian@ebb:~$ i2cdetect -l
i2c-1    i2c              OMAP I2C adapter              I2C adapter
i2c-2    i2c              OMAP I2C adapter              I2C adapter
i2c-0    i2c              OMAP I2C adapter              I2C adapter
```

If the circuit is wired as in Figure 8-2 with an ADXL345 and a DS3231 breakout board attached to the /dev/i2c-1 bus, then it can be probed for connected devices, which will result in the following output:

```
debian@ebb:~$ i2cdetect -y -r 1
     0  1  2  3  4  5  6  7  8  9  a  b  c  d  e  f
00:          -- -- -- -- -- -- -- -- -- -- -- -- --
10: -- -- -- -- -- -- -- -- -- -- -- -- -- -- -- --
20: -- -- -- -- -- -- -- -- -- -- -- -- -- -- -- --
30: -- -- -- -- -- -- -- -- -- -- -- -- -- -- -- --
40: -- -- -- -- -- -- -- -- -- -- -- -- -- -- -- --
50: -- -- -- 53 -- -- 56 -- -- -- -- -- -- -- -- --
60: -- -- -- -- -- -- -- -- 68 -- -- -- -- -- -- --
70: -- -- -- -- -- -- -- --
```

Hexadecimal addresses in the range 0x03 to 0x77 are displayed by default. Using -a will display the full range 0x00 to 0x7F. When -- is displayed, the address was probed, but no device responded. If UU is displayed, then probing was skipped, as the address is already in use by a driver.

The ADXL345 breakout board occupies address 0x53, and the DS3231 ZS-042 breakout board occupies addresses 0x68 and 0x56.[4] Each of the attached breakout boards defines its own addresses, which means that problems will arise if two slave devices with the same address are connected to a single bus. Many I²C devices provide an address selection option that often involves setting an additional input high/low, which is typically implemented on breakout boards by jumper connections or contact points that can be bridged with solder.

i2cdump

The i2cdump command can be used to read in the values of the registers of the device attached to an I²C bus and display them in a hexadecimal block form. You should not use this command without consulting the datasheet for the slave device, as in certain modes the i2cdump command will write to the device. The argument -y ignores a related warning. The devices in Figure 8-2 can be safely used, and when the address 0x68 is probed on the i2c-1 bus in byte mode (b), it results in the following output:

```
debian@ebb:~$ i2cdump -y 1 0x68 b
     0  1  2  3  4  5  6  7  8  9  a  b  c  d  e  f    0123456789abcdef
00: 19 02 03 06 25 10 02 00 00 00 00 00 00 00 1c 88    ????%??.......??
10: 00 17 00 XX XX XX XX XX XX XX XX XX XX XX XX XX    .?.XXXXXXXXXXXXX
```

---

[4]There is a 32Kb AT24C32 Serial EEPROM on the DS3231 ZS-042 breakout board. The A0, A1, and A2 pins on the breakout board can be used to adjust its address. Also, the SQW pin on the board can be used for an interrupt alarm signal or a square-wave output (1Hz, 1KHz, 4KHz, or 8KHz). The 32K pin provides a 32KHz clock signal.

If the device is probed again in quick succession, then a similar output results, but in this example the register value for address 0x00 changes from 19 to 41. This value actually represents the number of clock seconds (in decimal form) on the RTC module. Therefore, 22 seconds had elapsed between these two calls to the i2cdump command.

```
debian@ebb:~$ i2cdump -y 1 0x68 b
     0  1  2  3  4  5  6  7  8  9  a  b  c  d  e  f    0123456789abcdef
00: 41 02 03 06 25 10 02 00 00 00 00 00 00 00 1c 88    A???%??.......??
10: 00 17 00 XX XX XX XX XX XX XX XX XX XX XX XX XX    .?.XXXXXXXXXXXXX
```

To understand the meaning of such registers, you need to read the datasheet for the device. The datasheet for the DS3231 is available at `tiny.cc/beagle802`, and the most important registers are illustrated in Figure 8-3. In this figure, the hwclock function (see the feature on Utilizing Linux Hardware RTC Devices that follows) is used to display the time value from the RTC module. The i2cdump command is called (a few seconds later) to display the registers, allowing their meaning to be verified. Note that the Irish standard time (IST) time zone results in a shift of plus one hour from UTC/GMT.

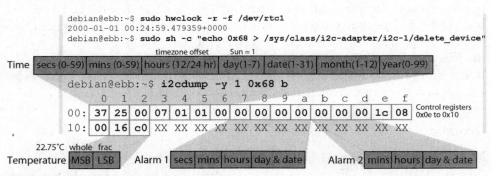

Figure 8-3: The DS3231 registers summary

UTILIZING LINUX HARDWARE RTC DEVICES

Linux supports the use of RTCs directly within the OS using LKMs. If a compatible LKM is available for your chosen RTC, then the RTC can be used to maintain the current time on the Beagle board without requiring you to write software. The first step is to associate the I²C device with a compatible LKM. The DS3231 is compatible with the `rtc-ds1307.ko` **LKM (see** `tiny.cc/beagle803`**) or built-in kernel code and can be associated with the bus device at address 0x68 using the following:**

```
debian@ebb:~$ sudo modprobe rtc-ds1307
debian@ebb:/sys/class/i2c-adapter/i2c-1$ sudo sh -c "echo →
ds1307 0x68 > new_device"
debian@ebb:/sys/class/i2c-adapter/i2c-1$ ls
1-0068        device    name        of_node   subsystem
```

```
delete_device  i2c-dev  new_device  power    uevent
debian@ebb:/sys/class/i2c-adapter/i2c-1$ dmesg|grep ds13
[  298.289697] rtc-ds1307 1-0068: registered as rtc1
[  298.294544] i2c i2c-1: Instantiated device ds1307 at 0x68
debian@ebb:/sys/class/i2c-adapter/i2c-1$ ls -l /dev/rtc
lrwxrwxrwx 1 root root 4 Jun 14 05:11 /dev/rtc -> rtc0
```

The RTC appears as device /dev/rtc1.

```
debian@ebb:/dev$ ls -l rtc*
lrwxrwxrwx 1 root root      4 Jun 14 05:11 rtc -> rtc0
crw------- 1 root root 251, 0 Jun 14 05:11 rtc0
crw------- 1 root root 251, 1 Jun 14 05:16 rtc1
debian@ebb:~$ sudo hwclock -r -f /dev/rtc1
2002-10-26 03:50:58.623563+0100
debian@ebb:~$ date
Fri Jun 15 04:31:10 IST 2018
debian@ebb:~$ sudo hwclock -r -f /dev/rtc1
2002-10-26 03:51:07.356274+0100
```

A new RTC device is now present in /dev. Note that a call to i2cdetect now displays UU instead of 68 for the RTC device, which indicates that probing is skipped for the address as it is in use by a driver.

```
debian@ebb:~$ i2cdetect -y -r 1
     0  1  2  3  4  5  6  7  8  9  a  b  c  d  e  f  ...
60: -- -- -- -- -- -- -- -- UU -- -- -- -- -- -- --   ...
```

The RTC device also contains a sysfs entry that you can use to display the time, as follows:

```
debian@ebb:~$ cd /sys/class/rtc/rtc1/
debian@ebb:/sys/class/rtc/rtc1$ ls
date  device         hctosys       name     since_epoch  time
dev   ds1307_nvram0  max_user_freq power    subsystem    uevent
debian@ebb:/sys/class/rtc/rtc1$ cat time
02:52:03
```

If necessary, you can delete the device using sysfs.

```
debian@ebb:~$ cd /sys/class/i2c-adapter/i2c-1
.../i2c-adapter/i2c-1$ sudo sh -c "echo 0x68 > delete_device"
.../i2c-adapter/i2c-1$ ls
delete_device  i2c-dev  new_device  power    uevent
device         name     of_node     subsystem
.../i2c-adapter/i2c-1$ ls /dev/rtc1
ls: cannot access '/dev/rtc1': No such file or directory
```

The hwclock utility can be used to read (-r) time from or write (-w) time to the RTC device. It can also use the RTC to set (-s) the system clock. Here's an example:

```
debian@ebb:~$ date
Fri Jun 15 04:33:32 IST 2018
```

```
debian@ebb:~$ sudo hwclock -r -f /dev/rtc1
2002-10-26 03:53:51.011882+0100
debian@ebb:~$ sudo hwclock -w -f /dev/rtc1
debian@ebb:~$ sudo hwclock -r -f /dev/rtc1
2018-06-15 04:34:18.153275+0100
debian@ebb:~$ sudo hwclock --set --date="2000-01-01
 00:00:00"  -f /dev/rtc1
debian@ebb:~$ sudo hwclock -r -f /dev/rtc1
2000-01-01 00:00:05.393018+0000
debian@ebb:~$ sudo hwclock -s -f /dev/rtc1
debian@ebb:~$ date
Sat Jan  1 00:00:17 GMT 2000
```

You can automate the process of using the RTC to set the system time on boot, by writing a systemd service and adding the LKM to the /etc/modules file. An example systemd service file is listed in the following code and in the directory chp08/i2c/systemd/:

```
debian@ebb:~$ tail -1 /etc/modules
rtc-ds1307
debian@ebb:/lib/systemd/system$ more ebb_hwclock.service
[Unit]
Description=EBB RTC Service
Before=getty.target
[Service]
Type=oneshot
ExecStartPre=/bin/sh -c "/bin/echo ds1307 0x68 > →
/sys/class/i2c-adapter/i2c-1/new_device"
ExecStart=/sbin/hwclock -s -f /dev/rtc1
RemainAfterExit=yes
[Install]
WantedBy=multi-user.target
```

Next, this custom service must be enabled and the current network time protocol (NTP) service disabled from starting on boot.

```
debian@ebb:/lib/systemd/system$ sudo systemctl enable ebb_hwclock
debian@ebb:/lib/systemd/system$ sudo reboot
```

On reboot you can check the service status, and you should see that the date and time are set according to the RTC module.

```
debian@ebb:~$ sudo systemctl status ebb_hwclock.service
• ebb_hwclock.service - EBB RTC Service
  Loaded: loaded (/lib/systemd/system/ebb_hwclock.service; enabled;
...
  Active: active (exited) since Sat 2000-01-01 00:09:17 GMT; 1min 56s
ago
  ...
```

```
debian@ebb:~$ date
Sat Jan  1 00:11:24 GMT 2000
```

To return the system to the way it was before this feature discussion, simply disable the custom RTC service and reboot.

```
debian@ebb:~$ sudo systemctl disable erpi_hwclock
debian@ebb:~$ sudo reboot
```

i2cget

The `i2cget` command can be used to read the value of a register to test the device or as an input for Linux shell scripts. For example, to read the number of seconds on the clock, you can use the following:

```
debian@ebb:~$ i2cget -y 1 0x68 0x00
0x30
```

The Analog Discovery digital logic analyzer functionality can be used to analyze the physical I²C bus to view the interaction of the SDA and SCL signals as data is written to and read from the I²C bus. The logic analyzer functionality has interpreters for I²C buses, SPI buses, CAN buses, and UART communication, which can display the numerical equivalent values of the serial data carried on the bus. Figure 8-4 captures the signal transitions of the `i2cget` command used in the preceding example. Here, you can see that the clock is running at *I²C standard data transfer mode* (i.e., 100kHz).

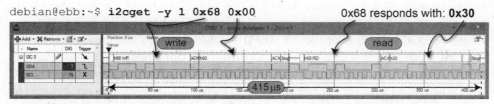

Figure 8-4: Using `i2cget` to read the number of seconds on the RTC from register 0x00

WARNING   A logic analyzer is used throughout this chapter to gain a deeper understanding of communication over I²C, SPI, CAN bus, and serial connections. Remember that you **should use a common ground connection** for the logic analyzer and the Beagle board in all cases. It is easy to forget to do this, but it can result in inconsistent readings, which may cause hours of frustration and confusion!

The ADXL345 accelerometer can be accessed in the same way as the RTC module. Figure 8-5 illustrates the important registers that are utilized in this chapter. To test that the ADXL345 is correctly connected to the bus, read the DEVID of the attached device, which should be returned as 0xE5.

```
debian@ebb:~$ i2cget -y 1 0x53 0x00
0xe5
```

You can see that the first value at address 0x00 is 0xE5, and this value corresponds to the DEVID entry in Figure 8-5—successful communication has been verified.

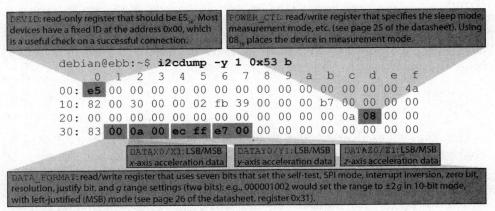

Figure 8-5: Important ADXL345 registers

i2cset

As previously stated, the datasheet for the ADXL345 from Analog Devices is available at www.analog.com/ADXL345. It is a comprehensive and well-written datasheet that details every feature of the device. In fact, the real challenge in working with new bus devices is in decoding the datasheet and the intricacies of the device's behavior. The ADXL345 has 30 public registers, and Figure 8-5 illustrates those that are accessed in this chapter. Other registers enable you to set power save inactivity periods, orientation offsets, and interrupt settings for free-fall, tap, and double-tap detection.

The x-, y-, and z-axis acceleration values are stored using a 10-bit or 13-bit resolution; therefore, two bytes are required for each reading. Also, the data is in 16-bit two's complement form (see Chapter 4). To sample at 13 bits, the ADXL345 must be set to the ±16 g range. Figure 8-6 (based on the ADXL345 datasheet) describes the signal sequences required to read and write to the device. For example, to write a single byte to a device register, the master/slave access pattern in the first row is used as follows:

1. The master sends a *start bit* (i.e., it pulls SDA low, while SCL is high).

2. While the clock toggles, the 7-bit slave address is transmitted one bit at a time.

3. A read bit (1) or write bit (0) is sent, depending on whether the master wants to read or write to/from a slave register.

4. The slave responds with an *acknowledge bit* (ACK = 0).

5. In write mode, the master sends a byte of data one bit at a time, after which the slave sends back an ACK bit. To write to a register, the register address is sent, followed by the data value to be written.

6. Finally, to conclude communication, the master sends a *stop bit* (i.e., it allows SDA to float high, while SCL is high).

The i2cset command can be used to set a register. This is required, for example, to take the ADXL345 out of power-saving mode, by writing 0x08 to the POWER_CTL register, which is at 0x2D. The value is written and then confirmed as follows:

```
debian@ebb:~$ i2cset -y 1 0x53 0x2D 0x08
debian@ebb:~$ i2cget -y 1 0x53 0x2D
0x08
```

The call to i2cset and i2cget invokes the handshaking sequences that are described in the ADXL345 datasheet and illustrated in Figure 8-6, which also identifies these numbered steps.

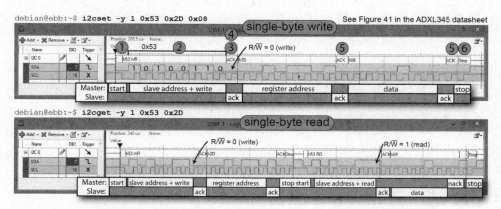

Figure 8-6: Capture and timings required for communication with the ADXL345 device

When the i2cdump command is subsequently used, the registers 0x32 through 0x37 (as identified in Figure 8-5) display the acceleration values, which change as the sensor is physically rotated and the i2cdump command is repeatedly called. The next step is to write program code that can interpret the values contained in the DS3231 and the ADXL345 registers.

I²C Communication in C

The first C program example, in Listing 8-1, reads in all of the DS3231 RTC registers and displays the current time and temperature. The time is contained in binary coded decimal (BCD) form in registers 0x00 (seconds), 0x01 (minutes), and 0x02 (hours). The temperature is in hexadecimal form in registers 0x11 (whole number temperature) and in the two most-significant bits of 0x12 (the fractional part—i.e., $00_2=0$, $01_2=¼$, $10_2=½$, and $11_2=¾$).

This is a useful first example because it is self-contained, will work on all generic embedded Linux platforms, and can be adapted for other I²C devices.

Listing 8-1: exploringbb/chp08/i2c/test/testDS3231.c

```c
#include<stdio.h>
#include<fcntl.h>
#include<sys/ioctl.h>
#include<linux/i2c.h>
#include<linux/i2c-dev.h>
#include<unistd.h>
#define BUFFER_SIZE 19      //0x00 to 0x13

// the time is in the registers in encoded decimal form
int bcdToDec(char b) { return (b/16)*10 + (b%16); }

int main(){
   int file;
   printf("Starting the DS3231 test application\n");
   if((file=open("/dev/i2c-1", O_RDWR)) < 0){
      perror("failed to open the bus\n");
      return 1;
   }
   if(ioctl(file, I2C_SLAVE, 0x68) < 0){
      perror("Failed to connect to the sensor\n");
      return 1;
   }
   char writeBuffer[1] = {0x00};
   if(write(file, writeBuffer, 1)!=1){
      perror("Failed to reset the read address\n");
      return 1;
   }
   char buf[BUFFER_SIZE];
   if(read(file, buf, BUFFER_SIZE)!=BUFFER_SIZE){
      perror("Failed to read in the buffer\n");
      return 1;
   }
   printf("The RTC time is %02d:%02d:%02d\n", bcdToDec(buf[2]),
          bcdToDec(buf[1]), bcdToDec(buf[0]));
```

```
        // note that 0x11 = 17 decimal and 0x12 = 18 decimal
        float temperature = buf[0x11] + ((buf[0x12]>>6)*0.25);
        printf("The temperature is %f°C\n", temperature);
        close(file);
        return 0;
    }
```

The code can be built and executed as follows:

```
debian@ebb:~/exploringbb/chp08/i2c/test$ gcc testDS3231.c -o testDS3231
debian@ebb:~/exploringbb/chp08/i2c/test$ ./testDS3231
Starting the DS3231 test application
The RTC time is 00:53:46
The temperature is 22.50°C
```

The temperature functionality is used to improve this RTC's accuracy by modeling the impact of environmental temperature on time keeping—it is updated every 64 seconds, and it is accurate only to ±3°C.

The ADXL345 digital accelerometer measures acceleration in three axes using analog sensors, which are internally sampled and filtered according to the settings that are placed in its registers. The acceleration values are then available for you to read from these registers. Therefore, the sensor performs timing-critical signal processing that would otherwise need to be performed by the Beagle board. However, further numerical processing is still required in converting the 16-bit two's complement values stored in its registers into values that describe angular pitch and roll. As such, C/C++ is a good choice for this type of numerical processing if real-time performance is required.

To display all the registers and to process the accelerometer values, a new program (chp08/i2c/test/ADXL345.cpp) is written that breaks the calls into functions, such as the readRegisters() function.

```
int readRegisters(int file){    // read all 64(0x40) registers to a buffer
    writeRegister(file, 0x00, 0x00);  // set address to 0x00 for block read
    if(read(file, dataBuffer, BUFFER_SIZE)!=BUFFER_SIZE){
        cout << "Failed to read in the full buffer." << endl;
        return 1;
    }
    if(dataBuffer[DEVID]!=0xE5){
        cout << "Problem detected! Device ID is wrong" << endl;
        return 1;
    }
    return 0;
}
```

This code writes the address 0x00 to the device, causing it to send back the full 64 (0x40) registers (BUFFER_SIZE). To process the two raw 8-bit acceleration registers, code to combine two bytes into a single 16-bit value is written as follows:

```
short combineValues(unsigned char upper, unsigned char lower){
    //shift the MSB left by 8 bits and OR with the LSB
    return ((short)upper<<8)|(short)lower;
}
```

The types of the data are vital in this function, as the register data is returned in two's complement form. If an int type (of size 32 bits, int32_t) were used instead of short 16-bit integral data (int16_t), then the sign bit would be located in the incorrect bit position (i.e., not at the MSB, bit 31). This function shifts the upper byte left (multiply) by eight places (equivalent to a multiplication by $2^8 = 256$) and ORs the result with the lower byte, which replaces the lower byte with eight zeros that are introduced by the shift. This results in a 16-bit signed value (int16_t) that has been created from two separate 8-bit values (uint8_t). When executed, the ADXL345.cpp application will give the following output, with the program updating the acceleration data on the same terminal shell line:

```
debian@ebb:~/exploringbb/chp08/i2c/test$ g++ ADXL345.cpp -o ADXL345
debian@ebb:~/exploringbb/chp08/i2c/test$ ./ADXL345
Starting the ADXL345 sensor application
The Device ID is: e5
The POWER_CTL mode is: 08
The DATA_FORMAT is: 00
X=40 Y=1 Z=276 sample=12
```

Additional code is required to convert these values into pitch and roll form. This is added to the C++ class in the next section. For your information, the logic analyzer indicates that it takes 4.19ms to read in the full set of 64 registers at a bus speed of 100kHz.

Wrapping I²C Devices with C++ Classes

Object-oriented programming is described in Chapter 5 as a suitable framework for developing code for embedded systems. A specific C++ class can be written to wrap the functionality of the ADXL345 accelerometer; because it is likely that you will need to write code to control several different types of I²C devices, it would be useful if the general I²C code could be extracted and placed in a parent class. To this end, a class has been written for this chapter called I2CDevice that captures the general functionality you would associate with an I²C bus device. You can extend this code to control any type of I²C device. It can be found in the I2CDevice.cpp and I2CDevice.h files in the chp08/i2c/cpp/ directory. The class has the structure described in Listing 8-2.

Listing 8-2: /exploringbb/chp08/i2c/cpp/I2CDevice.h

```cpp
class I2CDevice {
private:
  unsigned int bus, device;
  int file;
public:
  I2CDevice(unsigned int bus, unsigned int device);
  virtual int open();
  virtual int write(unsigned char value);
  virtual unsigned char readRegister(unsigned int registerAddress);
  virtual unsigned char* readRegisters(unsigned int number,
                                       unsigned int fromAddress=0);
  virtual int writeRegister(unsigned int registerAddress, unsigned
                            char value);
  virtual void debugDumpRegisters(unsigned int number);
  virtual void close();
  virtual ~I2CDevice();
};
```

The implementation code is available in the chp08/i2c/cpp/ directory. This class can be extended to control any type of I²C device, and in this case it is used as the parent of a specific device implementation class called ADXL345. Therefore, you can say that ADXL345 *is an* I2CDevice. This inheritance relationship means that any methods available in the I2CDevice class are now available in the ADXL345 class in Listing 8-3 (e.g., readRegister()).

Listing 8-3: /exploringbb/chp08/i2c/cpp/ADXL345.h

```cpp
class ADXL345:protected I2CDevice{
    // protected inheritance means that the public I2C methods are no
    //  longer publicly accessible by an object of the ADXL345 class
public:
    enum RANGE {          // enumerations are used to limit the options
       PLUSMINUS_2_G = 0,
       PLUSMINUS_4_G = 1,
       PLUSMINUS_8_G = 2,
       PLUSMINUS_16_G = 3
    };
    enum RESOLUTION { NORMAL = 0, HIGH = 1 };

private:
    unsigned int I2CBus, I2CAddress;
    unsigned char *registers;
    ADXL345::RANGE range;
    ADXL345::RESOLUTION resolution;
    short accelerationX, accelerationY, accelerationZ;
    float pitch, roll;  // in degrees
```

```
    short combineRegisters(unsigned char msb, unsigned char lsb);
    void calculatePitchAndRoll();
    virtual int updateRegisters();

public:
    ADXL345(unsigned int I2CBus, unsigned int I2CAddress=0x53);
    virtual int readSensorState();
    virtual void setRange(ADXL345::RANGE range);
    virtual ADXL345::RANGE getRange() { return this->range; }
    virtual void setResolution(ADXL345::RESOLUTION resolution);
    virtual ADXL345::RESOLUTION getResolution() {return this->resolution;}
    virtual short getAccelerationX() { return accelerationX; }
    virtual short getAccelerationY() { return accelerationY; }
    virtual short getAccelerationZ() { return accelerationZ; }
    virtual float getPitch() { return pitch; }
    virtual float getRoll() { return roll; }
    virtual void displayPitchAndRoll(int iterations = 600);
    virtual ~ADXL345();
};
```

The enumerations are used to constrain the range and resolution selections
to contain only valid options. A short example (application.cpp) can be used
to test this structure, as follows:

```
int main(){
    ADXL345 sensor(1,0x53);        // sensor is on bus 1 at the address 0x53
    sensor.setResolution(ADXL345::NORMAL);       //using 10-bit resolution
    sensor.setRange(ADXL345::PLUSMINUS_4_G);     //range is +/-4g
    sensor.displayPitchAndRoll();       // put the sensor in display mode
    return 0;
}
```

This code can be built and executed as follows, where the pitch and roll are
angular values that each vary between ±90°:

```
/chp08/i2c/cpp $ g++ application.cpp I2CDevice.cpp ADXL345.cpp -o ADXL345
debian@ebb:~/exploringbb/chp08/i2c/cpp$ ./ADXL345
Pitch:42.0089 Roll:-4.03966
```

You can use this approach to build wrapper classes for any type of I²C sensor
on any type of embedded Linux device.

SPI

The *Serial Peripheral Interface* (SPI) bus is a fast, full-duplex synchronous serial
data link that enables devices such as the Beagle board to communicate with
other devices over short distances. Therefore, like I²C, the SPI bus is synchronous,

but unlike the I²C bus, the SPI bus is *full duplex*. This means that it can transmit and receive data at the same time, by using separate lines for both sending data and receiving data.

In this section, the SPI bus is introduced, and two separate applications are developed. The first uses the SPI bus to drive a seven-segment LED display using the ubiquitous 74HC595 8-bit shift register. The second application interfaces to the ADXL345 accelerometer again, this time using its SPI bus instead of the I²C bus used previously.

SPI Hardware

SPI communication takes place between a single master device and one or more slave devices. Figure 8-7(a) illustrates a single slave example, where four signal lines are connected between the PocketBeagle master and slave devices. To communicate with the slave device, the following steps take place:

1. The *SPI master* defines the clock frequency at which to synchronize the data communication channels.

2. The SPI master pulls the *chip select* (CS) line low, which activates the client device—it is therefore said to be active low. This line is also known as *slave select* (SS).

3. After a short delay, the SPI master issues clock cycles, sending data out on the *master out - slave in* (MOSI) line and receiving data on the *master in - slave out* (MISO) line. The *SPI slave* device reads data from the MOSI line and transmits data on the MISO line. One bit is sent and one bit is received on each clock cycle. The data is usually sent in 1-byte (8-bit) chunks.

4. When complete, the SPI master stops sending a clock signal and then pulls the CS line high, deactivating the SPI slave device.

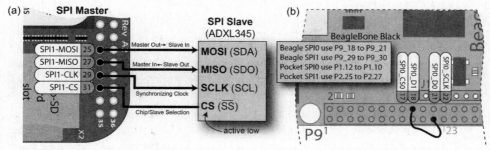

Figure 8-7: (a) Using SPI to connect to one slave device from the PocketBeagle, and (b) testing SPI using a loopback configuration on the BeagleBone

Unlike I²C, the SPI bus does not require pull-up resistors on the communication lines, so connections are straightforward. A summary comparison of I²C versus SPI is provided in Table 8-2.

Table 8-2: Comparison of I²C vs. SPI on the Beagle Board

	I²C	SPI
Connectivity	Two wires, to which up to 128 addressable devices can be attached.	Typically four wires and requires additional logic for more than one slave device.
Data rate	I²C fast mode is 400 kHz. It uses half-duplex communication.	Faster performance (~10MHz) on the Beagle boards. It uses full duplex (except the three-wire variant).
Hardware	Pull-up resistors required.	No pull-up resistors required.
Support	Fully supported with two external buses (plus one HDMI).	Fully supported with one bus. There are two slave selection pins on all boards.
Features	Can have multiple masters. Slaves have addresses, acknowledge transfer, and can control the flow of data.	Simple and fast, but only one master device, no addressing, and no slave control of data flow.
Application	Intermittently accessed devices, e.g., RTCs, EEPROMs.	For devices that provide data streams, e.g., ADCs.

The SPI bus operates using one of four different modes, which are chosen according to the specification defined in the SPI device's datasheet. Data is synchronized using the clock signal, and one of the *SPI communication modes* listed in Table 8-3 is set to describe how the synchronization is performed. The *clock polarity* defines whether the clock is low or high when it is idle (i.e., when CS is high). The *clock phase* defines whether the data on the MOSI and MISO lines is captured on the rising edge or falling edge of the clock signal. When a clock's polarity is 1, the clock signal is equivalent to an inverted version of the same signal with a polarity of 0. Therefore, a rising edge on one form of clock signal polarity is the equivalent of a falling edge on the other. You need to examine the datasheet for the slave device to determine the correct SPI mode to use.

Table 8-3: SPI Communication Modes

MODE	CLOCK POLARITY (CPOL)	CLOCK PHASE (CPHA)
0	0 (low at idle)	0 (data captured on the rising edge of the clock signal)
1	0 (low at idle)	1 (data captured on the falling edge of the clock signal)
2	1 (high at idle)	0 (data captured on the falling edge of the clock signal)
3	1 (high at idle)	1 (data captured on the rising edge of the clock signal)

The SPI protocol itself does not define a maximum data rate, flow control, or communication acknowledgment. Therefore, implementations vary from device to device, so it is important to study the datasheet of each type of SPI slave device. There are some three-wire SPI variants that use a single bidirectional MISO/MOSI line instead of two individual lines. For example, the ADXL345 sensor supports I²C, and both *four-wire* and *three-wire SPI* communication.

WARNING   Do not connect a 5V-powered SPI slave device to the MISO input on a Beagle board. Logic-level translation is discussed at the end of this chapter.

SPI on the Beagle Boards

The tables illustrated in Figure 6-6 and Figure 6-7 of Chapter 6 identify that the SPI buses are accessible from the GPIO headers as summarized in Table 8-4. Please note that SPI0 is not available by default on the BeagleBone and therefore must be enabled.

Table 8-4: Example SPI Pins on the Beagle Boards

	BBB SPI0	BBB SPI1	POCKET SPI0	POCKET SPI1
Chip Select	P9_17	P9_28	P1.06	P2.31
MOSI	P9_18	P9_29	P1.12	P2.25
MISO	P9_21	P9_30	P1.10	P2.27
Clock	P9_22	P9_31	P1.08	P2.29

The Linux devices are available in the /dev/ directory.

```
debian@ebb:/dev$ ls -l spi*
crw-rw---- 1 root spi 153, 0 Jan  1  2000 spidev0.0
crw-rw---- 1 root spi 153, 1 Jan  1  2000 spidev1.0
crw-rw---- 1 root spi 153, 2 Jan  1  2000 spidev1.1
```

Despite that there are two entries in /dev/ for spidev1, there exists only one SPI device for spidev1, which has two different enable modes (0 and 1).

Testing an SPI Bus

To test the SPI bus, you can use a program called spidev_test.c that is available from www.kernel.org. However, the latest version at the time of writing has added support for dual and quad data-wire SPI transfers, which are not supported on the Beagle boards. An older version of this code has been placed in /chp08/spi/spidev_test/ and can be built using the following:

```
.../chp08/spi/spidev_test$ gcc spidev_test.c -o spidev_test
```

If this code is executed without connecting to the SPI1 pins, then the output displayed by the spidev_test program will consist of a block of 0x00 or 0xFF values, depending on whether the MISO pin is configured in pull-down or pull-up configuration, respectively.

```
.../chp08/spi/spidev_test$ ./spidev_test -D /dev/spidev1.0
spi mode: 0
bits per word: 8
max speed: 500000 Hz (500 KHz)
FF FF FF FF FF FF
FF FF FF FF FF FF
FF FF FF FF FF FF
FF FF FF FF FF FF
FF FF FF FF FF FF
FF FF FF FF FF FF
FF FF
```

The source code for the spidev_test.c program includes a hard-coded array of values to test that the SPI communications line is working correctly. These values are as follows:

```
uint8_t tx[] = {
        0xFF, 0xFF, 0xFF, 0xFF, 0xFF, 0xFF,
        0x40, 0x00, 0x00, 0x00, 0x00, 0x95,
        0xFF, 0xFF, 0xFF, 0xFF, 0xFF, 0xFF,
        0xFF, 0xFF, 0xFF, 0xFF, 0xFF, 0xFF,
        0xFF, 0xFF, 0xFF, 0xFF, 0xFF, 0xFF,
        0xDE, 0xAD, 0xBE, 0xEF, 0xBA, 0xAD,
        0xF0, 0x0D,
};
```

if the SPI MOSI and SPI MISO pins are connected together, as illustrated in Figure 8-7(b) for SPI0. To test SPI0 on the BeagleBone, use P9_29 and P9_30, and on the PocketBeagle, use P2.25 and P2.27. When the test program is executed again, the output should be as follows:

```
.../chp08/spi/spidev_test$ ./spidev_test -D /dev/spidev1.0
spi mode: 0
bits per word: 8
max speed: 500000 Hz (500 KHz)
FF FF FF FF FF FF
40 00 00 00 00 95
FF FF FF FF FF FF
FF FF FF FF FF FF
FF FF FF FF FF FF
DE AD BE EF BA AD
F0 0D
```

This is the exact block of data that is defined in the `tx[]` array inside the `spidev_test.c` code. Therefore, in this case, the block of data has been successfully transmitted from SPI1 MOSI and received by SPI1 MISO. You can see the same stream of data captured using the logic analyzer in Figure 8-8. The clock frequency of SCLK is 500kHz.

This program can be executed on the SPI0 bus as follows:

```
.../chp08/spi/spidev_test$ ./spidev_test -D /dev/spidev0.0
```

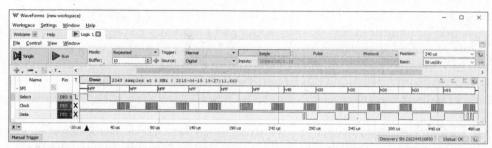

Figure 8-8: The SPI hardware loopback test on the PocketBeagle at 500kHz

A First SPI Application (74HC595)

The first circuit application to test the SPI bus is illustrated in Figure 8-9. It uses a 74HC595, which is an 8-bit shift register with latched outputs that can be supplied at 3.3V logic levels. The 74HC595 can typically be used at frequencies of 20MHz or greater, depending on the supply voltage V_{CC}. The circuit in Figure 8-9 uses a seven-segment display and resistors to create a circuit that can display seven-segment symbols.

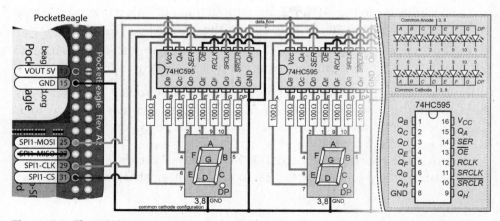

Figure 8-9: The 74HC595 seven-segment display SPI example (supports multiple display modules)

Seven-segment displays typically consist of eight LEDs that can be used to display decimal or hexadecimal numerals with a "decimal" point. They are available in a range of sizes and colors and are described as being either *common cathode* or *common anode* displays. This means the cathodes or anodes of the array of LEDs that make up the display are connected together as on the top right of Figure 8-9. You should not limit the current passing through the display by placing a single resistor on the common anode or the common cathode connection, as the limited current will be shared among the segments that are lighting. This results in an uneven light level, the intensity of which depends on the number of segments that are lit. Therefore, eight current-limiting resistors (or a resistor network) are required for each seven-segment display.

It is possible to drive these displays using eight GPIO pins per seven-segment module, but using serial shift registers and the SPI interface has the advantage of requiring only three SPI pins, regardless of the number of segments that are daisy chained together.

> **NOTE** For a video on serial-to-parallel conversion that explains the concept of output latching by comparing the 74HC164 to the 74HC595, see the chapter web page www.exploringbeaglebone.com/chapter8.

Wiring the 74HC595 Circuit

The 74HC595 is connected to the PocketBeagle using three of the four SPI lines, as a MISO response from the 74HC595 is not required. In addition to the 5V and GND inputs, the SPI connections are as follows:

- SPI1-CLK is connected to the Serial Clock input (pin 11) of the 74HC595. This line is used to synchronize the transfer of SPI data on the MOSI line.

- SPI1-MOSI is the MOSI line and is used to transfer the data from the PocketBeagle to the 74HC595 Serial Input (pin 14). This will send one byte at a time, which is the full capacity of the 74HC595.

- SPI-CS is connected to the Serial Register Clock input, which is used to latch the 74HC595 state to the output pins, thus lighting the LEDs.

To avoid the need for an external power supply, this circuit is powered using the board's 5V supply. However, this means that the circuit is now using 5V logic levels, and *it would damage your board if you were to connect any of the 74HC595 outputs (e.g., Q_H) back to the board.*

You can safely connect the board's MOSI line directly to the circuit, as a 3.3V output can be safely connected to a 5V input. However, strictly speaking, 3.3V is slightly below the threshold of 3.5V (i.e., 30 percent below 5V) required for an input to a 5V logic-level CMOS IC (see Figure 4-24 in Chapter 4). In practice, the circuit works fine; however, a 74LS595 (at V_{CC} = 5V) or a 74LVC595 (at V_{CC} = 3.3V) would be more appropriate, despite their high cost and lack of availability.

The LEDs on the seven-segment display will light according to the byte that is transferred. For example, sending 0xAA should light every second LED segment (including the dot) if the setup is working correctly, as 0xAA = 10101010_2. This circuit is useful for controlling eight outputs using a single serial data line, and it can be extended to further seven-segment displays by daisy chaining 74HC595 ICs together, as indicated in Figure 8-9.

Once the SPI device is enabled on the Beagle board, you can write directly to the device as follows to light *most* of the LEDs (-n suppresses the newline character, -e enables escape character interpretation, and \x escapes the subsequent value as hexadecimal):

```
debian@ebb:~$ echo -ne "\xFF" > /dev/spidev1.1
```

The following will turn *most* of the LEDs off.

```
debian@ebb:~$ echo -ne "\x00" > /dev/spidev1.1
```

This may not work exactly as expected, as the current SPI communication mode does not align by default with the operation of the 74HC595, as wired in Figure 8-9. However, it is a useful test to confirm that there is some level of response from the circuit. The transfer mode issue is resolved within the code example in the next section.

SPI Communication Using C

A C program can be written to control the seven-segment display. Basic open() and close() operations on the /dev/spidevX.Y devices work, but if you need to alter the low-level SPI transfer parameters, then a more sophisticated interface is required.

The following program uses the Linux user space SPI API, which supports reading and writing to SPI slave devices. It is accessed using Linux ioctl() requests, which support SPI through the sys/ioctl.h and linux/spi/spidev.h header files. A full guide on the use of this API is available at www.kernel.org/doc/Documentation/spi/.

The program in Listing 8-4 counts in hexadecimal (i.e., 0 to F) on a single seven-segment display using the encoded value for each digit. For example, 0 is obtained by lighting only the segments *A, B, C, D, E,* and *F* in Figure 8-10—this value is encoded as 0b00111111 in Listing 8-4, where *A* is the LSB (on the right) and *H* (the dot) is the MSB (on the left) of the encoded value. The transfer() function is the most important part of the code example, as it transfers each encoded value to the 74HC595 IC.

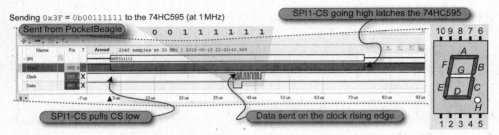

Figure 8-10: The 74HC595 SPI signal and output

Listing 8-4: /exploringbb/chp08/spi/spi595Example/spi595.c

```c
#include<stdio.h>
#include<fcntl.h>
#include<unistd.h>
#include<sys/ioctl.h>
#include<stdint.h>
#include<linux/spi/spidev.h>
#define SPI_PATH "/dev/spidev1.1"

// The binary data that describes the LED state for each symbol
// A(top)          B(top right) C(bottom right)  D(bottom)
// E(bottom left) F(top left)  G(middle)         H(dot)
const unsigned char symbols[16] = {                  //(msb) HGFEDCBA (lsb)
     0b00111111, 0b00000110, 0b01011011, 0b01001111,  // 0123
     0b01100110, 0b01101101, 0b01111101, 0b00000111,  // 4567
     0b01111111, 0b01100111, 0b01110111, 0b01111100,  // 89Ab
     0b00111001, 0b01011110, 0b01111001, 0b01110001   // CdEF
};

int transfer(int fd, unsigned char send[], unsigned char rec[], int len){
    struct spi_ioc_transfer transfer;        //transfer structure
    transfer.tx_buf = (unsigned long) send;  //buffer for sending data
    transfer.rx_buf = (unsigned long) rec;   //buffer for receiving data
    transfer.len = len;                       //length of buffer
    transfer.speed_hz = 1000000;              //speed in Hz
    transfer.bits_per_word = 8;               //bits per word
    transfer.delay_usecs = 0;                 //delay in us
    transfer.cs_change = 0;          // affects chip select after transfer
    transfer.tx_nbits = 0;           // no. bits for writing (default 0)
    transfer.rx_nbits = 0;           // no. bits for reading (default 0)
    transfer.pad = 0;                // interbyte delay - check version
```

```
   // send the SPI message (all of the above fields, inc. buffers)
   int status = ioctl(fd, SPI_IOC_MESSAGE(1), &transfer);
   if (status < 0) {
      perror("SPI: SPI_IOC_MESSAGE Failed");
      return -1;
   }
   return status;
}

int main(){
   int fd, i;                       // file handle and loop counter
   unsigned char null=0x00;         // sending only a single char
   uint8_t mode = 3;                // SPI mode 3

   // The following calls set up the SPI bus properties
   if ((fd = open(SPI_PATH, O_RDWR))<0){
      perror("SPI Error: Can't open device.");
      return -1;
   }
   if (ioctl(fd, SPI_IOC_WR_MODE, &mode)==-1){
      perror("SPI: Can't set SPI mode.");
      return -1;
   }
   if (ioctl(fd, SPI_IOC_RD_MODE, &mode)==-1){
      perror("SPI: Can't get SPI mode.");
      return -1;
   }
   printf("SPI Mode is: %d\n", mode);
   printf("Counting in hexadecimal from 0 to F now:\n");
   for (i=0; i<=15; i++)
   {
      // This function can send and receive data, just sending now
      if (transfer(fd, (unsigned char*) &symbols[i], &null, 1)==-1){
         perror("Failed to update the display");
         return -1;
      }
      printf("%4d\r", i);    // print the number in the terminal window
      fflush(stdout);        // need to flush the output, no \n
      usleep(500000);        // sleep for 500ms each loop
   }
   close(fd);               // close the file
   return 0;
}
```

The main() function sets the SPI control parameters. These are ioctl() requests that allow you to override the device's current settings for parameters such as the following, where xx is both RD (read) and RW (write):

▪ SPI_IOC_xx_MODE: The SPI transfer mode (0–3).

▪ SPI_IOC_xx_BITS_PER_WORD: The number of bits in each word.

- `SPI_IOC_xx_LSB_FIRST`: 0 is MSB first, 1 is LSB first.

- `SPI_IOC_xx_MAX_SPEED_HZ`: The maximum transfer rate in Hz.

The current Linux implementation provides for synchronous transfers only. When executed, this code results in the following output, where the count value continually increases (0 to F) on the one line of the terminal window:

```
debian@ebb:~/exploringbb/chp08/spi/spi595Example$ ./spi595
SPI Mode is: 3
Counting in hexadecimal from 0 to F now:
   5
```

At the same time, this code is sending signals to the 74HC595 as captured using the SPI interpreter of the logic analyzer in Figure 8-10, in which the symbol 0 is being displayed by the seven-segment display (i.e., 0b00111111). During this time period, the CS (SPI1-CS) line is pulled low, while the SCLK clock (SPI1-CLK) that is "high at idle" is toggled by the SPI master after a short delay. The data is then sent on the SDIO (SPI1-MOSI) line, MSB first, to the 74HC595, and it is transferred on the rising edge of the clock signal. This confirms that the SPI transfer is taking place in mode 3, as described in Table 8-3.

The data transfer takes ~9μs. This means that if the channel were held open, it would be capable of transferring a maximum of ~111kB/s (~0.9Mb/s) at a processor clock rate of 1MHz.

Bidirectional SPI Communication in C/C++

The 74HC595 example only sends data from the board to the 74HC595 and as such is a unidirectional communication example. In this section, a bidirectional communication example is developed that involves using the registers on the ADXL345 sensor. As discussed previously, the ADXL345 has both an I²C and an SPI communications interface. This makes it a useful device with which to examine bidirectional SPI communication, as the register structure is already described in detail earlier in this chapter.

NOTE For reference, the main guide for writing user space code for bidirectional SPI communication under Linux is available at `www.kernel.org/doc/Documentation/spi/spidev`.

The ADXL345 SPI Interface

SPI is not a formal standard with a standards body controlling its implementation, and therefore it is vital that you study the datasheet for the device that you want to attach to your Beagle board. In particular, the SPI communication timing diagram should be studied in detail. This is presented for the ADXL345 in Figure 8-11.

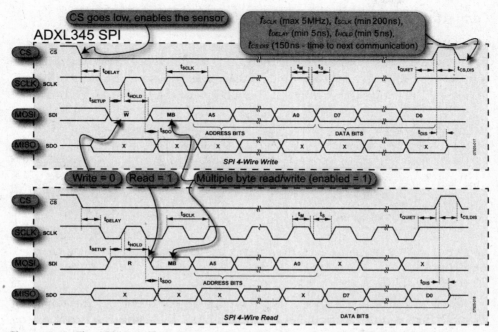

Figure 8-11: The ADXL345 SPI communication timing chart (from the ADXL345 datasheet)
Underlying image is courtesy of Analog Devices, Inc.

Note the following important points, which can be observed directly from the datasheet figure, as summarized in Figure 8-11:

- To write to an address, the first bit on the SDI line must be low. To read from an address, the first bit on the SDI line must be high.

- The second bit is called MB. From further analysis of the datasheet, this bit enables multiple byte reading/writing of the registers (i.e., send the first address and data will be continuously read from that register forward). This leaves six bits in the first byte for the address ($2^6 = 64_{10} = 40_{16}$), which is sufficient to cover the available registers.

- As shown in Figure 8-11, the SCLK line is high at rest, and data is transferred on the rising edge of the clock signal. Therefore, the ADXL345 device must be used in communications mode 3 (refer to Table 8-3).

- When writing (top figure), the address (with a leading 0) is written to SDI, followed by the byte value to be written to the address.

- When reading (bottom figure), the address (with a leading 1) is written to SDI. A second byte is written to SDI and will be ignored. While the second (ignored) byte is being written to SDI, the response will be returned on SDO detailing the value stored at the register address.

Connecting the ADXL345 to the Beagle Boards

The ADXL345 breakout board can be connected to the SPI bus as illustrated in Figure 8-12(a), where MOSI on the BBB is connected to SDA and MISO is connected to SDO. The clock lines and the slave select lines are also interconnected. Figure 8-12(b) shows the equivalent connection for the PocketBeagle board.

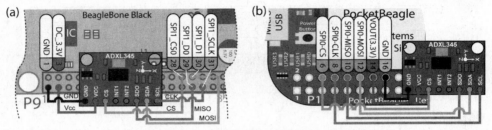

Figure 8-12: (a) BBB SPI connection to the ADXL345, and (b) PocketBeagle SPI connection to the ADXL345

Once again, a logic analyzer is useful for debugging problems that can occur with SPI bus communication. For example, Figure 8-13 captures a read operation at address 0x00. You may notice that the value that was sent was 0x80 and not 0x00. This is because (as detailed in Figure 8-11) the leading bit must be a 1 to read and a 0 to write from/to an address. Sending 0x00 is a write request to address 0x00 (which is not possible), and sending 0x80 (i.e., **1**0000000 + 00**000000**) is a request to read the value at address 0x00. The second bit is 0 in both cases, thus disabling multiple-byte read functionality for this example.

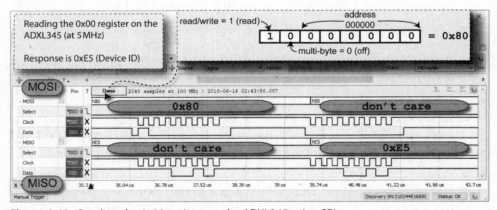

Figure 8-13: Reading the 0x00 register on the ADXL345 using SPI

The code in Listing 8-4 is adapted in /spi/spiADXL345/spiADXL345.c so that it reads the first register (0x00) of the ADXL345, which should return the DEVID, as illustrated in Figure 8-5. This value should be $E5_{16}$, which is 229_{10}. The maximum recommended SPI clock speed for the ADXL345 is 5MHz, so this value is used in the program code.

```
debian@ebb:~/exploringbb/chp08/spi/spiADXL345$ gcc spiADXL345.c -o spiADXL345
debian@ebb:~/exploringbb/chp08/spi/spiADXL345$ ./spiADXL345
spi mode: 0x3
bits per word: 8
max speed: 5000000 Hz (5000 KHz)
Return value: 229
```

Wrapping SPI Devices with C++ Classes

A C++ class is available in Listing 8-5 that wraps the software interface to the SPI bus, using the OOP techniques that are described in Chapter 5. This class is quite similar to the I2CDevice class that is described in Listing 8-2.

Listing 8-5: /chp08/spi/spiADXL345_cpp/SPIDevice.h

```
class SPIDevice {
public:
    enum SPIMODE{    //!< The SPI Mode
        MODE0 = 0,   //!< Low at idle,  capture on rising clock edge
        MODE1 = 1,   //!< Low at idle,  capture on falling clock edge
        MODE2 = 2,   //!< High at idle, capture on falling clock edge
        MODE3 = 3    //!< High at idle, capture on rising clock edge
    };
public:
    SPIDevice(unsigned int bus, unsigned int device);
    virtual int open();
    virtual unsigned char readRegister(unsigned int registerAddress);
    virtual unsigned char* readRegisters(unsigned int number, unsigned int
fromAddress=0);
    virtual int writeRegister(unsigned int registerAddress, unsigned char
value);
    virtual void debugDumpRegisters(unsigned int number = 0xff);
    virtual int write(unsigned char value);
    virtual int write(unsigned char value[], int length);
    virtual int setSpeed(uint32_t speed);
    virtual int setMode(SPIDevice::SPIMODE mode);
    virtual int setBitsPerWord(uint8_t bits);
    virtual void close();
    virtual ~SPIDevice();
    virtual int transfer(unsigned char read[], unsigned char write[], int
length);
    private:
        std::string filename; //!< The precise filename for the SPI device
        int file;             //!< The file handle to the device
        SPIMODE mode;         //!< The SPI mode as per the SPIMODE enumeration
```

```
   uint8_t bits;          //!< The number of bits per word
   uint32_t speed;        //!< The speed of transfer in Hz
   uint16_t delay;        //!< The transfer delay in usecs
};
```

The SPI class in Listing 8-5 can be used in a stand-alone form for any SPI device type. For example, Listing 8-6 demonstrates how to probe the ADXL345 device.

Listing 8-6: /chp08/spi/spiADXL345_cpp/SPITest.cpp

```cpp
#include <iostream>
#include <sstream>
#include "bus/SPIDevice.h"
#include "sensor/ADXL345.h"
using namespace std;
using namespace exploringBB;

int main(){
    SPIDevice spi(0,0);
    spi.setSpeed(5000000);
    cout << "The device ID is: " << (int) spi.readRegister(0x00) << endl;
    spi.setMode(SPIDevice::MODE3);
    spi.writeRegister(0x2D, 0x08);
    spi.debugDumpRegisters(0x40);
}
```

This will give the following output when built and executed ($0xE5 = 229_{10}$):

```
debian@ebb:~/exploringbb/chp08/spi/spiADXL345_cpp$ ./build
debian@ebb:~/exploringbb/chp08/spi/spiADXL345_cpp$ ./SPITest
The device ID is: 229
SPI Mode: 3
Bits per word: 8
Max speed: 5000000
Dumping Registers for Debug Purposes:
e5 00 00 00 00 00 00 00 00 00 00 00 00 00 00 4a
82 00 30 00 00 01 fe 08 00 00 00 ea 00 00 00 00
00 00 00 00 00 00 00 00 00 00 00 00 0a 08 00 00
02 0b 3a 00 db ff 17 01 00 00 00 00 00 00 00 00
```

The same SPIDevice class can be used as the basis for modifying the ADXL345 class in Listing 8-3 to support the SPI bus rather than the I²C bus. Listing 8-7 provides a segment of the class that is complete in the /chp08/spi/spiADXL345_cpp/ directory.

Listing 8-7: /chp08/spi/spiADXL345_cpp/ADXL345.h (Segment)

```cpp
class ADXL345{
public:
    enum RANGE {  ...  };
```

```
      enum RESOLUTION {   ...   };
private:
   SPIDevice *device;
   unsigned char *registers;
   ...
public:
   ADXL345(SPIDevice *busDevice);
   virtual int readSensorState();
   ...
   virtual void displayPitchAndRoll(int iterations = 600);
   virtual ~ADXL345();
};
```

The full class from Listing 8-7 can be used to build an example, as in Listing 8-8. This example helps demonstrate how an embedded device that is attached to one of the buses can be wrapped with a high-level OOP class.

Listing 8-8: /chp08/spi/spiADXL345_cpp/testADXL345.cpp

```
#include <iostream>
#include <sstream>
#include "bus/SPIDevice.h"
#include "sensor/ADXL345.h"
using namespace std;
using namespace exploringBB;

int main(){
   cout << "Starting EBB ADXL345 SPI Test" << endl;
   SPIDevice *busDevice = new SPIDevice(0,0);
   busDevice->setSpeed(5000000);
   ADXL345 acc(busDevice);
   acc.displayPitchAndRoll(100);
   cout << "End of EBB ADXL345 SPI Test" << endl;
}
```

When this program is executed, it displays the current accelerometer pitch and roll values on a single line of the terminal window.

```
debian@ebb:~/exploringbb/chp08/spi/spiADXL345_cpp$ ./build
debian@ebb:~/exploringbb/chp08/spi/spiADXL345_cpp$ ./testADXL345
Starting EBB ADXL345 SPI Test
Pitch:47.1902 Roll:-6.48042
```

Three-Wire SPI Communication

The ADXL345 supports a *three-wire SPI (half duplex)* mode. In this mode, the data is read and transmitted on the same SDIO line. To enable this mode on the ADXL345, the value 0x40 must be written to the 0x31 (DATA_FORMAT) register, and a 10kΩ resistor should be placed between SD0 and V_{CC} on the ADXL345. There is a draft project in place in the chp08/spi/spiADXL345/3-wire/ directory, but at the time of writing, there is a lack of support for this mode in current Linux distributions.

Multiple SPI Slave Devices

One of the advantages of the SPI bus is that it can be shared with *multiple slave devices*, provided that only one slave device is active when communication takes place. On most microcontrollers, GPIO pins can be used as slave selection pins, and a similar structure can be developed for the Beagle boards. While the Debian image has kernel support for multiple slave selection pins on the SPI bus through entries in the /dev/ directory, it is not fully realized on the Beagle boards. The idea is that multiple devices (0 and 1) are associated with SPI1, and each is activated by using one of the following entries:

```
debian@ebb:/dev$ ls -l spidev1*
crw-rw---- 1 root spi 153, 1 Jan  1  2000 spidev1.0
crw-rw---- 1 root spi 153, 2 Jan  1  2000 spidev1.1
```

If you want to allow the Linux SPI interface library code to retain control of the slave selection functionality, then a wiring configuration similar to Figure 8-14 could be used. This configuration uses OR gates and an inverter to ensure that only one CS input is pulled low at a single time. In Figure 8-14 (a), the ADXL345 slave device is active when CS = 0 and GPIO = 0, and in Figure 8-14 (b), the second slave device is active when CS = 0 and GPIO = 1.

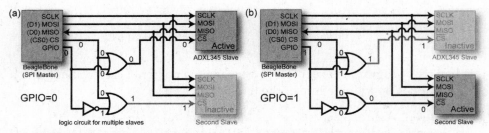

Figure 8-14: BBB control of more than one slave device using GPIO pins and additional logic

Depending on the particular slave devices being used, the GPIO output combined with a single inverter may be sufficient, as you could "permanently" pull the $\overline{CS}$ line low on the slave device, ignoring the CS output of the master. However, this would not work for the 74HC595 example, as the Beagle board's CS line is used to latch the data to the output LEDs.

For more than two slave devices, a 3-to-8 line decoder, such as the 74HC138, would be a good solution. It has inverted outputs, which means that only one of its eight outputs is low at a single point in time. This device could be controlled using three of the board's GPIOs, and it could enable one of eight slave devices ($2^3 = 8$). There are also 4-to-16 line decoders with inverting outputs, such as the 74HC4515, which would enable you to control 16 slave devices with only four GPIOs ($2^4 = 16$). For both of these devices, the Beagle board's CS output could be connected to their $\overline{E}$ enable input(s).

UART

A *Universal Asynchronous Receiver/Transmitter* (UART) is a microprocessor peripheral device used for the serial transfer of data, one bit at a time, between two electronic devices. UARTs were originally stand-alone ICs but now are often integrated with the host microprocessor/microcontroller. A UART is not, strictly speaking, a bus, but its capacity to implement serial data communications overlaps with similar capacities of the I²C and SPI buses described earlier. A UART is described as *asynchronous* because the sender does not need to send a clock signal to the recipient to synchronize the transmission; rather, a communication structure is agreed upon that uses start and stop bits to synchronize the transmission of data. Because no clock is required, the data is typically sent using only two signal lines. Just like a regular telephone line, the *transmit data connection* (*TXD*) from one end is connected to the *receive data connection* (*RXD*) on the other end of the connection, and vice versa.

Traditionally, UARTs have been used with level converters/line drivers to implement interfaces such as RS-232 or RS-485, but for short-distance communications, it is possible to use the original logic level for the UART outputs and inputs to enable two UARTs to communicate with each other. Note that this is a perfectly possible but nonstandardized use of UARTS.

The number of symbols per second is known as the *baud rate* or modulation rate. With certain encoding schemes, a symbol could be used to represent two bits (i.e., four states, for example, by using quadrature phase-shift keying [QPSK]). Then the *bit rate* would be twice the baud rate. However, for a simple bi-level UART connection, the baud rate is the same as the bit rate.

The transmitter and receiver agree upon a bit rate before communication begins. The *byte rate* is somewhat lower than 1/8th of the bit rate, as there are overhead bits associated with the serial transmission of data. Transmission begins when the transmitter sends a *start bit* (logic low), as shown in Figure 8-15. On the receiver's end, the falling edge of the start bit is detected, and then after 1.5 bit periods, the first bit value is sampled. Every subsequent bit is sampled after 1.0 bit periods, until the agreed-upon number of bits is transferred (typically seven or eight). The *parity bit* is optional (though both devices must be configured to either use it or not); if used, it can identify whether a transmission error has occurred. It would be high or low, depending on whether odd or even *parity checking* is employed. Finally, one *stop bit* is sent (or optionally two stop bits), which is always a logic high value. The examples that follow in this section all use a standard *8N1* form, which means that eight bits are sent in each frame, with no parity bits and one stop bit.

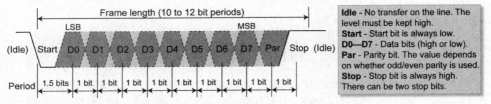

Figure 8-15: UART transmission format for a typical one-byte transfer

> **WARNING**   Again, it is important that you do not connect a 5V UART device to the UART RXD input of a Beagle board or you will damage the board. A solution to this problem is provided at the end of this chapter.

The Beagle Board UART

The Beagle boards each have four UARTs that are accessible via the GPIO Expansion headers at the pin locations listed in Table 8-5. In addition, UART3 is not broken out to the GPIO Headers.

Table 8-5: Beagle Board UART Header Pins (PocketBeagle in Brackets)

	UART0	UART1	UART2	UART4	UART5
TXD	n/a (P1.30)	P9_24 (P2.9)	P9_21 (P1.10)	P9_13 (P2.7)	P8_37 (n/a)
RXD	n/a (P1.32)	P9_26 (P2.11)	P9_22 (P1.8)	P9_11 (P2.5)	P8_38 (n/a)

For the following examples UART4 is used. As detailed in Table 8-5, the pins for UART4 are as follows:

- **UART4-TXD: P9_13** on the BeagleBone or **P2.7** on the PocketBeagle. This is an output that transmits data to a receiver.

- **UART4-RXD: P9_11** on the BeagleBone or **P2.5** on the PocketBeagle. This is an input that receives data from a transmitter.

Chapter 9 describes how you can add additional UARTs to the Beagle boards using USB devices, but this chapter focuses on the built-in UART. The first test is to connect these two pins together, as in Figure 8-16(a), so that the board UART is literally "talking to itself."

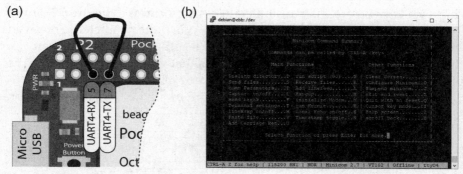

Figure 8-16: (a) Loopback testing the UART, and (b) configuring the minicom program settings

The /dev directory includes entries for ttyO0 to ttyO4 (letter *O*, not zero). This is the "teletype" (terminal) device, which is a software interface that enables you to send and receive data via the on-board UART. First, check that the terminal device is listed (on the PocketBeagle).

```
debian@ebb:/dev$ ls -l ttyO*
lrwxrwxrwx 1 root root 5 Jan  1  2000 ttyO0 -> ttyS0
lrwxrwxrwx 1 root root 5 Jan  1  2000 ttyO1 -> ttyS1
lrwxrwxrwx 1 root root 5 Jan  1  2000 ttyO2 -> ttyS2
lrwxrwxrwx 1 root root 5 Jan  1  2000 ttyO4 -> ttyS4
```

NOTE   The first human-computer interface was the teletypewriter, also known as the teletype or TTY, an electromechanical typewriter that can be used to send and receive messages. This terminology is still in use today!

To test the device, you can use the agetty (*a*lternative *getty*) command or the minicom terminal emulator, both of which enable you to send and receive data on the ttyO4 device. The minicom program enables you to dynamically change the serial settings while it is executing (e.g., number of bits in a frame, number of stop bits, parity settings) by pressing Ctrl+A followed by Z. Install and execute minicom using the following commands:

```
debian@ebb:/dev$ sudo apt install minicom
debian@ebb:/dev$ minicom -b 115200 -o -D /dev/ttyO4
Welcome to minicom 2.7
OPTIONS: I18n
Compiled on Apr 22 2017, 09:14:19.
Port /dev/ttyO4, 04:02:08
Press CTRL-A Z for help on special keys
```

At this point, you should press Ctrl+A followed by Z and then E to turn on local Echo. Now when the board is wired as in Figure 8-16(a) and you press a key, you should see the following output when you type letters:

```
hheelllloo  PPoocckkeettBBeeaaggllee
```

Whichever key you press is transmitted in binary form (as in Figure 8-17) from the TXD output and is echoed on the console. When the character is received on the RXD input, it is then displayed on the terminal. Therefore, if you can see the characters appearing twice for the keys that you are pressing, then the simple UART test is working correctly. You can verify this by briefly disconnecting one end of the TXD-RXD loopback wire in Figure 8-16(a), whereupon the key presses will appear only once.

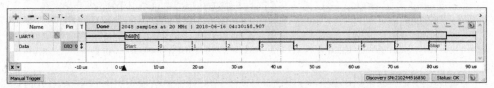

Figure 8-17: Logic analyzer display of the loopback serial transmission of the letter *h* (0x68) = 01101000_2 at 115,200 baud

The Analog Discovery has an interpreter that can be used for analyzing serial data communication. The logic analyzer can be connected in parallel to the TXD and RXD lines to analyze the transfer of data from the board to another device. An example of the resulting signals is displayed in Figure 8-17 for the loopback test in Figure 8-16(a) when only the letter "h" is being transmitted. The start and stop bits can be observed, along with the eight-bit data as it is sent, LSB first, from the TXD pin to the RXD pin, with a sample bit-period of 8.7μs. At a baud rate of 115,200, the effective byte rate will be somewhat lower because of the overhead of transmitting start, stop, and parity bits.

To this point, this chapter describes SPI and I²C communication as well as UART. However, using a UART connection is probably the most straightforward approach, and it has the additional advantage that there can be some degree of physical distance between the two controllers. Table 8-6 lists some advantages and disadvantages of using a UART in comparison to using I²C or SPI.

UART Examples in C

The next step is to write C code on the board that can communicate with the desktop computer using the USB-to-TTL 3.3V cable (see Chapter 2), as wired in Figure 8-19(a). You should first test your connection by opening a serial terminal connection on the desktop PC (e.g., using PuTTY) and then use minicom on the Beagle board to communicate with the desktop PC.

Table 8-6: Advantages and Disadvantages of UART Communication

ADVANTAGES	DISADVANTAGES
Simple, single-wire transmission and single-wire reception of data with error checking.	The typical maximum data rate is low compared to SPI (typically 460.8kb/sec).
Easy interface for interconnecting embedded devices and desktop computers, etc., especially when that communication is external to the device and/or over a significant distance—some tens of feet. I²C and SPI are not suited for external/distance communication.	Because it is asynchronous, the clock on both devices must be accurate, particularly at higher baud rates. You should investigate Controller Area Network (CAN) buses for high-speed external asynchronous data transfer (described later in this chapter).
Can be directly interfaced to popular RS-232 physical interfaces, enabling long-distance communication (15 meters or greater). The longer the cable, the lower the speed. RS-422/485 allows for 100-meter runs at greater than 1Mb/s.	UART settings need to be known in advance of the transfer, such as the baud rate, data size, and parity checking type.

Beagle Board Serial Client

The C program in Listing 8-9 sends a string to a desktop machine (or any other device) that is listening to the other end of the connection (e.g., using PuTTY). It uses the Linux *termios* library, which provides a general terminal interface that can control asynchronous communication ports.

Listing 8-9: exploringbb/chp08/uart/uartC/uart.c

```c
#include<stdio.h>
#include<fcntl.h>
#include<unistd.h>
#include<termios.h>
#include<string.h>

int main(int argc, char *argv[]){
    int file, count;
    if(argc!=2){
        printf("Please pass a message string to send, exiting!\n");
        return -2;
    }
    if ((file = open("/dev/ttyO4", O_RDWR | O_NOCTTY | O_NDELAY))<0){
        perror("UART: Failed to open the device.\n");
        return -1;
    }
```

```
struct termios options;
tcgetattr(file, &options);
options.c_cflag = B115200 | CS8 | CREAD | CLOCAL;
options.c_iflag = IGNPAR | ICRNL;
tcflush(file, TCIFLUSH);
tcsetattr(file, TCSANOW, &options);

// send the string plus the null character
if ((count = write(file, argv[1], strlen(argv[1])+1))<0){
    perror("UART: Failed to write to the output.\n");
    return -1;
}
close(file);
printf("Finished sending the message, exiting.\n");
return 0;
}
```

This code uses the `termios` structure, setting flags to define the type of communication that should take place. The `termios` structure has the following members:

- `tcflag_t c_iflag`: Sets the input modes
- `tcflag_t c_oflag`: Sets the output modes
- `tcflag_t c_cflag`: Sets the control modes
- `tcflag_t c_lflag`: Sets the local modes
- `cc_t c_cc[NCCS]`: Used for special characters

A full description of the `termios` functionality and flag settings is available by typing **man termios** at the Linux shell prompt.

```
debian@ebb:~/exploringbb/chp08/uart/uartC$ gcc uart.c -o uart
.../exploringbb/chp08/uart/uartC$ ./uart "Hello Desktop!"
Finished sending the message, exiting.
.../exploringbb/chp08/uart/uartC$ ./uart " From the PocketBeagle."
Finished sending the message, exiting.
.../exploringbb/chp08/uart/uartC$ echo " Using echo!" >> /dev/ttyO4
```

The output appears on the desktop PC as in Figure 8-18 when PuTTY is set to listen to the correct serial port (e.g., COM5 in my case). The C program functionality is similar to a simple echo to the terminal device; however, it does have access to set low-level modes such as the baud rate, parity types, and so on.

Figure 8-18: A PuTTY desktop COM terminal that is listening for messages from the Beagle board

LED Serial Server

For some applications, it can be useful to allow a desktop computer master to take control of a Beagle board slave. In this section, a serial server runs on the PocketBeagle and awaits commands from a desktop serial terminal. Once again, the USB-to-TTL 3.3V cable is used; however, it is important to note that a similar setup could be developed with wireless technologies, such as Bluetooth, infrared transmitter/receivers, and serial ZigBee (see Chapter 12).

In this example, the PocketBeagle is connected to a simple LED circuit and the USB-to-TTL cable, as illustrated in Figure 8-19(a). When the PuTTY client on the desktop computer issues simple string commands such as LED on and LED off, as illustrated in Figure 8-19(b), the hardware LED that is attached to the board performs a corresponding action. Importantly, this program permits safe remote control of the board, as it does not allow the serial client access to any other functionality on the board—in effect, the serial server behaves like a shell that has only three commands! Please note that you may have to turn on local echo in the terminal window (e.g., in PuTTY use Terminal ➪ Local echo and select the option "Force on").

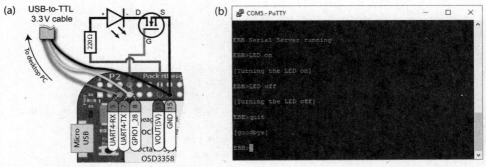

Figure 8-19: (a) The LED serial server circuit, and (b) PuTTY on the PC communicating to the LED serial server

The source code for the serial server is provided in Listing 8-10. The example uses sysfs to control the LED circuit (see Chapter 5). On execution, the server displays the following output when you provide the input strings that are captured in Figure 8-19(b):

```
debian@ebb:~/exploringbb/chp08/uart/server$ gcc server.c -o server
debian@ebb:~/exploringbb/chp08/uart/server$ ./server
EBB Serial Server running
LED on
Server>>>[Turning the LED on]
LED off
Server>>>[Turning the LED off]
quit
Server>>>[goodbye]
```

You can then add a new service entry for the server code in this section so that it starts on boot. If your intention is to run this program as a service, then you should, of course, remove the client-controlled "quit" functionality!

Listing 8-10: /exploringbb/chp08/uart/server/server.c

```c
#include<stdio.h>
#include<fcntl.h>
#include<unistd.h>
#include<termios.h>
#include<string.h>
#include<stdlib.h>
#define  LED_PATH  "/sys/class/gpio/gpio60/"

// Sends a message to the client and displays the message on the console
int message(int client, char *message){
   int size = strlen(message);
   printf("Server>>>%s\n", (message+1));   // print message with new line
   if (write(client, message, size)<0){
      perror("Error: Failed to write to the client\n");
      return -1;
   }
   write(client, "\n\rEBB>", 7);            // display a simple prompt
   return 0;                                // \r for a carriage return
}

void makeLED(char filename[], char value[]){
   FILE* fp;   // create a file pointer fp
   char  fullFileName[100];  // to store the path and filename
   sprintf(fullFileName, LED_PATH "%s", filename); // write path and filename
   fp = fopen(fullFileName, "w+"); // open file for writing
   fprintf(fp, "%s", value);  // send the value to the file
   fclose(fp);  // close the file using the file pointer
}

// Checks to see if the command is one that is understood by the server
int processCommand(int client, char *command){
   int val = -1;
   if (strcmp(command, "LED on")==0){
      val = message(client, "\r[Turning the LED on]");
      makeLED("value", "1");          // turn the physical LED on
   }
   else if(strcmp(command, "LED off")==0){
      val = message(client, "\r[Turning the LED off]");
      makeLED("value", "0");          // turn the physical LED off
   }
```

```
      else if(strcmp(command, "quit")==0){      // shutting down server!
         val = message(client, "\r[goodbye]");
      }
      else { val = message(client, "\r[Unknown command]"); }
      return val;
}

int main(int argc, char *argv[]){
   int client, count=0;
   unsigned char c;
   char *command = malloc(255);
   makeLED("direction", "out");              // the LED is an output
   if ((client = open("/dev/ttyO4", O_RDWR | O_NOCTTY | O_NDELAY))<0){
      perror("UART: Failed to open the file.\n");
      return -1;
   }
   struct termios options;
   tcgetattr(client, &options);
   options.c_cflag = B115200 | CS8 | CREAD | CLOCAL;
   options.c_iflag = IGNPAR | ICRNL;
   tcflush(client, TCIFLUSH);
   fcntl(STDIN_FILENO, F_SETFL, O_NONBLOCK);  // make reads non-blocking
   tcsetattr(client, TCSANOW, &options);
   if (message(client, "\n\rEBB Serial Server running")<0){
      perror("UART: Failed to start server.\n");
      return -1;
   }

   // Loop forever until the quit command is sent from the client or
   //  Ctrl-C is pressed in the server's terminal window
   do {
      if(read(client,&c,1)>0){
         write(STDOUT_FILENO,&c,1);
         command[count++]=c;
         if(c=='\n'){
            command[count-1]='\0';  // replace /n with /0
            processCommand(client, command);
            count=0;                     // reset the command string
         }
      }
      if(read(STDIN_FILENO,&c,1)>0){ // can send from stdin to client
         write(client,&c,1);
      }
   }
   while(strcmp(command,"quit")!=0);
   close(client);
   return 0;
}
```

UART Applications: GPS

A low-cost *Global Positioning System* (GPS) module has been chosen as an example device to demonstrate interconnection to Beagle board UART devices. The GY-GPS6MV2 breakout board (~$10) uses the u-blox NEO-6M series GPS module (tiny.cc/beagle804). It can be powered at 3.3V and therefore can be connected directly to a Beagle board's UART pins.

Figure 8-20 illustrates the board UART connection to the GPS module. As with all UART connections, ensure that you connect the transmit pin of the board to the receive pin of the device and connect the receive pin of the board to the transmit pin of the device.

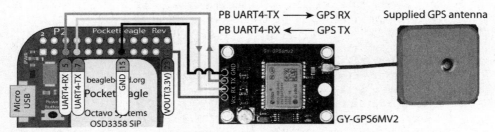

Figure 8-20: PocketBeagle UART connection to the GPS module

The GPS module is set for 9600 baud by default, so to connect to the module, you can use the following:

```
debian@ebb:~$ sudo minicom -b 9600 -o -D /dev/ttyO4
Welcome to minicom 2.7
OPTIONS: I18n
Compiled on Apr 22 2017, 09:14:19.
Port /dev/ttyO4, 23:40:20
Press CTRL-A Z for help on special keys
$GPRMC,133809.00,A,5323.12995,N,00615.36410,W,1.015,,190815,,,A*60
$GPVTG,,T,,M,1.015,N,1.879,K,A*21
$GPGGA,133809.00,5323.12995,N,00615.36410,W,1,08,1.21,80.2,M,52.9,M,,*73
$GPGSA,A,3,21,16,18,19,26,22,07,27,,,,,2.72,1.21,2.44*06
$GPGSV,4,1,14,04,07,227,17,07,24,306,16,08,33,278,09,13,05,018,*7A
$GPGSV,4,2,14,15,04,048,08,16,61,174,25,18,39,096,31,19,35,275,21*78
$GPGSV,4,3,14,20,12,034,08,21,36,061,23,22,29,142,21,26,32,159,12*71
$GPGSV,4,4,14,27,75,286,26,30,10,334,*75
$GPGLL,5323.12995,N,00615.36410,W,133809.00,A,A*78
```

The GPS module outputs NEMA 0183 sentences, which can be decoded to provide information about the sensor's position, direction, velocity, and so on. There is a lot of work involved in decoding the sentences, so it is best to use a client application to test the performance of your sensor. Here's an example:

```
debian@ebb:~$ sudo apt install gpsd-clients
debian@ebb:~$ gpsmon /dev/ttyO4
```

This results in the output shown in Figure 8-21 that provides an intuitive display of the NEMA 0183 sentences. An LED on the module flashes at a rate of 1 pulse per second (PPS) when it is capturing valid data. This pulse is extremely accurate and can therefore be used as a calibration method for other applications. The `gpsmon` application was executed in my office, which overlooks a courtyard, so I was surprised that the low-cost sensor achieved line of sight with 11 satellites.

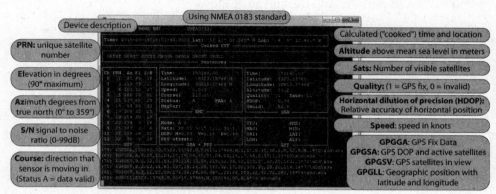

Figure 8-21: The `gpsmon` output display

Walter Dal Mut (`@walterdalmut`) has made a C library available for interfacing to GPS sensors. The library can be easily integrated within your project to utilize GPS, as follows:

```
debian@ebb:~$ git clone git://github.com/wdalmut/libgps
Cloning into 'libgps'...
debian@ebb:~$ cd libgps
debian@ebb:~/libgps$ make
/usr/bin/make -C src all
RUN TESTS SHOULD BE A GOOD IDEA...
make tests...
debian@ebb:~/libgps$ sudo make install
debian@ebb:~/libgps$ ls /usr/lib/libgps.a
/usr/lib/libgps.a
```

Once the library has been installed, you can use a straightforward C program to identify the GPS information, as in Listing 8-11.

Listing 8-11: /exploringbb/chp08/uart/gps/gps_test.c

```c
#include<stdio.h>
#include<stdlib.h>
#include<gps.h>


int main() {
   gps_init();                        // initialize the device
```

```
loc_t gps;                      // a location structure
gps_location(&gps);             // determine the location data
printf("The board location is (%lf,%lf)\n", gps.latitude, gps.longitude);
printf("Altitude: %lf m. Speed: %lf knots\n", gps.altitude, gps.speed);
return 0;
}
```

You can build and execute the code as follows:

```
.../exploringbb/chp08/uart/gps$ gcc gps_test.c -o gps_test -lgps -lm
.../exploringbb/chp08/uart/gps$ ./gps_test
The board location is (53.385511,-6.256224)
Altitude: 81.900000 m. Speed: 0.060000 knots
```

You can enter the coordinate pair in maps.google.com to find my office at Dublin City University (tiny.cc/beagle805)!

CAN Bus

Controller Area Network (CAN) was developed by Bosch for industrial communication applications. Similar to I²C, CAN supports multimaster messaging at rates of up to 1MB/sec. Unlike the other buses described in this chapter, CAN uses short messages called *frames*, as illustrated in Figure 8-22. These frames have an identifier that allows for priority messaging on the bus, where a lower value has the highest message priority. There are four frame types.

- Data Frame is a regular data transmission frame.

- Remote Frame is a request for transmission from another node.

- Error Frame is used when an error occurs (such as an incorrect checksum) and causes the original transmitter to resend the message.

- Overload Frame is used when a node is too busy. It inserts a delay into communications between each frame to give the node time to process.

CAN is designed primarily for distributed real-time control, particularly where security, cost, low latency, and high-error failsafe are important design criteria. As a result, CAN is used today in automotive and industrial control. CAN supports CSMA/CD+AMP, which means

- Carrier sense/multiple access (CSMA) allows a bus participant to wait for inactivity before a message is sent. Even with such sensing, two participants could begin transmitting at the same time.

- Collision detection with arbitration on message priority (CD + AMP) uses bitwise arbitration, where each participant places a frame on the bus bit -by bit and then checks its values. Higher-priority messages always win bus access, as the first bits to be transmitted in the frame represent the identifier.

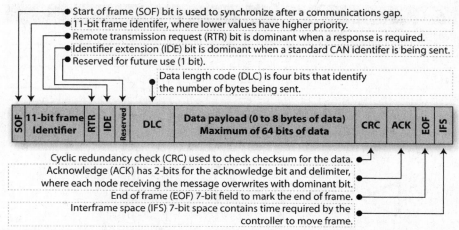

Figure 8-22: A standard CAN frame (extended CAN frames are also available that have an additional 18-bit identifier extension)

The buses described to this point in the chapter use single-ended signals, where a signal is sent on a data line and has a return path through GND. The CAN bus uses a differential communications model, where balanced signals are used to transmit the signal, as illustrated in Figure 8-23(a). Noise as a result of *electromagnetic interference* (EMI) is likely to affect both lines equally and is therefore canceled out. Differential signaling is also used in USB and Ethernet communications as it gives better signal voltage versus power consumption than single-ended communications.

Figure 8-23(b) illustrates the voltage levels used in 5V CAN bus signaling, where a dominant bit (a logic low) is transmitted by setting the CAN_H line to ~3.5V and the CAN_L line to ~1.5V. When the bus is idle, the bit is recessive (a logic high), and the line voltages are both weakly biased at approximately 2.5V.

Beagle Board CAN Bus

The AM335x SoC has a DCAN controller that provides two CAN bus devices (DCAN0 and DCAN1), which are accessible through the Expansion Headers as described in Table 8-7. The DCAN controller supports CAN protocol version 2.0 (A and B) at bit rates of up to 1Mbit/s. You will need to add CAN transceiver (transmitter and receiver) hardware to your Beagle board to drive the physical layer voltage levels, which are illustrated in Figure 8-23(b). Modules that use the TI SN65HVD230 CAN Bus Transceiver IC are popular for this task (`tiny.cc/beagle810`) as they operate at 3.3V logic levels, support data rates of up to 1Mbit/s, and are available in modular form for as little as $1 each.

Table 8-7: CAN Bus Pins on the Beagle Boards (All Mux Mode 2)

H/W BUS	POCKETBEAGLE	BEAGLEBONE
CAN0 RX	P1.28 or P1.30	P9_19
CAN0 TX	P1.26 or P1.32	P9_20
CAN1 RX	P2.09 or P2.25	P9_24
CAN1 TX	P2.11 or P2.27	P9_26

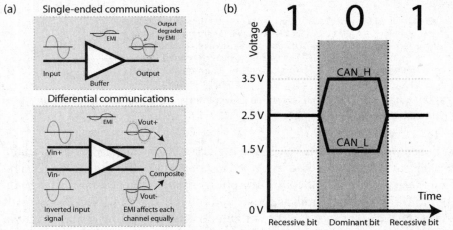

Figure 8-23: (a) Single-ended versus differential communications, and (b) voltage levels used in CAN bus signaling for 5V CAN (3.3V CAN is typically centered around 2.3V)

SocketCAN

Linux provides support for CAN through the networking subsystem and SocketCAN. SocketCAN is a hardware-independent CAN API that allows for multiuser userspace control of CAN devices. The advantage of this design is that users can easily write program code that typically sends and receives raw CAN frames to and from the bus. The downside is that this approach uses a full-stack networking approach for a bus that was designed for low-latency and that the packet scheduler is shared with other buses (e.g., heavy network traffic on Ethernet). You can configure the pins for DCAN0 as follows:

```
debian@ebb:~$ config-pin -q P1.28
P1_28 Mode: default Direction: in Value: 0
```

```
debian@ebb:~$ config-pin -q P1.26
P1_26 Mode: default Direction: in Value: 0
debian@ebb:~$ config-pin P1.28 can
debian@ebb:~$ config-pin P1.26 can
debian@ebb:~$ config-pin -q P1.28
P1_28 Mode: can
debian@ebb:~$ config-pin -q P1.26
P1_26 Mode: can
```

and DCAN1 as follows:

```
debian@ebb:~$ config-pin P2.9 can
debian@ebb:~$ config-pin P2.11 can
debian@ebb:~$ config-pin -q P2.9
P2_09 Mode: can
debian@ebb:~$ config-pin -q P2.11
P2_11 Mode: can
```

Load the LKMs for CAN (it is likely that only the last module is required) and then check that the LKM loaded correctly.

```
debian@ebb:~$ dmesg|grep can
[    1.210665] c_can_platform 481cc000.can: c_can_platform device
registered (regs=fa1cc000, irq=39)
[    1.211749] c_can_platform 481d0000.can: c_can_platform device
registered (regs=fa1d0000, irq=40)
[    1.328253] can: controller area network core (rev 20170425 abi 9)
debian@ebb:~$ sudo modprobe can
debian@ebb:~$ sudo modprobe can-dev
debian@ebb:~$ sudo modprobe can-raw
debian@ebb:~$ lsmod|grep can
can_raw              20480  0
debian@ebb:~$ dmesg|grep raw
[ 625.214610] can: raw protocol (rev 20170425)
```

The CAN Bus devices can then be brought up as follows, where a bit rate of 125Kbit/s is specified (this value can be as high as 1,000,000—i.e., 1Mbit/s):

```
debian@ebb:~$ sudo ip link set can0 up type can bitrate 125000
debian@ebb:~$ sudo ip link set can1 up type can bitrate 125000
debian@ebb:~$ sudo ifconfig can0 up
debian@ebb:~$ sudo ifconfig can1 up
debian@ebb:~$ ifconfig
can0: flags=193<UP,RUNNING,NOARP>  mtu 16
        unspec 00-00-00-00-00-00-00-00-00-00-00-00-00-00-00-00
        ...
        device interrupt 39
can1: flags=193<UP,RUNNING,NOARP>  mtu 16
        unspec 00-00-00-00-00-00-00-00-00-00-00-00-00-00-00-00
        ...
        device interrupt 40...
```

```
debian@ebb:~$ ip -details link show can0
2: can0: <NO-CARRIER,NOARP,UP,ECHO> mtu 16 qdisc pfifo_fast state DOWN
mode DEFAULT group default qlen 10
    link/can  promiscuity 0
    can state BUS-OFF (berr-counter tx 248 rx 0) restart-ms 0
          bitrate 125000 sample-point 0.875 ...
debian@ebb:~$ dmesg
[  727.310927] c_can_platform 481cc000.can can0: setting BTR=1c0b BRPE=0000
[  727.319229] IPv6: ADDRCONF(NETDEV_CHANGE): can0: link becomes ready
[  822.875931] c_can_platform 481d0000.can can1: setting BTR=1c0b BRPE=0000
[  822.883165] IPv6: ADDRCONF(NETDEV_CHANGE): can1: link becomes ready
```

VIRTUAL CAN (VCAN)

Linux also has virtual CAN driver support that can be used for testing purposes. You can enable it as follows and use it as a test device in much the same way that the real CAN devices are used in this chapter.

```
debian@ebb:~$ sudo modprobe vcan
debian@ebb:~$ lsmod |grep vcan
vcan                  16384  0
debian@ebb:~$ sudo ip link add dev vcan0 type vcan
debian@ebb:~$ sudo ip link set up vcan0
debian@ebb:~$ ifconfig
...
vcan0: flags=193<UP,RUNNING,NOARP>  mtu 72 ...
debian@ebb:/sys/class/net$ ls -l vcan*
lrwxrwxrwx 1 root root 0 Jun 20 01:48 vcan0 ->
   ../../devices/virtual/net/vcan0
debian@ebb:~$ cansend vcan0 123#de.ad.be.ef
```

And, simultaneously in a separate terminal window:

```
debian@ebb:~$ candump vcan0
  vcan0  123   [4]  DE AD BE EF
```

A CAN Bus Test Circuit

You can use both CAN buses on the PocketBeagle or BeagleBone to create a true hardware loopback test. You could also perform this test by using one CAN interface on two separate boards. Importantly, you will need to acquire and connect two CAN physical layer modules (e.g., TI SN65HVD230-based modules), as illustrated in Figure 8-24. Other third-party CAN bus devices can be added to the bus at this point.

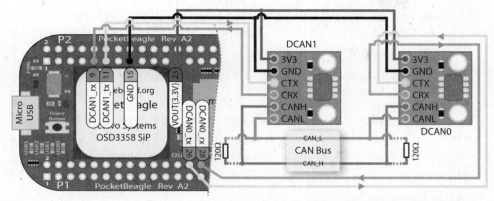

Figure 8-24: PocketBeagle CAN Bus test using DCAN0 and DCAN1 for a hardware loopback test with SN65HVD230 CAN modules

CAN Bus requires termination resistors on the CAN_H and CAN_L lines that match the nominal impedance of the cable. The ISO 11898 CAN standard requires a cable with a nominal impedance of 120Ω. You should place two such resistors on each end of the cable, as illustrated in Figure 8-24.

The device properties are available in /sysfs/ and /proc/ at the following locations:

```
debian@ebb:~$ ls /sys/class/net/
can0  can1  lo  usb0  usb1
debian@ebb:~$ ls /sys/class/net/can0/
addr_assign_type   dormant       name_assign_type   speed
address            duplex        netdev_group       statistics
addr_len           flag          operstate          subsystem  ...
debian@ebb:~$ cat /proc/net/can/version
rev 20170425 abi 9
debian@ebb:~$ cat /proc/net/can/stats
       0 transmitted frames (TXF)
       0 received frames (RXF)   ...
```

Linux CAN-utils

You can test the configuration in Figure 8-24 using the SocketCAN Can-utils tools (elinux.org/Can-utils). These are installed on the BeagleBoard.org Linux image by default in the /usr/bin/ directory.

```
debian@ebb:/usr/bin$ ls can*
canbusload          candump    cangen   canlogserver   cansend
can-calc-bit-timing canfdtest  cangw    canplayer      cansniffer
```

The cansend utility can be used to send messages to the CAN bus. You can specify the CAN device (e.g., can0) followed by the CAN ID and data payload in the form <can_id>#<data>.

```
debian@ebb:~$ cansend can1 123#11.22.33.44.55.66.77.88
debian@ebb:~$ cansend can0 123#11.22.33
```

The candump utility can be used to read messages from the bus. If you open two terminal windows (one for each CAN device) and run the candump utility in each window, you will see the following output when the cansend command is called:

```
debian@ebb:~$ candump can0
  can0   123   [8]   11 22 33 44 55 66 77 88
  can0   123   [3]   11 22 33

debian@ebb:~$ candump can1
  can1   123   [8]   11 22 33 44 55 66 77 88
  can1   123   [3]   11 22 33

debian@ebb:~$ cat /proc/net/can/stats
        42 transmitted frames (TXF)
        84 received frames (RXF)
        32 matched frames (RXMF) ...
```

A large number of messages is typically sent to an active bus, so the candump utility also supports *filters*, which enables you to receive only frames in a particular range. For example, to receive all frames between 0x100 and 0x2FF, use this:

```
debian@ebb:~$ candump can0,100:2FF
```

Figure 8-25 displays a capture of the CAN Bus in Figure 8-24 when the following message is transmitted to the bus. You can also see that the voltage level profile of the bus is consistent with Figure 8-23(b).[5]

```
debian@ebb:~$ cansend can0 123#11.22.33.44.55.66.77.88
```

A SocketCAN C Example

SocketCAN greatly simplifies the complexity of the code that is required to read and write CAN frames to the bus. It uses the same framework as is used for TCP/IP socket communication, except that the protocol family is PF_CAN and the packet is sent using the raw interface. A modified version of the standard SocketCAN example from the SocketCAN Wikipedia page (en.wikipedia.org/wiki/SocketCAN) is presented in Listing 8-12 for convenience.

---

[5]To use the Analog Discovery (AD) to interpret the CAN Bus you can connect the AD GND to the Beagle board GND, any DIO pin (e.g., DIO7) to the CAN_L line (as in Figure 8-24), set the polarity to "low," and set a trigger. This ensures that the DIO pin is maintained within voltage range for the AD. Do not connect the CAN_H line to the AD DIO pins as it may exceed acceptable voltage levels when using 5V CAN Bus connections.

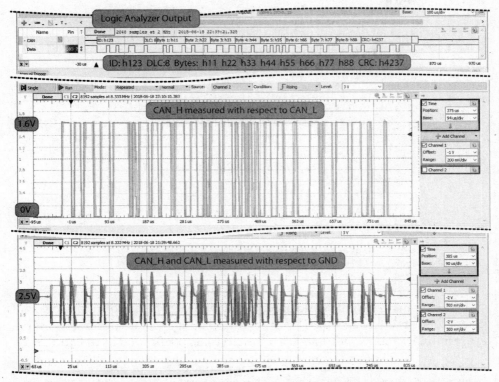

Figure 8-25: A logic analyzer and scope capture of the CAN Bus circuit in Figure 8-24 sending the message 123#11.22.33.44.55.66.77.88

Listing 8-12: /chp08/can/simpleCAN.c

```c
#include <stdio.h>
#include <stdlib.h>
#include <unistd.h>
#include <string.h>
#include <net/if.h>
#include <sys/types.h>
#include <sys/socket.h>
#include <sys/ioctl.h>
#include <linux/can.h>
#include <linux/can/raw.h>

int main(void) {
    int s, nbytes;
    struct sockaddr_can addr;
    struct can_frame frame;
    struct ifreq ifr;
    const char *ifname = "can0";
    if((s = socket(PF_CAN, SOCK_RAW, CAN_RAW)) < 0) {
        perror("Error while opening socket");
```

```
        return -1;
    }
    strcpy(ifr.ifr_name, ifname);
    ioctl(s, SIOCGIFINDEX, &ifr);
    addr.can_family  = AF_CAN;
    addr.can_ifindex = ifr.ifr_ifindex;
    printf("%s at index %d\n", ifname, ifr.ifr_ifindex);
    if(bind(s, (struct sockaddr *)&addr, sizeof(addr)) < 0) {
        perror("Error in socket bind");
        return -2;
    }
    frame.can_id  = 0x123;   // can0 123#11.22.33
    frame.can_dlc = 3;
    frame.data[0] = 0x11;
    frame.data[1] = 0x22;
    frame.data[2] = 0x33;
    nbytes = write(s, &frame, sizeof(struct can_frame));
    printf("Wrote %d bytes\n", nbytes);
    return 0;
}
```

The code can be compiled and executed as follows, whereupon a message will be sent to the bus and received by the candump utility that is running in a separate terminal window, provided that the circuit is configured as in Figure 8-24.

```
debian@ebb:~/exploringbb/chp08/can$ gcc simpleCAN.c -o simple
debian@ebb:~/exploringbb/chp08/can$ ./simple
can0 at index 2
Wrote 16 bytes
debian@ebb:~$ candump can0
  can0   123    [3]   11 22 33
```

Logic-Level Translation

As noted throughout this chapter, it is important that you are cognizant of the voltage levels used in communicating with the Beagle boards. If you connect a device that uses 5V logic levels, then when the device is sending a high state to the board, it will apply a voltage of 5V to the board's input pins. This would likely permanently damage the board. Many embedded systems have overvoltage-tolerant inputs, but the Beagle boards do not. Therefore, *logic-level translation* circuitry is required if you want to connect the buses to 5V or 1.8V logic-level circuits.

For *unidirectional data buses*, like four-wire SPI, logic-level translation can be achieved using a combination of diodes (using their ~0.6V forward-voltage drop characteristic) combined with resistors, or transistors. However, *bidirectional data buses* like the I²C bus are more complex because the level must be translated in both directions on a single line. This requires circuits that use devices such as N-channel MOSFETs (e.g., the BSS138). They are available in surface-mounted packages and, unfortunately, there are few through-hole alternatives. Fortunately, this is a common problem, and there are straightforward unidirectional and bidirectional breakout board solutions available from several suppliers, including the following:

- SparkFun Bi-directional Logic Level Converter (BOB-12009), which uses the BSS138 MOSFET (~$3).

- Adafruit Four-Channel Bi-directional Level Shifter (ID:757), which uses the BSS138 MOSFET (1.8V to 10V shifting) (~$4).

- Adafruit Eight-Channel Bi-directional Logic Level Converter (ID:395; ~$8), which uses the TI TXB0108 Voltage-Level Translator that automatically senses direction (1.2–3.6V or 1.65–5.5V translation). Note that it does not work well with I²C because of the pull-up resistors required. However, it can switch at frequencies greater than 10MHz.

- Watterott Four-Channel Level Shifter (20110451), which uses the BSS138 MOSFET (~$2).

Some of these products are displayed in Figure 8-26. With the exception of the Adafruit eight-channel converter, they all use BSS138 MOSFETs. A small test was performed to check the switching frequency of these devices, as displayed in Figure 8-27, and it is clear from the oscilloscope traces that there are data-switching performance limitations when using these devices that you must factor into your circuit design. In this test, the 3.3V input is switching a 5V level output using a square wave, and it is clear that the output signal is distorted at higher frequencies. For example, when switching at 1MHz, the distortion means that the output signal does not actually reach a 5V level.

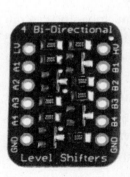

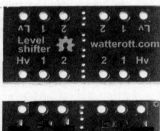

Figure 8-26: Adafruit four-channel, Adafruit eight-channel, and Watterott four-channel logic-level translators

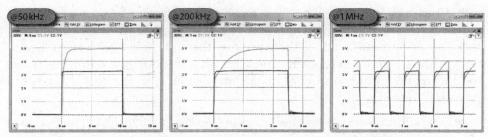

Figure 8-27: Switching BSS138-based translators from 3.3V to 5V logic levels at 50 kHz, 200kHz, and 1MHz

For further information on logic-level shifting techniques in I^{2}C-bus design, see the application notes from NXP (AN97055), which are linked on the chapter web page and also available at `tiny.cc/beagle806`.

Summary

After completing this chapter, you should be able to do the following:

- Describe the most commonly used buses or interfaces that are available on the Beagle boards and choose the correct bus to use for your application
- Configure the Beagle boards to enable I^{2}C, SPI, CAN bus, and UART capabilities
- Attach circuits to a Beagle board that interface to its I^{2}C bus and use the Linux I2C-tools to communicate with those circuits
- Build circuits that interface to the SPI bus using shift registers and write C code that controls low-level SPI communication
- Write C/C++ code that interfaces to and "wraps" the functionality of devices attached to the I^{2}C and SPI buses
- Communicate between UART devices using both Linux tools and custom C code
- Build a basic distributed system that uses UART connections to the board to allow it to be controlled from a desktop PC
- Interface to a low-cost GPS sensor using a UART connection
- Build circuits that interface to the Beagle board CAN buses and use Linux SocketCAN to send and receive messages to and from the bus
- Add logic-level translation circuitry to your circuits to communicate between devices with different logic-level voltages

Further Reading

Documents and links for further reading have been listed throughout this chapter, but here are some further reference documents:

- *The I²C Manual*, Jean-Marc Irazabal and Steve Blozis, Philips Semiconductors, TecForum at DesignCon 2003 in San Jose, CA, on January 27, 2003, at `tiny.cc/beagle807`

- *The Linux I²C Subsystem*, at `i2c.wiki.kernel.org`

- *Serial Programming Guide for POSIX Operating Systems*, 5th ed., Michael R. Sweet, 1994–1999, at `tiny.cc/beagle808`

- *Serial Programming HOWTO*, Gary Frerking, Revision 1.01, at `tiny.cc/beagle809`

Interacting with the Physical Environment

In this chapter, you will learn how to build on your knowledge of GPIO and bus interfacing. In particular, you can combine hardware and software to provide the Beagle boards with the ability to interact with their physical environments in the following three ways: First, by controlling actuators such as motors, the board can affect its environment, which is important for applications such as robotics and home automation. Second, the board can gather information about its physical environment by communicating with sensors. Third, by interfacing to display modules, the board can present information. This chapter explains how each of these interactions can be performed. Physical interaction hardware and software provides you with the capability to build advanced projects, such as to build a robotic platform that can sense and interact with its environment. The chapter finishes with a discussion on how you can build your own C/C++ code libraries and interact with them to build highly scalable projects.

EQUIPMENT REQUIRED FOR THIS CHAPTER:

- Beagle board, DMM, and oscilloscope
- DC motor and H-bridge interface board
- Stepper motor, EasyDriver interface board, and a 5V relay
- Op-amps (LM358, MCP6002/4), diodes, resistors, 5V relay
- TMP36 temperature sensor and Sharp infrared distance sensor

- MCP3208 SPI ADC, op-amp (MCP6002/4), diodes, and resistors
- LCD character display module
- MAX7219 seven-segment display module
- ADXL335 analog three-axis accelerometer

Further details on this chapter are available at www.exploringbeaglebone. com/chapter9/.

Interfacing to Actuators

Electric motors can be controlled by the Beagle boards to make physical devices move or operate. They convert electrical energy into mechanical energy that can be used by devices to act upon their surroundings. A device that converts energy into motion is generally referred to as an *actuator*. Interfacing a board to actuators provides a myriad of application possibilities, including robotic control, home automation (e.g., control of locks, controlling blinds), camera control, unmanned aerial vehicles (UAVs), 3D printer control, and many more.

Electric motors typically provide rotary motion around a fixed axis, which can be used to drive wheels, pumps, belts, electric valves, tracks, turrets, robotic arms, and so on. In contrast to this, *linear actuators* create movement in a straight line, which can be useful for position control in computer numerical control (CNC) machines and 3D printers. In some cases, they convert rotary motion into linear motion using a screw shaft that translates a threaded nut along its length as it rotates. In other cases, a solenoid moves a shaft linearly through the magnetic effects of an electric current.

Three main types of motors are commonly used with embedded Linux boards: servo motors, DC motors, and stepper motors. Table 9-1 provides a summary comparison of these motor types. Interfacing to servo motors (also known as *precision actuators*) through the use of PWM outputs is discussed in Chapter 6, so this section focuses on interfacing to DC motors and stepper motors.

Table 9-1: Summary Comparison of Common Motor Types

	SERVO MOTOR	DC MOTOR	STEPPER MOTOR
Typical application	When high torque, accurate rotation is required.	When fast, continuous rotation is required.	When slow and accurate rotation is required.
Control hardware	Position is controlled through PWM. No controller required. May require PWM tuning.	Speed is controlled through PWM. Additional circuitry required to manage power requirements.	Typically requires a controller to energize stepper coils. A Beagle board can perform this role, but an external controller is preferable and safer.

	SERVO MOTOR	DC MOTOR	STEPPER MOTOR
Control type	Closed-loop, using a built-in controller.	Typically closed-loop using feedback from optical encoders.	Typically open-loop, as movement is precise and steps can be counted.
Features	Known absolute position. Typically, limited angle of rotation.	Can drive large loads. Often geared to provide high torque.	Full torque at standstill. Can rotate a large load at low speeds. Tendency to vibrate.
Example applications	Steering controllers, camera control, and small robotic arms.	Mobile robot movement, fans, water pumps, and electric cars.	CNC machines, 3D printers, scanners, linear actuators, and camera lenses.

The applications discussed in this section often require a secondary power supply, which could be an external battery pack in the case of a mobile platform or a high-current supply for powerful motors. The boards need to be isolated from these supplies; as a result, generic motor controller boards are described here for interfacing to DC motors and stepper motors. Circuitry is also carefully designed for interfacing to relay devices.

WARNING   High-current inductive loads are challenging to interface with the Beagle boards—they invariably require more current than the boards can supply, and they generate voltage spikes that can be extremely harmful to the interfacing circuitry.

DC Motors

DC motors are used in many applications, from toys to advanced robotics. They are ideal motors to use when continuous rotation is required, such as in the wheels of an electric vehicle. Typically, they have only two electrical terminals to which a voltage is applied. The speed of rotation and the direction of rotation can be controlled by varying this voltage. The tendency of a force to rotate an object around its axis is called *torque*, and for a DC motor, torque is generally proportional to the current applied.

The higher the gear ratio, the slower the rotation speed, and the higher the stall torque. For example, the DC motor in Figure 9-1(a) has a no-load speed of 80 revolutions per minute (rpm) and a stall torque of 250oz·in (18 kg·cm).[1] Similarly, if a 70:1 gear ratio is used, the rotation speed becomes 150rpm, but the stall torque reduces to 200oz·in (14.4kg·cm). The DC motor in Figure 9-1(a) has a free-run current of 300mA at 12V, but it has a stall current of 5A—a large current that must be factored into the circuit design.

(a)   (b)

Figure 9-1: (a) A 12V DC motor with an integrated 131¼:1 gearbox ($40), and (b) an integrated counts per revolution (CPR) Hall Effect sensor shaft encoder

Most DC motors require more current than the Beagle boards can supply; therefore, you might be tempted to drive them from your board by simply using a transistor or FET. Unfortunately, this will not work well because of a phenomenon known as inductive kickback, which results in a large voltage spike that is caused by the inertia of current flowing through an inductor (i.e., the motor's coil windings) being suddenly switched off. Even for modest motor power supplies, this large voltage could exceed 1kV for a short period of time. The FETs discussed in Chapter 4 cannot have a drain-source voltage of greater than 60V and will therefore be damaged by such large voltage spikes.

One solution is to place a Zener diode across the drain-source terminals of the FET (or collector-emitter of a transistor). The Zener diode limits the voltage across the drain-source terminals to that of its reverse breakdown voltage. The downside of this configuration is that the ground supply has to sink a large current spike, which could lead to the type of noise in the circuit that is discussed in Chapter 4. With either of these types of protection in place, it is possible to use a Beagle board PWM output to control the speed of the DC motor.

---

[1]DC motor datasheets often do not use SI units, which would be newton-meters (N·m) in this case. It is therefore important to understand the meaning of 250oz·in: Imagine that you fixed a 1-inch metal bar to the motor shaft at 90degrees to the direction of rotation and rotated the shaft until the bar is horizontal to the surface of the Earth. Should you attach a weight of greater than 250ounces to the end of the 1-inch bar, this motor would not be able to rotate its shaft; this is called its stall torque limit. Because 250ounces = 7.08738kg and 1inch = 2.54cm, the conversion to metric units is 7.08738 × 2.54 = 18.002kg·cm (i.e., the torque effect of 18kg at the end of a 1cm bar is equivalent to 7.08738kg at the end of a 1-inch bar—the law of the lever). Also note that 70 × 150rpm = 131.25 × 80rpm = 10,500rpm (the 1:1 rotation speed of the motor). See tiny.cc/ beagle909.

With a PWM duty cycle of 50 percent, the motor will rotate at half the speed that it would if directly connected to the motor supply voltage.

The DC motor in Figure 9-1 has a 64 counts per revolution (CPR) quadrature encoder that is attached to the motor shaft, which means there are 64 × 131.25 = 8,400 counts for each revolution of the geared motor shaft. Shaft encoders are often used with DC motors to determine the position and speed of the motor. For example, the encoder has an output as illustrated in Figure 9-2(a) when rotating clockwise and Figure 9-2(b) when rotating counterclockwise. The frequency of the pulses is proportional to the speed of the motor, and the order of the rising edges in the two output signals describes the direction of rotation. Note that the Hall Effect sensor must be powered, so four of the six motor wires are for the encoder: *A* output (yellow), *B* output (white), encoder power supply (blue), GND (green). The remaining two wires are for the motor power supply (red and black).

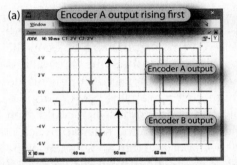 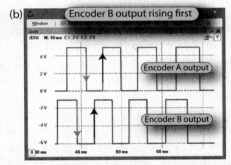

Figure 9-2: The output from the shaft encoder in Figure 9-1(b) when rotating: (a) clockwise, and (b) counterclockwise

An alternative to this configuration is to place a Zener diode across the drain-source terminals of the FET (or collector-emitter of a transistor). The Zener diode limits the voltage across the drain-source terminals to that of its reverse breakdown voltage. The downside of this alternative configuration is that the ground supply has to sink a large current spike, which could lead to the type of noise in the circuit that is discussed in Chapter 4. With either of these types of protection in place, it is possible to use a Beagle board PWM output to control the speed of the DC motor. With a PWM duty cycle of 50 percent, the motor will rotate at half the speed that it would if directly connected to the motor supply voltage.

For *bidirectional motor control*, a circuit configuration called an *H-bridge* can be used, which has a circuit layout in the shape of the letter *H*, as illustrated in Figure 9-3. Notice that it has Zener diodes to protect the four FETs. To drive the motor in a forward (assumed to be clockwise) direction, the top-left and bottom-right FETs can be switched on. This causes a current to flow from the positive to the negative terminal of the DC motor. When the opposing pair of FETs is switched on, current flows from the negative terminal to the positive terminal of the motor and the motor reverses (turns counterclockwise). The motor does not rotate if two opposing FETs are switched off (open circuit).

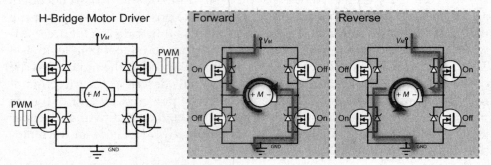

Figure 9-3: Simplified H-bridge description

Four Beagle board PWM header pins could be connected to the H-bridge circuit, but particular care must be taken to ensure that the two FETs on the left side or right side of the circuit are not turned on at the same time, as this would result in a large current (*shoot-through current*)—the motor supply would effectively be shorted (V_M to GND). As high-current capable power supplies are often used for the motor power supply, this is dangerous, as it could even cause a power supply or a battery to explode! An easier and safer approach is to use an H-bridge driver that has already been packaged in an IC, such as the SN754410, a quadruple high-current half-H driver, which can drive 1A at 4.5V to 36V per driver (see `tiny.cc/beagle901`).

Driving Small DC Motors (up to 1.5A)

There are many more recently introduced drivers that can drive even larger currents using smaller package sizes than the SN754410. In this example, a DRV8835 dual low-voltage motor driver carrier on a breakout board ($4) from `www.pololu.com` is used, as illustrated in Figure 9-4. The DRV8835 itself is only 2mm × 3mm in dimension and can drive 1.5A (max) per H-bridge at a motor supply voltage up to 11V. It can be driven with logic levels of 2V to 7V, which enables it to be used directly with a Beagle board.

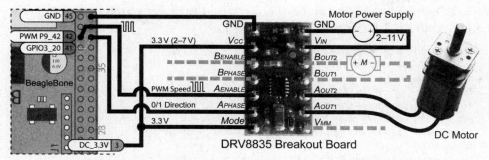

Figure 9-4: Driving a DC motor using an example H-Bridge driver breakout board

The DRV8835 breakout board can be connected to the BeagleBone as illustrated in Figure 9-4. This circuit uses four pins from the BeagleBone:

- P9_3 provides a 3.3V supply for the control logic circuitry.
- P9_45 provides a GND for the logic supply circuitry.
- P9_42 provides a PWM output from the BeagleBone that can be used to control the rotation speed of the motor, as it is connected to the A_{ENABLE} input on the DRV8835.
- P9_41 provides a GPIO output that can be used to set whether the motor is rotating clockwise or counterclockwise, as it is connected to the A_{PHASE} input.

The motor power supply voltage is set according to the specification of the DC motor that is chosen. By tying the *Mode* pin high, the DRV8835 is placed in PHASE/ENABLE mode, which means that one input is used for direction, and the other is used for determining the rotation speed.

> **WARNING** The DRV8835 IC can get hot enough to burn, even while operating within its normal operating parameters. This is a common characteristic of motor driver ICs—so be careful! Heat sinks can be added to dissipate heat, and they have the added advantage of extending the constant run time, as thermal protection circuitry will shut motor driver ICs down to prevent them from overheating when driving large loads.

Controlling a DC Motor Using sysfs

With a circuit wired as shown in Figure 9-4, the DC motor can be controlled using sysfs. In this example, P9_41 (GPIO3_20 = 116) is connected to the A_{PHASE}

input. Therefore, this pin can be enabled, and the motor's direction of rotation can be controlled using the following:

```
debian@ebb:~$ config-pin -a P9_41 out
debian@ebb:~$ config-pin -q P9_41
 P9_41 Mode: gpio Direction: out Value: 0
debian@ebb:~$ cd /sys/class/gpio/gpio116
debian@ebb:/sys/class/gpio/gpio116$ ls
active_low device direction edge label power subsystem uevent value
debian@ebb:/sys/class/gpio/gpio116$ echo out > direction
debian@ebb:/sys/class/gpio/gpio116$ echo 1 > value
debian@ebb:/sys/class/gpio/gpio116$ echo 0 > value
```

The speed of the motor can be controlled using a BeagleBone PWM output. The overlays can be loaded, and the motor can be controlled using the PWM overlay that is associated with P9_42, as follows:

```
debian@ebb:~$ config-pin -l P9_42
default gpio gpio_pu gpio_pd gpio_input spi_cs spi_sclk uart pwm pru_ecap
debian@ebb:~$ config-pin -a P9_42 pwm
debian@ebb:~$ config-pin -q P9_42 pwm
P9_42 Mode: pwm
debian@ebb:~$ cd /sys/class/pwm
debian@ebb:/sys/class/pwm$ ls
pwmchip0  pwmchip1  pwmchip3  pwmchip5  pwmchip6
```

As described in Chapter 6, P9_42 is connected to ECAP0, which is mapped to the pwmchip0 device. This device must be enabled and configured, whereupon modifying the duty cycle will control the rotation speed of the motor.

```
debian@ebb:/sys/class/pwm$ cd pwmchip0
debian@ebb:/sys/class/pwm/pwmchip0$ ls
device export npwm power subsystem uevent unexport
debian@ebb:/sys/class/pwm/pwmchip0$ echo 0 > export
debian@ebb:/sys/class/pwm/pwmchip0$ ls
device  export  npwm  power  pwm-0:0  subsystem  uevent  unexport
debian@ebb:/sys/class/pwm/pwmchip0$ cd pwm-0\:0/
debian@ebb:/sys/class/pwm/pwmchip0/pwm-0:0$ ls
capture  device  duty_cycle  enable  period  polarity  power  subsystem  uevent
debian@ebb:/sys/class/pwm/pwmchip0/pwm-0:0$ sudo sh -c "echo 4000 > period"
debian@ebb:/sys/class/pwm/pwmchip0/pwm-0:0$ sudo sh -c "echo 1000 > duty_cycle"
debian@ebb:/sys/class/pwm/pwmchip0/pwm-0:0$ cat polarity
normal
debian@ebb:/sys/class/pwm/pwmchip0/pwm-0:0$ sudo sh -c "echo 1 > enable"
debian@ebb:/sys/class/pwm/pwmchip0/pwm-0:0$ sudo sh -c "echo 2000 > duty_cycle"
debian@ebb:/sys/class/pwm/pwmchip0/pwm-0:0$ sudo sh -c "echo 4000 > duty_cycle"
debian@ebb:/sys/class/pwm/pwmchip0/pwm-0:0$ sudo sh -c "echo 0 > enable"
```

Here, the PWM frequency is set to 250kHz, and the duty cycle is adjusted from 25 percent to 50 percent and then to 100 percent, changing the rotation speed of the motor accordingly. As with servo motors, DC motors should be controlled with the PWM polarity set to `normal` (as opposed to `inversed`) so that the duty period represents the time when the pulse is high rather than low. The direction of rotation can be adjusted at any stage using the `gpio116` sysfs directory.

Driving Larger DC Motors (Greater than 1.5 A)

The Pololu *Simple Motor Controller* family ($30–$55), illustrated in Figure 9-5(a), supports powerful brushed DC motors with continuous currents of up to 23A and maximum voltages of 34V. It supports USB, TTL serial, analog, and hobby radio-control (RC) PWM interfaces. The controller uses 3.3V logic levels, but it is also 5V tolerant.

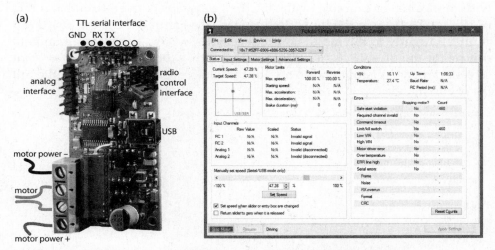

Figure 9-5: (a) The Pololu Simple Motor Controller, and (b) the associated motor configuration tool

Despite its name, this is an advanced controller that can be configured with settings such as maximum acceleration/deceleration, adjustable starting speed, electronic braking, over-temperature threshold/response, etc., which makes it a good choice for larger-scale robotic applications. The controller can be configured using a Windows GUI application, as illustrated in Figure 9-5(b), or by using a Linux command-line user interface. The Windows configuration tool can also be used to monitor motor temperature and voltage conditions and control the speed settings, braking, PWM, communications settings, and so on, over USB, even while the motor is connected to the Beagle board with a TTL serial interface.

The 3.3V TTL serial interface is likely the best option for embedded applications, as it can be used directly with a UART device. A UART device can be utilized for communication, as described in Chapter 8.

> **NOTE**   Connect a power supply to the Simple Motor Controller board before attempting serial communication. The power supply must be sufficient for the controller board, or the red LED will flash to indicate an error state. Also, configure the controller using a Windows machine before connecting it to the board and choose a fixed baud rate of 115,200, rather than choosing the auto-negotiate option.

The Simple Motor Controller can be configured to be in a serial ASCII mode, whereupon it can be controlled using a UART device from the Beagle board with minicom. For example, with ASCII mode enabled and a fixed baud rate of 115,200 (8N1) set in the Input Settings tab (see Figure 9-5(b)), the board can connect directly to the motor controller and issue text-based commands to control the motor, such as V (version), F (forward), B (brake), R (reverse), GO (exit safe-start mode), X (stop), and so on. See the comprehensive manual for the full list of commands (tiny.cc/beagle902).

```
debian@ebb:/dev$ minicom -b 115200 -o -D /dev/ttyO4
V
!161 01.04
GO
.
F 50%
.
B
?
GO
.
R 25%
.
```

The Simple Motor Controller can also be controlled directly using the C/C++ UART communications code that is described in Chapter 8. The configuration tool can be used to set the serial TTL mode to be Binary mode with a baud rate of 115,200. Assuming the motor controller is attached to /dev/ttyO4 (as shown previously), the motor.c code example in the /chp09/simple/ directory can be used to control the motor directly.

```
debian@ebb:~/exploringbb/chp09/simple$ gcc motor.c -o motor
debian@ebb:~/exploringbb/chp09/simple$ ./motor
Starting the motor controller example
Error status: 0x0000
Current Target Speed is 0.
Setting Target Speed to 3200.
```

Controlling a DC Motor Using C++

A C++ class that you can use to control a DC motor is available in the GitHub repository. The constructor expects a named PWM input, which has already been configured via sysfs, and a GPIO object or GPIO number. Listing 9-1 displays the C++ header file for the DCMotor class.

Listing 9-1: library/motor/DCMotor.h

```
class DCMotor {
public:
    enum DIRECTION{ CLOCKWISE, ANTICLOCKWISE };
private:
    ...
public:
    DCMotor(PWM *pwm, GPIO *gpio);
    DCMotor(PWM *pwm, int gpioNumber);
    DCMotor(PWM *pwm, GPIO *gpio, DCMotor::DIRECTION direction);
    DCMotor(PWM *pwm, int gpioNumber, DCMotor::DIRECTION direction);
    DCMotor(PWM *pwm, GPIO *gpio, DCMotor::DIRECTION direction, float speedPercent);
    DCMotor(PWM *pwm, int gpioNumber, DCMotor::DIRECTION direction, float speedPercent);
    virtual void go();
    virtual void setSpeedPercent(float speedPercent);
    virtual float getSpeedPercent() { return this->speedPercent; }
    virtual void setDirection(DIRECTION direction);
    virtual DIRECTION getDirection() { return this->direction; }
    virtual void reverseDirection();
    virtual void stop();
    virtual void setDutyCyclePeriod(unsigned int period_ns);
    virtual ~DCMotor();
};
```

An example application that uses the DCMotor class is provided in Listing 9-2. Notice that the header file is in the motor subdirectory.

Listing 9-2: /chp09/dcmotor/DCMotorApp.cpp

```
#include <iostream>
#include <unistd.h>
#include "motor/DCMotor.h"
using namespace std;
using namespace exploringBB;

int main(){
    cout << "Starting EBB DC Motor Example" << endl;
    DCMotor dcm(new PWM("pwmchip0/pwm-0:0/"), 116); // exports GPIO116
    dcm.setDirection(DCMotor::ANTICLOCKWISE);
```

```
    dcm.setSpeedPercent(50.0f);    //make it clear that a float is passed
    dcm.go();
    cout << "Rotating Anticlockwise at 50% speed" << endl;
    usleep(5000000);    //sleep for 5 seconds
    dcm.reverseDirection();
    cout << "Rotating clockwise at 50% speed" << endl;
    usleep(5000000);
    dcm.setSpeedPercent(100.0f);
    cout << "Rotating clockwise at 100% speed" << endl;
    usleep(5000000);
    dcm.stop();
    cout << "End of EBB DC Motor Example" << endl;
}
```

The build script assumes that the example application source is in /exporingbb/chp09/dcmotor/ and that the shared library and header files are in the directory /exploringbb/library/. This conforms to the directory structure of the GitHub repository. The code can be built using the build script that is in the dcmotor directory and executed using the following:

```
debian@ebb:~/exploringbb/chp09/dcmotor$ more build
#!/bin/bash
g++ DCMotorApp.cpp ../../library/libEBBLibrary.so -o DCApp -I "../../library"
debian@ebb:~/exploringbb/chp09/dcmotor$ ./build
debian@ebb:~/exploringbb/chp09/dcmotor$ ls
DCApp  DCMotorApp.cpp  build
debian@ebb:~/exploringbb/chp09/dcmotor$ sudo ./DCApp
Starting EBB DC Motor Example
Rotating Anti-clockwise at 50% speed
Rotating clockwise at 50% speed
Rotating clockwise at 100% speed
End of EBB DC Motor Example
```

At the end of this chapter a description is provided that shows how to build code into dynamic libraries, such as libEBBLibrary.so. This enables you to alter the library to suit your requirements.

Stepper Motors

Unlike DC motors, which rotate continuously when a DC voltage is applied, *stepper motors* normally rotate in discrete fixed-angle steps. For example, the stepper motor that is used in this chapter rotates with 200 *steps per revolution* and therefore has a *step angle* of 1.8°. The motor steps each time a pulse is applied to its input, so the speed of rotation is proportional to the rate at which pulses are applied.

Stepper motors can be positioned accurately, as they typically have a positioning error of less than 5 percent of a step (i.e., typically ±0.1°). The error does not accumulate over multiple steps, so stepper motors can be controlled in an open-loop form, without the need for feedback. Unlike servo motors, but like DC motors, the absolute position of the shaft is not known without the addition of devices like rotary encoders, which often include an absolute position reference that can be located by performing a single shaft rotation.

Stepper motors, as illustrated in Figure 9-6(a), have toothed permanent magnets that are fixed to a rotating shaft, called *the rotor*. The rotor is surrounded by coils (grouped into *phases*) that are fixed to the stationary body of the motor (*the stator*). The coils are electromagnets that, when energized, attract the toothed shaft teeth in a clockwise or counterclockwise direction, depending on the order in which the coils are activated, as illustrated in Figure 9-6(b) for full-step drive.

- **Full step:** Two phases always on (max torque).
- **Half step:** Double the step resolution. Alternates between two phases on and a single phase on (torque at about 3/4 max).
- **Microstep:** Uses sine and cosine waveforms for the phase currents to step the motor rather than the on/off currents illustrated in Figure 9-6(b) and thus allows for higher step resolutions (though the torque is significantly reduced).

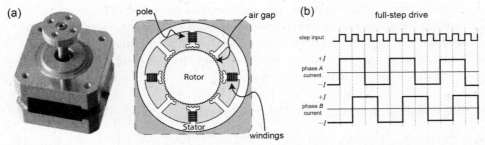

Figure 9-6: (a) Stepper motor external and internal structure; (b) full- and half-step drive signals

The EasyDriver Stepper Motor Driver

An easy way to generate the stepper motor pulse signals is to use a stepper-motor driver board. The EasyDriver board (illustrated in Figure 9-7) is a low-cost (~$15) open-hardware stepper motor driver board that is widely available. It can be used to drive four-, six-, and eight-wire stepper motors. The board has an output drive capability of between 7V and 30V at ±750mA per phase. The board uses the Allegro A3967 Microstepping Driver with Translator, which allows for full, half, quarter, and one-eighth step microstepping modes. In addition, the board can be driven with 5V or 3.3V logic levels, which makes it an ideal board for use with the Beagle boards. For 3.3V logic control levels, there is a jumper (SJ2) that has to be solder bridged.

WARNING   Do not disconnect a motor from the EasyDriver board while it is powered, as it may destroy the board.

Figure 9-7: Driving a stepper motor using the open-hardware EasyDriver board

The merit in examining this board is that many boards can be used for higher-powered stepper motors that have a similar design.

NOTE   If you don't have access to a datasheet for a stepper motor (e.g., you rescued it from an old printer), you can determine the connections to the coils by removing any power source, shorting pairs of wires, and rotating the motor. If there is noticeable resistance to rotation for a particular shorted pairing, then you have identified the connections to a coil. You cannot determine the coils using the colors of the wires alone, as there is no standard format.

A Beagle Board Stepper Motor Driver Circuit

The EasyDriver board can be connected to the PocketBeagle as illustrated in Figure 9-8, using GPIOs for each of the control signals. The pins on the EasyDriver board are described in Figure 9-7, and a table is provided in the figure for the MS1/MS2 inputs. A C++ class called `StepperMotor` is available that accepts alternative GPIO numbers.

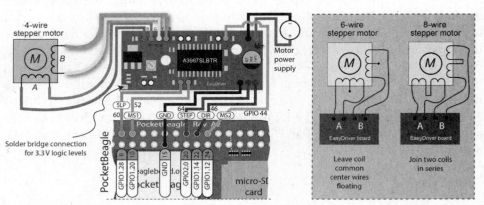

Figure 9-8: Driving a stepper motor using the PocketBeagle and the EasyDriver interface board

Controlling a Stepper Motor Using C++

Listing 9-3 presents the description of a class that can be used to control the EasyDriver board using five PocketBeagle GPIO pins. This code can be adapted to drive most types of stepper driver boards from any Beagle board.

Listing 9-3: /library/motor/StepperMotor.h (Segment)

```
class StepperMotor {
public:
    enum STEP_MODE { STEP_FULL, STEP_HALF, STEP_QUARTER, STEP_EIGHT };
    enum DIRECTION { CLOCKWISE, ANTICLOCKWISE };
private:
    // The GPIO pins MS1, MS2 (Microstepping options), STEP (The low->high step)
    // SLP (Sleep - active low) and DIR (Direction)
    GPIO *gpio_MS1, *gpio_MS2, *gpio_STEP, *gpio_SLP, *gpio_DIR;
    ...
public:
    StepperMotor(GPIO *gpio_MS1, GPIO *gpio_MS2, GPIO *gpio_STEP, GPIO *gpio_SLP,
             GPIO *gpio_DIR, int speedRPM = 60, int stepsPerRevolution = 200);
    StepperMotor(int gpio_MS1, int gpio_MS2, int gpio_STEP, int gpio_SLP,
             int gpio_DIR, int speedRPM = 60, int stepsPerRevolution = 200);
    virtual void   step();
    virtual void   step(int numberOfSteps);
    virtual int    threadedStepForDuration(int numberOfSteps, int duration_ms);
    virtual void   threadedStepCancel() { this->threadRunning = false; }
    virtual void   rotate(float degrees);
    virtual void   setDirection(DIRECTION direction);
    virtual DIRECTION getDirection() { return this->direction; }
    virtual void   reverseDirection();
    virtual void   setStepMode(STEP_MODE mode);
    virtual STEP_MODE getStepMode() { return stepMode; }
    virtual void   setSpeed(float rpm);
    virtual float  getSpeed() { return speed; }
    virtual void   setStepsPerRevolution(int steps) { stepsPerRevolution = steps; }
    virtual int    getStepsPerRevolution() { return stepsPerRevolution; }
    virtual void   sleep();
    virtual void   wake();
    virtual bool   isAsleep() { return asleep; }
    virtual ~StepperMotor();
    ...   //Full code available in /library/motor/StepperMotor.h
};
```

The library code is used in Listing 9-4 to create a `StepperMotor` object and rotate the motor counterclockwise 10 times at full-step resolution. It then uses a threaded step function to microstep the stepper motor clockwise for one full revolution over five seconds at one-eighth step resolution.

Listing 9-4: /chp09/stepper/StepperMotorApp.cpp

```cpp
#include <iostream>
#include <unistd.h>
#include "motor/StepperMotor.h"
using namespace std;
using namespace exploringBB;

int main(){
   cout << "Starting EBB Stepper Motor Example:" << endl;
   //Using 5 GPIOs, RPM=60 and 200 steps per revolution
   //MS1=52, MS2=44, STEP=64, SLP=60, DIR=46
   StepperMotor m(52,44,64,60,46,60,200);
   m.setDirection(StepperMotor::ANTICLOCKWISE);
   m.setStepMode(StepperMotor::STEP_FULL);
   m.setSpeed(100);   //rpm
   cout << "Rotating 10 times at 100 rpm anti-clockwise, full step..." << endl;
   m.rotate(3600.0f);    //in degrees
   cout << "Finished regular (non-threaded) rotation)" << endl;
   m.setDirection(StepperMotor::CLOCKWISE);
   cout << "Performing 1 threaded revolution in 5 seconds using micro-stepping:" << endl;
   m.setStepMode(StepperMotor::STEP_EIGHT);
   if(m.threadedStepForDuration(1600, 5000)<0){
      cout << "Failed to start the Stepper Thread" << endl;
   }
   cout << "Thread should now be running..." << endl;
      for(int i=0; i<10; i++){ // sleep for 10 seconds.
      usleep(1000000);
      cout << i+1 << " seconds has passed..." << endl;
   }
   m.sleep();    // cut power to the stepper motor
   cout << "End of Stepper Motor Example" << endl;
}
```

After calling the associated build script, the program can be executed and should result in the following output:

```
debian@ebb:~/exploringbb/chp09/stepper$ ./StepperApp
Starting EBB Stepper Motor Example:
Rotating 10 times at 100 rpm anti-clockwise, full step...
Finished regular (non-threaded) rotation)
Performing 1 threaded revolution in 5 seconds using micro-stepping:
Thread should now be running...
1 seconds has passed...
2 seconds has passed...
...
10 seconds has passed...
End of Stepper Motor Example
```

It is important to note that the threaded revolution completes the revolution after five seconds. The counter continues for a further five seconds, during which time a holding torque is applied. The final call to `m.sleep()` removes power from the stepper motor coils, thus removing holding torque.

It is possible to further reduce the number of pins that are used in this motor controller example by using 74HC595 ICs and the SPI bus, as described in Chapter 8.

Relays

Traditional relays are electromechanical switches that are typically used to control a high-voltage/high-current signal using a low-voltage/low-current signal. They are constructed to enable a low-powered circuit to apply a magnetic force to an internal movable switch. The internal switch can turn on or turn off a second circuit that often contains a high-powered DC or AC load. The relay itself is chosen according to the power requirements; whether the circuit is designed so that the high-powered circuit is normally powered or normally disabled; and the number of circuits being switched in parallel.

Electromechanical relays (EMRs) are prone to switch bounce and mechanical fatigue, so they have a limited life span, particularly if they are switched constantly at frequencies of more than a few times per minute. Rapid switching of EMRs can also cause them to overheat. More recent, solid-state relays (SSRs) are electronic switches that consist of FETs, thyristors, and opto-couplers. They have no moving parts and therefore have longer life spans and higher maximum switching frequencies (about 1kHz). The downside is that SSRs are more expensive, and they are prone to failure (often in the switched "on" state) because of overloading or improper wiring. They are typically installed with heat sinks and fast-blow fuses on the load circuit.

EMRs and SSRs are available that can switch high currents and voltages. That makes them particularly useful for applications such as smart home installations, the control of mains-powered devices, motor vehicle applications for switching high-current DC loads, and powering high-current inductive loads in robotic applications. **Importantly, wiring mains applications is for expert users only, as even low currents coupled with high voltages can be fatal. Please seek local professional advice if dealing in any way with high currents or high voltages, including, but not limited to, AC mains voltages.**

Figure 9-9(a) illustrates the type of circuit that can be used to interface the PocketBeagle to a relay. It is important that the relay chosen is capable of being switched at 5V and that, like the motor circuit in Figure 9-3, a flyback diode is placed in parallel to the relay's inductive load to protect the FET from damage. Pololu (www.pololu.com) sells a small SPDT relay kit (~$4), as illustrated in Figure 9-9(b), that can be used to switch 8A currents at 30V DC using an Omron G5LE power relay. The breakout board contains a BSS138 FET, the flyback diode, and LEDs that indicate when the relay is switched to enable—that is, close the circuit connected to the normally open (NO) output.

Figure 9-9: (a) Controlling a relay using the PocketBeagle; (b) example relay breakout boards

The relay can be connected to a regular GPIO for control. For example, if the relay were connected as shown in Figure 9-9(a) to P2.17 (GPIO2.1), which is GPIO 65, then it can be switched using the following:

```
debian@ebb:/sys/class/gpio/gpio65$ echo out > direction
debian@ebb:/sys/class/gpio/gpio65$ cat value
0
debian@ebb:/sys/class/gpio/gpio65$ echo 1 > value
debian@ebb:/sys/class/gpio/gpio65$ echo 0 > value
```

WARNING   The circuit in Figure 9-9(a) is intended for connection to low-voltage supplies only (e.g., 12V supplies). High voltages can be extremely dangerous to human health, and only suitably trained individuals with appropriate safety equipment and taking professional precautions should wire mains-powered devices. Suitable insulation, protective enclosures, or additional protective devices such as fuses or circuit breakers (possibly including both current-limiting circuit breakers and earth-leakage circuit breakers) may be required to prevent creating either a shock or a fire hazard. Seek advice from a qualified electrician before installing mains-powered home automation circuitry.

Interfacing to Analog Sensors

A *transducer* is a device that converts variations in one form of energy into proportional variations in another form of energy. For example, a microphone is an acoustic transducer that converts variations in sound waves into proportional variations in an electrical signal. In fact, actuators are also transducers, as they convert electrical energy into mechanical energy.

Transducers, the main role of which is to convert information about the physical environment into electrical signals (voltages or currents), are called *sensors*. Sensors may contain additional circuitry to further condition the electrical signal (e.g., by filtering out noise or averaging values over time), and this combination is often referred to as an *instrument*. The terms *sensor, transducer,* and *instrument* are in fact often used interchangeably, so too much should not be read into the distinctions between them. Interfacing to sensors enables you to build an incredibly versatile range of project types using the Beagle boards, some of which are described in Table 9-2.

Table 9-2: Example Analog Sensor Types and Applications

MEASURE	APPLICATIONS	EXAMPLE SENSORS
Temperature	Smart home, weather monitoring.	TMP36 temperature sensor. MAX6605 low-power temperature sensor.
Light Level	Home automation, display contrast adjustment.	Mini photocell/photodetector (PDV-P8001).
Distance	Robotic navigation, reversing sensing.	Sharp infrared proximity sensors (e.g., GP2D12).
Touch	User interfaces, proximity detection.	Capacitive touch. The AM335x ADC has touchscreen functionality.
Acceleration	Determine orientation, impact detection.	Accelerometer (ADXL335). Gyroscope (LPR530) detects change in orientation.
Sound	Speech recording and recognition, UV meters.	Electret microphone (MAX9814), MEMS microphone (ADMP401).
Magnetic Fields	Noncontact current measurement, home security, noncontact switches.	100A Non-invasive current sensor (SCT-013-000). Hall effect and reed switches. Linear magnetic field sensor (AD22151).
Motion Detection	Home security, wildlife photography.	PIR Motion Sensor (SE-10).

The ADXL345 I²C/SPI digital accelerometer is discussed in Chapter 8, and Table 9-2 identifies another accelerometer, the ADXL335, which is an analog accelerometer. Essentially, the ADXL345 digital accelerometer is an analog sensor that also contains filtering circuitry, analog-to-digital conversion, and input/output circuitry. It is quite often the case that both analog and digital sensors are available that can perform similar tasks. Table 9-3 provides a summary comparison of digital versus analog sensors.

Table 9-3: Comparison of Typical Digital and Analog Sensor Devices

DIGITAL SENSORS	ANALOG SENSORS
ADC is handled by the sensor, freeing up limited microcontroller ADC inputs.	Provide continuous voltage output and capability for fast sampling rates.
The real-time issues surrounding embedded Linux, such as variable sampling periods, are not as significant.	Typically less expensive but may require external components to configure the sensor parameters.
Often contain advanced filters that can be configured and controlled via registers.	Output is generally easy to understand without the need for complex datasheets.
Bus interfaces allow for the connection of many sensor devices.	Relatively easy to interface.
Less susceptible to noise.	

Digital sensors typically have more advanced features (e.g., the ADXL345 has double-tap and free-fall detection), but at a greater cost and level of complexity. Many sensors are not available in a digital package, so it is important to understand how to connect analog sensors to your Beagle board. Ideally, the analog sensor that you connect should not have to be sampled at a rate of thousands of times per second, or it will add significant CPU overhead.

> **WARNING**   You must be particularly careful when connecting powered sensors to the Beagle board ADC inputs, as the ADC contains sensitive circuitry that can be easily damaged by going outside its limits (e.g., 0V to 1.8V). You should not sink current to or source current from the ADC inputs or voltage reference pins.

Protecting the ADC Inputs

The Beagle board ADC is easily damaged as it is primarily intended to be a touchscreen controller for the AM335x, rather than a general-purpose ADC. In addition, many of the analog sensors that are described in Table 9-2 require 3.3V or 5V supplies. This is a particular concern when prototyping a new sensor interface circuit, as one connection mistake could physically damage the board. The ADC inputs do have some internal circuitry for protection, but it is not designed to carry even a modest current for more than short periods of time. The internal circuitry is mainly present for electrostatic discharge (ESD) protection, rather than to be relied on for clamping input signals. Therefore, external circuit protection is useful in preventing damage.

Diode Clamping

Figure 9-10(a) illustrates a simple *diode clamping* circuit that is typically used to limit voltage levels applied to ADCs. The circuit consists of two diodes and a current limiting resistor. The diodes are reverse biased when the voltage level is within the range 0V to *Vref*. Current flows to the notional AIN0 input, and the circuit behaves correctly as illustrated in Figure 9-10(b) when a sine wave is applied (V_{IN}) that oscillates within the 0V to *Vref* range. However, if V_{IN} exceeds the *Vref* level (plus the forward voltage drop of the diode), then the upper diode is forward biased and current would flow to the *Vref* rail. If *Vref* is 1.8V and silicon diodes are used (~0.7V forward voltage), then this signal will be clamped at 2.5V. For the lower diode, if V_{IN} falls below 0V–0.7V, then the diode will be forward biased and AGND will source current. The resistor *R* can be used to limit the upper current level. The resulting clamped output is illustrated in Figure 9-10(c) when a sine wave is applied to the input that exceeds the permitted range.

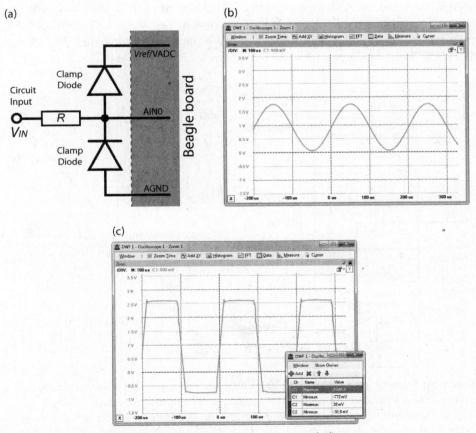

Figure 9-10: A typical diode clamping circuit (not recommended)

The clamping circuit in Figure 9-10(a) is not recommended for use with the AM335x for two reasons. First, the forward voltage drop of a typical silicon diode extends the nonclamped range to approximately -0.7V to 2.5V, which is well outside acceptable levels. More expensive Schottky diodes can be used that have a forward voltage drop of about 0.25V at 2mA and 25°C (e.g., the 1N5817G). These would bring the effective output range to about -0.25V to 2.05V, which is better but still not ideal. The second reason is that when clamping occurs, the current would need to be sourced from or sinked to the Beagle board's AGND or *Vref* rails. Sinking current to the *Vref* rail could damage the *Vref* input and/ or affect the reference voltage level. However, diode clamping is preferable to no protection whatsoever.

Op-Amp Clamping

A recommended circuit to protect the ADC circuitry is presented in Figure 9-11(a). While it appears complex, it is reasonably easy to connect, as it requires only three ICs and seven resistors to protect all seven or eight AINs. This voltage follower circuit uses a 5V powered single op-amp package to provide a 1.8V voltage reference source to an array of low-voltage op-amps. The Microchip MCP6001/2 or LM358 can be used for this voltage supply task.

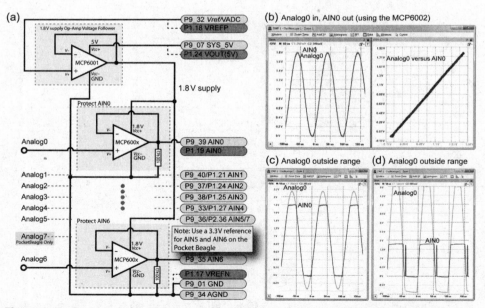

Figure 9-11: Protecting the ADC inputs using 1.8V powered op-amps (recommended); (a) the circuit to protect all analog inputs on the BeagleBone and PocketBeagle boards; (b) linear response characteristic; (c) clipped response to an out-of-range input; and (d) clipped response to a significantly out-of-range input

An array of modern op-amps, supplied at 1.8V (i.e., V_{CC+} = 1.8V), are config-ured in voltage follower configuration and placed in front of each of the ADC inputs AIN0 to AIN6/7. You can use a 3.3V reference voltage for the AIN5 and AIN6 inputs on the PocketBeagle.

These op-amps are supplied with $V_{DD} = V_{CC+} = 1.8V$ and $V_{SS} = V_{CC-}$ = GND, so it is not possible for their output voltage levels to exceed the range 0V to 1.8V. The MCP600x is a low-cost DIP packaged op-amp that is suitable for this role. In particular, the MCP6004 has four op-amps within the one package, so only two MCP6004s (plus the 1.8V supply circuit op-amp) are required to protect all seven/eight ADC inputs.

Figure 9-11(b) illustrates the behavior of this circuit when a 0.9V amplitude sine wave (biased at +0.9V) is applied to the Analog0 circuit input. The output signal overlays precisely on the input signal. Older op-amps (including the LM358) would have difficulty with this type of *rail-to-rail operation* (i.e., 0V to 1.8V) and would behave in a nonlinear way near the rail voltages. As shown in the plot of the Analog0 input versus the AIN0 output in Figure 9-11(b), there is a strong linear relationship, even at the supply rail voltage levels. Figure 9-11(c) and (d) illustrate the consequence of the input signal (accidently) exceeding the allowable range. In both cases the output is clamped to the 0V to 1.8V range and the AM335x ADC is protected, though (of course) the signal input to the ADC is distorted.

The circuit can be connected to the Beagle board as illustrated in Figure 9-11(a), and its impact can be evaluated in a terminal using the following steps (e.g., on the PocketBeagle):

```
debian@ebb:~$ cd /sys/bus/iio/devices/iio\:device0
debian@ebb:/sys/bus/iio/devices/iio:device0$ ls
buffer            in_voltage2_raw  in_voltage6_raw  power
dev               in_voltage3_raw  in_voltage7_raw  scan_elements
in_voltage0_raw   in_voltage4_raw  name             subsystem
in_voltage1_raw   in_voltage5_raw  of_node          uevent
```

Setting the DC voltage levels at Analog0 (P1.19) to be 0V (P1.19 connected to P1.17 VREFN), 0.9V, 1.8V, and 2.1V results in the respective raw input values from the 12-bit ADC (0-4095) as follows:

```
debian@ebb:/sys/bus/iio/devices/iio:device0$ cat in_voltage0_raw
0
debian@ebb:/sys/bus/iio/devices/iio:device0$ cat in_voltage0_raw
2107
debian@ebb:/sys/bus/iio/devices/iio:device0$ cat in_voltage0_raw
4026
debian@ebb:/sys/bus/iio/devices/iio:device0$ cat in_voltage0_raw
4024
```

The 100 kΩ resistor ensures that current flows to GND through the resistor rather than through the AINx input. (For your reference, the Touchscreen Controller

ADC functional block diagram is shown in Figure 12-2 of the *AM335x TRM*.) The AM335x datasheet at `tiny.cc/beagle903` provides further details about the limitations of the AM335x ADC.

EXTERNAL ANALOG TO DIGITAL CONVERTERS

The internal ADC circuitry described in this section can be easily damaged by incorrect usage (e.g., sourcing/sinking excessive current). Therefore, replaceable external ADCs are a good choice for prototyping work, even when an internal ADC is available.

There are ADCs available that can be used with the I²C bus (e.g., the ADS1015), but the SPI bus is preferable for this application, especially for sampling a sensor output at moderately high data rates. This discussion is focused on two families of SPI ADCs that are produced by Microchip, the MCP300x 10-bit and the MCP320x 12-bit families. Each of these families has discrete ICs with different numbers of input channels—for example, the MCP320x has one-channel (MCP3201), two-channel (MCP3202), four-channel (MCP3204), and eight-channel (MCP3208) variants.

The MCP3208 is the most capable device in the two families of ADCs as it supports eight 12-bit successive approximation ADC channels. It is chosen for this discussion for that reason and the fact that it is a low-cost (~$3) device that is widely available in PDIP form. It is suitable for interfacing to the Beagle boards as it can be powered at 3.3V and has an SPI interface. It is capable of sampling at ~75,000 samples per second (ksps) and has a differential nonlinearity of ±1 LSB. By default, the MCP3208 supports eight single-ended inputs, but it can be programmed to provide four pseudodifferential input pairs.[2] Table 9-4 describes the input/output pins of the 16-pin IC. The full datasheet is available at `tiny.cc/beagle904`.

Table 9-4: Input/Output Pins for the MCP3208

IC PINS	PIN TITLE	DESCRIPTION
Pins 1-8	CH0-CH7	The eight ADC input channels.
Pin 9	DGND	Digital ground—connected to the internal digital ground. Can be connected to the Beagle board GND.
Pin 10	CS/SHDN	Chip Select/Shutdown—used to initiate communication with the device when pulled low. When pulled high it ends the conversation. Must be pulled high between conversions.

---

[2]Single-ended ADC inputs share a common reference ground. Differential inputs are applied to the ADC in pairs (IN+, IN−), which are compared against each other to determine the ADC value. This is particularly beneficial for the common-mode rejection of coupled noise, which could cause single-ended inputs to exceed their range. Please note that there is also a MCP330x family of 13-bit differential input SPI ADCs that can also be used in the way that is described in this discussion.

IC PINS	PIN TITLE	DESCRIPTION
Pin 11	D_{IN} (MOSI)	Used to configure the ADC by selecting the input to use, and whether to use single-ended or differential inputs.
Pin 12	D_{OUT} (MISO)	The data output sends the results of the ADC back to the Beagle board. The data bit changes on the falling edge of the clock cycle.
Pin 13	CLK	The SPI clock is used to synchronize communication. A clock rate of greater than 10KHz should be maintained to avoid introducing linearity errors.
Pin 14	AGND	Analog ground—connected to the internal analog circuit GND.
Pin 15	V_{REF}	Reference voltage input.
Pin 16	V_{DD}	Voltage Supply (2.7V–5.5V). Can be connected directly to the Beagle board 3.3V supply rail, but not to the 5V supply without adding logic-level translation circuitry to the D_{OUT} pin.

The **TMP36** (`tiny.cc/beagle905`) **is a low-cost precision analog temperature sensor that provides a voltage output that is linearly proportional to the temperature. The TMP36 has a typical accuracy of ±1°C at +25°C. It can be powered at between 2.7V and 5.5V and is available in a three-pin TO-92 package, which makes it suitable for prototyping work.**

The TMP36 provides an output of 750mV at 25°C. It has a linear output, where the output scale factor is 10mV/°C. This means that the minimum output voltage is 0.75V – (65 × 0.01V) = 0.1V, and the maximum output voltage is 0.75V + (100 × 0.01V) = 1.75V. The sensor output current will be between 0µA and 50µA, depending on the input impedance of the device to which it is attached. The high input impedance of the MCP3208 ADC means that current supplied is only a few nanoamps.

The C/C++ code required to convert the ADC value to a temperature in degrees Celsius is expressed in C code as follows:

```
float getTemperature(int adc_value) {                 // from the datasheet
    float cur_voltage = adc_value * (3.30f/4096.0f); // Vcc = 3.3V, 12-bit
    float diff_degreesC = (cur_voltage-0.75f)/0.01f; // how many 0.01V steps?
    return (25.0f + diff_degreesC);
}
```

Figure 9-12 illustrates the circuit that can be used to connect the TMP36 to the PocketBeagle via the MCP3208 family of SPI ADCs. You can use a 10-bit ADC, but you will need to change the value in the temperature calculation code above from 4,096 (i.e., 2^{12}) to 1,024 (i.e., 2^{10}). The full code example is available in the code segment below. This code uses the `SPIDevice` C++ class that is described in Chapter 8.

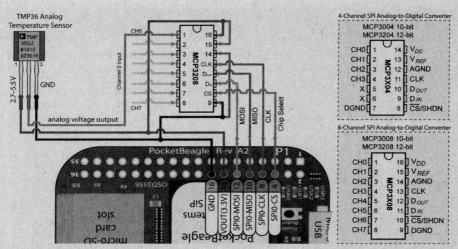

Figure 9-12: The PocketBeagle SPI ADC circuit and its connection to the TMP36 analog temperature sensor

```cpp
#include <iostream>
#include "bus/SPIDevice.h"
using namespace exploringBB;
using namespace std;

float getTemperature(int adc_value) {      // from the TMP36 datasheet
   float cur_voltage = adc_value * (3.30f/4096.0f); // Vcc = 3.3V, 12-bit
   float diff_degreesC = (cur_voltage-0.75f)/0.01f;
   return (25.0f + diff_degreesC);
}


int main(){
   std::cout << "Starting the TMP36 example" << std::endl;
   SPIDevice *busDevice = new SPIDevice(0,0);
   busDevice->setSpeed(5000000);
   busDevice->setMode(SPIDevice::MODE0);
   unsigned char send[3], receive[3];
   send[0] = 0b00000110;       // Reading single-ended input from channel 0
   send[1] = 0b00000000;
   busDevice->transfer(send, receive, 3);
   float temp = getTemperature(((receive[1]&0b00001111)<<8)|receive[2]);
   float fahr = 32 + ((temp * 9)/5);     // convert deg. C to deg. F
   cout << "Temperature is " << temp << "°C (" << fahr << "°F)" << endl;
   busDevice->close();
}
```

This code can be built and executed as follows:

```
debian@ebb:~/exploringbb/chp09/tmp36$ ./build
debian@ebb:~/exploringbb/chp09/tmp36$ ./tmp36
Starting the TMP36 example
Temperature is 23.1543°C (73.6777°F)
```

Analog Sensor Signal Conditioning

One of the problems with analog sensors is that they may have output signal voltage levels quite different from those required by the AM335x ADC. For example, the Sharp GP2D12 distance sensor that is used as an example in this section outputs a DC voltage of ~2.6V when it detects an object at a distance of 10cm and of ~0.4V when the object is detected at a distance of 80cm. If this sensor is connected to the clamping circuit in Figure 9-11(a), the AM335x ADC would not be damaged, but the sensing distance range would be reduced by clamping.

Signal conditioning is the term used to describe the manipulation of an analog signal so that it is suitable for the next stage of processing. To condition a sensor output as an input to the Beagle boards, this often means ensuring that the signal's range is less than 1.8V, with a DC bias of +0.9V.

Scaling Using Voltage Division

The voltage divider circuit described at the beginning of Chapter 4 can be used to condition a sensor output. If the output voltage from the sensor is greater than 1.8V but not less than 0V, then a voltage divider circuit can be used to linearly reduce the voltage to remain within a 0V–1.8V range.

Figure 9-13 illustrates a voltage division circuit and its integration with the 1.8V op-amp protection circuitry discussed in the previous section. Voltage follower circuits also act as *buffer* circuits. The maximum input impedance of the AM335x ADC inputs ranges from about 76kΩ at the highest frequencies to many megaohms at low frequencies.[3] The voltage divider circuit will further load the sensor output impedance (perhaps requiring further unity-gain buffers before the voltage divider). However, the MCP6002 will act as a buffer that prevents the sensor circuit from exceeding the maximum input impedance of the ADC (remember that ideal voltage follower circuits have infinite input impedance and zero output impedance). There are some important points to note about this circuit:

- Resistors have a manufacturing tolerance (often 5%–10% of the resistance value), which will affect the scaling accuracy of the voltage division circuit. You may need to experiment with combinations or use a potentiometer to adjust the resistance ratio.

- A capacitor C_1 can be added across V_{OUT} to reduce noise if required. The value of C_1 can be chosen according to the value of R_1 and the desired

---

[3]The input impedance varies according to the function: Impedance $(\Omega) = (1/((65.97 \times 10^{-12} \times f)))$ (Texas Instruments, 2013).

cutoff frequency f_C, according to the equation $R_{12}C_1 = 1 / (2\pi \times f_c)$, where $R_{12} = R_1 \| R_2$. (i.e., R_1 in parallel with R_2). There is an example in the next section.

- With multi-op-amp packages, unused inputs should be connected as shown in Figure 9-13 (in light gray) to avoid random switching noise.

This circuit works well for linearly scaling down an input signal, but it would not work for a zero-centered or negatively biased input signal. For that, a more general and slightly more complex op-amp circuit is required.

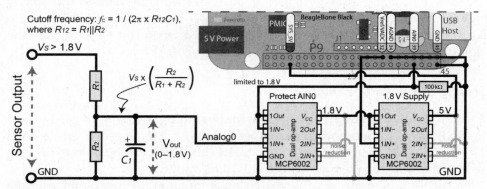

Figure 9-13: Scaling an input signal using voltage division with op-amp ADC protection in place

Signal Offsetting and Scaling

Figure 9-14(a) provides a general op-amp circuit that can be used to set the gain and offset of an input signal. Do not connect this circuit directly to the Beagle board—it is designed as an adjustable prototyping circuit to use in conjunction with an oscilloscope to design a fixed-signal conditioning circuit for your particular application. Some notes on this circuit:

- The *Vcc*- input of the op-amp is tied to GND, which is representative of the type of circuit that is built using the Beagle boards, as a –5V rail is not readily available.

- If an LM358 is used, then a load resistor is required to prevent the output from being clamped below 0.7V. According to the National Semiconductor Corporation (1994), "the LM358 output voltage needs to raise approximately one diode drop above ground to bias the on-chip vertical PNP transistor for output current sinking applications."

- The 1.8V level can be provided by the analog voltage reference on the Beagle boards, but do not connect it without the use of a voltage follower circuit as shown earlier. Alternatively, a voltage divider could be used with the 5V rail.

▪ A 100nF decoupling capacitor can be used on the V_{IN} input to remove the DC component of the incoming sensor signal. However, for many sensor circuits, the DC component of the sensor signal is important and should not be removed.

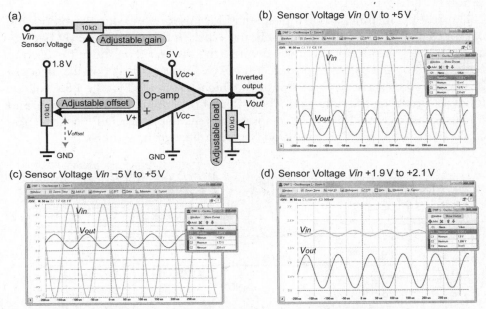

Figure 9-14: (a) A general op-amp signal conditioning circuit that inverts the input; (b) conditioned output when Vin is 0V to 5V; (c) output when Vin is −5V to +5V; (d) conditioned and amplified output when the input signal is 1.9V to 2.1V

The circuit in Figure 9-14(a) amplifies (or attenuates), offsets, and inverts the input signal according to the settings of the potentiometers:

▪ The gain is set using the adjustable gain potentiometer, where $V_- = G \times V_{IN}$.

▪ The offset is set using the adjustable offset potentiometer. This can be used to center the output signal at 0.9V.

▪ The output voltage is approximately $V_{OUT} = V_+ - V_- = offset - (G \times V_{IN})$. As such, the output is an inverted and scaled version of the input signal.

▪ The inversion of the signal (you can see that the output is at a maximum when the input is at a minimum) is a consequence of the circuit used. Non-inverting circuits are possible but they are more difficult to configure. The inversion can easily be corrected in software by subtracting the received ADC input value from 4,095.

In Figure 9-14(b), (c), and (d) the offset voltage is set to 0.9V, and the gain is adjusted to maximize the output signal (between 0 and 1.8V) without clipping the signal. In Figure 9-14(b), the gain and offset are adjusted to map a 0V to +5V signal to a 1.8V to 0V inverted output signal. In Figure 9-14(c), a −5V to +5V signal is mapped to a 1.8V to 0V signal. Finally, in Figure 9-14 (d), a 1.9V to 2.1V input signal is mapped to a 1.3V to 0V output (this is the limit for the LM358 in this case). The last case is applied to an example application in the next·section.

Figure 9-15 illustrates a full implementation of the op-amp signal conditioning circuit as it is attached to the BeagleBone board. In this example, only two op-amps are required in total. This is because the MCP6002 on the left is used to both condition the signal and protect the ADC input. This is possible because it is powered using a V_{CC} = 1.8V supply, which is provided by the 1.8V voltage follower circuit on the right side. The MCP6002 is a dual op-amp package, and it is used because the MCP6001 is not readily available in a DIP package. You could use the MCP6002 to condition two separate sensor signals.

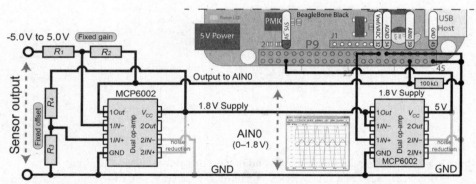

Figure 9-15: Signal conditioning circuit connected to the BBB with gain set using R_1 and R_2 and offset set using R_3 and R_4

The potentiometers in Figure 9-14 are replaced by fixed-value resistors in Figure 9-15 to demonstrate how a fixed offset and gain can be configured. In addition, the MCP6002 does not require a load resistor on the output, but a 100kΩ resistor is used to protect the ADC input.

If the input voltage is −5V to +5V, then this circuit will give an output of 0.048V to 1.626V with the resistor values R_1 = 9.1kΩ, R_2 = 1.5kΩ, R_3 = 4.7kΩ, and R_4 = 6.5kΩ. A general equation to describe the relationship between the input and output can be determined as follows:

$$V_{OUT} = 1.8 \times \left(\frac{R_3}{R_3 + R_4} \right) \left(\frac{R_1 + R_2}{R_1} \right) - V_{IN} \left(\frac{R_2}{R_1} \right)$$

At $V_{IN} = 5\text{V}$, $V_{OUT} = -0.05\text{V}$, and at $V_{IN} = -5\text{V}$, $V_{OUT} = 1.71\text{V}$.

Listing 9-5 displays a test program that can be used to read in 1,000 values from AIN0 at about 20Hz, with the output presented on a single line.

Listing 9-5: /exploringbb/chp09/testADC/testADC.cpp (Segment)

```cpp
#define LDR_PATH "/sys/bus/iio/devices/iio:device0/in_voltage"

int readAnalog(int number){
    stringstream ss;
    ss << LDR_PATH << number << "_raw";
    fstream fs;
    fs.open(ss.str().c_str(), fstream::in);
    fs >> number;
    fs.close();
    return number;
}

int main(int argc, char* argv[]){
    cout << "The value on the ADC is:" << endl;
    for(int i=0; i<1000; i++){
        int value = readAnalog(0);
        cout << "  = " << readAnalog(0) << "/4095    " << '\r' << flush;
        usleep(50000);
    }
    return 0;
}
```

When built and executed, this code gives the following output:

```
debian@ebb:~/exploringbb/chp09/testADC$ ./build
debian@ebb:~/exploringbb/chp09/testADC$ ./testADC
The value on the ADC is: = 2140/4095
```

If a sine wave is inputted at a frequency of 0.1Hz, then the output of the program will slowly increase and decrease between a value close to 0 and a value close to 4,095.

Analog Interfacing Examples

Now that the Beagle board's ADC inputs can be protected from damage using op-amp clamping, two analog interfacing examples are discussed in this section. The first example demonstrates how you can model the response of a sensor, and the second example employs signal offsetting and scaling.

Infrared Distance Sensing

Sharp infrared (IR) distance measurement sensors are useful for robotic navigation applications (e.g., object detection and line following) and proximity switches (e.g., automatic faucets and energy-saving switches). These sensors can also be attached to servo motors and used to calculate range maps (e.g., on the front of a mobile robot). They work well in indoor environments but have limited use in direct sunlight. They have a response time of ~39ms, so at 25–26 readings per second they will not provide dense range images. Figure 9-16(a) shows two aspect views of a low-cost sensor, the Sharp GP2D12.

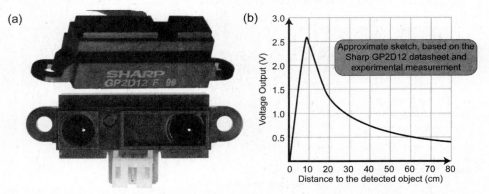

Figure 9-16: (a) Sharp infrared distance measurement sensor; (b) its analog output response

This is a good analog sensor integration example because four problems need to be resolved, which occur generally with other sensors.

1. The sensor response in Figure 9-16(b) is highly nonlinear so that two different distances can give the same sensor output. Thus, you need to find a way to disambiguate the sensor output. For example, if the sensor output is 1.5V, it could mean that the detected object is either 5cm or 17cm from the sensor. A common solution to this problem is to mount the sensor so that it is physically impossible for an object to be closer than 10cm from the sensor. This problem is not examined in further detail, and it is assumed here that the detected object cannot be closer than 10cm from the sensor.

2. The voltage value (0V to 2.6V) exceeds the ADC range. As shown, a signal conditioning circuit can be designed to solve this problem.

3. The output signal is prone to high-frequency noise. A low-pass RC filter can be designed to solve this problem.

4. Even for the assumed distances of 10cm or greater, the relationship between distance and voltage output is still nonlinear. A curve-fitting process can be employed to solve this problem if a linear relationship is required (e.g., threshold applications do not require a linear relationship—just a set value).

To solve the second problem, a voltage divider configuration can be employed to map the output voltage range from 0V–2.6V to 0V –1.8V. A 10kΩ potentiometer can be used for this task, as shown in Figure 9-17(a), where 69.2 percent (100 × 1.8V/2.6V) of the voltage needs to be dropped across the lower resistor. Therefore, if the total resistance is 10kΩ, then the lower resistor would be 6.92kΩ. If fixed-value resistors are to permanently replace the adjustable potentiometer, then 6.8kΩ and 3.3kΩ could be used. Accuracy is not vital, as the op-amp circuit protects the ADC input and the sensor is itself separately calibrated based on the actual resistor values used.

To solve the third problem, the circuit in Figure 9-17(a) includes a low-pass RC filter to remove high-frequency signal noise. The last step determined the series resistor to be approximately 3.3kΩ; therefore, a capacitor value must be chosen to suit the cutoff sampling frequency, which is about 52Hz (i.e., 2 × 26Hz) in this case (taking account of the Nyquist criterion). A capacitor value of 1 µF provides an appropriate value, given the equation $RC = 1 / (2\pi \times f_c)$.

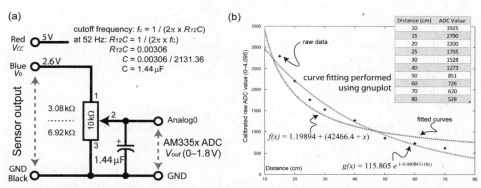

Figure 9-17: (a) A voltage divider circuit configured for the GP2D12 sensor; (b) the plot of the fitting data from gnuplot

To solve the final problem, a small test rig can be set up to calibrate the distance sensor. A measuring tape can be placed at the front of the sensor, and a large object can be positioned at varying distances from the sensor, between 10cm and 80cm. In my case, this provided the raw data for the table in Figure 9-17(b), which is plotted on the graph with the square markers.

This raw data is not sufficiently fine to determine the distance value represented by an ADC measurement intermediate between the values corresponding to the squares. Therefore, curve fitting can be employed to provide an expression that can be implemented in program code. The data can be supplied to the curve fitting tools that are freely available on the Wolfram Alpha website at www. wolframalpha.com. Using the following command string:

```
exponential fit {{3925,10}, {2790,15}, {2200,20}, {1755,25}, {1528,30},
{1273,40}, {851,50}, {726,60}, {620,70}, {528,80}}
```

results in the expression $distance = 115.804e^{-0.000843107v}$ (see `tiny.cc/beagle906`). This curve is plotted in Figure 9-17(b) with the triangular markers. It could also be modeled with a quadratic using the following command string:

```
quadratic fit {{3925,10}, {2790,15}, {2200,20}, {1755,25}, {1528,30},
{1273,40}, {851,50}, {726,60}, {620,70}, {528,80}}
```

which results in the expression $distance = 8.93664 \times 10^{-6} x^2 - 0.0572854x + 99.7321$ (see `tiny.cc/ebb907`).

FITTING DATA TO A CURVE USING GNUPLOT

In addition to plotting data, gnuplot can also be used to fit data to a curve using the nonlinear least-squares (NLLS) Marquardt-Levenberg algorithm. For example, the data in Figure 9-17(b) can be fitted to a function of the form 1/x using the following steps:

```
debian@ebb:~/exploringbb/chp09/sharp$ more data
3925 10
2790 15 ...
debian@ebb:~/exploringbb/chp09/sharp$ gnuplot
   G N U P L O T
    Version 5.0 patchlevel 5    last modified 2016-10-02...
gnuplot> f(x) = a + b/x
gnuplot> fit f(x) "data" using 1:2 via a,b
...
Final set of parameters            Asymptotic Standard Error
=======================            ==========================
a              = 1.19894           +/- 1.415         (118%)
b              = 42466.4           +/- 1335          (3.144%)
correlation matrix of the fit parameters:
               a       b
a              1.000
b             -0.862  1.000
...
```

The best fit function is therefore $f(x)=1.19894+(42466.4/x)$, where x is the captured ADC input value. The plot of the fitted function with respect to the calibration data is available in Figure 9-17(b).

You can also use gnuplot to fit the data against a function with the form of an exponential decay by continuing on from the previous steps. Providing an initial estimate of the c and d values can help the NLLS algorithm converge on a valid solution. For this, you can use the values that are identified by the output of Wolfram Alpha, or appropriate estimate values.

```
gnuplot> g(x) = c * exp(-x * d)
gnuplot> c = 115
gnuplot> d = 0.0008
gnuplot> fit g(x) "data" using 1:2 via c,d
...
```

```
Final set of parameters              Asymptotic Standard Error
=========================            ============================
c              = 115.805            +/- 7.696         (6.645%)
d              = 0.000843118        +/- 7.279e-05     (8.633%)
correlation matrix of the fit parameters:
                    c        d
c                 1.000
d                 0.898   1.000
gnuplot> set term postscript
Terminal type set to 'postscript'
Options are 'landscape enhanced defaultplex ...
gnuplot> set output "fittings.ps"
gnuplot> plot "data" using 1:2, f(x), g(x)
gnuplot> exit
debian@ebb:~/exploringbb/chp09/sharp$ sudo apt install ghostscript
debian@ebb:~/exploringbb/chp09/sharp$ ps2pdf fittings.ps
debian@ebb:~/exploringbb/chp09/sharp$ ls -l fittings*
-rw-r--r-- 1 debian debian  4515 Jun 30 21:39 fittings.pdf
-rw-r--r-- 1 debian debian 24326 Jun 30 21:38 fittings.ps
```

The best fit function is therefore $g(x) = 115.805e^{-0.000843118x}$, where x is the captured ADC input value. The standard error values in this case are lower, and Figure 9-17(b) indicates that the exponential decay function provides a slightly better fit, particularly at close distances.

Note that this process can be used for many analog sensor types to provide an expression that can be used to interpolate between the measured sensor values. What type of fitting curve best fits the data will vary according to the underlying physical process of the sensor. For example, you could use the linear fit command on the Wolfram Alpha website to derive an expression for the LDR described in Chapter 6. A C++ code example can be written to read in the ADC value and convert it into a distance, as shown in Listing 9-6, where the exponential fix expression is coded on a single line.

Listing 9-6: /exploringbb/chp09/IRdistance/IRdistance.cpp (Segment)

```cpp
...
int main(int argc, char* argv[]){
    cout << "Starting the IR distance sensor program:" << endl;
    for(int i=0; i<1000; i++){
        int value = readAnalog(0);
        float distance = 115.804f * exp(-0.000843107f * (float)value);
        cout << "The distance is: " << distance << " cm" << '\r' << flush;
        usleep(100000);
    }
    return 0;
}
```

When the code example is executed, it continues to output the distance of a detected object in centimeters, for about 100 seconds.

```
debian@ebb:~/exploringbb/chp09/IRdistance$ ./build
debian@ebb:~/exploringbb/chp09/IRdistance$ ./IRdistance
Starting the IR distance sensor program:
The distance is: 17.7579 cm
```

If the speed of execution of such code is vital in the application, then it is preferable to populate a lookup table (LUT) with the converted values. This means that each value is calculated once, either at the initialization stage of the program, or perhaps during code development, rather than every time a reading is made and has to be converted. When the program is in use, the subsequent memory accesses (for reading the LUT) are much more efficient than the corresponding floating-point calculations. This is possible because a 12-bit ADC can output only 4,096 unique values, and it is not unreasonable to store an array of the 4,096 possible outcomes in the memory associated with the program.

DISTANCE SENSING WITH OTHER SENSORS

Two low-cost distance sensors are described in detail in this book. The Sharp infrared distance measurement sensor is described in this chapter, and the HC-SR04 ultrasonic distance sensor is described in Chapter 10 and Chapter 15. Both of these sensors have quite limited precision and sample rates. Infrared sensors have a narrow beam but are prone to sunlight interference. Ultrasonic sensors perform well in sunlight but do not work well with sound-absorbing materials and are prone to ghost echo (e.g., sound reflections that hit more than one surface). These low-cost sensors perform well for obstacle avoidance applications, but for precision applications such as spatial mapping, you could investigate *light detection and ranging* (LiDAR) sensors. The laser-based LIDAR-Lite v2 ($115) sensor from www.pulsedlight3d.com has a 40 meter range capability, 1 cm resolution, ±2.5 cm accuracy, and is capable of 500 readings per second. It can be interfaced to the Beagle boards using their I²C buses.

ADXL335 Conditioning Example

The ADXL335 is a small three-axis accelerometer that outputs an analog signal that has undergone conditioning. It behaves just like the ADXL345 except that the output is from three analog pins, one for each axis.

When measuring in a range of ±1g, the x-axis outputs ~1.30V at 0°, ~1.64V at 90°, and ~1.98V at 180°. This means that the output signal of the breakout board is centered on 1.64V and has a variation of ±0.34V. A circuit can be designed as shown in Figure 9-18 to map the center point to 0.9V and to extend the variation over the full 1.8V range.

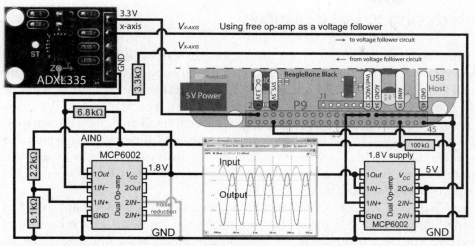

Figure 9-18: The ADXL335 analog accelerometer and its connection to the BBB with further signal conditioning

Unfortunately, there are output impedance problems with this particular ADXL335 breakout board, and the voltage divider circuit in the conditioning circuit will not function correctly. A buffer circuit is therefore required, and an op-amp in voltage follower configuration can be used. The 1.8V powered op-amp could not be used for this task, as the upper sensor output (at 1.98V) exceeds the 1.8V output limit of that op-amp and would thus have been clamped. The 1.8V supply op-amp IC on the right side has a limit of 5V, so it is used for this task.

This circuit is a little complex, and it may be overkill, as the amplification of a signal does not necessarily improve the information content of that signal—noise is amplified along with the signal. It is quite possible that the 12-bit ADC performs just as well over a linearly scaled 1.3V to 1.98V range as it does over the full 0V–1.8V range for this particular sensor. However, it is important that you are exposed to the process of offsetting and scaling a signal using op-amps, as it is required for many sensor types, particularly those that are centered on 0V, such as microphone audio signals.

The `testADC` program that was used previously can be used to print out the digitized AIN value from the accelerometer. In this case, the program prints out

```
debia@ebb:~/exploringbb/chp09/testADC$ ./testADC
The value on the ADC is:  = 2174/4095
```

at rest (90°), 250 at 0°, and 4,083 at +180°. A simple linear interpolation can be used to approximate the intermediate values.

Interfacing to Local Displays

As described in Chapter 1, many Beagle boards can be attached to computer monitors and digital televisions using the HDMI output connector. In addition, LCD Capes and SPI LCD displays can be connected to the expansion headers. The downsides of such displays are that they may not be practical, or they may be overly expensive for certain applications. When a small amount of information needs to be relayed to a user, a simple LED can be used; for example, the onboard power and activity LEDs are useful indicators that the board continues to function. For more complex information, two possibilities are to interface to low-cost LED displays and low-cost character LCD modules.

In Chapter 8, an example is provided for driving seven-segment displays using SPI and 74HC595 serial shift register ICs. That is a useful educational exercise, but the wiring can quickly become impractical for multiple digits. In the following sections more advanced solutions are described for adding low-cost onboard display to your board.

MAX7219 Display Modules

The Maxim Integrated MAX7219 is a serially interfaced eight-digit LED display driver that is widely available and built in to low-cost multi-seven-segment display modules. The module in Figure 9-19(a) ($2–$3) is a 5V eight-digit red LED display that contains the MAX7219 IC, which can be interfaced using SPI. The datasheet for the IC is available at tiny.cc/beagle908.

The module can be connected to the PocketBeagle using an SPI bus, which in this case is the SPI1 bus, as illustrated in Figure 9-19(a). Note that the module is powered using the 5V line but is controlled using 3.3V logic levels. Do not connect the DOUT line on the module directly back to the PocketBeagle SPI1-MISO input as you may damage your board!

In decode mode, the module can display eight digits consisting of the numeric values 0–9 (with a point), the letters *H, E, L, P*, a space, and a dash. The decode mode can also be disabled, permitting each of the seven-segments to be controlled directly. For example, the following steps that use the summary list of registers in Figure 9-19(b) can be used to test that the module is configured correctly by sending pairs of bytes to the device—the register address and data value to write:

1. Turn on the module and then place the module in test mode (i.e., all segments on).[4]

---

[4]As discussed with the echo command: -n means do not output a trailing newline character, -e means enable interpretation of backslash escape sequences, and \xHH means a byte with a hexadecimal value HH. Writing to /dev/spidev1.1 uses the SPI1-CS enable pin on the Beagle board. If you are having difficulty in getting the correct output using the command line, then execute the example in Listing 9-7 first.

(a)

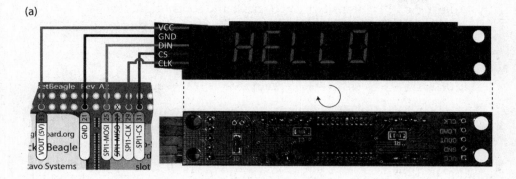

(b)

Register	Addr	Value
Digit 0	0x01	0x00 to 0x09 displays digits 0 to 9
Digit 1	0x02	0x0A = dash, 0x0F = blank space
...	...	0x0B = E, 0x0C=H, 0x0D=L, 0x0E=P
Digit 7	0x08	Set bit D7 to give a point (i.e., 0x8x)
Decode?	0x09	0x00 No decode, 0xFF decode digits 7-0
Intensity	0x0A	Min-Max (0x00 to 0x0F)
Scan Limit	0x0B	1 digit to 8 digits enabled (0x00 to 0x07)
Shutdown	0x0C	0x00 Shutdown, 0x01 Normal
Test	0x0F	0x01 Test Mode, 0x00 Normal

Figure 9-19: (a) The MAX7219 eight-digit seven-segment display module connected to the SPI1 bus on a PocketBeagle, and (b) a summary register table for the MAX7219

```
debian@ebb:/dev$ echo -ne "\x0C\x01" > /dev/spidev1.1
debian@ebb:/dev$ echo -ne "\x0F\x01" > /dev/spidev1.1
```

2. Take the module out of test mode (return to its previous state).

```
debian@ebb:/dev$ echo -ne "\x0F\x00" > /dev/spidev1.1
```

3. Change to eight-segment mode and display the number 6.5 using the last two digits (i.e., on the RHS).

```
debian@ebb:/dev$ echo -ne "\x09\xFF" > /dev/spidev1.1
debian@ebb:/dev$ echo -ne "\x01\x05" > /dev/spidev1.1
debian@ebb:/dev$ echo -ne "\x02\x86" > /dev/spidev1.1
```

4. Display the word "Hello   " (i.e., with three trailing spaces), as in Figure 9-19(a).

```
debian@ebb:/dev$ echo -ne "\x08\x0C" > /dev/spidev1.1
debian@ebb:/dev$ echo -ne "\x07\x0B" > /dev/spidev1.1
debian@ebb:/dev$ echo -ne "\x06\x0D" > /dev/spidev1.1
debian@ebb:/dev$ echo -ne "\x05\x0D" > /dev/spidev1.1
debian@ebb:/dev$ echo -ne "\x04\x00" > /dev/spidev1.1
debian@ebb:/dev$ echo -ne "\x03\x0F" > /dev/spidev1.1
debian@ebb:/dev$ echo -ne "\x02\x0F" > /dev/spidev1.1
debian@ebb:/dev$ echo -ne "\x01\x0F" > /dev/spidev1.1
```

5. Adjust the LED intensity to its darkest and to its brightest.

```
debian@ebb:/dev$ echo -ne "\x0A\x00" > /dev/spidev1.1
debian@ebb:/dev$ echo -ne "\x0A\x0F" > /dev/spidev1.1
```

6. Turn off the module.

```
debian@ebb:/dev$ echo -ne "\x0C\x00" > /dev/spidev0.1
```

The code in Listing 9-7 uses the SPIDevice class from Chapter 8 to create a high-speed counter. The display module is responsive at an SPI bus speed of 10MHz, updating the display 1,000,000 times in approximately 18 seconds. The output of the program in Listing 9-7 is displayed in Figure 9-20. The display is counting quickly, so the blurred digits on the RHS are caused by the update speed of the count relative to the camera shutter speed, which was used to capture this photograph.

Listing 9-7: chp09/max7219/max7219.cpp

```cpp
#include <iostream>
#include "bus/SPIDevice.h"
using namespace exploringBB;
using namespace std;

int main(){
   cout << "Starting the MAX7219 example" << endl;
   SPIDevice *max = new SPIDevice(1,1);
   max->setSpeed(10000000);               // max speed is 10MHz
   max->setMode(SPIDevice::MODE0);

   // turn on the display and disable test mode -- just in case:
   max->writeRegister(0x0C, 0x01);        // turn on the display
   max->writeRegister(0x0F, 0x00);        // disable test mode
   max->writeRegister(0x0B, 0x07);        // set 8-digit mode
   max->writeRegister(0x09, 0xFF);  // set decode mode on

   for(int i=1; i<9; i++){            // clear all digits to be dashes
      max->writeRegister((unsigned int)i, 0x0A);
   }
   for(int i=0; i<=100000; i++){      // count to 100,000
      int val = i;                    // need to display each digit
      unsigned int place = 1;         // the current decimal place
      while(val>0){                   // repeatedly divide and get remainder
        max->writeRegister( place++, (unsigned char) val%10);
        val = val/10;
      }
   }
   max->close();
   cout << "End of the MAX7219 example" << endl;
   return 0;
}
```

Figure 9-20: The MAX7219 eight-digit seven-segment display counting due to Listing 9-7 (photographed while counting)

Character LCD Modules

Character LCD modules are LCD dot matrix displays that feature pre-programmed font tables so that they can be used to display simple text messages without the need for complex display software. They are available in a range of character rows and columns (commonly 2×8, 2×16, 2×20, and 4×20) and usually contain an LED backlight, which is available in a range of colors. Recently, *OLED* (organic LED) versions and *E-paper* (e-ink) versions have been released that provide for greater levels of display contrast.

To understand the use of a character LCD module, you should study its datasheet. While most character LCD modules have common interfaces (often using a Hitachi HD44780 controller), the display modules from Newhaven have some of the best datasheets. The datasheet for a typical Newhaven display module is available at `tiny.cc/beagle910`. It is recommended that the datasheet be read in conjunction with this discussion. The datasheet for the HD44780 controller is available at `tiny.cc/beagle911`. The following code will work for all character LCD modules that are based on this controller.

There are character LCD modules available with integrated I²C and SPI interfaces, but the majority of modules are available with an eight-bit and four-bit parallel interface. By adding a 74HC595 to the circuit, it is possible to develop a custom SPI interface, which provides greater flexibility in the choice of modules. A generic character LCD module can be attached to the BBB using the wiring configuration illustrated in Figure 9-21.

You can interface to character LCD modules using either an eight-bit or a four-bit mode, but there is no difference in the functionality available with either mode. The four-bit interface requires fewer interface connections, but each eight-bit value has to be written in two steps—the lower four bits (*nibble*) followed by the higher four bits (nibble).

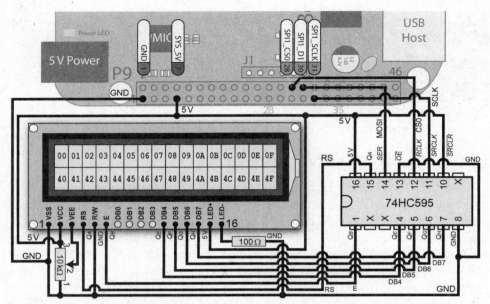

Figure 9-21: SPI interfacing to character LCD modules using a 74HC595 8-bit serial shift register

To write to the character LCD module two lines are required, the RS line (register select signal) and the E line (operational enable signal). The circuit in Figure 9-21 is designed to use a four-bit interface, as it requires only six lines rather than the 10 lines that would be required with the eight-bit interface. This means that a single eight-bit 74HC595 can be used to interface to the module when it is in four-bit mode. The downside is that the software is slightly more complex to write, as each byte must be written in two nibbles. The four-bit interface uses the inputs DB4–DB7, whereas the eight-bit interface requires the use of DB0–DB7.

It is possible to read data values from the display, but it is not required in this application; therefore, the R/W (read/write select signal) is tied to GND to place the display in write mode. The power is supplied using VCC (5V) and VSS (GND). VEE sets the display contrast level and must be at a level between VSS and VCC. A 10kΩ multi-turn potentiometer can be used to provide precise control over the display contrast. Finally, the LED+ and LED connections supply the LED backlight power.

WARNING Do not attempt to read data from this display module directly to your Beagle board, as it uses 5V logic levels.

The display character address codes are illustrated on the module in Figure 9-21. Using *commands* (on page 6 of the datasheet), *data* values can be sent to these addresses. For example, to display the letter *A* in the top-left corner, the following procedure can be used with the four-bit interface:

- Clear the display by sending the value 00000001 to D4–D7. This value should be sent in two parts: the lower nibble (0001), followed by the higher nibble (0000). The E line is set high and then low after each nibble is sent. A delay of 1.52ms (datasheet, page 6) is required. The module expects a *command* to be sent when the RS line is low. After sending this command, the cursor is placed in the top-left corner.

- Write data 01000001 = 65_{10} = A (datasheet, page 9) with the lower nibble sent first, followed by the upper nibble. The E line is set high followed by low after each nibble is sent. The module expects *data* to be sent when the RS line is set high.

A C++ class is available for you to use in interfacing the Beagle boards to display modules using SPI. The class assumes that the 74HC595 lines are connected as shown in Figure 9-21, and the data is represented as in Table 9-5. The code does not use bits 2 (Q_D) and 3 (Q_C) on the 74HC595, so it is possible for you to repurpose these for your own application. For example, one pin could be connected to the gate of a FET and used to switch the backlight on and off. The class definition is provided in Listing 9-8, and the implementation is in the associated `LCDCharacterDisplay.cpp` file.

Table 9-5: Mapping of the 74HC595 Data Bits to the Character LCD Module Inputs, as Required for the C++ LCDCharacterDisplay Class

	BIT 7 MSB	BIT 6	BIT 5	BIT 4	BIT 3	BIT 2	BIT 1	BIT 0 LSB
Character LCD module	D7	D6	D5	D4	Not used	Not used	E	RS
74HC595 pins	Q_H	Q_G	Q_F	Q_E	Q_D	Q_C	Q_B	Q_A

Listing 9-8: library/display/LCDCharacterDisplay.h

```
class LCDCharacterDisplay {
private:
    SPIDevice *device;
    int width, height;
    ...
public:
    LCDCharacterDisplay(SPIDevice *device, int width, int height);
    virtual void write(char c);
    virtual void print(std::string message);
    virtual void clear();
    virtual void home();
```

```
    virtual int  setCursorPosition(int row, int column);
    virtual void setDisplayOff(bool displayOff);
    virtual void setCursorOff(bool cursorOff);
    virtual void setCursorBlink(bool isBlink);
    virtual void setCursorMoveOff(bool cursorMoveOff);
    virtual void setCursorMoveLeft(bool cursorMoveLeft);
    virtual void setAutoscroll(bool isAutoscroll);
    virtual void setScrollDisplayLeft(bool scrollLeft);
    virtual ~LCDCharacterDisplay();
};
```

The constructor requires an SPIDevice object and details about the width and height of the character display module (in characters). The constructor provides functionality to position the cursor on the display and to describe how the cursor should behave (e.g., blinking or moving to the left/right). This class can be used as shown in Listing 9-9 to create an LCDCharacterDisplay object, display a string, and display a count from 0 to 10,000 on the module.

Listing 9-9: chp09/LCDcharacter/LCDApp.cpp

```cpp
#include <iostream>
#include <sstream>
#include "display/LCDCharacterDisplay.h"
using namespace std;
using namespace exploringBB;

int main(){
   cout << "Starting EBB LCD Character Display Example" << endl;
   SPIDevice *busDevice = new SPIDevice(2,0); //Using second SPI bus (both loaded)
   busDevice->setSpeed(1000000);      // Have access to SPI Device object
   ostringstream s;                   // Using this to combine text and int data
   LCDCharacterDisplay display(busDevice, 16, 2); // Construct 16x2 LCD Display
   display.clear();                   // Clear the character LCD module
   display.home();                    // Move the cursor to the (0,0) position
   display.print("EBB by D. Molloy"); // String to display on the first row
   for(int x=0; x<=10000; x++){       // Do this 10,000 times
      s.str("");                      // clear the ostringstream object s
      display.setCursorPosition(1,3); // move the cursor to second row
      s << "X=" << x;                 // construct a string that has an int value
      display.print(s.str());         // print the string X=*** on the LCD module
   }
   cout << "End of EBB LCD Character Display Example" << endl;
}
```

The code example in Listing 9-9 can be built and executed using the following steps:

```
debian@ebb:~/exploringbb/chp09/LCDcharacter$ ./build
debian@ebb:~/exploringbb/chp09/LCDcharacter$ ./LCDApp
```

The count incrementally updates on the display and finishes with the output illustrated in Figure 9-22.

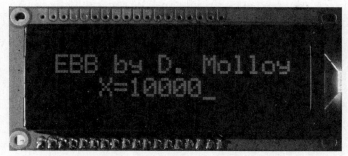

Figure 9-22: Output from Listing 9-9 on a Newhaven display module

It takes 26 seconds to display a count that runs from 0 to 10,000, which is approximately 385 localized screen updates per second. This means that you could potentially connect many display modules to a single SPI bus and still achieve reasonable screen refresh rates. You would require the type of multiple SPI slave circuitry that is discussed in Chapter 8, which would require $\lceil \log_2 x \rceil$ GPIOs for x modules. At its maximum refresh rate, the top command gives the following output:

```
  PID USER      PR  NI    VIRT   RES   SHR S  %CPU %MEM     TIME+  COMMAND
18227 root      20   0       0     0     0 S  34.6  0.0  25:02.50 spi2
20967 debian    20   0    2708   988   856 S  33.9  0.2   0:04.15 LCDApp
```

This indicates that the LCDApp program and its associated spi2 platform device are utilizing 68.5 percent of the available CPU time at this extreme module display refresh rate of 385 updates per second. To be clear, the display maintains its current display state without any Linux overhead, and refresh is only required to change the display contents.

Building C/C++ Libraries

In this chapter, a number of different actuators, sensors, and display devices are interfaced to the Beagle boards using stand-alone code examples. Should you embark upon a grand design project, it will quickly become necessary to combine such code examples together into a single software project. In addition, it would not be ideal if you had to recompile every line of code in the project each time you made a change. To solve this problem, you can build your own libraries of C/C++ code, and to assist you in this task, you can use makefiles, and better still, CMake.

Makefiles

As the complexity of your C/C++ projects grows, an IDE such as Eclipse can be used to manage compiler options and program code interdependencies. However, there are occasions when command-line compilation is required; and when projects are complex, a structured approach to managing the build process is necessary. A good solution is to use the `make` program and makefiles.

The process is best explained by using an example. To compile a `hello.cpp` program and a `test.cpp` program within a single project without makefiles, the build script can be as follows:

```
debian@ebb:~/exploringbb/chp09/makefiles$ more build
#!/bin/bash
g++ -o3 hello.cpp -o hello
g++ -o3 test.cpp -o test
```

The script works perfectly fine; however, if the project's complexity necessitated separate compilation, then this approach lacks structure. The following is a simple `Makefile` file that could be used instead (it is important to use the Tab key to indent the lines with the `<Tab>` marker shown here):

```
debian@ebb:~/exploringbb/chp09/makefiles$ more Makefile
all: hello test

hello:
<Tab> g++ -o3 hello.cpp -o hello

test:
<Tab> g++ -o3 test.cpp -o test

debian@ebb:~/exploringbb/chp09/makefiles$ rm hello test
debian@ebb:~/exploringbb/chp09/makefiles$ make
g++ -o3 hello.cpp -o hello
g++ -o3 test.cpp -o test
```

If the `make` command is issued in this directory, the `Makefile` file is detected, and a call to **make all** will automatically be invoked. That will execute the commands under the `hello:` and `test:` labels, which build the two programs. However, this `Makefile` file does not add much in the way of structure, so a more complete version is required, such as this:

```
debian@ebb:~/exploringbb/chp09/makefiles2$ more Makefile
CC       = g++
CFLAGS   = -c -o3 -Wall
LDFLAGS  =
```

```
all: hello test

hello: hello.o
<tab>    $(CC) $< -o $@
hello.o: hello.cpp
<tab>    $(CC) $(CFLAGS) $< -o $@
test: test.o
<tab>    $(CC) $(LDFLAGS) $< -o $@
test.o: test.cpp
<tab>    $(CC) $(CFLAGS) $< -o $@
clean:
<tab>    rm -rf *.o hello test
```

In this version, the compiler choice, compiler options, and linker options are defined at the top of the Makefile file. This enables the options to be easily altered for all files in the project. In addition, the object files (.o files) are retained, which dramatically reduces repeated compilation times when there are many source files in the project. There is some shortcut syntax in this Makefile file. For example, $< is the name of the first prerequisite (hello.o in its first use), and $@ is the name of the target (hello in its first use). The project can now be built using the following steps:

```
debian@ebb:~/exploringbb/chp09/makefiles2$ ls
hello.cpp  Makefile  test.cpp
debian@ebb:~/exploringbb/chp09/makefiles2$ make
g++ -c -o3 -Wall hello.cpp -o hello.o
g++ hello.o -o hello
g++ -c -o3 -Wall test.cpp -o test.o
g++  test.o -o test
debian@ebb:~/exploringbb/chp09/makefiles2$ ls
hello hello.cpp hello.o Makefile test test.cpp  test.o
debian@ebb:~/exploringbb/chp09/makefiles2$ make clean
rm -rf *.o hello test
debian@ebb:~/exploringbb/chp09/makefiles2$ ls
hello.cpp  Makefile  test.cpp
```

This description only scratches the surface of the capability of the make command and the use of makefiles. You can find a full GNU guide at tiny.cc/beagle912.

CMake

Unfortunately, makefiles can become overly complex for tasks such as building projects that have multiple subdirectories, or projects that are to be deployed to multiple platforms. Building complex projects is where CMake really shines; CMake is a cross-platform makefile generator. Simply put, CMake automatically generates the makefiles for your project. It can do much more than that too (e.g., build MS Visual Studio solutions), but this discussion focuses on the compilation of library code. The first step is to install CMake on your board.

```
debian@ebb:~$ sudo apt install cmake
debian@ebb:~$ cmake -version
cmake version 3.7.2
```

A Hello World Example

The first project to test CMake is available in the /chp09/cmake/ directory. It consists of the hello.cpp file and a text file called CMakeLists.txt, as provided in Listing 9-10.

Listing 9-10: /chp09/cmake/CMakeLists.txt

```
cmake_minimum_required(VERSION 3.7.2)
project (hello)
add_executable(hello hello.cpp)
```

The CMakeLists.txt file in Listing 9-10 consists of three lines.

- The first line sets the minimum version of CMake for this project, which is major version 3, minor version 7, and patch version 2 in this example. This version is somewhat arbitrary, but providing a version number allows for future support for your build environment. Therefore, you should use the current version of CMake on your system.
- The second line is the project() command that sets the project name.
- The third line is the add_executable() command, which requests that an executable is to be built using the hello.cpp source file. The first argument to the add_executable() function is the name of the executable to be built, and the second argument is the source file from which to build the executable.

The Hello World project can now be built by executing the cmake utility and by passing to it the directory that contains the source code and the CMakeLists.txt file. In this case, . refers to the current directory.

```
debian@ebb:~/exploringbb/chp09/cmake$ ls
CMakeLists.txt  hello.cpp
debian@ebb:~/exploringbb/chp09/cmake$ cmake .
-- The C compiler identification is GNU 6.3.0
-- The CXX compiler identification is GNU 6.3.0
...
debian@ebb:~/exploringbb/chp09/cmake$ ls
CMakeCache.txt  cmake_install.cmake  hello.cpp
CMakeFiles      CMakeLists.txt       Makefile
```

CMake identified the environment settings for the Linux device and created the `Makefile` for this project. You can view the content of this file, but do not make edits to it, because any edits will be overwritten the next time that the `cmake` utility is executed. You can now use the `make` command to build the project.

```
debian@ebb:~/exploringbb/chp09/cmake$ make
Scanning dependencies of target hello
[ 50%] Building CXX object CMakeFiles/hello.dir/hello.cpp.o
[100%] Linking CXX executable hello
[100%] Built target hello
debian@ebb:~/exploringbb/chp09/cmake$ ls -l hello
-rwxr-xr-x 1 debian debian 9144 Jul  1 02:38 hello
debian@ebb:~/exploringbb/chp09/cmake$ ./hello
Hello from the Beagle board!
```

This is a lot of additional effort to build a simple Hello World example, but as your project scales, this approach can be invaluable.

Building a C/C++ Library

The code that is utilized throughout this book can be grouped together and organized into a single directory structure so that you can use it within your project as a library of code. For example, selected code is organized in the `library` directory within the repository, as follows:

```
debian@ebb:~/exploringbb/library$ tree .
...
└── bus
|   └── BusDevice.cpp
|   └── BusDevice.h
|   └── I2CDevice.cpp
|   └── I2CDevice.h
|   └── SPIDevice.cpp
|   └── SPIDevice.h
└── CMakeLists.txt
└── display
|   └── LCDCharacterDisplay.cpp
|   └── LCDCharacterDisplay.h
|   └── SevenSegmentDisplay.cpp
|   └── SevenSegmentDisplay.h
...
25 directories, 93 files
```

A `build` directory (which should initially be empty) is used to contain the final binary library and any temporary files that are required for the build. The `CMakeLists.txt` file is created in the library root, as in Listing 9-11.

Listing 9-11: /library/CMakeLists.txt

```
debian@ebb:~/exploringbb/library$ more CMakeLists.txt
cmake_minimum_required(VERSION 3.7.2)
```

```
project(EBBLibrary)
find_package (Threads)
set(CMAKE_BUILD_TYPE Release)
#set(CMAKE_BUILD_TYPE Debug)

#Only available from version 2.8.9 on
set(CMAKE_POSITION_INDEPENDENT_CODE TRUE)

#Bring the headers, such as Student.h into the project
include_directories(bus display gpio motor network sensor)

#However, the file(GLOB...) will allow for wildcard additions:
file(GLOB_RECURSE SOURCES "./*.cpp")

#Can build statically to libEBBLibrary.a using the next line
#add_library(EBBLibrary STATIC ${SOURCES})

#Building shared library to libEBBLibrary.so using the next line
add_library(EBBLibrary SHARED ${SOURCES})

target_link_libraries(EBBLibrary ${CMAKE_THREAD_LIBS_INIT})

install (TARGETS EBBLibrary DESTINATION /usr/lib)
```

The important features of the CMakeLists.txt file in Listing 9-11 are as follows:

- The find_package(Threads) adds pthread support to the build.
- The set(CMAKE_BUILD_TYPE Release) function is used to set the build type. A Release build will have slightly improved execution performance. The next call to set() adds the -fPIC compile flag to the build so that the machine code is not dependent on being located at a specific memory address, which makes it suitable for inclusion in a library.
- The include_directories() function is used to bring the header files into the build environment.
- The file() command is used to add the source files to the project. GLOB (or GLOB_RECURSE) is used to create a list of all the files that meet the globbing expression (i.e., src/*.cpp) and add them to a variable SOURCES.
- This example uses the add_library() function. The library is built as a shared library using the SHARED flag (other options are STATIC or MODULE), and EBBLibrary is used as the name of the shared library.
- The last line uses the install() function to define an installation location for the library (in this case it is the /usr/lib/ directory). Deployment is invoked using a call to sudo make install in this case.

A STATICALLY LINKED LIBRARY (.A)

A statically linked library is created at compile time to contain all the code that relates to the library; essentially, the compiler makes copies of any dependency code, including that in other libraries. This results in a library that is typically larger in size than the equivalent shared library, but because all the dependencies are determined at compile time, there are fewer run-time loading costs, and the library may be more platform independent. Unless you are certain that you require a static library, you should use a shared library because there will be fewer code duplications and the shared library can be updated (e.g., for bug fix releases) without recompilation.

To build a static library using CMake, the steps are almost the same as in Listing 9-11; however, you must use the `add_library()` line entry that uses `STATIC`, rather than the line entry that uses `SHARED`. The steps that follow will then result in the creation of a static library with an `.a` extension:

```
debian@ebb:~/exploringbb/library$ ls -l *.a
-rw-r--r-- 1 debian debian 132378 May 13 00:14 libEBBLibrary.a
debian@ebb:~/exploringbb/library$ ar -t libEBBLibrary.a
SevenSegmentDisplay.cpp.o
LCDCharacterDisplay.cpp.o
```

Once the `CMakeLists.txt` file has been created, the library can be built as follows:

```
debian@ebb:~/exploringbb/library/build$ cmake ..
-- The C compiler identification is GNU 6.3.0
-- The CXX compiler identification is GNU 6.3.0
debian@ebb:~/exploringbb/library/build$ make
Scanning dependencies of target EBBLibrary
[  5%] Building CXX object ...
[100%] Built target EBBLibrary
debian@ebb:~/exploringbb/library/build$ ls -l *.so
-rwxr-xr-x 1 debian debian 95448 Jul  1 02:52 libEBBLibrary.so
```

NOTE Should an error arise in this library build, remove the libi2c-dev package using `sudo apt remove libi2c-dev` and retry the build steps.

The `CMakeLists.txt` file also includes a deployment step, which allows you to install the library in a suitably accessible location. Shared library locations can be added to the path, or if you want to make the libraries available for all users, then you can deploy them to the /usr/lib/ directory. This step requires root access to write to the /usr/lib/ directory. For example, the libEBBLibrary.so library can be installed for all users as follows:

```
debian@ebb:~/exploringbb/library/build$ sudo make install
[sudo] password for debian:
```

```
[100%] Built target EBBLibrary
Install the project...
-- Install configuration: "Release"
-- Installing: /usr/lib/libEBBLibrary.so
debian@ebb:~/exploringbb/library/build$ cd /usr/lib
debian@ebb:/usr/lib$ ls -l libEBB*
-rw-r--r-- 1 root root 132378 Jun 16 02:27 libEBBLibrary.a
-rw-r--r-- 1 root root  95448 Jul  1 02:52 libEBBLibrary.so
```

You will also find a file in the build directory, called install_manifest.txt, that describes the locations at which the make install command applied changes.

Using a Shared (.so) or Static (.a) Library

Once a library has been developed, the next question is how you use the library in your projects. To simplify this process, CMake can once again be used to generate the makefiles for your project.

Listing 9-12 provides the source code for a CMakeLists.txt file that can be used to build a program that links to your project library (either dynamically or statically). The libEBBLibrary.so shared library is used for this example. A short C++ program is available in Listing 9-13 that utilizes the functionality of the shared library, in this case to display a message on an LCD character display. This code is provided in the directory /chp09/libexample/.

Listing 9-12: /chp09/libexample/CMakeLists.txt

```
cmake_minimum_required(VERSION 3.0.2)
project (TestEBBLibrary)

#For the shared library:
set ( PROJECT_LINK_LIBS libEBBLibrary.so )
link_directories( ~/exploringbb/library/build )

#For the static library:
#set ( PROJECT_LINK_LIBS libEBBLibrary.a )
#link_directories( ~/exploringbb/library/build )

include_directories(~/exploringbb/library/)

add_executable(libtest libtest.cpp)
target_link_libraries(libtest ${PROJECT_LINK_LIBS} )
```

Listing 9-13: /chp09/libexample/libtest.cpp

```
#include <iostream>
#include <sstream>
#include "display/LCDCharacterDisplay.h"
using namespace exploringBB;
using namespace std;
```

```
int main() {
    cout << "Testing the EBB library" << endl;
    SPIDevice *busDevice = new SPIDevice(1,1);
    busDevice->setSpeed(1000000);       // access to SPI Device object
    ostringstream s;                    // using to combine text and ints
    LCDCharacterDisplay display(busDevice, 20, 2); // a 20x4 display
    display.clear();                    // Clear the character LCD module
    display.home();                     // Move to the (0,0) position
    display.print("   Exploring BB");
    cout << "End of the EBB library test" << endl;
    return 0;
}
```

There are only two files in the project (Listing 9-12 and Listing 9-13). The library of code (libEBBLibrary.so) and associated header files are assumed to be in the ~/exploringbb/library/ directory. The following steps can be used to build the executable:

```
debian@ebb:~/exploringbb/chp09/libexample$ ls
CMakeLists.txt  libtest.cpp
debian@ebb:~/exploringbb/chp09/libexample$ mkdir build
debian@ebb:~/exploringbb/chp09/libexample$ cd build
debian@ebb:~/exploringbb/chp09/libexample/build$ cmake ..
-- The C compiler identification is GNU 6.3.0
-- The CXX compiler identification is GNU 6.3.0
...
debian@ebb:~/exploringbb/chp09/libexample/build$ make
Scanning dependencies of target libtest
...
debian@ebb:~/exploringbb/chp09/libexample/build$ ls -l libtest
-rwxr-xr-x 1 debian debian 14324 Jul  1 03:19 libtest
debian@ebb:~/exploringbb/chp09/libexample/build$ ./libtest
Testing the EBB library
End of the EBB library test
```

It is important to note that any changes to the libtest.cpp program in List-ing 9-13 will not require recompilation of the library. Indeed, that is also true of other C/C++ files in the same project. For further information on CMake, see the www.cmake.org website. In particular, the CMake Documentation Index provides a useful list of available commands.

Summary

After completing this chapter, you should be able to do the following:

- Interface to actuators, such as DC motors, stepper motors, and relays
- Protect the AM335x ADC from damage using op-amp clamping
- Condition a sensor signal so that it can be interfaced to the Beagle board ADCs, regardless of the output voltage levels

- Interface analog sensors such as distance sensors and accelerometers to the Beagle boards
- Interface to low-cost display modules such as seven-segment displays and character LCD displays
- Build C/C++ code as a dynamic library to be used on a Linux SBC

Further Reading

The following additional links provide further information on the topics in this chapter:

- The Hitachi HD44780 datasheet: `tiny.cc/beagle913`

Real-Time Interfacing Using External Slave Processors

In this chapter, you are introduced to real-time interfacing with the Beagle board. Linux has difficulty performing certain real-time interfacing tasks, such as generating or sampling bit patterns on GPIOs at high speeds. The chapter describes how you can expand the number of available GPIOs and UART devices on the Beagle board. This chapter investigates the use of dedicated real-time external slave processors and associated communication frameworks. There are many suitable slave processors available, but this chapter is focused on just one platform—the Arduino. This chapter describes how a Beagle board can interface effectively to the Arduino using UART serial and I²C communication. Examples are provided of the Arduino in use as an input/output extender and as a dedicated high-speed slave processor.

EQUIPMENT REQUIRED FOR THIS CHAPTER:

- Any Beagle board
- GPIO expander ICs (MCP23017, MCP23S17)
- USB UART device (e.g., CP2102 or CH340G compatible)

- An Arduino Uno or equivalent (with a logic-level translator) and/or an Arduino Pro Mini with 3.3V or 5V logic levels

- Sensors: TMP36 analog temperature sensor and a HC-SR04 distance sensor

Further resources for this chapter are available at `www.exploringbeaglebone.com/chapter10/`.

Real-Time Beagle Board

The advantages of integrating the Linux OS with an embedded system are described throughout this book. The quantity and quality of device drivers, software packages, programming languages, and software APIs available for the Linux platform are immense. However, certain features that you may take for granted, on even low-cost microcontrollers, may be absent—the most notable of which is the capability to perform input/output operations in a time-critical manner. Systems are described as being *real-time* if they can guarantee a valid response within a specified time frame (often of the order of ms/µs), regardless of their system load.

Real-time systems are often used for mission-critical applications. *Hard real-time systems* are used in applications for which a total systems failure could result from missing a deadline (e.g., power-steering, self-balancing robots). *Soft real-time systems* are used in applications that require meeting deadlines. In such applications, missing a deadline might result in a reduced quality of service, but certainly not systems failure (e.g., live video transmission, mobile phone communication). The mainline Linux kernel can typically meet soft real-time requirements (e.g., playing desktop audio), but it is not designed to meet hard real-time requirements.

Real-Time Kernels

The use of the Beagle board GPIOs is described in detail in Chapter 6, as are the switching frequency limitations that are present when using sysfs. In particular, Figure 6-5 illustrates the result of a shell script that is switching a GPIO output at approximately 1.8kHz, in which it is clear that the output signal suffers from *jitter* (i.e., a deviation from true periodicity of a periodic signal). When a more sophisticated C/C++ program is used in Chapter 6 to increase the switching frequency, the same jitter issue arises. It could be time for a GPIO to be toggled in a time-critical manner, but the Linux process scheduler may already have determined that the Apache web server should execute. Therefore, the toggling of the GPIO will be delayed and signal jitter arises.

Preemptive scheduling means that kernel scheduling is based on the priority of the tasks to be executed. Therefore, if the GPIO toggle task is designated to be of a higher priority than the Apache web server, then the Apache task will be interrupted, even though its kernel service time has not expired. For hard real-time systems, the *preemption period* is typically of the order of microseconds or lower. The *latency* of a task is the key measurement of the real-time performance of the system, and it is largely dependent on the tasks that are running at equal or higher priorities on the same machine.

As described in Chapter 7, one way to implement preemptive scheduling on the Beagle board is to apply the RT-Preempt patch (aka PREEMPT_RT) to a Linux kernel build. This patch converts the mainline Linux kernel into a fully preemptive system (with the exception of interrupt handling and certain regions that are guarded by spinlocks). To apply the patch, you must rebuild the Linux kernel and add CONFIG_PREEMPT_RT_FULL=y to the build configuration (see tiny.cc/beagle1001 for further details). When applied to the Beagle board, the RT-Preempt patch typically results in worst-case latency times of double-digit milliseconds, when executing C/C++ real-time applications.

Xenomai (www.xenomai.org) provides a different type of solution. It supplements mainline Linux with a real-time co-kernel, called Cobalt, which is responsible for performing all time-critical activities. The co-kernel has higher priority than Linux—it processes hardware interrupts and passes virtual interrupts to the underlying Linux kernel. The Machinekit (machinekit.io) Debian distribution is a good way to get started with Xenomai on the BeagleBone, as it is based on the official BeagleBoard.org Debian release. The distribution is targeted specifically at computer numerical control (CNC) and 3D printing applications.

Note also that the Beagle boards can be used without mainline Linux. For example, the following platforms can be downloaded without cost:

- **StarterWare for ARM-based TI Sitara processors:** This is a *no-OS* platform for devices such as the AM335x. It provides a device abstraction layer (e.g., for UART, SPI, I²C, LCD, Ethernet) that can be programmed using open-source tools and C-based library APIs to build applications that can perform peripheral configuration and I/O. See tiny.cc/beagle1002 for further details.

- **QNX Neutrino RTOS on OMAP and Sitara:** This is a full-featured real-time OS (RTOS) that is available with AM335x reference designs for in-car, digital instrument, and smart home displays. See tiny.cc/beagle1003 and tiny.cc/beagle1004.

While suitable for hard real-time applications, both of these commercial offerings are not general-purpose OSs and require significant expertise.

Real-Time Hardware Solutions

Later in this chapter a communications framework is described that can be used to offload real-time processing to low-cost microcontrollers, such as the Arduino, Atmel AVR, and TI MSP platforms. The framework uses a UART device and I²C buses for communication. Using this framework, a set of microcontrollers could be connected to a Beagle board and used to take responsibility for hard real-time processing and interfacing. The Beagle board could then be used for centralized high-level tasks, such as GUI display, network communication, data aggregation/storage, and algorithmic tuning.

Sophisticated capes are available for the BBB that can be used for real-time processing, the most notable being the *Valent F(x) LOGi-Bone-2 FPGA development board*.[1] Hardware description languages (HDLs), such as Verilog or VHDL, can be used in programming *field-programmable gate arrays* (FPGAs) to create high-speed logic circuits. FPGAs are particularly useful for parallel processing, as they can perform many thousands of operations in a single clock cycle. Unfortunately, not all tasks are suitable for a parallel implementation, and there is a steep learning curve in developing FPGA software. The LOGi-Bone-2 cape provides a good introduction to FPGA development, as the associated applications are open source and a growing community of users is working on this platform. The guide at `tiny.cc/beagle1005` provides a detailed overview of the steps required to interface the cape to the BBB. In the next section, GPIO extenders are examined that can provide a small degree of input/output programmability through the use of interrupt masks.

The AM335x processor has two programmable real-time units (PRUs) that can be used for certain real-time interfacing operations, and these are the focus of Chapter 15.

Extended GPIO Availability

The use of the Beagle board GPIOs is described in detail in Chapter 6, where it is discussed that there are a large number of GPIOs available on the multiplexed header pins; however, these pins are quickly consumed by functions such as HDMI, which require a significant number of pins (e.g., for the connection of an LCD panel to the board).

It is possible to use low-cost I/O expanders, such as the Microchip 16-bit MCP23017 I²C I/O Expander and the 16-bit MCP23S17 SPI Expander, which are both available in PDIP form for $1–$2. Figure 10-1(a) illustrates the connection

---

[1] Uses a Xilinx Spartan 6 LX9 TQFP-144 FPGA with 9,152 logic cells, 11,440 CLB flip-flops, 16 DSP48A1 slices, and 576Kb RAM. The board also contains a 256Mb SDRAM, Arduino compatible headers, and is accessed using GPMC, SPI, or I²C from the BBB.

of the MCP23017 to the I²C bus, and Figure 10-1(b) illustrates the connection of the MCP23S17 to the SPI bus. These are different physical devices, but their pin layouts are consistent, which assists with design for possible bus interchange. In fact, both devices are described by a single datasheet: `tiny.cc/beagle1006`.

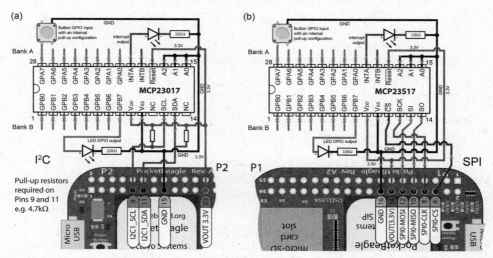

Figure 10-1: Adding GPIOs to the PocketBeagle using (a) the MCP23017 I²C GPIO expander and (b) the MCP23S17 SPI GPIO expander

These are some physical features of each device that should be noted:

- The MCP23017 has three address pins (A0–A2) that allow up to eight ICs to be connected to a single I²C bus, which facilitates the addition of up to 128 GPIOs to each I²C bus. The device supports 100kHz, 400kHz, and 1.7MHz bus speeds.

- The MCP23S17 also has three address pins (A0–A2) that are used to address separate devices, which have been daisy chained together as a single SPI device (discussed shortly). This facilitates the addition of up to 256 GPIOs to the single SPI bus on the Beagle board by using both chip select pins. The MCP23S17 supports SPI bus speeds of up to 10MHz.

It is worth noting up front that these are capable devices that are surprisingly complex. For example, the GPIO pins can be configured as inputs/outputs, internal pull-up/pull-down resistor configuration is possible, input polarity is selectable, and different types of interrupt conditions can be configured. This is all useful functionality that can greatly improve the I/O capabilities of the Beagle boards (and of other embedded devices), so it is worth the effort involved in becoming familiar with their configuration and use.

The internal register configuration of both devices is consistent. They have two banks of registers (A and B), each associated with eight configurable GPIOs. In addition, the devices have two interrupt pins (INTA and INTB) that can be configured to react to a programmable set of input conditions.

The illustrations in Figure 10-1 each include three test circuits that are used in this section to help explain the capability of these devices:

- A pushbutton circuit is connected to GPA7, which is configured shortly to have an internal pull-up resistor enabled.

- An LED circuit is connected to GPB7, which is configured to be an output. The LED lights when GPB7 is high.

- An LED circuit is connected to the interrupt pin, INTA, which is used to test the interrupt capabilities of the devices.

The I²C device is investigated first because the Linux i2c-tools (see Chapter 8) are useful for familiarizing yourself with the registers on a new device.

The MCP23017 and the I²C Bus

The MCP23017 appears on the bus at address 0x20 by default. You can alter this address by tying A0, A1, and A2 high or low. For example, if A0 and A1 are tied to the 3.3V line, then the device address becomes 0x23. In the default configuration, as in Figure 10-1(a) you can verify the device address.

```
debian@ebb:~$ i2cdetect -y -r 1
     0  1  2  3  4  5  6  7  8  9  a  b  c  d  e  f
00:          -- -- -- -- -- -- -- -- -- -- -- --
10: -- -- -- -- -- -- -- -- -- -- -- -- -- -- -- --
20: 20 -- -- -- -- -- -- -- -- -- -- -- -- -- -- -- ...
```

The registers can then be displayed as in Figure 10-2 using the i2cdump command. This figure identifies the name and role of each of the registers, which are organized into pairs so as to align against the two 8-bit ports (Port A and Port B) on the devices.

To become familiar with the use of these devices, a good starting point is to use the i2cset and i2cget commands to control the LED circuit and the push-button circuit, both of which are illustrated in Figure 10-1(a).

IODIRA	0x00	Input/Output direction Port A Register (1=input, 0=output)
IODIRB	0x01	Input/Output direction Port B Register (1=input, 0=output)
IPOLA	0x02	Set the polarity of Port A (invert inputs) (1=invert, 0=regular)
IPOLB	0x03	Set the polarity of Port B (invert inputs) (1=invert, 0=regular)
GPINTENA	0x04	Interrupt-on-change control register Port A (1=enable, 0=disable)
GPINTENB	0x05	Same but for Port B—must have DEFVALx and INTCONx set
DEFVALA	0x06	Default compare register for interrupt-on-change INTA
DEFVALB	0x07	Same for Port B. If pin level opposite from register then trigger interrupt.
INTCONA	0x08	Interrupt control register to choose whether interrupt-on-change (1)
INTCONB	0x09	is set or on-compare is set (0) with DEFVALx.
IOCONA	0x0A	Configuration and control register Port A
IOCONB	0x0B	Same but for Port B (settings typicallly mirrored)

IOCONx

Bit	IOCONx	
7	Bank control	1 different bank 0 same bank
6	Mirror INT pins	1 connected 0 not connected
5	Sequential operation	1 disabled 0 enabled
4	Slew rate control	1 disabled 0 enabled
3	h/w addr. enable (SPI)	1 enabled 0 disabled
2	Open-drain output	1 open-drain 0 active driver
1	Interrupt polarity	1 active-high 0 active-low
0	N/A	1 ignored 0 ignored

Use: 00111010 (0x3A) in the examples in this section

```
debian@ebb.../chp10/gpioExpander$ ./testI2C
debian@ebb.../chp10/gpioExpander$ i2cdump -y 1 0x20 b

     0  1  2  3  4  5  6  7  8  9  a  b  c  d  e  f
00: 00 ff 00 00 00 ba 00 00 00 00 54 54 00 00 00 00
10: 00 00 00 00 00 00 ...
```

GPPUA	0x0C	Input pull-up resistor config for Port A (1=pull-up, 0=pull-down)
GPPUB	0x0D	Input pull-up resistor config for Port B (1=pull-up, 0=pull-down)
INTFA	0x0E	Interrupt flag register—indicates GPIOs on A that triggered interrupt (1)
INTFB	0x0F	Interrupt flag register—indicates GPIOs on B that triggered interrupt (1)
INTCAPA	0x10	Captures Port A values when interrupt occurs
INTCAPB	0x11	Captures Port B values when interrupt occurs
GPIOA	0x12	GPIO input register—current input state (writing affects OLATx)
GPIOB	0x13	GPIO input register for Port B
OLATA	0x14	Output latch for setting outputs on Port A
OLATB	0x15	Output latch for setting outputs on Port B

Figure 10-2: The MCP23x17 registers

Controlling the GPIO LED Circuit

The output LED is attached to Port B Pin 7 (GPB7), as in Figure 10-1(a). To set the state of the LED, you first need to perform the following steps:

1. Set the IOCONB configuration and control register state (0x0B) to be 0x3A, as determined on the right side of Figure 10-2:

    ```
    debian@ebb:~$ i2cset -y 1 0x20 0x0B 0x3A
    ```

2. Set GPB7 in the IODIRB (0x01) direction register to be in output mode by setting bit 7 to be low (note that the following call will set all eight GPB pins to be outputs):

    ```
    debian@ebb:~$ i2cset -y 1 0x20 0x01 0x00
    ```

3. To light the LED that is attached to GPB7, you can set bit 7 on the OLATB output latch register (0x15) high. You can then read the current Port B state using the GPIOB register (0x13) as follows:

    ```
    debian@ebb:~$ i2cset -y 1 0x20 0x15 0x80
    debian@ebb:~$ i2cget -y 1 0x20 0x13
    0x80
    ```

4. At this point, the LED is lighting, and the GPIO bit 7 (0b10000000 = 0x80) is set. The LED can be turned off by setting bit 7 low.

```
debian@ebb:~$ i2cset -y 1 0x20 0x15 0x00
debian@ebb:~$ i2cget -y 1 0x20 0x13
0x00
```

Note that all the previous operations affect all the GPB input/outputs. For example, turning the LED off by writing the value 0x00 also sets GPB0–GPB6 low. To solve this problem, you can read in the current state of the outputs using the GPIOB registers (0x13), modify the value of the desired bit, and then write it back to the OLATB register (0x15). For example, if a read of GPIOB returned 0x03, then GPB0 and GPB1 are high. To retain this state and to set GPB7 high, you should OR the two values together (i.e., 0x03|0x80), which results in a value of 0x83. If this value is written to OLATB, all three pins are now set high (GPB0, GPB1, and GPB7).

Reading the GPIO Button State

To read the pushbutton state that is attached to Bank A pin 7 (GPA7), you can use a similar method:

1. Set the IOCONA control register to be 0x3A, as illustrated on the right side of Figure 10-2:

```
debian@ebb:~$ i2cset -y 1 0x20 0x0A 0x3A
```

2. Set GPA7 to be an input using the IODIRA register (0x00):

```
debian@ebb:~$ i2cset -y 1 0x20 0x00 0x80
```

3. Set GPA7 to be in a pull-up mode using the GPPUA input pull-up configuration register (0x0C):

```
debian@ebb:~$ i2cset -y 1 0x20 0x0C 0x80
```

4. Read the Port A state using the GPIOA input register (0x12):

```
debian@ebb:~$ i2cget -y 1 0x20 0x12
0x80
debian@ebb:~$ i2cget -y 1 0x20 0x12
0x00
```

When the button is not pressed, the state is 0b10000000 (0x80), and when the button is pressed, the state is 0b00000000 (0x00), indicating that the button circuit is working correctly and that it has a pull-up configuration.

An Interrupt Configuration Example (Advanced)

The devices can be programmed to activate an interrupt output (INTA or INTB) when one of two configurable conditions arises:

1. The input state changes from its current state, where a mask can be set using the GPINTENx register to check or ignore individual bits.

2. The input state differs from a defined value, which is set using the DEFVALx register.

The INTA and INTB output pins can be configured to activate individually, or they can be programmed to both activate if either port causes the interrupt.

The use of interrupts is best explained with an example, which is once again illustrated in Figure 10-1(a). In this example, the device is configured so that if the pushbutton that is attached to GPA7 is pressed (or released), the LED attached to the INTA pin will light.

- Set up the pushbutton to be an input, as described in the previous example. Remember that the button is in a pull-up configuration so that when the button is not pressed, the output is as follows:

```
debian@ebb:~$ i2cget -y 1 0x20 0x12
0x80
```

- Set the GPINTENA interrupt-on-change control register (0x04) to enable GPB7. The DEFVALA default interrupt-on-change compare value (0x06) should be set to 0x80, and the INTCONA interrupt control register (0x08) should also be set to 0x80.

```
debian@ebb:~$ i2cset -y 1 0x20 0x04 0x80
debian@ebb:~$ i2cset -y 1 0x20 0x06 0x80
debian@ebb:~$ i2cset -y 1 0x20 0x08 0x80
```

- Reading the output clears the interrupt. If the INTA LED is currently lighting, then displaying the Port A state using the GPIOA input register (0x12) should cause it to turn off.

```
debian@ebb:~$ i2cget -y 1 0x20 0x12
0x80
```

- Pressing the button at this point should trigger the interrupt and cause the INTA LED to light. You can then use the INTFA interrupt flag register (0x0E) to identify which input caused the interrupt, and you can use the INTCAPA capture register (0x10) to determine the Port A state when the interrupt occurred.

```
debian@ebb:~$ i2cget -y 1 0x20 0x0E
0x80
debian@ebb:~$ i2cget -y 1 0x20 0x10
0x00
```

- Reading the value of INTCAPA clears the interrupt. So, it is once again ready to trigger an interrupt when the button is pressed.

Clearly, you do not need such a complex arrangement to trigger an LED when a button is pressed! However, it is possible to configure the device so that a particular bit pattern on all the Port A and Port B pins is used to trigger the interrupt. My tests indicate that in this example the LED lights 190ns after the button is pressed, which is extremely fast in comparison to the response times reported for the Beagle board GPIOs in Chapter 6. Clearly, it is possible to build a hardware circuit using logic gates that can react to a bit pattern even more quickly, but it is important to remember that this behavior is software configurable and can be changed dynamically at run time.

A code example is introduced shortly to facilitate the structured use of these devices.

The MCP23S17 and the SPI Bus

The MCP23S17 SPI version of the MCP23017 I²C device has the same register configuration, and therefore the input/output circuits that are illustrated in Figure 10-1(a) and Figure 10-1(b) are identical.

The registers on the SPI device are accessed using the same techniques as described in Chapter 8. However, there is one important difference in the way that this device operates in comparison to other SPI bus devices examined to this point—it implements a custom internal device addressing architecture. Figure 10-3 illustrates how up to eight MCP23S17 devices can be attached to a single SPI bus as a single SPI device. The address lines A0–A2 are used to assign each device a unique 3-bit hardware address, which each device uses to decide whether it should act upon or ignore messages on the bus.

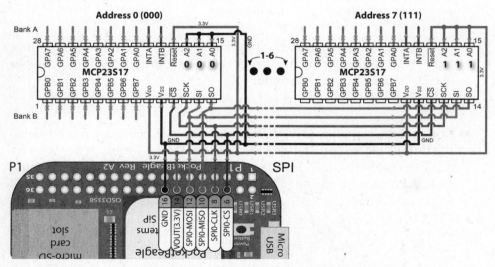

Figure 10-3: Daisy chaining up to eight MCP23S17s as a single SPI bus device

As illustrated in Figure 10-3, all the devices share the same MOSI, MISO, CLK, and CS lines, which means that all data read/write requests are simultaneously sent to all the daisy-chained devices. Each device must identify which requests it should act upon and which requests it should ignore based on its hardware-defined address (A0–A2) and addressing information that is contained within the SPI data message. Therefore, the structure of the SPI message is different than those described in Chapter 8. For example, each write request must contain the device address, the register address, and the data to write to the register address. Figure 10-4 illustrates an example data write transaction taking place, which has the following form: "on device 000 set the IOCONA control register (0x0A) to have the value 0x3A."

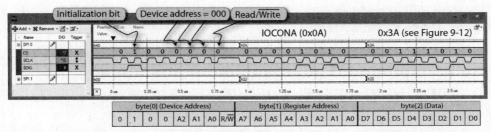

Figure 10-4: An SPI write request to the MCP23S17 at device address 000 to set the IOCONA register to 0x3A

A C++ Class for the MCP23x17 Devices

A C++ class that simplifies the use of the MCP23x17 devices is provided in Listing 10-1 and is available in the /chp10/gpioExpander/ directory. The class wraps the register functionality that is illustrated in Figure 10-2 and provides a framework for accessing the general functionality and interrupt functionality of the MCP23017 and MCP23S17 devices.

Listing 10-1: /chp10/gpioExpander/gpioExpander.h (Segment)

```cpp
class GPIOExpander {
private:
    I2CDevice *i2cDevice;
    SPIDevice *spiDevice;
    bool isSPIDevice;
    unsigned char spiAddress; configRegister;

public:
    enum PORT { PORTA=0, PORTB=1 };
    int writeDevice(unsigned char address, unsigned char value);
    unsigned char readDevice(unsigned char address);
    GPIOExpander(I2CDevice *i2cDevice);
    GPIOExpander(SPIDevice *spiDevice, unsigned char address=0x00);
```

```
                // 16-bit -- PORTA is LSB (8-bits), PORTB is MSB (8-bits)
                virtual int setGPIODirections(PORT port, unsigned char value);
                virtual int setGPIODirections(unsigned short value);

                virtual unsigned char getOutputValues(PORT port);
                virtual unsigned short getOutputValues();
                virtual std::string getOutputValuesStr();
                virtual int setOutputValues(PORT port, unsigned char value);
                virtual int setOutputValues(unsigned short value);

                virtual unsigned char getInputValues(PORT port);
                virtual unsigned short getInputValues();
                virtual std::string getInputValuesStr();
                virtual int setInputPolarity(PORT port, unsigned char value);
                virtual int setInputPolarity(unsigned short value);

                // Pull-up resistors for the input ports -- 100k Ohm value
                virtual int setGPIOPullUps(PORT port, unsigned char value);
                virtual int setGPIOPullUps(unsigned short value);
                virtual int updateConfigRegister(unsigned char value);
                virtual int setInterruptOnChange(PORT port, unsigned char value);
                virtual int setInterruptOnChange(unsigned short value);

                // Get the value on the port when interrupt occurs
                virtual unsigned char getInterruptCaptureState(PORT port);
                virtual unsigned short getInterruptCaptureState();
                virtual std::string getInterruptCaptureStateStr();

                // Sets if the interrupt is configured on change or on comparison
                virtual int setInterruptControl(PORT port, unsigned char value);
                virtual int setInterruptControl(unsigned short value);

                // Sets the default comparison register
                virtual int setDefaultCompareValue(PORT port, unsigned char value);
                virtual int setDefaultCompareValue(unsigned short value);

                // Get the interrupt flag register
                virtual unsigned char getInterruptFlagState(PORT port);
                virtual unsigned short getInterruptFlagState();
                virtual std::string getInterruptFlagStateStr();
                virtual void dumpRegisters();  ...
        };
```

An example is provided in Listing 10-2 that uses the GPIOExpander class to perform the same test operations as described with the Linux i2c-tools to control the circuit that is illustrated in Figure 10-1.

Listing 10-2: /chp10/gpioExpander/example.cpp

```
int main(){
    cout << "Starting the GPIO Expander Example" << endl;
    SPIDevice *spiDevice = new SPIDevice(0,0);
```

```
   spiDevice->setSpeed(10000000);                    // MCP23S17 bus speed
   spiDevice->setMode(SPIDevice::MODE0);

// I2CDevice *i2cDevice = new I2CDevice(1, 0x20);    // for an I2C device
// GPIOExpander gpio(i2cDevice);                     // for an I2C device
   GPIOExpander gpio(spiDevice, 0x00);               // SPI dev. addr. 000
   cout << "The GPIO Expander was set up successfully" << endl;

   // PORTA are inputs and PORTB are outputs -- can mix bits
   gpio.setGPIODirections(GPIOExpander::PORTA, 0b11111111); // input=1
   gpio.setGPIODirections(GPIOExpander::PORTB, 0b00000000); // output=0
   gpio.setGPIOPullUps(GPIOExpander::PORTA, 0b10000000);    // pullup GPA7
   gpio.setInputPolarity(GPIOExpander::PORTA, 0b00000000);  // non-inverted

   // Example: get the values of PORTA and set PORTB accordingly
   unsigned char inputValues = gpio.getInputValues(GPIOExpander::PORTA);
   cout << "The values are in the form [B7,..,B0,A7,..,A0]" << endl;
   cout << "The PORTA values are: [" << gpio.getInputValuesStr() << "]\n";
   cout << "Setting PORTB to be " << (int)inputValues << endl;
   gpio.setOutputValues(GPIOExpander::PORTB, inputValues);

   // Example: attach on-change interrupt to GPIOA GPA7
   cout << "Interrupt flags[" << gpio.getInterruptFlagStateStr() << "]\n";
   cout << "Capture state[" << gpio.getInterruptCaptureStateStr() << "]\n";
   gpio.setInterruptControl(GPIOExpander::PORTA, 0b00000000);  // on change
   gpio.setInterruptOnChange(GPIOExpander::PORTA, 0b10000000); // to GPA7
   gpio.dumpRegisters();                             // display the registers
   cout << "End of the GPIO Expander Example" << endl;
}
```

The code example reads the state of the Port A inputs and sets Port B accordingly (remember that GPA7 is in a pull-up configuration, so it is high when the button is not pressed). In addition, an interrupt-on-change configuration is set for INTA, which lights the LED that is attached to INTA when the button is pressed:

```
debian@ebb:~/exploringbb/chp10/gpioExpander $ ./example
Starting the GPIO Expander Example
The GPIO Expander was set up successfully
The values are in the form [B7,..,B0,A7,..,A0]
The PORTA values are: [1000000010000000]
Setting PORTB to be 128
Interrupt flags[0000000000000000]
Capture state[0000000000000000]
Register Dump:
Register IODIRA  :    255  B: 0
Register IPOLA   :      0  B: 0
Register GPINTENA:    128  B: 0
Register DEFVALA :      0  B: 0
Register INTCONA :      0  B: 0
Register IOCONA  :     58  B: 58
Register GPPUA   :    128  B: 0
```

```
Register INTFA    :      0  B: 0
Register INTAPA   :      0  B: 0
Register GPIOA    :    128  B: 128
Register OLATA    :      0  B: 128
End of the GPIO Expander Example
```

At this point, the program has run to completion, but it is important to note that the interrupt will still trigger at any future point. The MCP23x17 is programmed to handle the interrupt independently of the Beagle board.

If the button is pressed, the interrupt is triggered, and a call to the display program in the same directory displays the register states. In this example, the interrupt flag register (INTFA) indicates that GPA7 caused the interrupt (i.e., $128_{10} = 0b10000000$):

```
debian@ebb:~/exploringbb/chp10/gpioExpander $ ./display
Starting the SPI GPIO Expander Example
Register Dump:
Register IODIRA   :    255  B: 0
Register IPOLA    :      0  B: 0
Register GPINTENA:     128  B: 0
Register DEFVALA  :      0  B: 0
Register INTCONA  :      0  B: 0
Register IOCONA   :     58  B: 58
Register GPPUA    :    128  B: 0
Register INTFA    :    128  B: 0
Register INTAPA   :      0  B: 0
Register GPIOA    :    128  B: 128
Register OLATA    :      0  B: 128
End of the GPIO Expander Example
```

The display program reads the GPIOx registers, so the interrupt is once again primed, even without executing the example program again. Also, if you hold the pushbutton and simultaneously execute the display program, then the interrupt is triggered when you release the button, which demonstrates that an interrupt-on-change condition is configured.

Adding External UARTs

As described in Chapter 8, UART devices provide a mechanism for serial communication to discrete modules such as GPS units, microprocessors, microcontrollers, sensor modules, actuator modules, and much more. In addition, UARTs can be combined with line driver hardware, such as RS-485 modules, to communicate over long distances—RS-485 supports a network of up to 32 devices communicating at distances of up to 4,000ft (1,200m) using a single pair of twisted-pair wires and a common ground connection.[2]

---

[2]See `tiny.cc/beagle1008` for further details.

It is possible to use the SPI or I²C bus to add UART devices to the Beagle boards. For example, the SparkFun SC16IS750 module ($15) supports high-speed (up to 921,600 baud) communication using the NXP chip of the same name. You can interface this device to the Beagle boards using approaches similar to those described in this chapter. However, a much easier solution is to use the USB ports and USB-to-TTL converters, which have Linux driver support.

There are several low-cost USB-to-TTL converters available, many of which have stable Linux driver support. Figure 10-5 illustrates three such devices that are available from as little as $1–$2. They can be attached directly to the Beagle board USB port or to a multi-port USB hub; however, be careful to ensure that the pins from one adapter do not touch the pins or the tracks on the base of the adapter that is inserted into an adjacent USB hub slot.

Figure 10-5: Three low-cost USB-to-TTL converters

Modern Linux kernels support USB hot plugging, which allows USB devices to be plugged in to the Beagle board after it has booted. The kernel then loads the correct LKM for the device. You can use the `dmesg` command to display system-level driver messages, which can help you in diagnosing any device driver problems. You can then list the attached USB devices using the `lsusb` command, whereupon a new device is displayed:

```
debian@ebb:~$ lsusb
...
Bus 001 Device 004:ID 1a86:7523 QinHeng Elec HL-340 USB-Serial adapter
```

There are also new LKMs loaded that are associated with this device:

```
debian@ebb:~$ lsmod | grep ch34
ch341                  4921  0 ...
```

With three devices plugged into the board, each USB device has its own device entry in the `/dev/` directory.

```
debian@ebb:~$ lsusb
Bus 001 Device 004: ID 1a86:7523 QinHeng Elec HL-340 USB-Serial adapter
Bus 001 Device 006: ID 1a86:7523 QinHeng Elec HL-340 USB-Serial adapter
Bus 001 Device 005: ID 10c4:ea60 Cygnal Integrated Products, CP210x UART ...
debian@ebb:~$ ls -l /dev/ttyUSB*
crw-rw---T 1 root dialout 188, 0 Aug 30 15:40 /dev/ttyUSB0
crw-rw---T 1 root dialout 188, 1 Aug 30 15:44 /dev/ttyUSB1
crw-rw---T 1 root dialout 188, 2 Aug 30 15:44 /dev/ttyUSB2
```

Several of the available USB devices have built-in logic-level translation circuitry, which is useful for interfacing to both 3.3V and 5V tolerant devices. For example, the YP-02 has a jumper that you can move to bridge its VCC and 5V pins, or the VCC and 3V3 pins, as illustrated in Figure 10-5. The Baite module has a slider selector switch on its side that can be used to select either logic level.

USB DEVICES AND UDEV RULES

When you unplug the USB device that is associated with `/dev/ttyUSB0`, then the other device names will be updated to close any numbering "gaps":

```
debian@ebb:~$ ls -l /dev/ttyUSB*
crw-rw---T 1 root dialout 188, 0 Aug 30 15:40 /dev/ttyUSB0
crw-rw---T 1 root dialout 188, 1 Aug 30 16:49 /dev/ttyUSB1
```

This can cause difficulty for your software applications because they will not be aware of the update (e.g., a serial motor controller could become connected to a serial sensor module). You can solve this problem using udev rules. Each USB device has a vendor, a product ID, and sometimes a unique serial number. This information can be used to construct a rule that associates the USB adapter with a custom device name. You can find the adapter's details using `lsusb` (as shown earlier) and/or by using the `udevadm` command.

```
debian@ebb:~$ sudo udevadm info -a -n /dev/ttyUSB1 | grep idVendor
    ATTRS{idVendor}=="10c4" ...
debian@ebb:~$ sudo udevadm info -a -n /dev/ttyUSB1 | grep idProduct
    ATTRS{idProduct}=="ea60" ...
debian@ebb:~$ sudo udevadm info -a -n /dev/ttyUSB1 | grep serial
    ATTRS{serial}=="0001" ...
```

You can then write a rule to create a custom device entry when the USB adapter is plugged in. For example, if a motor was attached to the CP210x device (ID 10c4:ea60), you could write the following rule to create a custom device entry (note that `==` is for comparison, and `=` is for assignment):

```
debian@ebb:/etc/udev/rules.d$ sudo nano 98-ebb.rules
debian@ebb:/etc/udev/rules.d$ more 98-ebb.rules
SUBSYSTEM=="tty", ATTRS{idVendor}=="10c4", ATTRS{idProduct}=="ea60", →
ATTRS{serial}=="0001", SYMLINK+="ebb_motor"
```

On reboot a new device appears in `/dev/` that is automatically linked to the correct `ttyUSBx` device whenever the CP210x device is plugged in.

```
debian@ebb:/etc/udev/rules.d$ ls -l /dev/er*
lrwxrwxrwx 1 root root 7 Jan  1  1970 /dev/ebb_motor -> ttyUSB1
```

The symbolic link is automatically removed if the device is unplugged and will appear again if the device is reinserted (hot plugged). Clearly, you should use the `/dev/ebb_motor` symbolic link within your code.

The serial number can usually be used to distinguish between two identical devices. Unfortunately, these low-cost adapters often do not have unique serial numbers. There are tools available to write serial numbers onto USB devices, but they can destroy the devices. An alternative solution is to use the physical USB slot to identify the device, but it is not straightforward. Please see `tiny.cc/beagle1007` for more information on writing udev rules. If your device does not have a definite serial number or you cannot seem to get the udev rule to work correctly when adding the apparent serial number for your device, try to remove that portion from the udev rules file. For example, for the YP-02 adapter in Figure 10-5, use the following:

```
SUBSYSTEM=="tty", ATTRS{idVendor}=="1a86", ATTRS{idProduct}=="7523", →
SYMLINK+="ebb_serial"
```

The Arduino

The *Arduino* (`www.arduino.cc`) is a popular, low-cost, and powerful microcontroller that can be used as a capable companion controller for a Beagle board. The Arduino was designed as an introductory platform for embedded systems. It is programmed using the Arduino programming language, in the Arduino development environment, which are both designed to be as user friendly as possible.

An in-depth introduction to the Arduino is beyond the scope of this book; instead, this chapter focuses on possible interactions between the Arduino and the Beagle board platform. In particular, the Arduino is used to develop a framework for Beagle board applications that distributes high-speed embedded systems workload to slave processors, while still maintaining high-level control.

NOTE There are videos on getting started with the Arduino on the web page associated with this chapter: `www.exploringbeaglebone.com/chapter10/`.

In addition, a comprehensive book on the Arduino is available in this Wiley miniseries, called *Exploring Arduino*, by Jeremy Blum. See `www.exploringarduino.com` for more details.

Figure 10-6 illustrates to relative scale two Arduino models. The Arduino UNO in Figure 10-6(a) is a popular version of the Arduino that contains a replaceable ATmega IC in a DIP format. The Arduino Pro Mini in Figure 10-6(b) is a smaller, lower-cost version of the same platform; however, the ATmega IC is surface mounted and cannot be easily replaced should it be accidentally damaged.

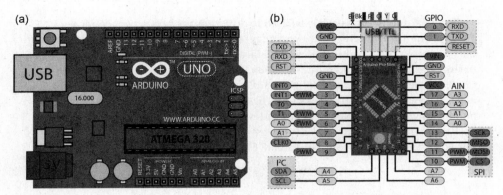

Figure 10-6: Arduino boards (to relative scale): (a) the Arduino UNO and (b) the Arduino Pro Mini (3.3V or 5V)

Because the Arduino is open-source hardware, it is available in many different forms. However, an open hardware Arduino Pro Mini (ATmega168 or ATmega328) is chosen as the focus of this chapter for the following reasons:

- A 3.3V version is available, which simplifies communication with the Beagle boards, because no logic-level translation circuitry is required. The more commonplace 5V version is also used throughout this chapter.

- It is a low-cost, open-hardware device ($5–$10) that is only 1.3"× 0.7" (33mm × 18mm) in size; therefore, you can connect several boards to a single Beagle board while still maintaining a modest footprint.

- There is no USB input on the board (reducing size and cost), but it can be programmed using a UART connection.

- The principles described for this board can be easily adapted for any Arduino model.

> **WARNING**   Pay special attention to voltage levels in this chapter. As discussed in Chapter 8, you have to be careful when connecting 5V microcontrollers to the Beagle board inputs and outputs. Read the section in Chapter 8 on logic-level translation carefully before building the interfacing circuits in this chapter. Arduino board models can look similar but have quite different input/output configurations. If you have any doubts, measure the voltage levels on an output line before connecting it to your Beagle board.

Figure 10-7 illustrates the Arduino programming environment as it is used to develop a program to flash the onboard LED that is attached to pin 13 on most Arduino boards (see Listing 10-3). The program sends the string "Hello from the Arduino" to the desktop machine when the program begins. An Arduino sketch has the extension .INO (previous versions used .PDE), but it is essentially a C++ program that is parsed by the Arduino preprocessor.

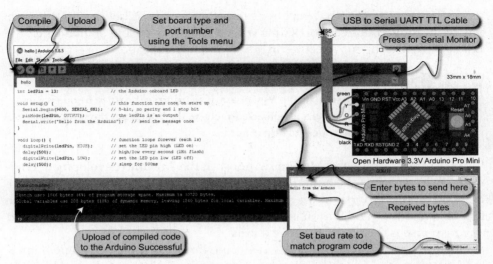

Figure 10-7: The Arduino platform "Hello World" example and the Arduino Pro Mini programming configuration

The Arduino Pro Mini can be programmed from a desktop machine by attaching a USB-to-Serial TTL cable/device, as illustrated in Figure 10-7. Check the connections for your board; different models vary slightly. The same cable can be used to provide serial monitoring capabilities, which is extremely useful in debugging program code. The low-cost USB-to-Serial TTL devices described in this chapter can also be used to program the Arduino from the desktop machine. In addition, several have selectable 5V/3.3V levels using either a jumper connection or an onboard switch. Use a USB-to-Serial cable/device that matches the logic-level voltages of your chosen Arduino.

Listing 10-3: `/chp10/hello/hello.ino`

```
int ledPin = 13;                    // the Arduino onboard LED

void setup() {                      // this function runs once on start up
  Serial.begin(9600, SERIAL_8N1);   // 8-bit, no parity and 1 stop bit
  pinMode(ledPin, OUTPUT);          // the ledPin is an output
  Serial.write("Hello from the Arduino");   // send the message once
}

void loop() {                       // function loops forever (each 1s)
  digitalWrite(ledPin, HIGH);       // set the LED pin high (LED on)
  delay(500);                       // high/low every second (1Hz flash)
  digitalWrite(ledPin, LOW);        // set the LED pin low (LED off)
  delay(500);                       // sleep for 500ms
}
```

The `setup()` function in Listing 10-3 is called once when the program is started. It configures the serial port to use 9,600 baud (8N1 form). The program flashes the onboard LED (attached to pin 13) forever at a rate of 1 Hz. It does this using the `loop()` function, which repeats as fast as it possibly can. In this case, it is programmed to sleep for 500ms when the LED is on and 500ms when the LED is off, so each loop executes in approximately 1 second.

> **NOTE**   It is important that you choose the correct Arduino board in the Tools menu, especially when using the Pro Mini board. If an incorrect board or frequency is chosen, the code may compile and upload correctly to the board, but the serial communication channel may appear to be corrupt.

You can open the Serial Monitor window in the Arduino development environment by pressing the button in the upper-right corner. Choose the baud rate that corresponds to that in the program code. When a string is entered in the text field and the Send button is pressed, the string is sent to the Arduino, and any response is displayed in the text area.

One method of overcoming the real-time limitations of the Beagle boards that are discussed in earlier chapters is to outsource some of the workload to other embedded controllers, such as those provided by the Arduino, Microchip PIC, TI SimpleLink MCU, and TI MSP430. These embedded microcontrollers share common communication interfaces with the Beagle boards that could be used for this task, including UART devices, I²C, and SPI. The following sections describe how the Arduino can be used as a slave processor to control different types of circuits and devices and how it can be interfaced using UART and I²C communications protocols. The same approaches can be used for all other microcontroller families.

An Arduino Serial Slave

Using a UART connection between a Beagle board and an Arduino is probably the most straightforward method of establishing a slave-processor framework. As discussed in Chapter 8, UART communication has the advantage that there can be some degree of physical distance between the two devices.

> **WARNING**   Do not connect a 5V Arduino to the Beagle boards using the UART connection or you will damage your board. The Arduino Pro 3.3V can be connected directly to your board, but if you are connecting a 5V device, then be sure to use a logic-level translator or a simple voltage divider technique.

The following examples can use either the onboard UART device or a USB-to-TTL adapter. However, you *must* stop any `serial-getty` services for the UART device you want to use.

A UART Echo Test Example

The Arduino Pro Mini is used to test the UART communication capability of a Beagle board, first by using the `minicom` program and then by writing a C program to echo information to/from the Arduino. This approach is further developed to create a serial client/server command control framework.

Echoing Minicom (with LED Flash)

Listing 10-4 provides an Arduino program that waits until serial data is available on the RXD pin. When it is, the LED is turned on, and a character is read in from the pin. The character is then written to the Arduino TXD pin. The program sleeps for 100ms to ensure that the LED flash is visible. The program then loops in preparation for the next character to be received on the RXD pin.

Listing 10-4: /chp10/uart/echo/echo.ino

```
int ledPin = 11;    // LED that flashes when a key is pressed

void setup() {                         // called once on start up
   // A baud rate of 115200 (8-bit with No parity and 1 stop bit)
   Serial.begin(115200, SERIAL_8N1);
   pinMode(ledPin, OUTPUT);            // the LED is an output
}

void loop() {                          // Loops forever
   byte charIn;
   digitalWrite(ledPin, LOW);          // set the LED to be off
   if(Serial.available()){             // a byte has been received
      charIn = Serial.read();          // read character in from the Beagle
      Serial.write(charIn);            // send character back to the Beagle
      digitalWrite(ledPin, HIGH);      // light the LED
      delay(100);                      // delay so the LED is visible
   }
}
```

This program should be uploaded to the Arduino, where it will then execute, awaiting communication on its RXD pin. This program is stored in the EEPROM of the Arduino and will begin to execute as soon as power is applied.

WARNING   The Arduino Pro Mini is a useful board, but there are many variants available. You need to manually check the voltages on the *Vin* and *Vcc* pins to verify the logic levels. For example, some 5V boards take a raw *Vin* of 5V, but that level is regulated to a *Vcc* of 3.3V, and logic levels are set at 3.3V.

The next step is to disconnect the USB-to-Serial TTL cable/device and connect the Arduino to the Beagle board, as illustrated in Figure 10-8 for the Pocket-Beagle board, ensuring that the TXD pin on the board is connected to the RXD pin on the Arduino and that the RXD pin on the board is connected to the TXD pin on the Arduino.

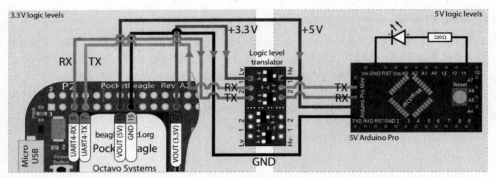

Figure 10-8: UART communication between the PocketBeagle and the Arduino UNO/Pro Mini 5V with a PWM LED example

When you are modifying the Arduino source code and uploading it to the Arduino, you should disconnect the UART connection to the Beagle board each time; otherwise, the process of programming the Arduino will likely fail.[3]

NOTE   If you are having communication problems, check carefully that you have selected the correct Arduino board type. Having the incorrect board type (e.g., wrong clock frequency) can result in consistent errors on only some character transmissions.

Once the Arduino is attached to the Beagle board, the next step is to open the `minicom` program and test the connection. The baud rate is set at 115,200 in the Arduino code, so the same setting must be passed to the `minicom` command. If the connection is displaying incorrect data, reduce the baud rate in the Arduino code to a lower rate, such as 57,600, 19,200, or 9,600:

```
debian@ebb:~$ minicom -b 115200 -o -D /dev/tty04
Welcome to minicom 2.7
OPTIONS: I18n
Compiled on Apr 22 2017, 09:14:19.
Port /dev/tty04, 15:10:57
Press CTRL-A Z for help on special keys
TTeessttiinngg  KKeeyypprreessss  AArrdduuiinnoo
```

---

[3]You can typically leave the USB-to-Serial TTL cable attached to the Arduino if you do not connect the (red) power pin from the desktop machine, but you still have to disconnect the Beagle board RX/TX pins before programming.

The characters appear twice when the minicom local echo feature is enabled—once as a result of the local key press and then again after the transmitted character is echoed by the Arduino. In addition, the LED that is connected to Arduino Pin 11 in Figure 10-8 flashes briefly each time a key is pressed.

The Analog Discovery Logic Analyzer can be connected in parallel to the TXD and RXD lines to analyze the transfer of data from the PocketBeagle to the Arduino. An example of the resulting signals is displayed in Figure 10-9(a) when only the letter H is being transmitted. The start and stop bits can be observed, along with the 8-bit data as it is sent, LSB first, from the PocketBeagle to the Arduino, at a sample bit-period of 8.7μs. At a baud rate of 115,200, the effective byte rate will be somewhat lower because of the overhead of transmitting start, stop, and parity bits. The Arduino response delay is the time it takes for the Arduino to read the character from its RXD input and transmit it back to its TXD output. Test the voltage levels on the receive line from the Arduino before connecting it to the PocketBeagle directly, as illustrated in Figure 10-9(b).

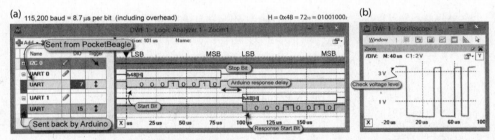

Figure 10-9: Analysis of the UART communication between the PocketBeagle and the Arduino Pro Mini: (a) the logic analyzer and (b) the same letter H on the oscilloscope

UART Echo Example in C

The next step is to write C code on the Beagle board that can communicate with the Arduino program. The Arduino code in Listing 10-4 must be adapted slightly to remove the LED flash, because this slows down communication.

The C program in Listing 10-5 sends a string to the Arduino and reads the responding echo. It uses the Linux termios library (see Chapter 8), which provides a general terminal interface for the control of asynchronous communication ports. This example uses the tty04 UART device. Adapt the source code accordingly for your chosen device (e.g., tty01, ttyUSB0).

Listing 10-5: /chp10/uart/echoC/echo.c

```
#include<stdio.h>
#include<fcntl.h>
#include<unistd.h>
#include<termios.h>    // using the termios.h library
```

```
int main() {
    int file, count;
    if ((file = open("/dev/ttyO4", O_RDWR | O_NOCTTY | O_NDELAY))<0){
        perror("UART: Failed to open the file.\n");
        return -1;
    }
    struct termios options;        // the termios structure is vital
    tcgetattr(file, &options);     // sets the parameters for the file

    // Set up the communications options:
    // 115200 baud, 8-bit, enable receiver, no modem control lines
    options.c_cflag = B115200 | CS8 | CREAD | CLOCAL;
    options.c_iflag = IGNPAR | ICRNL;    // ignore parity errors
    tcflush(file, TCIFLUSH);             // discard file information
    tcsetattr(file, TCSANOW, &options);  // changes occur immmediately
    unsigned char transmit[20] = "Hello Beagle board!";  // send string
    if ((count = write(file, &transmit, 20))<0){          // transmit
        perror("Failed to write to the output\n");
        return -1;
    }
    usleep(100000);              // give the Arduino a chance to respond
    unsigned char receive[100]; //declare a buffer for receiving data
    if ((count = read(file, (void*)receive, 100))<0){   //receive data
        perror("Failed to read from the input\n");
        return -1;
    }
    if (count==0) printf("There was no data available to read!\n");
    else printf("The following was read in [%d]: %s\n",count,receive);
    close(file);
    return 0;
}
```

This program can be built and executed as follows, where the circuit is wired as in Figure 10-8:

```
debian@ebb:~/exploringbb/chp10/uart/echoC$ gcc echo.c -o echo
debian@ebb:~/exploringbb/chp10/uart/echoC$ ./echo
The following was read in [20]: Hello Beagle Board!
```

UART Command Control of an Arduino

The Arduino code in Listing 10-4 is adapted as shown in Listing 10-6 to create a simple LED brightness controller on the Arduino slave. The program on the Arduino expects to receive string commands from a master that have the format LED followed by a space, and then an integer value between 0 and 255. The integer value defines the brightness of an LED that is attached to the PWM output (pin 11) on the Arduino. The program checks that the value is within range and issues an error if it is not. If the command string is not recognized, the Arduino program echoes it back to the sender. This program will continue to run on the Arduino forever.

Listing 10-6: /chp10/uart/command/command.ino

```
int ledPin = 11;            // LED with PWM brightness control

void setup() {              // called once on start up
   // A baud rate of 9600 (8-bit with No parity and 1 stop bit)
   Serial.begin(9600, SERIAL_8N1);
   pinMode(ledPin, OUTPUT);         // the LED is an output
}

void loop() {               // loops forever
   String command;
   char buffer[100];        // stores the return buffer on each loop
   if (Serial.available()>0){              // bytes received
      command = Serial.readStringUntil('\0'); // C strings end with \0
      if(command.substring(0,4) == "LED "){  // begins with "LED "?
         String intString = command.substring(4, command.length());
         int level = intString.toInt();      // extract the int
         if(level>=0 && level<=255){         // is it in range?
            analogWrite(ledPin, level);      // yes, write out
            sprintf(buffer, "Set brightness to %d", level);
         }
         else{                               // no, error message back
            sprintf(buffer, "Error: %d is out of range", level);
         }
      }                                      // otherwise, unknown cmd
      else{ sprintf(buffer, "Unknown command: %s", command.c_str()); }
      Serial.print(buffer);           // send buffer to PocketBeagle
   }
}
```

The C program that is provided in Listing 10-7 is a general test program that sends its command-line argument over the UART connection to the Arduino. It has the same syntax as the echo example in the previous section.

Listing 10-7: /chp10/uart/command/command.c

```
#include<stdio.h>
#include<fcntl.h>
#include<unistd.h>
#include<termios.h>
#include<string.h>

int main(int argc, char *argv[]){
   int file, count;
   if(argc!=2){
      printf("Invalid number of arguments, exiting!\n");
      return -2;
   }
   if ((file = open("/dev/ttyO4", O_RDWR | O_NOCTTY | O_NDELAY))<0){
      perror("UART: Failed to open the file.\n");
      return -1;
   }
```

```
struct termios options;
tcgetattr(file, &options);
options.c_cflag = B9600 | CS8 | CREAD | CLOCAL;
options.c_iflag = IGNPAR | ICRNL;
tcflush(file, TCIFLUSH);
tcsetattr(file, TCSANOW, &options);
// send the string plus the null character
if ((count = write(file, argv[1], strlen(argv[1])+1))<0){
   perror("Failed to write to the output\n");
   return -1;
}
usleep(100000);
unsigned char receive[100];
if ((count = read(file, (void*)receive, 100))<0){
   perror("Failed to read from the input\n");
   return -1;
}
if (count==0) printf("There was no data available to read!\n");
else {
   receive[count]=0;  //There is no null character sent by the Arduino
   printf("The following was read in [%d]: %s\n",count,receive);
}
close(file);
return 0;
}
```

This program can be built and executed as follows, whereupon the LED changes brightness according to the integer value supplied. In addition, the transfer of data can be observed on a logic analyzer, as in Figure 10-10.

```
debian@ebb:~/exploringbb/chp10/uart/command$ gcc command.c -o command
debian@ebb:~/exploringbb/chp10/uart/command$ ./command "LED 255"
The following was read in [21]: Set brightness to 255
debian@ebb:~/exploringbb/chp10/uart/command$ ./command "LED 50"
The following was read in [20]: Set brightness to 50
debian@ebb:~/exploringbb/chp10/uart/command$ ./command "LED 10"
The following was read in [20]: Set brightness to 10
debian@ebb:~/exploringbb/chp10/uart/command$ ./command "LED 0"
The following was read in [19]: Set brightness to 0
debian@ebb:~/exploringbb/chp10/uart/command$ ./command "LED 699"
The following was read in [26]: Error: 699 is out of range
debian@ebb:~/exploringbb/chp10/uart/command$ ./command "wrong"
The following was read in [22]: Unknown command: wrong
```

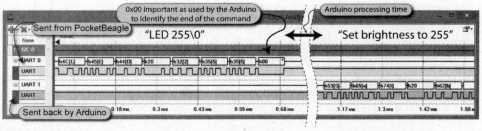

Figure 10-10: Sending the command "LED 255\0" to the Arduino and receiving the response string "Set brightness to 255" at 115,200 baud

The performance of this code could be improved by defining a list of single-byte commands and responses to minimize data transfer time. This framework could be used to create a simple distributed embedded controller platform, and it is limited only by the number of available UART devices on your Beagle board.

An Arduino I²C Slave

Chapter 8 describes how digital devices, such as the ADXL345 accelerometer and a real-time clock, can be attached to a Beagle board using the I²C bus. It describes how you can use the bus to control these devices by reading from and writing to device registers. The Arduino can be configured as an I²C slave, which effectively allows you to create your own I²C digital sensors and controllers. This architecture is useful for a number of reasons.

- A large number of Arduino microcontrollers can be connected to a single Beagle board using each of its I²C buses.[4]
- The Arduino can be intermixed with other I²C devices on the same bus. Each Arduino can be assigned any address.
- As described in Chapter 8, there is a good framework in place for reading from and writing to I²C devices by using registers.
- Using the two-wire interface (TWI) on the Arduino allows it to perform other functions without having to explicitly check for incoming communications.

Relative to SPI or UART serial communications, one disadvantage of I²C is the maximum data rate; however, a master/slave arrangement typically performs the high-speed interfacing work on the slave device and only management commands and status information is passed between the master and the slave devices. Given these considerations, I²C communication is a strong choice for a master/slave arrangement.

An I²C Test Circuit

Figure 10-11 illustrates a test circuit that is used in several of the following sections to demonstrate the capabilities of the I²C master/slave arrangement. It uses a TMP36 analog temperature sensor, which is attached to a 10-bit analog input on the Arduino. In addition, an LED is attached to the PWM output on pin 11. Several of the examples that follow in this chapter use this configuration to demonstrate how you can read data from the temperature sensor and write a value to control the LED brightness.

---

[4]You can connect up to 112 Arduino microcontrollers per I²C bus, as there are 16 reserved addresses (111 1xxx and 000 0xxx) out of the 128 possible 7-bit addresses (2^7). However, the total interconnection cable length is the most likely limiting factor. See tiny.cc/beagle1009. Remember to add pull-up resistors to the bus.

> **NOTE**   Despite warnings on logic voltage levels at the beginning of this chapter, it may be possible to connect a 5V Arduino to the I²C bus on the Beagle board. That is because the pull-up resistors can be tied to 3.3V and the Arduino typically does not have onboard pull-up resistors. This means that the high-level voltage that is used during communication is determined by the Beagle board, not the Arduino. However, if the Arduino (or other device) has onboard pull-up resistors, you cannot use it without bidirectional logic-level translation hardware or the physical removal of the slave device's pull-up resistors.

A desktop PC can be used to program the Arduino using a USB-to-TTL cable or one of the USB-to-TTL adapters described earlier in this chapter. Do not connect the voltage supply pin (red) to the TTL adapter, as this configuration uses the Beagle board to power the Arduino. In this example, a 5V Arduino Pro Mini is utilized, but you will notice that there is no logic-level translation circuitry employed. As previously discussed, the pull-up resistors are connected to 3.3V, and there are no pull-up resistors on this particular Arduino. Therefore, the Arduino can be safely attached to the Beagle board because the SDA and SCL lines can only be pulled high to a maximum of 3.3V. However, if the Arduino model you are using has onboard pull-up resistors, this configuration would damage your board; if in doubt, use a logic-level translator that is compatible with bidirectional data transfer, such as one of those described at the end of Chapter 8.

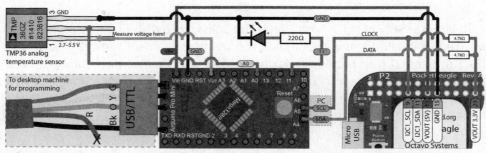

Figure 10-11: The Arduino I²C slave test circuit with a TMP36 analog temperature sensor

I²C Register Echo Example

The first example does not require the temperature sensor or LED circuit; instead, it is a test of I²C communication itself. This section uses Linux i2c-tools on the PocketBeagle to ensure that communication is taking place with the Arduino, before examining a C code example.

Listing 10-8 is an Arduino sketch that configures the Arduino as a slave device using the Arduino Wire library and the two-wire interface (TWI) of the ATmega.[5] In this example, the `setup()` function explicitly sets a clock frequency that aligns with the I²C baud rate of the PocketBeagle. The `setup()` function configures the Arduino to have the arbitrary I²C bus address of 0x44. It then registers two communication listener functions: `receiveRegister()`, which is called whenever data is written to the device using the I²C bus; and `respondData()`, which is called whenever data is read from the device. Importantly, you do not need to call these functions directly from the `loop()` function; instead, they are called automatically.

Listing 10-8: /chp10/i2c/echo/echo.ino

```
#include <Wire.h>                        // Uses the Two-Wire Interface (TWI)

const byte slaveAddr = 0x44;             // the slave address of the Arduino
int registerAddr;                        // the shared register addr variable

void setup() {                           // the setup function -- called once
  TWBR=100000L;                          // the i2c clk freq: 100000L = 100kHz
  Wire.begin(slaveAddr);                 // set Arduino as an I2C slave device
  Wire.onReceive(receiveRegister);       // register receive listener below
  Wire.onRequest(respondData);           // register respond listener below
}

void loop() {
  delay(1000);                           // loop each second -- reduce load
}

void receiveRegister(int x){             // handler called when data available
  registerAddr = Wire.read();            // read in one-byte address from PB
}

void respondData(){                      // handler that is called on response
  Wire.write(registerAddr);              // i.e., send the data back to the PB
}
```

In this example, the Arduino code reads the request byte that comes from the PocketBeagle master (into the `registerAddr` variable) and writes it back as the response. This means the Arduino echoes the address value that is requested as the response data.

When the Arduino is attached to the PocketBeagle as described in Figure 10-11 (even without the LED and temperature sensor), a call to the `i2cdump` command results in the following output:

```
debian@ebb:~/exploringbb/chp10/i2c/echo$ i2cdetect -y -r 1
     0  1  2  3  4  5  6  7  8  9  a  b  c  d  e  f
...
40: -- -- -- -- 44 -- -- -- -- -- -- -- -- -- -- --
```

---

[5]There is a detailed description of the Arduino Wire library at `tiny.cc/beagle1010`.

```
debian@ebb:~/exploringbb/chp10/i2c/echo$ i2cdump -y 1 0x44 b
     0  1  2  3  4  5  6  7  8  9  a  b  c  d  e  f    0123456789abcdef
00: 00 01 02 03 04 05 06 07 08 09 0a 0b 0c 0d 0e 0f   .?????????????????
10: 10 11 12 13 14 15 16 17 18 19 1a 1b 1c 1d 1e 1f   ??????????????????
...
f0: f0 f1 f2 f3 f4 f5 f6 f7 f8 f9 fa fb fc fd fe ff   ??????????????????.
```

You can see from this output that the Arduino program is designed to simply respond with the address that is requested. So, when the PocketBeagle requests the data at address 0x0A, the Arduino returns the data value 0x0A. This is a useful test to perform before continuing to the next section.

I²C Temperature Sensor Example

The next example uses the Arduino as an I²C slave device that wraps the TMP36 analog temperature sensor with a digital interface.

In this example, the Arduino uses its 10-bit ADC to read the analog output of the TMP36 sensor and then calculates the temperature in degrees Celsius by using the formula that is provided in the TMP36 datasheet. The temperature is then stored in two byte values: one for the whole value part and one for the fractional part of the temperature.

This example is similar to the TMP36 example in Chapter 9, except that all the processing is performed on the Arduino slave processor, rather than on the Beagle board. In fact, the Arduino also performs the conversion from degrees Celsius to degrees Fahrenheit and makes the converted value available at two further register addresses. The importance of this example is that the same approach can be applied to any analog sensor attached to the Arduino, facilitating you in building your own digital sensors.

Listing 10-9 provides the Arduino sketch that interfaces to the TMP36 analog temperature sensor that is attached to pin A0 (analog input 0) as illustrated in Figure 10-11. The Arduino calculates the temperature every five seconds and stores the Celsius value in bytes `data[0]` and `data[1]` and stores the Fahrenheit value in bytes `data[2]` and `data[3]`. The indexes of these `data[]` values align with the register values that are requested by the PocketBeagle and returned by the `respondData()` listener function.

Listing 10-9: /chp10/i2c/i2cTMP36/i2cTMP36.ino

```
#include <Wire.h>                  // uses the Two-Wire Interface (TWI)
const byte slaveAddr = 0x44;       // the slave address of the Arduino
int registerAddr;                  // the shared register addr variable
const int analogInPin = A0;        // analog input for the TMP36
int data[4];                       // the data registers 00 to 0x03
```

```
void setup(){
  TWBR=100000L;                      // set the i2c clk freq e.g. 100000L
  Wire.begin(slaveAddr);             // set up the Arduino as an I2C slave
  Wire.onReceive(receiveRegister);   // register receive listener below
  Wire.onRequest(respondData);       // register respond listener below
}

void loop(){                                 // update registers every five seconds
  int adcValue = analogRead(analogInPin);         // using a 10-bit ADC
  float curVoltage = adcValue * (5.0f/1024.0f);   // Vcc = 5.0V, 10-bit
  float tempC = 25.0 + ((curVoltage-0.75f)/0.01f); // from datasheet
  float tempF = 32.0 + ((tempC * 9)/5);           // deg. C to F
  data[0] = (int) tempC;                          // whole deg C (0x00)
  data[1] = (int) ((tempC - data[0])*100);        // fract C     (0x01)
  data[2] = (int) tempF;                          // whole deg F (0x02)
  data[3] = (int) ((tempF - data[2])*100);        // fract F     (0x03)
  delay(5000);                                    // delay 5 seconds
}

void receiveRegister(int x){        // passes the number of bytes
  registerAddr = Wire.read();       // read in the one-byte address
}

void respondData(){                 // respond function
  byte dataValue = 0x00;            // default response value is 0x00
  if ((registerAddr >= 0x00) && (registerAddr <0x04)){
    dataValue = data[registerAddr];
  }
  Wire.write(dataValue);            // send the data back to the PB
}
```

Note that the two listener functions act independently of the `loop()` function, only called upon when the PocketBeagle makes a request. In other words, the `loop()` function does not need to explicitly check for a data request on each iteration, which was necessary in the UART example.

Once the code is compiled and deployed to the Arduino, you can then use the `i2cdump` command to view the register values:

```
debian@ebb:~/exploringbb/chp10/i2c/i2cTMP36$ i2cdump -y 1 0x44 b
    0  1  2  3  4  5  6  7  8  9  a  b  c  d  e  f   0123456789abcdef
00: 17 49 4a 47 00 00 00 00 00 00 00 00 00 00 00 00   ?IJG............
10: 00 00 00 00 00 00 00 00 00 00 00 00 00 00 00 00   ................
...
debian@ebb:~/exploringbb/chp10/i2c/i2cTMP36$ i2cget -y 1 0x44 0x00 b
0x17
debian@ebb:~/exploringbb/chp10/i2c/i2cTMP36$ i2cget -y 1 0x44 0x01 b
0x49
```

The values are in hexadecimal form; therefore, the temperature value in this example is $23.73°C_{10}$ (i.e., $17.49°C_{16}$), which is $74.71°F_{10}$ (i.e., $4A.47°F_{16}$).

I²C Temperature Sensor with a Warning LED

The next example builds on the previous example with the addition of a warning LED that lights when the room temperature exceeds a user-defined threshold. The importance of this example is that it demonstrates how you can send data to the Arduino from the PocketBeagle—in effect, by writing a value to a register on the I²C device. Figure 10-11 illustrates the warning LED circuit for this example.

From the perspective of the PocketBeagle, the whole-number alert threshold value is stored at address 0x04 on the Arduino. For example, if the value 0x20 is written to the address 0x04, then the warning LED will remain off unless the temperature exceeds 0x20 = 32°C. This value is appropriate for testing, as you can achieve this temperature by holding the TMP36 sensor with your fingers.

Listing 10-10 is the Arduino sketch required to read the alert threshold value from the PocketBeagle and to store it in the byte data[4]. The receiveRegister (int x) listener function checks to see whether the PocketBeagle is accessing register 0x04 and whether exactly two bytes of data have been passed (i.e., the address and value). If so, then the second byte (the value) that is passed is stored in data[4]. The example also contains some commented-out code to write to the Arduino serial console. You can enable these lines of code to help you in debugging any changes.

Listing 10-10: /chp10/i2c/i2cTMP36warn/i2cTMP36warn.ino

```
#include <Wire.h>                     // uses the Two-Wire Interface (TWI)
const byte slaveAddr = 0x44;          // the slave address of the Arduino
int registerAddr;                     // the shared register address variable
const int analogInPin = A0;           // analog input pin for the TMP36
int data[5];                          // the data registers 00 to 0x04
int alertTemp = 0xFF;                 // alert temperature not set by default
int ledPin = 11;                      // the warning light LED

void setup(){
   pinMode(ledPin, OUTPUT);           // LED provides a visible temp alert
   TWBR=100000L;                      // set the i2c clk freq e.g. 100000L
   Wire.begin(slaveAddr);             // set up the Arduino as an I2C slave
   Wire.onReceive(receiveRegister);   // register receive listener below
   Wire.onRequest(respondData);       // register respond listener below*/
   //Serial.begin(115200, SERIAL_8N1);  // remove for debug
}

void loop(){                          // update registers every five seconds
   int adcValue = analogRead(analogInPin);        // using a 10-bit ADC
   //Serial.print("\nThe ADC value is: ");         // remove for debug
   //Serial.print(adcValue);                       // remove for debug
   float curVoltage = adcValue * (3.3f/1024.0f);   // Vcc = 3.3V, 10-bit
   float tempC = 25.0 + ((curVoltage-0.75f)/0.01f);  // from datasheet
```

```
    float tempF = 32.0 + ((tempC * 9)/5);        // deg. C to deg. F
    data[0] = (int) tempC;                       // whole deg C (0x00)
    data[1] = (int) ((tempC - data[0])*100);     // fract deg C (0x01)
    data[2] = (int) tempF;                       // whole deg F (0x02)
    data[3] = (int) ((tempF - data[2])*100);     // fract deg F (0x03)
    data[4] = alertTemp;                         // alert tmp C (0x04)
    if (alertTemp <= tempC) {                    // test alert?
        digitalWrite(ledPin, HIGH);              // yes, set LED on
    }
    else {
        digitalWrite(ledPin, LOW);               // else LED off
    }
    delay(5000);
}

void receiveRegister(int x){         // passes the number of bytes
    registerAddr = Wire.read();      // read in the one-byte address
    if(registerAddr==0x04 && x==2){  // if writing the alert value
        alertTemp = Wire.read();     // read in the alert temperature
    }
}

void respondData(){                  // respond function
    byte dataValue = 0x00;           // default response value is 0x00
    if ((registerAddr >= 0x00) && (registerAddr <= 0x04)){
        dataValue = data[registerAddr];
    }
    Wire.write(dataValue);           // send the data back to the PB
}
```

Once this program is uploaded to the Arduino, the Linux i2c-tools can be used to query the registers. You can see a fifth register at 0x04, which has the initial value of 0xFF.

```
.../chp10/i2c/i2cTMP36warn$ i2cdump -y 1 0x44 b
     0  1  2  3  4  5  6  7  8  9  a  b  c  d  e  f    0123456789abcdef
00: fd c5 19 35 ff 00 00 00 00 00 00 00 00 00 00 00    ???5............
...
```

You can alter this value using the i2cset command, as follows:

```
.../chp10/i2c/i2cTMP36warn$ i2cget -y 1 0x44 0x04 b
0xff
.../chp10/i2c/i2cTMP36warn$ i2cset -y 1 0x44 0x04 0x20
.../chp10/i2c/i2cTMP36warn$ i2cget -y 1 0x44 0x04 b
0x20
```

These transactions are captured by the logic analyzer in Figure 10-12. In my case, the LED is currently off because the room temperature is approximately 27°C; however, once the sensor is pinched between my fingers, the temperature quickly rises above 32°C (0x20), and the warning LED turns on.

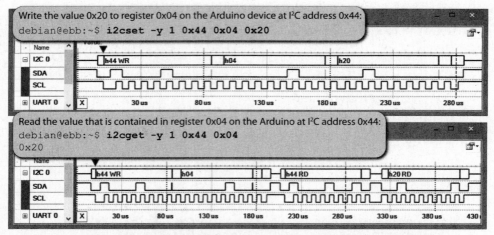

Figure 10-12: Writing to and reading from the 0x04 register that has been created on the Arduino

Importantly, the code in the loop() function continues completely independently of the Beagle board. For example, it can take a few seconds for the LED to turn on or off after a new temperature threshold is set. That is because the main loop in the Arduino code has a five-second delay between readings, and the threshold comparison takes place at the end of the loop. It is important that you keep the listener functions (i.e., receiveRegister() and respondData()) as short as possible because otherwise I²C communication may be somewhat unresponsive.

Arduino Slave Communication Using C/C++

C/C++ code examples for reading from and writing to I²C devices are presented in Chapter 8, but another example is provided here for completeness. Listing 10-11 is a C program for reading from and/or writing to the Arduino slave device.

Listing 10-11: /chp10/i2c/i2cTMP36warn/i2cTMP36.c

```c
#include<stdio.h>
#include<fcntl.h>
#include<unistd.h>
#include<sys/ioctl.h>
#include<linux/i2c.h>
#include<linux/i2c-dev.h>
#define BUFFER_SIZE 5        //0x00 to 0x04

int main(int argc, char **argv){
    int file, i, alert=0xFF;
    printf("Starting the Arduino I2C temperature application\n");
```

```
         // check if alert temperature argument passed
         if(argc==2){            // convert argument string to int value
            if (sscanf(argv[1],"%i",&alert)!=1) {
               perror("Failed to read the alert temperature\n");
               return 1;
            }
            if (alert>255 || alert<0) {
               perror("Alert temperature is outside of range\n");
               return 1;
            }
         }
         if((file=open("/dev/i2c-1", O_RDWR)) < 0){
            perror("failed to open the bus\n");
            return 1;
         }
         if(ioctl(file, I2C_SLAVE, 0x44) < 0){
            perror("Failed to connect to the Arduino\n");
            return 1;
         }
         char rec[BUFFER_SIZE], send;
         for(i=0; i<BUFFER_SIZE; i++){        // sending char by char
            send = (char) i;
            if(write(file, &send, 1)!=1){
               perror("Failed to request a register\n");
               return 1;
            }
            if(read(file, &rec[i], 1)!=1){
               perror("Failed to read in the data\n");
               return 1;
            }
         }
         printf("The temperature is %d.%d°C\n", rec[0], rec[1]);
         printf(" which is %d.%d°F\n", rec[2], rec[3]);
         printf("The alert temperature is %d°C\n", rec[4]);

         if(alert!=0xFF) {
            char alertbuf[] = {0x04, 0};      // writing alert to 0x04
            alertbuf[1] = (char) alert;       // value read as argument
            printf("Setting alert temperature to %d°C\n", alert);
            if(write(file, alertbuf, 2)!=2){
               perror("Failed to set the alert temperature!\n");
               return 1;
            }
         }
         close(file);
         return 0;
}
```

This program can be built and executed as follows:

```
debian@ebb:.../chp10/i2c/i2cTMP36warn$ gcc i2cTMP36.c -o i2cTMP36
debian@ebb:.../chp10/i2c/i2cTMP36warn$ ./i2cTMP36
```

```
The temperature is 17.67°C which is 63.81°F
The alert temperature is 30°C
debian@ebb:.../chp10/i2c/i2cTMP36warn$ ./i2cTMP36 40
The temperature is 17.67°C which is 63.81°F
The alert temperature is 30°C
Setting alert temperature to 40°C
debian@ebb:.../chp10/i2c/i2cTMP36warn$ ./i2cTMP36
The temperature is 17.67°C which is 63.81°F
The alert temperature is 40°C
```

When an argument is provided, the program converts the value from a string to an integer and writes it to the register 0x04 on the Arduino using the I²C bus. This value then becomes the alert threshold temperature that triggers the LED to light should it be exceeded. If no argument is provided, the program displays the properly formatted current state of the Arduino slave device.

An I²C Ultrasonic Sensor Application

The HC-SR04 is a low-cost ($2–$5) ultrasonic sensor that you can use to determine the distance to an obstacle using the speed of sound. The sensor has a range of approximately 1″ (2.5cm) to 13′ (4m). Unlike the IR distance sensor that is used in Chapter 10, it is not affected by sunlight, but it does not perform well with soft materials that do not reflect sound well (e.g., clothing and soft furnishings). Figure 10-13 illustrates how this sensor can be connected to the PocketBeagle via an Arduino UNO. The use of the Arduino UNO is purely illustrative, and a 5V Arduino PRO mini can equivalently be used.

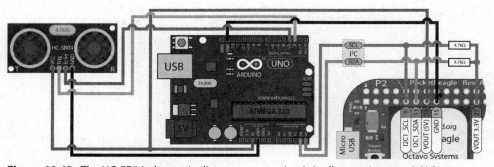

Figure 10-13: The HC-SR04 ultrasonic distance sensor circuit (pull-up resistors to 3.3V)

Figure 10-14 illustrates how interaction takes place with this sensor. A 10µs trigger pulse is sent to the Trig input of the sensor; the sensor then responds on its Echo output with a pulse that has a width that corresponds to the distance of an obstacle (approximately 150µs to 25ms, or 38ms if no obstacle is in range). The maximum number of samples per second is approximately 20 for a single sensor.

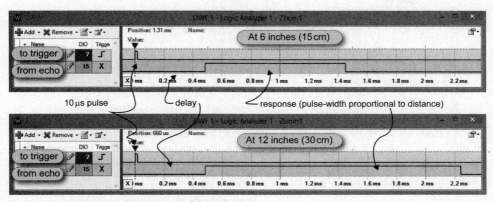

Figure 10-14: The signal response of the HC-SR04

It is possible but difficult to get accurate results directly from Linux userspace using regular GPIOs with this sensor. There are UART versions of this sensor that contain a microcontroller, but they are much more expensive. The solution that is presented here is fast enough to allow you to connect several such sensors to a single Arduino—a single trigger signal could be sent to many sensors simultaneously, and different GPIOs could be used to measure the response signals from each sensor. Listing 10-12 is the Arduino code for this example. The code builds on Listing 10-10 with code to generate the trigger pulse and read the width of the echo pulse response.

Listing 10-12: /chp10/i2c/sr04/sr04.ino

```
#include <Wire.h>                  // uses the Two-Wire Interface (TWI)
const byte slaveAddr = 0x55;       // the slave address of the Arduino
int registerAddr;                  // the shared register addr variable
int triggerPin = 2;                // connected to trig
int echoPin = 3;                   // connected to echo
int ledPin = 13;                   // the onboard LED
byte data[4];                      // the data registers 0x00 to 0x03

void setup() {
   // Serial.begin(115200);        // for debugging
   pinMode(triggerPin, OUTPUT);    // the pin to send a 10us pulse
   pinMode(echoPin, INPUT);        // the response pin to measure
   pinMode(ledPin, OUTPUT);        // the onboard LED indicator
   TWBR=100000L;                   // set the i2c clk freq e.g. 100000L
   Wire.begin(slaveAddr);          // set up the Arduino as an I2C slave
   Wire.onReceive(receiveRegister); // register receive listener below
   Wire.onRequest(respondData);    // register respond listener below
}
```

```
void loop() {                      // loop 20 times per second
  int duration;                    // the response pulse width
  float distancecm, distancein;    // the converted value

  digitalWrite(triggerPin, HIGH);  // send the 10us pulse
  delayMicroseconds(10);
  digitalWrite(triggerPin, LOW);
  duration = pulseIn(echoPin, HIGH);  // measure response pulse (in us)

  distancecm = (float) duration / 58.0;    // time converted to cm
  data[0] = (int) distancecm;              // whole part (0x00)
  data[1] = (int) ((distancecm - data[0])*100); // fract part (0x01)
  distancein = (float) duration / 148.0;   // time converted to in
  data[2] = (int) distancein;              // whole part (0x02)
  data[3] = (int) ((distancein - data[2])*100); // fract part (0x03)

  // code that can be added for debugging the program
  // Serial.print(distancecm);  Serial.println(" cm");
  // Serial.print(distancein);  Serial.println(" inches");
  digitalWrite(ledPin, LOW);       // LED off
  delay(50);                       // 20 samples per second
  digitalWrite(ledPin, HIGH);      // give a slight flash
}

void receiveRegister(int x){       // passes the number of bytes
  registerAddr = Wire.read();      // read in the one-byte address
}

void respondData(){                // respond function
  byte dataValue = 0x00;           // default response value is 0x00
  if ((registerAddr >= 0x00) && (registerAddr <0x04)){
    dataValue = data[registerAddr];
  }
  Wire.write(dataValue);           // send the data back to the PB
}
```

Once this program is built and uploaded to the Arduino, it can be tested from the PocketBeagle using the following calls:

```
debian@ebb:... /chp10/i2c/sr04$ i2cdetect -y -r 1
     0  1  2  3  4  5  6  7  8  9  a  b  c  d  e  f
...
50: -- -- -- -- -- 55 -- -- -- -- -- -- -- -- -- --
...
debian@ebb:.../chp10/i2c/sr04$ i2cdump -y 1 0x55 b
     0  1  2  3  4  5  6  7  8  9  a  b  c  d  e  f    0123456789abcdef
00: 0a 1b 04 02 00 00 00 00 00 00 00 00 00 00 00 00    ????............
...
```

With a one-line script you can find the decimal value represented by these registers using the following calls. (Ensure that you use a ` rather than a ` in wrapping the i2cget call; it is often on the keyboard directly below Esc.)

```
.../sr04$ printf "Distance is %d.%02d cm\n" `i2cget -y 1 0x55 0x00` →
`i2cget -y 1 0x55 0x01`
Distance is 10.27 cm
.../sr04$ printf "Distance is %d.%02d inches\n" `i2cget -y 1 0x55 0x02` →
`i2cget -y 1 0x55 0x03`
Distance is 4.02 inches
```

The C program in Listing 10-11 can be adapted to read the register values for the HC-SR04 Arduino program. Such a program would easily be able to communicate with a Beagle board over I²C and read the calculated register values at the maximum rate possible for the sensor (a rate of ~20Hz). Please note that the HC-SR04 is used again in Chapter 15 with the AM335x PRU-ICSS onboard real-time microcontrollers.

Summary

After completing this chapter, you should be able to do the following:

- Describe real-time kernel and hardware solutions that can be used on a Beagle board
- Increase the number of available GPIOs on the Beagle board using both I²C and SPI GPIO expanders, and utilize the interrupt functionality that is available on such devices
- Increase the number of available serial UART devices on a Beagle board using low-cost USB-to-TTL devices with a USB hub
- Interface a Beagle board to the Arduino using a UART serial connection to create a master/slave communications framework
- Interface a Beagle board to the Arduino using the I²C bus and use a register-based framework to read and write values to/from the Arduino
- Build high-speed, real-time interfacing application examples that utilize this I²C register-based framework

Further Reading

There are many links to websites and documents provided throughout this chapter. Additional links and further information on the topics in this chapter are provided at www.exploringbeaglebone.com/chapter10/.

Advanced Beagle Board Systems

In This Part

Chapter 11: The Internet of Things
Chapter 12: Wireless Communication and Control
Chapter 13: Beagle Board with a Rich User Interface
Chapter 14: Images, Video, and Audio
Chapter 15: Real-Time Interfacing with the PRU-ICSS
Chapter 16: Embedded Kernel Programming

The Internet of Things

This chapter describes how the Beagle boards can be used as a core building block of the Internet of Things (IoT). In this chapter, you are introduced to the concepts of network programming, the IoT, and the connection of sensors to the internet. Several different communications architectures are described: The first architecture configures the Beagle board to be a web server that uses various server-side scripting techniques to display sensor data. Next, custom C/ C++ code is described that can push sensor data to the internet and to platform as a service (PaaS) offerings, such as ThingSpeak and the Adafruit IO service using MQTT. Finally, a client/server pair for high-speed Transmission Control Protocol (TCP) socket communication is described. The latter part of the chapter introduces some techniques for managing distributed Beagle board sensors, and physical networking topics: setting the Beagle board to have a static IP address and using Power over Ethernet (PoE) with the Beagle board. By the end of this chapter you should be able to build your own connected embedded IoT devices.

EQUIPMENT REQUIRED FOR THIS CHAPTER:

- Beagle board (any model with a valid internet connection)
- TMP36 temperature sensor and an LED circuit

Further details on this chapter are available at `www.exploringbeaglebone` `.com/chapter11/`.

The Internet of Things

The terms *Internet of Things* (IoT) and *cyber-physical systems* (CPS) are broadly used to describe the extension of the web and the internet into the physical realm, by the connection of distributed embedded devices. Currently, the internet is largely an internet of people—the IoT concept envisions that if physical sensors and actuators can be linked to the internet, then a whole new range of applications and services are possible. For example, if sensors in a home environment could communicate with each other and the internet, then they could be "smart" about how they function—a home heating system that could retrieve the weather forecast may be more efficient and could provide a more comfortable environment (the Google Nest thermostat as an example). Within smart homes, IoT devices should be able to automate laborious tasks; manage security; and improve energy efficiency, accessibility, and convenience. However, the IoT also has broad application to many large-scale industries, such as energy management, security, healthcare, transport, and logistics.

In Chapter 9, interaction with the physical environment is discussed in detail. When the physical world can be acted upon by devices that are attached to the internet, such as actuators, then the devices are often called CPS. The terms IoT and CPS are often used interchangeably, with certain industries such as smart manufacturing favoring the term CPS. However, it is not unreasonable to consider a CPS to be a constituent building block, which when combined with web sensors and large-scale communications frameworks forms the IoT.

In this chapter, the implementation of several software communication architectures that can be used to realize IoT or CPS is described. Figure 11-1 summarizes the different communication architectures that are implemented in this chapter.

Each of the architectures in Figure 11-1 has a different structure, and each can be applied to different communications applications.

1. **A Beagle board web server:** A board that is connected to a sensor and running a web server can be used to present information to the web when it is requested to do so by a web browser. Communications take place using the *Hypertext Transfer Protocol* (HTTP).

2. **A Beagle board web client:** A Beagle board can initiate contact with a web server using HTTP requests to send and receive data. A C/C++ program is written that uses TCP sockets to build a basic web browser, which can communicate over HTTP or, if necessary, securely over *secure HTTP* (HTTPS).

3. **A Beagle board TCP client/server:** A custom C++ client and server are presented that can intercommunicate at high speeds with a user-defined communications protocol.

4. **A Beagle board web sensor using a PaaS:** Code is written to enable the Beagle board to use HTTP and MQTT to send data to, and receive data

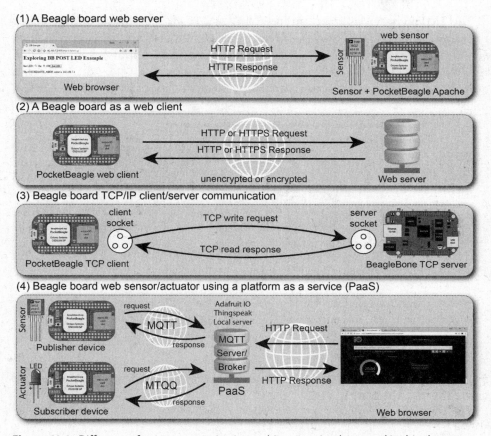

Figure 11-1: Different software communication architectures implemented in this chapter

from, web services such as ThingSpeak and Adafruit IO. This code enables you to build large arrays of sensors that can intercommunicate and store data on remote servers. In addition, these web services can be used to visualize the data that is stored.

Before examining these communication architectures, you need a *thing* to connect to the internet, for which you can use any sensor from earlier in the book.

A Beagle Board IoT Sensor

This book is filled with examples of sensors and actuators that you can use to create *things*. For example, the Beagle board can be turned into a *thing* by attaching a TMP36 temperature sensor directly to an ADC input to create a room temperature sensor.

The TMP36 provides an output of 750mV at 25°C. It has a linear output, where the output scale factor is 10mV/°C. This means that the minimum output voltage at −40°C is $0.75V - (65 \times 0.01V) = 0.1V$, and the maximum output voltage at +125°C is $0.75V + (100 \times 0.01V) = 1.75V$. It is therefore safe to connect it to a 1.8V ADC input as in Figure 11-2 as long as your room temperature does not exceed +130°C (266°F)[1]!

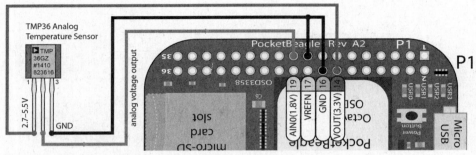

Figure 11-2: The PocketBeagle TMP36 temperature sensor circuit

You can read the current temperature from the TMP36 sensor as follows using the AIN0 input, which is attached to `in_voltage0_raw`:

```
debian@ebb:/sys/bus/iio/devices/iio:device0$ cat in_voltage0_raw
1748
```

The temperature in degrees Celsius and degrees Fahrenheit can be calculated using the code in Listing 11-1.

Listing 11-1: /chp11/tmp36adc/tmp36adc.cpp

```cpp
#include <iostream>
#include <sstream>
#include <fstream>
using namespace std;

#define ADC_PATH "/sys/bus/iio/devices/iio:device0/in_voltage"
#define ADC 0

float getTemperature(int adc_value) {        // from the TMP36 datasheet
   float cur_voltage = adc_value * (1.80f/4096.0f); // Vcc = 1.8V, 12-bit
   float diff_degreesC = (cur_voltage-0.75f)/0.01f;
   return (25.0f + diff_degreesC);
}

int readAnalog(int number){
   stringstream ss;
   ss << ADC_PATH << number << "_raw";
```

---

[1]The TMP36 has a rated temperature range from −40°C to +125°C, but it does operate up to +150°C. See the TMP35/36/37 datasheet for further information (www.analog.com/media/en/technical-documentation/data-sheets/TMP35_36_37.pdf).

```
    fstream fs;
    fs.open(ss.str().c_str(), fstream::in);
    fs >> number;
    fs.close();
    return number;
}

int main(){
    std::cout << "Starting the TMP36 example" << std::endl;
    std::cout << "The ADC value input is: " << readAnalog(ADC) << endl;
    float temp = getTemperature(readAnalog(ADC));
    float fahr = 32 + ((temp * 9)/5);    // convert deg. C to deg. F
    cout << "Temperature is " << temp << "°C (" << fahr << "°F)" << endl;
}
```

The code can be built and executed as follows:

```
debian@ebb:~/exploringbb/chp11/tmp36adc$ g++ tmp36adc.cpp -o tmp36adc
debian@ebb:~/exploringbb/chp11/tmp36adc$ ./tmp36adc
Starting the TMP36 example
The ADC value input is: 1735
Temperature is 26.2891°C (79.3203°F)
```

You can use any sensor in place of the TMP36, for example the LDR analog circuit from Chapter 6.

The Beagle Board as a Sensor Web Server

One significant advantage of an embedded Linux device over more traditional embedded systems is the vast amount of open-source software that is available. In this section, a web server is installed and configured on the Beagle board. It is a straightforward process compared to the steps involved for a typical non-Linux embedded platform. In fact, one of the more difficult challenges is choosing which Linux web server to use! There are low-overhead servers available such as lighttpd, Boa, Monkey, and Nginx, and there are full-featured web servers such as the popular Apache server. The Apache web server is a sufficiently lightweight server that has an overhead that is suitable for running on a Beagle board. It is installed by default on the BeagleBoard.org Debian image distribution, which makes it a good choice for this section.

Running a web server on a Beagle board provides you with a number of application possibilities, including the following:

- Present general web content to the world
- Integrate sensors and display their values to the world
- Integrate sensors and use the web server to intercommunicate between devices
- Provide web-based interfaces to tools that are running on a Beagle board

Installing and Configuring a Web Server

As just mentioned, the Apache server is currently present in the BeagleBoard.org Debian Linux distribution. You can use the following commands to install or upgrade the Apache server:

```
debian@ebb:~$ dpkg --get-selections|grep apache
apache2                                       install
apache2-bin                                   install
apache2-data                                  install
apache2-utils                                 install
debian@ebb:~$ sudo apt update
debian@ebb:~$ sudo apt install apache2
... apache2 is already the newest version (2.4.25-3+deb9u4).
```

On the BeagleBoard.org Debian image, the Apache web server is running on port number 8080 by default. A *port number* is an identifier that can be combined with an IP address to provide an endpoint for a communications session. It is effectively used to identify the software service running on a server that is required by a client. For example, you can find out the list of services that are listening to ports on your board by using the network statistics (netstat) and systemctl commands:

```
debian@ebb:~$ hostname -I
192.168.7.2 192.168.6.2
debian@ebb:~$ sudo netstat -tlpn
Active Internet connections (only servers)
Proto   Local Address    Foreign Address    State    PID/Program name
tcp6    :::80            :::*               LISTEN   1/init
tcp6    :::8080          :::*               LISTEN   982/apache2
tcp6    :::53            :::*               LISTEN   1112/dnsmasq
tcp6    :::22            :::*               LISTEN   920/sshd     ...
debian@ebb:~$ systemctl -all list-sockets
LISTEN              UNIT                    ACTIVATES
[::]:1880           node-red.socket         node-red.service
[::]:3000           cloud9.socket           cloud9.service
[::]:80             bonescript.socket       bonescript.service ...
```

Therefore, when a network request is received for port 8080, it is directed to the apache2 web server application (process ID 982). The usual port number for unsecured web traffic is 80—this is assumed when you enter a URL in your web browser—and is currently directed to init. The init process then calls upon bonescript.service to provide the Bone101 web pages to the client browser. You can also see that traffic for port 22 is directed to the SSH server (sshd), and traffic for port 3000 is directed to the cloud9.service, which is demonstrated in Chapter 2.

```
debian@ebb:~$ service --status-all
 [ + ]  apache-htcacheclean
 [ + ]  apache2
 ...
```

You can also get information about changes that you make to the server configuration before you perform a server restart, as follows:

```
debian@ebb:~$ apachectl configtest
Syntax OK
debian@ebb:~$ sudo service apache2
Usage: apache2 {start|stop|graceful-stop|restart|reload|force-reload}
debian@ebb:~$ apachectl
Usage: /usr/sbin/apachectl start|stop|restart|graceful|graceful-
  stop|configtest|status|fullstatus|help
        /usr/sbin/apachectl <apache2 args>
        /usr/sbin/apachectl -h     (for help on <apache2 args>)
```

These tests are particularly useful in identifying configuration problems.

Configuring the Apache Web Server

Apache can be configured using the files in the /etc/apache2/ directory.

```
debian@ebb:/etc/apache2$ ls
apache2.conf    conf-enabled  magic           mods-enabled  sites-available
conf-available  envvars       mods-available  ports.conf    sites-enabled
```

where the key configuration files are as follows:

- apache2.conf is the main configuration file for the server.
- ports.conf is for configuring virtual server port numbers (set to port 8080 by default on the BeagleBoard.org Debian image).
- The sites-available directory contains the configuration files for any virtual sites, and the sites-enabled directory should contain a symbolic link to a configuration file in the sites-available directory to activate a site. The a2ensite and a2dissite commands should be used to enable and disable sites. There is an example configuration file present, in which you should set the ServerAdmin e-mail address and the document root (the default is /var/www).

In addition to the configuration files, the functionality of Apache can be further extended (e.g., to provide Python support) with the use of modules (see tiny.cc/beagle1101 for a full list). You can identify the current modules that have been compiled into Apache using the following:

```
debian@ebb:~$ apache2 -l
Compiled in modules:  core.c  mod_so.c     mod_watchdog.c   http_core.c
         mod_log_config.c   mod_logio.c  mod_version.c    mod_unixd.c
```

Creating Web Pages and Web Scripts

To create a simple web page for a Beagle board web server, you can use the nano text editor and some basic HTML syntax as follows:

```
debian@ebb:/var/www/html$ sudo nano index.html
debian@ebb:/var/www/html$ more index.html
<HTML><TITLE>Beagle Board First Web Page</TITLE>
<BODY><H1>Beagle Board First Page</H1>
The Beagle board's test web page.
</BODY></HTML>
```

Now when you connect to the web server on the board using a web browser, you will see the output displayed as in Figure 11-3.

Figure 11-3: The first web page from the Apache web server running on port 8080

Web pages are ideal for the presentation of *static web content*, and by using an editor like KompoZer, CoffeeCup, or Notepad++, you can quickly build HTML content for a personal web server. You could then use the port forwarding functionality of your home router, as well as a dynamic DNS service, to share your static web content with the world.

More advanced *dynamic web content* can also be developed for the Beagle platform that interfaces to the physical environment for such tasks as reading sensor data or actuating motors. One relatively straightforward method of doing this is to use *Common Gateway Interface* (CGI) scripts. The configuration file (or linked to) in the `sites-enabled` directory specifies a directory location in which scripts can be placed so that they can be executed via a web browser request. The default location is the `/usr/lib/cgi-bin/` directory, where a simple script can be created as follows (see `/chp11/cgi-bin/test.cgi` in the GitHub repository):

```
debian@ebb:~$ cd /usr/lib/cgi-bin/
debian@ebb:/usr/lib/cgi-bin$ sudo nano test.cgi
debian@ebb:/usr/lib/cgi-bin$ more test.cgi
#!/bin/bash
printf "Content-type: text/html\n\n"
printf "<html><head>"
printf "<meta charset=\"UTF-8\">"
printf "<title>Hello Beagle Board</title></head>"
printf "<body><h1>Hello Beagle Board</h1><para>"
hostname
printf " has been up "
uptime
printf "</para></html>"
```

The script must then be made executable and can be tested as follows:

```
debian@ebb:/usr/lib/cgi-bin$ sudo chmod ugo+x test.cgi
debian@ebb:/usr/lib/cgi-bin$ ./test.cgi
Content-type: text/html
<html><head><meta charset="UTF-8"><title>Hello Beagle Board</title>
</head><body><h1>Hello Beagle Board</h1><para>ebb has been up
02:48:42 up 3 days,  1:41,  2 users,  load average: 0.04, 0.02, 0.00
```

Next, you must enable Apache to serve CGI scripts. To do this, perform the following steps:

```
.../usr/lib/cgi-bin$ cd /etc/apache2/mods-enabled/
.../etc/apache2/mods-enabled$ sudo ln -s ../mods-available/cgi.load
.../etc/apache2/mods-enabled$ ls -l cgi.load
lrwxrwxrwx 1 root root 26 Jul  7 02:36 cgi.load -> ../mods-available/cgi.load
```

And then restart the apache2 service.

```
debian@ebb:/etc/apache2/mods-enabled$ sudo service apache2 reload
```

Finally, you can test the web server using the `curl` command, which connects to the web server in just the same way that a web browser does.

```
debian@ebb:~$ curl localhost:8080/cgi-bin/test.cgi
<html><head><meta charset="UTF-8"><title>Hello Beagle Board</title>
</head><body><h1>Hello Beagle Board</h1><para>ebb has been up
02:55:15 up 3 days,  1:48,  2 users,  load average: 0.01, 0.01, 0.00
```

NOTE If you see errors on the web page, for example, a "500 Internal Server Error," then you should check the log files in `/var/log/apache2/error.log`.

The script code is quite verbose, but you can see that it is easy to use it to call system commands (e.g., `hostname` and `uptime`). When the script is tested in the terminal window, its output displays HTML source code. However, when this output is viewed using a web browser, as in Figure 11-4, the HTML is rendered and presented correctly.

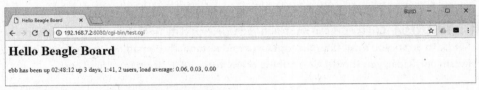

Figure 11-4: The output from a simple CGI script

As well as calling Linux system commands, you can also execute programs that have been written in C/C++. To demonstrate this capability, the `tmp36adc.cpp` program from Listing 11-1 can be modified so that it only outputs the raw temperature in degrees Celsius when it is executed. This new binary executable, called `tmp36raw`, can then be copied to the `/usr/local/bin/` directory so that it is "permanently" installed on the board.

```
debian@ebb:~/exploringbb/chp11/tmp36adc$ g++ tmp36raw.cpp -o tmp36raw
debian@ebb:~/exploringbb/chp11/tmp36adc$ sudo cp tmp36raw /usr/local/bin
debian@ebb:~/exploringbb/chp11/tmp36adc$ cd /usr/local/bin/
debian@ebb:/usr/local/bin$ ./tmp36raw
26.2012
```

The CGI script can then be modified to output the temperature value directly from the TMP36 sensor as follows (see `chp11/cgi-bin/temperature.cgi`):

```
debian@ebb:/usr/lib/cgi-bin$ sudo nano temperature.cgi
debian@ebb:/usr/lib/cgi-bin$ sudo chmod ugo+x temperature.cgi
debian@ebb:/usr/lib/cgi-bin$ more temperature.cgi
#!/bin/bash
printf "Content-type: text/html\n\n"
printf "<html><head>"
printf "<meta charset=\"UTF-8\">"
printf "<title>Beagle Board Temperature</title></head>"
printf "<body><h1>Beagle Board Temperature</h1><para>"
printf "The temperature in the room is "
/usr/local/bin/tmp36raw
printf " degrees Celsius</para></html>"
```

This script results in the output displayed in Figure 11-5. If you are experiencing difficulties with your CGI scripts, the log files that can help you diagnose problems are stored in `/var/log/apache2/`, which can be viewed with super user access.

Figure 11-5: Temperature sensor web page

> **WARNING** CGI scripts can be structured to accept data from the web by using form fields. To do so, you must filter the input to avoid potentially damaging cross-site scripting. In particular, you should filter out the characters <>&*?./ from form field entry.

PHP on the Beagle Board

CGI scripts work well for the short scripts used in the previous section—these are lightweight and easy to edit. However, as well as security concerns (e.g., attacks via URL manipulations), they do not scale very well (e.g., for interfacing with databases). One alternative is to use the PHP server-side scripting language. PHP is a reasonably lightweight open-source scripting language with a C-like syntax that can be written directly within HTML pages. It is capable of complex website delivery and is particularly well known as the language in which several content management systems (CMS), such as WordPress, are written. It can be installed for Apache as follows:

```
debian@ebb:~$ sudo apt install libapache2-mod-php7.0
debian@ebb:~$ sudo a2enmod php7.0
...
Module php7.0 already enabled
```

To test the server is working correctly, you can copy the example `hello.php` from Listing 11-2 (see `chp11/php/hello.php`) to the `/var/www/html/` directory (the location in which you previously wrote your first web page `index.html`).

```
debian@ebb:/var/www/html$ sudo cp ~/exploringbb/chp11/php/hello.php .
debian@ebb:/var/www/html$ ls -l
total 8
-rw-r--r-- 1 root root 317 Jul  7 03:27 hello.php
-rw-r--r-- 1 root root 138 Jul  7 00:27 index.html
```

Similarly to the CGI script, it interfaces to the TMP36 sensor by executing the `tmp36raw` program, resulting in the output shown in Figure 11-6.

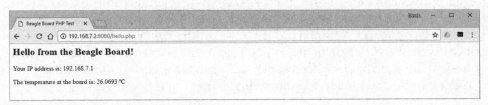

Figure 11-6: A PHP temperature sensor example

Listing 11-2: /chp11/php/hello.php

```
<?php $temperature = shell_exec('/usr/local/bin/tmp36raw'); ?>
<html><head><title>Beagle Board PHP Test</title></head>
<body>
 <h2>Hello from the Beagle Board!</h2>
 </p>Your IP address is: <?php echo $_SERVER['REMOTE_ADDR']; ?></p>
 </p>The temperature at the board is: <?php echo $temperature ?> &#186C</p>
 </body>
</html>
```

NOTE   To enter a Unicode symbol using nano, you can press Ctrl-Shift-u and then type the Unicode value, e.g., **00b0** for degrees (°). Then press Enter and the symbol will appear. Also, you can use 00a9=©, 00b1=±, 00b5=µ, 00d7=×, and 00f7=÷.

GNU Cgicc Applications (Advanced)

CGI allows a web browser to pass environment and application information to a script/program using HTTP POST or GET requests. Almost all programming languages can be used to build CGI applications, as their only roles in the transaction are to parse the input that is sent to these by the server and to construct a suitable HTML output response.

The GNU Cgicc is a C++ library for building CGI applications. It is powerful, and it greatly simplifies the process of building applications that allow you to interact with a Beagle board over the internet using an HTML form-based interface. It could be argued that this is a "dated approach" to solving the problem of having an embedded system web server interact with a web browser client—it has been around since the 1990s. To some extent that is true. There are powerful alternatives available such as Java servlets, Node.js, Dart, and PHP; however, this approach:

- has a very low overhead on the Beagle board, as the code is compiled rather than interpreted
- permits direct access to system calls
- can interface readily with hardware using code libraries

The downside is that it is not really suitable for novice programmers, the output format syntax can be verbose, and session management is complex. Even with that, it is worth pointing out that some large-scale web applications, including those by Google and Amazon, do use C++ on their servers for performance-critical systems. A Beagle board is not a high-end server, so any performance optimizations are always welcome, perhaps even at the cost of added complexity.

Cgicc can be downloaded and installed using the following steps:[2]

```
debian@ebb:~$ mkdir cgicc
debian@ebb:~$ cd cgicc/
debian@ebb:~/cgicc$ wget ftp://ftp.gnu.org/gnu/cgicc/cgicc-3.2.19.tar.gz
debian@ebb:~/cgicc$ tar xvf cgicc-3.2.19.tar.gz
debian@ebb:~/cgicc$ cd cgicc-3.2.19/
debian@ebb:~/cgicc/cgicc-3.2.19$ ./configure --prefix=/usr
debian@ebb:~/cgicc/cgicc-3.2.19$ make
debian@ebb:~/cgicc/cgicc-3.2.19$ sudo make install
debian@ebb:~/cgicc/cgicc-3.2.19$ ls /usr/lib/libcgi*
/usr/lib/libcgicc.a    /usr/lib/libcgicc.so     /usr/lib/libcgicc.so.3.2.10
/usr/lib/libcgicc.la   /usr/lib/libcgicc.so.3
```

As an example application, Cgicc can be used to control an LED that is attached to a GPIO on a Beagle board. Using the circuit from Figure 6-3 in Chapter 6, the LED can be attached to the Beagle board on GPIO1_28 (i.e., GPIO 60) and a web interface can be developed, as illustrated in Figure 11-7 to control the LED using only a web browser—this interface can be used from anywhere in the world!

---

[2]You can use a web browser to connect to the `ftp://ftp.gnu.org/gnu/cgicc/` FTP site to identify the most recent version of Cgicc.

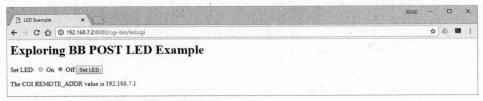

Figure 11-7: The LED Cgicc form post example

Listing 11-3 provides a form POST example. The form can contain elements such as checkboxes, radio components, buttons, and text fields. The code dynamically generates the HTML web form in Figure 11-7 and updates the page output to display the current state of the LED by selecting the appropriate radio component.

The listing uses Cgicc functions such as `HTTPHTMLHeader()`, `html()`, and `body()` to generate the HTML content for the output. In addition, the example demonstrates how to interact with radio buttons, within HTML forms. It is important that the form data is parsed at the beginning of the program code, as the form data that was previously submitted needs to be propagated into the new output. Clearly, the first time this form is requested there is no data present, and the code at the beginning of the program assigns a default value (e.g., `cmd="off"`). If this is not performed, then the program will result in a segmentation fault. From that point onward, the form output needs to maintain the state, and that is why these values appear in the HTML generation code.

Listing 11-3: /chp11/cgicc/led.cpp

```cpp
#include <iostream>        // for the input/output
#include <stdlib.h>        // for the getenv call
#include <sys/sysinfo.h>   // for the system uptime call
#include <cgicc/Cgicc.h>   // the cgicc headers
#include <cgicc/CgiDefs.h>
#include <cgicc/HTTPHTMLHeader.h>
#include <cgicc/HTMLClasses.h>
#define LED_GPIO "/sys/class/gpio/gpio60/"
using namespace std;
using namespace cgicc;

void writeGPIO(string filename, string value){
   fstream fs;
   string path(LED_GPIO);
   fs.open((path + filename).c_str(), fstream::out);
   fs << value;
   fs.close();
}

int main(){
   Cgicc form;                     // the CGI form object
   string cmd;                     // the Set LED command
   writeGPIO("direction", "out");
```

```
    // get the state of the form that was submitted - script calls itself
    bool isStatus = form.queryCheckbox("status");
    form_iterator it = form.getElement("cmd");  // the radio command
    if (it == form.getElements().end() || it->getValue()==""){
       cmd = "off";                     // if it is invalid use "off"
    }
    else { cmd = it->getValue(); }      // otherwise use submitted value
    char *value = getenv("REMOTE_ADDR");    // The remote IP address

    // generate the form but use states that are set in the submitted form
    cout << HTTPHTMLHeader() << endl;        // Generate the HTML form
    cout << html() << head() << title("LED Example") << head() << endl;
    cout << body() << h1("Exploring BB POST LED Example") << endl;;
    cout << "<form action=\"/cgi-bin/led.cgi\" method=\"POST\">\n";
    cout << "<div>Set LED: <input type=\"radio\" name=\"cmd\" value=\"on\""
         << ( cmd=="on" ? "checked":"") << "/> On ";
    cout << "<input type=\"radio\" name=\"cmd\" value=\"off\""
         << ( cmd=="off" ? "checked":"") << "/> Off ";
    cout << "<input type=\"submit\" value=\"Set LED\"/>";
    cout << "</div></form>";

    // process the form data to change the LED state
    if (cmd=="on") writeGPIO("value", "1");            // turn on
    else if (cmd=="off") writeGPIO("value", "0");      // turn off
    else cout << "<div> Invalid command! </div>";      // not possible
    cout << "<div> The CGI REMOTE_ADDR value is " << value << "</div>";
    cout << body() << html();
    return 0;
}
```

You can build and deploy this application as follows:

```
debian@ebb:~/exploringbb/chp11/cgicc$ g++ led.cpp -o led.cgi -lcgicc
debian@ebb:~/exploringbb/chp11/cgicc$ ls -l led.cgi
-rwxr-xr-x 1 debian debian 33356 Jul  7 15:42 led.cgi
debian@ebb:~/exploringbb/chp11/cgicc$ sudo cp led.cgi /usr/lib/cgi-bin/
debian@ebb:~/exploringbb/chp11/cgicc$ sudo chmod +s /usr/lib/cgi-bin/led.cgi
```

This example just scratches the surface of what can be performed using CGI and C++ on the Beagle board. For complex applications you may be better placed to examine other frameworks, but for simple high-performance web interfaces, the GNU Cgicc library provides a perfectly appropriate solution.

It is worth noting that there is one important limitation with the current example. It is a single session solution—if two users access the led.cgi script at the same time, then the LED state that is displayed will be inconsistent. For more complex applications, session management is important.

For more information on the Cgicc library, please see the GNU Cgicc library documentation at tiny.cc/beagle1102. By browsing the Class List, you will see that the library is capable of handling cookies, file transfers, and much more.

Replacing Bone101 with Apache

The Bone101 web server provides valuable information about getting started with your Beagle board; however, it occupies the default web port (port 80). If you want to replace Bone101 with your custom web server, you can shut down the `bone-script` service and configure the custom server to use port 80. To shut down the `bonescript` service, you can use the following steps. The first call is shown here:

```
debian@ebb:~$ systemctl list-units -t service | grep bonescript
 bonescript-autorun.service  loaded active running Bonescript autorun
 bonescript.service          loaded active running Bonescript server
```

It confirms that `bonescript.service` is running. To stop the service, you need to stop `bonescript.socket` first, and then you can disable the service, as follows:

```
debian@ebb:~$ sudo systemctl stop bonescript.socket
debian@ebb:~$ sudo systemctl stop bonescript.service
debian@ebb:~$ sudo systemctl disable bonescript.socket
Removed /etc/systemd/system/sockets.target.wants/bonescript.socket.
debian@ebb:~$ sudo systemctl disable bonescript.service
```

You can then configure the Apache2 server to use port 80 by modifying the `ports.conf` file to listen to port 80 as follows:

```
debian@ebb:/etc/apache2$ sudo nano ports.conf
debian@ebb:/etc/apache2$ more ports.conf | grep 80
Listen 80
```

And restart the Apache2 server as follows:

```
debian@ebb:/etc/apache2$ sudo systemctl restart apache2.service
```

LAMP AND MEAN

In addition to web servers, it is possible to install a database such as MySQL onto the Beagle board, forming a LAMP (Linux, Apache/Nginx, MySQL, PHP) server. This allows you to further install content management systems (CMSs) such as WordPress or Drupal, allowing you to create advanced web content that can even include hardware interaction.

MEAN is a full stack JavaScript framework for web application development that consists of MongoDB, Express, AngularJS, and Node.js. Essentially, MEAN is a more modern version of LAMP. MEAN is lightweight enough to be deployed on a Beagle board and provide a full framework for application development; however, developing software for a full MEAN framework is beyond what is possible in this text. However, a simple Node.js with Express example is presented here to get you started.

Node.js is introduced in Chapter 3. Express (`expressjp.com`) is a fast, minimalist web framework for Node.js that can be used to build feature-rich web applications. To install Express using the following steps, you must first ensure that your Node.js installation is up-to-date:

```
debian@ebb:~$ sudo npm cache clean
debian@ebb:~$ sudo npm install -g n
```

```
debian@ebb:~$ sudo n stable
debian@ebb:~$ node -v
v10.6.0
debian@ebb:~$ mkdir express
debian@ebb:~$ cd express/
debian@ebb:~/express$ sudo npm install express --save
debian@ebb:~/express$ cp ~/exploringbb/chp11/express/* .
debian@ebb:~/express$ ls -l
total 24
-rw-r--r--  1 debian debian   331 Jul  7 16:21 hello.js
drwxr-xr-x 50 root   root    4096 Jul  7 16:20 node_modules
-rw-r--r--  1 root   root   13438 Jul  7 16:20 package-lock.json
debian@ebb:~/express$ more hello.js
var express = require('express');
var app = express();

app.get('/', function (req, res) {
  res.send('Hello from the Beagle board!');
});

var server = app.listen(5050, function () {
  var host = server.address().address;
  var port = server.address().port;
  console.log('Application listening at http://%s:%s', host, port);
});
debian@ebb:~/express$ nodejs hello.js
Application listening at http://:::5050
```

The Node.js code results in an Express server that listens for connections on port 5050. You can use a web browser to connect to the server, as illustrated in Figure 11-8.

Figure 11-8: Express hello world example

To really appreciate the power of this framework, you need to investigate the use of express-generator, AngularJS, and MongoDB. Please see www.mean.io for further information.

A C/C++ Web Client

Installing a web server on a Beagle board provides it with a simple, intuitive way to present information to a client web browser application. It is important to understand that the distinction between a *client* and a *server* has nothing to do with the hardware capability of the interconnected devices; rather, it relates to the role of each device at that particular point in time. For example, when retrieving a web page from the Beagle board using its Apache web server, a desktop computer's web browser is a client of the Beagle board's web server. Table 11-1 summarizes the characteristics of the two types of application, which when used together is termed the *client-server model*.

Table 11-1: Characteristics of Server vs. Client Applications

SERVER APPLICATIONS	CLIENT APPLICATIONS
Special-purpose applications that are typically dedicated to one service.	Typically become a client temporarily, but perform other computation locally.
Typically invoked on system startup and they attempt to run forever.	Typically invoked by a user for a single session.
Wait passively, and potentially forever, for contact from client applications.	Actively initiate contact with the server. The client must know the address of the server.
Accept contact from client applications.	Can access several servers simultaneously.
Typically run on a shared machine.	Typically run on a local machine.

When a Beagle board acts as a server, it waits passively for a connection from a client machine, but there are many cases when the board might need to actively contact a server on another machine. In such cases, the board must act as a client of that server. At this point in the book you have already used many such client network applications on the board, such as `ping`, `wget`, `ssh`, `sftp`, and so on, and these applications can be used within shell scripts. However, it would also be useful if you could generate client requests from within program code, and for this you can use network sockets.

Network Communications Primer

A *socket* is a network endpoint that is defined using an IP address and a port number. An *IP address* (version 4) is simply a 32-bit number, which is represented as four eight-bit values (e.g., 192.168.7.2), and a *port number* is a 16-bit unsigned integer (0–65,535) that can be used to enable multiple simultaneous communications to a single IP address. Ports under 1,024 are generally restricted to root access to prevent users from hijacking core services (e.g., 80 for HTTP, 20/21 for FTP, 22 for SSH, 443 for HTTPS).

The description of a socket must also define the *socket type*, indicating whether it is a *stream socket* or a *datagram socket*. Stream sockets use the *Transmission Control Protocol* (TCP), which provides for reliable transfer of data where the time of transmission is not a critical factor. Its reliability means that it is used for services such as HTTP, e-mail (SMTP), and FTP, where data must be reliably and correctly transferred. The second type of socket is a datagram socket that uses the *User Datagram Protocol* (UDP), which is less reliable but much faster than TCP, as there is no error-checking for packets. Time-critical applications such as voice over IP (VoIP) use UDP, as errors in the data will be presented in the output as noise, but the conversation will not be paused awaiting lost data to be resent.

When communication is established between two network sockets, it is called a *connection*. Data can then be sent and received on this connection using write and read functions. It is important to note that a connection could also be created between two processes (programs) that are running on a single machine and thus used for *inter-process communication*.

A C/C++ Web Client

Full C/C++ support for socket communication can be added to your program by including the sys/socket.h header file. In addition, the sys/types.h header file contains the data types that are used in system calls, and the netint/in.h header file contains the structures needed for working with internet domain addresses.

Listing 11-4 is the C source code for a basic web browser application that can be used to connect to an HTTP web server, retrieve a web page, and display it in raw HTML form—like a regular web browser but without the pretty rendering. The code performs the following steps:

1. The server name is passed to the program as a string argument. The program converts this string into an IP address (stored in the hostent structure) using the gethostbyname() function.

2. The client creates a TCP socket using the socket() system call.

3. The hostent structure and a port number (80) are used to create a sock-addr_in structure that specifies the endpoint address to which to connect the socket. This structure also sets the address family to be IP-based (AF_INET) and the network byte order.

4. The TCP socket is connected to the server using the connect() system call—the communications channel is now open.

5. An HTTP request is sent to the server using the write() system call and a fixed-length response is read from the server using the read() system call. The HTML response is displayed.

6. The client disconnects, and the socket is closed using close().

Listing 11-4: /chp11/webbrowser/webbrowser.c

```
#include <stdio.h>
#include <sys/socket.h>
#include <sys/types.h>
#include <netinet/in.h>
```

```c
#include <netdb.h>
#include <strings.h>
#include <unistd.h>

int main(int argc, char *argv[]){
    int     socketfd, portNumber, length;
    char    readBuffer[2000], message[255];
    struct sockaddr_in serverAddress; //describes endpoint to a socket
    struct hostent *server;           //stores information about host name

    // The command string for a HTTP request to get / (often index.html)
    sprintf(message, "GET / HTTP/1.1\r\nHost: %s\r\nConnection: 
            close\r\n\r\n", argv[1]);
    printf("Sending the message: %s", message);
    if (argc<=1){  // must pass the hostname
        printf("Incorrect usage, use: ./webBrowser hostname\n");
        return 2;
    }
    // gethostbyname accepts a string name and returns host name struct
    server = gethostbyname(argv[1]);
    if (server == NULL) {
        perror("Socket Client: error - unable to resolve host name.\n");
        return 1;
    }
    // Create the socket of IP address type, SOCK_STREAM is for TCP
    socketfd = socket(AF_INET, SOCK_STREAM, 0);
    if (socketfd < 0){
        perror("Socket Client: error opening TCP IP-based socket.\n");
        return 1;
    }
    // clear the data in the serverAddress sockaddr_in struct
    bzero((char *) &serverAddress, sizeof(serverAddress));
    portNumber = 80;
    serverAddress.sin_family = AF_INET; //set the addr. family to be IP
    serverAddress.sin_port = htons(portNumber);    //set port num to 80
    bcopy((char *)server->h_addr,(char *)&serverAddress.sin_addr.s_addr,
        server->h_length); //set the addr. to the resolved hostname addr.

    // try to connect to the server
    if (connect(socketfd, (struct sockaddr *) &serverAddress,
        sizeof(serverAddress)) < 0){
        perror("Socket Client: error connecting to the server.\n");
        return 1;
    }
    // send the HTTP request string
    if (write(socketfd, message, sizeof(message)) < 0){
        perror("Socket Client: error writing to socket");
        return 1;
    }
    // read the HTTP response to a maximum of 2000 characters
    if (read(socketfd, readBuffer, sizeof(readBuffer)) < 0){
        perror("Socket Client: error reading from socket");
        return 1;
    }
```

```
        printf("**START**\n%s\n**END**\n", readBuffer);  //display response
        close(socketfd);                                  //close socket
        return 0;
}
```

This code can be built and executed as follows. In this example, the simple web page from the local Beagle board Apache web server is requested, by using *localhost*, which essentially means "this device," and it uses the Linux *loopback virtual network interface* (lo), which has the IP address 127.0.0.1:

```
debian@ebb:~/exploringbb/chp11/webbrowser$ gcc webbrowser.c -o webbrowser
debian@ebb:~/exploringbb/chp11/webbrowser$ ./webbrowser localhost
Sending the message: GET / HTTP/1.1
Host: localhost
Connection: close

**START**
HTTP/1.1 200 OK
Date: Sat, 07 Jul 2018 16:17:34 GMT
Server: Apache/2.4.25 (Debian)
Last-Modified: Fri, 06 Jul 2018 23:27:01 GMT
ETag: "8a-5705d0030eb6b"
Accept-Ranges: bytes
Content-Length: 138
Vary: Accept-Encoding
Connection: close
Content-Type: text/html

<HTML><TITLE>Beagle Board First Web Page</TITLE>
<BODY><H1>Beagle Board First Page</H1>
The Beagle board's test web page.
</BODY></HTML>
**END**
```

The example works correctly, returning the index.html file from the /var/www/ directory that is sent through the Apache server. It can also connect to other web servers (e.g., call ./webbrowser www.google.com).

Secure Communication Using OpenSSL

One of the limitations of the TCP socket application in the previous section is that all communications are sent "in the clear" across IP networks. This may not be of concern for home networks, but if your client and server are on different physical networks, then the data that is transferred can be easily viewed on intermediary networks. Sometimes it is necessary to communicate securely between a client and a server—for example, if you are sending a username and password to an online service. In addition, particular care should be taken in applications where the Beagle board can actuate motors or relays—a malicious attack could cause physical destruction. One way to implement secure communications is to use the OpenSSL toolkit.

OpenSSL (www.openssl.org) is a toolkit that implements *Secure Sockets Layer* (SSL), *Transport Layer Security* (TLS), and a cryptography library. This library can be installed using the following:

```
debian@ebb:~$ sudo apt install openssl libssl-dev
```

OpenSSL is a complex and comprehensive toolkit that can be used to encrypt all types of communications. This section presents one example application to illustrate its use. For this example, the C/C++ web client code is modified to support SSL communications as shown in Listing 11-5. The code involved in this example is the same as in Listing 11-4, except for the following:

1. The TCP socket connection is formed to the *HTTP secure* (i.e., *HTTPS*) port, which is port 443 by default.

2. The *SSL library* is initialized using the SSL_Library_init() function.

3. An *SSL context object* is used to establish the TLS/SSL connection. The security and certificate options can be set in this object.

4. The network connection is assigned to an SSL object and a handshake is performed using the SSL_connect() function.

5. The SSL_read() and SSL_write() functions are used.

6. The SSL_free() function is used to shut down the TLS/SSL connection, freeing the socket and SSL context objects.

Listing 11-5: /chp11/webbrowserSSL/webbrowserSSL.c (Segment)

```c
/*** After the connection to the server is formed:  ***/
// Register the SSL/TLS ciphers and digests
SSL_library_init();
// Create an SSL context object to establish TLS/SSL enabled connections
SSL_CTX *ssl_ctx = SSL_CTX_new(SSLv23_client_method());
// Attach an SSL Connection to the socket
SSL *conn = SSL_new(ssl_ctx); // create an SSL structure for an SSL session
SSL_set_fd(conn, socketfd);   // Assign a socket to an SSL structure
SSL_connect(conn);            // Start an SSL session with a remote server
// send data across a SSL session
if (SSL_write(conn, message, sizeof(message)) < 0){ ... }
// read data scross a SSL session
if (SSL_read(conn, readBuffer, sizeof(readBuffer)) < 0){ ... }
printf("**START**\n%s\n**END**\n", readBuffer);   //display the response
SSL_free(conn);                              //free the connection
close(socketfd);                             //close the socket
SSL_CTX_free(ssl_ctx);                       //free the SSL context
```

The full source code is in the /chp11/webbrowserSSL/ directory. It can be compiled and tested using the following commands:

```
.../chp11/webbrowserSSL$ gcc webbrowserSSL.c -o webbrowserSSL -lcrypto -lssl
.../chp11/webbrowserSSL$ ls -l webbrowserSSL
```

```
-rwxr-xr-x 1 debian debian 9188 Jul  7 17:33 webbrowserSSL
.../chp11/webbrowserSSL$ ./webbrowserSSL www.google.com
```

The application can successfully communicate with the SSL port (443) on secured web servers (e.g., www.google.com). The current code does not verify the authenticity of the server owner, but it does encrypt communications.

A Beagle Board as a "Thing"

Earlier in this chapter a web server was configured on the Beagle board so that it can send temperature information to the internet. This mechanism is useful, as it provides a snapshot in time of sensor outputs. To provide trend data, it would be possible to store the data in flat files or to install a lightweight database on a Beagle board (e.g., MongoDB). PHP charting tools such as *phpChart* and *pChart* could be used to visually represent the data.

An alternative way of performing the collection and visualization of web sensor information is to connect a Beagle board to online data aggregation services, which enable you to push sensor data to the cloud, directly from the board. In this section, online services are utilized directly from within C/C++ programs that are executing on a board. This enables you to develop lightweight operations that can leverage internet services to intercommunicate between several different boards on different networks. It also enables the collection of sensor data from many "web sensors" at the same time on different physical networks.

ThingSpeak

ThingSpeak is an open-source IoT application and API that can be used to store data from web sensors (*things*). Using HTTP, the sensors can push numeric or alphanumeric data to the server, where it can be processed and visualized. The ThingSpeak application can be installed on a server that is running the *Ruby on Rails* web application framework and an SQL database.

In this example, the Beagle board pushes room temperature data to a hosted free service at www.thingspeak.com, where data can also be visualized as shown in Figure 11-9. Once you set up a free MathWorks account, you can then create a new *channel* on ThingSpeak, which provides you with read and write API keys for the channel.

A C++ SocketClient is available for this example. This class simply wraps the C code that is used for the C/C++ web browser application in Listing 11-4. Listing 11-6 provides the class interface definition.

Figure 11-9: A ThingSpeak web sensor example using the TMP36 sensor circuit in Figure 11-2

Listing 11-6: /chp11/thingSpeak/network/SocketClient.h

```
class SocketClient {
private:
    int         socketfd;
    struct      sockaddr_in    serverAddress;
    struct      hostent        *server;
    std::string serverName;
    int         portNumber;
    bool        isConnected;
public:
    SocketClient(std::string serverName, int portNumber);
    virtual int connectToServer();
    virtual int disconnectFromServer();
    virtual int send(std::string message);
    virtual std::string receive(int size);
    bool isClientConnected() { return this->isConnected; }
    virtual ~SocketClient();
};
```

The code example in Listing 11-7 uses this `SocketClient` class. The example reads the temperature sensor and pushes it to the hosted ThingSpeak server using an HTTP POST request.

Listing 11-7: /chp11/thingSpeak/thingSpeak.cpp

```
#include <iostream>
#include <sstream>
#include <fstream>
#include "network/SocketClient.h"
#define ADC_PATH "/sys/bus/iio/devices/iio:device0/in_voltage"
#define ADC 0
using namespace std;
using namespace exploringBB;
```

```
float getTemperature(int adc_value) {        // from the TMP36 datasheet
    float cur_voltage = adc_value * (1.80f/4096.0f); // Vcc = 1.8V, 12-bit
    float diff_degreesC = (cur_voltage-0.75f)/0.01f;
    return (25.0f + diff_degreesC);
}

int readAnalog(int number){
    stringstream ss;
    ss << ADC_PATH << number << "_raw";
    fstream fs;
    fs.open(ss.str().c_str(),fstream::in);
    fs >> number;
    fs.close();
    return number;
}

int main() {
    ostringstream head, data;
    cout << "Starting ThingSpeak Example" << endl;
    SocketClient sc("api.thingspeak.com",80);
    data << "field1=" << getTemperature(readAnalog(ADC)) << endl;
    cout << "Sending the temperature:" <<
            getTemperature(readAnalog(ADC)) << endl;
    sc.connectToServer();
    head << "POST /update HTTP/1.1\n"
       << "Host: api.thingspeak.com\n"
       << "Connection: close\n"
       // This key is available from the API keys tab in Fig 11-9
       << "X-THINGSPEAKAPIKEY: G6MTQ21IVBFGYEBB\n"
       << "Content-Type: application/x-www-form-urlencoded\n"
       << "Content-Length:" << string(data.str()).length() << "\n\n";
    sc.send(string(head.str()));
    sc.send(string(data.str()));
    string rec = sc.receive(1024);
    cout << "[" << rec << "]" << endl;
    cout << "End of ThingSpeak Example" << endl;
}
```

To send data to the server at regular time intervals, POSIX threads and `sleep()` calls can be added to the code in Listing 11-7. However, an easier alternative is to use the Linux cron time-based job scheduler. The code in Listing 11-7 can be built and executed as follows:

```
.../chp11/thingSpeak$ g++ thingSpeak.cpp network/SocketClient.cpp →
    -o thingSpeak
.../chp11/thingSpeak$ ./thingSpeak
Starting ThingSpeak Example
Sending the temperature: 27.168
[HTTP/1.1 200 OK
Content-Type: text/html; charset=utf-8
Content-Length: 1  ....
```

The Linux Cron Scheduler

The Linux *cron* daemon (named after Chronos, the Greek god of time) is a highly configurable utility for scheduling tasks to be performed at specific times and dates. It is typically used for system administration tasks, such as backing up data, clearing temporary files, rotating log files, updating package repositories, or building software packages during off-peak times.

When sensors or actuators are interfaced to a Beagle board, cron can also be useful for applications such as logging data from these sensors at fixed intervals over long periods of time. On a Beagle board, you could use the scheduler for tasks such as collecting sensor data, building a stepper-motor clock, time-lapse photography, setting security alarms, and so on.

System crontab

Cron wakes once every minute and checks its configuration files, called *crontabs*, to see whether any commands are scheduled to be executed. It can be used to schedule tasks to run with a maximum frequency of once per minute down to a minimum frequency of once per year. Configuration files for cron can be found in the /etc/ directory.

```
debian@ebb:~$ cd /etc/cron.<Tab><Tab>
cron.d/   cron.daily/   cron.hourly/   cron.monthly/   cron.weekly/
```

The crontab file contains scheduling instructions for the cron daemon, according to the crontab fields that are listed in Table 11-2. Each line of the crontab file specifies the time at which the command field should execute. A wildcard value (*) is available—for example, if it is placed in the hour field, then the command should execute at each and every hour of the day.

Table 11-2: Crontab Fields

FIELD	RANGE	DESCRIPTION
m	0–59	The minute field
h	0–23	The hour field
dom	1–31	Day of the month field
mon	1–12 or name	Month of the year (first three letters can be used)
dow	0–7 or name	0 or 7 is Sunday (first three letters can be used)
user		Can specify the user that executes the command
command		The command to be executed at this point in time

Ranges are permitted (e.g., 1-5 for Monday to Friday) and so are lists of times (e.g., 1, 3, 5). In addition, strings can be used in place of the first five fields:

@reboot, @yearly, @annually, @monthly, @weekly, @daily, @midnight, and @hourly. The custom `crontab` file in Listing 11-8 provides some examples. There are comments in the file to explain the functionality of the entries.

Listing 11-8: /etc/crontab

```
# /etc/crontab: system-wide crontab
SHELL=/bin/sh
PATH=/usr/local/sbin:/usr/local/bin:/sbin:/bin:/usr/sbin:/usr/bin

# m h dom mon dow user          command
# Go to bed message, every night at 1am, sent to all users using wall
0  1    * * *   root    echo Go to bed! | wall
# Extra reminder, every work day night (i.e. 1:05am Monday-Friday)
5  1    * * 1-5 root    echo You have work in the morning! | wall
# Perform a task each day (same as 0 0  * * *). Clear the /tmp directory
@daily          root    rm -r /tmp/*

# The following are present in the default Debian crontab file:
17 *    * * *   root    cd / && run-parts --report /etc/cron.hourly
25 6    * * *   root    test -x /usr/sbin/anacron || ( cd / && run-parts
--report /etc/cron.daily ) ...
```

Examples are added to the `crontab` file to send messages and to clear the /tmp directory (see the listing comments). You can also specify that a command should be executed every 10 minutes by using `*/10` in the minutes field.

You may have also noticed other entries in the `crontab` file that refer to an `anacron` command. *Anacron* (anachronistic cron) is a specialized cron utility for devices, such as laptop computers and embedded systems that are not expected to be running 24/7. If regular cron were configured to back up files every week but the Beagle board happened to be powered off at that exact moment, then the backup would never be performed. However, with anacron the backup will be performed when the Beagle board next boots (i.e., jobs are queued). You can install anacron using the following:

```
debian@ebb:~$ sudo apt install anacron
```

Now there will be a new /etc/anacrontab file that performs the same role as `crontab` does for cron. The configuration file for anacron can be found in /etc/init/anacron.conf.

One problem with having both cron and anacron installed on one system is that it is possible for cron to run a job that anacron has already run, or vice versa. That is the reason for the `crontab` entries at the end of Listing 11-8. These entries ensure that `run-parts` is executed only if anacron is not installed on the Beagle board. This is tested by the call to `test -x /usr/sbin/anacron`, which returns 0 if the `anacron` command is present, and 1 if it is not. Calling `echo $?` displays the output value.

An alternative to adding an entry directly to the `crontab` file is to add a script to one of the directories: `cron.daily`, `cron.hourly`, `cron.monthly`, or `cron.weekly` in the `/etc/` directory. Any scripts in these directories are executed by cron. For example, you could create a script in the `cron.hourly` directory to update the temperature on ThingSpeak as follows:

```
.../chp11/thingSpeak$ sudo cp thingSpeak /usr/local/bin
.../chp11/thingSpeak$ cd /etc/cron.hourly/
debian@ebb:/etc/cron.hourly$ sudo nano thingSpeakTemp
debian@ebb:/etc/cron.hourly$ more thingSpeakTemp
#!/bin/bash
/usr/local/bin/thingSpeak
debian@ebb:/etc/cron.hourly$ sudo chmod a+x thingSpeakTemp
debian@ebb:/etc/cron.hourly$ ls -l
-rwxr-xr-x 1 root root 38 Jul  8 00:16 thingSpeakTemp
```

An alternative to this is to execute the binary directly within the user account using *user crontab*, which is described in the next section.

User crontab

Each user account can have its own `crontab`. These files are placed in the `/var/spool/cron/crontabs` directory, but they should not be edited in this location. The following creates a `crontab` for the debian user:

```
debian@ebb:~$ crontab -e
no crontab for debian - using an empty one
```

You can edit the user `crontab` file to upload the room temperature to Thing-Speak every 15 minutes by adding the following line:

```
# m  h  dom mon dow   command
*/15 *  *   *   *     /usr/local/bin/thingSpeak > /dev/null 2>&1
```

The end of this command redirects the standard output to `/dev/null`. The call `2>&1` redirects the standard error to the standard output and therefore also to `/dev/null`. If this were not present, then by default the output of the `thingSpeak` command would be e-mailed to the system administrator (if mail is configured on the board). You can back up your crontab file as follows:

```
debian@ebb:~$ crontab -l > crontab-backup
debian@ebb:~$ ls -l crontab-backup
-rw-r--r-- 1 debian debian 954 Jul  8 00:26 crontab-backup
```

To reinstate this backup file with crontab, use the following:

```
debian@ebb:~ $ crontab crontab-backup
```

The administrator account can control which users have access to cron by placing either a `cron.allow` or `cron.deny` file in the `/etc/` directory. Under Debian all users can have their own crontab by default. Use the following to remove this capability:

```
debian@ebb:/etc$ more cron.deny
debian
debian@ebb:~ $ crontab -e
You (debian) are not allowed to use this program (crontab)
```

With the previous crontab entry, the `thingSpeak` program uploads sensor temperature data to the ThingSpeak server every 15 minutes, as illustrated in the plot in Figure 11-9. ThingSpeak also supports MATLAB server-side code execution. For example, Figure 11-10 illustrates a short MATLAB program to convert the most recent temperature from degrees Celsius to degrees Fahrenheit. The example is structured to populate the converted result into another ThingSpeak data channel.

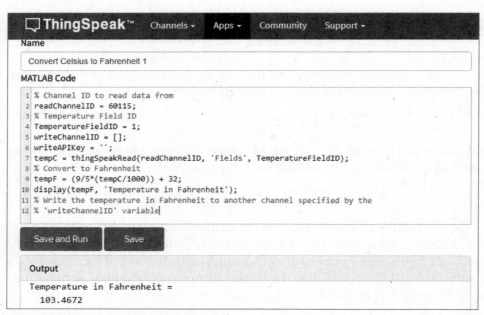

Figure 11-10: A ThingSpeak MATLAB example

Sending E-mail from the Beagle Board

It can be useful to send e-mail directly from a Beagle board so that detected system problems are relayed to a potentially remote administrator. In addition, it is useful for an e-mail to be sent when a sensor event occurs—for example, an e-mail could be sent if the room temperature exceeds 30°C. There are many mail client applications, but if you are using a secure *Simple Mail Transfer Protocol*

(SMTP) server, like Gmail, then the `ssmtp` program works well. Install `ssmtp` using the following command:

```
debian@ebb:~$ sudo apt install ssmtp mailutils
```

Configure the e-mail settings in the file /etc/ssmtp/ssmtp.conf. For example, to configure your board to send e-mail through a Gmail account, replace the account name and password fields in the following and change the hostname to localhost:

```
debian@ebb:/etc/ssmtp$ more ssmtp.conf
# Config file for sSMTP sendmail
root=MyName@gmail.com
mailhub=smtp.gmail.com:587
AuthUser=MyName@gmail.com
AuthPass=MyPassword
AuthMethod=LOGIN
UseTLS=YES
UseSTARTTLS=YES
TLS_CA_File=/etc/ssl/certs/ca-certificates.crt
rewriteDomain=gmail.com
hostname=localhost
```

GMAIL SECURITY SETTINGS

To use Gmail as the e-mail relay for your Beagle board, it may be necessary for you to reduce the security settings of your Gmail account. To do this, go to myaccount. google.com/security and select the "Allow less secure apps" option to be ON, as illustrated in Figure 11-11. In addition, you may have to use a password without characters that would typically need to be escaped (e.g., # or ""). Remember that it is easy to set up a specific Gmail account just for your Beagle board.

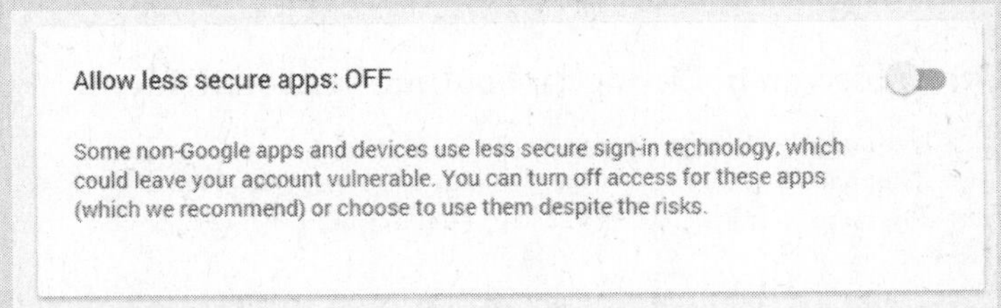

Allow less secure apps: OFF

Some non-Google apps and devices use less secure sign-in technology, which could leave your account vulnerable. You can turn off access for these apps (which we recommend) or choose to use them despite the risks.

Figure 11-11: The Gmail settings security option

The settings can be tested by sending an e-mail from the terminal:

```
debian@ebb:~ $ ssmtp toname@destination.com
To: toname@destination.com
From: myaccountname@gmail.com
Subject: Testing 123
Hello World!
^d
```

Typing Ctrl+D at the end of the message sends the e-mail. An alternative to this is to place the message text, which is the same as that just shown (including the To/From/Subject lines), in a file (e.g., ~/.message) and then send it using the following call:

```
debian@ebb:~ $ ssmtp toname@destination.com < ~/.message
```

Or, you can use the `mail` tool directly (from the `mailutils` package):

```
debian@ebb:~ $ echo "Test Body" | mail -s "Test Subject" →
    toname@destination.com
```

All messages are sent using the user Gmail account. This command can be added to scripts or encapsulated within a C++ program that uses a `system()` call, as in Listing 11-9. C or C++ could be used for this example, but C++ strings make this task more straightforward.

Listing 11-9: /chp11/cppMail/cppMail.cpp

```
#include <iostream>
#include <sstream>
#include <stdlib.h>
using namespace std;

int main(){
   string to("xxx@yyy.com");
   string subject("Hello Derek");
   string body("Test Message body...");
   stringstream command;
   command << "echo \""<< body <<"\" | mail -s \""<< subject <<"\" "<< to;
   int result = system(command.str().c_str());
   cout << "Command: " << command.str() << endl;
   cout << "The return value was " << result << endl;
   return result;
}
```

When executed, the program in Listing 11-9 outputs the following:

```
.../chp11/cppMail $ g++ cppMail.cpp -o cppMail
.../chp11/cppMail $ ./cppMail
Command: echo "Test Message body..." | mail -s "Hello Derek" x@y.com
The return value was 0
```

Here the value 0 indicates success. As well as sending notification messages, e-mail can be used to trigger other types of events using web services such as www.ifttt.com, which is discussed in the next section.

If This Then That

If This Then That (IFTTT) is a web service that enables you to create connections between online channels, such as Twitter, LinkedIn, Google Calendar, iPhone/Android Integration, YouTube, Adafruit IO, and many more. It works by connecting *triggers* and *actions* using the simple statement: "If *this*, then *that*," where the trigger is the *this*, and the action is the *that*. For example, "If *it is night time* then *mute my phone ringer*," or "If *the weather forecast is for rain tomorrow* then *send me an Android or iOS notification*." These statements are called *recipes*, and they can be activated in an IFTTT account and even shared with other users.

IFTTT can be triggered using an e-mail message that is sent to `trigger@applet.ifttt.com` from a linked Gmail account. Hashtags (e.g., `#EBB`) can be used to differentiate events, and the subject and body of the e-mail message can be used as *ingredients* for the recipe. For example, the recipe in Figure 11-12(a) states, "If *send trigger@applet.ifttt.com an email tagged #EBB from xxx@gmail.com, then Send me an SMS at 00353xxx.*" The body of the e-mail can be passed as an ingredient to the SMS message, which enables personalized messages to be sent from the Beagle board via SMS messaging (in many cases at no cost).

```
If send trigger@applet.ifttt.com an email tagged #EBB from x@gmail.com,
then send me an SMS at 00353xxxxxxxx
```

The recipe should have the following body text:

```
Beagle: {{Body}} {{AttachmentUrl}}
```

The recipe can then be triggered by sending an e-mail from the Beagle board.

```
debian@ebb:~ $ ssmtp trigger@applet.ifttt.com
To: trigger@applet.ifttt.com
From: xxxxxx@gmail.com
Subject: #EBB
Hello Derek!
^d
```

This results in a text message being received that contains the recipe message and the e-mail body (i.e., "`Beagle: Hello Derek!`"), as in Figure 11-12(b).

(a)   (b)

Figure 11-12: (a) Example IFTTT recipe, and (b) an SMS message received based on this recipe

IFTTT enables you to construct quite sophisticated interactions by simply sending e-mails from the Beagle board when certain events occur. For example, if a motion sensor is triggered, then you can message someone. Certain physical devices can also be triggered using IFTTT, such as Nest devices, smart phones, Automatic/Dash car OBD sensors, WeMo switches, Fitbit Flex healthcare devices, Lifx RGB smart lighting, SmartThings devices, Ubi voice control, and the Quirky+GE Aros smart air conditioner.

Some example recipes for the IoT include the following:

- Receive an emergency call if motion is detected.
- At sunrise, turn the security lights off.
- Remotely set your Nest thermostat to. . . .
- Delay watering your garden if it is going to rain tomorrow.
- Every day at . . . turn the lights on.

IFTTT supports Webhooks (`ifttt.com/maker_webhooks`) that allow a URL request to be made directly on a web server for DIY projects. For example, you could use Google Home Assistant to call a CGI script on a web server that is running on the Beagle board (similar to Listing 11-3). The only complication is that your Beagle board must be visible to the internet and addressable (e.g., via Dynamic DNS) outside of your home network.

IoT Frameworks

The ThinkSpeak solution that is presented in this chapter is a useful introduction to hosted platform as a service (PaaS) offerings, and it demonstrates some underlying communication technologies that are required to connect a Beagle board to the IoT. However, connecting single devices to the internet to log data does not solve all IoT challenges—in fact, it is only the starting point of the IoT. Figure 11-13 illustrates some of the large-scale interactions required to more fully realize an IoT platform.

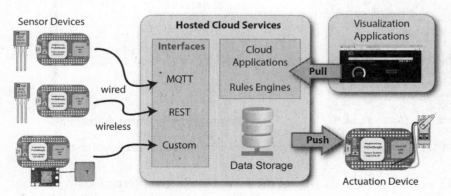

Figure 11-13: A typical IoT solution architecture

In the not too distant future, the IoT will involve tens of billions of devices interchanging trillions of messages, and this must be performed in a secure and scalable manner. The challenges involved are immense, and some of the world's largest cloud solutions providers are involved in the development of solutions. IBM released the Bluemix IoT service in August 2015, and in October 2015 Amazon launched the AWS IoT platform for building, managing, and analyzing the IoT. These are both enterprise-level solutions with price plans that scale according to usage. For example, Amazon charges ~$1 per billion messages that are interchanged by IoT devices, but it charges separately for device shadow and registry ($1 per million operations) and for rules engine calls ($1 per million rules triggered).

In this section, MQTT messaging APIs and servers are used to ensure vendor portability for your application.

MQ Telemetry Transport

Message Queueing Telemetry Transport (MQTT) is a lightweight connectivity protocol for machine-to-machine (M2M) communications. It was conceived in 1999 and has been used by industry since then; however, its applicability to the emerging IoT domain has placed it firmly in the spotlight, and in 2014 MQTT (version 3.1.1) became an OASIS standard. The lightweight nature of MQTT means that it can be used with low-level embedded devices and that it makes efficient use of network resources, while still providing reliable transactions. TCP/IP port 1883 is reserved for the MQTT protocol, and 8883 is reserved for the protocol over SSL. In addition to SSL, MQTT supports username/password transactions.

MQTT uses a publish/subscribe design model, where the publisher and subscriber are fully decoupled. A *publisher client* sends a message on a named *topic* (e.g., "ebb/temp") to a *broker*, and the broker responds with an acknowledgment message and a status code. Any *subscriber clients* connected to the broker that are listening for messages on the named topic then receive the message from the broker. Figure 11-14 illustrates the architecture that is implemented in this section. The publisher does not know at the time of messaging how many subscribers there are (if any) on a particular topic. The *topics* are essentially message queues that the broker maintains, along with subscriptions to these queues as part of a session.

MQTT achieves efficient and reliable communication through the use of small message sizes (as little as two bytes) and different Quality of Service (QoS) configurations:

- QoS Level 0: There will be at most one delivery, and no acknowledgment is required (fire and forget).

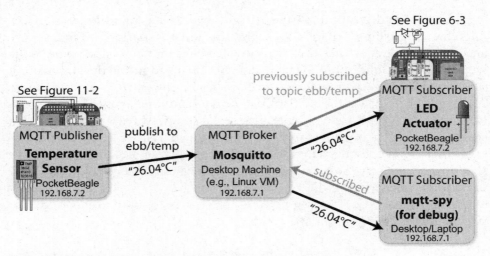

Figure 11-14: The MQTT messaging architecture used in this section

- QoS level 1: Acknowledgment is required, so there will be at least one message delivery (but possibly more). Message IDs can be used to identify duplicates.

- QoS Level 2: Acknowledgment is required, and there will be exactly one message delivery.

MQTT uses TCP, which has built-in QoS functionality. However, it is important to remember that IoT implementations often involve wireless devices that are operating in unreliable networks, with frequent power outage, or signal range issues. Therefore, these application layer QoS configurations can greatly improve communication reliability. For example, if a message with QoS Level 1 is sent from the broker to a subscriber and no acknowledgment is received, then the broker will continue to re-issue the message (with a duplicate flag set and an identical message ID) until an acknowledgment (with the corresponding message ID) is received. Importantly, the broker employs back-off schemes to ensure that it does not flood the (possibly stressed) network with duplicate messages and thus exacerbate network problems.

MQTT supports *retain messaging* that allows a publisher to flag a message to be retained by a broker on a topic, which is sent to a subscriber when it first subscribes to that topic. This is particularly important if a publisher sends infrequent messages or sends messages only when there is a change in the sensor value (*delta messaging*); for example, a passively powered thermostat might only send a message every hour. Without retain messaging, if a heating system subscriber was to connect to the broker, it may have to wait for up to one hour before receiving a sensor reading. With retain messaging, a message with the last known temperature value would be sent immediately to the heating system.

The MQTT message may also contain a username, password, and a *last will* message. The *last will* message can be used to notify other clients should this client be abruptly disconnected. This is particularly important for sensing failure conditions—for example, a home alarm sensor might have stored a *last will* message with the broker to lock the doors in case of its disconnection from the network.

Figure 11-14 illustrates an MQTT messaging architecture that is implemented in this chapter. It uses the Mosquitto MQTT server running on a desktop machine to broker all messages. An MQTT publisher client running on a Beagle board can use the TMP36 circuit illustrated in Figure 11-2 to send messages on the arbitrary topic ebb/temp, which contain the current temperature. The broker then sends these messages to any MQTT subscriber that has previously subscribed to this topic. In this example, the LED Actuator PocketBeagle will light an LED if the temperature value exceeds a defined threshold. Separately, the mqtt-spy subscriber is used for debugging.

MQTT Server/Broker

You will need to install the Mosquitto server (also known as Mosquitto broker) on your desktop machine for this task. If you are running Windows, it is possible to install the Mosquitto server directly without Linux. However, I recommend you install VirtualBox and a Debian guest OS on your machine if you are running Windows or macOS, as it can be difficult to integrate software libraries at a later stage.

```
molloyd@desktop:~$ sudo apt update
molloyd@desktop:~$ sudo apt install mosquitto
...
The following additional packages will be installed:
  libev4 libwebsockets8
molloyd@desktop:~$ sudo apt install mosquitto-clients net-tools
```

The server will usually be executed automatically at this point. In this case, you should see that the MQTT server is bound to port 1883 on your Linux desktop machine.

```
molloyd@desktop:~$ netstat -at
Active Internet connections (servers and established)
Proto Recv-Q Send-Q Local Address      Foreign Address       State
tcp       0      0 0.0.0.0:1883        0.0.0.0:*             LISTEN
tcp       0      0 desktop:34682       ftp-nyc.osuosl.org:http TIME_WAIT
tcp6      0      0 [::]:1883           [::]:*                LISTEN
```

If it does not start automatically, you should be able to start it using sudo start mosquitto. The configuration files for the Mosquitto server are located as follows, should you need these:

```
molloyd@desktop:~$ cd /etc/mosquitto/
molloyd@desktop:/etc/mosquitto$ ls -l
drwxr-xr-x 2 root root 4096 Jul  7 23:15 ca_certificates
drwxr-xr-x 2 root root 4096 Jul  7 23:15 certs
drwxr-xr-x 2 root root 4096 Jul  7 23:15 conf.d
-rw-r--r-- 1 root root  348 Dec 22  2017 mosquitto.conf
```

You can test that the broker is working correctly using the Mosquitto client applications on the desktop machine:

- `mosquitto_pub`: A publisher client that sends messages (`-m`) to a broker host (defaults to `localhost`) on a topic (`-t`) of choice. It also supports QoS levels and authenticated messaging.

- `mosquitto_sub`: A subscriber client that listens to a broker (defaults to `localhost`) for messages on a defined topic (`-t`). It supports wildcard subscriptions (e.g., + and #)[3].

In the example displayed in Figure 11-15, the subscriber client on the right side is subscribed to the topic `ebb/test`. The publisher client on the left side publishes six different messages, but only those that are published on topic `ebb/test` are received by the subscriber. Importantly, the publisher and subscriber are not connected to each other directly but are connected via the Mosquitto broker.

Figure 11-15: The Mosquitto publisher client sending four messages on the topic ebb/test and the subscriber receiving only the relevant messages

---

NAT PORT FORWARDING

If you are using a Linux virtual machine (VM) as the MQTT broker, then your Beagle board will need to be able to see the VM on the network. The easiest way to do this is to configure the VM to use network address translation (NAT) with port forwarding for port 1883. In this case, if a connection is made to your desktop machine (e.g., the Windows host OS) on port 1883, then it will pass on the connection to the VM (e.g., the Linux guest OS). This configuration is illustrated in Figure 11-16. You may have to shut down and restart your VM before these changes will propagate fully.

---

[3]The + wildcard is a single-level wildcard. For example, `ebb/+/temp` will subscribe to both `ebb/sensor1/temp` and `ebb/sensor2/temp`, but not `ebb/sensor3/bright`. The # wildcard is a multi-level wildcard. For example, `ebb/#` will subscribe to `ebb/sensor1/temp`, `ebb/sensor2/temp`, `ebb/sensor3/bright`, but not `ebb2/sensor1`.

You can install a SSH server on your desktop Linux machine as a test service and to allow you to SSH from your Beagle board to your VM.

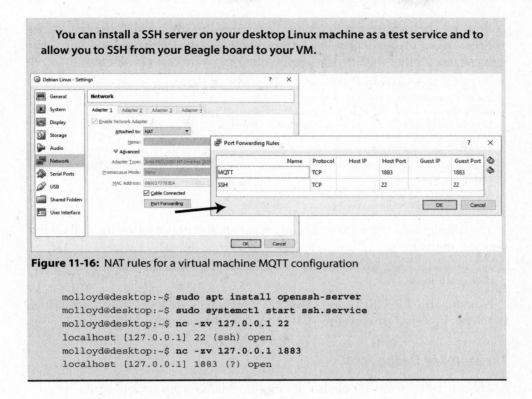

Figure 11-16: NAT rules for a virtual machine MQTT configuration

```
molloyd@desktop:~$ sudo apt install openssh-server
molloyd@desktop:~$ sudo systemctl start ssh.service
molloyd@desktop:~$ nc -zv 127.0.0.1 22
localhost [127.0.0.1] 22 (ssh) open
molloyd@desktop:~$ nc -zv 127.0.0.1 1883
localhost [127.0.0.1] 1883 (?) open
```

MQTT Publisher/Subscriber on a Beagle Board

Before writing your own code on a Beagle board, you should first test that your board can see the MQTT broker on your network. Begin by installing the Mosquitto client applications on your board and testing that you can send and receive messages on a topic, where -x specifies the address of your desktop machine (see the feature on port forwarding):

```
debian@ebb:~$ sudo apt install mosquitto-clients nmap
debian@ebb:~$ nmap -T4 192.168.7.1
Starting Nmap 7.40 ( https://nmap.org ) at 2018-07-08 17:57 IST
Nmap scan report for 192.168.7.1
Host is up (0.0073s latency).
Not shown: 996 closed ports
PORT     STATE SERVICE
22/tcp   open  ssh
135/tcp  open  msrpc
139/tcp  open  netbios-ssn
445/tcp  open  microsoft-ds ...
```

NOTE   Please note that you may have to disable Windows Defender Firewall for network traffic to pass from the Beagle board through to your Linux VM. If an nmap scan does not return any results, then this is the likely problem.

You can then subscribe to a topic (ebb/test) on the broker, identifying its address using the -h option. It is advisable to use the debug mode (-d) so that you can see all the MQTT messages to identify connection problems.

```
debian@ebb:~$ mosquitto_sub -v -t 'ebb/test' -h 192.168.7.1 -d
Client mosqsub/25610-ebb sending CONNECT
Client mosqsub/25610-ebb received CONNACK
Client mosqsub/25610-ebb sending SUBSCRIBE(Mid:1,Topic:ebb/test,QoS:0)
Client mosqsub/25610-ebb received SUBACK
Subscribed (mid: 1): 0
Client mosqsub/25610-ebb received PUBLISH(d0,q0,r0,m0,'ebb/test',32bytes)
ebb/test Message from the desktop machine
Client mosqsub/25610-ebb sending PINGREQ
Client mosqsub/25610-ebb received PINGRESP
```

The highlighted message was received as a result of the following call on the desktop machine:

```
molloyd@desktop:~$ mosquitto_pub -t 'ebb/test' -m 'Message from the
   desktop machine'
```

Note that the PINGREQ and PINGRESP messages are used by the subscriber in the background to keep the TCP connection to the broker alive.

The mqtt-spy Debug Tool

There are many useful tools for debugging MQTT applications, but I recommend the cross-platform mqtt-spy application. You can download it from tiny. cc/beagle1104. It is a Java application, so you will need a JVM (e.g., Oracle JDK) on your machine. You should be able to double-click the .jar file to execute it. Once you open it, you can configure a connection to your MQTT broker that is running on your Linux (or VirtualBox Linux) host. In my case, the IP address of the broker is 192.168.7.1:1883, so the connection can be configured as in Figure 11-17. Please note that you must hit the Enter key when you change a value in any of the fields or the changes will not persist.

(a)   (b)

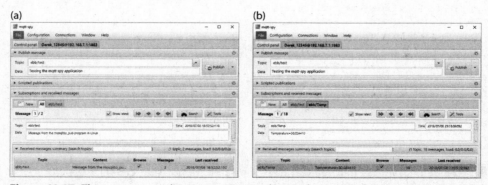

Figure 11-17: The mqtt-spy application running under Windows: (a) publishing and subscribing to the ebb/test topic; and (b) subscribing to the ebb/Temp topic

Writing MQTT Code

The Eclipse *Paho project* (www.eclipse.org/paho/) provides open-source implementations of MQTT in C/C++, Java, Python, JavaScript, and other languages that can be used to build small footprint, reliable MQTT client applications. In addition, the Eclipse IoT Working Group (iot.eclipse.org) provides strong support documentation and tools for developing open-source IoT solutions.

To download, build, and install the Paho libraries on a Beagle board, use the following steps:

```
debian@ebb:~$ sudo apt install libssl-dev git
debian@ebb:~$ git clone http://github.com/eclipse/paho.mqtt.c
Cloning into 'paho.mqtt.c'...
debian@ebb:~$ cd paho.mqtt.c/
debian@ebb:~/paho.mqtt.c$ make
```

There may be warnings during the make process, but there should be no errors. You can test that the libraries are in the correct location using the following:

```
debian@ebb:~/paho.mqtt.c$ sudo make install
debian@ebb:~/paho.mqtt.c$ ls /usr/local/lib/libpaho*
/usr/local/lib/libpaho-mqtt3a.so  /usr/local/lib/libpaho-mqtt3c.so
...
```

A Paho MQTT Publisher Example

Listing 11-10 is a Paho publisher example that sends temperature sensor messages to the broker in text format. It utilizes the circuit in Figure 11-2 to connect to the TMP36 sensor. This code is adapted from the examples that are distributed with the Paho libraries.

The listing begins by defining the fields that are required for connection to the broker, such as its address, the topic to publish against, the client ID, and authentication data if required. It is easy to configure the Mosquitto server to require authentication data, but it is unnecessary in a first example. Later code examples use authentication fields to connect to the Adafruit IO server.

Listing 11-10: /chp11/mqtt/publish.cpp

```
#include <iostream>
#include <sstream>
#include <fstream>
#include <string.h>
#include "MQTTClient.h"
using namespace std;

//Please replace the following address with the address of your server
#define ADDRESS     "tcp://192.168.7.1:1883"
#define CLIENTID    "Beagle1"       // any ID is fine
#define TOPIC       "ebb/Temp"      // this is the topic for messages
```

```
#define QOS         1               // at least one message received
#define TIMEOUT    10000L
#define ADC_PATH   "/sys/bus/iio/devices/iio:device0/in_voltage"
#define ADC 0                       // change to your ADC

float getTemperature(int adc_value) {  // from the TMP36 datasheet
   float cur_voltage = adc_value * (1.80f/4096.0f); // Vcc = 1.8V, 12-bit
   float diff_degreesC = (cur_voltage-0.75f)/0.01f;
   return (25.0f + diff_degreesC);
}

int readAnalog(int number){
   stringstream ss;
   ss << ADC_PATH << number << "_raw";
   fstream fs;
   fs.open(ss.str().c_str(), fstream::in);
   fs >> number;
   fs.close();
   return number;
}

int main(int argc, char* argv[]) {
   char str_payload[100];          // Set your max message size here
   MQTTClient client;
   cout << "Starting Beagle board MQTT Publish Example" << endl;
   MQTTClient_connectOptions opts = MQTTClient_connectOptions_initializer;
   MQTTClient_message pubmsg = MQTTClient_message_initializer;
   MQTTClient_deliveryToken token;
   MQTTClient_create(&client, ADDRESS, CLIENTID,
                     MQTTCLIENT_PERSISTENCE_NONE, NULL);
   opts.keepAliveInterval = 20;
   opts.cleansession = 1;
   int rc;
   if ((rc = MQTTClient_connect(client, &opts)) != MQTTCLIENT_SUCCESS) {
      cout << "Failed to connect, return code " << rc << endl;
      return -1;
   }
   sprintf(str_payload, "Temperature=%f", getTemperature(readAnalog(ADC)));
   pubmsg.payload = str_payload;
   pubmsg.payloadlen = strlen(str_payload);
   pubmsg.qos = QOS;
   pubmsg.retained = 0;
   MQTTClient_publishMessage(client, TOPIC, &pubmsg, &token);
   cout << "Waiting for up to " << (int)(TIMEOUT/1000) <<
         " seconds for publication of " << str_payload <<
         " \non topic " << TOPIC << " for ClientID: " << CLIENTID << endl;
   rc = MQTTClient_waitForCompletion(client, token, TIMEOUT);
   cout << "Message with token " << (int)token << " delivered." << endl;
   MQTTClient_disconnect(client, 10000);
   MQTTClient_destroy(&client);
   return rc;
}
```

This code can be built and executed as follows, where the "classic" Paho synchronous library is used (asynchronous libraries are also available):

```
.../chp11/mqtt$ g++ publish.cpp -o publish -lpaho-mqtt3c
.../chp11/mqtt$ ./publish
Starting Beagle board MQTT Publish Example
Waiting for up to 10 seconds for publication of Temperature=28.354490
on topic ebb/Temp for ClientID: Beagle1
Message with token 1 delivered.
.../chp11/mqtt$ ./publish
Starting Beagle board MQTT Publish Example
Waiting for up to 10 seconds for publication of Temperature=30.024410
on topic ebb/Temp for ClientID: Beagle1
Message with token 1 delivered.
```

Each time the program is executed, the current room temperature value is published to the ebb/Temp topic on the broker. Any clients that are subscribed to this topic will then receive the messages. For example, mqtt-spy is subscribed to this topic, and the output is visible in Figure 11-17(b).

A Paho MQTT Subscriber Example

Listing 11-11 is a client example that can be used to subscribe to a topic on the MQTT broker. In this example, my broker is running at 192.168.7.1 at port 1883, and the client is subscribing to the ebb/Temp topic.

In this example, an LED that is attached to GPIO 60 (see Figure 6-3 in Chapter 6) will light if the temperature exceeds 30°C—a value that can be exceeded by pinching the sensor with your fingers. It is important to remember that the publisher is sending messages to the broker and the subscriber is receiving messages from the broker, as in Figure 11-14—they are not communicating directly to each other.

NOTE The MQTT publisher and subscriber clients can be run on the same Beagle board, which is useful as a learning exercise, but it is not representative of a typical real-world implementation where many devices will work together.

Listing 11-11: /chp11/mqtt/subscribe.cpp

```cpp
#include <iostream>
#include <fstream>
#include <stdio.h>
#include <stdlib.h>
#include <string.h>
#include "MQTTClient.h"
using namespace std;

#define ADDRESS    "tcp://192.168.7.1:1883"
#define CLIENTID   "Beagle2"        // Could be a different board
#define TOPIC      "ebb/Temp"       // The MQTT topic
```

```
#define QOS          1
#define TIMEOUT      10000L
#define LED_GPIO     "/sys/class/gpio/gpio60/"
#define THRESHOLD    30                      // LED triggered if Temp>30

// Use this function to control the LED
void writeGPIO(string filename, string value){
   fstream fs;
   string path(LED_GPIO);
   fs.open((path + filename).c_str(), fstream::out);
   fs << value;
   fs.close();
}


volatile MQTTClient_deliveryToken deliveredtoken;

void delivered(void *context, MQTTClient_deliveryToken dt) {
    printf("Message with token value %d delivery confirmed\n", dt);
    deliveredtoken = dt;
}


// Called each time a message arrives for the stated topic
int msgarrvd(void *context, char *topicName, int topicLen,
            MQTTClient_message *message) {
    int i;
    char* payloadptr;
    printf("Message arrived\n");
    printf("    topic: %s\n", topicName);
    printf("  message: ");
    payloadptr = (char*) message->payload;

    //Hack offset ptr by 12 -- the message is the form "temperature=x.xxxx"
    float temperature = atof(payloadptr+12);   //float at 12th character in
    printf("The temperature is %f\n", temperature);
    temperature>THRESHOLD ? writeGPIO("value", "1"):writeGPIO("value", "0");
    MQTTClient_freeMessage(&message);
    MQTTClient_free(topicName);
    return 1;
}

void connlost(void *context, char *cause) {
    printf("\nConnection lost\n");
    printf("     cause: %s\n", cause);
}

int main(int argc, char* argv[]) {
    MQTTClient client;
    MQTTClient_connectOptions opts = MQTTClient_connectOptions_initializer;
    int rc;
    int ch;
    writeGPIO("direction", "out");
```

```
MQTTClient_create(&client, ADDRESS, CLIENTID,
                  MQTTCLIENT_PERSISTENCE_NONE, NULL);
opts.keepAliveInterval = 20;
opts.cleansession = 1;

MQTTClient_setCallbacks(client, NULL, connlost, msgarrvd, delivered);
if ((rc = MQTTClient_connect(client, &opts)) != MQTTCLIENT_SUCCESS) {
    printf("Failed to connect, return code %d\n", rc);
    exit(-1);
}
printf("Subscribing to topic %s\nfor client %s using QoS%d\n\n"
       "Press Q<Enter> to quit\n\n", TOPIC, CLIENTID, QOS);
MQTTClient_subscribe(client, TOPIC, QOS);

do {
    ch = getchar();
} while(ch!='Q' && ch != 'q');
MQTTClient_disconnect(client, 10000);
MQTTClient_destroy(&client);
return rc;
}
```

This code can be built and executed as before, whereupon the subscriber client will listen to the broker forever until a message is published on the ebb/Temp topic. In fact, the subscriber client will send "hidden" messages to the broker in order to keep the TCP connection alive, as was illustrated previously using the debug mode (-d) of the mosquitto_sub tool.

```
debian@ebb:~/exploringbb/chp11/mqtt$ ./subscribe
Subscribing to topic ebb/Temp for client Beagle2 using QoS1
Press Q<Enter> to quit
Message arrived
    topic: ebb/Temp
  message: The temperature is 26.860350
Message arrived
    topic: ebb/Temp
  message: The temperature is 26.728512
Message arrived
    topic: ebb/Temp
  message: The temperature is 30.024410
```

Adafuit IO

Adafruit is well regarded in the Maker community for selling electronics hardware and for developing high-quality modules and associated software libraries. To support emerging connected embedded devices, Adafruit has developed online IoT data logging and communication services that are aimed in particular at the Maker community. This section examines the use of MQTT for communicating to the Adafruit IO platform.

At the time of writing, Adafruit IO has a free-tier platform that supports up to 30 messages per minute for 10 unique feeds, 5 visualization dashboards, with 30 days of storage. The Adafruit IO+ subscription service supports unlimited feeds, unlimited dashboards, higher data rates, and a longer data storage duration for $10 per month. Interestingly, you can connect your Adafruit IO account to your IFTTT account, whereby you can use an Adafruit IO feed as a trigger for and IFTTT event. This functionality would allow you to easily build a PocketBeagle burglar alarm that texted your phone when the alarm sensor is activated.

Figure 11-18 illustrates the outcome from the instruction in this section, in which the Adafruit IO account is configured to work with the MQTT publisher client code in the previous section to create a temperature sensor logging platform. A separate MQTT subscriber client on a Beagle board can then connect to the Adafruit IO service to retrieve sensor measurements.

Figure 11-18: The Adafruit IO platform in operation

Configuring the Adafruit IO Account

The following steps must be performed to create this application:

1. Create an Adafruit user account on the Adafruit IO platform at io.adafruit.com. There is no requirement for payment.

2. Use the Feeds menu in Figure 11-19 to create a new feed. In this case, the feed is called temperature in the weather group. This feed is known as weather.temperature on the Adafruit IO platform and in your program code.

3. Identify your AIO key and keep this value safe (e.g., do not share it in a book!). You can generate a new key if it is compromised, but you will have to update this value in any existing programs. This key is used in the program code examples in the next sections.

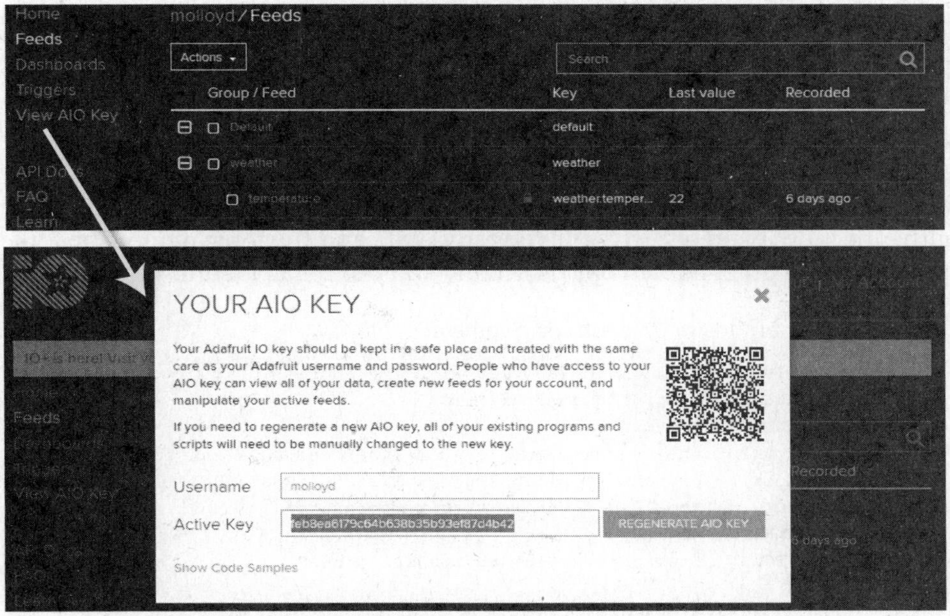

Figure 11-19: Creating an Adafruit IO feed and identifying the AIO key

4. Create a new dashboard to visualize your IoT data as in Figure 11-20. This dashboard contains blocks, which are visualization glyphs that can be used to represent the data that you pass to the Adafruit IO server. In Figure 11-18 I use a Gauge and a Line Chart block. These dashboards can be shared publicly as long as the feeds are also public.

Once these steps are complete, you can write program code that publishes and subscribes to the feeds on the Adafruit IO platform.

Figure 11-20: Creating an Adafruit IO dashboard and adding visualization blocks

Connecting to Adafruit IO with MQTT

The code in the previous section can be adapted to connect to the Adafruit IO platform instead of a local MQTT broker. The code alterations are relatively straightforward and largely involve activating the authentication functionality of the Paho API. Listing 11-12 provides a segment of code, which captures the alterations required to Listing 11-11. The code identifies my username, my private authentication token (which is no longer valid!), and the topic name. The topic name must be prefixed by your username and the feeds identifier.

Listing 11-12: /chp11/adafruit/publish.cpp (Segment)

```
//Please replace the following address with the address of your server
#define ADDRESS     "tcp://io.adafruit.com"
#define CLIENTID    "Beagle1"
//Please note that the username must precede the feed name and that
// "feeds" must be present. Topic groupings are dot separated.
#define TOPIC       "molloyd/feeds/weather.temperature"
#define AUTHMETHOD  "molloyd"
#define AUTHTOKEN   "feb8ea6179c64b638b35b93ef87d4b42"
...
float getTemperature(int adc_value) { ... }
int readAnalog(int number){ ... }

int main(int argc, char* argv[]) {
   char str_payload[100];          // Set your max message size here
   MQTTClient client;
   cout << "Starting Beagle board MQTT Adafruit publish Example" << endl;
   MQTTClient_connectOptions opts = MQTTClient_connectOptions_initializer;
   MQTTClient_message pubmsg = MQTTClient_message_initializer;
   MQTTClient_deliveryToken token;
   MQTTClient_create(&client, ADDRESS, CLIENTID,
                     MQTTCLIENT_PERSISTENCE_NONE, NULL);
   opts.keepAliveInterval = 20;
   opts.cleansession = 1;
   opts.username = AUTHMETHOD;
   opts.password = AUTHTOKEN;
   int rc;
   if ((rc = MQTTClient_connect(client, &opts)) != MQTTCLIENT_SUCCESS) {
      cout << "Failed to connect, return code " << rc << endl;
      return -1;
   }
   sprintf(str_payload, "%f", getTemperature(readAnalog(ADC)));
   ...
   if(rc == MQTTCLIENT_SUCCESS) {
      cout << "Message with token " << (int)token << " delivered." << endl;
   }
   else {
      cout << "Did not complete with error code: " << rc << endl;
      // MQTTCLIENT_SUCCESS 0           MQTTCLIENT_FAILURE -1
      // MQTTCLIENT_DISCONNECTED -3     MQTTCLIENT_MAX_MESSAGES_INFLIGHT -4
      // MQTTCLIENT_BAD_UTF8_STRING -5  MQTTCLIENT_NULL_PARAMETER -6
```

```
    // MQTTCLIENT_TOPICNAME_TRUNCATED -7   MQTTCLIENT_BAD_STRUCTURE -8
    // MQTTCLIENT_BAD_QOS    -9        MQTTCLIENT_SSL_NOT_SUPPORTED    -10
  }
}
```

Listing 11-12 also provides a list of error codes and their meanings to aid you in debugging your connection to the Adafruit IO server. The code can be built and executed as follows:

```
debian@ebb:~/exploringbb/chp11/adafruit$ ./build
debian@ebb:~/exploringbb/chp11/adafruit$ ./publish
Starting Beagle board MQTT Adafruit Publish Example
Waiting for up to 10 seconds for publication of 25.366211
on topic molloyd/feeds/weather.temperature for ClientID: Beagle1
Message with token 1 delivered.
debian@ebb:~/exploringbb/chp11/adafruit$ ./publish
Starting Beagle board MQTT Adafruit Publish Example
Waiting for up to 10 seconds for publication of 25.454098
on topic molloyd/feeds/weather.temperature for ClientID: Beagle1
Message with token 1 delivered.
```

The chp11/Adafruit/ folder also contains a subscriber.cpp example that is similar to Listing 11-11, but with the addition of authentication code. This code can be executed in a second Linux terminal window, whereupon it will connect to the Adafruit IO platform and subscribe to the desired feed, as follows:

```
debian@ebb:~/exploringbb/chp11/adafruit$ ./subscribe
Subscribing to topic molloyd/feeds/weather.temperature
for client Beagle2 using QoS1
Press Q<Enter> to quit
Message arrived
    topic: molloyd/feeds/weather.temperature
  message: The temperature is 25.366211
Message arrived
    topic: molloyd/feeds/weather.temperature
  message: The temperature is 25.454098
```

Similar to the program in Listing 11-11, the subscribe program is also configured to light the LED that is attached to GPIO 60, as illustrated in Chapter 6's Figure 6-3, should the temperature exceed 30°C.

An MQTT Node.js Publish Example

The code in Listing 11-13 uses Node.js to read the temperature sensor in Figure 11-2 and send its value to the Adafruit IO platform using MQTT. The importance of this example is that it demonstrates how to connect a sensor on the Beagle board to the Adafruit IO platform using a different programming language but still using the same MQTT configuration.

Listing 11-13: /chp11/adafruitjs/adafruit.js

```javascript
// This example uses mqtt.js to upload the TMP36 val to Adafruit IO
var mqtt       = require('mqtt');   // required module
var fs         = require('fs')
var DEVID      = 'Beaglejs';        // the individual device id
var AUTHTOKEN  = 'feb8ea6179c64b638b35b93ef87d4b42';  // auth token
var PORT       = 1883;              // reserved MQTT port
var BROKER     = 'io.adafruit.com';
var URL        = 'mqtt://' + BROKER + ':' + PORT;
var AUTHMETH   = 'molloyd';         // using username
var client     = mqtt.connect(URL, { clientId: DEVID,
                   username: AUTHMETH, password: AUTHTOKEN });
var TOPIC      = 'molloyd/feeds/weather.temperature';
var TEMP       = '/sys/bus/iio/devices/iio:device0/in_voltage0_raw'

console.log(URL);
console.log('Starting the Beagle MQTT Adafruit IO Example');

// Convert ADC value into a temperature
function getTemperature(adc_value) {       // from TMP36 datasheet
    var cur_voltage = (parseInt(adc_value) * 1.80) / 4096;
    var diff_degreesC = (cur_voltage-0.75)/0.01;
    return (25.0 + diff_degreesC);
}

client.on('connect', function() {
    setInterval(function(){
        var tempStr = 'invalid', temp;
        try {
           tempStr = fs.readFileSync(TEMP, 'utf8');
           temp = getTemperature(tempStr).toFixed(4);
        }
        catch (err){
           console.log('Failed to Read the temperature sensor.');
        }
        console.log('Sending Temp: ' + temp.toString() + '°C to Adafruit IO');
        client.publish(TOPIC, temp.toString());
    }, 10000);                  // publish data every ten seconds
});
```

To use this code example, you must first install the Node.js MQTT module. The code can then be executed, whereupon it connects to the IoT platform using the MQTT settings. When the adafruit.js script is executed, the data points appear in the Adafruit dashboard visualization, as previously illustrated in Figure 11-18.

```
debian@ebb:~/exploringbb/chp11/adafruitjs$ npm install mqtt --save
... + mqtt@2.18.2 ...
debian@ebb:~/exploringbb/chp11/adafruitjs$ node adafruit.js
mqtt://io.adafruit.com:1883
Starting the Beagle MQTT Adafruit IO Example
Sending Temp: 24.9268°C to Adafruit IO
Sending Temp: 24.8828°C to Adafruit IO
Sending Temp: 29.0137°C to Adafruit IO
...
```

The C++ Client/Server

The C/C++ client application described earlier in this chapter uses HTTP and HTTPS to connect to a web server and retrieve a web page. In this section, a TCP server is described, to which a TCP client can connect to exchange information, which does not have to be in HTTP form. The same `SocketClient` class that is used earlier in the chapter is reused in this section, and a new class called `SocketServer` is described. The importance of this example is that it allows for high-speed communications between the client and server, which is suitable for the transmission of video, audio, and real-time state data and is limited only by the speed of your network connection.

Figure 11-21 illustrates the steps that take place during communication in this client/server example:

1. In step 1, a TCP server that is running on the Beagle board at IP address 192.168.7.2 begins listening to a user-defined TCP port (54321). It will listen to this port forever, awaiting contact from a client.

2. In step 2, a TCP client application is executed. The client application must know the IP address and port number of the server to which it is to connect. The client application opens a client socket, using the next available Linux port allocation. The server, which can be running on a different Beagle board (or the same Beagle board in a different terminal window), accepts a connection request from the client. It then retrieves a reference to the client IP address and port number. A connection is formed, and the client writes a message to this connection, which is "Hello from the Client."

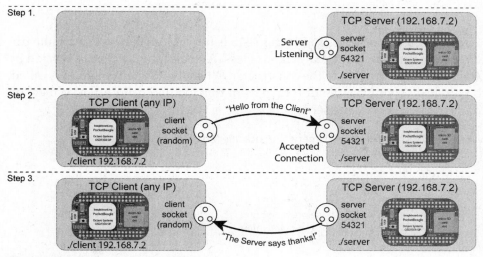

Figure 11-21: A client/server example

3. In step 3, the server reads the message from the connection and sends back a new message to the client, which is "The Server says thanks!" The client reads the response message and displays it to the terminal. Then the client and server both close the network sockets. The programs run asynchronously—in this case running to completion.

The full example is provided in the `chp11/clientserver/` directory. The `client.cpp` program in Listing 11-14 uses the `SocketClient` class from the network subdirectory (see Listing 11-6).

Listing 11-14: /chp11/clientserver/client.cpp

```cpp
#include <iostream>
#include "network/SocketClient.h"
using namespace std;
using namespace exploringBB;

int main(int argc, char *argv[]){
    if(argc!=2){
        cout << "Incorrect usage: " << endl;
        cout << "    client server_name" << endl;
        return 2;
    }
    cout << "Starting Beagle Board Client Example" << endl;
    SocketClient sc(argv[1], 54321);
    sc.connectToServer();
    string message("Hello from the Client");
    cout << "Sending [" << message << "]" << endl;
    sc.send(message);
    string rec = sc.receive(1024);
    cout << "Received [" << rec << "]" << endl;
    cout << "End of Beagle Board Client Example" << endl;
}
```

The `SocketServer` class in Listing 11-15 is new, and it behaves in a quite different manner than the `SocketClient` class. An object of the class is created by passing the port number to the constructor. When the `listen()` method is called, the program counter will not return from this method call until a connection has been accepted by the server.

Listing 11-15: /chp11/clientserver/network/SocketServer.h

```cpp
class SocketServer {
private:
    int     portNumber;
    int     socketfd, clientSocketfd;
    struct  sockaddr_in    serverAddress;
    struct  sockaddr_in    clientAddress;
    bool    clientConnected;
```

```
public:
    SocketServer(int portNumber);
    virtual int listen();
    virtual int send(std::string message);
    virtual std::string receive(int size);
    virtual ~SocketServer();
};
```

The `server.cpp` code example in Listing 11-16 creates an object of the `ServerSocket` class and awaits a client connection.

Listing 11-16: /chp11/clientserver/server.cpp

```cpp
#include <iostream>
#include "network/SocketServer.h"
using namespace std;
using namespace exploringBB;

int main(int argc, char *argv[]){
    cout << "Starting Beagle Board Server Example" << endl;
    SocketServer server(54321);
    cout << "Listening for a connection..." << endl;
    server.listen();
    string rec = server.receive(1024);
    cout << "Received from the client [" << rec << "]" << endl;
    string message("The Server says thanks!");
    cout << "Sending back [" << message << "]" << endl;
    server.send(message);
    cout << "End of Beagle Board Server Example" << endl;
    return 0;
}
```

The code for this example can be built using the `build` script in the `chp11/clientserver/` directory. The server can then be executed.

```
debian@ebb:~/exploringbb/chp11/clientserver$ ./server
Starting Beagle Board Server Example
Listening for a connection...
```

The server will wait at this point until a client request has been received. To execute the client application, a separate terminal session on the same Beagle board, another Beagle board, or a Linux desktop machine can be used.[4] The client application can be executed by passing the IP address of the server. The port number (54321) is defined within the client program code.

```
debian@ebb:~/exploringbb/chp11/clientserver$ ./client localhost
Starting Beagle Board Client Example
Sending [Hello from the Client]
```

---

[4]When the server terminates it can take a short period of time for the Linux kernel to free the server socket and TCP port for re-use. This TIME-WAIT state in TCP prevents delayed packets from one connection being accepted by a later connection. As a result, you may have to wait a few seconds before the server application will restart, as you will receive an "Address already in use" error message.

```
Received [The Server says thanks!]
End of Beagle Board Client Example
```

When the client connects to the server, both the client and server execute simultaneously, resulting in the preceding and following output:

```
debian@ebb:~/exploringbb/chp11/clientserver$ ./server
Starting Beagle Board Server Example
Listening for a connection...
Received from the client [Hello from the Client]
Sending back [The Server says thanks!]
End of Beagle Board Server Example
```

This code is further improved later in the book to add threading support and to enable it to communicate with a better structure than simple strings. However, it should be clear that this code enables you to intercommunicate between Linux client/servers that are located anywhere in the world. The client/server pair communicates by sending and receiving bytes; therefore, communication can take place at very high data rates and is limited only by the physical network infrastructure.

IoT Device Management

One of the difficulties with remote web sensors is that they may be in physically inaccessible and/or distant locations. In addition, a period of system downtime may lead to a considerable loss of sensing data. If the problem becomes apparent, you can SSH into the Beagle board and restart the application or perform a system reboot. In this section, two quite different management approaches are described—the first is manual web-based monitoring, and the second is automatic, through the use of Linux watchdog timers.

Remote Monitoring of a Beagle Board

One of the advantages of installing a web server in this chapter is that it supports a number of additional open-source services. One such example is a remote monitoring service called *Linux-dash*. For simplicity, the following steps use Node.js as the server:

```
debian@ebb:~$ sudo git clone https://github.com/afaqurk/linux-dash.git
debian@ebb:~$ cd linux-dash/
debian@ebb:~/linux-dash $ sudo npm install
```

Use an environment variable to configure Linux-dash to use a different number than port 80 (e.g., 81 in this case).

```
debian@ebb:~/linux-dash$ sudo -i
root@ebb:~# cd /home/debian/linux-dash
```

```
root@ebb:/home/debian/linux-dash# export LINUX_DASH_SERVER_PORT=81
root@ebb:/home/debian/linux-dash# echo $LINUX_DASH_SERVER_PORT
81

root@ebb:/home/debian/linux-dash# bin/linux-dash
Linux Dash Server Started on port 81!
```

These steps result in a service running on the Beagle board using the chosen port number; e.g., http://192.168.7.2:81/. You can then remotely connect to the Beagle board with a web browser to view system information, as shown in Figure 11-22. This approach can help you quickly identify system problems, such as unusual loads, network traffic, and so on, but it still requires that you manually check the web page.

Figure 11-22: Beagle board remote monitoring using Linux Dash

Beagle Board Watchdog Timers

One solution to automatically determine whether there has been a significant problem with your application is to use a watchdog timer. The AM335x has full support for a hardware watchdog timer, which can be used to automatically reset a board should it lock up. Having a watchdog timer can be important in IoT applications if the board is inaccessible or performing an important role that should not be halted (e.g., a PocketBeagle-based intruder alarm). You can examine its functionality using the following steps:

```
debian@ebb:/dev$ ls -l watchdog
crw------- 1 root root 10, 130 Jul  1 17:21 watchdog
debian@ebb:/dev$ sudo -i
root@ebb:/dev# cat > watchdog
Testing but quitting now ^C
```

The preceding steps should not cause the board to reboot. However, if you write anything to watchdog, do not close the file, and wait for 50 seconds after the last Return key is pressed, then the board will reboot!

```
root@ebb:/dev# cat > watchdog
This will reboot the BBB 50 seconds after I hit Return. Now!
Even if I type really slowly on this line but don't hit Return
```

This is because the watchdog has been activated, held open, and not "fed" for 50 seconds, which is the default watchdog time on the Debian distribution.

Watchdog timers can be integrated directly into program code. For example, Listing 11-17 is a watchdog timer example that opens the watchdog device and writes to it every time you "feed the dog" by pressing f. If you do not write to the device for more than 30 seconds (the user-defined interval in the code listing), then the board will reboot.

Listing 11-17: /chp11/watchdog/watchdog.c

```c
#include<stdio.h>
#include<stdlib.h>
#include<sys/fcntl.h>
#include<sys/ioctl.h>
#include<sys/stat.h>
#include<unistd.h>
#include<linux/watchdog.h>
#define WATCHDOG "/dev/watchdog"

int main(){
   int fd, interval=30, state;
   if ((fd = open(WATCHDOG, O_RDWR))<0){
     perror("Watchdog: Failed to open watchdog device\n");
     return 1;
   }                 // set the timing interval to 30 seconds
   if (ioctl(fd, WDIOC_SETTIMEOUT, &interval)!=0){
     perror("Watchdog: Failed to set the watchdog interval\n");
     return 1;
   }
   printf("Press f to feed the dog, h to say hello and q to quit:\n");
   do{
      state = getchar();
      switch(state){
      case 'f':
         printf("[feed!]");
         ioctl(fd, WDIOC_KEEPALIVE, NULL);
         break;
      case 'h':
         printf("[hello]");
         break;
      }
   } while (state!='q');
   printf("Closing down the application\n");
   close(fd);
   return 0;
}
```

If you build the principles of this code into an application, then you should "feed the dog" each time an important block of code executes. For example, if a sensor value were read every 15 seconds in your code example, then you would also "feed the dog" each time you read the sensor value. That way, if the application locks up, then the board would reboot automatically. Having a watchdog timer can be important in IoT applications if the board is inaccessible or performing an important role that should not be halted.

```
debian@ebb:~/exploringbb/chp11/watchdog$ sudo ./watchdog
Press f to feed the dog, h to say hello and q to quit:
f
[feed!]   <board reboots 30 seconds later>
```

Static IP Addresses

The Beagle boards are configured by default to use the *Dynamic Host Configuration Protocol* (DHCP) for the allocation of its wired and wireless IP addresses. Network routers typically run a DHCP server that allocates a pool of addresses to devices attached to the network. While DHCP works well for most devices on a local network, it can cause difficulties if you want to make a Beagle board visible outside a home firewall via port forwarding. This is because DHCP devices may receive a different IP address each time they boot (depending on the router's lease time). *Port forwarding* (aka *port mapping*) means that a particular port on a Beagle board (e.g., port 80) can be mapped to a port that is visible outside your firewall, thus making a service on the board visible to the world. Many router/firewalls require the Beagle board to have a static IP address to set up a port forward to it.

To allocate a static IP address to a network adapter, you can alter the /etc/network/ interfaces configuration file to manually specify the address (e.g., 192.168.1.33), the network mask, and the network gateway, with the following format:

```
debian@ebb:/etc/network $ more interfaces
# The primary network interface
auto eth0
allow-hotplug eth0
iface eth0 inet static
   address 192.168.1.33
   netmask 255.255.255.0
   gateway 192.168.1.1
```

The Beagle board then has a static IP address after reboot. A similar procedure applies to other adapter entries, such as the wlan0 wireless Ethernet adapter except that it uses connman, as described in Chapter 12. Do not pick a static address that is within the DHCP pool or assigned to another device, or it could result in IP conflicts on the network.

Power over Ethernet

One common difficulty in using the Beagle board as a web sensor is related to the provision of power. It is possible to power the Beagle board using batteries, and there are many *USB battery pack* solutions available that can perform this role. For example, the *IntoCircuit Portable Charger 26.8Ah* (~$44) is a popular choice that could in theory power the board for 30 to 50 hours at an average load (this duration will fall dramatically if Wi-Fi is used). For example, such a battery configuration could be used for a mobile robot platform.

When a fixed installation is required in a remote location (e.g., in a garden, gate/entrance) where power sockets are not readily available, then *power over Ethernet* (PoE) is a good option. Regular Ethernet cables (Cat 5e or Cat 6) contain four pairs of wires that are twisted together to cancel out electromagnetic interference from external power sources. Low-cost *unshielded twisted pair* (UTP) cables can therefore transmit data (and power) over long distances of up to 100m/328ft.

For standard Ethernet (100Base-T), only two of the twisted pair wires are actually used for data transfer; therefore, the other two pairs are available to carry power. However, it is also possible to inject a *common-mode voltage* onto the pair of wires that carry the data signals. This is possible because Ethernet over twisted pair (similar to CAN bus, USB, and HDMI) uses *differential signaling*, which means that the receiver reads the difference between the two signals, rather than their voltage level with respect to ground. External interference affects both of the paired wires in the same way, so its impact is effectively canceled out by the differential signaling. PoE can therefore use the network cable to deliver power to attached devices. This structure is commonly used by VoIP phones and IP cameras so that they do not need a separate mains power point.

The Beagle boards do not support PoE internally, so two main external options are available:

- **Use a pseudo-PoE cabling structure:** Adafruit sell a *Passive PoE Injector Cable Set* (~$6), illustrated in Figure 11-23, for which you can use a regular 5V mains supply to inject power into the unused twisted pair wires and then draw that power at the other end of the cable. You can use the crimp tool that is described in Chapter 4 to terminate the DC power connector with a DuPont connector so that it can be attached to the Beagle board GPIO header. **Do not connect such cables to a true PoE switch!**

- **Use a true PoE (IEEE 802.3af) switch:** To send power over long distances, PoE switches provide a 48V DC supply. Therefore, a *PoE power extraction module* is required to *step down* this voltage to a level that is acceptable by a Beagle board.

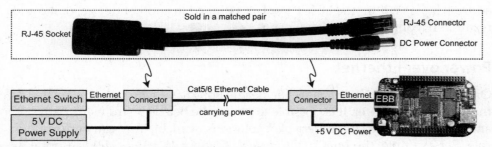

Figure 11-23: Adafruit pseudo-PoE cable

PoE Power Extraction Modules (Advanced Topic)

One problem with the arrangement in Figure 11-23 is that the 5V supply voltage will drop as the cable length increases due to the impact of cable resistance. Recently, low-cost network switches have become available that offer PoE functionality. *Power extraction modules* (PEMs) can be purchased to step down the 48V DC voltage that is supplied by these switches to lower, fixed DC levels (e.g., 3.3V, 5V, 12V). The low-cost ($10–$15) PEM that is used in this section is the PEM1305 (`tiny.cc/ebb1103`), which can be used to supply 5V to a Beagle board. PoE (802.3af) switches can provide up to 15.4W of power per attached device. The IEEE 802.3af standard (IEEE Standards Association, 2012) requires that true-PoE devices support two types of PoE:

- **Type-B PoE:** Uses the spare pair of wires to carry power. The data pairs are untouched.

- **Type-A PoE:** Uses a 48V common-mode DC voltage on the data wires to carry power. The spare pairs are unused.

Gigabit Ethernet uses all four pairs of wires to transmit data, so it is likely that Type-A PoE will be dominant in future PoE network switches.

Figure 11-24 illustrates a circuit that can be used to power the Beagle board using a PoE (IEEE 802.3af) supply. The PEM1305 can extract power from type-A and type-B PoE configurations. However, you must connect the module to DC isolation transformers to extract the power from the data wires. To do this, you can use a *MagJack* (a jack with integrated magnetics) with center-tapped outputs (e.g., the Belfuse 0826-1X1T-GJ-F). The MagJack contains the isolation transformers that are required to provide the 48V supply to the PoE PEM and to deliver the data pair safely to the Beagle board Ethernet jack at Ethernet signal voltage levels.

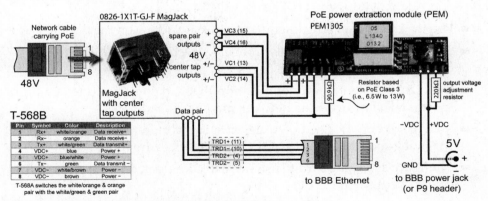

Figure 11-24: True PoE connection for the T-568B wiring scheme

The resistor that is placed on the input side of the PEM1305 is used to select the power output level of the PoE switch—accurately selecting the power output level results in a more power-efficient implementation. The output voltage adjustment resistor can further refine the PEM output voltage level. The PEM pin outputs can be connected directly to the BBB power jack or to the supply pins on the PocketBeagle headers.

NOTE   Be careful in your choice of PoE power extraction module and MagJack. For example, the PEM1205 module appears to be similar to the PEM1305, but it does not have rectifier bridges on the input, so you would need to add these yourself (otherwise, the circuit could not handle Ethernet cross-over cables). Also, many Ethernet MagJacks do not have center-tap outputs from the isolation transformers and so are unsuitable for use with PoE PEMs.

Summary

After completing this chapter, you should be able to do the following:

- Install and configure a web server on a Beagle board and use it to display static HTML content
- Enhance the web server to send dynamic web content that uses CGI scripts and PHP scripts to interface to Beagle board sensors
- Write the code for a C/C++ client application that can communicate using either HTTP or HTTPS
- Build a full local MQTT architecture using Mosquitto and Paho
- Interface to platform as a service (PaaS) offerings, such as ThingSpeak and Adafruit IO, using HTTP and MQTT
- Use the Linux cron scheduler to structure workflow on the Beagle board
- Send e-mail messages directly from a Beagle board and utilize them as a trigger for web services such as IFTTT
- Build a C++ client/server application that can communicate at a high speed and a low overhead between any two TCP devices
- Manage remote Beagle board devices, using monitoring software and watchdog code, to ensure that deployed services are robust
- Configure a Beagle board to use static IP addresses, and wire it to utilize Power over Ethernet (PoE)

## CHAPTER 12

Wireless Communication and Control

This chapter describes how a Beagle board can be configured to wirelessly communicate to the internet and to wirelessly interface to devices and sensors using different communication standards. The chapter begins with a description of how Bluetooth communications can be used to develop a wireless remote-control framework using mobile apps. Next, a description is provided about how the board can be configured to connect to the internet using USB Wi-Fi adapters. The discussion on Wi-Fi continues with a description of how the low-cost NodeMCU (ESP8266) Wi-Fi microcontroller can be used to build a local network of wireless things, which can communicate sensor values to the Beagle board and to an IoT PaaS. The ZigBee protocol is then used to build peer-to-peer wireless networks that use the popular XBee ZigBee devices. Finally, NFC/RFID is used to build a simple security access control system. By the end of this chapter, you should be able to choose an appropriate wireless communication standard to suit your needs, and you should be able to build sophisticated wireless IoT applications.

EQUIPMENT REQUIRED FOR THIS CHAPTER:

- Beagle board (any model)
- BeagleBone Black Wireless or USB Bluetooth adapter

- Access to an Android mobile device
- BeagleBone Black Wireless or USB Wi-Fi adapter
- NodeMCU microprocessor (ESP8266 version 2)
- ZigBee modules (ideally the Digi XBee S2/S2C ZigBee model)
- An XBee USB Explorer and two XBee-to-breadboard adapters
- An RFID card reader (ideally PN532 NFC compatible)
- TMP36 temperature sensor (or other analog sensors)

Further details on this chapter are available at `www.exploringbeaglebone` `.com/chapter12/`.

Introduction to Wireless Communications

The addition of wireless capabilities to a Beagle board further enhances its application possibilities in areas such as robotics, environmental sensing, and remote imaging. The BeagleBone Black Wireless (BBBW) has onboard wireless capabilities, and by using USB devices and interfacing communication modules, many different communication types can be realized on all Beagle boards. For example, low-cost USB Wi-Fi and Bluetooth adapters are widely available, many of which have Linux driver support. In addition, other communication standards such as *ZigBee* and *near field communication* (NFC) can be realized by interfacing modules that have serial-UART connections. There is no single best solution for all projects; rather, each of the wireless communication standards has different advantages and disadvantages.

- *Bluetooth* (802.15.1) is a popular standard for interfacing to computer peripherals, audio devices, *personal area networks* (PANs), and mobile devices—all applications where the data rate is not a critical factor. It has a low cost and low power consumption profile, which makes it particularly suitable for battery-powered devices. Bluetooth *low energy* (LE) supports very low-power applications while maintaining comparable communication ranges.
- *Wi-Fi* (802.11) communication is more suitable than Bluetooth for full-scale networking applications in which a high data rate is critical; therefore, it is popular with media-rich internet-attached devices and laptop computers. Unfortunately, Wi-Fi has heavy power consumption costs (as much as 40 times the power consumption of Bluetooth for comparable communication tasks[1]) and slow connection setup times.

---

[1]Rahul Balani, "Energy Consumption Analysis for Bluetooth, WiFi and Cellular Networks," Networked and Embedded Systems Laboratory, University of California, Los Angeles, Technical Report, 2007.

- The *ZigBee* (802.15.4 based) communication standard can also be utilized by the Beagle boards, usually by interfacing via a UART device to *XBee modules*. XBee devices are designed to have a low power profile and can communicate over significant distances, forming mesh network arrangements to further extend the network range. Unfortunately, the maximum data rates are quite limited in comparison to Bluetooth and Wi-Fi; however, the low communications latency and fast connection setup times mean that the standard is suitable for real-time control. ZigBee sits on 802.15.4 and provides additional routing, authentication, and encryption functionality. It is important to note that there are other such 802.15.4 frameworks, most notably 6LoWPAN, which provides an IPv6 stack on top of 802.15.4 and is particularly useful if you want to configure a device to be directly accessible from the internet.

- NFC (SO/IEC 14443/18000-3) is a short-range radio communication standard that builds on *radio frequency identification* (RFID) communications. It supports a communication range of up to 8 inches and enables very high data rates when the devices are almost touching (i.e., less than 2 inches). NFC supports communication with unpowered devices using *inductive coupling*.

The general characteristics of different wireless standards are summarized in Table 12-1. Clearly, the data rate and communications range are important factors in the choice of module. In this chapter, each of these technologies is interfaced to a Beagle board so that you have a starting point from which to work.

Table 12-1: Summary Comparison of Different Wireless Standards

	BLUETOOTH	WI-FI	ZIGBEE	NFC/RFID
Standard	IEEE 802.15.1	IEEE 802.11	IEEE 802.15.4	ISO/IEC
Range	10m to 100m	50m to 100m	30m to 100m+	<20cm
Power	Low	High	Very low	Very low
Data Rate	<2.1 Mb/s	10 to 300Mb/s	<250kb/s	Up to 20Mb/s
Topology	Star	Star	Mesh/star	Point-to-point
Organization	Bluetooth SIG	Wi-Fi Alliance	ZigBee Alliance	NFC Forum

Bluetooth Communications

Bluetooth is a popular wireless communication system that was created by Ericsson and is now managed by the Bluetooth *Special Interest Group* (SIG). Bluetooth was designed as an open standard to enable different device types to communicate wirelessly over short distances. It is often used for the digital transfer of data for audio headsets, keyboards, computer mice, medical devices, and many more applications. Only the BBBW has support for onboard Bluetooth, but support can be added to other Beagle board models using low-cost USB Bluetooth adapters.

Installing a Bluetooth Adapter

The choice of USB Bluetooth adapter is important; not every adapter has Linux driver support. Ideally, you should determine in advance of purchase that there is Linux support and that the device works with your board. Unfortunately, that is not always possible; furthermore, as Linux device driver support is usually chipset-dependent, it may even be the case that two devices with the same model number and ostensibly the same functionality have different chipsets, leaving one supported by Linux and the other not. The USB Bluetooth adapter used in this section is the Kinivo BTD-400 Bluetooth 4.0 USB adapter (~$15), shown in Figure 12-1. It is commonly available, and the current version uses a Broadcom chipset that has good Linux support.

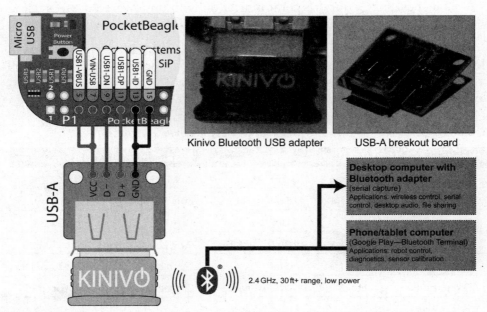

Figure 12-1: Bluetooth connected to the PocketBeagle board through a USB-A breakout board

The first step is to install the packages that are required for Bluetooth connectivity on all Beagle board models, which may already be the latest version:

```
debian@ebb:~$ sudo apt update
debian@ebb:~$ sudo apt install bluetooth bluez
bluetooth is already the newest version (5.43-2+deb9u1).
bluez is already the newest version (5.43-2+deb9u1).
```

After installation, the USB adapter can be "hot plugged" into the Beagle board USB socket, or custom USB socket for the PocketBeagle, as illustrated in Figure 12-1. You can list the USB modules that are currently connected to the board using the following command, where the Broadcom Corp. listing indicates that the USB adapter has been detected:

```
debian@ebb:~$ lsusb
Bus 002 Device 002: ID 0a5c:2198 Broadcom Corp. Bluetooth 3.0 Device
Bus 002 Device 001: ID 1d6b:0002 Linux Foundation 2.0 root hub
Bus 001 Device 001: ID 1d6b:0002 Linux Foundation 2.0 root hub
```

Checking the LKM

As discussed in previous chapters, a Linux *loadable kernel module* (LKM) is a mechanism for adding code to the Linux kernel at run time. The LKMs are ideal for device drivers, enabling the kernel to communicate with the hardware without it having to know how the hardware works. The alternative to LKMs would be to build the code for each and every driver into the Linux kernel, which would lead to an impractical kernel size and constant kernel recompilations. LKMs are loaded at run time, but these modules do not exist in user space—they are essentially part of the kernel. When the Bluetooth adapter is plugged into the Beagle board (or onboard Bluetooth is enabled on the BBBW), you can use the lsmod command to find out which modules are loaded. For example, with a USB Bluetooth adapter, you can see the btusb module is loaded:

```
debian@ebb:~$ lsmod
Module            Size  Used by
bnep             28672  2
btusb            49152  0
btrtl            16384  1 btusb
btbcm            16384  1 btusb
btintel          16384  1 btusb
bluetooth       540672  26 btrtl,btintel,bnep,btbcm,btusb ...
```

The modprobe command enables you to add or remove an LKM to or from the Linux kernel at run time. However, if everything has worked correctly, the module should have loaded automatically. You can check dmesg for errors that may have arisen. Using cat /proc/modules provides similar information about the modules that are loaded, but it is in a less readable form. You can then test the status of the Bluetooth service under systemd as follows:

```
debian@ebb:~$ dmesg
[  130.206616] Bluetooth: Core ver 2.22 ...
[  131.219889] usbcore: registered new interface driver btusb
[  198.523584] Bluetooth: BNEP (Ethernet Emulation) ver 1.3
[  198.523602] Bluetooth: BNEP filters: protocol multicast
[  198.523659] Bluetooth: BNEP socket layer initialized
```

```
debian@ebb:~$ systemctl status bluetooth
● bluetooth.service - Bluetooth service
   Loaded: loaded (/lib/systemd/system/bluetooth.service; enabled; vendor preset
   Active: active (running) since Wed 2018-07-18 18:42:10 IST; 3 weeks 5 days ag
     Docs: man:bluetoothd(8)
 Main PID: 1501 (bluetoothd)
   Status: "Running"
    Tasks: 1 (limit: 4915)
   CGroup: /system.slice/bluetooth.service
           └─1501 /usr/lib/bluetooth/bluetoothd
```

Configuring a Bluetooth Adapter

The hcitool command is used to configure Bluetooth connections, and if the dev argument is passed, it provides information about the local Bluetooth device.

```
debian@ebb:~$ hcitool dev
Devices: hci0    00:02:72:CB:C3:53
```

This is the hardware device address of the adapter that was connected to my board. Using this command you can scan for devices, display connections, display power levels, and perform many more functions—check man hcitool for more details.

At this point, you should be able to scan for Bluetooth devices in the vicinity. Ensure that the devices are *discoverable*—that they can be found when a scan takes place. For example, under Windows you have to explicitly make an adapter discoverable, by using Windows Settings ⇨ Devices ⇨ Bluetooth & other devices ⇨ and enabling On. You can scan for Bluetooth devices in the vicinity of the board and test communication by sending an echo request using the BlueZ l2ping tool (use Ctrl+C to quit).

```
debian@ebb:~$ hcitool scan
Scanning ...
        00:21:04:F9:35:8E        S68H
        40:E2:30:13:CA:09        DEREK-OFFICE-PC
debian@ebb:~$ sudo l2ping 40:E2:30:13:CA:09
Ping: 40:E2:30:13:CA:09 from 00:02:72:CB:C3:53 (data size 44) ...
0 bytes from 40:E2:30:13:CA:09 id 0 time 5.17ms
0 bytes from 40:E2:30:13:CA:09 id 1 time 10.18ms ...
```

This means that the adapter on the PocketBeagle has discovered my desktop computer, DEREK-OFFICE-PC (the hcitool scan command may activate Bluetooth devices in nearby rooms that use Bluetooth remote controls—e.g., smart televisions may magically activate!). The board can interrogate the available services on the desktop computer using the following:

```
debian@ebb:~$ sdptool browse 40:E2:30:13:CA:09
Browsing 40:E2:30:13:CA:09 ...
Service Name: Service Discovery
```

```
Service Description: Publishes services to remote devices
Service Provider: Microsoft
Service RecHandle: 0x0 ...
```

This output is followed by a long list of available services, such as an AV remote, voice gateway, audio source, audio sink, FTP server, printing service, and so on, each having its own unique channel number. Chapter 13 examines how you can pair a user-interface device to the board; however, this discussion focuses on how you can send commands to a Beagle board from a desktop machine, tablet computer, or mobile phone. Such a framework is suitable for localized wireless remote control of the board for applications such as robotic control or home automation.

Making the Beagle Board Discoverable

If the Beagle board is to act as a wireless server, it is vital that it is discoverable by the client machines. The hciconfig command can configure the Bluetooth device (hci0) to enable page and inquiry scans, as follows:

```
debian@ebb:~$ hciconfig
hci0:    Type: Primary  Bus: USB
         BD Address: 00:02:72:CB:C3:53  ACL MTU: 1021:8  SCO MTU: 64:1
         UP RUNNING
         RX bytes:4480 acl:25 sco:0 events:108 errors:0
         TX bytes:3389 acl:22 sco:0 commands:70 errors:0
debian@ebb:~$ sudo hciconfig hci0 piscan
debian@ebb:~$ sudo hciconfig hci0 name PocketBeagle
debian@ebb:~$ sudo hciconfig hci0 name
hci0:    Type: Primary  Bus: USB
         BD Address: 00:02:72:CB:C3:53  ACL MTU: 1021:8  SCO MTU: 64:1
         Name: 'PocketBeagle'
```

A *Serial Port Profile* (SPP) is required on the board to define how virtual serial ports are connected via Bluetooth connections. The sdptool can be used to configure a profile for a *serial port* (SP) on Bluetooth channel 22 and find details about available services using the following:

> **NOTE**   To get the next step to work correctly on some boards, I had to start the bluetoothd **process with a** --compat **(compatibility) option for my adapter. This should be resolved over time.**

```
debian@ebb:/lib/systemd/system $ more bluetooth.service
...
ExecStart=/usr/lib/bluetooth/bluetoothd --compat
debian@ebb:/lib/systemd/system$ sudo systemctl restart bluetooth.service
```

You must restart the Bluetooth service after making this file edit.

```
debian@ebb:~$ sudo sdptool add --channel=22 SP
Serial Port service registered
debian@ebb:~$ sudo sdptool browse local
```

```
Browsing FF:FF:FF:00:00:00 ...
Service Name: Serial Port
Service Description: COM Port
Service Provider: BlueZ
Service RecHandle: 0x10005
Service Class ID List:  "Serial Port" (0x1101)
Protocol Descriptor List:
   "L2CAP" (0x0100)  "RFCOMM" (0x0003) Channel: 22 ...
```

At this point, a desktop computer or a tablet/phone device can be used to scan for devices, as illustrated in Figure 12-2(a) (using an Android mobile phone). The Beagle board should be detected with the hostname defined earlier in this section (i.e., `PocketBeagle`). However, to allow for communication between the board and the desktop PC or mobile device, a serial connection needs to be established to channel 22. The board must run a service that can listen for incoming connections on that specific Bluetooth channel, for example, by using the `rfcomm` tool.

```
debian@ebb:~$ sudo rfcomm listen /dev/rfcomm0 22
Waiting for connection on channel 22
```

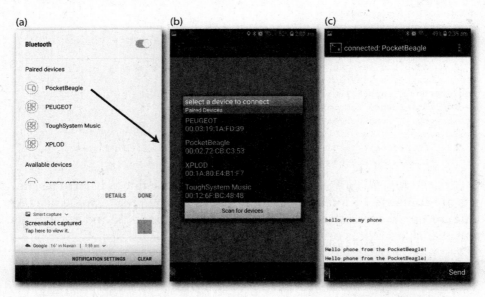

Figure 12-2: An Android mobile phone connecting to the PocketBeagle using Bluetooth: (a) device pairing, (b) a Bluetooth terminal application setup, and (c) terminal communication

You can then use a serial terminal on the desktop machine with the associated COM port, or you can use a Bluetooth Terminal App (e.g., the app by Qwerty), as illustrated in Figure 12-2(b), to connect to the PocketBeagle `rfcomm` device (i.e., `/dev/rfcomm0`).

A serial terminal can then be opened from the phone or tablet computer, as illustrated in Figure 12-2(c). When a connection is formed to the PocketBeagle, the SSH window displays the following:

```
debian@ebb:~$ sudo rfcomm listen /dev/rfcomm0 22
Waiting for connection on channel 22
Connection from D0:B1:28:55:BD:78 to /dev/rfcomm0
Press CTRL-C for hangup
```

Do *not* stop this service. While the service is listening, open a second SSH terminal to the PocketBeagle. In the second SSH terminal, you can cat and echo to the device associated with the Bluetooth serial connection rfcomm0.

```
debian@ebb:~$ cat /dev/rfcomm0
hello from my phone^C
debian@ebb:~$ echo "Hello phone from the PocketBeagle!" > /dev/rfcomm0
debian@ebb:~$ echo "Hello phone from the PocketBeagle!" > /dev/rfcomm0
```

Figure 12-2(c) captures the resulting communication from the mobile device's perspective. At this point, it is clear that the device is working, and you can connect a minicom terminal to the mobile app or Windows terminal as follows (turn on local echo in minicom):

```
debian@ebb:~$ minicom -b 115200 -o -D /dev/rfcomm0
Welcome to minicom 2.7
OPTIONS: I18n
Port /dev/rfcomm0, 06:01:34
Hello from the Android device
Hello from the PocketBeagle
```

The resulting conversation is bidirectional, and a message is sent whenever the Enter key is pressed. Once you have established serial communication between two devices, there is no limit to the number of possible applications. One such application is the command control of a Beagle board using a graphical user interface (GUI) that is running on an Android mobile device—this is outlined in the next section.

Android App Development with Bluetooth

Many resources available for Bluetooth mobile application development with both Android and iOS. Mobile apps could be used for projects such as the remote control of a robotic platform. For example, the app graphical user interface could have forward, backward, left, and right buttons that send string messages to a custom serial server that is running on a PocketBeagle. Code for such a server is provided in Chapter 8 in the section titled "LED Serial Server."

A great place to start with mobile application development is the MIT App Inventor (appinventor.mit.edu/). It consists of an innovative web-based graphical programming language (similar to MIT Scratch) for mobile application development. You can pair an Android tablet or phone with the App Inventor environment and view your code developments live on your mobile device. The App Inventor API has Bluetooth client and server libraries that can be integrated with your program code. Applications that are developed with App Inventor 2 can be distributed like regular applications (e.g., using .apk files to be side-loaded on Android devices).

Wi-Fi Communications

Bluetooth is perfectly suited to local wireless remote control of your Beagle board, but Wi-Fi is more suitable for high data rate wireless applications. Wi-Fi can also be used for wireless remote control of your board, but it requires a complex controller such as a cell phone/tablet. As discussed, there are low-cost Bluetooth remote control devices available that can be paired with the Beagle boards and used for remote control applications, as discussed in Chapter 8 (see the section titled "LED Serial Server"). However, if you want to connect your board wirelessly to the internet, then Wi-Fi is the clear solution, despite its complexity and power consumption cost.

Installing a Wi-Fi Adapter

Various popular low-profile USB *Wi-Fi adapters* and the BeagleBone Black Wireless (BBBW) onboard adapter[2] are tested in this section, with the adapters and summary results illustrated in Figure 12-3. The table lists indicative performance results that may not be repeatable, as product revisions and Linux updates may affect the outcomes.

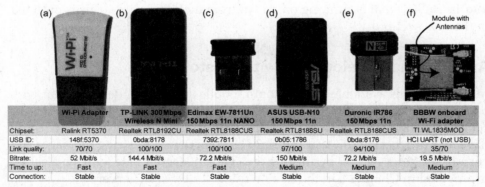

	Wi-Pi Adapter	TP-LINK 300 Mbps Wireless N Mini	Edimax EW-7811Un 150 Mbps 11n NANO	ASUS USB-N10 150 Mbps 11n	Duronic IR786 150 Mbps 11n	BBBW onboard Wi-Fi adapter
Chipset:	Ralink RT5370	Realtek RTL8192CU	Realtek RTL8188CUS	Realtek RTL8188SU	Realtek RTL8188CUS	TI WL1835MOD
USB ID:	148f:5370	0bda:8178	7392:7811	0b05:1786	0bda:8176	HCI UART (not USB)
Link quality:	70/70	100/100	100/100	97/100	94/100	35/70
Bitrate:	52 Mbit/s	144.4 Mbit/s	72.2 Mbit/s	150 Mbit/s	72.2 Mbit/s	19.5 Mbit/s
Time to up:	Fast	Fast	Fast	Medium	Medium	Medium
Connection:	Stable	Stable	Stable	Stable	Stable	Stable

Figure 12-3: A selection of Wi-Fi adapters and test results

---

[2]The BBBW uses a TI WL18xxMOD WiLink 8 single band combo 2x2 MIMO Wi-Fi, Bluetooth & Bluetooth Smart module.

Once a USB Wi-Fi adapter is inserted (hot plugged) into the Beagle board, you can confirm that the network adapter is being detected using the `lsusb` command, which should result in an output of the following form:

```
debian@ebb:~$ lsusb
Bus 001 Device 002: ID 148f:5370 Ralink Tech, Corp. RT5370 Wireless Adapter
```

The adapter should be detected by the board and its chipset identified. Sometimes you may need to search for the latest firmware that is available for the adapter:

```
debian@ebb:~$ sudo apt update
debian@ebb:~$ apt-cache search RTL8188
firmware-realtek - Binary firmware for Realtek wired/wifi/BT adapters
debian@ebb:~$ sudo apt install firmware-realtek
firmware-realtek is already the newest version ...
```

In all cases, the `dmesg` command will give you useful information about the operation status of a USB device that was plugged into your board.

```
[ 1381.345612] usb 1-1: new high-speed USB device number 2 using musb-hdrc
[ 1381.504867] usb 1-1: New USB device found, idVendor=148f, idProduct=5370
[ 1381.504889] usb 1-1: New USB device strings: Mfr=1, Product=2,
SerialNumber=3
[ 1381.504898] usb 1-1: Product: 802.11 n WLAN
[ 1381.504906] usb 1-1: Manufacturer: Ralink
[ 1381.504913] usb 1-1: SerialNumber: 1.0
[ 1381.717635] usb 1-1: reset high-speed USB device number 2 using musb-hdrc
...
```

NOTE   If your USB device does not appear when you type `lsusb`, use `dmesg` to help identify the problem. A common issue that arises with the PocketBeagle and other boards is that a Wi-Fi adapter may have power requirements that are greater than the board configuration can supply. The following type of message is indicative of such a problem:

```
debian@ebb:~$ sudo udevadm trigger
debian@ebb:~$ dmesg
[  304.281103] usb 2-1: new high-speed USB device number 14 using musb-hdrc
[  304.409165] usb 2-1: device descriptor read/64, error -71
```

A powered USB hub or a different board power configuration may be required in this case.

The latest version of the BeagleBoard.org Linux distribution utilizes the ConnMan daemon for managing internet connections. ConnMan is specially tailored to manage internet communications for embedded devices by consolidating multiple networking services into a single service. You can configure Wi-Fi on a Beagle board using ConnMan as follows:

```
debian@ebb:~$ sudo connmanctl
connmanctl> enable wifi
Error wifi: Already enabled
connmanctl> scan wifi
Scan completed for wifi
connmanctl> services
    Tesla        wifi_f45eab38d5f9_5465736c76_managed_psk
    Galileo      wifi_f45eab38d5f9_47616c696c665f_managed_psk
```

Because your network connection is likely encrypted, you will also have to provide the passphrase.

```
connmanctl> agent on
Agent registered
connmanctl> connect wifi_f45eab38d5f9_47616c696c665f_managed_psk
Agent RequestInput wifi_f45eab38d5f9_47616c696c665f_managed_psk
  Passphrase = [ Type=psk, Requirement=mandatory, Alternates=[ WPS ] ]
  WPS = [ Type=wpspin, Requirement=alternate ]
Passphrase? MySecretPassword
connmanctl> exit
```

You can then use ifconfig to test your network connections. In this case, my BBBW is connected at the address 192.168.1.116.

```
debian@ebb:~$ ifconfig
SoftAp0: flags=4163<UP,BROADCAST,RUNNING,MULTICAST>  mtu 1500 ...
lo: flags=73<UP,LOOPBACK,RUNNING>  mtu 65536 ...
usb0: flags=4163<UP,BROADCAST,RUNNING,MULTICAST>  mtu 1500 ...
usb1: flags=4099<UP,BROADCAST,MULTICAST>  mtu 1500 ...
wlan0: flags=-28605<UP,BROADCAST,RUNNING,MULTICAST,DYNAMIC>  mtu 1500
        inet 192.168.1.116  netmask 255.255.255.0  broadcast 192.168.1.255
        inet6 fe80::f65e:abff:fe38:d5f9  prefixlen 64  scopeid 0x20<link>
        ether f4:5e:ab:38:d5:f9  txqueuelen 1000  (Ethernet) ...
```

The current IP addresses associated with the board can be listed using the hostname command, which includes an IPv6 address if available.

```
debian@ebb:~$ hostname -I
192.168.7.2 192.168.6.2 192.168.1.116 192.168.8.1
fd4d:a035:2d8d:1:f65e:abff:fe38:d5f9
```

If problems arise with the previous steps, then you can use the following commands to gain insight into your network configuration. For example, you can use the iwlist command to list the available access points and to get information about signal strength.

```
debian@ebb:~$ sudo iwlist wlan0 scan
wlan0     Scan completed :
          Cell 01 - Address: 98:FC:11:B5:32:96
                    Channel:11
                    Frequency:2.462 GHz (Channel 11)
                    Quality=34/70  Signal level=-76 dBm
                    Encryption key:on
```

```
              ESSID:"Galileo"
              Bit Rates:1 Mb/s; 2 Mb/s; 5.5 Mb/s; ...
```

You can restart the ConnMan service if necessary and check its status using `systemctl`. Here's an example:

```
debian@ebb:~$ sudo systemctl restart connman
debian@ebb:~$ sudo systemctl status connman
• connman.service - Connection service
   Loaded: loaded (/lib/systemd/system/connman.service; enabled; vendor preset:
   Active: active (running) since Sun 2018-08-19 23:07:53 UTC; 37s ago
 Main PID: 2748 (connmand)
    Tasks: 1 (limit: 4915)
   CGroup: /system.slice/connman.service
           └─2748 /usr/sbin/connmand -n --nodnsproxy
```

If these commands fail, then you should use `dmesg` to check for problems (e.g., `dmesg|grep wlan0|more`). If the adapter still fails to function correctly, then you may need to build drivers for the board. For example, for Realtek adapters you can download custom driver source code from www.realtek.com.tw/downloads/ and build them on the Beagle board. You can also get useful information about your adapter configuration using `iwconfig`.

```
debian@ebb:~$ iwconfig wlan0
wlan0     IEEE 802.11  ESSID:"Galileo"
          Mode:Managed  Frequency:2.462 GHz  Access Point: 98:FC:11:B5:32:69
          Bit Rate=19.5 Mb/s   Tx-Power=20 dBm ...
```

Similarly, you can use the following command to present a display of the signal strength properties, which updates the display every second:

```
debian@ebb:~$ watch -n 1 cat /proc/net/wireless
Inter-| sta-|  Quality       |Discarded packets          |Missed| WE
 face | tus |link level noise |nwid crypt  frag retry misc|beacon| 22
 wlan0: 0000 34.  -77.  -256  0      0      0    17     8    0
```

Alternatively, you can use the `wavemon` application (`sudo apt install wavemon`) to format that data appropriately for a Linux terminal.

One key advantage of Linux on an embedded device is the ease with which a device can be connected to the internet using the vast choice of low-cost Wi-Fi adapters. Clearly the web server code, IoT code, and high-speed client/server code examples from Chapter 11 are all directly applicable to a wireless Linux device. Using Wi-Fi you can build untethered IoT devices and robots, typically for indoor applications, that connect directly to the internet.

The NodeMCU Wi-Fi Slave Processor

In Chapter 10, the Arduino is used as a slave processor for the Beagle board, where the Beagle board can take control of its GPIOs and read analog values from its ADCs. The Arduino can be extended with a Wi-Fi shield ($30+), or the Arduino Yún ($75) can be used to build a wireless slave processor. However, there is a cheaper option with a small footprint that can be interfaced directly to a Beagle board as a wireless slave processor: the NodeMCU.

The NodeMCU (nodemcu.com) uses the low-cost ESP8266 Wi-Fi microcontroller module ($2–$3) to create a low-cost Lua-based development platform for IoT applications. The NodeMCU version 2 ($5–$10) is breadboard ready and can be programmed over micro USB, which makes it a suitable prototyping platform for the development of wireless slave devices. Figure 12-4 illustrates the bottom and top of the NodeMCU processor along with its various input/output capabilities, including ADC, GPIO, PWM, SPI, software-based I²C, and serial UART.

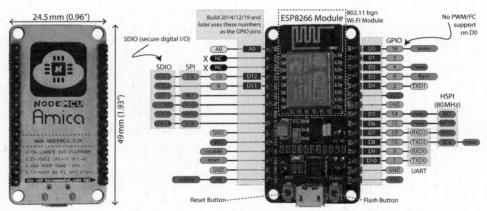

Figure 12-4: The bottom and top views of the low-cost NodeMCU (version 2) Wi-Fi slave processor

The ESP8266 module itself contains the microcontroller, and it is affixed on top of the NodeMCU prototyping platform as a tiny daughterboard. It is possible to use the ESP8266 without the NodeMCU, but the ESP8266 module must be affixed to a breakout board to make it breadboard compatible. The documentation for the NodeMCU is available at tiny.cc/beagle1201, and the datasheet for the ESP8266 is available at tiny.cc/beagle1202.

THE ESP32

There is a newer version of the ESP8266 with a Tensilica Xtensa LX6 dual-core microprocessor and 520KiB of SRAM. It is faster than the ESP8266 and provides additional support for CAN bus, security, touchscreen devices; it also provides a greater range of

I/O capabilities. NodeMCU supports the ESP32 device, which makes it a great option if you need a more powerful wireless slave processor at modest additional cost.

Flashing with the Latest Firmware

The NodeMCU variant boards implement internal USB-to-UART conversion using the CP2102 or CH340 serial chipsets. There is typically built-in driver support for these chipsets in Linux and Windows.[3] The most straightforward method of upgrading the firmware on the NodeMCU is to download the open-source NodeMCU firmware programmer from github.com/nodemcu/nodemcu-flasher (in one of the release subdirectories).

You can build a custom version of NodeMCU to suit your application using the builder tool at nodemcu-build.com. In the following example ADC, file, GPIO, HTTP, net, node, UART, timer, SPI, I²C, MQTT, and Wi-Fi support were selected. Click "Start your Build" when you are finished your selection. The build server will notify you a few minutes later when your build is complete, providing you with a firmware file. The "integer" version without floating-point support is used in this section as it has a much lower resource footprint, and it is useful to investigate the limitations of not having floating-point operation support.

The NodeMCU should appear as a device on your host OS, as illustrated for Windows in Figure 12-5(a). Figure 12-5(b) illustrates the NodeMCU firmware programmer in action. Note that you may have to press the reset button on the NodeMCU to begin the firmware update.

(a)   (b)

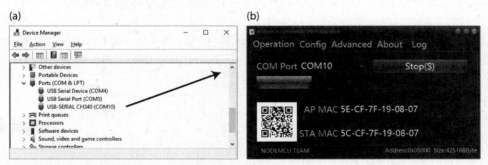

Figure 12-5: (a) The NodeMCU device profile under Windows, and (b) the NodeMCU firmware programmer captured while writing the image

---

[3]If device support is not available or requires an update, then see tiny.cc/beagle1203.

Connecting the NodeMCU to Wi-Fi

Once the NodeMCU has been flashed with the latest firmware, you can use PuTTY or `minicom` to connect to the device at 115,200 baud (use 9,600 baud for older builds). Alternatively, you can use the ESPlorer tool from `tiny.cc/beagle1204` to connect to the module over a serial port (COM10/COM11), as illustrated in Figure 12-6. This tool allows you to communicate with the device and also includes a Lua editor, which makes software development straightforward. On connecting to the board the available modules are listed on the right side, as in Figure 12-6. In this figure you can see listed modules that correspond to the earlier image build options.

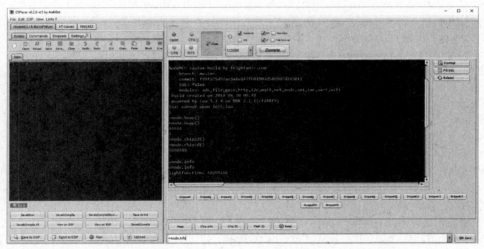

Figure 12-6: ESPlorer window communicating with the NodeMCU ESP8266 device

You can also attach the NodeMCU directly to the Beagle board using a USB-to-micro-USB cable. Press the reset button on the NodeMCU after connecting it via USB; you should see the following output:

```
debian@ebb:~$ lsusb
Bus 001 Device 097: ID 1a86:7523 QinHeng Electronics HL-340 USB-Serial
adapter
Bus 001 Device 001: ID 1d6b:0002 Linux Foundation 2.0 root hub
debian@ebb:~$ ls -l /dev/ttyUSB*
crw-rw---- 1 root dialout 188, 0 Aug 19 21:37 /dev/ttyUSB0
debian@ebb:~$ sudo apt install minicom
debian@ebb:~$ sudo minicom -b 115200 -o -D /dev/ttyUSB0 -s
```

Press the reset button on the NodeMCU; a few strange characters may appear. Do *not* enable local echo in `minicom`, and be sure that you disable hardware flow control.

> **NOTE** You must disable hardware flow control in `minicom` to connect to the NodeMCU device directly from the Beagle board via USB. You do this by pressing Ctrl+A followed by Z and O, select Serial port setup and then press F (to set Hardware Flow Control to No). The `-s` option can be used when executing `minicom` to place you directly in this menu. If the NodeMCU displays the reset message but remains unresponsive, it is a symptom of incorrect hardware flow control settings.

If all goes well, you are now able to issue commands to the NodeMCU using Lua scripting via either ESPlorer or the Beagle board direct connection. As discussed in Chapter 5, Lua has a low overhead, which makes it suitable for use on this device. The first step you should take is to configure the NodeMCU so that it can connect to your Wi-Fi network.

```
NodeMCU custom build by frightanic.com
modules: adc,file,gpio,http,i2c,mqtt,net,node,spi,tmr,uart,wifi
  build created on 2018-08-20 00:48
powered by Lua 5.1.4 on SDK 2.2.1(cfd48f3)
lua: cannot open init.lua
>station_cfg={}
>station_cfg.ssid="MySSID"
>station_cfg.pwd="MyPassword"
>station_cfg.save=true
>=wifi.sta.config(station_cfg)
true
>wifi.sta.connect()
>=wifi.sta.getip()
192.168.1.119  255.255.255.0  192.168.1.1
>=wifi.sta.getmac()
5c:cf:7f:19:08:29
>=wifi.sta.status()
5
```

You should see a message that the board cannot open `init.lua`. At this point, you do not want to have your scripts execute automatically on a power cycle until they are fully working.

The final value of 5 in the output of `wifi.sta.status()` indicates that the NodeMCU "station" now has an IP address. These Wi-Fi settings persist on the NodeMCU after it has been power cycled as the line `station_cfg.save=true` is used previously.

Programming the NodeMCU

To upload Lua programs to the NodeMCU, you can use the ESPlorer tool (Figure 12-6) or `luatool` directly from a Linux machine (including a Beagle board). The `luatool` can be downloaded and installed as follows:

```
debian@ebb:~$ git clone https://github.com/4refr0nt/luatool
Cloning into 'luatool'...
```

```
debian@ebb:~$ cd luatool/luatool/
debian@ebb:~/luatool/luatool$ ls
init.lua  luatool.py  main.lua  telnet_srv.lua
```

You can install the tool for all users on the Linux machine by placing it in the /usr/local/bin/ directory:

```
debian@ebb:~/luatool/luatool$ sudo cp luatool.py /usr/local/bin
```

An example program is provided in /chp12/nodemcu/test/ and in Listing 12-1 that establishes a simple web server on the NodeMCU. The simple web server listens for TCP socket connections on port 80 and returns an HTML "hello world" message to the web client.

You can also use ESPlorer to upload this directly, as in Figure 12-7, whereby both methods result in the web page as shown in the web browser window in Figure 12-7.

Listing 12-1: /chp12/nodemcu/test/main.lua

```lua
-- a simple http server
srv=net.createServer(net.TCP)
gpio.mode(1,gpio.INPUT)
srv:listen(80,function(conn)
    conn:on("receive",function(conn,payload) print(payload)
        conn:send("HTTP/1.1 200 OK\n\n")
        conn:send("<html><body><h1> Hello from the NodeMCU.</h1>")
        conn:send("<h2> GPIO 1 = ")
        conn:send(gpio.read(1))
        conn:send("</h2></body></html>")
        conn:on("sent",function(conn) conn:close() end)
    end)
end)
```

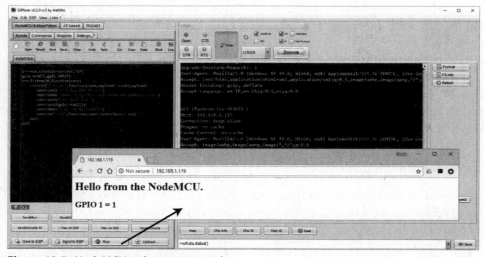

Figure 12-7: NodeMCU web server example

You must disconnect the `minicom` communications session to use the `luatool` to upload the program to the NodeMCU device—the two programs cannot share the same UART device connection. Because the `luatool` is installed in the `/usr/local/bin/` directory, you can execute it directly from the book's repository directory, as follows:

```
debian@ebb.../chp12/nodemcu/test$ ls
main.lua
debian@ebb.../chp12/nodemcu/test$ luatool.py -p /dev/ttyUSB0 -b 115200
->file.open("main.lua", "w") -> ok
->file.close() -> ok
->file.remove("main.lua") -> ok
->file.open("main.lua", "w+") -> ok
->file.writeline([==[-- a simple http server]==]) -> ok
->file.writeline([==[srv=net.createServer(net.TCP)]==]) -> ok  ...
--->>> All done <<<---
```

After a successful upload, you can once again connect to the NodeMCU using `minicom`. The program is named `main.lua` on the NodeMCU, so the warning message remains in relation to the absence of `init.lua`. This is perfectly fine—you should only write an `init.lua` script that automatically invokes `main.lua` on startup when you are certain that it is functioning correctly. For the moment, it is best to manually call the `main.lua` script as follows so that you can observe any output errors within the `minicom` session:

```
debian@ebb:~$ minicom -b 115200 -o -D /dev/ttyUSB0 -s
NodeMCU custom build by frightanic.com ...
lua: cannot open init.lua
> node.restart()
...
powered by Lua 5.1.4 on SDK 2.2.1(cfd48f3)
lua: cannot open init.lua
> =node.info()
2  2  0  1640489  1458400  4096  2  40000000
> =wifi.sta.getip()
192.168.1.119  255.255.255.0  192.168.1.1
```

You can then execute the program as follows:

```
> dofile("main.lua")
```

Once the program has started, you can open a web browser on your desktop machine and direct it at the IP address of the NodeMCU device (192.168.1.119 in my case). In addition to the hello message, the Lua program displays the state of the D1 pin (GPIO 5). If you tie this pin high (to 3.3V) or low (to GND), you will see that the web page changes to display the current GPIO state when the Reload button is clicked on the web browser.

The NodeMCU Web Server Interface

The NodeMCU can be used as a wireless slave processor for your Beagle board, whereby communication takes place over TCP/IP, using the socket-based techniques that are described in Chapter 11. A circuit is illustrated in Figure 12-8(a) that can be used to read from a GPIO, write to a GPIO, and read from the 10-bit ADC on the NodeMCU. The NodeMCU uses 3.3V logic levels, despite being powered at 5V using the Vin pin. However, while the NodeMCU is tethered to your Beagle board (or PC) using the USB cable, no external power supply is required. Remember, though, that communication, such as that illustrated in Figure 12-8(b), is taking place over Wi-Fi, not via the USB cable. Once development is complete, the USB cable can be removed, and the NodeMCU can be powered by an external supply, such as a 5V battery, using the Vin and GND pins.

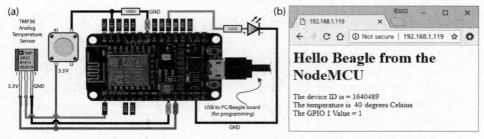

Figure 12-8: NodeMCU Wi-Fi slave test (a) the test circuit, and (b) the web page output

The code for this example is provided in Listing 12-2. The program converts the ADC value presented by the TMP36 sensor into a temperature value; however, it does this using integer-based calculation only. As discussed, the firmware without floating-point support has a lower footprint and better performance. Should you need floating-point support, you can download and flash the NodeMCU with the floating-point firmware, as described previously in this chapter.

The LED flashes each time a request is received. Note that it flashes twice when the Chrome browser in Figure 12-8(b) sends a request, as the browser actually sends two requests: one for the HTML page and another for the website icon.

Listing 12-2: /chp12/nodemcu/web/main.lua

```
srv=net.createServer(net.TCP)
gpio.mode(1,gpio.INPUT)                    -- the button
gpio.mode(7,gpio.OUTPUT)                   -- the LED
srv:listen(80,function(conn)
    conn:on("receive",function(conn,payload) print(payload)
        gpio.write(7, gpio.HIGH)
        conn:send("HTTP/1.1 200 OK\n\n")
        conn:send("<html><body><h1> Hello Beagle from the NodeMCU</h1>")
        conn:send("<div> The device ID is = ")
        conn:send(node.chipid())
```

```
         -- using integers only! float version uses more memory
         raw_voltage = adc.read(0) - 233      -- 233 is 25C
         diff_degC   = raw_voltage / 6        -- 6 steps is 1C
         temperature = diff_degC + 25         -- add/sub from 25
         conn:send("<div> The temperature is ")
         conn:send(temperature)
         conn:send(" degrees Celsius</div>")
         conn:send("<div> The GPIO 1 Value = ")
         conn:send(gpio.read(1))
         conn:send("</div></body></html>")
         gpio.write(7, gpio.LOW)
         conn:on("sent",function(conn) conn:close() end)
    end)
end)
```

You can upload this program, start it, and test it using the steps described in the previous section. You can also test the output directly from the Beagle board using the web browser code described in Chapter 11. Here's an example:

```
debian@ebb:.../chp11/webbrowser$ ./webbrowser 192.168.1.119
Sending the message: GET / HTTP/1.1
Host: 192.168.1.119
Connection: close
**START**
HTTP/1.1 200 OK

<html><body><h1> Hello Beagle from the NodeMCU</h1><div> The device ID is
= 1640489<div> The temperature is 40 degrees Celsius</div><div> The
GPIO 1 Value = 1</div></body></html>
**END**
```

This provides you with a method of writing code on the Beagle board that can communicate to the NodeMCU slave processor to retrieve information over TCP/IP. However, it would be a better solution if the data was easier to parse than the HTML output in this example—for this you could use JSON.

JSON

JSON is a lightweight data-interchange format that supports serialization and deserialization of data values from strings. It is relatively straightforward to format a message for transmission, but it is more difficult to parse the received message. *JsonCpp* is a lightweight C++ library that can be used for this task, but first it must be built and deployed on the Beagle board. It is useful to note that the library also has Python bindings. You can install the JsonCpp library on the Beagle board as follows:

```
debian@ebb:~$ git clone https://github.com/open-source-parsers/jsoncpp.git
Cloning into 'jsoncpp'...
debian@ebb:~$ cd jsoncpp/
debian@ebb:~/jsoncpp$ sudo apt install cmake
```

```
debian@ebb:~/jsoncpp$ mkdir -p build/debug
debian@ebb:~/jsoncpp$ cd build/debug/
debian@ebb:~/jsoncpp/build/debug$ cmake -DCMAKE_BUILD_TYPE=debug →
 -DBUILD_STATIC_LIBS=ON -DBUILD_SHARED_LIBS=OFF -DARCHIVE_INSTALL_DIR=. →
 -G "Unix Makefiles" ../..
-- The C compiler identification is GNU 6.3.0 ...
debian@ebb:~/jsoncpp/build/debug$ make
debian@ebb:~/jsoncpp/build/debug$ sudo make install
```

Listing 12-3 is a short JSON data file that can be used to test the JsonCpp library on the Beagle board. The file contains two fields: a floating-point temperature value and a Boolean value that describes the state of a button.

Listing 12-3: /chp12/json/data.json

```
{
    "temperature" : 28.5,
    "button" : true
}
```

Listing 12-4 is a C++ example program that uses the JsonCpp library to parse the data.json file in Listing 12-3.

Listing 12-4: /chp12/json/json_test.cpp

```cpp
#include "json/json.h"
#include<iostream>
#include<fstream>
using namespace std;

int main(){
   Json::Value root;               // the parsed data is at the root
   Json::CharReaderBuilder builder;
   ifstream data("data.json",  ifstream::binary);
   string error;
   bool success = parseFromStream(builder, data, &root, &error);
   if(!success){                   // has the parsing failed?
      cout << "Failed: " << error << endl;
   }
   // the deserialized data can be converted to a float and a bool
   float temperature = root.get("temperature", "UTF-8").asFloat();
   bool button = root.get("button", "UTF-8").asBool();
   cout << "The temperature is " << temperature << "°C" << endl;
   cout << "The button is " << (button ? "pressed":"not pressed") << endl;
   return 0;
}
```

Once the data file is open, the call root.get("temperature", "UTF-8").asFloat() is used to get the temperature field value. It is important to note that the deserialized return value is of the type float. The JSON library has performed all the work involved in parsing the file, identifying the temperature field, and deserializing the data. The program can be built and executed as follows:

```
.../chp12/json$ g++ json_test.cpp /usr/local/lib/libjsoncpp.a -o test
.../chp12/json$ ls -l test
-rwxr-xr-x 1 debian debian 1132704 Aug 22 04:39 test
.../chp12/json$ ./test
The temperature is 28.5°C
The button is pressed
```

JSON is used again later in this chapter for communicating between XBee devices and also features in the next chapter for data communication.

The NodeMCU and MQTT

The NodeMCU firmware has full built-in support for MQTT. Therefore, the MQTT frameworks that are described in Chapter 11 can be used for brokered communication between the NodeMCU and Beagle boards. For example, the NodeMCU could publish sensor data to an IoT Platform as a Service (PaaS) and the Beagle board could subscribe to the same data stream. Listing 12-5 provides an MQTT example that runs directly on the NodeMCU. To use this example, you must create an account on the MQTT PaaS using the instructions in Chapter 11. The following example connects to the Adafruit IO platform from the NodeMCU using MQTT.

The Lua code in Listing 12-5 uses these properties to connect the NodeMCU to Adafruit IO. The program opens an MQTT connection and publishes ten samples from the temperature sensor at ten-second intervals. Once ten samples have been sent, the program closes the connection to Adafruit IO. The program uses the same circuit that is illustrated in Figure 12-8(a).

Listing 12-5: /chp12/nodemcu/mqtt/main.lua

```lua
-- a simple NodeMCU MQTT publish example for AdaFruit IO
BROKER  = "io.adafruit.com"
BRPORT  = 1883
BRUSER  = "molloyd"
BRPWD   = "feb8ea6179c64b638b35b93ef87d4b42"
DEVID   = "NodeMCU1"
TOPIC   = "molloyd/feeds/weather.temperature"
count   = 0                -- used to count the number of samples sent

gpio.mode(7, gpio.OUTPUT)
gpio.write(7, gpio.HIGH)
print("Starting the NodeMCU MQTT client test")
print("Current heap is: " .. node.heap())   -- .. appends strings
m = mqtt.Client(DEVID, 120, BRUSER, BRPWD)   -- keep alive time 120s
m:connect(BROKER, BRPORT, 0, function(conn)  -- secure off
    print("Connected to MQTT Broker: " .. BROKER)
    tmr.alarm(0, 10000, 1, function()        -- repeat is on
        publish_sample()
        print("Time for another sample")
```

```
        count = count + 1
    end)
end)

function publish_sample()
    raw_voltage = adc.read(0) - 233      -- 233 is 25C
    diff_degC  = raw_voltage / 6         -- 6 steps is 1C
    temp        = diff_degC + 25         -- add/sub from 25
    msg = string.format("%d", temp)
    m:publish(TOPIC, msg, 0, 0, function(conn)
        print("Published a message: " .. msg)
        print("Value of count is: " .. count)
        if count>=10 then
          .close()
            timer.cancel(0)
        end
    end)
end

function close()
    m:close()
    print("End of the NodeMCU MQTT Example")
    gpio.write(7, gpio.LOW)
end
```

This program can be uploaded from the PC/Beagle board and executed on the NodeMCU as follows:

```
debian@ebb .../chp12/nodemcu/mqtt $ luatool.py -p /dev/ttyUSB0 -b 115200
NodeMCU 0.9.6 build 20150704  powered by Lua 5.1.4 on SDK 2.2.1(cfd48f3)
lua: cannot open init.lua
> node.restart()
> dofile("main.lua")
Starting the NodeMCU MQTT client test
Current heap is: 37464
Connected to MQTT Broker: io.adafruit.com
Time for another sample
Published a message: 33
 Value of count is: 1
...
Published a message: 34
 Value of count is: 10
End of the NodeMCU MQTT Example
```

The LED attached to the NodeMCU turns on when the program begins and turns off when the communication transaction has completed.

This final application of the NodeMCU demonstrates the numerous possibilities of IoT frameworks—it is possible to have many low-cost devices such as the NodeMCU wirelessly publishing sensor data to a cloud platform, whereupon the cloud platform can execute programs to analyze the data and trigger events on other such devices that are subscribed to data streams. The computationally powerful nature of the Beagle boards means that it can aggregate data locally and/or perform advanced interactions (e.g., using computer vision techniques to recognize a face) for IoT applications. Finally, the example also confirms the low-overhead nature of MQTT, as it can clearly be used on a low-cost microcontroller such as the ESP8266 for persistent data communications.

TEXAS INSTRUMENTS SIMPLELINK DEVICES AND CONTIKI

There are strong alternatives to the ESP8266, ESP32, and Arduino devices, such as the TI SimpleLink family of devices that support communication using Bluetooth, Sub-1GHz, Wi-Fi, Thread/OpenThread, ZigBee, and Wired channels. For example, the TI CC2650/2 (www.ti.com/product/cc2650) is a multistandard MCU that can support either Bluetooth, ZigBee, or 6LoWPAN using a reconfigurable RF core. It is based on an ARM Cortex M3 with AES, ADC, and strong I/O support for ultralow power applications. The MCU is available in a low-cost LaunchPad and SensorTag configuration, which makes it easy to get started in building interfacing applications.

Importantly, while such devices have low power consumption (and excellent sleep characteristics), they are also powerful enough to run an operating system. For example, Contiki (www.contiki-os.org) and TI-RTOS are popular choices for low-power edge computing on the TI SimpleLink family of devices. The key advantage of operating system implementations (including Linux on the Beagle boards) is that the code base in your project can be transported to a new platform without having to rewrite register access operations. Usefully, Linux developers will feel at home with the type of development required on these edge computing operating systems.

ZigBee Communications

ZigBee is a global standard for power-efficient, low data rate, embedded wireless communication. It supports the concept of wireless mesh networking, in which nodes cooperate to relay data. This allows the range of the network to be extended far beyond what is possible with the single access point model. In addition, the mesh network can heal itself should a node in the network be lost. The ZigBee standard is maintained by the *ZigBee Alliance* (zigbee.org), a nonprofit association of approximately 450 members, who promote the use of ZigBee.

Introduction to XBee Devices

Digi (digi.com) *XBee* devices, such as those illustrated in Figure 12-9(a), are possibly the best known hardware realization of the ZigBee standard. However, not all XBee devices are actually ZigBee compatible. In fact, Digi also manufactures devices that use a proprietary *DigiMesh* protocol for mesh networking, which is not compatible with ZigBee.[4] Care must be taken in choosing your devices. The ZigBee protocol defines three types of nodes:

- *Coordinators.* There is one coordinator in each network that is used to establish the network and to distribute security keys. For Beagle board applications, the coordinator is usually connected directly to the board via a UART connection.

- *Routers.* These nodes relay data from device to device and are not permitted to sleep.

- *End devices.* These devices are the leaf nodes in the network. They take information from sensor devices and transmit the information to routers and coordinators. The end devices cannot relay data from other nodes but are permitted to sleep.

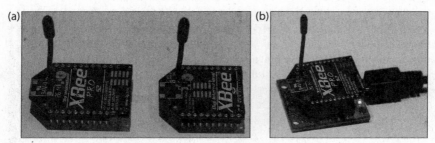

Figure 12-9: (a) The XBee Pro S2/S2C and XBee S2/S2C devices with wire antennas, and (b) the SparkFun XBee USB Explorer

In contrast, the DigiMesh protocol simplifies the mesh structure by using only one type of node that can take on any of the ZigBee roles. Unfortunately, it is not compatible with the ZigBee protocol or other vendor solutions. A separate *XBee 802.15.4* standard version is also available, but it only supports point-to-point or point-to-multipoint networking—it does not support mesh networking. The model numbering scheme used by Digi is confusing, but once you understand the difference between ZigBee and DigiMesh you can choose a module accordingly. Table 12-2 summarizes these differences and lists the current naming convention for devices, which all operate at 2.4GHz and are in a through-hole package.

---

[4]A white paper is available at `tiny.cc/beagle1205` that describes the differences between ZigBee and DigiMesh in detail.

Table 12-2: Comparison of XBee Models

XBEE NAME	PROTOCOL/ TOPOLOGY	DESCRIPTION
Series 2 ZigBee	ZigBee/Mesh	Standardized and interoperable with other vendor solutions. This model supports AT and API modes. There must be one coordinator in each network. Coordinators and routers cannot sleep.
XBee3	Multi standard	Enhanced Series 2 modules in a range of form factor that support dual-mode radio, multiple protocols, and frequencies. The devices can be easily configured using XCTU and can be programmed using MicroPython.
Series 1 802.15.4	802.15.4/ Multipoint	Good point-to-point and point-to-multipoint support.
Series 1 DigiMesh	DigiMesh/Mesh	Uses firmware to implement proprietary mesh networking on Series 1 modules. Only one type of node is required.

Source: www.digi.com/lp/xbee

The XBee Pro S2/S2C and XBee S2/S2C devices are shown side by side in Figure 12-9(a). These devices have compatible pin layouts, but the XBee Pro S2/S2C is physically longer. The Pro version is somewhat more expensive (~$29 versus ~$19) and uses greater power levels (63mW versus 2mW), but it is capable of free-space communication distances of up to 1 mile, whereas the non-Pro version is limited to approximately 400 feet. The versions in Figure 12-9(a) include an on-board wire antenna, which is a delicate but convenient option. Alternative configurations include PCB trace antennas or external u.FL/RP-SMA antennas. The latter are particularly useful if you intend to place your project inside a metal and/or weather-sealed box. Most XBee devices (including the XBee3 form factor), like Wi-Fi devices, operate at 2.4GHz. This band of frequencies does not need a license, as transmissions in this band do not interfere with licensed frequency bands, such as those used for radio broadcast and cellular phones.

Note that the 2mm pin spacing on XBee modules is not compatible with 0.1-inch (2.5mm) breadboard spacing, which means that an adapter board ($2–$3) is required for prototyping work. Also, remember to purchase at least two XBee modules—they are not much use on their own!

AT versus API Mode

XBee devices can be used in two modes, and it is important that you understand the distinction.

- *AT command mode.* *AT*tention commands are instructions that are used to control serial devices such as modems. These devices relay data precisely, but when a certain string of characters is sent to the device, it enters a special AT mode. This is the default mode of operation on XBee devices, and it hides much of the underlying communications complexity. In effect, two XBee devices configured in this mode behave somewhat like a wireless serial UART connection. However, in this mode, XBee devices enter AT command mode when the characters +++ are sent to the device. Subsequent AT commands, which are prefixed by the characters AT, can then be issued. For example, ATID returns the network ID (PAN ID). This topic is discussed in more detail shortly.

- *API mode.* The Digi XBee devices can also be used in API mode, which is used to transmit structured frames of data. The frames of data can be addressed and sent to an individual module without having to reprogram the device. In addition, API mode facilitates interaction with the input/output (I/O) capabilities of an XBee module, and it provides support for the receipt of data transfer acknowledgements.

API mode is much more capable than AT mode, but it is more complex to program. In the following sections, an application is developed in both modes.

XBee Configuration

Once you have XBee devices, the first step is to configure them using your desktop computer and a device such as the SparkFun XBee USB Explorer, which is illustrated in Figure 12-9(b). The most intuitive way to configure an XBee device is to use the *XCTU* software platform from Digi.

XCTU

XCTU is a full-featured GUI-based configuration platform for XBee devices that is provided by Digi. It can discover modules that are attached to your desktop computer using the XBee USB Explorer, as illustrated in Figure 12-10(a), and configure the network properties, such as the PAN ID, as illustrated in Figure 12-10(b). XCTU is available for free on Windows, macOS, and Linux. You can download it from www.digi.com/xctu.

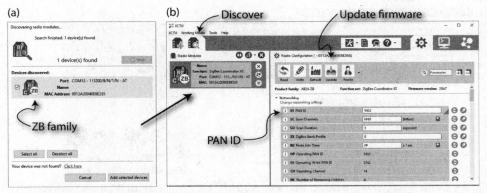

Figure 12-10: The Digi XCTU software: (a) device discovery using an XBee USB adapter, and (b) the device configuration window

Configuring an XBee Network Using XCTU

The first thing you should do with XCTU is to update the XBee modules to the latest firmware. Click the Update Firmware button (see Figure 12-10b) and then choose the product family, function set, and firmware version. There are different firmware versions depending on whether you are using AT or API mode and whether you are setting up a coordinator, router, or end device. These options are described throughout this section.

To configure an AT or API-based network, you must set a *PAN ID*. The *personal area network ID* is a 16-bit address that allows you to configure a set of XBee devices to be on the same network. This network ID facility allows you to create multiple networks of devices that are independent from each other, even at the same physical location. To establish a network, ensure that all the devices have the same PAN ID.

The two examples that follow provide step-by-step instructions on configuring XBee devices in AT and API mode. Each example identifies and utilizes different firmware versions, which necessitates the use of XCTU in reprogramming the firmware of the devices.

RESETTING OLDER/GENERIC XBee USB EXPLORERS

You may have a SparkFun XBee USB Explorer from an older project or you may have purchased a generic XBee USB Explorer that does not have a reset button. If so, you may see a message such as the one in Figure 12-11(a) when you use it to update the firmware. You can add a pushbutton to the RST and GND pins on your XBee USB Explorer, as illustrated in Figure 12-11(b).

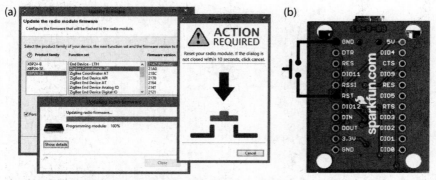

Figure 12-11: (a) XCTU firmware update reset warning and (b) a reset pushbutton modification for the XBee USB Explorer

An XBee AT Mode Example

In this example, an Arduino is configured to be a wireless temperature sensor for the PocketBeagle. The Arduino takes an analog reading from the TMP36 temperature sensor and converts the voltage value into degrees Celsius (or Fahrenheit). One XBee router module in AT mode is connected to the Arduino (termed XBeeA). A second XBee coordinator module in AT mode is connected to the PocketBeagle (termed XBeePB). To be clear, both modules are physically identical, but they will have different roles as a result of the firmware that is written to them. The final circuit is illustrated in Figure 12-13, but you should not connect it at this point, as the modules must be configured. In AT mode the XBee modules behave like a wireless UART connection, but you must first pair the devices to establish communication. Each device must be configured with the destination address set to that of the other XBee module.

Setting Up the Arduino XBee Device (XBeeA)

Place the XBeeA module in the XBee USB Explorer and attach it to your desktop machine—ensure that you align the pin numbers on the XBee module and the XBee USB Explorer. Click the Discover button in XCTU (as indicated in Figure 12-10b); the device appears in the list of available modules. In my case, XBeeA has the MAC address 0013A200 40C8B460.

In XCTU, perform the following configuration steps:

- Update to the latest firmware for a ZigBee Router AT.
- Change the PAN ID to 5432. Both XBee devices will use this address.
- Change the serial baud rate (BD) to 115,200. XCTU updates the device settings when you write this value to the XBee.
- Read the destination address (DH/DL) from the bottom of the XBeePB (see Figure 12-12a) and enter it as the destination address for XBeeA: DH as 0013A200 and DL as 40E8E355 in my case, as illustrated in Figure 12-12(b).

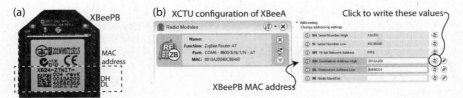

Figure 12-12: Configuring the Arduino XBee to connect to the PocketBeagle XBee Device: (a) the PocketBeagle XBee, and (b) Arduino XBee XCTU settings

Connect XBeeA to the Arduino as illustrated in Figure 12-13(a) but do not connect the RX and TX lines at this point. Listing 12-6 is an Arduino sketch that interfaces to analog input pin A0, reads in the voltage present, and converts it to degrees Celsius (as described in Chapter 10). The code then sends a JSON string out on the serial connection. You can change `tempC` to `tempF` to transmit the temperature in degrees Fahrenheit.

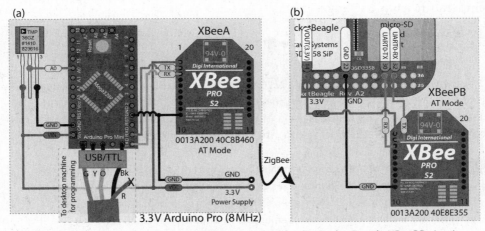

Figure 12-13: (a) The XBeeA circuit configuration, and (b) the PocketBeagle XBeePB circuit configuration

> **NOTE**   You must disconnect the TX and RX lines from the Arduino to the XBee device when you are programming the Arduino or you will have communication problems. If you are doing this regularly, then it might be worth adding two slider switches to your breadboard circuit.

Listing 12-6: /chp12/xbee/at/xbee.ino

```
const int analogInPin = A0;              // analog input for the TMP36

void setup(){
   pinMode(13, OUTPUT);
   Serial.begin(115200, SERIAL_8N1);
}
```

```
void loop(){                             // update registers every five secs
  digitalWrite(13, HIGH);                            // LED briefly on
  delay(100);                                        // 100ms + processing
  int adcValue = analogRead(analogInPin);            // using a 10-bit ADC
  float curVoltage = adcValue * (3.3f/1024.0f);      // Vcc = 5.0V, 10-bit
  float tempC = 25.0 + ((curVoltage-0.75f)/0.01f);   // from datasheet
  float tempF = 32.0 + ((tempC * 9)/5);              // deg. C to F
  Serial.print("{ \"Temperature\" : ");              // Send as JSON msg
  Serial.print(tempC);                               // The temperature
  Serial.println(" }");                              // close JSON message
  digitalWrite(13, LOW);                             // LED off
  delay(4900);                                       // delay ~5 secs total
}
```

Write the program to the Arduino using a USB-to-UART cable as described in Chapter 10. Then, open the serial console on the Arduino programming environment (use a baud rate of 115,200); you should see the following JSON format messages every five seconds. If you hold the TMP36 sensor, then the temperature should change.

```
{ "Temperature" : 22.19 }
{ "Temperature" : 22.19 }
{ "Temperature" : 24.44 }
```

You can now connect the RX/TX pins from the Arduino to the XBee as illustrated in Figure 12-13(a). You can leave the Arduino Serial Console open. The on-board LED acts as a status indicator, flashing briefly each time a reading is transmitted. The Arduino XBee configuration is complete.

> **NOTE** Several of the examples in this chapter use a USB-to-UART adapter. These adapters are described in Chapter 10 as a convenient alternative to the on-board UART devices (e.g., /dev/ttyS0) when 5V logic level communication is required. If you use the on-board UART device, remember to disable any associated serial-getty service that runs by default—this step is performed in the next section for the PocketBeagle.

Setting Up the PocketBeagle XBee Device (XBeePB)

The second XBee module, XBeePB, must be configured to have XBeeA as the communications destination. Place the XBeePB module in the XBee USB Explorer and attach it to your desktop machine. Click the Discover button in XCTU; in my case, the module appears with the MAC address 0013A200 40E8E355 as expected. Then perform the following steps using XCTU:

1. Update the firmware on the device to ZigBee Coordinator AT. Note that this module should be set to be a *coordinator*, unlike the XBeeA *router*.

2. Change the PAN ID to 5432 and set the baud rate to 115,200 to conform to the settings of XBeeA.

3. Set the destination address DH and DL values according to the MAC address of XBeeA (0013A200 40C8B460 in my case).

With the XBeePB module still in the XBee USB Explorer, you can click the Discover Radio Nodes button, and the XBeeA should appear in the list. You cannot view or configure the settings because the devices are in AT mode; however, you can switch to the Console working mode and click Connect, whereupon you should see an output similar to Figure 12-14. The output indicates that the Arduino is successfully communicating with the XBeePB module, and you are now ready to connect it to the PocketBeagle board.

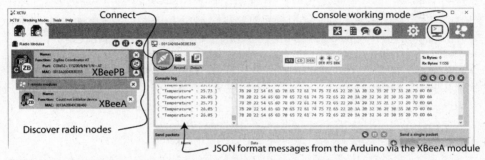

Figure 12-14: The XCTU Console working mode receiving JSON messages from the Arduino XBee device

The XBeePB can be removed from the XBee USB Explorer and attached to the PocketBeagle, as described in Figure 12-13(b). The connection can be tested by using minicom as follows (please note that you must disable the serial debug service if it is bound to UART0):

```
debian@ebb:~$ sudo systemctl stop serial-getty@ttyS0.service
debian@ebb:~$ sudo minicom -b 115200 -o -D /dev/ttyS0
Welcome to minicom 2.7
OPTIONS: I18n
Compiled on Apr 22 2017, 09:14:19.
Port /dev/ttyS0, 05:56:43
Press CTRL-A Z for help on special keys
{ "Temperature" : 25.73 }
{ "Temperature" : 26.05 } ...
```

A new JSON format temperature reading appears after each five-second interval. The Arduino UART code from Chapter 10 can be used to read these values in C/C++, and the JSON code earlier in this chapter can be used to parse the data strings.

Remember, this circuit is a bidirectional communication channel—the UART Command Control code can also be used to control the Arduino, as described in Chapter 10.

XBee AT COMMANDS

A useful exercise at this point is to become familiar with AT commands. Leave the `minicom` session running, but disconnect the power to the XBeeA module to halt the incoming data stream to the PocketBeagle board. Then, using the `minicom` terminal, enter some AT commands:

- To turn on AT mode, type +++ (don't press Enter); OK will appear as the response.
- Then display the network ID (PAN ID) by typing **ATID** (i.e., ID prefixed by AT) and pressing Enter.

For example, the following is an AT conversation to read the settings for the network ID, serial number (high and low parts), and destination address (high and low parts). Ensure that local echo is enabled in `minicom`, and note that AT mode ends ten seconds after you type the last valid AT command—you have to be quick!

```
debian@ebb:~$ sudo minicom -b 115200 -o -D /dev/ttyS0
+++OK
ATID
5432
ATSH
13A200
ATSL
40E8E355
ATDH
13A200
ATDL
40C8B460
```

To change a setting, you should append the new value to the command. For example, to set a new network ID 1234 (and then set it back to 5432), type the following:

```
ATID1234
OK
ATID
1234
ATID5432
OK
ATID
5432
```

A full list of AT commands is visible in the configuration entries of XCTU (see Figure 12-10b) and in the *XBee Command Reference Tables* at `tiny.cc/beagle1206`.

An XBee API Mode Example

Unfortunately, XBee AT mode does not provide access to the advanced features that are available on a ZigBee device. In the previous example, the source and destination points are manually configured for the two devices. XBee API mode uses data frames, each with a software-configurable address that allows other modules in API mode to selectively receive the data.

Setting Up the PocketBeagle XBee Device (XBee1)

In this section, two identical XBee S2/S2C ZigBee devices are configured into API mode by writing new firmware to them. As illustrated in Figure 12-15, XBee1 is configured as a ZigBee Coordinator (API mode), and XBee2 is configured as a ZigBee Router (API mode). In this example, the coordinator is attached to the PocketBeagle, but the XBee router is utilized as a stand-alone microcontroller, as illustrated in Figure 12-16.

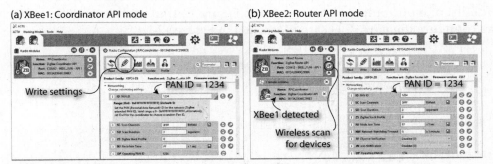

Figure 12-15: (a) Configuring XBee1 as a coordinator with PAN ID 1234 and (b) configuring XBee2 as a router with PAN ID 1234

The PAN ID is set to 1234 for both devices. Once the PAN ID is set for XBee1, it can be disconnected from the XBee USB Explorer and attached to the PocketBeagle, as illustrated in Figure 12-16(a).

Setting Up the Stand-Alone XBee Device (XBee2)

The XBee2 can be placed in the XBee USB Explorer and programmed with ZigBee router firmware. A scan can then be performed by clicking the Wireless Scan for Devices button (as identified in Figure 12-15b). The XBee1 coordinator device that is attached to the PocketBeagle should be detected, and because the devices are both in API mode, it is possible to wirelessly change the settings on the XBee1 device.

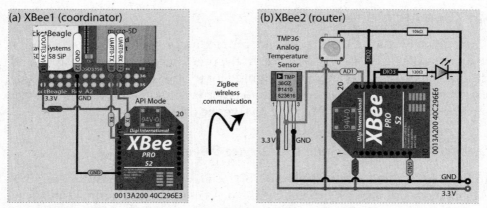

Figure 12-16: (a) The XBee1 PocketBeagle coordinator circuit and (b) the stand-alone XBee2 router circuit with sample I/O connections

In this example, the XBee2 router device is not attached to an Arduino; rather, it is used as a stand-alone microcontroller, as illustrated in Figure 12-16(b). The full list of input/outputs is illustrated in Figure 12-17(a), and the settings used to configure them in XCTU are illustrated in Figure 12-17(b).

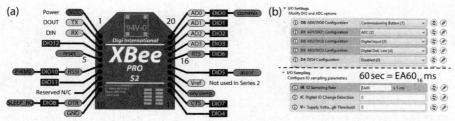

Figure 12-17: (a) The XBee S2/S2C pinout and (b) the XCTU I/O settings for an XBee S2/S2C module

At this point, you might try to use `minicom` to connect to the XBee1 device on the PocketBeagle—unfortunately, it will not work, as the XBee device is configured in API mode and therefore expects data frames. However, it is possible to interact with the XBee module using code that is written in several different languages, including Node.js and C/C++.

XBee API Mode and Node.js

The `xbee-api` Node.js module (`tiny.cc/beagle1207`) is a quick and effective way of writing applications that utilize the XBee devices in API mode. The module fully supports the XBee Series 2/2C (ZigBee) devices that are used in this section. To utilize the Node.js module, you must begin by ensuring that you have a recent version of Node.js. (See the "LAMP and MEAN" feature in Chapter 11 for instructions on updating Node.js.)

Listing 12-7 is a Node.js program that displays the Node Identifier (NI) information and any data frames that are sent on PAN ID 1234.

Listing 12-7: /chp12/xbee/nodejs/test.js

```
// From the example code at www.npmjs.com/package/xbee-api
var util       = require('util');
var SerialPort = require('serialport');
var xbee_api   = require('xbee-api');
var C          = xbee_api.constants;

var xbeeAPI = new xbee_api.XBeeAPI({ // two API modes are available
  api_mode: 1
});

var serialport = new SerialPort("/dev/ttyS0", {
  baudRate: 9600,                    // default baud rate
});

serialport.pipe(xbeeAPI.parser);
xbeeAPI.builder.pipe(serialport);

serialport.on("open", function() {    // uses the serialport module
  var frame_obj = {                   // AT Request to be sent...
    type: C.FRAME_TYPE.AT_COMMAND,    // Prepare for an AT command
    command: "NI",                    // Node identifier command
    commandParameter: [],             // No parameters needed
  };
  xbeeAPI.builder.write(frame_obj);
});

// The data frames received are outputted by this function
xbeeAPI.parser.on("data", function(frame) {
    console.log("Object> ", frame);
});
```

To execute this code, you must first use the Node package manager (npm) to install the required xbee-api and serialport modules as follows:

```
debian@ebb:.../chp12/xbee/nodejs$ npm update -g
debian@ebb:.../chp12/xbee/nodejs$ npm install serialport
debian@ebb:.../chp12/xbee/nodejs$ npm install xbee-api
debian@ebb:.../chp12/xbee/nodejs$ sudo node test.js
Object>  { type: 136,
  id: 1,
  command: 'NI',
  commandStatus: 0,
  commandData: <Buffer 20 52 50 69 43 6f 6f 72 64 69 6e 61 74 6f 72> }
Object>  { type: 146,
```

```
remote64: '0013a20040c296e6',
remote16: '885e',
receiveOptions: 1,
digitalSamples: { DIO2: 1, DIO3: 1, DIO4: 1 },
analogSamples: { AD1: 601 },
numSamples: 1 }
```

The program outputs the Node Identifier information, and then every 60 seconds (as configured in Figure 12-17(b)) the XBee2 router device reads its ADC input and transmits the value to the XBee1 coordinator node. You can see that the value received here is 601 (i.e., from a 10-bit ADC) and that the button (DIO2) is pressed.

Each time a new frame of data is received, the `xbeeAPI.on()` function is called and the frame is passed to it. The frame describes the following:

- `type` refers to the frame type. In this case, it is 146 (0x92), which is an "IO Data Sample Rx Indicator."
- `remote64` is the address of the node that transmitted the data, which corresponds to the address of the XBee2 in Figure 12-16(b).
- `remote16` is the network address of the device that transmitted the data, which is 0x885E in this example.

The interactive *XBee API Frame generator* utility is available in the Tools menu of XCTU. It describes the contents of such a frame in detail.

You can see that the Node.js output is in JSON format. JSON support is built in to Node.js, and the `JSON.parse()` method can be used to transform the string into usable data values.

XBee and C/C++

A C/C++ library called libxbee is available to support the use of XBee API mode devices. It is not as straightforward to use as the Node.js module, but it has full support for API mode transmissions. To get started with the library, you can download and build it using the following steps:

```
debian@ebb:~$ git clone https://github.com/attie/libxbee3
debian@ebb:~$ cd libxbee3/
```

Running `make configure` will copy a generic configuration file into the main build directory. You should disable RTS/CTS support before building on the Beagle board by uncommenting the `XBEE_NO_RTSCTS` line as follows:

```
debian@ebb:~/libxbee3$ make configure
debian@ebb:~/libxbee3$ nano config.mk
debian@ebb:~/libxbee3$ more config.mk |grep RTSCTS
OPTIONS+=       XBEE_NO_RTSCTS
debian@ebb:~/libxbee3$ make
debian@ebb:~/libxbee3$ sudo make install
```

Using the same circuit configuration as in Figure 12-16, you can execute the `simple.c` program in `/chp12/xbee/cpp/` to test the library (remember to set the XBee UART device in the `simple.c` file):

```
debian@ebb:~/exploringbb/chp12/xbee/cpp$ gcc simple.c -o simple -lxbee
debian@ebb:~/exploringbb/chp12/xbee/cpp$ sudo XBEE_LOG_LEVEL=100 ./simple
 20#[xbee.c:160] xbee_vsetup() 0x1296128: Created new libxbee instance ...
  5#[rx.c:212] xbee_rxHandler() 0x1296128: connectionless 'Transmit Status'
 12#[rx.c:203] xbee_rxHandler() 0x1296128: received 'I/O' type packet...
  5#[rx.c:212] xbee_rxHandler() 0x1296128: connectionless 'I/O' packet...
 10#[conn.c:181] xbee_conLogAddress() 0x1296128:address @ 0xb6624ce4...
 10#[conn.c:182] xbee_conLogAddress() 0x1296128:broadcast: No
 10#[conn.c:184] xbee_conLogAddress() 0x1296128:16-bit addr:0x885E
 10#[conn.c:191] xbee_conLogAddress() 0x1296128:64-bit:0x13A20040C296E6
 10#[conn.c:198] xbee_conLogAddress() 0x1296128:endpoints: --
 10#[conn.c:203] xbee_conLogAddress() 0x1296128:profile ID: ----
 10#[conn.c:208] xbee_conLogAddress() 0x1296128:cluster ID: ----
```

The libxbee C/C++ library requires detailed study to understand how to parse the resulting data frames. A guide to getting started is available at `tiny.cc/beagle1208`, and the full documentation for the library is available at `github.com/attie/libxbee3/`.

Near Field Communication

Near field communication (NFC) is a wireless technology that allows two devices that are physically close to each other to communicate bidirectionally. NFC is a specialized high-frequency version of *radio frequency identification* (RFID) that supports secure communication and peer-to-peer communication. For example, NFC is the core technology involved in contactless payments using mobile devices and is also used for phone-to-phone information sharing (e.g., by tapping two devices together). NFC devices operate at the same frequency as high-frequency RFID (13.56MHz), which means that many NFC devices can also interface to passive or actively powered RFID devices. Commonly available RFID cards do not have a power supply; rather, the RFID cards contain a wire coil. The NFC device uses a magnetic field to generate power in the wire coils to initiate communication.

One of the difficulties of developing software for NFC/RFID is the complexity and large number of proprietary solutions. The open-source libnfc (`nfc-tools.org`) is a platform-independent, low-level software development kit for NFC/RFID, and it can be installed on the Beagle boards. However, you also need NFC/RFID hardware. The circuit that is illustrated in Figure 12-18 can be used for this task—it uses the Philips PN532 NFC controller.

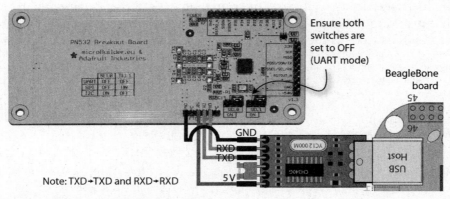

Figure 12-18: The Adafruit NFC/RFID interface for the BeagleBone using a 5V USB-to-UART module

The Philips PN532 NFC controller (`tiny.cc/beagle1209`) supports contactless communication at 13.56MHz using the ISO14443A/MIFARE and FeliCa communication schemes. It supports SPI, I²C, and serial UART interfaces; however, it is available only in a surface mount package and must be attached to an external antenna. Thankfully, Adafruit and others have developed breakout boards that simplify development with this technology. There is an Arduino shield and a stand-alone interface board, both retailing at approximately $40. There are other very low-cost PN532 controllers available—ensure that you purchase one that makes a UART connection available, such as those illustrated in Figure 12-19(a). In addition, passively powered 13.56MHz RFID/NFC stickers, cards, keyrings, buttons, plastic nails, bracelets, and laundry tags are also available at low cost, which opens up the application possibilities—see Figure 12-19(b).

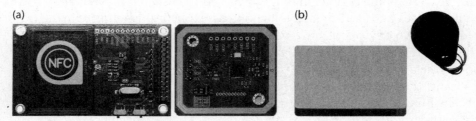

Figure 12-19: (a) Low-cost PN532 NFC breakout boards ($5–$16); (b) RFID cards and key chain tags

The latest version of libnfc can be downloaded and configured as follows:

```
debian@ebb:~$ lsusb
Bus 002 Device 002: ID 1a86:7523 QinHeng Electronics HL-340 USB-Serial
adapter
Bus 002 Device 001: ID 1d6b:0002 Linux Foundation 2.0 root hub
```

```
Bus 001 Device 001: ID 1d6b:0002 Linux Foundation 2.0 root hub
debian@ebb:~$ ls -l /dev/ttyUSB*
crw-rw---- 1 root dialout 188, 0 Aug 22 08:54 /dev/ttyUSB0
debian@ebb:~$ git clone https://github.com/nfc-tools/libnfc
debian@ebb:~/libnfc$ cd libnfc/
debian@ebb:~/libnfc$ sudo apt install libusb-dev
debian@ebb:~/libnfc$ sudo mkdir /etc/nfc
debian@ebb:~/libnfc$ sudo cp libnfc.conf.sample /etc/nfc/libnfc.conf
```

The last step in this set of commands copies a sample configuration file onto the board that can be used to identify the NFC device configuration. In Figure 12-18, a USB-to-UART device is used to interface to the board so as to take care of logic level issues, so this must be specified in the configuration file as follows:

```
debian@ebb:~/libnfc$ sudo nano /etc/nfc/libnfc.conf
debian@ebb:~/libnfc$ more /etc/nfc/libnfc.conf
device.name = "microBuilder.eu"
device.connstring = "pn532_uart:/dev/ttyUSB0"
```

Once the configuration file is in place, you can build libnfc for the Beagle board as follows. The `ldconfig` step is used to update the shared library cache.

```
debian@ebb:~/libnfc$ cmake .
debian@ebb:~/libnfc$ make
debian@ebb:~/libnfc$ sudo make install
debian@ebb:~/libnfc$ sudo ldconfig -v
debian@ebb:~/libnfc$ ls /usr/local/lib/libnfc*
libnfc.so        libnfc.so.5.0.1      libnfc.so.5
debian@ebb:~/libnfc$ ls /usr/local/bin/nfc*
/usr/local/bin/nfc-anticol   /usr/local/bin/nfc-list ...
```

If the interface board is now attached as in Figure 12-18, then you can test your configuration using the binary tools that are provided with libnfc.

```
debian@ebb:~$ sudo nfc-list
nfc-list uses libnfc 1.7.1
NFC device: microBuilder.eu opened
```

If you get a shared library error, then check the `ldconfig` step. (You can use the `ldd` tool that is described in Chapter 5 in the section "Static and Dynamic Compilation" to test shared library dependencies.) Now, when two individual RFID cards are used with the circuit, you will see different but consistent IDs presented.

```
debian@ebb:~$ sudo nfc-poll
nfc-poll uses libnfc 1.7.1
NFC reader: microBuilder.eu opened
NFC device will poll during 30000 ms (20 pollings of 300 ms for 5
modulations)
ISO/IEC 14443A (106 kbps) target:
    ATQA (SENS_RES): 00  04
       UID (NFCID1): 9a  1b  24  2b
```

```
        SAK (SEL_RES): 08 ...
debian@ebb:~$ sudo nfc-poll
nfc-poll uses libnfc 1.7.1
NFC reader: microBuilder.eu opened
NFC device will poll during 30000 ms (20 pollings of 300 ms for 5
modulations)
ISO/IEC 14443A (106 kbps) target:
    ATQA (SENS_RES): 00  04
       UID (NFCID1): e9  6b  7b  9e
      SAK (SEL_RES): 08 ...
```

A sample C program is available in `/chp12/nfc/nfc_test.c` that can be used to build your own NFC access control program. The program stores a UID as an array of characters (`char secretCode[] = {0x9a, 0x1b, 0x24, 0x2b};`), which is compared against the individual RFID values that are read from different RFID cards. The program grants notional access when the correct card with that "secret" ID is presented, as can be observed in the following test example:

```
debian@ebb:~/exploringbb/chp12/nfc$ ./build
debian@ebb:~/exploringbb/chp12/nfc$ ./nfc_test
EBB NFC reader: microBuilder.eu opened
 Waiting for you to use an RFID card or tag....
The following tag was found:
  UID (NFCID1): 9a  1b  24  2b
 *** EBB Access allowed! ***
debian@ebb:~/exploringbb/chp12/nfc$ ./nfc_test
EBB NFC reader: microBuilder.eu opened
 Waiting for you to use an RFID card or tag....
The following tag was found:
  UID (NFCID1): e9  6b  7b  9e
 *** EBB Access NOT allowed! ***
```

Summary

After completing this chapter, you should be able to do the following:

- Choose an appropriate wireless communication protocol and associated hardware for your projects
- Configure a USB Bluetooth adapter for your Beagle board and connect to it from a mobile device for the purpose of building a basic remote-control application
- Install a USB Wi-Fi adapter on a Beagle board and configure the board to connect to a secured Wi-Fi network
- Use the NodeMCU device to build a distributed wireless network of things that is controlled by a Beagle board

- Build on skills developed in Chapter 11 to create IoT devices that can be wireless
- Use the ZigBee protocol with XBee adapters in AT mode to establish a wireless serial data link
- Investigate ZigBee using XBee devices that are configured in API mode, which allows for the use of advanced ZigBee features, such as mesh networking
- Use NFC/RFID devices to build a basic access control system

## CHAPTER 13

Beagle Board with a Rich User Interface

In this chapter, you are introduced to rich user interface (UI) architectures and application development on the Beagle board platform. Rich UIs allow for a depth of interaction with an application that is not possible with command-line interfaces (CLIs). In particular, the addition of graphical display elements can result in easier-to-use applications. Also introduced are different Beagle board architectures that can support rich UIs, such as general-purpose computing, touchscreen display modules, and virtual network computing (VNC). Different software application frameworks are examined for rich UI development, such as GTK+ and Qt. The Qt framework is the focus of the discussion, largely because of its comprehensive libraries of code. An example rich UI application is developed for a Beagle board that uses the TMP36 temperature sensor. Finally, a feature-rich remote fat-client application framework is developed, and two example applications are described—one that uses the TMP36 sensor and a second that uses the ADXL345 accelerometer.

EQUIPMENT REQUIRED FOR THIS CHAPTER:

- Beagle board (ideally one with a HDMI output)
- Analog Devices TMP36 temperature sensor

- USB/HDMI accessories from Chapter 1 (optional)
- ADXL345 accelerometer (optional)

Further resources for this chapter are available at `www.exploringbeaglebone` `.com/chapter13/`.

Rich UI Beagle Board Architectures

In Chapter 9, low-cost LED displays and character LCD displays were introduced. They can be coupled with sensors, switches, or keyboard modules to form simple low-cost UI architectures that are sufficient for many applications, such as for configuration or interaction with hardware devices (e.g., vending machines, printer control interfaces, etc.). However, Beagle boards have a powerful processor, which when coupled with the Linux OS is capable of providing sophisticated user interfaces—similar to those to which you are accustomed on your desktop machine and/or mobile devices.

The BeagleBone Black's (BBBs) LCD controller and HDMI framer enable it to be connected directly to a physical display (e.g., a monitor, television, or LCD touchscreen) to create a sophisticated self-contained physical UI device. This is one application of the BBB that demonstrates the strength of embedded Linux in particular, as it supports open-source UI development frameworks such as GTK+ and Qt. These frameworks provide libraries of visual components (aka *widgets*) that you can combine to create applications with considerable depth of interaction.

Before examining software development frameworks, this section introduces four UI hardware architectures that are available on a BBB board:

- **General-purpose computing:** By connecting the BBB to a monitor/ television by HDMI and connecting a keyboard and mouse by USB, it can be used as a general-purpose computer.

- **LCD touchscreen display:** By attaching an LCD touchscreen cape to the BBB P8/P9 headers, it can be used as a stand-alone UI device.

- **Virtual network computing (VNC):** By using remote access and control software on a network-attached Beagle board, it can control UIs on a virtual display.

- **Remote fat-client applications:** By using custom client/server programming with a network-attached Beagle board, it can interact with remote UIs by sending and receiving messages.

These architectures are described in detail in this section, but to give the discussion some context, Table 13-1 summarizes the strengths and weaknesses of each approach when used with a Beagle board.

Table 13-1: Strengths and Weaknesses of Different UI Architectures

APPROACH	STRENGTHS	WEAKNESSES
As a general-purpose computer (via HDMI)	Low-cost computing platform with low power consumption. Ideal for a network-attached information display point application, by connecting it to a TV/monitor. Can interact with it using a USB keyboard and mouse.	Requires a dedicated monitor/TV. Beagle boards lack the processing power to replace a modern desktop computer. BBB HDMI has a limited resolution and uses a large number of the P8/P9 header pins.
With an LCD touchscreen (via header pins)	Portable interactive display that can be battery powered. Ideal for custom UI process controls. A range of display sizes are available.	Expensive. Occupies many of the header pins (remainder not carried forward). Typically resistive touch, rather than capacitive touch.
VNC (via network)	No display required on the board (frees header pins). Board could be battery powered and wireless.	Requires a desktop computer/tablet device and network connection. Display update over the network connection can be sluggish.
Fat-client applications (via network)	No display is required on the board. Board could be battery powered and wireless. Low processor overhead, as the display is updated by the desktop computer. Many simultaneous displays possible.	Requires custom application development (e.g., using TCP socket programming). Requires network connection and a device on which to run the fat-client applications.

Beagle Boards as General-Purpose Computers

The Beagle boards are capable embedded devices, largely because of their generous processor and memory specifications. When a HDMI video output capability is present on a board, it can be directly connected to a monitor/television, enabling it to be configured as a general-purpose desktop computer. For example, Figure 13-1(a) illustrates the use of a micro-HDMI adapter (described in Chapter 1) alongside the Kinivo Bluetooth adapter, together providing support for video output and keyboard/mouse input. Figure 13-1(b) displays a low-cost Bluetooth keyboard/touchpad that is used for this example—it is a compact device that is displayed to scale with the BBB.

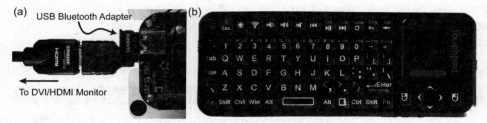

Figure 13-1: (a) Connection to an HDMI and a Bluetooth adapter, (b) a Bluetooth keyboard/ touchpad

The Ethernet connector (or internet over USB) can be used to provide network support, and a powered USB hub can be connected to a Beagle board to provide support for more devices, such as Wi-Fi adapters or separate keyboard and mouse peripherals. Figure 13-2 displays a screen capture of the BBB display output when connected directly to a computer monitor using the HDMI interface.

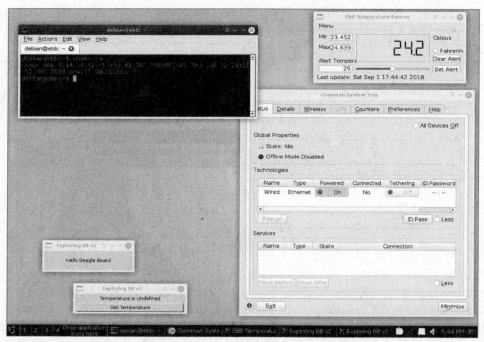

Figure 13-2: Screen capture of the BBB monitor display in Figure 13-1

To be clear, this display is running on a stand-alone monitor, and the screen was captured on a BBB using a Linux tool called *scrot* that can be installed and executed from the CLI using the following:

```
debian@ebb:~$ sudo apt install scrot
debian@ebb:~$ scrot screenshot.png
```

Connecting a Bluetooth Input Peripheral

A regular USB keyboard and mouse can be directly connected to a Beagle board for this architecture. Bluetooth keyboard/touchpads are also useful, as they can be reused in other applications, such as wireless robotic control and home automation. The BeagleBone Black Wireless (BBBW) or any BeagleBone with the Kinivo Bluetooth adapter (see Chapter 9) can directly interface to devices such as the handheld *iPazzPort Bluetooth keyboard and touchpad* (~$20). Devices can be configured using the following steps:

```
debian@ebb:~$ sudo apt install bluez bluetooth
bluetooth is already the newest version (5.43-2+deb9u1).
bluez is already the newest version (5.43-2+deb9u1).
debian@beaglebone:~$ sudo bluetoothctl
[NEW] Controller 38:D2:69:E0:BB:06 beaglebone #2 [default]
[NEW] Controller 00:02:72:CB:C3:53 beaglebone
[bluetooth]# agent KeyboardOnly
Agent registered
[bluetooth]# default-agent
Default agent request successful
[bluetooth]# scan on
Discovery started
[CHG] Controller 38:D2:69:E0:BB:06 Discovering: yes
[CHG] Device 54:46:6B:01:E2:13 Name: bluetooth iPazzport
[CHG] Device 54:46:6B:01:E2:13 Alias: bluetooth iPazzport ...
[bluetooth]# pair 54:46:6B:01:E2:13
Attempting to pair with 54:46:6B:01:E2:13
[CHG] Device 54:46:6B:01:E2:13 Connected: yes
[agent] PIN code: 218596
```

To pair the device, a pin code of 218596 is presented by the tool in the preceding instructions, so 218596 must also be keyed on the Bluetooth keyboard device (followed by Enter), which results in the following output:

```
[CHG] Device 54:46:6B:01:E2:13 Paired: yes
Pairing successful
[CHG] Device 54:46:6B:01:E2:13 ServicesResolved: no
[CHG] Device 54:46:6B:01:E2:13 Connected: no
[bluetooth]# trust 54:46:6B:01:E2:13
[CHG] Device 54:46:6B:01:E2:13 Trusted: yes
Changing 54:46:6B:01:E2:13 trust succeeded
[bluetooth]# connect 54:46:6B:01:E2:13
Attempting to connect to 54:46:6B:01:E2:13
[CHG] Device 54:46:6B:01:E2:13 Connected: yes
Connection successful
[CHG] Device 54:46:6B:01:E2:13 ServicesResolved: yes
[bluetooth iPazzport]# info 54:46:6B:01:E2:13
Device 54:46:6B:01:E2:13
        Name: bluetooth iPazzport        Alias: bluetooth iPazzport
        Class: 0x002540                  Icon: input-keyboard
        Paired: yes                      Trusted: yes
        Blocked: no                      Connected: yes
```

The Bluetooth keyboard/touchpad is now attached to the BBBW, and it will automatically connect from then on. It can control the general-purpose computing environment that is displayed in Figure 13-2.

> **NOTE**   Linux allows *virtual consoles* (aka *virtual terminals*) to be opened while an X Window System (windowing display) is executing. Use Ctrl+Alt+F1 to open a virtual console—there are six virtual text-based consoles (F1 to F6). Use Ctrl+Alt+F7 to return to the X Window System. Using Alt+Left arrow and Alt+Right arrow switches in order between the consoles.
>
> Also, you can kill a frozen SSH session by typing **Enter ~ .** in sequence (i.e., the Return key followed by the tilde followed by a period). Use **Enter ~ ?** to display a list of the escape sequences that are available within an SSH session.

BeagleBone with a LCD Touchscreen Cape

The AM335x system on a chip (SoC) includes an *LCD controller* (LCDC) that is capable of driving LCD modules (up to 2,048 × 2,048 with a 24-bits-per-pixel active TFT configuration) using TI Linux LCDC and backlight drivers. An LCD touchscreen display, such as the LCD4 cape discussed in Chapter 1, can be attached to the BBB as illustrated in Figure 13-3. The LCD4's 4.3″ TFT display has a resolution of 480 × 272 pixels, which limits the desktop space for general-purpose computing applications. The cape also occupies many of the P8/P9 header pins, including the ADC inputs, which are used for the touch interface and the control buttons. Despite these limitations, it can be used to build sophisticated UI applications.

> **NOTE**   A full video example of the type of rich UI applications that are possible when using this cape is available at the chapter web page: www.exploring-beaglebone.com/chapter13/.

The LCD capes from CircuitCo are fully compatible with the BBB, and the BeagleBoard.org Debian image does not require specific software configuration to use them. The touchscreen interface must be calibrated on its first use—for this task, and for general usage, a nylon-tipped stylus is a useful accessory, as pressure must be applied to resistive touchscreens that can result in scratches. The Bluetooth keyboard/touchpad from the last section can also be used to control the BBB when it is attached to an LCD display, which is useful because entering text using on-screen touch keyboards can be frustrating.

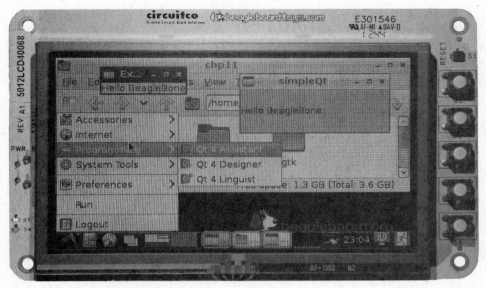

Figure 13-3: The CircuitCo LCD4 cape

Virtual Network Computing

Virtual network computing (VNC) enables desktop applications on one computer (the server) to be shared and remotely controlled from another computer (the client). Keystrokes and mouse interactions on the VNC client are transmitted to the VNC server over the network. The VNC server determines the impact of these interactions and then updates the remote *frame buffer* (RAM containing bitmap image data) on the VNC client machine. VNC uses the *remote frame buffer protocol*, which is similar to the *remote desktop protocol* (RDP) that is tightly coupled to the Windows OS, but because VNC works at the frame buffer level, it is available for many OSs.

A Beagle board does not require a physical display to act as a VNC server, which means that any header pins that are allocated to HDMI output can be retasked. Importantly, with VNC the Linux applications are executing on the board using its processor, but the frame buffer display is being updated on the remote machine.

VNC Using VNC Viewer

Many VNC client applications are available, but VNC Viewer is described here because it is available for Windows, macOS, and Linux platforms. It can be downloaded and installed free from www.realvnc.com. Once it is executed,

Part III ■ Advanced Beagle Board Systems

a login screen appears that requests the VNC server address. However, for this configuration you must ensure that your board is running a VNC server before you can log in. The *tightvncserver* is available under the BeagleBoard.org Debian distribution by default. The first time you execute the server, you will be prompted to define a password for remote access, as follows:

```
debian@ebb:~$ sudo apt install tightvncserver
debian@ebb:~$ tightvncserver
You will require a password to access your desktops.
Password: MyPassword
Verify: MyPassword
Would you like to enter a view-only password (y/n)? n
New 'X' desktop is ebb:1
Starting applications specified in /home/debian/.vnc/xstartup
Log file is /home/debian/.vnc/ebb:1.log
```

> **NOTE** If you are using the BeagleBoard.org IoT image, then you will have to install a window manager, such as LXQt. Please note you require at least 900MB of free space on your board to complete this installation.
>
> ```
> debian@ebb:~$ sudo apt update
> debian@ebb:~$ sudo apt install xorg lxqt
> ```

To start a graphical display manually from a console, where you have a physical monitor, keyboard, and mouse connected to the board, use:

```
debian@ebb:~$ startx
```

Once the server is running, you can check the process description to determine the port number—here it is running on port 5901:

```
debian@ebb:~$ ps aux | grep vnc
debian 1914 1.3 1.3 7928 6516 pts/0 S 03:00 0:00 Xtightvnc :1 -desktop
X -auth /home/debian/.Xauthority -geometry 1024x768 -depth 24 -rfbwait
120000 -rfbauth /home/debian/.vnc/passwd -rfbport 5901 -fp ...
```

The VNC Viewer session can then be started on your desktop machine using the server address and its port number (e.g., 192.168.7.2:5901). The Beagle board desktop is contained within a window frame, as displayed in Figure 13-4.

VNC with Xming and PuTTY

The Xming X Server (`tiny.cc/beagle1301`) for Windows, in combination with PuTTY, is a different approach to the same task; however, it does not require that a VNC server is running on the Beagle board. Once Xming is installed and executed, it appears only in the Windows taskbar with an "X" icon. The PuTTY Beagle board session can be configured using Connection ⇨ SSH ⇨ X11 to set "Enable SSH X11 forwarding" to the local X display location and to set the X display location to be :0.0.

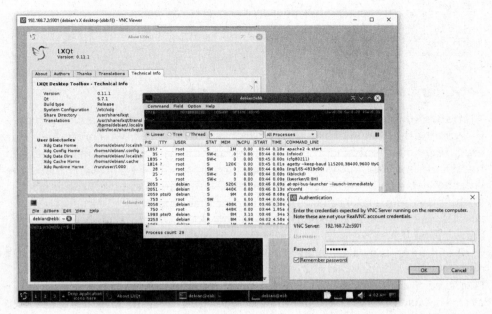

Figure 13-4: VNC Viewer on Windows connected to the LXQt window manager on a Beagle board

When an SSH session is opened to a Beagle board, you can simply perform the following instructions, which result in the display of an xterm and xeyes display. The *xterm* window is the standard terminal emulator for the X Window System, and the "magical" *xeyes* follow your mouse cursor around the desktop computer. Remember that the xeyes display is being updated by the Beagle board, not the desktop computer.

```
debian@ebb:~$ sudo apt-get install x11-apps xterm
debian@ebb:~$ xterm &
debian@ebb:~$ xeyes &
```

One advantage of this approach is that you can seamlessly integrate Beagle board applications and Windows applications on the desktop display. You can also start the board's *LXQt standard panel* by calling `lxqt-panel`, which results in the bottom-bar menu display (refer to Figure 13-4).

VNC with a Linux Desktop Computer

If you are running Linux as your desktop OS (e.g., Debian x64 on a VM), then you can usually start a VNC session using the following steps, where -x enables X11 forwarding and -c requests that compression is used in the transmission of frame buffer data.

```
molloyd@debian:~$ ssh -XC debian@192.168.7.2
debian@192.168.7.2's password: MyPassword
debian@ebb:~$ xeyes &
debian@ebb:~$ xterm &
```

Fat-Client Applications

At the beginning of Chapter 11, the Beagle board is configured as a web server—essentially, the Beagle board is serving data to a *thin-client* web browser that is executing on a client machine. The temperature sensor application executes on the Beagle board, and the data is served to the client's web browser using the Apache web server and CGI/PHP scripts. With thin-client applications, most of the processing takes place on the server machine (*server-side*). In contrast, *fat-client* (aka *thick-client*) applications execute on the client machine (client-side) and send and receive data messages to and from the server.

Recent computing architecture design trends have moved away from fat-client architectures and toward thin-client (and cloud) browser-based frameworks. However, the latter frameworks are usually implemented on a powerful cluster of server machines and are unsuitable for deployment on embedded devices. When working with the Beagle boards, it is likely that the client desktop machine is the more computationally powerful device.

A fat-client application is typically more complex to develop and deploy than a thin-client application, but it reduces the demands on the server while allowing for advanced functionality and user interaction on the client machine. Later in this chapter, fat-client UI applications are developed that execute on a desktop computer and communicate to the Beagle board via TCP sockets. In turn, the Beagle board interfaces to the TMP36 temperature sensor and the ADXL345 accelerometer and serves their sensor data to the remote UI applications. Importantly, the fat-client applications use the resources of the desktop computer for graphical display, and therefore there is a minimal computational cost on the Beagle board. As such, it is possible for many fat-client applications on different desktop computers to simultaneously communicate with a single Beagle board.

Rich UI Application Development

Once a display framework is available to your board, a likely next step is to write rich UI applications that can utilize its benefits. Such applications are termed *graphical user interface* (GUI) applications; if you have used desktop computers, tablet computers, or smartphones, then you are familiar with their use. There are many different ways to implement GUI applications on the Beagle boards—for example, Java has comprehensive built-in support for GUI development with its abstract windowing toolkit (AWT) libraries, and Python has libraries such as pyGTK, wxPython, and Tkinter.

To develop GUI applications under C/C++ for the Beagle board, there are two clear options: the *GIMP Toolkit* (*GTK+*) and the *Qt* cross-platform development framework. This section describes how you can get started with both of these options. It is important to note that the applications in this section will function regardless of whether they are used directly on the Beagle board (i.e., general-purpose computer or touchscreen form) or through VNC. GTK+ and Qt can also be used as the basis for building fat-client applications, which is covered later in this chapter.

Introduction to GTK+ on the Beagle Boards

GTK+ (www.gtk.org) is a cross-platform toolkit for creating GUI applications. It is most well-known for its use in the Linux GNOME desktop and the *GNU Image Manipulation Program* (GIMP). Figure 13-5 illustrates a sample GTK+ application running on the Beagle board using VNC. The same application also works perfectly if the application is running on the Beagle board directly.

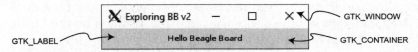

Figure 13-5: The GTKsimple application

The "Hello World" GTK+ Application

The code for the application shown in Figure 13-5 is provided in Listing 13-1. The application consists of a single label, which contains the text "Hello Beagle Board" that has been added to a GTK+ window. Each line of the code has been commented in the listing to explain the important steps.

Listing 13-1: /exploringbb/chp13/gtk/GTKsimple.cpp

```
#include<gtk/gtk.h>    // the GTK+ library header file

int main(int argc, char *argv[]){
             // This application will have a window and a single label
   GtkWidget *window, *label;
             // Initialize the GTK+ toolkit, pass the command-line arguments
   gtk_init(&argc, &argv);
             // Create the top-level window (not yet visible)
   window = gtk_window_new(GTK_WINDOW_TOPLEVEL);
             // Set the title of the window to "Exploring BB v2"
   gtk_window_set_title ( GTK_WINDOW (window), "Exploring BB v2");
```

```
                    // Create a label
      label = gtk_label_new ("Hello Beagle Board");
                    // Add the label to the window
      gtk_container_add(GTK_CONTAINER (window), label);
                    // Make the label visible (must be performed for every widget)
      gtk_widget_show(label);
                    // Make the window visible on the display
      gtk_widget_show(window);
                    // Runs the main loop until gtk_main_quit() is called
      gtk_main(); // for example, if Ctrl C is typed
      return 0;
}
```

The application can be compiled using the following call, which is also captured in the Git repository build script (use the grave accent character `, not the single opening quotation mark character, ʼ):

```
.../chp13/gtk$ sudo apt install gtk+-2.0 glib-2.0 libgtk2.0-dev
.../chp13/gtk$ g++ `pkg-config --libs --cflags glib-2.0 gtk+-2.0` →
  GTKsimple.cpp -o gtksimple
.../chp13/gtk$ ./gtksimple
```

This call uses *pkg-config*, a tool that is useful when building applications and libraries under Linux, as it inserts the correct system-dependent options. It does this by collecting metadata about the libraries that are installed on the Linux system. For example, to get information about the current GTK+ library, you can use the following:

```
debian@ebb:~$ pkg-config --modversion gtk+-2.0
2.24.31
```

The application in Figure 13-5 does not quit when the X button (top-right corner) is clicked—the window itself disappears, but the program continues to execute. This is because the preceding code has not defined that something should happen when the X button is clicked—you need to associate a "close" function with the signal that is generated when the button is clicked.

The Event-Driven Programming Model

GUI applications typically use an *event-driven programming model*. Under this model, the application waits in its main loop until an event (e.g., the user action of clicking a button) is detected, which triggers a callback function to be performed. In GTK+, a user action causes the main loop to deliver an event to GTK+, which is initialized by the call to gtk_init(). GTK+ then delivers this event to the graphical widgets, which in turn emit signals. These signals can be attached to callback functions of your own design or to windowing functions. For example, the following GTK+ code quits the application if the window X button is clicked:

```
g_signal_connect(window, "destroy", G_CALLBACK (gtk_main_quit), NULL);
```

The signal is attached to the `window` handle so that when a signal named `destroy` is received, the `gtk_main_quit()` function is called, which causes the application to exit. The last argument is `NULL` because no data is required to be passed to the `gtk_main_quit()` function.

The GTK+ Temperature Application

Listing 13-2 provides the full source code for a more complete GTK+ application, which executes on the Beagle board as shown in Figure 13-6. It uses the same TMP36 temperature sensor and ADC configuration used in Chapter 11 (Figure 11-2 and Listing 11-1). This example is a GUI application that reads the Beagle board ADC when a button is clicked and then displays the temperature in a label. In this example, a signal is connected to the `button` object, so when it is clicked, the callback function `getTemperature()` is called.

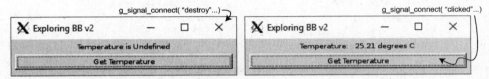

Figure 13-6: The GTKtemperature application

Listing 13-2: /exploringbb/chp13/gtk/GTKtemperature.cpp (Segment)

```cpp
#include<gtk/gtk.h>
...
#define LDR_PATH "/sys/bus/iio/devices/iio:device0/in_voltage"

// Same function as in Chp. 11 to read the ADC value (Listing 11-1)
int readAnalog(int number){ ... }

// The callback function associated with the button. A pointer to the
// label is passed, so that the label can display the temperature
static void getTemperature(GtkWidget *widget, gpointer temp_label){
    // cast the generic gpointer into a GtkWidget label
    GtkWidget *temperature_label = (GtkWidget *) temp_label;
    int adc_value = readAnalog(0);
    float cur_voltage = adc_value * (1.80f/4096.0f);
    float diff_degreesC = (cur_voltage-0.75f)/0.01f;
    float temperature = 25.0f + diff_degreesC;
    stringstream ss;
    ss << "Temperature: "  << temperature << " degrees C";
    // set the text in the label
    gtk_label_set_text( GTK_LABEL(temp_label), ss.str().c_str());
    ss << endl;  // add a \n to the string for the standard output
    g_print(ss.str().c_str());  // output to the terminal (std out)
}
```

```
int main(int argc, char *argv[]){
    GtkWidget *window, *temp_label, *button, *button_label;
    gtk_init(&argc, &argv);
    window = gtk_window_new(GTK_WINDOW_TOPLEVEL);
    gtk_window_set_title(GTK_WINDOW (window), "Exploring BB v2");

    // Fix the size of the window so that it cannot be resized
    gtk_widget_set_size_request(window, 220, 50);
    gtk_window_set_resizable(GTK_WINDOW(window), FALSE);
    // Place a border of 5 pixels around the inner window edge
    gtk_container_set_border_width (GTK_CONTAINER (window), 5);

    // Quit application if X button is pressed
    g_signal_connect(window, "destroy", G_CALLBACK (gtk_main_quit), NULL);

    // Set up the window to contain two vertically stacked widgets using a vbox
    GtkWidget *vbox = gtk_vbox_new(FALSE, 5);  // spacing of 5
    gtk_container_add (GTK_CONTAINER (window), vbox); // add vbox to window
    gtk_widget_show (vbox);                    // set the vbox visible

    // This is the label in which to display the temperature
    temp_label = gtk_label_new ("Temperature is Undefined");
    gtk_widget_show(temp_label);               // make it visible
    gtk_label_set_justify( GTK_LABEL(temp_label), GTK_JUSTIFY_LEFT);
    // Add the label to the vbox
    gtk_box_pack_start (GTK_BOX (vbox), temp_label, FALSE, FALSE, 0);

    // Create a button and connect it to the getTemperature() callback function
    button = gtk_button_new();
    button_label = gtk_label_new ("Get Temperature"); // label for text on button
    gtk_widget_show(button_label);                    // show label
    gtk_widget_show(button);                           // show button
    gtk_container_add(GTK_CONTAINER (button), button_label);  // label for button
    // Connect the callback function getTemperature() to the button press
    g_signal_connect(button, "clicked",
                     G_CALLBACK (getTemperature), (gpointer) temp_label);
    // Add the button to the vbox
    gtk_box_pack_start (GTK_BOX (vbox), button, FALSE, FALSE, 0);
    gtk_widget_show(window);
    gtk_main();
    return 0;
}
```

Introduction to Qt for the Beagle Board

Qt (pronounced "cute") is a powerful cross-platform development framework
that uses standard C++. It provides libraries of C++ code for GUI application
development and for database access, thread management, networking, and more.

Importantly, code developed under this framework can be executed under Windows, Linux, macOS, Android, and iOS, as well as on embedded platforms, such as the Beagle board. Qt can be used under open-source or commercial terms, and it is supported by freely available development tools, such as qmake and Qt Creator. The capability and flexibility of this framework make it an ideal candidate for GUI applications that are to run directly on the Beagle board or on devices that control the board.

Qt is described in greater detail in the next section, but it is useful to get started using a simple "hello world" example, as illustrated in Figure 13-7, which can be compiled and executed on the Beagle board either directly or using VNC.

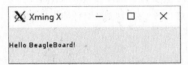

Figure 13-7: Qt "hello world" Beagle board example executing using VNC

Installing Qt Development Tools

The first step is to install the Qt development tools on the Beagle board. The last command in the following code snippet installs a full suite of tools (~20MB to 200MB of storage required depending on your current configuration). The middle command identifies the constituent components of the suite.

```
debian@ebb:~$ sudo apt update
debian@ebb:~$ apt-cache search qt5
debian@ebb:~$ sudo apt install qt5-default
```

You can then test the version of the installation using the following:

```
debian@ebb:~$ qmake -version
QMake version 3.0
Using Qt version 5.7.1 in /usr/lib/arm-linux-gnueabihf
```

The "Hello World" Qt Application

Listing 13-3 is a concise Qt application that can be used as a test—it does not represent good Qt programming practice! It uses an object of the QLabel class, which is a subclass of the QWidget class, to display a message in the application. A *widget* is the primary UI element that is used for creating GUIs with Qt. The parent QWidget class provides the code required to render (draw) the subclass object on the screen display.

Listing 13-3: /exploringbb/chp13/simpleQt/simpleQt.cpp

```
#include <QApplication>
#include <QLabel>
int main(int argc, char *argv[ ]){
    QApplication app(argc, argv);
    QLabel label("Hello BeagleBoard!");
    label.resize(200, 100);
    label.show();
    return app.exec();
}
```

The `simpleQt.cpp` file in Listing 13-3 is the only file required in a directory before the following steps take place. The *qmake* cross-platform makefile generator can then be used to create a default project.

```
debian@ebb:~/exploringbb/chp13/simpleQt$ ls
simpleQt.cpp
debian@ebb:~/exploringbb/chp13/simpleQt$ qmake -project
debian@ebb:~/exploringbb/chp13/simpleQt$ ls
simpleQt.cpp  simpleQt.pro
```

Edit the project file to specify that you are using the nondefault `widgets` module by adding the line highlighted here:

```
debian@ebb:~/exploringbb/chp13/simpleQt$ more simpleQt.pro
######################################################################
# Automatically generated by qmake (3.0) Tue Aug 28 00:28:43 2018
######################################################################

TEMPLATE = app
TARGET = simpleQt
QT +=widgets
INCLUDEPATH += .

# Input
SOURCES += simpleQt.cpp
```

This project `.pro` file describes the project settings; if required, it can be edited manually to add additional dependencies. The `qmake` makefile generator can then be executed again, this time with no `-project` argument:

```
debian@ebb:~/exploringbb/chp13/simpleQt$ qmake
Info: creating stash file .../chp13/simpleQt/.qmake.stash
debian@ebb:~/exploringbb/chp13/simpleQt$ ls
Makefile  simpleQt.cpp  simpleQt.pro
```

This step results in a `Makefile` file being created in the current directory that allows the executable to be built using a call to `make`, which in turn uses g++ to build the final application.

```
debian@ebb:~/exploringbb/chp13/simpleQt$ make
g++ -c -pipe -O2 -Wall -W -fPIC ... -o simpleQt.o simpleQt.cpp ...
```

The executable is now present in the directory and can be executed as follows, which results in the visual display shown earlier in Figure 13-7:

```
debian@ebb:~/exploringbb/chp13/simpleQt$ ls
Makefile  simpleQt  simpleQt.cpp  simpleQt.o  simpleQt.pro
debian@ebb:~/exploringbb/chp13/simpleQt$ ./simpleQt
```

Clearly, there are additional steps involved in using qmake to build a Qt application, but these are necessary to take advantage of the cross-platform nature of Qt. For example, you can perform similar steps on your desktop machine to build the same application, regardless of its OS.

Qt Primer

Qt is a full cross-platform development framework that is written in C/C++. It is used in the preceding section for UI programming, but it also provides support for databases, threads, timers, networking, multimedia, XML processing, and more. Qt extends C++ by adding macros and *introspection*, code that examines the type and properties of an object at run time, which is not natively available in C++. It is important to note that *all the code is still just plain C++!*

Qt Concepts

Qt is built in modules, each of which can be added to your project by including the requisite header files in your C++ program and by identifying that the module is used in the project .pro file. For example, to include the classes in the QtNetwork module, you add #include<QtNetwork> to your program code and link against the module by adding QT += network to the qmake .pro file. Table 13-2 provides a list of important Qt modules.

Table 13-2: Summary of the Important Qt Modules

NAME	DESCRIPTION
QtCore	Contains the core non-GUI classes, such as QString, QChar, QDate, QTimer, and QVector. It is included by default in Qt projects, as all other Qt modules rely on this module.
QtGui	Core module that adds GUI support to the QtCore module, with classes such as QDialog, QWidget, QToolbar, QLabel, QTextEdit, and QFont. This module is included by default—if your application has no GUI, then you can add Qt -= gui to your .pro file.
QtMultimedia	Contains classes for low-level multimedia functionality, such as QVideoFrame, QAudioInput, and QAudioOutput. To use this module, add #include <QtMultimedia> to your source file and QT += multimedia to your .pro file.

Continues

Table 13-2 (*continued*)

NAME	DESCRIPTION
QtNetwork	Contains classes for network communication over TCP and UDP, including SSL communications, with classes such as `QTcpSocket`, `QFtp`, `QLocalServer`, `QSslSocket`, and `QUdpSocket`. As earlier, use `#include <QtNetwork>` and `QT += network`.
QtOpenGL	The *Open Graphics Library* (*OpenGL*) is a cross-platform application programming interface (API) for 3-D computer graphics, which is widely used in industrial visualization and computer gaming applications. This module makes it straightforward to contain OpenGL in your application with classes such as `QGLBuffer`, `QGLWidget`, `QGLContext`, and `QGLShader`. As earlier, use `#include <QtOpenGL>` and `QT += opengl`. The AM335x has OpenGL hardware acceleration capability, but it is difficult to utilize.
QtScript	Enables you to make your Qt application *scriptable*. *Scripts* are used in applications such as Microsoft Excel and Adobe Photoshop to enable users to automate repetitive tasks. QtScript includes a JavaScript engine, which you can use within the core application to interlink functionality in scripts. It can also be used to expose the internal functionality of your application to users, enabling them to add new functionality without the need for C++ compilation. As earlier, use `#include <QtScript>` and `QT += script`.
QtSql	Contains classes for interfacing to databases using the SQL programming language, such as `QSqlDriver`, `QSqlQuery`, and `QSqlResult`. As earlier, use `#include <QtSql>` and `QT += sql`.
QtSvg	Contains classes for creating and displaying scalar vector graphics (SVG) files, such as `QSvgWidget`, `QSvgGenerator`, and `QSvgRenderer`. As earlier, use `#include <QtSvg>` and `QT += svg`.
QtTest	Contains classes for unit testing Qt applications using the QTestLib tool, such as `QSignalSpy` and `QTestEventList`. As earlier, use `#include <QtTest>` and `QT += testlib`.
QtWebKit	Provides a web browser engine and classes for rendering and interacting with web content, such as `QWebView`, `QWebPage`, and `QWebHistory`. As earlier, use `#include <QtWebKit>` and `QT += webkit`.
QtXml	Extensible markup language (XML) is a human-readable document format that can be used to transport and store data. The QtXml module provides a stream reader and writer for XML data, with classes such as `QXmlReader`, `QDomDocument`, and `QXmlAttributes`. As earlier, use `#include <QtXml>` and `QT += xml`.

The QObject Class

The QObject class is the base class of almost all the Qt classes and all the widgets.[1] This means most Qt classes share common functionality for handling memory management, properties, and event-driven programming.

Qt implements introspection by storing information about every class that is derived from QObject using a QMetaObject object within its *Meta-Object System*. When you build projects using Qt you will see that new .cpp files appear in the build directory—these are created by the *Meta-Object Compiler* (*moc*).[2] The C++ compiler will then compile these files into a regular C/C++ objective file (.o), which is ultimately linked to create an executable application.

Signals and Slots

Similar to GTK+, Qt has an event-driven programming model that enables events and state changes to be interconnected with reactions using a mechanism termed *signals and slots*. For example, a Qt button widget can be configured so that when it is clicked, it generates a *signal*, which has been connected to a *slot*. The slot, which is somewhat like a callback function, performs a user-defined function when it receives a signal. Importantly, the signals and slots mechanism can be applied to non-GUI objects—it can be used for intercommunication between any object that is in any way derived from the QObject class. Signals and slots provide a powerful mechanism that is possibly the most unique feature of the Qt framework.

A full-featured Qt temperature sensor application is developed shortly that makes extensive use of signals and slots. For example, the application updates the temperature display every five seconds by reading the ADC value; Figure 13-8 illustrates how this takes place. In this example, the QTimer class has a signal called timeout() that is emitted whenever an object called timer "times out" (which it does after five seconds). This signal is connected to the on_updateTemperature() slot on an object of the QMainWindow class called mainWindow. The connection is made by a call of the following form:

```
QObject::connect(source,SIGNAL(signature),destination,SLOT(signature));
```

---

[1] Java programmers will notice that this is similar to the Object class in Java; however, in Qt, classes requiring object instances that can be copied do not subclass QObject (e.g., QString, QChar).

[2] At compile time, the moc uses information from the class header files (e.g., if the class is a descendent of QObject) to generate a "marked-up" version of the .cpp file. For example, if you have a class X that is defined in the files X.h and X.cpp, the moc will generate a new file called moc-X.cpp, which contains the meta-object code for the class X.

where `source` and `destination` are objects of classes that are derived from the `QObject` class. The `signature` is the function name and argument types (without the variable names).

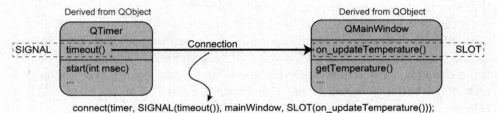

Figure 13-8: QTimer signals and slots example

The website www.qt.io provides an excellent detailed description of the behavior of signals and slots, but here are some further summary points on signals, slots, and connections that will get you started:

- Signals can be connected to any number of slots.
- Signals are defined in the signals section of the code (under a `signals:` label, which is usually in the class header file).
- Signal "methods" must return `void` and may not have any implementation.
- A signal can be explicitly emitted using the `emit` keyword.
- Slots can be connected to any number of signals.
- Slots are defined in the slots section of the code (under a `slots:` label that can be public, private, or protected).
- Slots are regular methods with a full implementation.
- Connections can be explicitly formed (as in the timer example shown earlier) or automatically created when using the Qt graphical design tools in the next section.

Qt Development Tools

The Qt framework also has associated development tools. As well as the qmake tool, there is a full-featured IDE called *Qt Creator*, which is similar in nature to Eclipse, except that it is specifically tailored for Qt development. The IDE, which is illustrated in Figure 13-9, is available for Linux, Windows, and macOS, and its *Qt Designer* tool can even execute on the Beagle board directly. Qt Creator can be used to build native applications, or it can be used to cross-compile applications for the board by installing a cross-platform toolchain (similar to Eclipse).

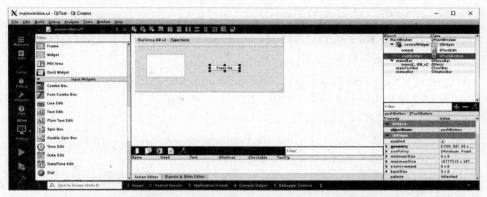

Figure 13-9: Qt Creator IDE visual design editor running directly on the Beagle board (via VNC)

To install and execute Qt Creator on the Beagle board (e.g., via VNC), use the following steps, whereupon the IDE appears as in Figure 13-9. Qt Creator needs approximately 400MB of installation space.

```
debian@ebb:~$ sudo apt install qtcreator
debian@ebb:~$ qtcreator &
```

One of the key features that Qt Creator provides is its *visual design editor*, which enables you to interactively drag and drop widgets onto window designs, called *forms*. The interface enables the properties of the widgets to be configured easily, and it provides a straightforward way of enabling signals and associating slots against the UI components. For example, to write code that executes when the Press Me button is clicked (refer to Figure 13-9), you can simply right-click the button and choose "Go to slot," which provides a dialog with a list of available signals (such as `clicked()`, `pressed()`, and `released()`).[3] Once a signal is chosen, the IDE will automatically enable the signal, provide a slot code template, and associate the signal with the slot. The form UI's properties are stored in an XML file and associated with the project (e.g., `mainwindow.ui`).

> **NOTE** When using Qt Creator, unusual problems can arise (e.g., changes to the code not appearing in the application build), particularly when switching projects. In such cases, go to the Build menu and choose Clean All.
>
> In addition, "unresolved external" link errors (e.g., when adding new classes) can often be resolved by selecting "Run qmake" from the Build menu.

---

[3]A click is a press and a release—code can be associated with the complete click action and/or the constituent actions.

A First Qt Creator Example

You can create a simple Qt GUI application on a Beagle board using Qt Creator by following these steps:

- Using VNC or by developing on the Beagle board directly, start Qt Creator with the following call:

```
debian@ebb:~$ qtcreator &
```

- Create a new project of type Qt Widgets Application. Call it QtTest and create it in the /home/debian/ directory.

- Select the Desktop kit and choose the default class information. This results in a new project being created within Qt Creator, which appears as in Figure 13-9 when you double-click the mainwindow.ui form entry.

- In this window view, add a Push Button component and a Text Edit (QTextEdit) component, as illustrated in Figure 13-9.

- Right-click the text edit box and choose Change objectName. Change the object name to be output.

- Retitle the button to Press Me and then right-click the button. Choose Go to Slot and then pick a signal such as clicked(). This creates a new function in the mainwindow.cpp file called on_pushButton_clicked(). See Figure 13-10.

- You can then add a line of code to this method that sets the text of the output QTextEdit component, which is accessed via the ui main window.

```
void MainWindow::on_pushButton_clicked() {
    ui->output->setText("Hello from the Beagle Board!");
}
```

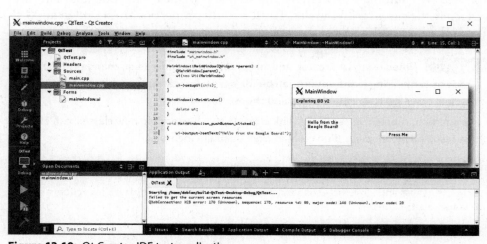

Figure 13-10: Qt Creator IDE test application

The application can be executed by clicking the Play button on the bottom-left side of Figure 13-10. The application window appears on the right side of the same figure. When the Press Me button is clicked, then the text "Hello from the Beagle Board!" appears in the output QTextEdit component.

> **NOTE** If you are having difficulties with the steps in this section, please ensure that you have the following packages installed: g++ and libglu1-mesa-dev. In addition, if there are errors reported by Qt Creator in relation to the Build Kit, choose **Projects** ⇨ **Manage Kits and ensure that the C++ compiler is pointing at** /usr/bin/arm-linux-gnueabihf-g++, **the C compiler is pointing at** /usr/bin/arm-linux-gnueabihf-gcc, **and CMake is pointing at** /usr/bin/make.

A Qt Temperature Sensor GUI Application

In this section, the Qt Creator IDE is used to build a full-featured GUI temperature sensor application, as illustrated in Figure 13-11. This application executes directly on a Beagle board, regardless of the UI architecture used. This application demonstrates some of the capabilities of Qt on a Beagle board, while being cognizant of the volume of code to be studied. It could be greatly extended. For example, it could also provide historical charting or fancy display dials. This example application supports the following features:

- A timer thread takes a reading every five seconds from a Beagle board ADC input using the TMP36 temperature sensor (see Chapter 11's Figure 11-2).
- An LCD-style floating-point temperature display is used.
- A display of the minimum and maximum temperature is provided.
- A slider is used that enables you to choose a temperature at which to activate an alert. An alert triggers the display of a dialog box.
- A mechanism is provided to convert the main display from a Celsius scale to a Fahrenheit scale by clicking the Fahrenheit radio widget.
- A status display is used at the bottom of the window.

The full source code and executable for this application are available in the Git repository's /exploringbb/chp13/QtTemperature/ directory.

There are three important source files to describe for this application, the first of which is in Listing 13-4. It provides the main() starting point for the application in which an instance of the QApplication and MainWindow classes are created. The QApplication class manages the GUI application control flow (the main loop). The MainWindow class is defined in Listings 13-5 and 13-6.

Listing 13-4: /exploringbb/chp13/QtTemperature/main.cpp

```
#include "mainwindow.h"
#include <QApplication>
```

```
int main(int argc, char *argv[]){
    QApplication a(argc, argv); // manages GUI application control flow
    MainWindow w;               // the user-defined class
    w.show();                   // shows the user-defined class UI
    return a.exec();            // without a.exec() the program would end here
}                               // it is the main loop that processes events
```

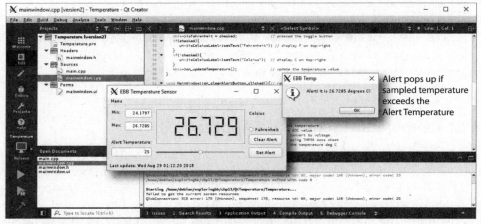

Figure 13-11: The Qt TMP36 temperature sensor GUI application

The `MainWindow` class is a child of the `QMainWindow` class (which is a child of `QWidget` and ultimately `QObject`). This means any methods that are available in the parent classes are also available in the `MainWindow` class.

Figure 13-12 illustrates the relationship between the UI components and the slots that are declared in Listing 13-5 and defined in Listing 13-6. The fimer code is also summarized—it is not a GUI component, but it does generate a `timeout()` signal, which is connected to the `on_updateTemperature()` slot. The exact nature of the code in Listings 13-5 and 13-6 is described by the comments. However, the clearest way to fully understand the code is to edit it and see what impact your edits have. You do not require the temperature sensor to execute the code, but the temperature display will remain fixed at 25°C in its absence.

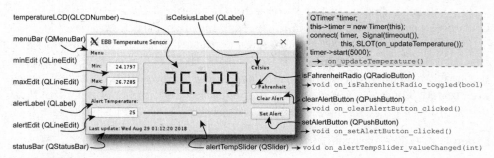

Figure 13-12: The UI components and associated slots

Listing 13-5: /exploringbb/chp13/QtTemperature/mainwindow.h

```cpp
#include <QMainWindow>        // for the main GUI interface
#include <QTimer>            // for a timer that periodically reads temperature
#include <QDateTime>         // to find out the date/time of the sample
#include <QMessageBox>       // for pop-up message boxes - e.g., alert!

namespace Ui {
   class MainWindow;        // Places class MainWindow in UI namespace
}

class MainWindow : public QMainWindow    // a child of the QMainWindow class
{
   // This macro must appear in the private section of a class that
   // declares its own signals and slots
   Q_OBJECT
public:
   explicit MainWindow(QWidget *parent = 0);      // constructor
   ~MainWindow();                                 // destructor
private slots:
   void on_setAlertButton_clicked();
   void on_isFahrenheitRadio_toggled(bool checked);
   void on_clearAlertButton_clicked();
   void on_alertTempSlider_valueChanged(int value);  // if alert slider moved
   void on_updateTemperature();   // this slot is triggered by the timer
private:
   Ui::MainWindow *ui;            // the main user interface
   QTimer *timer;                 // timer thread that triggers after a delay
   bool  isFahrenheit;            // is the main display deg C or deg F
   int   alertTemperature;        // the alert temperature value
   bool  isAlertSet;              // is the alert set?
   float minTemperature, maxTemperature;          // min and max temp values
   float celsiusToFahrenheit(float valueCelsius); // function for conversion
   float getTemperature();        // get the temperature from the sensor
   int   readAnalog(int number);  // used by getTemperature to read the ADC
};
```

Listing 13-6: /exploringbb/chp13/QtTemperature/mainwindow.cpp

```cpp
#include "mainwindow.h"
#include "ui_mainwindow.h"
#include <fstream>
#include <sstream>
using namespace std;
#define LDR_PATH   "/sys/bus/iio/devices/iio:device0/in_voltage"

// Constructor used to set up the default values for the created object
MainWindow::MainWindow(QWidget *parent) :
   QMainWindow(parent), ui(new Ui::MainWindow)  {
   ui->setupUi(this);
   this->isFahrenheit = false;                // default to Celsius
   this->isAlertSet = false;                  // no alert set
```

```
      statusBar()->showMessage("No alert set");    // status at bottom of window
      this->timer = new QTimer(this);              // create a new timer
        // when the timer times out, call the slot on_updateTemperature()
      connect(timer, SIGNAL(timeout()), this, SLOT(on_updateTemperature()));
      this->maxTemperature = -100.0f;              // pick an impossible min
      this->minTemperature = 200.0f;               // pick an impossible max
      this->on_updateTemperature();          // explicitly update the display
      timer->start(5000);                    // set the time out to be 5 sec
}

MainWindow::~MainWindow() { delete ui; }       // destructor, destroys UI

void MainWindow::on_setAlertButton_clicked() { // set the alert temperature
   int sliderValue = ui->alertTempSlider->value();  // get the slider value
   if(sliderValue < getTemperature()){          // lower than current temp?
      QMessageBox::warning(this, "EBB Temperature",
                        "Alert setting too low!", QMessageBox::Discard);
   }
   else{                                         // alert value fine
      QString tempStr("Alert is set for: ");   // form a message
      tempStr.append(QString::number(sliderValue)); // with the alert temp
      statusBar()->showMessage(tempStr);        // display the message
      this->isAlertSet = true;                  // alert is set
      this->alertTemperature = sliderValue;     // alert temp set
   }
}

void MainWindow::on_isFahrenheitRadio_toggled(bool checked){
   this->isFahrenheit = checked;                // pressed the toggle button
   if(checked){
      ui->isCelsiusLabel->setText("Fahrenheit"); // display F on top-right
   }
   if(!checked){
      ui->isCelsiusLabel->setText("Celsius");   // display C on top-right
   }
   this->on_updateTemperature();                // update the temperature value
}

void MainWindow::on_clearAlertButton_clicked(){// remove the alert
   this->isAlertSet = false;
   statusBar()->showMessage("No alert set");
}

void MainWindow::on_alertTempSlider_valueChanged(int value) {
   ui->alertEdit->setText(QString::number(value)); // update alert text field
}

float MainWindow::getTemperature(){ ... }       // same as Chp.10 code (10-5)
```

```
int MainWindow::readAnalog(int number){ ... }    // same as Chp.10 code (10-5)

float MainWindow::celsiusToFahrenheit(float valueCelsius){
   return ((valueCelsius * (9.0f/5.0f)) + 32.0f);
}

// slot for the timer, called every 5 sec, and also explicitly in the code.
void MainWindow::on_updateTemperature() {     // called whenever temp updated
   float temperature = this->getTemperature();
   QDateTime local(QDateTime::currentDateTime()); // display sample time
   statusBar()->showMessage(QString("Last update: ").append(local.toString()));
   if(temperature >= this->maxTemperature){    // is this the max temperature?
      this->maxTemperature = temperature;
      ui->maxEdit->setText(QString::number(temperature));
   }
   if(temperature <= this->minTemperature){    // is this the min temperature?
      this->minTemperature = temperature;
      ui->minEdit->setText(QString::number(temperature));
   }
   if(this->isFahrenheit){                       // is the display in Fahrenheit?
      ui->temperatureLCD->display((double)this->celsiusToFahrenheit(temperature));
   }
   else{                                         // must be Celsius
      ui->temperatureLCD->display((double)temperature);
   }
   if(this->isAlertSet){                         // is the alert enabled?
      if(temperature>=this->alertTemperature){   // does it exceed alert temp?
         QString message("Alert! It is ");
         message.append(QString::number(temperature)).append(" degrees C!");
         QMessageBox::information(this, "EBB Temp", message, QMessageBox::Ok);
      }
   }
}
```

The code can be executed on the Beagle board from within Qt Creator or manually from a terminal window as follows:

```
molloyd@desktop:~$ ssh -XC debian@192.168.7.2
debian@ebb:~$ cd ~/exploringbb/chp13/QtTemperature/
debian@ebb:~/exploringbb/chp13/QtTemperature$ ./Temperature
```

Remote UI Application Development

In Chapter 11, a C++ client/server application was introduced that can be used for direct intercommunication between two processes that are running on two different machines (or the same machine) using TCP sockets. The machines could be situated on the same physical/wireless network or could even be on different continents. Direct socket communication requires programmers to frame their own intercommunication protocol. This results in programming overhead, but it also leads to efficient communication, which is only really limited by the speed of the network.

In this section, the functionality of the Qt temperature sensor GUI application and the C++ client/server application (from Chapter 11) are combined. This enables the creation of a fat-client GUI temperature application that can intercommunicate with a temperature service, which is running on the Beagle board. The temperature service server code is enhanced from that presented in Chapter 11, by making it multithreaded. This change enables many client applications to attach to the server at the same time. The architecture is illustrated in Figure 13-13.

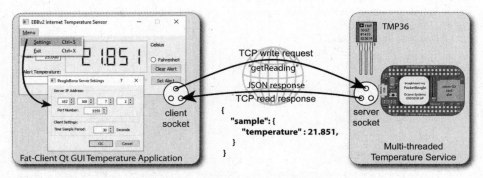

Figure 13-13: The Qt fat-client GUI application client/server architecture

The full source code for the Qt GUI application is available in the chp13/ QtSocketsTemperature directory, and the server source code is available in the chp13/threadedTemperatureServer directory.

Fat-Client Qt GUI Application

In this section, the Qt temperature sensor GUI application from earlier in this chapter is modified so that it becomes "internet enabled." This change means the application does not have to execute on the Beagle board; rather, the GUI application can run on a desktop machine and communicate to the board sensor using TCP sockets. To achieve this outcome, the following changes are made to the GUI application code:

1. A new dialog window is added to the application that can be used to enter the server IP address, the service port number, and the reading refresh frequency. This dialog is illustrated in Figure 13-14.

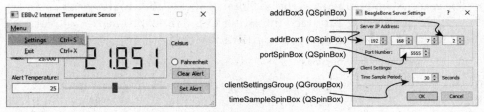

Figure 13-14: The Menu and the Server Settings dialog

2. Rather than read from the Beagle board ADC, the GUI application must open a TCP socket and communicate to the Beagle board server application. The client application sends the string "getTemperature" to the server. The server is programmed to respond with the temperature, which it reads from the TMP36 sensor that is attached to an ADC input. The temperature is encoded in a JSON format.

3. A menu is enabled on the application UI that can be used to open the Server Settings dialog or to quit the application. The respective key sequences Ctrl+S and Ctrl+X can also be used.

The first change involves adding a new class to the project called Server-SettingsDialog, as described in Listing 13-7, which is associated with the dialog (and its serversettingsdialog.ui XML file). The role of this class is to act as a wrapper for the values that are entered in the dialog—for example, it will return the IPv4 address that a user entered in the QSpinBox widgets, by returning a single 32-bit unsigned int (quint32) when its getIPAddress() method is called.

Listing 13-7: /chp13/QtSocketsTemperature/serversettingsdialog.h

```
class ServerSettingsDialog : public QDialog
{
    Q_OBJECT                              // the Qt macro required for
public:
    explicit ServerSettingsDialog(QWidget *parent = nullptr); //pass ref to mainwindow
    ~ServerSettingsDialog();
    quint32 virtual getIPAddress();       // return the IP address as a 32-bit int
    int virtual getTimeDelay() { return timeDelay; }  // the sample time
    int virtual getServerPort() { return serverPortNumber; } // the port number
private slots:
    void on_buttonBox_accepted();         // OK button is pressed
    void on_buttonBox_rejected();         // Cancel button is pressed
private:
    Ui::ServerSettingsDialog *ui;         // pointer to the UI components
    int serverPortNumber;                 // port number (default 5555)
    int timeDelay;                        // time delay sec (default 30)
    int address[4];                       // IP address (default 192.168.7.2)
};
```

The second change involves the addition of socket code to the `getSensorTemperature()` method, as provided in Listing 13-8. This code uses the QtNetwork module, which requires that you add the following:

```
QT          += core gui network
```

to the `SocketsTemperature.pro` project file so that the project links to that module. The `QTcpSocket` class is used to create a client connection to the Beagle board TCP temperature server. Regular TCP sockets are used on the Beagle board, which does not cause any difficulty in the transaction of string data. Interestingly, you could equivalently use Java socket code on either end of a connection—just be careful to ensure that the byte order is preserved.

Listing 13-8: /chp13/QtSocketsTemperature/mainwindow.cpp (Segment)

```cpp
int MainWindow::getSensorTemperature(){
    // Get the server address and port from the settings dialog box
    int serverPort = this->dialog->getServerPort();  // get from the dialog box
    quint32 serverAddr = this->dialog->getIPAddress();   // from the dialog box
    QTcpSocket *tcpSocket = new QTcpSocket(this);     // create socket
    tcpSocket->connectToHost(QHostAddress(serverAddr), serverPort); // connect
    if(!tcpSocket->waitForConnected(1000)){    //wait up to 1s for a connection
        statusBar()->showMessage("Failed to connect to server...");
        return 1;
    }
    // Send the message "getTemperature" to the server
    tcpSocket->write("getTemperature");
    if(!tcpSocket->waitForReadyRead(1000)){    // wait up to 1s for the server
        statusBar()->showMessage("Server did not respond...");
        return 1;
    }
    // If the server has sent bytes back to the client
    if(tcpSocket->bytesAvailable()>0){
        int size = tcpSocket->bytesAvailable(); // how many bytes are ready?
        char data[20];                          // upper limit of 20 chars
        tcpSocket->read(&data[0], static_cast<qint64>(size)); // read the number of
bytes rec.
        data[size]='\0';                        // termintate the string
        //this->curTemperature = atof(data);      // string -> float conversion
        cout << "Received the data [" << this->curTemperature << "]" << endl;
        this->parseJSONData(QString(data));
    }
    else{
        statusBar()->showMessage("No data available...");
    }
    return 0;     // the on_updateTemperature() slot will update the display
}
```

```
void MainWindow::createActions(){
    QAction *exit = new QAction("&Exit", this);
    exit->setShortcut(QKeySequence(tr("Ctrl+X")));
    QAction *settings = new QAction("&Settings", this);
    settings->setShortcut(QKeySequence(tr("Ctrl+S")));
    QMenu *menu = menuBar()->addMenu("&Menu");
    menu->addAction(settings);
    menu->addAction(exit);
    connect(exit, SIGNAL(triggered()), qApp, SLOT(quit()));    //quit application
    connect(settings, SIGNAL(triggered()), this, SLOT(on_openSettings()));
}

void MainWindow::on_openSettings(){
    this->dialog->exec();                                    // display the dialog box
    this->timer->start(1000*this->dialog->getTimeDelay()); //update timer delay
}

int MainWindow::parseJSONData(QString str){
    QJsonDocument doc = QJsonDocument::fromJson(str.toUtf8());
    QJsonObject obj = doc.object();
    QJsonObject sample = obj["sample"].toObject();
    this->curTemperature = sample["temperature"].toDouble();
    cout << "The temperature is " << this->curTemperature << endl;
    return 0;
}
```

The third change is implemented by the `createActions()` method in List-ing 13-8, which creates the GUI menu when it is called by the class constructor. It adds two actions to the menu: The Exit item quits the application, and the Settings item triggers the execution of the `on_openSettings()` slot, which opens the Server Settings dialog.

The Beagle board does not have to update the client-side GUI of the application in this architecture. Rather, it manages TCP socket connections, processes strings, and reads values from an ADC input. Such operations have a low overhead on the Beagle board, and therefore it is capable of simultaneously handling many client requests. Unfortunately, the server code that is presented in Chapter 11 is not capable of handling multiple *simultaneous* requests; instead, it processes requests in sequence and would reject a connection if it is presently occupied.

Multithreaded Server Applications

For many server applications it is important that the server can handle multiple simultaneous requests. For example, if the Google search engine web page could handle requests only sequentially, then there might be a long queue and/or many rejected connections! Figure 13-15 illustrates the steps that must take place for a multithreaded server application on a BBB to communicate simultaneously with two individual client applications. The steps are as follows:

1. TCP Client 1 requests a connection to the BBB TCP server. It must know the server's IP address (or name) and the port number.

2. The BBB TCP server creates a new thread (connection handler 1) and passes the TCP client's IP address and port number to it. The BBB TCP server immediately begins listening for new connections (on port 5555). The connection handler 1 thread then forms a connection to the TCP client 1 and begins communicating.

3. TCP client 2 requests a connection to the BBB TCP server. The connection handler 1 thread is currently communicating to TCP client 1, but the BBB TCP server is also listening for connections.

4. The BBB TCP server creates a new thread (connection handler 2) and passes the second TCP client's IP address and port number to it. The BBB TCP server immediately begins listening for new connections. The connection handler 2 thread then forms a connection to the TCP client 2 and begins communication.

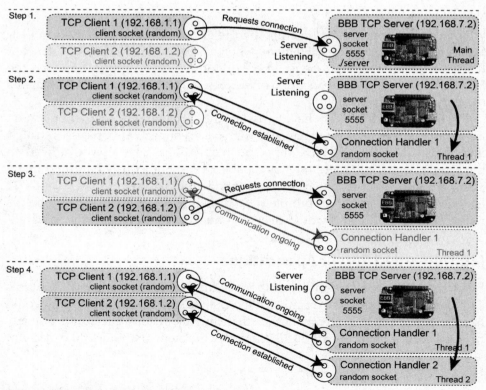

Figure 13-15: A multithreaded server on the BBB

At this point, communication is simultaneously taking place between both client/connection handler pairs, and the server main thread is listening for new connections. The client/connection handler communication session could persist for a long time—for example, for video streaming internet services such as YouTube or Netflix.

If the connection handler objects were not implemented as threads, then the server would have to wait until the client/connection handler communication is complete before it could listen again for new connections. With the structure described, the server is unavailable only while it is constructing a new connection handler threaded object. Once the object is created, the server returns to a listening state. Client socket connections have a configurable timeout limit (typically of the order of seconds), so a short processing delay by the server should not result in rejected connections.

A C++ multithreaded client/server example is available in the `chp13/threadedclientserver` directory. An artificial five-second delay is present in the `ConnectionHandler` class to prove conclusively that simultaneous communication is taking place. For example, you can open three terminal sessions on the board and start the server.

```
~/exploringbb/chp13/threadedclientserver$ ls
build  client  client.cpp  network  server  server.cpp
~/exploringbb/chp13/threadedclientserver$ ./server
Starting EBB Server Example
Listening for a connection...
```

Then start TCP client 1 in the next terminal.

```
~/exploringbb/chp13/threadedclientserver$ ./client localhost
Starting EBB Client Example
Sending [Hello from the Client]
```

Then start TCP client 2 in the last terminal (quickly—the delay is five seconds!).
```
~/exploringbb/chp13/threadedclientserver$ ./client localhost
Starting EBB Client Example
Sending [Hello from the Client]
```

The fact that the second client is able to connect while the first client is awaiting an (artificially delayed) response means that the server must be multithreaded. The final output of the server is as follows:

```
~/exploringbb/chp13/threadedclientserver$ ./server
Starting EBB Server Example
Listening for a connection...
Received from the client [Hello from the Client]
Sending back [The Server says thanks!]
  but going asleep for 5 seconds first....
Received from the client [Hello from the Client]
Sending back [The Server says thanks!]
  but going asleep for 5 seconds first....
```

Both clients will display the same final output.

```
~/exploringbb/chp13/threadedclientserver$ ./client localhost
Starting EBB Client Example
Sending [Hello from the Client]
Received [The Server says thanks!]
End of EBB Client Example
```

The class definition for the ConnectionHandler class is provided in Listing 13-9. This class has a slightly complex structure so that a thread is created and started when an object of the class is created. This code can be used as a template—just rewrite the threadLoop() implementation.

Listing 13-9: /chp13/threadedclientserver/network/ConnectionHandler.h

```
class SocketServer;  // class declaration, due to circular reference problem
                     // and C/C++ single definition rule.
class ConnectionHandler {
public:
   // Constructor expects a reference to the server that called it and
   // the incoming socket and file descriptor
   ConnectionHandler(SocketServer *server, sockaddr_in *in, int fd);
   virtual ~ConnectionHandler();
   int  start();
   void wait();
   void stop() { this->running = false; }  // stop the thread loop
   virtual int send(std::string message);  // send a message to the client
   virtual std::string receive(int size);  // receive a message
protected:
   virtual void threadLoop();     // the user-defined thread loop
private:
   sockaddr_in  *client;          // a handle to the client socket
   int          clientSocketfd;   // the client socket file desc.
   pthread_t    thread;           // the thread
   SocketServer *parent;          // a handle to the server object
   bool         running;          // is the thread running (default true)

   // static method to set the thread running when an object is created
   static void * threadHelper(void * handler){
         ((ConnectionHandler *)handler)->threadLoop();
         return NULL;
   }
};
```

A Multithreaded Temperature Service

The code in the previous section is modified in this section to create the multithreaded temperature service in Listing 13-10, which is available in the chp13/threadedTemperatureServer/ directory. It is unlikely that you will need to check the room temperature every fraction of a second. Therefore, a multithreaded approach is overkill in this example. However, this structure is important for applications that stream data, so it is useful to be exposed to it.

Listing 13-10: /threadedTemperatureServer/network/ConnectionHandler.cpp

```
int ConnectionHandler::readAnalog(int number){ ... // same as before }

float ConnectionHandler::getTemperature(int adc_value){ ... // same as before }

void ConnectionHandler::threadLoop(){
    cout << "*** Created a Temperature Connection Handler threaded Function" << endl;
    string rec = this->receive(1024);
    if (rec == "getTemperature"){
        cout << "Received from the client [" << rec << "]" << endl;
        stringstream ss;
        ss << " { \"sample\": { \"temperature\" : ";
        ss << this->getTemperature(this->readAnalog(0)) << " } } ";  //JSON string
        this->send(ss.str());
        cout << "Sent [" << ss.str() << "]" << endl;
    }
    else {
        cout << "Received from the client [" << rec << "]" << endl;
        this->send(string("Unknown Command"));
    }
    cout << "*** End of the Temperature Connection Handler Function" << endl;
    this->parent->notifyHandlerDeath(this);
}
```

The temperature server code can be tested by using the temperatureClientTest CLI test application, which is in the same directory as the server, by using the following:

```
.../chp13/threadedTemperatureServer$ ./temperatureServer
Starting EBB Server Example
Listening for a connection...
```

Then execute the test client in a different terminal.

```
.../.../threadedTemperatureServer$ ./temperatureClientTest localhost
Starting EBB Temperature Client Test
Sending [getTemperature]
Received [ { "sample": { "temperature" : 21.4551 } } ]
End of EBB Temperature Client Test
```

The final output of the server is as follows:

```
.../chp13/threadedTemperatureServer$ ./temperatureServer
Starting EBB Server Example
Listening for a connection...
Starting the Connection Handler thread
```

```
*** Created a Temperature Connection Handler threaded Function
Received from the client [getTemperature]
Sent [ { "sample": { "temperature" : 21.4551 } } ]
*** End of the Temperature Connection Handler Function ...
```

The localhost hostname is resolved to the loopback address 127.0.0.1, which enables the board to communicate with itself. If the client application outputs a temperature (e.g., 21.4551°C), then this test is successful and the Qt fat-client GUI application should also connect to the server, as illustrated in Figure 13-14.

Parsing Stream Data

The obvious approach to sending data between a server and a client is to use byte data and to *marshal* and *unmarshal* the data values. This can be performed by manually converting numeric data into string values; however, manual conversion is prone to parsing errors, particularly as the complexity of communication increases. One solution to this problem is to use an XML format to communicate between the client and the server. For example, the sample data could be structured as a simple XML message format.

```
<sample><temperature>21.4551</temperature></sample>
```

The Qt framework has full support for XML parsing in the QtXml module by using the QXmlStreamReader class.

An alternative solution is to use *JavaScript Object Notation* (JSON), which is also a human-readable format and is commonly used to transmit data between server and web applications. As you will have noticed, the sample data in the Qt temperature client/server application is transmitted in the JSON format as follows:

```
{
    "sample": {
        "temperature" : 21.4551,
    }
}
```

The Qt framework also has full support for parsing JSON data using the QJsonDocument class. Listing 13-11 is a segment of code from the Qt temperature client application that parses the JSON data format and retrieves the floating-point temperature value. By converting the byte data into an sample object of the QJsonObject class, the data values can be retrieved by calling sample["name"] .toDouble(), where name is the string name of the value to be retrieved. There are similar functions for other data types, for example, toInt(), toString(), toBool(), and toArray().

Listing 13-11: /chp13/QtSocketsTemperature/mainwindow.cpp (Segment)

```
int MainWindow::parseJSONData(QString str){
   QJsonDocument doc = QJsonDocument::fromJson(str.toUtf8());
   QJsonObject obj = doc.object();
   QJsonObject sample = obj["sample"].toObject();
   this->curTemperature = sample["temperature"].toDouble();
   cout << "The temperature is " << this->curTemperature << endl;
   return 0;
}
```

This framework is flexible and can be applied to many client/server applications on the Beagle board. In fact, it can even be reversed so that the Beagle board is the client and a desktop/server machine acts as the TCP server. Regardless, the same multithreading and data interchange principles can be used.

The Fat Client as a Server

In the previous example, the Qt fat-client GUI application initiates contact with the temperature service using the IP address (or hostname) of the server and the port number of the service. It is possible to reverse this relationship, by programming the GUI application to be the server and the Beagle board to be a client. Clearly, such a change would mean that the Beagle board is responsible for establishing communication with the GUI application, so it would therefore need to know the desktop computer's IP address and service port number.

For a single-client-to-single-server arrangement, the choice of which device is to be the server is not that important. The choice is likely resolved by deciding which party is most likely to initiate contact and then choosing it as the client. In fact, it would be possible to build client and server functionality into both parties, but that would add significant complexity to the program design. However, for single-party-to-multiple-party relationships, the decision is clearer. For example, the temperature service application is designed so that many client applications can make contact with a single server. It would be extremely difficult to reverse the client/server relationship in that case, as the Beagle board temperature sensor would have to somehow identify and push the temperature reading to each and every GUI application.

There are applications for which it is appropriate for the GUI application to be the server and for the Beagle board to act as the client. This is especially the case if one GUI application is responsible for aggregating sensor readings from many services and/or Beagle board devices. Figure 13-16 illustrates one such example. In this example a BBB is attached to the ADXL345 accelerometer using the I²C bus. The BBB streams accelerometer data to the GUI application, which provides a "live" graphical display of the ADXL345's pitch and roll values. For brevity, this example uses one BBB client, but it could easily be adapted to use multiple clients and either display multiple GUI interfaces or average the sample data.

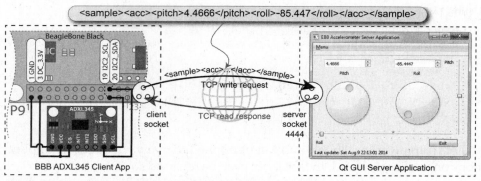

Figure 13-16: The Qt accelerometer client/server application

In this example, the controls on the Qt GUI Server application are *not used for input*; rather, they dynamically change according to the ADXL345's pitch and roll values—the only input controls on the GUI application are the Exit button and the menu. The current pitch and roll values are each described by three Qt widgets: a `QDoubleSpinBox` at the top, which displays the value as a `double`; a `QDial`, which rotates as the value changes from −90° to +90° (0° is when the dial indicator is at the very top); and a graduated `QSlider`, which slides from −90° to +90° (0° is the center value). This application differs from the previous Qt GUI application in a number of ways.

- The BBB is the client, and the GUI application is the server.
- The BBB sends a continuous stream of 1,000 readings, each sent every 50ms. The GUI display is updated instantly without latency problems (geographical distance would have an impact).
- The GUI application is threaded so that it can be "lively." A thread object is created to handle communication with the client so that the main loop can continue its role. If a thread were not used, then you would not be able to exit by clicking the Exit button.
- The messaging protocol is much more sophisticated, as it uses XML data to communicate. This issue is discussed shortly.

The Qt GUI server application is available in the Git repository directory /chp13/QtSocketsAccelerometer, and the BBB client application is available in the directory /chp13/ADXL345Client. Listing 13-12 provides the core thread loop that is used to communicate with the ADXL345 sensor client. Using threads in this way means that the code structure could be easily adapted for simultaneous communication with many client devices.

Listing 13-12: /chp13/QtSocketsAccelerometer/serverthread.cpp (Segment)

```
void ServerThread::run(){              // the main thread loop
    QTcpSocket clientSocket;           // the clientSocket object
    this->running = true;              // the main thread loop bool flag
```

```
   if (!clientSocket.setSocketDescriptor(socketDescriptor)){ //set up socket
      qDebug() << "Failed to set up the Socket";  // debug output
   }
   while(running){                             // loop forever until flag changes
      if(!clientSocket.waitForReadyRead(1000)){ // wait for up to 1 sec.
         this->running = false;                 // failed - exit the loop
      }
      while(clientSocket.bytesAvailable()>0)     // are bytes available?
      {
         int x = clientSocket.bytesAvailable();  // how many?
         qDebug() << "There are " << x << " bytes available"; // debug
         char data[2000];                        // capacity for up to 2000 bytes
         x = (qint64) clientSocket.read(&data[0], (qint64) x);
         data[x] = '\0';                         // add null in case of print output
         this->parse(&data[0]);                  // parse the XML string
      }
   }
   clientSocket.close();                         // if loop finished, close socket
   qDebug() << "The client just disconnected";   // debug output
}
```

The Qt GUI Server application has a number of classes, as illustrated in
Figure 13-17. The `QMainWindow` object is created when the application is executed. Its primary role is to update the UI, which it performs using a slot called
`sampleConsume()` that receives an object of the `SensorSample` class when data
is sent to the server. The `SensorSample` object contains a pitch value and a roll
value, which are used to update the UI components.

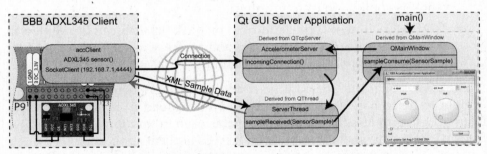

Figure 13-17: The Qt accelerometer client/server application program structure

When the `QMainWindow` object is created, it instantiates an object of the
`AccelerometerServer` class (child of `QTcpServer`). This server object awaits an
incoming connection; and when it receives one, it creates an object of the `Ser-
verThread` class (child of `QThread`). The `ServerThread` object then forms a read/
write connection with the BBB ADXL345 client application. The client application sends the accelerometer data in XML form, which the `ServerThread` object
parses to create a `SensorSample` object. If the data is parsed successfully, a signal
is triggered that passes the `SensorSample` object to the `sampleConsume()` slot.

> **NOTE** Both GUI client/server applications could be executed on a single Beagle board by using the loopback address (127.0.0.1) as the server IP address.

Parsing Stream Data with XML

As described earlier when discussing JSON, sending string data back and forth between the client and the server is prone to parsing errors, particularly as the complexity of communication increases. This example utilizes an XML format to communicate between the client and the server. This example uses a simple XML message to pass the sample data:

```
<sample><acc><pitch>4.4666</pitch><roll>-85.447</roll></acc></sample>
```

The Qt framework has full support for XML parsing in the `QtXml` module by using the `QXmlStreamReader` class. It can be used to efficiently convert such an XML string into a data structure, which offers the following advantages:

- It is possible to recover from communication errors should the data stream be corrupted—for example, by searching for the next valid tag in the stream.

- Having a human-readable format can greatly help in debugging code.

- Additional tags can be added to the stream, and it will not affect legacy applications that are reading the stream. For example, a new `<gyro> ... </gyro>` tag could be introduced to the `<sample>` tag, and it would not prevent this application from running.

- A DTD (document type definition) or XML Schema can be written to describe the rules (e.g., nesting and occurrence of elements) for the XML, to formally support third-party communication.

The downside is that the additional tag information increases the amount of data to be transmitted, and there is an overhead in processing XML. Listing 13-13 provides the source code that is used in this application to parse the XML data that is sent from the BBB ADXL345 client application.

Listing 13-13: /chp13/QtSocketsAccelerometer/serverthread.cpp (Segment)

```
int ServerThread::parse(char *data){
  QXmlStreamReader xml(data);
  while(!xml.atEnd() && !xml.hasError()){
    if((xml.tokenType()==QXmlStreamReader::StartElement) &&     // found <sample>
      (xml.name()=="sample")){
      // this is a data sample <sample> - need to loop until </sample>
      float pitch = 0.0f, roll = 0.0f;
      xml.readNext();                                      // read next token
      while(!((xml.tokenType()==QXmlStreamReader::EndElement)&&     // </sample>
```

```
                          (xml.name()=="sample"))){
            qDebug() << "Found a sample";
            if((xml.tokenType()==QXmlStreamReader::StartElement)      // <acc>
                    &&(xml.name()=="acc")){
              xml.readNext();
              qDebug() << "-- it has an acceleration element";
              while(!((xml.tokenType()==QXmlStreamReader::EndElement)  // </acc>
                      &&(xml.name()=="acc"))){
                if(xml.tokenType() == QXmlStreamReader::StartElement){ // <pitch>
                  if(xml.name() == "pitch") {
                    QString temp = xml.readElementText();     // read the value
                    pitch = (temp).toFloat();                 // convert to float
                  }
                  if(xml.name() == "roll") {                            // <roll>
                    QString temp = xml.readElementText();
                    roll = (temp).toFloat();
                  }
                }
                xml.readNext();
              }
            }
            xml.readNext();
          }
          SensorSample sample(pitch, roll);        // create a sample object and
          emit sampleReceived(sample);             // emit it as a signal -- caught
        }                                          // by a slot in mainWindow, which
      xml.readNext();                              // updates the display widgets
    }
  return 0;
}
```

An alternative solution is to use a JSON format once again. The same accelerometer data could be transmitted in the JSON format as follows:

```
{
    "acc": {
        "pitch": 32.55,
        "roll": 65.55
    }
}
```

The Beagle Board Client Application

In this application example, the more complex programming is in the Qt GUI server application and not in the client. In fact, the code for the client application (provided in Listing 13-14) is quite straightforward. It uses the library of code that is developed throughout this book, as well as simple string processing to structure the XML messages that are transmitted.

Listing 13-14: /exploringbb/chp13/ADXL345Client/accClient.cpp

```cpp
#include <iostream>
#include "network/SocketClient.h"        // using the EBB library
#include "bus/I2CDevice.h"               // I2CDevice class see CHP8
#include "sensor/ADXL345.h"              // ADXL345 see CHP8
#include "sstream"                       // to format the string
#include <unistd.h>                      // for the usleep()
using namespace std;
using namespace exploringBB;

int main(int argc, char *argv[]){
   if(argc!=2){
      cout << "Usage:  accClient server_name" << endl;
      return 2;
   }
   cout << "Starting EBB ADXL345 Client Example" << endl;
   I2CDevice i2c(1,0x53);                     // the I2C device P9_19 P9_20
   ADXL345 sensor(&i2c);                      // pass device to ADXL const.
   sensor.setResolution(ADXL345::NORMAL);     // regular resolution
   sensor.setRange(ADXL345::PLUSMINUS_4_G);   // regular +/- 2G
   SocketClient sc(argv[1], 4444);            // server addr and port number
   sc.connectToServer();                      // connect to the server
   for(int i=0; i<1000; i++){                 // going to send 1000 samples
      stringstream ss;                        // use a stringstream for msg.
      sensor.readSensorState();               // update the sensor state
      float pitch = sensor.getPitch();        // get pitch and roll
      float roll = sensor.getRoll();          // structure as XML string
      ss << "<sample><acc><pitch>" << pitch << "</pitch>";
      ss << "<roll>" << roll << "</roll></acc></sample>";
      cout << ss.str() << '\xd';              // print to output on one line
      cout.flush();                           // flush to update the display
      sc.send(ss.str());                      // send the same str to server
      usleep(50000);                          // 50ms between samples
   }
   cout << "End of EBB Client Example" << endl;
}
```

The code can be built using the build script and can be executed by providing the address of the server machine, which is 192.168.7.1 in this case:

```
debian@ebb:~/.../ADXL345Client$ ./accClient 192.168.7.1
Starting EBB ADXL345 Client Example
<sample><acc><pitch>0.493899</pitch><roll>0.493899</roll></acc></sample>
```

The display continually updates on the same line while sending data to the server application. The use of XML messages and server threads means that the client application can be stopped and restarted without requiring the server application to be restarted.

Summary

After completing this chapter, you should be able to do the following:

- Configure the Beagle board as a general-purpose computing device and use Bluetooth peripherals to control it
- Acquire hardware for LCD touchscreen display applications
- Use virtual network computing (VNC) to remotely execute graphical user interface (GUI) applications on a Beagle board
- Build rich user interface (UI) applications that execute directly on a Beagle board using the GTK+ and Qt frameworks
- Build Qt applications with advanced interfaces that interface to hardware sensors on a Beagle board
- Build fat-client remote Qt applications that communicate using TCP sockets to a server that is executing on a Beagle board
- Enhance TCP server code to be multithreaded to allow multiple simultaneous connections from TCP client applications
- Build remote Qt GUI server applications that communicate, using TCP sockets and XML, to a client application on a Beagle board

Further Reading

The following additional links provide further information on the topics in this chapter:

- Chapter web page: www.exploringbeaglebone.com/chapter13
- Core documentation on GTK+2.0: tiny.cc/beagle1302
- Qt Signals and Slots: tiny.cc/beagle1303

Images, Video, and Audio

In this chapter, USB peripherals are attached to the Beagle board so that it can be used for capturing image, video, and audio data using low-level Linux drivers and APIs. It describes Linux applications and tools that can be used to stream captured video and audio data to the internet. Open Source Computer Vision (OpenCV) image processing and computer vision approaches are investigated that enable the Beagle board to draw inferences from the information content of the captured image data. Capture and playback of audio streams are described, along with the use of Bluetooth audio. The chapter also covers some applications of audio on the Beagle board, including streaming audio, internet radio, and text-to-speech.

EQUIPMENT REQUIRED FOR THIS CHAPTER:

- A Beagle board (preferably one with HDMI and USB)
- Linux USB webcam (ideally the Logitech HD Pro C920)
- USB audio and/or Bluetooth adapter

Further resources for this chapter are available at www.exploringbeaglebone
.com/chapter14/.

Capturing Images and Video

In this section, the Beagle board is used as a platform for capturing image and video data from USB webcams and saving the data on the board's file system. This is useful for Beagle board applications such as robotics, home security, home automation, and aeronautics, when networked image streaming is not an available option—for example, if the application is untethered and distant from a wireless network. With suitable peripherals, the board can be used to capture high-quality video streams, which can be viewed asynchronously. The durations of the video streams are limited only by the available storage on the board. (Chapter 3 describes an approach for mounting a high-capacity micro-SD card or USB memory device on the file system.) Alternatively, the video can be streamed to the network, which is discussed in the next section of this chapter.

NOTE A full video on video capture and image processing on the BBB is available at `tiny.cc/beagle1401`. This video enables you to personally evaluate the quality of the video data described in this chapter.

USB Webcams

The main focus in this section is USB webcams, as they are widely available and can be reused as a general-purpose desktop peripheral. The Logitech HD C270 ($26), HD C310 ($30), and HD Pro C920 ($70), shown in Figure 14-1, are chosen, as they are commonly available HD cameras that are known to function under Linux. In fact, for the following tests the three cameras are connected simultaneously to the Beagle board using the USB hub displayed in Chapter 1. It is not a powered USB hub, but the board is connected to a 5V 2A supply in this case.

WARNING Similar to Wi-Fi adapters, many problems with USB webcams are caused by low power. The camera LED may indicate that the camera is working, but the lack of power may result in data transmission problems. Ideally, you should use a powered USB hub or power the Beagle board using an external 5V power supply when working with webcams.

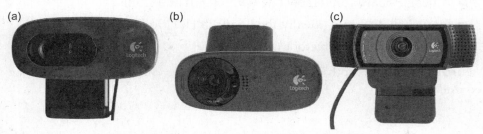

(a) (b) (c)

Figure 14-1: Logitech USB HD webcams (a) C270, (b) C310, and (c) C920

When the three USB cameras are connected to the board at the same time using a USB hub, the "list USB devices" utility provides the following output:

```
debian@ebb:~$ lsusb
Bus 001 Device 002: ID 1a40:0201 Terminus Technology Inc. FE 2.1 7-port Hub
Bus 001 Device 001: ID 1d6b:0002 Linux Foundation 2.0 root hub
Bus 002 Device 001: ID 1d6b:0002 Linux Foundation 2.0 root hub
Bus 001 Device 003: ID 046d:082d Logitech, Inc. HD Pro Webcam C920
Bus 001 Device 004: ID 046d:0825 Logitech, Inc. Webcam C270
Bus 001 Device 005: ID 046d:081b Logitech, Inc. Webcam C310
```

The output lists the device IDs for the cameras, two USB sound adapters, and a Bluetooth adapter. The fact that "Logitech" is listed against the device IDs indicates that some level of Linux support is already present on the board for these devices. If this is not the case, then you will have to source proprietary Linux drivers from the webcam manufacturer. Typically, such drivers would be built and deployed on the board before the webcam could be used.

Full information about the modes that are available on the USB cameras can be displayed using the following:

```
debian@ebb:~$ lsusb -v | less
```

This command results in detailed and verbose output. In addition, the loadable kernel modules (LKMs) that are currently loaded against these peripherals can be listed using the following command:

```
debian@ebb:~$ lsmod
Module               Size   Used by
snd_usb_audio        184320  0
uvcvideo             90112  0
snd_hwdep            20480  1 snd_usb_audio
videobuf2_vmalloc    16384  1 uvcvideo
videobuf2_memops     16384  1 videobuf2_vmalloc
snd_rawmidi          32768  1 snd_usbmidi_lib
videobuf2_v4l2       24576  1 uvcvideo
videobuf2_core       45056  2 uvcvideo,videobuf2_v4l2 ...
```

The uvcvideo LKM supports UVC (USB video class) compliant devices, such as the webcam that is attached. The videobuf2_vmalloc LKM is the memory allocator for the Video4Linux video buffer. If everything is working as expected, there should be new video and audio devices available, which can be listed using the following:

```
debian@ebb:~$ ls /dev/{vid,aud}*
/dev/audio    /dev/audio2  /dev/video0   /dev/audio1  /dev/video2
/dev/audio3   /dev/video1
```

The device /dev/audio is mapped to the HDMI audio device, which will appear only if the HDMI virtual cape is enabled. The other audio devices are mapped to USB audio adapters and USB webcams.

Video4Linux2 (V4L2)

Video4Linux2 (V4L2) is a video capture driver framework that is tightly integrated with the Linux kernel and is supported by the uvcvideo LKM. It provides drivers for video devices, such as webcams, PCI video capture cards, and TV (DVB-T/S) tuner cards/peripherals. V4L2 primarily supports video (and audio) devices through the following types of interfaces:

- **Video capture interface:** Used to capture video from capture devices, such as webcams, TV tuners, or video capture devices
- **Video output interface:** For video output devices, e.g., video transmission devices or video streaming devices
- **Video overlay interface:** Enables the direct display of the video data without requiring the data to be processed by the CPU
- **Video blanking interval (VBI) interface:** Provides access to legacy data that is transmitted during the VBI of an analog video signal (e.g., teletext)
- **Radio interface:** Provides access to AM/FM tuner audio streams

V4L2 provides support for many types of devices, and simply put, it is complex! In addition to supporting video input/output, the V4L2 API also has stubs for codec and video effect devices, which enable manipulation of the video stream data. The focus in this section is on the capture of video data from webcam devices using V4L2 by performing the following steps (not necessarily in this order):

- Opening the V4L2 device
- Changing the device properties (e.g., camera brightness)
- Agreeing on a data format and input/output method
- Performing the transfer of data
- Closing the V4L2 device

The main source of documentation on V4L2 is available from www.kernel .org at tiny.cc/beagle1402, and the V4L2 API specification is available at tiny .cc/beagle1403.

> **NOTE** The examples that follow in this chapter are written with the assumption that you have configured a display for your Beagle board, as described in Chapter 13. For example, a VNC client/server (e.g., Xming or VNC Viewer) allows the output images to be displayed on your desktop machine. An alternative approach is to sftp image files back and forth between the desktop machine and the Beagle board.

Image Capture Utility

The first step is to install the V4L2 development libraries, abstraction layer, utilities, and a simple webcam application for V4L2-compatible devices. Always update the package lists to get information about the newest packages and their dependencies, before installing a system library:

```
debian@ebb:~$ sudo apt-get update
debian@ebb:~$ apt-cache search v4l2
libv4l-dev - Collection of video4linux support libraries..
```

Then, install the packages that are required for this section:

```
debian@ebb:~$ sudo apt-get install fswebcam gpicview libav-tools libv4l-dev
```

The fswebcam application can then be used to test that the attached web camera is working correctly. It is a surprisingly powerful and easy-to-use application that is best used by writing a configuration file, as shown in Listing 14-1, which contains settings for choosing the device, capture resolution, output file type, and the addition of a title banner. It can even be used on a continuous loop by adding a `loop` entry that specifies the time in seconds between frame captures.

Listing 14-1: /exploringbb/chp14/fswebcam/fswebcam.conf

```
device /dev/video0
input 0
resolution 1280x720
bottom-banner
font /usr/share/fonts/truetype/ttf-dejavu/DejaVuSans.ttf
title "Exploring BeagleBone v2"
timestamp "%H:%M:%S %d/%m/%Y (%Z)"
png 0
save exploringBB.png
```

The fswebcam application can be configured with these settings by passing it the configuration filename on execution:

```
.../chp14/fswebcam$ ls
fswebcam.conf
.../chp14/fswebcam$ sudo fswebcam -c fswebcam.conf
--- Opening /dev/video0... Trying source module v4l2...
/dev/video0 opened. --- Capturing frame...  ...
```

The image can then be viewed using gpicview, which requires that you have attached a display to the Beagle board, such as a VNC connection:

```
.../chp14/fswebcam$ gpicview exploringBB.png
```

This will result in output like that in Figure 14-2(a). The image data has been modified to include a formatted bottom text banner, which contains a title and the date and time of image capture. Sample full-resolution capture images are available on the chapter web page.

> **NOTE** You can output a live view of the webcam by using the command `mplayer tv://` or by installing **Cheese** (`sudo apt install cheese`) **and executing it using** `cheese`, **as illustrated in Figure 14-2(b).**

(a)   (b)

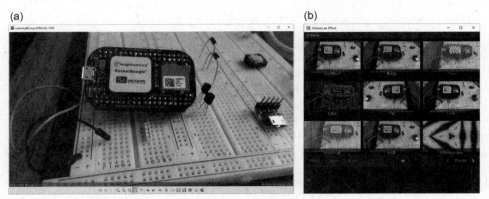

Figure 14-2: (a) The fswebcam webcam capture (1280 × 720) displayed using gpicview via VNC; (b) the Cheese application displaying some available image filters

Interestingly, the fswebcam application could be executed on a loop and combined with the Apache web server (as described in Chapter 11) to create a simple web camera, which uses a web page that links to the captured image file present on the Beagle board file system.

Video4Linux2 Utilities

V4L2 provides a set of user-space utilities that can be used for obtaining information about connected V4L2-compatible devices. It is also possible to use the user-space utilities to change camera settings; however, it is possible that executed applications will be programmed to override such changes. The most important role of these tools is to verify that connected V4L2 devices are functioning correctly. You can list the available V4L2 devices using the following:

```
debian@ebb:~$ v4l2-ctl --list-devices
HD Pro Webcam C920 (usb-musb-hdrc.1-1):    /dev/video0
```

The devices appear in the order in which they are attached to the USB hub. You can get information about a particular device by listing its modes (where `-d 0` refers to the HD Pro C920 in this instance).

```
debian@ebb:~$ v4l2-ctl --all -d 0
Driver Info (not using libv4l2):
        Driver name    : uvcvideo
        Card type      : HD Pro Webcam C920
        Bus info       : usb-musb-hdrc.1-1
        Driver version : 4.14.54
        Capabilities   : 0x84200001 Video Capture Streaming
```

Certain controls can be used to configure a camera, which can be accessed using the --list-ctrls option, as follows:

```
debian@ebb:~$ v4l2-ctl --list-ctrls -d 0
 brightness (int)  : min=0 max=255 step=1 default=128 value=128
 contrast (int)    : min=0 max=255 step=1 default=128 value=128
 saturation (int)  : min=0 max=255 step=1 default=128 value=128
 white_balance_temperature_auto (bool)  : default=1 value=1
 gain (int)        : min=0 max=255 step=1 default=0   value=255 ...
```

For the C920, other controls include white balance, color temperature, sharpness, backlight compensation, exposure (auto or absolute), focus, zoom, and support for pan/tilt. For example, to change the brightness on device 0 to 100 (currently 128 as shown in the preceding snippet), you can use the following:

```
debian@ebb:~$ v4l2-ctl --set-ctrl=brightness=100 -d 0
debian@ebb:~$ v4l2-ctl --list-ctrls -d 0 | grep brightness
 brightness (int)  : min=0 max=255 step=1 default=128 value=100
```

You can also list the modes of the cameras. In this case, there are three different video capture pixel formats, with *fourcc* color space video codes: YUYV (a common broadcast format with one luminance and two chrominance channels), H264 (a common modern interframe video compression format), and MJPG (a common, but older, intraframe-only motion JPEG video compression format). The listing is obtained using the following:

```
debian@ebb:~$ v4l2-ctl --list-formats -d 0
ioctl: VIDIOC_ENUM_FMT
    Index        : 0              Type  : Video Capture
    Pixel Format: 'YUYV'          Name  : YUYV 4:2:2
    Index        : 1              Type  : Video Capture
    Pixel Format: 'H264' (compressed) Name  : H.264
    Index        : 2              Type  : Video Capture
    Pixel Format: 'MJPG' (compressed) Name  : Motion-JPEG
```

The C270 and C310 cameras do not have H.264 mode, but they both have YUYV and MJPG compressed pixel formats at indices 0 and 1, respectively. It is possible to explicitly set the resolution and pixel format of a camera as follows:

```
~$ v4l2-ctl --set-fmt-video=width=1920,height=1080,pixelformat=1 -d 0
~$ v4l2-ctl --all -d 0
```

```
Driver Info (not using libv4l2):
        Driver name   : uvcvideo
        Card type     : HD Pro Webcam C920
        Bus info      : usb-musb-hdrc.1-1
        Driver version: 4.14.54        ...
        Capabilities  : 0x84000001     Video Capture    Streaming
Format Video Capture:
        Width/Height  : 1920/1080      Pixel Format  : 'H264'
        Field         : None           Bytes per Line : 3840
        Size Image    : 4147200        Colorspace    : SRGB
Crop Capability Video Capture:
        Bounds        : Left 0, Top 0, Width 1920, Height 1080
        Default       : Left 0, Top 0, Width 1920, Height 1080
        Pixel Aspect  : 1/1
Video input : 0 (Camera 1: ok)
Streaming Parameters Video Capture:
        Capabilities  : timeperframe   Frames per second: 30.000 (30/1)
        Read buffers  : 0              Priority: 2
```

This output provides useful state information, such as the resolution, video frame image size, frame rate, and so on.

Writing Video4Linux2 Programs

As with other devices in Linux (e.g., SPI in Chapter 8), it is possible to send data to and receive data from a video device by opening its /dev/videoX file system entry by using a call to file open(). Unfortunately, such an approach would not provide the level of control or performance that is required for video devices. Instead, low-level input/output control (ioctl()) calls are required to configure the settings of the device, and memory map (mmap()) calls are used to perform image frame memory copy, rather than using a byte-by-byte serial transfer.

The Git repository contains programs in the /chp14/v4l2/ directory that use V4L2 and its low-level ioctl() calls to perform video frame capture and video capture tasks.

- grabber.c: Grabs raw image frame data from a webcam into memory using libv4l2. The images can be written to the file system.

- capture.c: Grabs raw video data to a stream or file. It does this quickly enough to be used for real-time video capture.

These code examples are almost entirely based on the samples that are provided by the V4L2 project team. The code is too long to display here, but you can view it in the Git repository. To build and execute the code examples, use the following steps:

```
~/exploringbb/chp14/v4l2$ sudo apt install libv4l-dev
.../chp14/v4l2$ ls *.c
capture.c  grabber.c
.../chp14/v4l2$ gcc -O2 -Wall `pkg-config --cflags --libs libv4l2` →
 grabber.c -o grabber
```

```
.../chp14/v4l2$ gcc -O2 -Wall `pkg-config --cflags --libs libv4l2` →
 capture.c -o capture
.../chp14/v4l2$ ./grabber
.../chp14/v4l2$ ls *.ppm
grabber000.ppm  grabber005.ppm  grabber010.ppm  grabber015.ppm ...
.../chp14/v4l2$ gpicview grabber000.ppm
```

The .ppm file format describes an uncompressed color image format, which gpicview will display. You can use the "forward" button on gpicview to step through the 20 image frames. To capture data using the capture.c program, use a selection of the following options:

```
.../chp14/v4l2$ ./capture -h
Usage: ./capture [options]
Version 1.3    Options:
-d | --device name   Video device name [/dev/video0] ...
-f | --format        Force format to 640x480 YUYV
-F | --formatH264    Force format to 1920x1080 H264
-c | --count         Number of frames to grab [100] - use 0 for infinite
Example usage: capture -F -o -c 300 > output.raw
Captures 300 frames of H264 at 1920x1080. Use raw2mpg4 script to convert to mpg4
```

If you have the C920 camera, you can capture 100 frames of H.264 data using the first of the following commands. A second command then converts the .raw file to a .mp4 file format, which can be played on a desktop machine.

```
.../chp14/v4l2$ ./capture -d /dev/video0 -F -o -c 100 > output.raw
Force Format 2
.............................................................
.../chp14/v4l2$ avconv -f h264 -i output.raw -vcodec copy output.mp4
.../chp14/v4l2$ ls -l output*
-rw-r--r-- 1 debian debian 1355695 Sep  3 22:23 output.mp4
-rw-r--r-- 1 debian debian 1353801 Sep  3 22:23 output.raw
```

The file sizes are almost identical because the video data is actually captured in a raw H.264 format. The conversion is performed using the avconv (Libav) utility, which is a fork of the FFmpeg project that is well supported by the Debian Linux distribution. The -vcodec copy option enables the video to be copied without transcoding the video data format.

The capture.c program can also be used with cameras such as the C270 and C310, which do not have hardware H.264 functionality; however, the capabilities are more limited.

```
...$ v4l2-ctl --set-fmt-video=width=1280,height=720,pixelformat=1 -d 1
...$ v4l2-ctl --all -d 1
Format Video Capture: Width/Height:1280/720   Pixel Format:'MJPG'
.../chp14/v4l2$ ./capture -d /dev/video1 -o -c 100 > output.raw
Force Format 0 .............................................
.../chp14/v4l2$ ls -l output.raw
-rw-r--r-- 1 debian debian 4476448 Sep  3 01:58 output.raw
```

```
.../chp14/v4l2$ avconv -f mjpeg -i output.raw output.mp4
.../chp14/v4l2$ ls -l output.mp4
-rw-r--r-- 1 debian debian 1456040 Sep  3 02:06 output.mp4
```

True video conversion using avconv can take quite some time on the Beagle board! In this example, you can see that the H.264 video file requires significantly less space than the MJPEG file, as it is a more efficient interframe video-encoding format.

> **NOTE** A common problem arises when using the `capture.c` program. The camera returns a "select timeout" error. If this arises, then you need to change the timeout properties of the uvcvideo LKM as follows:
>
> ```
> debian@ebb:~$ sudo rmmod uvcvideo
> debian@ebb:~$ sudo modprobe uvcvideo nodrop=1 timeout=5000
> debian@ebb:~$ lsmod | grep uvcvideo
> uvcvideo             90112  0
> videobuf2_vmalloc    16384  1 uvcvideo
> videobuf2_v4l2       24576  1 uvcvideo
> videobuf2_core       45056  2 uvcvideo,videobuf2_v4l2
> ```

Streaming Video

It is possible to use a Beagle board to capture and stream live video. The Logitech C920 is particularly useful for this purpose, as it has a built-in H.264 hardware encoder. The raw 1080p H.264 data can be passed directly from the camera stream to the network stream without transcoding, which means that the computational load on the Beagle board is reasonably low. Streaming scripts are available in the /chp14/v4l2/ repository directory. For example, Listing 14-2 provides a script for sending H.264 video data over UDP to a desktop PC at 192.168.7.1 using the C920 webcam.

Listing 14-2: /exploringbb/chp14/v4l2/streamVideo

```
#!/bin/bash
echo "Video Streaming for the Beaglebone - Exploring BeagleBone v2"
v4l2-ctl --set-fmt-video=width=1920,height=1080,pixelformat=1
v4l2-ctl --set-parm=15
./capture -F -o -c300000|avconv -i - -vcodec copy -f rtp rtp://192.168.7.1:8090/
```

This script pipes the raw video output from the capture program to the avconv application, which "copies" the raw data to the network stream using RTP. There is an additional script to multicast the video stream to multiple network points (streamVideoMulti) using the broadcast network address 226.0.0.1.

A full video on my YouTube channel describes the steps involved in detail: tiny.cc/beagle1404.

You can execute this script directly, but you must also copy the text highlighted here from its output and paste it into a new text file (you can name this new file stream.sdp) and place it on your host machine.

```
debian@ebb:~/exploringbb/chp14/v4l2$ ./streamVideo
Frame rate set to 15.000 fps
Force Format 2 ...
Output #0, rtp, to 'rtp://192.168.7.1:8090/':
  Metadata:
    encoder         : Lavf57.56.101
    Stream #0:0: Video: h264 (Constrained Baseline), yuvj420p(pc, prog),
    1920x1080 [SAR 1:1 DAR 16:9], q=2-31, 30 fps, 30 tbr, 90k tbn, 30 tbc
SDP:
v=0
o=- 0 0 IN IP4 127.0.0.1
s=No Name
c=IN IP4 192.168.7.1
t=0 0
a=tool:libavformat 57.56.101
m=video 8090 RTP/AVP 96
a=rtpmap:96 H264/90000
a=fmtp:96 packetization-mode=1; sprop-parameter-
sets=Z0JAKLtAPAES8uAokAAAAwAQAAADA8YEAALcbAAtx73vheEQjUA=,aM44gA==;
profile-level-id=424028

Stream mapping:
  Stream #0:0 -> #0:0 (copy)...
  frame= 1120 fps= 34 q=-1.0 Lsize=13901kB ... bitrate=3052.5kbits/s
video:13756kB audio:0kB subtitle:0kB other streams:0kB ...
```

You can then open this file stream.sdp using a media player such as VLC, whereupon you will see a live video stream from the Beagle board on which the streamVideo script is executed.

It is possible to build a custom Qt application that can receive the video stream on a desktop computer. This can be combined with the Qt client/server applications in Chapter 11 to provide network control and support for video streaming. Further details are available at tiny.cc/beagle1405.

A second Beagle board can be used to receive the network video stream; however, it does not have sufficient capability to render the HD video stream to a display in real time. Interestingly, it is possible to use a Raspberry Pi 2/3 to capture the UDP stream and display it using a video player that takes advantage of the Raspberry Pi's H.264 hardware decoder. For example, the OMXplayer supports hardware decoding, and it can be used to open the network broadcast stream using the following:

```
molloyd@raspberryPI$ omxplayer -o hdmi udp://226.0.0.1:123
```

The Raspberry Pi can decode the C920 video stream and display it live on a monitor, albeit with a varying degree of latency.

Image Processing and Computer Vision

Once a USB camera or camera cape is attached to the Beagle board, it is possible to capture images and process them using a comprehensive high-level library called Open Source Computer Vision (OpenCV). OpenCV (www.opencv.org) provides a cross-platform library of functions for computer vision, such as gesture recognition, motion understanding, motion tracking, augmented reality, and structure-from-motion. It also provides supporting libraries for applications such as artificial neural networks, support vector machines, classification, and decision tree learning. OpenCV is written in C/C++ and is optimized for real-time applications, including support for multicore programming. The OpenCV libraries can be installed using this:

```
debian@ebb ~ $ sudo apt install libopencv-dev
```

Image Processing with OpenCV

OpenCV supports V4L2 and provides a high-level interface for capturing image data, which can be used instead of the grabber.c program. Listing 14-3 is an OpenCV application that captures data from a webcam and filters it using some simple image processing techniques. The steps that it performs are as follows:

1. Capture of the image from the webcam.

2. Conversion of the image into grayscale form.

3. Blurring of the image to remove high-frequency noise.

4. Detecting regions in the image where the image brightness changes sharply. This is achieved using an image processing operator known as an *edge detector*—the Canny edge detector in this example.

5. Storage of the image files to the Beagle board file system.

OpenCV uses a file-naming convention whereby an .hpp file extension is used for header files that contain C++ code. This convention enables a C version of a header file (e.g., opencv.h) to coexist alongside a C++ header file (e.g., opencv.hpp). Because OpenCV mixes both C and C++ code, this is an appropriate way to distinguish one form from the other.

Listing 14-3: /exploringbb/chp14/openCV/boneCV.cpp

```
#include<iostream>
#include<opencv2/opencv.hpp>    // C++ OpenCV include file
```

```
using namespace std;
using namespace cv;              // using the cv namespace too

int main()
{
    VideoCapture capture(0);     // capturing from /dev/video0
    cout << "Started Processing - Capturing Image" << endl;
    // set any  properties in the VideoCapture object
    capture.set(CV_CAP_PROP_FRAME_WIDTH,1280);    // width in pixels
    capture.set(CV_CAP_PROP_FRAME_HEIGHT,720);    // height in pixels
    capture.set(CV_CAP_PROP_GAIN, 0);             // enable auto gain
    if(!capture.isOpened()){     // connect to the camera
        cout << "Failed to connect to the camera." << endl;
    }
    Mat frame, gray, edges;     // original, grayscale and edge image
    capture >> frame;           // capture the image to the frame
    if(frame.empty()){          // did the capture succeed?
        cout << "Failed to capture an image" << endl;
        return -1;
    }
    cout << "Processing - Performing Image Processing" << endl;
    cvtColor(frame, gray, CV_BGR2GRAY);     // convert to grayscale
    blur(gray, edges, Size(3,3));           // blur image using a 3x3 kernel
    // use Canny edge detector that outputs to the same image
    // low threshold = 10, high threshold = 30, kernel size = 3
    Canny(edges, edges, 10, 30, 3);         // run Canny edge detector
    cout << "Finished Processing - Saving images" << endl;

    imwrite("capture.png", frame);     // store the original image
    imwrite("grayscale.png", gray);    // store the grayscale image
    imwrite("edges.png", edges);       // store the processed edge image
    return 0;
}
```

This example can be built and executed as follows, which results in the output displayed in Figure 14-3:

```
.../chp14/openCV$ g++ -O2 `pkg-config --cflags --libs opencv` →
  boneCV.cpp -o boneCV
.../chp14/openCV$ ./boneCV
Started Processing - Capturing Image
Processing - Performing Image Processing
Finished Processing - Saving images
.../chp14/openCV$ ls *.png
capture.png  edges.png  grayscale.png
.../chp14/openCV$ gpicview capture.png
.../chp14/openCV$ gpicview edges.png
```

(a)   (b)

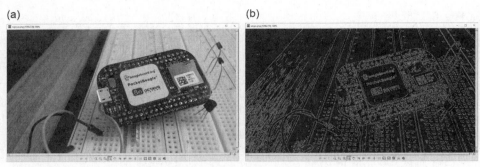

Figure 14-3: The OpenCV image processing example: (a) the webcam image; (b) the edge-processed image

A second example application in the same directory can be used to test the performance of using OpenCV for image processing. In each iteration, it performs an image capture at a 640 × 480 resolution, converts the image to grayscale form, and performs an edge detection operation. The program performs 100 iterations, after which the execution time is measured.

```
debian@ebb:~/exploringbb/chp14/openCV$ ./boneCVtiming
It took 12.3263 seconds to process 100 frames
Capturing and processing 8.11274 frames per second
```

During this test the application uses 95 percent of CPU and 6 percent of memory capacity.

> **NOTE**   The AM335x has a NEON single-instruction multiple-data (SIMD) engine that allows you to perform certain instructions in parallel on multiple data values. The engine is capable of greatly accelerating image processing operations; however, utilizing the engine may require that inline assembly language code is written in your C/C++ programs. Details of the NEON SIMD engine are available at `tiny .cc/beagle1406`. Since the release of OpenCV 3.0 in June 2015, more than 40 basic functions have been accelerated using the NEON intrinsics, which has also resulted in the acceleration of high-level functions.

Computer Vision with OpenCV

Image processing involves manipulating images by filters (e.g., smoothing, contrast enhancement) or transformations (e.g., scaling, rotation, stretching) for purposes such as enhancing or even reducing the information content of digital images. Image processing is one tool that is used in *computer vision*, which often has the goal of "understanding" the information content within digital images.

Computer vision applications often try to replicate the capabilities of human vision by drawing inferences, making decisions, and taking actions based on visual data. For example, the OpenCV application described in this section uses the BeagleBone to process image data and apply computer vision techniques to determine whether a human face is present in a webcam image frame or an image file. Importantly, the approach is designed for face detection, not face recognition. Face detection can be used for applications such as security and photography; however, the processing required has a significant computational overhead and is not suitable for high frame rates on a Beagle board.

Listing 14-4 provides an example computer vision application that uses OpenCV for face detection. It uses a Harr feature-based cascade classifier, which uses a characterization of adjacent rectangular image regions to identify regions of interest—for example, in human faces the region near the eyes has a darker intensity than the region containing the cheeks. Human faces can be detected using such observations. Usefully, OpenCV provides some codified rules for detecting human faces, which have been used in this example.

Computer vision is an entire research domain, and it requires a significant time investment before you will be able to perform some of its more complex operations. The "Further Reading" section provides links to resources to get you started.

Listing 14-4: /exploringbb/chp14/openCV/face.cpp

```cpp
#include <iostream>
#include <opencv2/highgui/highgui.hpp>
#include <opencv2/objdetect/objdetect.hpp>
#include <opencv2/imgproc/imgproc.hpp>
using namespace std;
using namespace cv;

int main(int argc, char *args[])
{
   Mat frame;
   VideoCapture *capture; //capture needs full scope of main(), using ptr
   cout << "Starting face detection application" << endl;
   if(argc==2){  // loading image from a file
      cout << "Loading the image " << args[1] << endl;
      frame = imread(args[1], CV_LOAD_IMAGE_COLOR);
   }
   else {
      cout << "Capturing from the webcam" << endl;
      capture = new VideoCapture(0);
      // set any  properties in the VideoCapture object
      capture->set(CV_CAP_PROP_FRAME_WIDTH,1280);   // width pixels
      capture->set(CV_CAP_PROP_FRAME_HEIGHT,720);   // height pixels
      if(!capture->isOpened()){   // connect to the camera
         cout << "Failed to connect to the camera." << endl;
         return 1;
      }
      *capture >> frame;     // populate the frame with captured image
      cout << "Successfully captured a frame." << endl;
```

```
    }
    if (!frame.data){
        cout << "Invalid image data... exiting!" << endl;
        return 1;
    }
    // loading the face classifier from a file (standard OpenCV example)
    CascadeClassifier faceCascade;
    faceCascade.load("haarcascade_frontalface.xml");

    // faces is a STL vector of faces - will store the detected faces
    std::vector<Rect> faces;
    // detect objects in the scene using the classifier above (frame,
    // faces, scale factor, min neighbors, flags, min size, max size)
    faceCascade.detectMultiScale(frame, faces, 1.1, 3,
                    0 | CV_HAAR_SCALE_IMAGE, Size(50,50));
    if(faces.size()==0){
        cout << "No faces detected!" << endl;       // display the image
    }
    // draw oval around the detected faces in the faces vector
    for(int i=0; i<faces.size(); i++)
    {
        // Using the center point and a rectangle to create an ellipse
        Point cent(faces[i].x+faces[i].width*0.5,
                   faces[i].y+faces[i].height*0.5);
        RotatedRect rect(cent, Size(faces[i].width,faces[i].width),0);
        // image, rectangle, color=green, thickness=3, linetype=8
        ellipse(frame, rect, Scalar(0,255,0), 3, 8);
        cout << "Face at: (" << faces[i].x << "," <<faces[i].y << ")" << endl;
    }
    imshow("EBB OpenCV face detection", frame);  // display image results
    imwrite("faceOutput.png", frame);       // save image too
    waitKey(0);                             // dislay image until key press
    return 0;
}
```

The face detection example can be built and executed using the following commands:

```
.../chp14/openCV$ g++ -O2 `pkg-config --cflags --libs opencv` face.cpp -o face
.../chp14/openCV$ ./face
Starting face detection application
Capturing from the webcam
Successfully captured a frame.
Face at: (697,470)  Face at: (470,152)   Face at: (82,192) Face at: (966,296)
.../chp14/openCV$ ./face Lena.png
Starting face detection application
Loading the image Lena.png
Face at: (217,201)
```

When executed, it results in the display of the image in Figure 14-4(a) (if an X Window session is configured), with ellipses identifying any faces that are detected in the image.

(a)   (b)

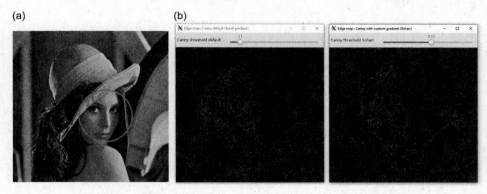

Figure 14-4: (a) OpenCV face detection on with the Lena image file, and (b) OpenCV3 examples in operation

There is a myriad of OpenCV3 examples available in the source code repositories and at `tiny.cc/beagle1408`. The examples can be built and executed on the Beagle board as follows:

```
.../chp14/openCV3$ g++ -O2 `pkg-config --cflags --libs opencv` edge.cpp -o edge
.../chp14/openCV3$ ls
build  edge  edge.cpp  fruits.jpg
.../chp14/openCV3$ ./edge fruits.jpg
```

This directly results in the interactive threshold edge detection windows in Figure 14-4(b).

Boost

Similar to OpenCV, Boost (`www.boost.org`) provides a comprehensive free library of C++ source code that can be used for many applications on the Beagle board. There are libraries for multithreading, data structures, algorithms, regular expressions, memory management, mathematics, and more. The range of libraries available is too exhaustive to detail here, but a full listing is available at `www.boost.org/doc/libs/`. Boost can be installed on the board using the following:

```
debian@ebb:~$ sudo apt install libboost-dev
... Unpacking libboost-dev:armhf (1.62.0.1) ...
```

Listing 14-5 provides an example of usage of the Boost library for calculating the geometric distance between two 2-D points.

Listing 14-5: /exploringbb/chp14/boost/testBoost.cpp

```
#include <boost/geometry.hpp>
#include <boost/geometry/geometries/point_xy.hpp>
using namespace boost::geometry::model::d2;
```

```
#include <iostream>

int main(){
    point_xy<float> p1(1.0,2.0), p2(3.0,4.0);
    float d = boost::geometry::distance(p1,p2);
    std::cout << "The distance between points is: " << d << std::endl;
    return 0;
}
```

Similarly to OpenCV, it utilizes an `.hpp` extension form. It also makes extensive use of C++ namespaces. The preceding code can be built and executed using the following:

```
debian@ebb:~/exploringbb/chp14/boost$ g++ testBoost.cpp -o testBoost
debian@ebb:~/exploringbb/chp14/boost$ ./testBoost
Distance between points is: 2.82843
```

BeagleBone Audio

There are several approaches to utilizing audio inputs and outputs with Beagle boards, including the following:

- **HDMI audio:** This output is enabled by default on the BeagleBone boards and allows audio signals to be sent to a television via HDMI (not DVI).

- **USB audio:** Low-cost USB adapters can be attached to Beagle boards that have Linux driver support for the input/output of audio. In addition, USB webcams can be used as audio input devices.

- **Bluetooth audio:** A Linux-compatible Bluetooth adapter can be used to input from, or output to, external Bluetooth recorder/speaker devices.

- **Multichannel audio serial port (McASP):** Several Beagle boards have header pins for McASP that can be used to interface to McASP-capable audio codecs (e.g., the TI TLV320AIC series). This is a complex task that requires proprietary (typically SMT) components.

It is also possible to use the built-in ADC inputs to capture audio events at low sample rates. For example, the SparkFun electret microphone breakout board (BOB-09964) can be connected via an op-amp circuit to the Beagle board ADC (with a 10kΩ potentiometer on the GND line) and used for tasks such as impact detection (e.g., a door knock). The sample rate of such a microphone circuit could be improved by using an external ADC that has an SPI interface, such as the low-cost ($3) MCP3008, which has eight 10-bit ADCs. In addition, the TI ADS8326 16-bit 250kS/s SPI out could be interfaced to the PRU-ICSS, which is described in Chapter 15.

In this section, the most common approaches are examined, as is software that enables you to perform basic audio input/output tasks.

Core Audio Software Tools

The following tools are used in this section of the book:

- **MPlayer:** A movie player for Linux that has optimized built-in support for audio devices. It works well as an MP3 audio stream player on a Beagle board.

- **ALSA utilities:** Contains tools for configuring and using ALSA (advanced Linux sound architecture) devices. It includes the `aplay`/`arecord` utilities for the playback and recording of audio streams, the `amixer` tool for controlling volume levels, and the `speaker-test` utility.

- **Libav:** Contains libraries and programs for handling multimedia data. In particular, `avconv` is a fast video and audio conversion tool that can also be used to capture audio data from devices or to stream data to the network (see `libav.org/avconv.html`).

To install these tools, ensure that your package lists are up-to-date and install the tools as follows:

```
debian@ebb:~$ sudo apt-get update
debian@ebb:~$ sudo apt-get install mplayer alsa-utils libav-tools
```

Audio Devices for the Beagle Boards

After you have the core software installed, the next step is to utilize an audio device that is connected to a Beagle board. In this section, an example is used in which several audio devices are attached simultaneously to the Beagle board—the HDMI audio interface, a webcam, and two USB audio adapters. Remember that the HDMI virtual cape must be enabled to utilize the HDMI audio output.

HDMI and USB Audio Playback Devices

Figure 14-5(a) illustrates the USB hub with three USB devices attached—the two USB audio adapters and the Bluetooth adapter. When the three webcams are also attached to the Velleman USB hub, then a call to `lsusb` results in the following:

```
Linux ebb 4.14.54-ti-rt-r63 #1 SMP PREEMPT RT ...
debian@ebb:~$ lsusb
Bus 001 Device 005: ID 0d8c:013c C-Media Elec CM108 Audio Controller
Bus 001 Device 004: ID 041e:30d3 Creative Tech, Sound Blaster Play!
Bus 001 Device 006: ID 0a5c:2198 Broadcom Corp. Bluetooth 3.0 Device
Bus 001 Device 003: ID 046d:082d Logitech, Inc. HD Pro Webcam C920
Bus 001 Device 002: ID 1a40:0201 Terminus TechFE 2.1 7-port Hub
Bus 001 Device 001: ID 1d6b:0002 Linux Foundation 2.0 root hub
```

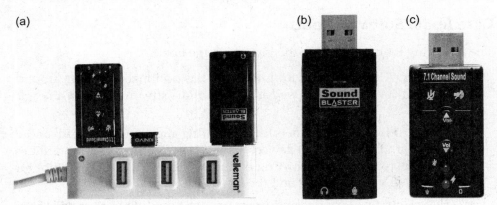

Figure 14-5: (a) Seven-port USB hub with multiple adapters, (b) the Sound Blaster audio adapter; (c) the Dynamode USB audio adapter

The USB hub in Figure 14-5(a) is not a powered hub; however, the board is powered via the 5V connector using a 2 A power supply, which provides sufficient power to use all these devices simultaneously. The Sound Blaster ($20) and Dynamode ($5) USB adapters are illustrated in Figure 14-5(b) and (c), respectively. These adapters can be hot-plugged into the board, where their LKMs can be dynamically loaded and unloaded during Linux execution.

When the various adapters are connected to the Beagle board, you can obtain information about them as follows:

```
debian@ebb:~$ cat /proc/asound/pcm
00-00: davinci-mcasp.0-i2s-hifi i2s-hifi-0 :  : playback 1
01-00: USB Audio : USB Audio : capture 1
02-00: USB Audio : USB Audio : playback 1 : capture 1
03-00: USB Audio : USB Audio : playback 1 : capture 1
```

In this case, the HDMI adapter is capable of playback only, the two USB adapters are capable of playback and capture, and the USB webcam is capable only of capture. An alternative approach is to use the aplay utility to list the available playback devices.

```
debian@ebb:~$ aplay -l
**** List of PLAYBACK Hardware Devices ****
card 0: Black [TI BeagleBone Black], device 0: davinci-mcasp.0-i2s-hifi ...
  Subdevices: 0/1
  Subdevice #0: subdevice #0
card 2: U0x41e0x30d3 [USB Device 0x41e:0x30d3], device 0: USB Audio ...
  Subdevices: 0/1
  Subdevice #0: subdevice #0
card 3: Device [USB PnP Sound Device], device 0: USB Audio ...
  Subdevices: 0/1
  Subdevice #0: subdevice #0
```

Once you have identified the devices, you can play back an audio file on the Dynamode and Creative Sound Blaster USB adapters, respectively, using the mplayer and aplay utilities, as follows:

```
.../chp14/audio$ mplayer -ao alsa:device=hw=2 320sample.mp3
.../chp14/audio$ mplayer -ao alsa:device=hw=3 320sample.mp3
.../chp14/audio$ aplay -D plughw:2,0 cheering.wav
```

The sound quality is audibly richer on the Sound Blaster adapter (card 2) than the Dynamode adapter (card 3). However, the quality of the Dynamode adapter is good for its price, and its manual volume control feature is useful.

The HDMI device adapter can also be used, either by connecting a Beagle board directly to an HDMI receiver or HDMI television (or a monitor with built-in speakers) or by using a VGA adapter to extract the HDMI audio channel to a 3.5mm stereo audio jack. The quality of the audio that is extracted from the latter devices can be quite variable and can suffer from auto-gain line noise when no audio stream is being played back.

To test an output device, you can use the speaker-test utility (where -c2 indicates two channels are to be tested).

```
../chp14/audio$ speaker-test -D plughw:2,0 -c2
```

The ALSA utilities also provide you with detailed information about the capabilities of a USB device. For example, amixer can be used to get and set an adapter's available properties. Using amixer on the Sound Blaster device provides its current state information:

```
debian@ebb:~/exploringbb/chp14/audio$ amixer -c 2
Simple mixer control 'Speaker',0
  Capabilities: pvolume pswitch pswitch-joined
  Playback channels: Front Left - Front Right
  Limits: Playback 0 - 151
  Mono: Front Left: Playback 44 [29%] [-20.13dB] [on]
  Front Right: Playback 44 [29%] [-20.13dB] [on]
Simple mixer control 'Mic',0
  Capabilities: pvolume pvolume-joined cvolume cvolume-joined pswitch
    pswitch-joined cswitch cswitch-joined
  Playback channels: Mono      Capture channels: Mono
  Limits: Playback 0 - 32 Capture 0 - 16
  Mono: Playback 23 [72%] [34.36dB] [off] Capture 0 [0%] [0.00dB] [on]
Simple mixer control 'Auto Gain Control',0
  Capabilities: pswitch pswitch-joined
  Playback channels: Mono      Mono: Playback [on]
```

To get its available control settings, use the following:

```
debian@ebb:~/exploringbb/chp14/audio$ amixer -c 2 controls
numid=3,iface=MIXER,name='Mic Playback Switch'
numid=4,iface=MIXER,name='Mic Playback Volume'
numid=7,iface=MIXER,name='Mic Capture Switch'
numid=8,iface=MIXER,name='Mic Capture Volume' ...
```

Therefore, to control the Speaker Playback Volume setting, you can use this:

```
...$ amixer -c 2 cset iface=MIXER,name='Speaker Playback Volume' 10,10
numid=6,iface=MIXER,name='Speaker Playback Volume'
  ; type=INTEGER,access=rw---R--,values=2,min=0,max=151,step=0
  : values=10,10 | dBminmax-min=-28.37dB,max=-0.06dB
```

This adjusts the volume on the speaker output of the Sound Blaster USB card—the 10,10 values are the left and right volume percentage settings, so 0,30 would turn off the left channel and set the volume level at 30 percent for the right channel.

Internet Radio Playback

You can play internet radio channels using the same mplayer application. For example, by using www.internet-radio.com, you can search for a radio station of your preference to determine its IP address. You can then stream the audio to your USB adapter using the following:

```
.../chp14/audio$ mplayer -ao alsa:device=hw=2 http://178.18.137.246:80
MPlayer 1.3.0 (Debian), built with gcc-6.2.1 (C) 2000-2016 MPlayer Team
do_connect: could not connect to socket
connect: No such file or directory
Failed to open LIRC support. You will not be able to use your remote control.
Playing http://178.18.137.246:80.
Resolving 178.18.137.246 for AF_INET6...
Couldn't resolve name for AF_INET6: 178.18.137.246
Connecting to server 178.18.137.246[178.18.137.246]: 80...
Name    : Pinguin Radio          Genre  : Alternative
Website: http://www.pinguinradio.com
Public : yes                     Bitrate: 320kbit/s
Cache size set to 320 Kbytes     Cache fill:  0.00% (0 bytes)
ICY Info: StreamTitle='Placebo & David Bowie  - Without You I'm Nothing
';StreamUrl='http://www.pinguinradio.com';  ...
```

This stream runs at 10 percent CPU and 5 percent memory usage on a BBB with good sound quality (regardless of what you might think of the music itself!). In fact, with multiple sound output devices, there is no difficulty in configuring a Beagle board to connect to multiple internet radio streams simultaneously and streaming audio to separate audio adapters.

Recording Audio

The USB adapters and the USB webcams can be used to capture audio directly to the Beagle board file system. You can use the arecord utility to provide a list of the available devices—for example, with one webcam and the two USB audio adapters connected:

```
debian@ebb:~$ arecord -l
**** List of CAPTURE Hardware Devices ****
```

```
card 1: C920 [HD Pro Webcam C920], device 0: USB Audio [USB Audio]
  Subdevices: 1/1    Subdevice #0: subdevice #0
card 2: U0x41e0x30d3 [USB Device 0x41e:0x30d3], device 0: USB Audio ...
  Subdevices: 1/1    Subdevice #0: subdevice #0
card 3: Device [USB PnP Sound Device], device 0: USB Audio [USB Audio]
  Subdevices: 1/1    Subdevice #0: subdevice #0
```

These devices are also indexed at the following /proc location:

```
debian@ebb:~$ cat /proc/asound/cards
 0 [Black      ]: TI_BeagleBone_B - TI BeagleBone Black
 1 [C920       ]: USB-Audio - HD Pro Webcam C920
 2 [U0x41e0x30d3]: USB-Audio - USB Device 0x41e:0x30d3
 3 [Device     ]: USB-Audio - USB PnP Sound Device
```

You can record audio from each of the audio capture devices using the arecord utility and the device's address. Interestingly, the LED does not light on the webcams described when they are recording only audio!

```
debian@ebb:~/tmp$ arecord -f cd -D plughw:2,0 -d 20 test.wav
Recording WAVE 'test.wav' : Signed 16 bit Little Endian, Rate 44100 Hz
```

The waveform audio file format (WAV) stores uncompressed audio data, which will quickly consume your file storage free space. To avoid this, you can compress WAV files into the popular MP3 compressed format using the LAME MP3 encoder, as follows:

```
debian@ebb:~$ sudo apt install lame
debian@ebb:/tmp$ lame test.wav output.mp3
LAME 3.99.5 32bits (http://lame.sf.net)
Using polyphase lowpass filter, transition band: 16538 Hz - 17071 Hz
Encoding test.wav to output.mp3
Encoding as 44.1 kHz j-stereo MPEG-1 Layer III (11x) 128 kbps qval=3
    Frame      | CPU time/estim | REAL time/estim | play/CPU | ETA
    767/767(100%)|  0:09/    0:09|   0:09/    0:09|  2.1909x| 0:00
```

A recording test was performed on the BBB that uses each of the two USB adapters. A Zoom H1 Handy Recorder (www.zoom.co.jp) was used to capture my voice. The analog stereo line output of the Zoom H1 was connected to the analog stereo line in of each adapter, and the following steps were used to record the audio for each adapter:

```
.../audio/testMicrophone$ arecord -f cd -D plughw:2,0 -d 45 testX.wav
.../chp14/audio/testMicrophone$ lame -b 128 testX.wav testX.mp3
```

A digital copy of the audio (i.e., digitally copied off the Zoom H1) is also provided in the Git repository for comparison. All three files are encoded at a sampling rate of 44.1kS/sec with a bit rate of 128Kb/sec. You can play these files directly on your desktop computer using the address tiny.cc/beagle1407.

```
.../chp14/audio/testMicrophone$ ls
ZoomH1DigitalSource.mp3  testCreative.mp3  testDynamode.mp3
```

Line noise is audible in both versions when compared to the original digital audio data, but there is not a significant difference in the quality of the audio recording from each USB audio adapter.

Audio Network Streaming

Earlier in this chapter, a description is provided of video streaming to the network using avconv. It is also possible to use the same application to stream audio as it is captured by an audio device, live to the network. For example, here is the command required to stream audio from a device attached to the address 2,0 using UDP to a desktop computer (at 192.168.7.1):

```
debian@ebb:/tmp$ avconv -ac 1 -f alsa -i hw:2,0 -acodec libmp3lame →
 -ab 32k -ac 1 -f mp3 udp://192.168.7.1:12345
ffmpeg version 3.2.12-1~deb9u1 Copyright (c) 2000-2018 the FFmpeg developers
 built with gcc 6.3.0 (Debian 6.3.0-18+deb9u1) 20170516  ...
Guessed Channel Layout for Input Stream #0.0 : mono
Input #0, alsa, from 'hw:2,0':
 Duration: N/A, start: 1536103924.360745, bitrate: 768 kb/s
   Stream #0:0: Audio: pcm_s16le, 48000 Hz, mono, s16, 768 kb/s
Output #0, mp3, to 'udp://192.168.7.1:12345':
 Metadata: TSSE : Lavf57.56.101
   Stream #0:0: Audio: mp3 (libmp3lame), 48000 Hz, mono, s16p, 32 kb/s
   Metadata: encoder : Lavc57.64.101 libmp3lame
Stream mapping: Stream #0:0 -> #0:0 (pcm_s16le (native) -> mp3 (libmp3lame))
Press [q] to stop, [?] for help
size=      73kB time=00:00:18.52 bitrate=  32.1kbits/s speed=0.993x
```

A desktop player such as VLC can be used to open the network UDP stream. For example, in VLC use Media ➪ Open Network Stream and set the network URL to be: udp://@:12345.

NOTE Wireshark (www.wireshark.org) **is a great tool for debugging network connection and communications problems that might occur in audio/video streaming and network socket programming (as in Chapters 11 and 12).**

Bluetooth A2DP Audio

The use of a Bluetooth adapter is first introduced in Chapter 12 for general-purpose serial communication. It is used again in Chapter 13 to attach peripherals to the BBB. Here again, Bluetooth can be used with a Beagle board—this time to communicate with audio devices.

One of the most common uses of the Bluetooth wireless communication system is for the connection of smartphones to in-car audio systems or to home entertainment centers. For this purpose, the Bluetooth *Advanced Audio Distribution*

Profile (A2DP) can be used to stream high-quality stereo audio from a media source to a media sink. The *source device* (SRC) acts as the source of a digital audio stream (e.g., Bluetooth headset, smartphone media player), which is sent in a compressed format to a *sink device* (SNK) (e.g., Bluetooth headphones, stereo receiver, in-car receiver).

When connected to a USB Bluetooth adapter, the Beagle board can be configured to act as an A2DP SRC or SNK. In this example, the board is configured as the SRC that is connected to a Hi-Fi system and Windows PC SNK. There are many low-cost A2DP audio receivers available that provide audio output on a 3.5mm stereo jack, which can be used to retrospectively add A2DP capability to Hi-Fi systems. However, the Sony Hi-Fi system that is used as the test platform has built-in A2DP support.

> **NOTE** It is recommended that you go through the process of connecting a smartphone to a Bluetooth A2DP SNK before attempting to connect the Beagle board. This will help you to verify that a connection is possible and help you to become familiar with the steps that are required to pair A2DP devices.

After a Bluetooth adapter is attached to the board, the first step is to install the necessary packages, configure it to support A2DP, and test that the Bluetooth audio SNKs are visible.

```
debian@ebb:~$ hcitool scan
Scanning ...   40:E2:30:13:CA:09       HOMEOFFICE-PC
               00:1D:BA:2E:BC:36       CMT-HX90BTR
               00:21:04:F9:35:8E       S68H
```

The board has detected the desktop PC, a Samsung device, and the Sony Hi-Fi system (CMT-HX90BTR).

An additional Linux service called PulseAudio, a background process that reroutes all audio streams, is required for recent A2DP services. It aims to support legacy devices, as well as to provide support for network audio (e.g., for VNC). PulseAudio is installed by default on the latest BeagleBoard.org Debian images. It provides useful user-interface tools, such as pavucontrol, which can be installed using the following:

```
debian@ebb:~$ sudo apt install pulseaudio pavucontrol →
 pulseaudio-module-bluetooth
debian@ebb:~$ pulseaudio --version
pulseaudio 10.0
debian@ebb:~$ pulseaudio --dump-modules
```

PulseAudio can be configured as follows:

```
debian@ebb:/etc/pulse$ sudo nano default.pa
```

The service can be started and stopped using the following (note: no `sudo`):

```
debian@ebb:~$ pulseaudio --kill
debian@ebb:~$ pulseaudio --start
```

One of the best ways to debug problems with PulseAudio is to kill the service and start the service using `pulseaudio -v` to get a verbose output.

Once you have ensure that PulseAudio is working correctly, you can execute it in daemon mode and begin the process of pairing the board with the Bluetooth device.

```
debian@ebb:~$ pulseaudio -D
debian@ebb:~$ sudo bluetoothctl
[bluetooth]# scan on
Discovery started ...
[CHG] Device 00:1D:BA:2E:BC:36 Name: CMT-HX90BTR
[CHG] Device 00:1D:BA:2E:BC:36 Alias: CMT-HX90BTR
[CHG] Device 00:1D:BA:2E:BC:36 LegacyPairing: yes
```

You can then connect to the SNKs using the following commands (you will likely have to enter a code [e.g., 0000] on both devices to pair the devices in the first step):

```
[bluetooth]# pair 00:1D:BA:2E:BC:36
Attempting to pair with 00:1D:BA:2E:BC:36
[CHG] Device 00:1D:BA:2E:BC:36 Connected: yes
[CHG] Device 00:1D:BA:2E:BC:36 Paired: yes
[bluetooth]# trust 00:1D:BA:2E:BC:36
[CHG] Device 00:1D:BA:2E:BC:36 Trusted: yes
Changing 00:1D:BA:2E:BC:36 trust succeeded
[bluetooth]# paired-devices
Device 00:1D:BA:2E:BC:36 CMT-HX90BTR
[bluetooth]# info 00:1D:BA:2E:BC:36
Device 00:1D:BA:2E:BC:36
        Name: CMT-HX90BTR       Alias: CMT-HX90BTR
        Class: 0x240428         Icon: audio-card
        Paired: yes             Trusted: yes
        Blocked: no             Connected: no
        LegacyPairing: yes      UUID: Audio Sink  ...
[bluetooth]# connect 00:1D:BA:2E:BC:36
Attempting to connect to 00:1D:BA:2E:BC:36
[CHG] Device 00:1D:BA:2E:BC:36 Connected: yes
Connection successful
```

Now if you use the PulseAudio sound configuration tool, `pacmd`, you can see that the Bluetooth device is now available as a sound sink.

```
debian@ebb:~$ pacmd
Welcome to PulseAudio 10.0! Use "help" for usage information.
>>> list-sinks
3 sink(s) available ...
index: 2      name: <bluez_sink.00_1D_BA_2E_BC_36> ...
>>> set-default-sink 2
```

You can then play audio files to the Bluetooth device by using PulseAudio as the device.

```
debian@ebb:~/exploringbb/chp14/audio$ aplay -D pulse cheering.wav
Playing WAVE 'cheering.wav' : Unsigned 8 bit, Rate 11025 Hz, Mono
```

Text-to-Speech

Once you have a working playback adapter connected to your Beagle board, you can then utilize Linux tools and online services to perform some interesting audio applications. One such application is text-to-speech (TTS)—it is possible to generate audio from text using tools such as eSpeak, FestVox Festival, and pico2wave. Currently, pico2wave must be built from source, but eSpeak and Festival are available in binary form in the Debian distribution.

You can install and get eSpeak to output audio to the aplay application as follows:

```
debian@ebb:~$ sudo apt install espeak
debian@ebb:~$ espeak "Hello Pocket Beagle" --stdout | aplay -D plughw:2,0
Playing WAVE 'stdin' : Signed 16 bit Little Endian, Rate 22050 Hz, Mono
```

You can install Festival and use it to output a text file to a WAV format file as follows:

```
debian@ebb:~$ sudo apt install festival festival-freebsoft-utils
debian@ebb:~$ nano hello.txt
debian@ebb:~$ more hello.txt
Hello Pocket Beagle
debian@ebb:~$ text2wave hello.txt -o hello.wav
debian@ebb:~$ ls -l *.wav
-rw-r--r-- 1 debian debian 52528 Sep  5 02:05 hello.wav
debian@ebb:~$ aplay -D plughw:2,0 hello.wav
Playing WAVE 'hello.wav' : Signed 16 bit Little Endian, Rate 16000 Hz, Mono
```

Text can be piped to the text2wave application as follows:

```
debian@ebb:~$ echo 'Hello Beagle' | text2wave -o test.wav
debian@ebb:~$ aplay -D plughw:2,0 test.wav
Playing WAVE 'test.wav' : Signed 16 bit Little Endian, Rate 16000 Hz, Mono
```

TTS engines can be integrated into your own applications. For example, you can use the output from a binary application as follows for the date application to provide dynamic speech output:

```
debian@ebb:~$ echo $(date +"It is %M minutes past %l %p") | →
    text2wave -o test.wav
debian@ebb:~$ aplay -D plughw:2,0 test.wav
Playing WAVE 'test.wav' : Signed 16 bit Little Endian, Rate 16000 Hz, Mono
debian@ebb:~$ lame test.wav test.mp3
debian@ebb:~$ mplayer -ao alsa:device=hw=2 test.mp3
```

```
debian@ebb:~$ ls -l test*
-rw-r--r-- 1 debian debian  7992 Sep  5 02:09 test.mp3
-rw-r--r-- 1 debian debian     0 Apr  5 01:46 test.txt
-rw-r--r-- 1 debian debian 81966 Sep  5 02:08 test.wav
```

Finally, it is also possible to install the CMU Sphinx Speech Recognition Toolkit on the Beagle board. Open-source speech recognition tools are notoriously difficult to train when compared to commercial offerings such as Nuance's Dragon NaturallySpeaking. However, with some time investment, PocketSphinx can be trained to provide good results.

Summary

After completing this chapter, you should be able to do the following:

- Capture image and video data on the Beagle board using USB webcams combined with Linux Video4Linux2 drivers and APIs.
- Use Video4Linux2 utilities to get information from and adjust the properties of video capture devices.
- Stream video data to the internet using Linux applications and UDP, multicast, and RTP streams.
- Use OpenCV to perform basic image processing on an embedded Linux device.
- Use OpenCV to perform a computer vision face-detection task.
- Utilize the Boost C++ libraries on the Beagle board.
- Play audio data using HDMI audio and USB audio adapters. The audio data can be raw waveform data or compressed MP3 data from the board file system or from internet radio streams.
- Record audio data using USB audio adapters or webcams.
- Stream audio data to the internet using UDP.
- Play audio to Bluetooth A2DP audio devices, such as Hi-Fi systems.
- Use text-to-speech (TTS) approaches to verbalize the text output of commands that are executed on the Beagle board.

Further Reading

There are many links to websites and documents provided throughout this chapter. Additional links and further information on the topics are provided at www.exploringbeaglebone.com/chapter14/ and the following:

- Video4Linux2 core documentation: tiny.cc/beagle1402
- V4L2 API Specification: tiny.cc/beagle1403

- The Boost C++ Libraries, Boris Schäling: `theboostcpplibraries.com`
- Computer Vision Cascaded Classification: `tiny.cc/beagle1409`
- CVonline: The Evolving, Distributed, Non-Proprietary, On-Line Compendium of Computer Vision, at `tiny.cc/beagle1410`

Real-Time Interfacing with the PRU-ICSS

The Beagle board AM335x SoC contains two programmable real-time units (PRUs) that can be used for certain real-time operations, and these are the focus of this chapter. The chapter begins with input and output examples that help explain the operation of the PRUs and their encompassing industrial communication subsystem (PRU-ICSS). The real-time capabilities of the AM335x are demonstrated using two applications—the first generates custom waveforms on a GPIO, and the second uses a low-cost ultrasonic distance sensor that requires precise timing to communicate the distance to an obstacle.

EQUIPMENT REQUIRED FOR THIS CHAPTER:

- Any Beagle board
- LED, FET (e.g., BS270), push button, capacitors, and resistors
- Oscilloscope (optional but useful)
- HC-SR04 ultrasonic sensor and logic-level translator board

Further resources for this chapter are available at www.exploringbeaglebone .com/chapter15/.

The PRU-ICSS

The Programmable Real-Time Unit and Industrial Communication Subsystem (PRU-ICSS) on the Beagle board's AM335x SoC contains two 32-bit 200MHz RISC cores, called PRUs. These PRUs have their own local memory allocation, but they can also use the BeagleBone P8/P9 or PocketBeagle P1/P2 header pins and share memory with the Linux host device.

The PRU-ICSS is a valuable addition to a general embedded Linux platform, as it can provide support for interfacing applications that have hard real-time constraints. It is important to note that the PRU-ICSS is not a hardware accelerator—it cannot be used to improve the general performance of code that is executing on the Linux host device. Rather, it can be used to manipulate inputs, outputs, and memory-mapped data structures to implement custom communication interfaces (e.g., simple I/O manipulation, bit-banging, SPI, UARTs). For example, in this chapter the PRU-ICSS is used to interface to an ultrasonic distance sensor by accurately measuring PWM signal properties.

The PRU-ICSS Architecture

Figure 15-1 outlines the PRU-ICSS architecture. There are two independent 32-bit RISC PRU cores (PRU0 and PRU1), each with 8KB of program memory and 8KB of data memory. The program memory stores the instructions to be executed by each PRU, and the data memory is typically used to store individual data values or data arrays that are manipulated by the program instructions. The PRU0 uses Data RAM0, and the PRU1 uses Data RAM1; however, each PRU can access the data memory of the other PRU, along with a separate 12KB of general-purpose shared memory.

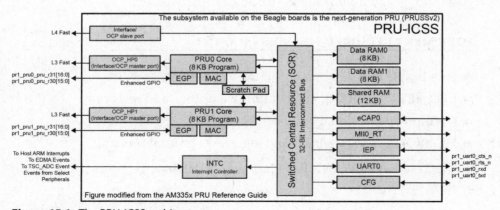

Figure 15-1: The PRU-ICSS architecture
Customized for the Beagle boards from an image that is courtesy of Texas Instruments

The PRU-ICSS subsystem that is available on the AM335x is the second-generation PRUSSv2, but not all its features are available on the Beagle board platform. In addition to the PRU cores and memory blocks, the most important blocks are illustrated in Figure 15-1, including the following:

- **Enhanced GPIO (EGP):** The PRU subsystem has a specific set of fast GPIOs, many of which are accessible via the BBB P8/P9 and PocketBeagle P1/P2 headers.

- **OCP master port:** Facilitates access to external Linux host memory. For example, this block also allows the PRUs to manipulate the state of GPIOs that are used in Chapter 6.

- **Multiplier with optional accumulation (MAC):** This block can be used to multiply two 32-bit operands and provide a 64-bit result.

- **Interrupt controller (INTC):** An interrupt controller can be used to notify each PRU that an event has occurred or to notify the host device of events (e.g., that the PRU executable program has run to completion).

- **Scratch pad (SPAD):** This provides three banks of 30 × 32-bit registers that are shared between the two PRU cores.

- **UART0:** A UART device with a dedicated 192MHz clock is available on the Beagle board headers.

The Switched Central Resource (SCR) connects the PRUs to the other resources inside the PRU-ICSS. PRUs have access to resources on the AM335x (e.g., regular GPIOs) using the Interface/OCP master port. Linux host memory can also be used by the PRUs; however, its use is several times slower than using PRU memory, as memory access needs to be routed external to the PRU-ICSS, and back in via the PRU-ICSS Interface/OCP slave port.

The Remote Processor Framework

The Linux remote processor framework, *remoteproc*, is designed to allow heterogeneous multiprocessor SoCs (HMPSoCs) to control the various remote/slave processors in a unified manner. The AM335x is an HMPSoC, as the PRU-ICSS has a different hardware architecture than the Arm Cortex-A8 main processor.

The remoteproc framework allows a main processor that is running Linux to control the slave processors via OS device bindings. For example, by using the following simple commands on a Beagle board, you can turn off, load new firmware, and turn on a PRU device:

```
root@ebb:/sys/class/remoteproc/remoteproc1# echo 'stop' > state
root@ebb:/sys/class/remoteproc/remoteproc1# cat state
offline
```

```
root@ebb:.../remoteproc1# echo 'am335x-pru0-fw' > firmware
root@ebb:.../remoteproc1# echo 'start' > state
root@ebb:.../remoteproc1# cat state
running
```

In this example, PRU0 is controlled, and the firmware from the `/lib/firmware/am335x-pru0-fw` file is loaded into the PRU. You can change this file at run time and thereby load new binary firmware (presently this must be in ELF32 form) to the PRU. The PRU must be stopped before you can write new PRU programs (i.e., firmware) to the device.

The remoteproc framework provides advanced features such as a *remote processor messaging framework* (rpmsg) that allows kernel drivers to communicate with processors. Each rpmsg device is a communication channel, termed *channel*, and the remote device is termed the *destination* rpmsg address. A driver listens to a channel, in which the receive callback is associated with a unique address value. When messages arrive, they are then dispatched by the *rpmsg core* to the registered driver.

> **NOTE** Linux kernel and device support for remoteproc and rpmsg is only just emerging and is currently subject to frequent updates. These updates may alter paths and commands, so check the following list of important documents for changes.

Important Documents

The most important documents that are available to describe the PRU-ICSS are listed here and at the chapter web page:

- **The PRU-ICSS Reference Guide:** This document is the main reference for the PRU-ICSS hardware: `tiny.cc/beagle1501`
- **The PRU-ICSS Getting Started Guide on Linux:** `tiny.cc/beagle1502`
- **The PRU Debugger User Guide:** `tiny.cc/beagle1503`
- **The Remote Processor Framework:** `tiny.cc/beagle1504`
- **The Processor Messaging Framework:** `tiny.cc/beagle1505`

The descriptions in this chapter refer to the preceding documents repeatedly, so it is useful to have them on hand.

Development Tools for the PRU-ICSS

Two tools must be installed to build and test the example applications that are described in this chapter, the PRU CGT and the PRU Debugger.

The PRU Code Generation Tools

Texas Instruments released the PRU Code Generation Tools (CGT) in May 2017. These development tools have full support for the remote processor framework.

- The *compiler* (clpru) takes in C/C++ (C89/C99) source code and produces assembly language code.
- The *assembler* (built in to clpru) translates assembly language code into machine object (.object) files.
- The *linker* (lnkpru) combines the object files into a single executable object file (.out). This single executable object file can be executed directly on a PRU device.

The compiler can be invoked and has the general usage:

```
clpru [options] [filenames] [--run_linker [link_options] [object files]]
```

where source filenames must be placed before the --run_linker option, and all linker options must be placed after this option. In this chapter, the clpru is called from within a Makefile file because of the significant number of required configuration options. There is further detail on the CGT at tiny.cc/beagle1506 and the compiler at tiny.cc/beagle1507.

The first step is to install the compiler on your Beagle board. Browse to www .ti.com/tool/download/PRU-CGT-2-1/ and determine the link to the latest download version. At the time of writing, this is version 2.1.5, which can be installed as follows:

```
debian@ebb:~$ wget http://software-dl.ti.com/codegen/esd/cgt_publ →
ic_sw/PRU/2.1.5/ti_cgt_pru_2.1.5_armlinuxa8hf_busybox_installer.sh
...~$ chmod ugo+x ti_cgt_pru_2.1.5_armlinuxa8hf_busybox_installer.sh
...~$ sudo ./ti_cgt_pru_2.1.5_armlinuxa8hf_busybox_installer.sh
Installing PRU Code Generation tools version 2.1.5 into /
  please wait, or press CTRL-C to abort
Extracting archive
Installing files
[####################] 100%
Installed successfully into /
debian@ebb:~$ clpru --compiler_revision
2.1.5
debian@ebb:~$ whereis clpru
clpru: /usr/bin/clpru
```

The PRU Debugger

The PRU Debugger, prudebug (sourceforge.net/projects/prudebug/), is a useful tool for identifying problems with your PRU program code. It can be executed in a separate terminal and used to view the registers when the PRU program is halted. For example, it can display the registers as follows (please note that the unusual register values in R00 to R07 result from an example in this chapter):

```
root@ebb:~# prudebug
PRU Debugger v0.25
(C)2011, 2013 by Arctica Technologies.  All rights reserved.
Written by Steven Anderson
Using /dev/mem device.
Processor type          AM335x
PRUSS memory address    0x4a300000
PRUSS memory length     0x00040000
   offsets below are in 32-bit word addresses (not ARM byte addr)
   PRU          Instruction     Data         Ctrl
   0            0x0000d000      0x00000000   0x00008800
   1            0x0000e000      0x00000800   0x00009000
PRU0> r
Register info for PRU0
   Control register: 0x00000001+
   Reset PC:0x0000 STOPPED, FREE_RUN, COUNTER_DISABLED, NOT_SLEEPING,
   PROC_DISABLED    Program counter: 0x003b
   Current instruction: HALT
   R00: 0x00010008  R08: 0xd767338a  R16: 0x00000020  R24: 0x80000000
   R01: 0xebbfeed0  R09: 0xfcccfbf7  R17: 0xffffff50  R25: 0x733c6942
   R02: 0xebbfeed1  R10: 0xbaff8256  R18: 0x00000403  R26: 0x3a8215cd
   R03: 0xebbfeed2  R11: 0x43935b82  R19: 0x00091e38  R27: 0xaa7935e9
   R04: 0xebbfeed3  R12: 0x5097debd  R20: 0xc0490000  R28: 0xff5fe5dd
   R05: 0xebbfeed4  R13: 0xb3b7db2e  R21: 0x40490000  R29: 0xe6b79da6
   R06: 0xebbfeed5  R14: 0x00000003  R22: 0x00000000  R30: 0x00000000
   R07: 0xebbfeed6  R15: 0x0000003b  R23: 0x00000000  R31: 0x00000000
```

The PRU debugger can also be used to load binaries into the PRUs, display instruction/data memory spaces, disassemble instruction memory space, and start/halt or single-step a PRU. This is useful, as it is difficult to debug programs that are running on the PRU because of the absence of a standard output. For example, you can switch PRU using the following:

```
PRU0> pru 1
Active PRU is PRU1.
```

Or, you can display the current values in PRU data memory:

```
PRU0> DD
Absolute addr = 0x0000, offset = 0x0000, Len = 16
[0x0000] 0xebbfeed0 0xebbfeed1 0x00000000 0x00000000
[0x0004] 0x00000000 0x00000000 0x00000000 0x00000000
[0x0008] 0x00000000 0x00000000 0x00000000 0x00000000
[0x000c] 0x00000000 0x00000000 0x00000000 0x00000000
```

Use Q to quit the debugger, RESET to reset the current PRU, SS to single step, G to start the processor, and BR to set a breakpoint. The debugger is revisited shortly in the first PRU program example.

Using the AM335x PRU-ICSS

The PRU-ICSS is not configured for use on the Beagle boards by default; therefore, you must first enable it and test that it is working.

Setting Up the Board for Remoteproc

There are virtual capes available for the Beagle board that allow you to easily enable the PRU. The /boot/uEnv.txt configuration file allows you to choose between two PRU interfacing models, remoteproc and UIO. UIO was used in the first edition of this book but is no longer supported under the latest kernel versions.

> **NOTE** It is highly recommended that you use the remoteproc framework rather than UIO so as to retain future support and kernel compatibility. If for some reason you must use UIO, please see the /chp15/uio/ directory for example code from the previous edition of this book.

Edit the /boot/uEnv.txt file as follows to uncomment the pru_rproc line, which should be edited to identify the device tree binary (.dtbo) for the kernel version you are currently running. In my case, I am running Linux 4.14.67, which means I must choose AM335X-PRU-RPROC-4-14-TI-00A0.dtbo from the /lib/firmware/ directory.

```
root@ebb:/boot# uname -r
4.14.67-ti-rt-r73
root@ebb:/boot# ls /lib/firmware/AM335X-PRU*
/lib/firmware/AM335X-PRU-RPROC-4-14-TI-00A0.dtbo
/lib/firmware/AM335X-PRU-RPROC-4-14-TI-PRUCAPE-00A0.dtbo
/lib/firmware/AM335X-PRU-RPROC-4-4-TI-00A0.dtbo
...
/lib/firmware/AM335X-PRU-UIO-00A0.dtbo
root@ebb:/boot# more uEnv.txt
...
###PRUSS OPTIONS
###pru_rproc (4.4.x-ti kernel)
#uboot_overlay_pru=/lib/firmware/AM335X-PRU-RPROC-4-4-TI-00A0.dtbo
uboot_overlay_pru=/lib/firmware/AM335X-PRU-RPROC-4-14-TI-00A0.dtbo
###pru_uio (4.4.x-ti, 4.14.x-ti & mainline/bone kernel)
#uboot_overlay_pru=/lib/firmware/AM335X-PRU-UIO-00A0.dtbo
...
```

The PRU pins are listed in Figure 6-8 and Figure 6-9 of Chapter 6, where they are prefixed by pr1_pru0_ or pr1_pru1_. For example, P9_27/P2.34 in Figure 6-9 can be configured as a PRU input in Mode6 (pr1_pru0_pru_r31_0) and an output in Mode5 (pr1_pru0_pru_r30_0). This notation is described shortly. However, you will notice that many of the PRU pins, particularly on the BeagleBone P8 header, are already allocated to HDMI. At this point, you may also want to edit the uEnv.txt file to disable the video virtual cape.

```
root@ebb:~$ more /boot/uEnv.txt
...
###Disable auto loading of virtual capes (emmc/video/wireless/adc)
#disable_uboot_overlay_emmc=1
disable_uboot_overlay_video=1
...
```

On reboot you can use the dmesg command to check for errors that have arisen as a result of your edits to the uEnv.txt configuration file. For example, a fully functioning PRU-ICSS will result in similar boot messages to the following:

```
root@ebb:~# dmesg |grep pru
[  279.649950] pruss 4a300000.pruss: creating PRU cores and →
other child platform devices
[  279.823196] remoteproc remoteproc1: 4a334000.pru is available
[  279.823424] pru-rproc 4a334000.pru: PRU rproc node →
/ocp/pruss_soc_bus@4a326004/pruss@0/pru@34000 probed successfully
[  279.919415] remoteproc remoteproc2: 4a338000.pru is available
[  279.919695] pru-rproc 4a338000.pru: PRU rproc node →
/ocp/pruss_soc_bus@4a326004/pruss@0/pru@38000 probed successfully
```

Note that 4a334000.pru (PRU0) is associated with Linux remoteproc1 and that 4a338000.pru (PRU1) is associated with Linux remoteproc2. A call to lsmod will also list the associated LKMs.

```
debian@ebb:~$ lsmod|grep pru
pruss_soc_bus          16384  0
pru_rproc              28672  0
pruss                  16384  1 pru_rproc
pruss_intc             20480  1 pru_rproc
```

Testing Remoteproc under Linux

Remoteproc binds to a number of locations under sysfs, providing a straightforward mechanism for loading firmware and interacting with the individual PRUs. Once loaded, the PRUs should appear as follows, where once again 0x4a334000 is the address of PRU0 and 0x4a338000 is the address of PRU1.

```
root@ebb:/sys/bus/platform/drivers/pru-rproc# ls -l
lrwxrwxrwx 1 root root    0 Sep  6 05:54 4a334000.pru ...
lrwxrwxrwx 1 root root    0 Sep  6 05:54 4a338000.pru ...
```

```
lrwxrwxrwx 1 root root    0 Sep  6 05:54 module ...
--w------- 1 root root 4096 Nov  3  2016 uevent
root@ebb:/sys/bus/platform/drivers/pru-rproc# cd 4a334000.pru
root@ebb:/sys/bus/platform/drivers/pru-rproc/4a334000.pru# ls
driver     driver_override  modalias  of_node  power  remoteproc
subsystem  uevent
```

> **NOTE**   Please note that some of the paths used in this chapter are accessible only if you have switched to a root shell, for example, by using `sudo -i`.

Each PRU can be controlled using its `/sys/kernel/debug/` binding. For example, the following calls show the structure of these bindings, where `remoteproc1` is bound to PRU0 and `remoteproc2` is bound to PRU1. The entry for `remoteproc0` relates to the Wakeup M3 (CM3) remoteproc driver that helps with low-power tasks on the Cortex M3 co-processor in the AM33xx family of devices—it has no role in controlling the PRU-ICSS.

```
root@ebb:/sys/kernel/debug/remoteproc# ls
remoteproc0  remoteproc1  remoteproc2
root@ebb:/sys/kernel/debug/remoteproc# cd remoteproc1
root@ebb:/sys/kernel/debug/remoteproc/remoteproc1# ls -l
-r-------- 1 root root 0 Sep  6 05:51 carveout_memories
-r-------- 1 root root 0 Sep  6 05:51 name
-r-------- 1 root root 0 Sep  6 05:51 recovery
-r-------- 1 root root 0 Sep  6 05:51 regs
-r-------- 1 root root 0 Sep  6 05:51 resource_table
-rw------- 1 root root 0 Sep  6 05:51 single_step
```

USING THE REMOTEPROC LINUX REGISTER VIEWER

The `/sys/kernel/debug/remoteproc/` binding for each PRU provides useful tools, such as a register viewer that displays the current state of each PRU, including the full set of general-purpose and control registers.

```
root@ebb:~# cd /sys/kernel/debug/remoteproc/remoteproc1
root@ebb:/sys/kernel/debug/remoteproc/remoteproc1# cat regs
=============== Control Registers ===============
CTRL       := 0x00000001
STS (PC)   := 0x0000003b (0x000000ec)
WAKEUP_EN := 0x00000000
CYCLE      := 0x00000000
STALL      := 0x00000000
CTBIR0     := 0x00000000
CTBIR1     := 0x00000000
CTPPR0     := 0x00000000
CTPPR1     := 0x00000000
================ Debug Registers ================
```

```
GPREG0   := 0x00010008    CT_REG0   := 0x00020000
GPREG1   := 0xebbfeed0    CT_REG1   := 0x48040000
GPREG2   := 0xebbfeed1    CT_REG2   := 0x4802a000
GPREG3   := 0xebbfeed2    CT_REG3   := 0x00030000
GPREG4   := 0xebbfeed3    CT_REG4   := 0x00026000
GPREG5   := 0xebbfeed4    CT_REG5   := 0x48060000
GPREG6   := 0xebbfeed5    CT_REG6   := 0x48030000
GPREG7   := 0xebbfeed6    CT_REG7   := 0x00028000
...
GPREG31  := 0x00000000    CT_REG31  := 0x80000000
```

Note that this provides a view of the registers that is consistent with the earlier output in this chapter from the PRU Debugger.

You can also control each PRU using its `/sys/class/remoteproc/` binding, which allows you to update firmware and start and stop each PRU.

```
root@ebb:/sys/class/remoteproc# ls
remoteproc0  remoteproc1  remoteproc2
root@ebb:/sys/class/remoteproc# tree remoteproc1
remoteproc1
├── device -> ../../../4a334000.pru
├── firmware
├── power
│   ├── async
│   ├── autosuspend_delay_ms
│   ├── control
│   ├── runtime_active_kids
│   ├── runtime_active_time
│   ├── runtime_enabled
│   ├── runtime_status
│   ├── runtime_suspended_time
│   └── runtime_usage
├── state
├── subsystem -> ../../../../../../../../class/remoteproc
└── uevent
```

For example, to start and stop a PRU, you can use the following commands:

```
root@ebb:/sys/class/remoteproc/remoteproc1# echo 'stop' > state
root@ebb:/sys/class/remoteproc/remoteproc1# echo 'start' > state
root@ebb:/sys/class/remoteproc/remoteproc1# echo 'start' > state
-bash: echo: write error: Device or resource busy
```

The PRU cannot be started twice and will give the error shown earlier should you try to do so or to write firmware to the device while it is running.

A First PRU Example

A "Hello World" LED flashing application is developed in this section so that you can quickly get started with the PRU-ICSS. The subsequent sections provide more detailed instruction and more complex examples.

PRU-ICSS Enhanced GPIOs

Each PRU has a set of GPIOs that have enhanced functionality, such as parallel-to-serial conversion. Their internal signal names have the following naming convention: pr1_pru**x**_pru_r3**y**_**z**, where **x** is the PRU number (0 or 1), **y** defines whether the pin is an input (1) or an output (0), and **z** is the pin number (0–16). For example, pr1_pru0_pru_r30_5 is output 5 for PRU0, and pr1_pru0_pru_r31_3 is input 3 for PRU0.

In Chapter 6, Figures 6-8 and 6-9 list the enhanced GPIO pins that are available on the P8/P9 and P1/P2 headers. It is clear from these figures that the pin mux must be configured in Mode5 or Mode6 using the config-pin tool to utilize these inputs/outputs. Not all the pins are exported to the P8/P9 headers on the BeagleBone or the P1/P2 headers on the PocketBeagle.

A circuit is illustrated in Figure 15-2 that uses two enhanced PRU pins. This circuit is used for several of the examples in this chapter.

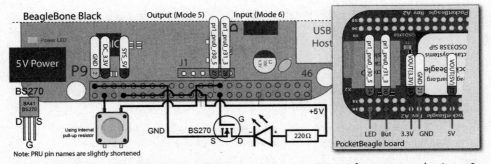

Figure 15-2: An example PRU0 circuit that uses pr1_pru0_pru_r30_5 for output and pr1_pru0_pru_r31_3 for input on the BBB and PocketBeagle boards

The pins must be configured to be in PRU mode. In this example, P9_27 (or P2.34 on the PocketBeagle) must be configured as a PRU output, as follows:

```
debian@ebb:~$ config-pin -l P9_27
default gpio gpio_pu gpio_pd gpio_input qep pruout pruin
debian@ebb:~$ config-pin P9_27 pruout
debian@ebb:~$ config-pin -q P9_27
P9_27 Mode: pruout
```

And, P9_28 (or P2.30 on the PocketBeagle) must be configured as a PRU input:

```
debian@ebb:~$ config-pin -l P9_28
default gpio gpio_pu gpio_pd gpio_input spi_cs pwm pwm2 pruout pruin
debian@ebb:~$ config-pin P9_28 in-
debian@ebb:~$ config-pin -q P9_28
P9_28 Mode: gpio_pd Direction: in Value: 0
debian@ebb:~$ config-pin P9_28 pruin
debian@ebb:~$ config-pin -q P9_28
P9_28 Mode: pruin
```

AUTOMATIC PIN CONFIGURATION ON BOOT

It would be useful if you could configure pins automatically on boot, rather than use manual configuration or a setup script. One way to achieve this is to write a script that is automatically executed on boot. The following steps write and test a basic script:

```
debian@ebb:/usr/bin$ sudo nano config-pru-pins.sh
debian@ebb:/usr/bin$ more config-pru-pins.sh
#!/bin/bash
config-pin P9_27 pruout
config-pin P9_28 pruin
debian@ebb:/usr/bin$ sudo chmod ugo+x config-pru-pins.sh
debian@ebb:/usr/bin$ ls -l config-*
-rwxr-xr-x 1 root root 41663 Aug  3 13:33 config-pin
-rwxr-xr-x 1 root root    59 Sep 21 02:22 config-pru-pins.sh
debian@ebb:/usr/bin$ ./config-pru-pins.sh
debian@ebb:/usr/bin$ ./config-pin -q P9_27
P9_27 Mode: pruout
debian@ebb:/usr/bin$ ./config-pin -q P9_28
P9_28 Mode: pruin
```

Next, you need a systemd service that will run on boot to call this script. Placing the service after `generic-board-startup.service` means that it will be one of the last boot services to run at boot time.

```
.../lib/systemd/system$ sudo nano ebb-set-pru-pins.service
.../lib/systemd/system$ more ebb-set-pru-pins.service
[Unit]
Description=Enable the PRU pins on boot
After=generic-board-startup.service

[Service]
Type=simple
User=root
WorkingDirectory=/usr/bin
ExecStart=/usr/bin/config-pru-pins.sh

[Install]
WantedBy=multi-user.target
```

Test and install the service.

```
...:~$ sudo systemd-analyze verify ebb-set-pru-pins.service
...:~$ sudo systemctl daemon-reload
...:~$ sudo systemctl enable ebb-set-pru-pins.service
Created symlink /etc/systemd/system/multi-user.target.wants/ebb-set
 -pru-pins.service → /lib/systemd/system/ebb-set-pru-pins.service.
```

Finally, reboot and test that all is working.

```
Debian GNU/Linux comes with ABSOLUTELY NO WARRANTY, to the extent
permitted by applicable law.
debian@ebb:~$ config-pin -q P9_27
P9_27 Mode: pruout
debian@ebb:~$ config-pin -q P9_28
P9_28 Mode: pruin
debian@ebb:~$ sudo systemctl status ebb-set-pru-pins.service
[sudo] password for debian:
● ebb-set-pru-pins.service - Enable the PRU pins on boot
   Loaded: loaded (/lib/systemd/system/ebb-set-pru-
   pins.service; enabled; vendor
   Active: inactive (dead) since Fri 2018-09-21 IST; 3min 8s ago
   Process: 1619 ExecStart=/usr/bin/config-pru-pins.sh
    (code=exited, status=0/SUC
  Main PID: 1619 (code=exited, status=0/SUCCESS)
Sep 21 02:41:04 ebb systemd[1]: Started Enable PRU pins on boot.
```

One useful tool to analyze boot times is `systemd-analyze blame`, which lists the time taken to execute each startup service. You can even plot the results, as illustrated in Figure 15-3, where the custom service can be analyzed against the entire boot sequence.

```
debian@ebb:~$ sudo systemd-analyze blame
    1min 44.791s generic-board-startup.service
        29.523s dev-mmcblk0p1.device
         6.060s loadcpufreq.service
         ...
debian@ebb:~$ sudo systemd-analyze plot > ~/boot_plot.svg
debian@ebb:~$ ls -l ~/boot_plot.svg
-rw-r--r-- 1 debian debian 266714 Sep 21 02:59 /home/debian/boot_plot.svg
```

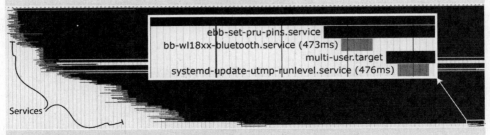

Figure 15-3: The output of the systemd analyze plot command with the `ebb-set-pru-pins.service` highlighted

A First PRU Program

The first PRU program is designed to flash the LED that is connected to pr1_pru0_pru_r30_5 (P9_27/P2.34) until a button that is connected to pr1_pru0_pru_r31_3 (P9_28/P2.30) is pressed (refer to Figure 15-2). This example is provided in C and in assembly language form.

A First PRU Program in C

The code for the PRU program is provided in Listing 15-1. This C code looks a little different than regular C code as it does not execute in Linux userspace; rather, it executes on a PRU. The LED is controlled by bit 5 in the register r30, which is accessed as hexadecimal 0x0000 0020 (i.e., 100000_2). Similarly, the button is controlled by bit 3 in the register r31, which is accessed as hexadecimal 0x0000 0008 (i.e., 1000_2). Please refer to the "Bit Manipulation in C/C++" feature in Chapter 6 for further details on the bitwise operations, which are performed in these examples.

Listing 15-1: /exploringbb/chp15/pru/ledFlash/ledFlash.c

```
/* Source Modified by Derek Molloy for Exploring BeagleBone Rev2
 * Based on the examples distributed by Texas Instruments  */

#include <stdint.h>
#include <pru_cfg.h>
#include "resource_table_empty.h"

volatile register uint32_t __R30;    // output gpio register
volatile register uint32_t __R31;    // input gpio register

void main(void) {
    volatile uint32_t led, button;  // for bit identifiers

    // Use pru0_pru_r30_5 as an output i.e., 100000 or 0x0020
    led = 0x0020;

    // Use pru0_pru_r31_3 as a button i.e., 1000 or 0x0008
    button = 0x0008;

    // Stop the loop when the button is pressed
    while (!(__R31 && button)) {     // while button bit not set
        __R30 ^= led;                // invert/flash the LED bit
        // delay for approx. 0.25s (one quarter second)
        __delay_cycles(50000000);
    }
    __halt();                        // end the program
}
```

The C program in Listing 15-1 is placed in a project directory with the following files:

- Makefile has all the build options for the project. You can call make, make clean to clear build files, and make install_PRUx to deploy the binary executable to a PRU.

- AM335x_PRU.cmd is a linker command file for linking PRU programs built with the compiler. It contains the memory map and definition for the PRU architecture.

- resource_table_empty.h is required by remoteproc to define the required resource table for the PRU cores.

```
debian@ebb:~/exploringbb/chp15/pru/ledFlashC$ ls -l
-rw-r--r-- 1 debian debian 3505 Sep  7 05:29 AM335x_PRU.cmd
-rw-r--r-- 1 debian debian 2326 Sep 18 00:09 ledFlash.c
-rw-r--r-- 1 debian debian 3616 Sep  7 05:29 Makefile
-rw-r--r-- 1 debian debian 2789 Sep  7 05:29 resource_table_empty.h
```

This project can be built using the Makefile file as follows:

```
.../chp15/pru/ledFlashC$ make
Building project: ledFlashC
Building file: ledFlash.c
Invoking: PRU Compiler
/usr/bin/clpru --include_path=/usr/lib/ti/pru-software-support-package/
include
--include_path=/usr/lib/ti/pru-software-support-package/include --
include_path=/usr/lib/ti/pru-software-support-package/include/am335x -v3 -O2
--display_error_number --endian=little --hardware_mac=on --obj_directory=gen
--pp_directory=gen -ppd -ppa -fe gen/ledFlash.object ledFlash.c
Building target: gen/ledFlashC.out
Invoking: PRU Linker
/usr/bin/clpru -v3 -O2 --display_error_number --endian=little
--hardware_mac=on
--obj_directory=gen --pp_directory=gen -ppd -ppa -z
-i/usr/lib/ti/pru-software-support-package/lib
-i/usr/lib/ti/pru-software-support-package/include --reread_libs
--warn_sections --stack_size=0x100 --heap_size=0x100 -o gen/ledFlashC.out
gen/ledFlash.object -mgen/ledFlashC.map ./AM335x_PRU.cmd --library=libc.a
--library=/usr/lib/ti/pru-software-support-package/lib/rpmsg_lib.lib
<Linking>
Finished building target: gen/ledFlashC.out
Output files can be found in the "gen" directory
Finished building project: ledFlashC
```

and then deployed to PRU0 using `make install_PRU0`:

```
.../chp15/pru/ledFlashC$ sudo make install_PRU0
Stopping current PRU0 application (/sys/class/remoteproc/remoteproc1)
Stop...  Installing firmware... Deploying firmware...
am335x-pru0-fw... Starting new PRU0 application... Start
```

Effectively, this `Makefile` builds a binary `ledFlashC.out` in the `gen/` directory, which is then copied to `/lib/firmware/am335x-pru0-fw` (hence the superuser requirement). In the same manner as previously described in this chapter, the PRU0 is stopped, the firmware file is written to PRU0 program memory, and then it is restarted.

```
.../chp15/pru/ledFlashC$ cd gen
.../chp15/pru/ledFlashC/gen$ ls
ledFlashC.map  ledFlashC.out  ledFlash.object  ledFlash.pp
.../chp15/pru/ledFlashC/gen$ ls -l ledFlashC.out
-rw-r--r-- 1 debian debian 32284 Sep 18 01:15 ledFlashC.out
.../chp15/pru/ledFlashC/gen$ cd ..
.../chp15/pru/ledFlashC$ ls -l /lib/firmware/am335x-pru0-fw
-rw-r--r-- 1 root root 32284 Sep 18 01:14 /lib/firmware/am335x-pru0-fw
```

A First PRU Program in Assembly

It is also possible to write this program in assembly language, which is sometimes more straightforward when designing timing-critical programs. The assembly code has the extension `.asm`, but you still require a C container program, such as that provided in Listing 15-2.

Listing 15-2: /exploringbb/chp15/pru/ledFlashASM/main.c

```c
#include <stdint.h>
#include <pru_cfg.h>
#include "resource_table_empty.h"

// the function is defined in ledFlashASM.asm in same dir
// declaration is here, definition is linked to the .asm

extern void start(void);  // not defined here, but in the .asm

void main(void) {
    START();                // call START in ledFlashASM.asm
}
```

The flash LED code in the project `ledFlashASM.asm` uses raw assembly code in Listing 15-3. The LED is turned on for 50ms and then off for 50ms, which means that the LED will flash at 10Hz (i.e., 10 times per second), resulting in the output shown in Figure 15-4.

Listing 15-3: /exploringbb/chp15/pru/ledFlashASM/ledFlashASM.asm

```
        .cdecls "main.c"
        .clink
        .global START
        .asg "5000000",  DELAY    ; hard define the DELAY
START:
        SET    r30, r30.t5      ; set the output LED pin (LED on)
        LDI32  r0, DELAY        ; load the delay value into REG0
DELAYON:
        SUB    r0, r0, 1        ; subtract 1 from the REG0 value
        QBNE   DELAYON, r0, 0   ; loop to DELAYON, unless REG0=0
LEDOFF:
        CLR    r30, r30.t5      ; clear the output pin (LED off)
        LDI32  r0, DELAY        ; Reset REG0 to the length of the delay
DELAYOFF:
        SUB    r0, r0, 1        ; decrement REG0 by 1
        QBNE   DELAYOFF, r0, 0  ; loop to DELAYOFF, unless REG0=0
        QBBC   START, r31, 3    ; is the button pressed? If not, loop
END:
        HALT                    ; halt the pru program
```

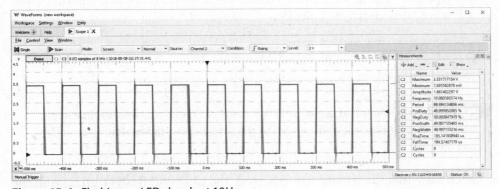

Figure 15-4: Flashing an LED cleanly at 10Hz

Details about the available assembly language instructions are provided later in this chapter, but the important instructions that are used in Listing 15-3 are as follows:

■ `SET r30.t5`: Sets bit 5 on register 30 to be high. REG30 is used to set the PRU0 GPIO pins high. Bit 5 specifically controls the `pr1_pru0_pru_r30_5` pin output.

- ▪ LDI32 r0, DELAY: Loads the 32-bit delay value (i.e., 5,000,000) in the register REG0. Registers are used here, just as variables are used in C. Assembly operations are performed on registers.

- ▪ DELAYON: A user-defined label to which the code can branch.

- ▪ SUB r0, r0, 1: Subtracts 1 from REG0 and stores the result in REG0. It is essentially the same as the code REG0 = REG0 - 1.

- ▪ QBNE DELAYON, r0, 0: Performs a quick branch if REG0 is not equal to 0. This creates a loop that loops these two instructions 5,000,000 times (taking exactly 50ms!).

- ▪ CLR r30, r30.t5: Clears bit 5 on register 30, setting the output low and turning the LED off.

- ▪ QBBC START, r31.t3: Does a quick branch to START if the r31.t3 bit is clear (i.e., 0). REG31 is the input register that is used to read the state of the input—t3 is bit 3, which is connected to the pr1_pru0_pru_r31_3 pin. As the button input pin is configured to have a pull-down resistor enabled, it will return 0 when it is not pressed and 1 when it is pressed. If the button is not pressed, then the program loops forever, continually flashing the LED. When the button is first found to be in the pressed state at this point during program execution, then the program continues to the next line.

- ▪ The program then ends with the call to HALT.

This program can be built using a call to the make command and then deployed to a PRU of your choice as follows:

```
.../chp15/pru/ledFlashASM$ make
.../chp15/pru/ledFlashASM$ sudo make install_PRU0
```

resulting in a file ledFlashASM.out in the gen/ directory.

> **NOTE** Remember that using nano -c ledFlashASM.asm displays line numbers, which is helpful in locating errors, as the compiler and linker identify errors by line number.

Each time that the program is executed, the LED will flash at 10Hz until the button is pressed. One impressive feature of this application is the regularity of the output signal, which can be observed when the circuit is connected to an oscilloscope. Figure 15-4 illustrates the output and the frequency measurements, and it is clear from the measurements that the signal does not suffer from the jitter issues that affect a similar circuit in Chapter 6. Also, the program is running with almost no Linux overhead.

The PRU-ICSS in Detail

It is useful to have a working example in place, but some features of the PRU-ICSS must be covered in more detail to ensure that you can write your own applications that build on the preceding example.

Registers

In the previous example, one register (REG0) is used as the memory location in which to store and decrement the time delay. *Registers* provide the fastest way to access data—assembly instructions are applied to registers, and they complete in a single clock cycle. However, each PRU core has 32 registers (0–31). Registers REG1 to REG29 are general-purpose registers, whereas REG30 and REG31 are special-purpose registers, and REG0 is used for indexing (or as a general-purpose register). It should be noted that 30 general-purpose registers is a generous number for a microcontroller, as these registers can be reused repeatedly. For example, in the previous PRU program, both delays are performed using a single register.

Register values are 32-bit variables that can be accessed using a suffix notation, which is illustrated in Figure 15-5. In Listing 15-3, shown earlier, bit 5 of REG30 is accessed using r30.t5. There are three suffixes.

- word .w*n* (where *n* is 0. . .2)
- byte .b*n* (where *n* is 0. . .3)
- bit .t*n* (where *n* is 0. . .31)

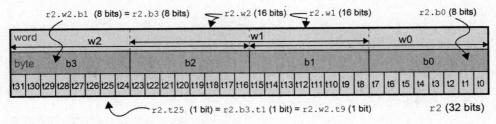

Figure 15-5: PRU register bit field notation

It is important to note that there are three word indices—w1 is offset by eight bits and therefore overlaps half the contents of w0 and w2. Figure 15-5 also provides some usages—for example, r2.w1.b1 requests byte 1 of word 1, which is eight bits in length (i.e., bits 16 to 23 of r2). This is equivalent to a request for r2.b2 (eight bits), but it is *not* equivalent to r2.w2, which has the same starting address but is 16 bits in length. Examples of illegal register calls include `r2.w2.b2`, `r2.t4.b1`, `r2.w1.t16`, and `r2.b0.b0`.

REG31 is called the *PRU Event/Status Register* (r31). It is a particularly complex register, which behaves differently depending on whether you are writing to it or reading from it. When writing to REG31, it provides a mechanism for sending output events to the Interrupt Controller (INTC). By writing an event number (0 to 31) to the five LSBs (`PRU_VEC[4:0]`) and setting bit 5 (`PRU_VEC_VALID`) high, an output event can be sent to the Linux host.

When reading from REG31, it provides the state of the enhanced GPIO inputs. For example, in Listing 15-3, the line `QBBC START, r31.t3` reads bit 3 from REG31 to determine whether the button is in a pressed state. Essentially, it reads the state of the GPIO that is connected to bit 3.

REG30 is used by the PRU to set enhanced GPIO outputs. For example, in Listing 15-3, the line `SET r30.t5` is used to set bit 5 of REG30 high. In turn, this results in the associated GPIO output switching the LED on.

Local and Global Memory

The PRUs have general-purpose local memory that can be used by PRU programs to store and retrieve data. Because this local PRU memory is mapped to a global address space on the Linux host, it can also be used to share data between PRU programs and programs running on the Linux host. Figure 15-6 illustrates the memory mappings.

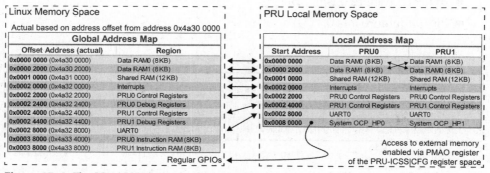

Figure 15-6: The PRU-ICSS memory address maps
Image created from data that is courtesy of Texas Instruments

It is important to note that there is a slight difference between the PRU memory spaces. PRU0 accesses its primary memory (Data RAM0) at address 0x00000000, and PRU1 also accesses its primary memory (Data RAM1) at address 0x00000000. However, each PRU can also access the data RAM of the other PRU at address 0x00002000. In addition, 12KB of shared memory can be used by both PRUs at the local address 0x00010000. The PRU cores can also use the global memory map, but there is latency as access is routed through the OCP slave port (refer to Figure 15-1).

Listing 15-4 is a short C program that uses PRU0 to write seven 32-bit values to three different memory locations, PRU0 memory, PRU1 memory, and the shared PRU memory. The addresses of each of these memory locations is illustrated in Figure 15-6. The values were chosen to be clearly identifiable, that is, 0xEBBFEEDx.

Listing 15-4: /exploringbb/chp15/pru/pruTest/pruTest.c

```c
#include <stdint.h>
#include <pru_cfg.h>
#include "resource_table_empty.h"

#define PRU0_DRAM   0x00000000
volatile uint32_t *pru0Mem = (unsigned int *) PRU0_DRAM;
#define PRU1_DRAM   0x00002000
volatile uint32_t *pru1Mem = (unsigned int *) PRU1_DRAM;
#define SHARE_MEM   0x00010000
volatile uint32_t *shared =  (unsigned int *) SHARE_MEM;

extern void start(void);

void main(void) {
    pru0Mem[0] = 0xEBBFEED0;
    pru0Mem[1] = 0xEBBFEED1;
    pru1Mem[0] = 0xEBBFEED2;
    pru1Mem[1] = 0xEBBFEED3;
    shared[0]  = 0xEBBFEED4;
    shared[1]  = 0xEBBFEED5;
    shared[2]  = 0xEBBFEED6;
    start();
}
```

The code in Listing 15-5 is a PRU program that is started by the call to start() in Listing 15-4. This assembly program simply loads the registers r1 to r7 with the values in the different memory locations. The register r0 is used as a temporary register that stores the address value to load.

Listing 15-5: /exploringbb/chp15/pru/pruTest/pruTest.asm

```asm
    .cdecls "pruTest.c"
    .clink
        .global start
start:
    LDI32   r0, 0x00000000   ; load r0 with the PRU0 address to load
    LBBO    &r1, r0, 0, 4    ; load r1 with value at r0 EBBFEED0
    LDI32   r0, 0x00000004   ; load r0 with the next PRU0 address
    LBBO    &r2, r0, 0, 4    ; load r2 with the EBBFEED1
```

```
LDI32    r0, 0x00002000    ; load r0 with the PRU1 address to load
LBBO     &r3, r0, 0, 4     ; load r3 with value at r0 EBBFEED2
LDI32    r0, 0x00002004    ; load r0 with the next PRU1 address
LBBO     &r4, r0, 0, 4     ; load r4 with the EBBFEED3

LDI32    r0, 0x00010000    ; load r0 with the shared address
LBBO     &r5, r0, 0, 4     ; load r5 with the EBBFEED4
LDI32    r0, 0x00010004    ; load r0 with the next shared address
LBBO     &r6, r0, 0, 4     ; load r6 with the EBBFEED5
LDI32    r0, 0x00010008    ; load r0 with the next shared address
LBBO     &r7, r0, 0, 4     ; load r7 with the EBBFEED6

HALT
```

The project can be built and executed using the following:

```
debian@ebb:~/exploringbb/chp15/pru/pruTest$ make
debian@ebb:~/exploringbb/chp15/pru/pruTest$ sudo make install_PRU0
```

Once this code is executed, you can access the memory addresses from Linux userspace using the devmem2 tool and the address map in Figure 15-6, which results in the following:

```
debian@ebb:~/exploringbb/chp15/pru/pruTest$ sudo -i
root@ebb:~# /home/debian/devmem2 0x4a300000
Memory mapped at address 0xb6f6a000.
... Value at address 0x4A300000 (0xb6f6a000): 0xEBBFEED0
root@ebb:~# /home/debian/devmem2 0x4a300004
... Value at address 0x4A300004 (0xb6fe8004): 0xEBBFEED1
root@ebb:~# /home/debian/devmem2 0x4a302000
... Value at address 0x4A302000 (0xb6fe3000): 0xEBBFEED2
root@ebb:~# /home/debian/devmem2 0x4a302004
... Value at address 0x4A302004 (0xb6f03004): 0xEBBFEED3
root@ebb:~# /home/debian/devmem2 0x4a310000
... Value at address 0x4A310000 (0xb6fae000): 0xEBBFEED4
root@ebb:~# /home/debian/devmem2 0x4a310004
... Value at address 0x4A310004 (0xb6f51004): 0xEBBFEED5
root@ebb:~# /home/debian/devmem2 0x4a310008
... Value at address 0x4A310008 (0xb6feb008): 0xEBBFEED6
```

The preceding values confirm that the mappings in Figure 15-6 are correct and that devmem2 is useful for verifying that the values in memory are as expected. Remember that it can also be used to write to memory locations.

You can use the remoteproc register view to confirm that the registers have been loaded, as described in Listing 15-5.

```
root@ebb:/sys/kernel/debug/remoteproc/remoteproc1# cat regs
============== Control Registers ==============
```

```
CTRL       := 0x00000001
STS (PC)   := 0x0000003b (0x000000ec)
...

=============== Debug Registers ===============
GPREG0  := 0x00010008   CT_REG0  := 0x00020000
GPREG1  := 0xebbfeed0   CT_REG1  := 0x48040000
GPREG2  := 0xebbfeed1   CT_REG2  := 0x4802a000
GPREG3  := 0xebbfeed2   CT_REG3  := 0x00030000
GPREG4  := 0xebbfeed3   CT_REG4  := 0x00026000
GPREG5  := 0xebbfeed4   CT_REG5  := 0x48060000
GPREG6  := 0xebbfeed5   CT_REG6  := 0x48030000
GPREG7  := 0xebbfeed6   CT_REG7  := 0x00028000 ...
```

You can also use the PRU debugger to confirm the same register and memory values.

```
root@ebb:~# prudebug
PRU Debugger v0.25
(C)2011, 2013 by Arctica Technologies. All rights reserved.
Written by Steven Anderson
Using /dev/mem device.
Processor type      AM335x
PRUSS memory address    0x4a300000
PRUSS memory length     0x00040000
offsets below are in 32-bit word addresses (not ARM byte addresses)
        PRU         Instruction     Data        Ctrl
        0           0x0000d000      0x00000000  0x00008800
        1           0x0000e000      0x00000800  0x00009000
PRU0> dd
Absolute addr = 0x0000, offset = 0x0000, Len = 16
[0x0000] 0xebbfeed0 0xebbfeed1 0x00000000 0x00000000
...
PRU0> r
Register info for PRU0
  Control register: 0x00000001
   Reset PC:0x0000  STOPPED, FREE_RUN, COUNTER_DISABLED,
     NOT_SLEEPING, PROC_DISABLED
  Program counter: 0x003b
   Current instruction: HALT
  R00: 0x00010008  R08: 0xd767338a  R16: 0x00000020  R24: 0x80000000
  R01: 0xebbfeed0  R09: 0xfcccfbf7  R17: 0xffffff50  R25: 0x733c6942
  R02: 0xebbfeed1  R10: 0xbaff8256  R18: 0x00000403  R26: 0x3a8215cd
  R03: 0xebbfeed2  R11: 0x43935b82  R19: 0x00091e38  R27: 0xaa7935e9
  R04: 0xebbfeed3  R12: 0x5097debd  R20: 0xc0490000  R28: 0xff5fe5dd
  R05: 0xebbfeed4  R13: 0xb3b7db2e  R21: 0x40490000  R29: 0xe6b79da6
  R06: 0xebbfeed5  R14: 0x00000003  R22: 0x00000000  R30: 0x00000000
  R07: 0xebbfeed6  R15: 0x0000003b  R23: 0x00000000  R31: 0x00000000
```

The PRUs have a *constants table,* which contains a list of commonly used addresses that are often used in memory load and store operations. This reduces the time required to load memory pointers into registers. Most of the constants are fixed, but some are programmable by using PRU control registers. The constants table is utilized later so that the PRU can access regular GPIOs that are outside the PRU-ICSS.

PRU Assembly Instruction Set

The PRU-ICSS has a relatively small RISC *instruction set architecture* (ISA), with approximately 45 instructions that can be categorized as arithmetic operations, logical operations, register load and store, and program flow control. A summary description of each of the instructions is provided in Figure 15-7. The full description of each instruction is available in the *PRU-ICSS Reference Guide*.

Instructions consist of an *operation code* (*opcode*) and a variable number of operands, where the third operand can often be a register or an *immediate value* (a simple number or an expression that evaluates to a constant value). Here's an example:

```
ADD REG1, REG2, OP(255)
```

where ADD is a mnemonic that evaluates to an opcode (e.g., 0x01 for ADD), REG1 is the target register, REG2 is a source register, and OP(255) can be another register field or an immediate value—it must be, or evaluate to, the range of 0_{10} to 255_{10} for the ADD operation. Here are some example usages (see the `chp15/pru/testASM/` project):

```
LDI32   r1, 0x25        ; set r1 = 0x25 = 37 (dec)
LDI32   r2, 4           ; set r2 = 4 (dec)
ADD     r1, r1, 5       ; set r1 = r1 + 5 = 42 (dec)
ADD     r2, r2, 1<<4    ; set r2 = r2 + 10000 (bin) = 20 (dec)
ADD     r1, r2, r1.w0   ; set r1 = r2 + r1.w0 = 20 + 42 = 62 (dec)
LDI32   r0, 0x00002000  ; place PRU1 data RAM1 base address in r0
SBBO    &r1, r0, 4, 4   ; write r1 to the address that is stored in r0
                        ; offset = 4 bytes, size of data = 4 bytes
```

If this example is run on PRU0, the value of r1 (62_{10} = 0x3e) is written to the PRU1 Data RAM1, which is at address 0x00002000 in the PRU1 memory space, and is at 0x4A302000 in Linux host memory space. The value is written at an offset of four bytes, so it appears at the address 0x4A302004 in the Linux host memory space. This code segment does not overwrite the 0xEBBFEED2 value (from the previous example) when an offset of four bytes is used:

```
root@ebb:~# /home/debian/devmem2 0x4a302000
Value at address 0x4A302000 (0xb6fd9000): 0xEBBFEED2
root@ebb:~# /home/debian/devmem2 0x4a302004
Value at address 0x4A302004 (0xb6f85004): 0x3E
```

Arithmetic Operations

	Short Description:	Definition:	Full Description:
ADD	Unsigned integer add	ADD REG1, REG2, OP(255)	Performs 32-bit add on two 32-bit zero extended source values
ADC	Unsigned integer add (carry)	ADC REG1, REG2, OP(255)	Performs 32-bit add on two 32-bit zero extended source values, plus a stored carry bit
SUB	Unsigned integer subtract	SUB REG1, REG2, OP(255)	Performs 32-bit subtract on two 32-bit zero extended source values
SUC	Unsigned integer subtract (carry)	SUC REG1, REG2, OP(255)	Performs 32-bit subtract on two 32-bit zero extended source values with carry (borrow)
RSB	Reverse unsigned int subtract	RSB REG1, REG2, OP(255)	Performs 32-bit subtract on two 32-bit zero extended source values. Source values reversed
RSC	Reverse unsigned integer subtract (carry)	RSC REG1, REG2, OP(255)	Performs 32-bit subtract on two 32-bit zero extended source values with carry (borrow). Source values reversed

Logical Operations

LSL	Logical shift left	LSL REG1, REG2, OP(31)	Performs 32-bit shift left of the zero extended source value
LSR	Logical shift right	LSR REG1, REG2, OP(31)	Performs 32-bit shift right of the zero extended source value
AND	Bitwise AND	AND REG1, REG2, OP(255)	Performs 32-bit logical AND on two 32-bit zero extended source values
OR	Bitwise OR	OR REG1, REG2, OP(255)	Performs 32-bit logical OR on two 32-bit zero extended source values
XOR	Bitwise XOR	XOR REG1, REG2, OP(255)	Performs 32-bit logical XOR on two 32-bit zero extended source values
NOT	Bitwise NOT	NOT REG1, REG2	Performs 32-bit logical NOT on the 32-bit zero extended source value
MIN	Copy minimum	MIN REG1, REG2, OP(255)	Compares two 32-bit zero extended source values and copies the smaller to REG1
MAX	Copy maximum	MAX REG1, REG2, OP(255)	Compares two 32-bit zero extended source values and copies the larger to REG1
CLR	Clear bit	CLR REG1, REG2, OP(31)	Clears the specified bit in the source and copies the result to the destination Also: CLR REG1, OP(31) CLR REG1, Rn.tx CLR Rn.tx
SET	Set bit	SET REG1, REG2, OP(31)	Sets the specified bit in the source and copies the result to the destination Also: SET REG1, OP(31) SET REG1, Rn.tx SET Rn.tx
SCAN	Register field scan	SCAN Rn, OP(255)	The SCAN instruction scans the register file for a particular value. It includes a configurable field width and stride. The width of the field to match can be set to 1, 2, or 4 bytes.
LMBD	Left-most bit detect	LMBD REG1, REG2, OP(255)	Scans REG2 from its left-most bit for a bit value matching bit 0 of OP(255), and writes the bit number in REG1 (writes 32 to REG1 if the bit is not found)

Register Load and Store

MOV	Copy value	MOV REG1, OP(65535)	Moves the value from OP(65535), zero extends it, and stores it into REG1
LDI	Load immediate	LDI REG1, IM(65535)	The LDI instruction moves value from IM(65535), zero extends it, and stores it into REG1
MVIB	Move register file indirect (8)	MVIB [*&]REG1, [*&]REG2	The MVIx instruction family moves a value from the source to the destination. The source, destination, or both can be register pointers.
MVIW	Move register file indirect (16)	MVIW [*&]REG1, [*&]REG2	
MVID	Move register file indirect (32)	VID [*&]REG1, [*&]REG2	
LBBO	Load byte burst	LBBO REG1, Rn2, OP(255), IM(124) LBBO REG1, Rn2, OP(255), bn	The LBBO instruction is used to read a block of data from memory into the register file. The memory address to read from is specified by a 32-bit register, using an optional offset.
SBBO	Store byte burst	SBBO REG1, Rn2, OP(255), IM(124) SBBO REG1, Rn2, OP(255), bn	The SBBO instruction is used to write a block of data from the register file into memory. The memory address to which to write is specified by a 32-bit register, using an optional offset.
LBCO	Load byte burst with constant table offset	LBCO REG1, Cn2, OP(255), IM(124) LBCO REG1, Cn2, OP(255), bn	The LBCO instruction is used to read a block of data from memory into the register file. The memory address from which to read is specified by a 32-bit constant register (Cn2), using an optional offset from an immediate or register value
SBCO	Store byte burst with constant table offset	SBCO REG1, Cn2, OP(255), IM(124) SBCO REG1, Cn2, OP(255), bn	The SBCO instruction is used to write a block of data from the register file into memory. The memory address to write to is specified by a 32-bit constant register (Cn2), using an optional offset from an immediate or register value
ZERO	Clear register space	ZERO IM(123), IM(124)	This pseudo-op is used to clear space in the register file. Also: ZERO &REG1, IM(124)

Program Flow Control

JMP	Unconditional jump	JMP OP(65535)	Unconditional jump to a 16-bit instruction address, specified by register or immediate value
JAL	Unconditional jump and link	JAL REG1, OP(65535)	Unconditional jump to a 16-bit instruction address, specified by register or immediate value. Address following the JAL instruction is stored into REG1, so that REG1 can later be used as a "return" address
CALL	Call procedure	CALL OP(65535)	The CALL instruction is designed to emulate a subroutine call on a stack-based processor
RET	Return from procedure	RET	The RET instruction is designed to emulate a subroutine return on a stack-based processor
QBGT	Quick branch if >	QBGT LABEL, REG1, OP(255)	Jumps if the value of OP(255) is greater than REG1
QBGE	Quick branch if ≥	QBGE LABEL, REG1, OP(255)	Jumps if the value of OP(255) is greater than or equal to REG1
QBLT	Quick branch if <	QBLT LABEL, REG1, OP(255)	Jumps if the value of OP(255) is less than REG1
QBLE	Quick branch if ≤	QBLE LABEL, REG1, OP(255)	Jumps if the value of OP(255) is less than or equal to REG1
QBEQ	Quick branch if =	QBEQ LABEL, REG1, OP(255)	Jumps if the value of OP(255) is equal to REG1
QBNE	Quick branch if ≠	QBNE LABEL, REG1, OP(255)	Jumps if the value of OP(255) is NOT equal to REG1
QBA	Quick branch always	QBA LABEL	Jump always. This is similar to the JMP instruction, only QBA uses an address offset and thus can be relocated in memory
QBBS	Quick branch if bit is set	QBBS LABEL, REG1, OP(31)	Jumps if the bit OP(31) is set in REG1. Also: QBBS LABEL, Rn.tx
QBBC	Quick branch if bit is clear	QBBC LABEL, REG1, OP(31)	Jumps if the bit OP(31) is clear in REG1. Also: QBBC LABEL, Rn.tx
WBS	Wait until bit set	WBS REG1, OP(31) WBS Rn.tx	The WBS instruction is a pseudo op that uses the QBBC instruction. It is used to poll on a status bit, spinning until the bit is set
WBC	Wait until bit clear	WBC REG1, OP(31) WBC Rn.tx	The WBC instruction is a pseudo op that uses the QBBS instruction. It is used to poll on a status bit, spinning until the bit is clear
HALT	Halt operation	HALT	The HALT instruction disables the PRU. This instruction is used to implement software breakpoints in a debugger
SLP	Sleep operation	SLP IM(1)	The SLP instruction will sleep the PRU, causing it to disable its clock. This instruction can specify either a permanent sleep or a "wake on event"

See: http://processors.wiki.ti.com/index.php/PRU_Assembly_Instructions for further information.

REG, REG1, REG2, ...	A register field from 8 to 32 bits	bn	A field that must be b0 to b3
Rn, Rn1, Rn2, ...	A 32-bit register field (r0 to r31)	LABEL	A valid label
Rn.tx	A 1-bit register field	IM(n)	An immediate value from 0 to n
Cn, Cn1, Cn2, ...	A 32-bit constant constant register (c0 to c31)	OP(n)	Operand - either a REG or IM(n)

Figure 15-7: Summary of the PRU instruction set

Image created from information that is courtesy of Texas Instruments

PRU-ICSS Applications

In this section, several example applications are developed to test the performance of the PRU-ICSS and to illustrate how you can build Linux host applications that interact with it. Each application introduces additional features of the PRU-ICSS, so it is important that you read each one, even if you do not intend to build that particular type of application.

PRU-ICSS Performance Tests

In Chapter 6, a test is described that evaluates the performance of a Linux user space C/C++ application that lights an LED when a button is pressed. A similar set of tests is presented here that use the PRU-ICSS. All these tests use the circuit illustrated in Figure 15-2. The tests are as follows:

- The *assembly button press, LED response test* is available in the /chp15/pru/ perfTestASM/ directory and in Listing 15-6. This test aims to evaluate the fastest response of a PRU to an input when the code is written in assembly language.

- The *C button press, LED response test* is available in the /chp15/pru/perfTest/ directory and in Listing 15-7. This test aims to evaluate the fastest response of a PRU to an input when the code is written in the C programming language.

- The *high-frequency LED flash test* is available in the /chp15/pru/blinkLED/ directory and in Listing 15-8. This test aims to consistently flash an LED at a frequency of 1MHz.

These tests stretch the capabilities of the Analog Discovery (5MHz, 50MSPS). The sample values are represented by "x" markers in Figure 15-8, which are spaced at 10ns intervals (curve fitting is used to display the outputs). Despite the shortcomings of the Analog Discovery, the graphs are indicative of the high-performance capability of the PRU-ICSS.

Each of these tests is an individual project and executable binary. The comments in each code listing describe how the test is performed.

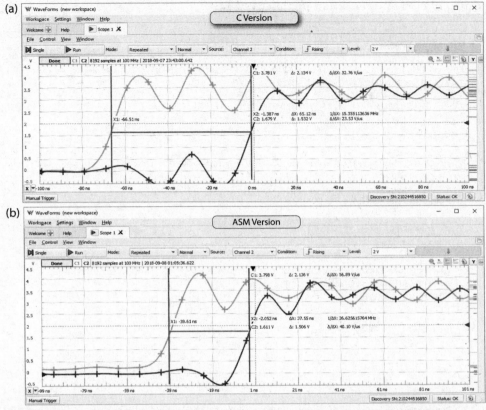

Figure 15-8: The button press LED response test, written in (a) C and (b) assembly language

Listing 15-6: /chp15/pru/perfTestASM/perfTestASM.asm

```
        .cdecls "perfTestContainer.c"
        .clink
        .global start
start:
        CLR     r30, r30.t5     ; turn off the LED
        WBS     r31, 3          ; wait bit set - i.e., button press
        SET     r30, r30.t5     ; set the output bit - turn on the LED

        HALT
```

Listing 15-7: /chp15/pru/perfTest/perfTest.c

```c
#include <stdint.h>
#include <pru_cfg.h>
#include "resource_table_empty.h"

volatile register uint32_t __R30;
volatile register uint32_t __R31;

void main(void) {
    volatile uint32_t led, button;

    // Use pru0_pru_r30_5 as an output i.e., 100000 or 0x0020
    led = 0x0020;
    // Use pru0_pru_r31_3 as a button i.e., 1000 or 0x0008
    button = 0x0008;

    // Turn the LED off
    __R30 &= !led;

    // Stop the loop when the button is pressed
    while (!(__R31 && button)) {
        // Do nothing
    }
    // Turn the LED on
    __R30 ^= led;

    __halt();
}
```

Listing 15-8: /chp15/pru/perfTestLED/perfTestLED.asm

```
        .cdecls "main.c"
        .clink
        .global START
        .asg "48",  DELAY          ; needs to account for control logic
START:
        SET     r30, r30.t5
        LDI32   r0, DELAY
DELAYON:
        SUB     r0, r0, 1
        QBNE    DELAYON, r0, 0    ; loop to DELAYON, unless REG0=0
LEDOFF:
        CLR     r30, r30.t5       ; clear the output bin (LED off)
        LDI32   r0, DELAY         ; reset REG0 to the length of the delay

DELAYOFF:
        SUB     r0, r0, 1         ; decrement REG0 by 1
```

```
        QBNE    DELAYOFF, r0, 0  ; loop to DELAYOFF, unless REG0=0
        QBBC    START, r31, 3    ; is the button pressed? If not, loop
END:                             ; notify the calling app that finished
        HALT                     ; halt the pru program
```

The results for each of the tests are as follows:

1. For the pure assembly program in Listing 15-7, the LED lights approximately 39 ns after the button is pressed (31 ns when a high-resolution oscilloscope is used)—see Figure 15-8(b). To put this number in context, in this time a light pulse would have traveled approximately 9 meters through free space (at 3×10^8 m/s) and sound would have traveled 100th of a mm in air (340 m/s at sea level). The latter means that this time resolution, coupled with suitable acoustic sensor(s), makes accurate distance measurements feasible with the PRU-ICSS. Figure 15-9(a) confirms the measurement of the Analog Discovery using a higher bandwidth oscilloscope.

2. For the C program, the LED lights approximately 67 ns after the button is pressed—see Figure 15-8(a). This is an impressive result for code that has been automatically compiled to assembly.

3. The LED test, as indicated in Figure 15-9(b), indicates that each PRU can be used to output user-configurable signals at very high frequencies (note that the PRU-ICSS also has dedicated clock outputs—e.g., a 192 MHz UART clock).

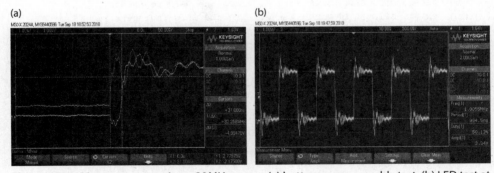

Figure 15-9: Measurements using a 20 MHz scope: (a) button press assembly test, (b) LED test at a blink frequency of 1 MHz

Importantly, none of these tests has a significant CPU or memory load on the Linux host. To run these tests, choose the test directory (`perfTest`, `perfTestASM`, or `perfTestLED`) and then use the following:

```
debian@ebb:.../chp15/pru/perfTestASM$ make
debian@ebb:.../chp15/pru/perfTestASM$ sudo make install_PRU0
```

Utilizing Regular Linux GPIOs

Each PRU is attached to an OCP master port, as illustrated in Figure 15-1, which permits access to memory addresses on the Linux host device. This functionality allows the PRUs to manipulate the state of the regular GPIOs that are used in Chapter 6. The first step is to enable the OCP master port using the following instructions:

```
LBCO   &r0, C4, 4, 4   ; load SYSCFG reg into r0 (use c4 const addr)
CLR    r0,  r0, 4      ; clear bit 4 (STANDBY_INIT)
SBCO   &r0, C4, 4, 4   ; store the modified r0 back at the load addr
```

Here, c4 refers to entry 4 in the constants table, which is the PRU_ICSS CFG (local) address. Therefore, offset 4 refers to the SYSCFG register. The CLR instruction sets bit 4 (STANDBY_INIT) to be 0, thus enabling the OCP master ports when r0 is written back to the SYSCFG register using the SBCO (store byte burst with constant table offset) instruction.

The next step is to determine the explicit Linux host memory addresses for the GPIOs—this is described in the feature "Memory-Based GPIO Switching" in Chapter 6. The GPIO bank addresses and states can be defined using the following addresses and offsets:

```
.asg  0x44e07000, GPIO0        ; GPIO Bank 0, See the AM335x TRM
.asg  0x4804c000, GPIO1        ; GPIO Bank 1, Table 2.2 Peripheral Map
.asg  0x481ac000, GPIO2        ; GPIO Bank 2,
.asg  0x481ae000, GPIO3        ; GPIO Bank 3,
.asg  0x190, GPIO_CLRDATAOUT;  for clearing the GPIO registers
.asg  0x194, GPIO_SETDATAOUT;  for setting the GPIO registers
.asg  0x138, GPIO_DATAIN       ; for reading the GPIO registers
.asg  1<<30, GPIO0_30          ; P9_11 gpio0[30] Output - bit 30
.asg  1<<31, GPIO0_31          ; P9_13 gpio0[31] Input - bit 31
```

The PRU code is provided in Listing 15-9. It is similar to Listing 15-8, with the exception that the GPIO addresses must be loaded into registers and manipulated at the bit level. The C code is not listed here, as it is similar to Listing 15-2. However, the full project is available in the /chp15/pru/ledFlashASM_OCP/ repository directory.

Listing 15-9: /chp15/pru/ledFlashASM_OCP/ledFlashASM_OCP.asm

```
; This program flashes an LED on P9_11/P2.05 until a button that is
; attached to P9_13/P2.07 is pressed.
.cdecls "main.c"
.clink
.global START
.asg  "5000000",  DELAY
.asg  0x44e07000, GPIO0        ; GPIO Bank 0, See the AM335x TRM
.asg  0x4804c000, GPIO1        ; GPIO Bank 1, Table 2.2 Peripheral Map
```

```
.asg   0x481ac000, GPIO2        ; GPIO Bank 2,
.asg   0x481ae000, GPIO3        ; GPIO Bank 3,
.asg   0x190, GPIO_CLRDATAOUT   ; for clearing the GPIO registers
.asg   0x194, GPIO_SETDATAOUT   ; for setting the GPIO registers
.asg   0x138, GPIO_DATAIN       ; for reading the GPIO registers
.asg   1<<30, GPIO0_30          ; P9_11/P2.05 gpio0[30] Output - bit 30
.asg   1<<31, GPIO0_31          ; P9_13/P2.07 gpio0[31] Input - bit 31
.asg   32, PRU0_R31_VEC_VALID   ; allows notification of program completion
.asg   3, PRU_EVTOUT_0          ; the event number that is sent back

START:
    ; Enable the OCP master port
    LBCO    &r0, C4, 4, 4     ; load SYSCFG reg into r0 (use c4 const addr)
    CLR     r0,  r0, 4        ; clear bit 4 (STANDBY_INIT)
    SBCO    &r0, C4, 4, 4     ; store the modified r0 back at the load addr

MAINLOOP:
    LDI32   r1, (GPIO0|GPIO_SETDATAOUT)  ; load addr for GPIO Set data r1
    LDI32   r2, GPIO0_30       ; write GPIO0_30 to r2
    SBBO    &r2, r1, 0, 4      ; write r2 to the r1 address value - LED ON
    LDI32   r0, DELAY          ; store the length of the delay in REG0
DELAYON:
    SUB     r0, r0, 1
    QBNE    DELAYON, r0, 0     ; Loop to DELAYON, unless REG0=0
LEDOFF:
    LDI32   r1, (GPIO0|GPIO_CLRDATAOUT)  ; load addr for GPIO Clear data
    LDI32   r2, GPIO0_30       ; write GPIO_30 to r2
    SBBO    &r2, r1, 0, 4      ; write r2 to the r1 address - LED OFF
    LDI32   r0, DELAY          ; Reset REG0 to the length of the delay
DELAYOFF:
    SUB     r0, r0, 1          ; decrement REG0 by 1
    QBNE    DELAYOFF, r0, 0    ; Loop to DELAYOFF, unless REG0=0

    LDI32   r5, (GPIO0|GPIO_DATAIN)    ; load read addr for DATAOUT
    LBBO    &r6, r5, 0, 4      ; Load the value at r5 into r6
    QBBC    MAINLOOP, r6, 31   ; is the button pressed? If not, loop
END:                          ; notify that finished
    LDI32   R31, (PRU0_R31_VEC_VALID|PRU_EVTOUT_0)
    HALT                      ; halt the pru program
```

There are two regular GPIO pins, P9_11/P2.05 (output) and P9_13/P2.07 (input). The P9_11/P2.05 pin should be connected to the FET gate input, and P9_13/P2.07 should be connected to the button, as described in Figure 15-2. Ensure that the GPIOs are configured as follows, before the application is executed:

```
root@ebb:~/PRU# config-pin -a P9_11 out
root@ebb:~/PRU# config-pin -q P9_11
P9_11 Mode: gpio Direction: out Value: 0
root@ebb:~/PRU# config-pin -a P9_11 hi
root@ebb:~/PRU# config-pin -a P9_11 lo
```

```
root@ebb:~/PRU# config-pin -q P9_13 in-
P9_13 Mode: default Direction: in Value: 0
```

When executed, the code will provide output similar to that shown in Figure 15-9(b).

```
.../chp15/pru/ledFlashASM_OCP$ make
.../chp15/pru/ledFlashASM_OCP$ sudo make install_PRU0
```

A PRU PWM Generator

As described in Chapter 6, PWM has many applications, such as motor and lighting control, and there is hardware PWM support available on the Beagle boards that can be accessed directly from Linux user space. However, sysfs is slow at adjusting the duty cycle, and it is prone to the same type of latency issues as regular GPIOs. In the next section, PWM is used to output a sine wave signal by rapidly changing the duty cycle of a high-frequency switched digital output cyclically as a function of time. In this section, we prepare for that application by setting up a square waveform with a constant duty cycle.

Listing 15-10 is the Linux container code for the assembly code. It also uses the main() function to transfer the PWM duty cycle percentage and the delay factor (i.e., how many instructions × 5 ns there should be for each of the 100 samples per period). The values passed by the code in Listing 15-10 result in a PWM signal with a duty cycle of 75 percent and a period of approximately 11 µs (i.e., 100 samples per period × 10 delay steps per sample × 2 instructions per delay × 5 ns per instruction + looping overhead).

Listing 15-10: /exploringbb/chp15/pru/pwm/main.c

```c
#include <stdint.h>
#include <pru_cfg.h>
#include <pru_ctrl.h>
#include "resource_table_empty.h"

#define PRU0_DRAM   0x00000
volatile unsigned int *shared = (unsigned int *)(PRU0_DRAM);

extern void START(void);

void main(void) {
   // Copy the PWM percentage (0-100) and delay factor into PRU memory
   shared[0] = 75;
   // Delay factor -- write it into the next word location in
   // memory (i.e.,4-bytes later)
   shared[1] = 10;
   START();
}
```

The assembly code is provided in Listing 15-11. It consists of a main loop that loops once for each signal period, until a button that is attached to r31 .t3 is pressed. Within the main loop are two nested loops. One iterates for the number of samples that the signal is high, and the second iterates for the number of samples that the signal is low. The total number of nested iterations is 100, where each iteration has a user-configurable delay.

Listing 15-11: /exploringbb/chp15/pru/pwm/pwm.asm

```
; Written for Exploring BeagleBone v2 by Derek Molloy
; This program uses the PRU as a PWM controller based on the values in
; 0x00000000 (percentage) and 0x00000004 (delay)
  .cdecls "main.c"
  .clink
  .global START
  .asg   32, PRU0_R31_VEC_VALID  ; allows notification of program completion
  .asg   3,  PRU_EVTOUT_0         ; the event number that is sent back

START:
        ; Reading the memory that was set by the C program into registers
        ; r1 - Read the PWM percent high (0-100)
        LDI32   r0, 0x00000000     ; load the memory location
        LBBO    &r1, r0, 0, 4      ; load the percent value into r1
        ; r2 - Load the sample time delay
        LDI32   r0, 0x00000004     ; load the memory location
        LBBO    &r2, r0, 0, 4      ; load the step delay value into r2
        ; r3 - The PWM percent that the signal is low (100-r1)
        LDI32   r3, 100            ; load 100 into r3
        SUB     r3, r3, r1         ; subtract r1 (high) away from 100
MAINLOOP:
        MOV     r4, r1             ; start counter at number of steps high
        SET     r30, r30.t5        ; set the output P9_27/P2.34 high
SIGNAL_HIGH:
        MOV     r0, r2             ; the delay step length - load r2 above
DELAY_HIGH:
        SUB     r0, r0, 1          ; decrement delay loop counter
        QBNE    DELAY_HIGH, r0, 0  ; repeat until step delay is done
        SUB     r4, r4, 1          ; the signal was high for a step
        QBNE    SIGNAL_HIGH, r4, 0 ; repeat until signal high steps are done
        ; Now the signal is going to go low for 100%-r1% - i.e., r3
        MOV     r4, r3             ; number of steps low loaded
        CLR     r30, r30.t5        ; set the output P9_27/P2.34 low
SIGNAL_LOW:
        MOV     r0, r2             ; the delay step length - load r2 above
DELAY_LOW:
        SUB     r0, r0, 1          ; decrement loop counter
        QBNE    DELAY_LOW, r0, 0   ; repeat until step delay is done
```

```
        SUB      r4, r4, 1              ; the signal was low for a step
        QBNE     SIGNAL_LOW, r4, 0      ; repeat until signal low % is done

        QBBS     END, r31, 3            ; quit if button on P9_28/P2.30 is pressed
        QBA      MAINLOOP               ; otherwise loop forever
END:                                    ; end of program, send back interrupt
        LDI32    R31, (PRU0_R31_VEC_VALID|PRU_EVTOUT_0)
        HALT                            ; halt the pru program
```

The circuit is wired as shown in Figure 15-2, and the same pin configuration is used for this example. The output of the circuit is displayed in Figure 15-10. A simple low-pass filter is added to the P9_27/P2.34 output pins, and it results in the "Low-pass filtered output" signal in Figure 15-2. In this example, the RC filter consists of a 4.7 kΩ resistor that is connected to P9_27/P2.34 and a 0.1 µF capacitor connected from the output side of the resistor to GND (i.e., *not* between P9_27/P2.34 directly and GND). The RC filter results in a time-averaged output, which is representative of the duty cycle. For example, if the PWM duty cycle is 75 percent, then the output voltage of the RC filter is approximately 0.75 × 3.3 V = 2.625 V, as illustrated in Figure 15-10.

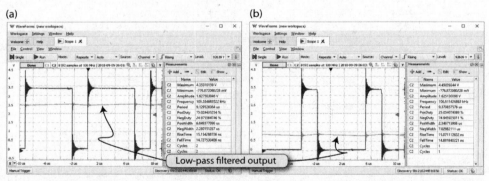

Figure 15-10: The PWM generator output: (a) 75% duty cycle (~2.5V) and (b) 25% duty cycle (0.8V)

The same example is built using C code in Listing 15-12, and the code is perhaps easier to follow.

Listing 15-12: /exploringbb/chp15/pru/pwmC/pwmC.c

```
#include <stdint.h>
#include <pru_cfg.h>
#include "resource_table_empty.h"

// Delay factor which defines the PWM frequency
#define DELAYFACTOR 10
volatile register uint32_t __R30;
volatile register uint32_t __R31;
```

```
void main(void) {
    volatile uint32_t gpio, button;
    uint32_t percent, count;

    // The PWM percentage (0-100) for the positive cycle
    percent = 75;
    // Use pru0_pru_r30_5 as an output i.e., 100000 or 0x0020
    gpio = 0x0020;
    // Use pru0_pru_r31_3 as a button i.e., 1000 or 0x0008
    button = 0x0008;

    // Stop the loop when the button is pressed
    while (!(__R31 && button)) {
        for(count=0; count<100; count++) {
            // Use two comparisons to equalize the timing
            if(count<=percent) { __R30 |= gpio;       }
            if(count> percent) { __R30 &= (~gpio);   }
            __delay_cycles(DELAYFACTOR);
        }
    }
    __halt();
}
```

Interestingly, this example shows the challenges of writing code for the PRU in C while trying to maintain precise timing. For example, these lines of code:

```
if(count<=percent) { __R30 |= gpio;       }
if(count> percent) { __R30 &= (~gpio); }
```

would usually be written as this:

```
if(count<=percent) { __R30 |= gpio;       }
else { __R30 &= (~gpio);   }
```

However, on testing the latter code, the timing is not consistent and results in a bias that is proportional to the duty cycle. By using two `if()` statements, the timing is balanced for the full range of duty cycles.

Figure 15-11 shows the PWM C program in operation, where the high-bandwidth oscilloscope is used to confirm the consistency observed in Figure 15-10.

(a)   (b)

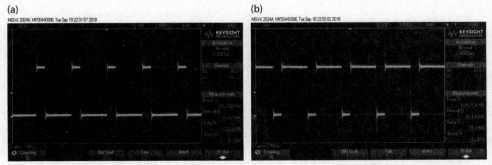

Figure 15-11: The PWM generator output with the PWM C program: (a) 25% duty cycle, (b) 75% duty cycle

A PRU Sine Wave Generator

The PRU PWM generator code in the previous section can be adapted to generate user-defined waveforms on a GPIO pin. This is achieved by altering the PWM signal duty cycle rapidly over time and passing the output through a low-pass filter. Figure 15-10 illustrates the output of such as circuit, where a 4.7 kΩ resistor and a 4.7 nF capacitor are used to form the requisite low-pass filter. The smoothing is effectively of shorter duration than the previous RC component values. Figure 15-12(a) displays the PWM signal with a duty cycle that changes over time. The low-pass filtered output is displayed in Figure 15-12(b), where it is clearly a good approximation to a sine waveform signal. The full project is available in the `chp15/pru/sineWave/` directory.

The PRU C code is provided in Listing 15-13. The main novelty in this code is the generation of a set of 100 values representing a single cycle of a sine waveform. The values of the sine wave cycle are designed to have an amplitude of 50 and an offset of +50 so that the output can be directly used as the duty cycle percentage values for the PWM generator code described in the previous section.

(a)   (b)

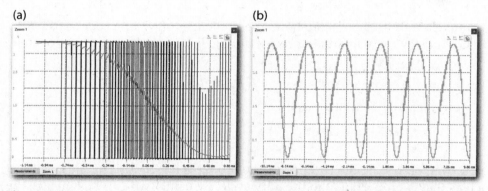

Figure 15-12: User-defined sine waveform output at different time bases: (a) with PWM signal present, and (b) low-pass output only

Listing 15-13: /exploringbb/chp15/pru/sineWave/sineWave.c

```
#include <stdint.h>
#include <pru_cfg.h>
#include "resource_table_empty.h"
#include <math.h>

// Delay factor which defines the PWM frequency
#define DELAYFACTOR 0
volatile register uint32_t __R30;
volatile register uint32_t __R31;

void main(void) {
   volatile uint32_t gpio, button;
```

```
uint32_t count, i;
uint32_t waveform[100];
float gain = 50.0f;                  // want the full range 0-99
float phase = 0.0f;                  // phase can be changed
float bias = 50.0f;                  // center on 1.65V, full range
float freq = 2.0f * 3.14159f / 100.0f;
for (i=0; i<100; i++){               // general sine wave equation
   waveform[i] = (unsigned int)(bias + (gain * sin((i * freq) + phase)));
}
// Use pru0_pru_r30_5 as an output i.e., 100000 or 0x0020
gpio = 0x0020;
// Use pru0_pru_r31_3 as a button i.e., 1000 or 0x0008
button = 0x0008;

// Stop the loop when the button is pressed
while (!(__R31 && button)) {
   for(i=0; i<100; i++){
      for(count=0; count<100; count++){
         // Use two comparisons to equalize the timing
         if(count<=waveform[i]) { __R30 |=  gpio;      }
         if(count> waveform[i]) { __R30 &= (~gpio); }
         __delay_cycles(DELAYFACTOR);
      }
   }
}
__halt();
}
```

The PRU code in Listing 15-13 builds on the PWM code in Listing 15-12. The main difference is an additional loop that loads a PWM duty cycle for each data array value. The code will output any periodic waveform that is passed to it, with a maximum periodic sample length of just under 8 KB (PRU0 RAM0) in this example. The code could be improved to extend this limit or to iterate with fewer instructions. However, the code demonstrates the principle that a PRU can be used to generate arbitrary custom analog waveforms using its digital GPIO outputs.

An Ultrasonic Sensor Application

As described in Chapter 10, the HC-SR04 is a low-cost (~$5) ultrasonic sensor that can be used to determine the distance to an obstacle using the speed of sound. The sensor has a range of approximately 1″ (2.5 cm) to 13′ (4 m). It is a 5 V sensor, so logic-level translation circuitry is required (as described at the end of Chapter 8). The final circuit is illustrated in Figure 15-13. It uses the same pin configuration that is described earlier in this chapter.

Figure 15-14 illustrates how interaction takes place with this sensor. A 10 μs trigger pulse is sent to the "Trig" input of the sensor; the sensor then responds on its "Echo" output with a pulse that has a width that corresponds to the distance of an obstacle (approximately 150 μs to 25 ms, or 38 ms if no obstacle is in range).

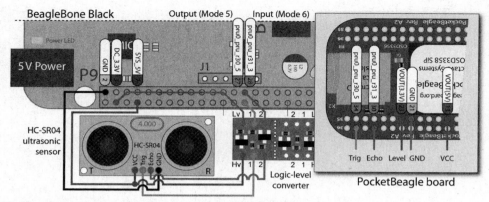

Figure 15-13: The HC-SR04 ultrasonic distance sensor circuit

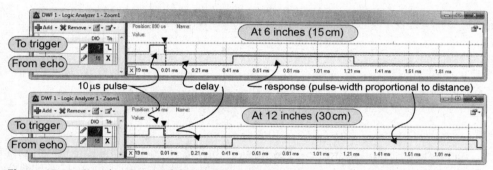

Figure 15-14: Signal response of the HC-SR04

The nondeterministic nature of Linux means that it would be difficult to use this sensor directly from Linux user space using regular GPIOs. There are UART versions of this sensor that contain a microcontroller, but they are much more expensive. In fact, the solution that is presented here is fast enough to enable you to connect ten or more such sensors to a single PRU—a single trigger signal could be sent to many sensors simultaneously, and different enhanced GPIOs could be used to measure the response signals from each sensor. Assembly language code is developed for this application with the following structure:

1. Initialization takes place to set up shared memory.

2. The main loop begins.

3. A pulse is sent to the output pin. The output pin (P9_27/P2.34) is set high, and the code delays for exactly 10 μs before switching low.

4. The input pin (P9_28/P2.30) is then polled until it goes high. At that point, a "width" timer counts until the input pin goes low.

5. The width timer value is written into shared memory. The main loop begins again.

The project code is available in the directory /chp15/pru/ultrasonic/.

Listing 15-14: /exploringbb/chp15/pru/ultrasonic/main.c

```c
#include <stdint.h>
#include <pru_cfg.h>
#include <pru_ctrl.h>
#include "resource_table_empty.h"

#define PRU0_DRAM    0x00000000
volatile unsigned int *shared = (unsigned int *)(PRU0_DRAM);

extern void START(void);

void main(void) {
    // The number of samples
    shared[0] = 5000;
    // Sample delay in ms
    shared[1] = 2;
    START();
}
```

The PRU code is provided in Listing 15-15. The program loops as described and stores the current value in memory on each iteration.

Listing 15-15: /exploringbb/chp15/pru/ultrasonic/ultrasonic.asm

```asm
; Written for Exploring BeagleBone v2 by Derek Molloy
; This program uses the PRU as an ultrasonic controller based on the
; values in 0x00000000 (percentage) and 0x00000004 (delay)
    .cdecls "main.c"
    .clink
    .global START
    .asg  32, PRU0_R31_VEC_VALID  ; allows notification of program completion
    .asg  3,   PRU_EVTOUT_0       ; the event number that is sent back
    .asg  1000, TRIGGER_COUNT     ;
    .asg  100000, SAMPLE_DELAY_1MS

; Using register 0 for all temporary storage (reused multiple times)
START:
    ; Read number of samples to read and inter-sample delay
    LDI32   r0, 0x00000000        ; load the memory location, number of samples
    LBBO    &r1, r0, 0, 4         ; load the value into memory - keep r1
    ; Read the sample delay
    LDI32   r0, 0x00000004        ; the sample delay is in the second 32-bits
    LBBO    &r2, r0, 0, 4         ; the sample delay is stored in r2

MAINLOOP:
    LDI32   r0, TRIGGER_COUNT     ; store length of the trigger pulse delay
    SET     r30, r30.t5           ; set the trigger high

TRIGGERING:                       ; delay for 10us
    SUB     r0, r0, 1             ; decrement loop counter
    QBNE    TRIGGERING, r0, 0     ; repeat loop unless zero
```

```
    CLR     r30, r30.t5             ; 10us over, set the triger low - pulse sent
    ; clear the counter and wait until the echo goes high
    LDI32   r3, 0                   ; r3 will store the echo pulse width
    WBS     r31, 3                  ; wait until the echo goes high


    ; start counting (measuring echo pulse width)  until the echo goes low
COUNTING:
    ADD     r3, r3, 1               ; increment the counter by 1
    QBBS    COUNTING, r31, 3        ; loop if the echo is still high
    ; at this point the echo is now low - write the value to shared memory
    LDI32   r0, 0x00000008          ; going to write the result to this address
    SBBO    &r3, r0, 0, 4           ; store the count at this address
    ; one more sample iteration has taken place
    SUB     r1, r1, 1               ; take 1 away from the number of iterations
    MOV     r0, r2                  ; need a delay between samples

SAMPLEDELAY:                        ; do this loop r2 times (1ms delay each time)
    SUB     r0, r0, 1               ; decrement counter by 1
    LDI32   r4, SAMPLE_DELAY_1MS    ; load 1ms delay into r4

DELAY1MS:
    SUB     r4, r4, 1
    QBNE    DELAY1MS, r4, 0         ; keep going until 1ms has elapsed
    QBNE    SAMPLEDELAY, r0, 0      ; repeat loop unless zero
    QBNE    MAINLOOP, r1, 0         ; loop if the no of iterations has not passed

END:                                ; end of program, send back interrupt
    LDI32   R31, (PRU0_R31_VEC_VALID|PRU_EVTOUT_0)
    HALT                            ; halt the pru program
```

The C code in Listing 15-16 is a separate Linux userspace program that accesses the PRU memory location 0x4a30 0008 and reads the current timing value. It then uses the displayDistance() function to convert this value into its equivalent distance in inches and centimeters.

Listing 15-16: /exploringbb/chp15/pru/ultrasonic/readDistance.c

```
#include <stdio.h>
...
#include <sys/mman.h>

#define MAP_SIZE 4096UL
#define MAP_MASK (MAP_SIZE - 1)

void displayDistance(unsigned int raw_distance) {
    float distin = ((float)raw_distance / (100 * 148));
    float distcm = ((float)raw_distance / (100 * 58));
    printf("Distance is %f inches (%f cm)                   \r", distin, distcm);
}

int main(int argc, char **argv) {
```

```
int fd, i, j;
void *map_base, *virt_addr;
unsigned long read_result, writeval;
unsigned int numberOutputSamples = 1;
off_t target = 0x4a300008;

if((fd = open("/dev/mem", O_RDWR | O_SYNC)) == -1){
    printf("Failed to open memory!\n");
    return -1;
}
fflush(stdout);
map_base = mmap(0, MAP_SIZE, PROT_READ | PROT_WRITE, MAP_SHARED,
                fd, target& ~MAP_MASK);
if(map_base == (void *) -1) {
    printf("Failed to map base address\n");
    return -1;
}
fflush(stdout);

for(j=0; j<1000; j++){
    for(i=0; i<numberOutputSamples; i++){
        virt_addr = map_base + (target & MAP_MASK);
        read_result = *((unsigned long *) virt_addr);
        //printf("Value at address 0x%X is: 0x%X\n", target, read_result);
        displayDistance((unsigned int)read_result);
        usleep(500000);
    }
    fflush(stdout);
}
if(munmap(map_base, MAP_SIZE) == -1) {
    printf("Failed to unmap memory");
    return -1;
}
close(fd);
return 0;
}
```

The code example can be built using the build script and results in the following output when executed:

```
debian@ebb:~/exploringbb/chp15/pru/ultrasonic$ make
debian@ebb:~/exploringbb/chp15/pru/ultrasonic$ sudo make install_PRU0
debian@ebb:~/exploringbb/chp15/pru/ultrasonic$ sudo ./readDistance
Distance is 5.335135 inches (13.551244 cm)
```

The program output updates on a single shell console line whenever it is sampled. This continues until the program is exited. The signal output is displayed in Figure 15-15. The sampling rate is variable in this example. It could be altered to a fixed sample period if required; however, a fixed sampling rate would have to account for the 38 ms pulse that the sensor returns when no obstacle is detected.

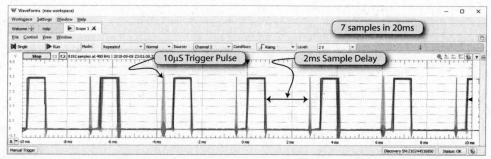

Figure 15-15: Signal response of the HC-SR04 with the ultrasonic project example

Summary

After completing this chapter, you should be able to do the following:

- Describe real-time kernel and hardware solutions that can be used on the Beagle boards
- Use tools such as the PRU Debugger and Texas Instruments' PRU Code Generation Tools (CGT) for PRU-ICSS application development
- Write a PRU program that can flash an LED and transfer it to the PRU-ICSS using remoteproc
- Describe the important features of the PRU-ICSS, such as its structure, registers, memory addressing, and assembly language instructions
- Write a PRU program that shares memory with a Linux host application
- Write a PRU program that interfaces to regular GPIOs that are in Linux host space
- Write a PRU program that generates PWM signals and adapts it to output user-defined analog waveforms on a GPIO pin
- Apply the PRU to sensor interfacing applications for which time measurement is important, such as interfacing to ultrasonic distance sensors

Further Reading

There are many links to websites and documents provided throughout this chapter. Additional links and further information on the topics in this chapter are provided at www.exploringbeaglebone.com/chapter15/.

Prof. Mark A. Yoder, co-author of the *BeagleBone Cookbook,* has developed a *PRU Cookbook,* which is an excellent resource for those who are planning to develop PRU applications. See `markayoder.github.io/PRUCookbook/`.

Mark A.Yoder, Jason Kridner, *BeagleBone Cookbook: Software and Hardware Problems and Solutions,* O'Reilly Media Inc., ISBN: 1491905395, 2015.

## CHAPTER 16

Embedded Kernel Programming

In this chapter, you are introduced to Linux kernel programming on an embedded device such as a Beagle board. Kernel programming is an advanced topic that requires in-depth study of the source code for the Linux kernel; however, this chapter is structured as a practical step-by-step guide to the focused task of writing Linux loadable kernel modules (LKMs) that interface to general-purpose inputs/outputs (GPIOs). The first example is a straightforward "Hello World" module that can be used to establish a configuration for LKM development on the board. The second LKM example introduces interrupt service routines (ISRs) and interfaces a simple GPIO button and LED circuit to Linux kernel space. Two further examples are provided that introduce the kobject interface and the use of kernel threads to build kernel-space sysfs devices for the board. By the end of this chapter, you should be familiar with the steps required to write kernel code, and appreciate the programming constraints that such development entails.

EQUIPMENT REQUIRED FOR THIS CHAPTER:

- Beagle board (any model) running Linux 4.x.x or greater

Further details on this chapter are available at `www.exploringbeaglebone` `.com/chapter16/`.

Introduction

As introduced in Chapter 3, a loadable kernel module (LKM) is a mechanism for adding code to, or removing code from, the Linux kernel at run time. LKMs are ideal for device drivers, enabling the kernel to communicate with the hardware without it having to know how the hardware works. Without this modular capability, the Linux kernel would be large because it would have to support every driver that would ever be needed on the board. You would also have to rebuild the kernel every time you want to add new hardware or update a device driver. The downside of LKMs is that driver files have to be maintained for each device. LKMs are loaded at run time, but they do not execute in user space; they are essentially part of the kernel.

Kernel modules run in kernel space and applications run in user space, as illustrated in Figure 16-1. Both kernel space and user space have their own unique memory address spaces that do not overlap. This approach ensures that applications running in user space have a consistent view of the hardware, regardless of the hardware platform. The kernel services are then made available to the user space in a controlled way through the use of system calls. The kernel also prevents individual user space applications from conflicting with each other or from accessing restricted resources through the use of protection levels (e.g., superuser versus regular user permissions).

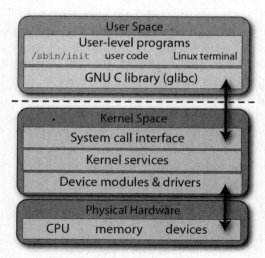

Figure 16-1: The Linux kernel and user space architecture

Why Write Kernel Modules?

When interfacing to electronics circuits under embedded Linux, you are exposed to sysfs and the use of low-level file operations for interfacing to electronics circuits. This approach can appear to be inefficient (especially if you have experience of traditional embedded systems); however, these file entries are memory mapped, and the performance is sufficient for many applications. As discussed in Chapter 6, it is possible to achieve response times of about one-third of a millisecond, with negligible CPU overhead, from within Linux user space by using pthreads, callback functions, and sys/poll.h.

Also described in Chapter 6 is an approach for bypassing the Linux kernel on the AM335x, using direct memory manipulation to take control of the SoC inputs and outputs. Unfortunately, this approach means your programs will not be portable to other embedded Linux platforms that do not use the AM335x. In addition, because the Linux kernel is unaware of such direct memory manipulations, you could potentially generate resource conflicts.

An alternative approach is to use kernel code, which has support for interrupts. However, kernel code is difficult to write and debug. My advice is that you should always try to accomplish your task in Linux user space unless you are certain that there is no other possible way!

Loadable Kernel Module Basics

The run-time life cycle of a typical computer program is reasonably straightforward: a loader allocates memory for the program and loads the program with any required shared libraries. Instruction execution then begins at some entry point (typically identified by the main() point in C/C++ programs), statements are executed, exceptions are thrown, dynamic memory is allocated and deallocated, and the program eventually runs to completion. On program exit, the operating system frees the memory that was allocated to the program back to the heap memory pool.

Kernel modules are written in C, but they are not programs; for a start, there is no main() function! Some of the key differences are that kernel modules:

- **Do not execute sequentially:** A kernel module registers itself to handle requests using its initialization function, which runs and then terminates. The type of requests that it can handle are defined within the module code. This is quite similar to the event-driven programming model that is commonly utilized in graphical user interface (GUI) applications.

- **Do not clean up automatically:** Any resources that are allocated to the module must be manually released when the module is unloaded, or they may be unavailable until a system reboots.

- **Do not have printf() functions:** Kernel code cannot access libraries of code that is written for the Linux user space. The kernel module lives and runs in kernel space, which has its own memory address space. The interface between kernel space and user space is clearly defined and controlled.

However, a `printk()` function is available that can be used to output information, which can be viewed from within user space.

▪ **Can be interrupted:** One conceptually difficult aspect of kernel modules is that they can be used by several different programs/processes at the same time. Modules must be constructed so that they have a consistent and valid behavior when they are interrupted. The BeagleBoard X15 has a multicore processor, which means you also have to consider the issues involved in simultaneous access from multiple processes.

▪ **Have a higher level of execution privilege:** Typically, more CPU cycles are allocated to kernel modules than to user space programs. This sounds like an advantage; however, you have to be careful that your module does not adversely affect the overall performance of your system.

▪ **Do not have floating-point support:** It is kernel code that uses traps to transition from integer to floating-point mode for your user space applications. However, it is difficult to perform these traps in kernel space. The alternative is to manually save and restore floating-point operations—a task that is best avoided and left to user space code.

A First LKM Example

The concepts just described are a lot to digest, and it is important that they are all addressed, but not all in the first example! Listing 16-1 provides the code for a first example LKM. When no kernel argument is provided, the code uses the `printk()` function to display "Hello world!" in the kernel logs. If the argument "Derek" is provided, then the logs display "Hello Derek!" The comments in Listing 16-1, which are written using a Doxygen format (see Chapter 7), describe the role of each statement. Further description is available after the code listing.

WARNING   It is easy to crash the Beagle board when you are writing and testing LKMs. It is always possible that such a system crash could corrupt your file system; it is unlikely, but it is possible. Performing a `sudo reboot` or holding the power button (see Chapter 1) will usually put everything back in order. Should something go wrong, the eMMC or SD card can easily be re-flashed, which makes it a good practice platform for LKM development. For your information, I have yet to corrupt any embedded Linux device file system as a result of a system crash, despite my being the cause of many!

Listing 16-1: /exploringbb/chp16/hello/hello.c

```
/**
 * @file    hello.c
 * @author  Derek Molloy
```

```
 * @date      10 September 2018
 * @version 0.1
 * @brief  An introductory "Hello World!" loadable kernel module (LKM)
 * that can display a message in the /var/log/kern.log file when the
 * module is loaded and removed. The module can accept an argument when
 * it is loaded -- the name, which appears in the kernel log files.
*/

#include <linux/init.h>       // macros to mark up functions e.g. __init
#include <linux/module.h>     // core header for loading LKMs
#include <linux/kernel.h>     // contains kernel types, macros, functions

MODULE_LICENSE("GPL");        // the license type (affects behavior)
MODULE_AUTHOR("Derek Molloy");  // The author visible with modinfo
MODULE_DESCRIPTION("A simple Linux LKM for the Beagle."); // desc.
MODULE_VERSION("0.1");        // the version of the module

static char *name = "world"; // example LKM argument default is "world"
// param description charp = char pointer, defaults to "world"
module_param(name, charp, S_IRUGO); // S_IRUGO can be read/not changed
MODULE_PARM_DESC(name, "The name to display in /var/log/kern.log");

/** @brief The LKM initialization function
 * The static keyword restricts the visibility of the function to within
 * this C file. The __init macro means that for a built-in driver (not
 * a LKM) the function is only used at initialization time and that it
 * can be discarded and its memory freed up after that point.
 * @return returns 0 if successful  */
static int __init helloEBB_init(void) {
   printk(KERN_INFO "EBB: Hello %s from the Beagle LKM!\n", name);
   return 0;
}

/** @brief The LKM cleanup function
 * Similar to the initialization function, it is static. The __exit
 * macro notifies that if this code is used for a built-in driver (not
 * a LKM) that this function is not required.     */
static void __exit helloEBB_exit(void) {
   printk(KERN_INFO "EBB: Goodbye %s from the Beagle LKM!\n", name);
}

/** @brief A module must use the module_init() module_exit() macros from
 * linux/init.h, which identify the initialization function at insertion
 * time and the cleanup function (as listed above).     */
module_init(helloEBB_init);
module_exit(helloEBB_exit);
```

In addition to the points described by the comments in Listing 16-1, there are some additional points worth noting.

- The statement MODULE_LICENSE("GPL") provides information (via modinfo) about the licensing terms of the module that you have developed, thus allowing users of your LKM to ensure that they are using free software.

Because the kernel is released under the GPL, your license choice impacts upon the way that the kernel treats your module. You can choose `"Proprietary"` for non-GPL code, but the kernel will be marked as "tainted," and a warning will appear. There are nontainted alternatives to GPL, such as `"GPL v2"`, `"GPL and additional rights"`, `"Dual BSD/GPL"`, `"Dual MIT/GPL"`, and `"Dual MPL/GPL"`. See `linux/module.h` for more information.

- The `name` (`char *`) is declared as static and is initialized to contain the string "world". You should avoid using global variables in kernel modules; it is even more important than in application programming because global variables are shared kernel wide. You should use the `static` keyword to restrict a variable's scope to within the module. If you must use a global variable, add a prefix that is unique to the module that you are writing.

- The `module_param(name, type, permissions)` macro has three parameters: `name` (the parameter name displayed to the user and the variable name in the module), `type` (the type of the parameter—i.e., one of `byte`, `int`, `uint`, `long`, `ulong`, `short`, `ushort`, `bool`, an inverse Boolean `invbool`, or a char pointer `charp`), and permissions (this is the access permissions to the parameter when using sysfs and is covered later). A value of `0` disables the entry, but `S_IRUGO` allows read access for user/group/others; see the *Mode Bits for Access Permissions Guide* at `tiny.cc/beagle1601`.

- The functions in the module can have whatever names you like (e.g., `helloEBB_init()` and `helloEBB_exit()`); however, the same names must be passed to the special macros `module_init()` and `module_exit()` at the end of Listing 16-1.

- The `printk()` is similar in usage to the familiar `printf()` function, and you can call it from anywhere within the kernel module code. The only significant difference is that you should specify a log level when you call the function. The log levels are defined in `linux/kern_levels.h` as one of `KERN_EMERG`, `KERN_ALERT`, `KERN_CRIT`, `KERN_ERR`, `KERN_WARNING`, `KERN_NOTICE`, `KERN_INFO`, `KERN_DEBUG`, and `KERN_DEFAULT`. This header is included via the `linux/kernel.h` header file, which includes it via `linux/printk.h`.

Essentially, when this module is loaded, the `helloEBB_init()` function executes, and when the module is unloaded, the `helloEBB_exit()` function executes.

The LKM Makefile

A `Makefile` file is required to build the kernel module; in fact, it is a special kbuild Makefile. The kbuild Makefile required to build the kernel module can be viewed in Listing 16-2. (Remember that there must be a Tab character in front of the calls to `make` in the `Makefile` file.)

Listing 16-2: /exploringbb/chp16/hello/Makefile

```
obj-m+=hello.o

all:
    make -C /lib/modules/$(shell uname -r)/build/ M=$(PWD) modules
clean:
    make -C /lib/modules/$(shell uname -r)/build/ M=$(PWD) clean
```

The first line of the `Makefile` file is called a goal definition, and it defines the module to be built (`hello.o`). The syntax is surprisingly intricate. For example, `obj-m` defines a loadable module goal, whereas `obj-y` indicates a built-in object goal. The syntax becomes more complex when a module is to be built from multiple objects, but Listing 16-2 is sufficient to build this example LKM.

The remainder of the `Makefile` file is similar to a regular Makefile. The `$(shell uname -r)` is a useful call to return the current kernel build version; this ensures a degree of portability for a Makefile. The `-C` option switches the directory to the kernel directory before performing any make tasks. The `M=$(PWD)` variable assignment tells the `make` command where the actual project files exist. The modules target is the default target for external kernel modules. An alternative target is `modules_install`, which would install the module. (The `make` command would have to be executed with superuser permissions, and the module installation path is required.)

Building the LKM on a Beagle Board

The process of building an LKM on the latest Debian Linux images is straightforward thanks to work that the BeagleBoard.org Foundation has put into maintaining kernel releases and kernel headers. To build a LKM, you must first install the Linux kernel headers on your board. The Linux kernel headers are C header files that define the interfaces between the different kernel modules and the kernel and user space. These header files are required to build external LKMs, and they must be the same version as the kernel for which you want to build a module.

The first thing to do is to install Linux kernel header files that perfectly align with the Linux kernel distribution on your device or machine. The `uname` command provides a long description (`-a` for all) and a kernel release output (`-r` for release) as follows:

```
debian@ebb:~$ uname -a
Linux ebb 4.14.67-ti-rt-r73 #1 SMP PREEMPT RT ... armv7l GNU/Linux
debian@ebb:~$ uname -r
4.14.67-ti-rt-r73
```

The kernel release output can be used to search for the appropriate Linux header files:

```
debian@ebb:~$ apt-cache search linux-headers-$(uname -r)
linux-headers-4.14.67-ti-rt-r73 - →
 Linux kernel headers for 4.14.67-ti-rt-r73 on armhf
debian@ebb:~$ sudo apt install linux-headers-$(uname -r)
```

At this point, the headers should be installed in /lib/modules/$(uname -r)/build/, which should likely be a symbolic link to the location /usr/src/ linux/$(uname -r)/. For historical reasons, an additional symbolic link is usually available at /usr/src/linux/.

```
debian@ebb:/usr/src$ ls -l
drwxr-xr-x 24 root root 4096 Sep 9 linux-headers-4.14.67-ti-rt-r73
...
debian@ebb:/lib/modules/4.14.67-ti-rt-r73$ ls -l build
lrwxrwxrwx ... build -> /usr/src/linux-headers-4.14.67-ti-rt-r73
```

Once the Linux kernel headers are in place, you can build the hello LKM using the Makefile file from Listing 16-2. Here's an example:

```
debian@ebb:~/exploringbb/chp16/hello$ make
make -C /lib/modules/4.14.67-ti-rt-r73/build/ →
  M=/home/debian/exploringbb/chp16/hello modules
make[1]: Entering dir '/usr/src/linux-headers-4.14.67-ti-rt-r73'
  CC [M]  /home/debian/exploringbb/chp16/hello/hello.o
  Building modules, stage 2.
  MODPOST 1 modules
  CC      /home/debian/exploringbb/chp16/hello/hello.mod.o
  LD [M]  /home/debian/exploringbb/chp16/hello/hello.ko
make[1]: Leaving dir '/usr/src/linux-headers-4.14.67-ti-rt-r73'
```

At this point, the LKM has been created with the name hello.ko in the current directory. Note that this LKM can be executed only on your Beagle board and is applicable only to the current kernel version. The instructions for how to test this module are provided next.

```
debian@ebb:~/exploringbb/chp16/hello$ ls -l
total 32
-rw-r--r-- 1 debian debian 2202 Sep 10 01:01 hello.c
-rw-r--r-- 1 debian debian 4828 Sep 10 01:01 hello.ko
-rw-r--r-- 1 debian debian ·921 Sep 10 01:01 hello.mod.c
-rw-r--r-- 1 debian debian 2340 Sep 10 01:01 hello.mod.o
-rw-r--r-- 1 debian debian 3092 Sep 10 01:01 hello.o
-rw-r--r-- 1 debian debian  154 Sep 10 01:00 Makefile
-rw-r--r-- 1 debian debian   53 Sep 10 01:01 modules.order
-rw-r--r-- 1 debian debian    0 Sep 10 01:01 Module.symvers
```

Testing the First LKM Example

The "Hello World!" LKM can then be tested on the Beagle board by loading it into the kernel. Once again, these steps require superuser permissions:

```
debian@ebb:~/exploringbb/chp16/hello$ sudo -i
root@ebb:~# cd /home/debian/exploringbb/chp16/hello
root@ebb:/home/debian/exploringbb/chp16/hello# ls
hello.c  hello.ko  hello.mod.c  hello.mod.o  hello.o
```

```
Makefile  modules.order  Module.symvers
root@ebb:/home/debian/exploringbb/chp16/hello# ls -l *.ko
-rw-r--r-- 1 debian debian 4828 Sep 10 01:01 hello.ko
```

The LKM can be loaded using the `insmod` program to insert a module into the Linux kernel:

```
root@ebb:.../exploringbb/chp16/hello# insmod hello.ko
root@ebb:.../exploringbb/chp16/hello# lsmod | grep hello
Module                   Size  Used by
hello                   16384  0
```

You can get information about the loaded LKM using the `modinfo` command, which identifies the description, author, and any module parameters that are defined by the LKM source code.

```
root@ebb:/home/debian/exploringbb/chp16/hello# modinfo hello.ko
filename:   /home/debian/exploringbb/chp16/hello/hello.ko
version:    0.1
description:A simple Linux LKM for the Beagle.
author:     Derek Molloy
license:    GPL
srcversion: B8B4B178374781B4A6AB86B
depends:
name:       hello
vermagic:   4.14.67-ti-rt-r73 SMP preempt mod_unload ARMv7 p2v8
parm:       name: The name to display in /var/log/kern.log (charp)
```

You can see that the kernel version is compiled into the module and any module parameters are visible, such as `name` in this instance. The module can be removed from the Linux kernel using the `rmmod` program.

```
root@ebb:.../exploringbb/chp16/hello# rmmod hello.ko
```

You can repeat these steps and view the output live in the kernel log as a result of the use of the `printk()` function in Listing 16-1. I recommend that you use a second terminal window and view the live output as your LKM is loaded and unloaded, as follows:

```
root@ebb:/var/log# tail -f kern.log
...[328594.240926] hello: loading out-of-tree module taints kernel.
...[328594.247654] EBB: Hello world from the Beagle LKM!
...[328717.701464] EBB: Goodbye world from the Beagle LKM!
```

NOTE   The Linux kernel can be *tainted* in several ways, such as by using a non-GPL-compatible kernel module or by using modules that are not part of the mainline Linux kernel source code. The latter can be safely ignored, but such a taint indication can help system managers in troubleshooting kernel problems.

```
debian@ebb:~$ dmesg | grep -i taint
[328594.240926] hello: loading out-of-tree module taints kernel
```

```
[754433.963405] CPU:0 PID:6302 Comm:insmod Tainted:G O 4.14.67
debian@ebb:~$ cat /proc/sys/kernel/tainted
4608
```

This value is the sum of 4096 (an out-of-tree module has been loaded) and 512 (a kernel warning has occurred). The list of kernel taint values is available at www.kernel.org/doc/Documentation/sysctl/kernel.txt.

Testing the LKM Parameter

The code in Listing 16-1 contains a custom LKM parameter that can be set when the module is being loaded. Here's an example:

```
root@ebb:.../chp16/hello# insmod hello.ko name=Derek
```

If you view /var/log/kern.log at this point, the message Hello Derek appears in place of Hello world:

```
root@ebb:.../exploringbb/chp16/hello# tail -f /var/log/kern.log
... [330060.720442] EBB: Hello Derek from the Beagle LKM!
```

However, you can also see information about the kernel module that is loaded, as follows:

```
root@ebb:/home/debian/exploringbb/chp16/hello# cd /proc
root@ebb:/proc# cat modules | grep hello
hello 16384 0 - Live 0xbf191000 (O)
```

This is the same information that is provided by the lsmod command, but it also provides the current kernel memory offset for the loaded module, which is useful for debugging.

The LKM also has an entry under /sys/module/, which provides you with direct access to the custom parameter state. Here's an example:

```
root@ebb:/proc# cd /sys/module
root@ebb:/sys/module# ls -l | grep hello
drwxr-xr-x 6 root root 0 Sep 10 01:35 hello
root@ebb:/sys/module# cd hello/
root@ebb:/sys/module/hello# ls
coresize   initsize   notes        refcnt     srcversion  uevent
holders    initstate  parameters   sections   taint       version
root@ebb:/sys/module/hello# cat version
0.1
root@ebb:/sys/module/hello# cat taint
O
```

The version value is 0.1 as per the MODULE_VERSION("0.1") entry in Listing 16-1 and the taint value is O as per the license that has been chosen, which is MODULE_LICENSE("GPL").

The custom parameter value can be viewed as follows:

```
root@ebb:/sys/module/hello# cd parameters/
root@ebb:/sys/module/hello/parameters# ls -l
```

```
total 0
-r--r--r-- 1 root root 4096 Sep 10 01:38 name
root@ebb:/sys/module/hello/parameters# cat name
Derek
```

Using this directory structure, you can see that the state of the name variable is displayed. Superuser permissions are not required to read the value because of the S_IRUGO argument that is used in defining the module parameter. It is possible to configure this value for write access, but your module code will need to detect such a state change and act accordingly. Finally, you can remove the module and observe the output.

```
root@ebb:/sys/module/hello/parameters# cd ~/
root@ebb:~# rmmod hello.ko
root@ebb:~# tail /var/log/kern.log -n 2
... [330060.720442] EBB: Hello Derek from the Beagle LKM!
... [330255.806194] EBB: Goodbye Derek from the Beagle LKM!
```

It is important that you move away from any directory associated with the LKM before you unload it, because otherwise you can cause a kernel panic with something as simple as a call to ls.

An Embedded LKM Example

Now that you have built a first LKM, more sophisticated device drivers can be developed. For example, see the chapter web page on how to build a character device. However, the remaining examples in this chapter focus on interfacing LKM code to simple hardware circuits using kernel-based GPIO code. A single circuit is used for this chapter, as illustrated in Figure 16-2(a). The hardware configuration is similar to the user space GPIO circuits that are described in Chapter 6.

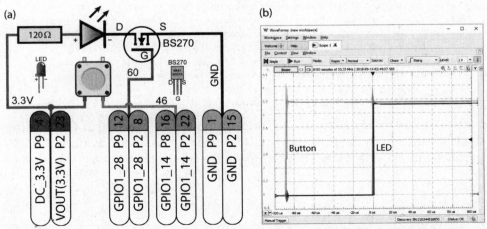

Figure 16-2: (a) An LED and pushbutton circuit for testing the GPIO LKM using the BBB and PocketBeagle, (b) LKM performance results (with software debouncing disabled)

Unlike Linux user space, the Linux kernel space has full support for interrupts. The first example in this section demonstrates how you can write an LKM that uses GPIOs and interrupts to achieve a faster response time than is possible in user space. I am not suggesting that you write all your GPIO code in kernel space, but these examples may provide inspiration for discrete tasks that you can perform in kernel space; the higher-level code can still be written in Linux user space.

First test that your circuit is working correctly by setting up GPIO60 (P9_12/P2.8) as an output and testing the LED and by setting up GPIO46 (P8_16/P2.22) as an input and testing that the button works correctly.

```
debian@ebb:/sys/class/gpio$ config-pin -q P9_12
P9_12 Mode: default Direction: out Value: 0
debian@ebb:/sys/class/gpio$ cd gpio60/
debian@ebb:/sys/class/gpio/gpio60$ echo out > direction
debian@ebb:/sys/class/gpio/gpio60$ echo 1 > value
debian@ebb:/sys/class/gpio/gpio60$ echo 0 > value
debian@ebb:/sys/class/gpio/gpio60$ cd ..
debian@ebb:/sys/class/gpio$ config-pin -q P8_16
P8_16 Mode: default Direction: in Value: 0
debian@ebb:/sys/class/gpio$ cd gpio46
debian@ebb:/sys/class/gpio/gpio46$ cat value
0
debian@ebb:/sys/class/gpio/gpio46$ cat value
1
```

Interestingly, the steps to control the GPIOs in Linux kernel space are similar to the previous steps. Linux GPIOs can easily be accessed and controlled from kernel space using the functions that are described in `linux/gpio.h`. Here are some of the most important functions that are available through the inclusion of this kernel header file:

```
/usr/src/linux-headers-4.14.67-ti-rt-r73/include/linux$ more gpio.h
static inline bool gpio_is_valid(int number)
static inline int  gpio_request(unsigned gpio, const char *label)
static inline int  gpio_direction_input(unsigned gpio)
static inline int  gpio_get_value(unsigned gpio)
static inline int  gpio_direction_output(unsigned gpio, int value)
static inline int  gpio_set_debounce(unsigned gpio, unsigned debounce)
static inline int  gpio_sysfs_set_active_low(unsigned gpio, int value)
static inline void gpio_free(unsigned gpio)
static inline int  gpio_to_irq(unsigned gpio)
```

Importantly, you can associate an interrupt request (IRQ) with a GPIO using the last function in the previous list. IRQs enable you to build efficient, high-performance code that detects a change in the input state.

Interrupt Service Routines

An interrupt is a signal that is sent to a microprocessor from an attached hardware device, software application, or circuit to indicate that an event has occurred that requires attention. Interrupts are high-priority conditions; the term essentially implies "interrupt what you are currently doing and do something instead." The processor suspends its current activities, saves the current state, and executes an interrupt handler function, which is also known as an *interrupt service routine* (ISR). Once the handler function has run to completion, the processor reloads its previous state and continues with its previous activities.

The LKM driver must register a handler function for the interrupt, which defines the actions that the interrupt should perform. In this example, the handler function is called `ebb_gpio_irq_handler()`, and it has the following form:

```
static irq_handler_t ebb_gpio_irq_handler(unsigned int irq,
   void *dev_id, struct pt_regs *regs) {
   // the actions that the interrupt should perform
   ... }
```

This handler function is then registered with an interrupt request (IRQ) using the `request_irq()` function as follows:

```
result = request_irq(irqNumber,           // the interrupt number
   (irq_handler_t) ebb_gpio_irq_handler,// pointer to the handler
   IRQF_TRIGGER_RISING,                  // interrupt on rising edge
   "ebb_gpio_handler",                   // used to identify the owner
   NULL);                   // *dev_id for shared interrupt lines, NULL
```

The `irqNumber` is determined automatically in the code example in Listing 16-3 by using the interrupt number that is associated with the respective GPIO number. Importantly, the GPIO number is not the interrupt number; however, there is a direct one-to-one mapping.

To undo the IRQ request, there is also a `free_irq()` function. In this first example, the `free_irq()` function is called from within the `ebb_gpio_exit()` function, which is invoked when the LKM is unloaded.

In this example, a simple momentary push button (as illustrated in Figure 16-2(a)) is used to generate an interrupt on the rising edge of a button press. It is also possible to generate the interrupt on the falling edge. (A full set of interrupt definitions is available in `/include/linux/interrupt.h`.) These flags can be combined using the bitwise OR operator to provide precise control over interrupt configuration.

The full source code for the first GPIO LKM is provided in Listing 16-3. The comments in the listing provide a description of the role of each function.

> **NOTE** Listing 16-3 uses a `gpio_set_bounce()` function call to ignore repeated edge transitions for a time period (typically of the order of 100ms to 200ms), once a single transition is detected. You should remove the `gpio_set_debounce()` function call if you want to use this code to detect multiple edge transitions on a "clean" digital signal, because software debouncing severely limits detection performance.

Listing 16-3: .../chp16/gpio/gpio_test.c

```c
#include <linux/init.h>
#include <linux/module.h>
#include <linux/kernel.h>
#include <linux/gpio.h>                 // for the GPIO functions
#include <linux/interrupt.h>            // for the IRQ code

MODULE_LICENSE("GPL");
MODULE_AUTHOR("Derek Molloy");
MODULE_DESCRIPTION("A Button/LED test driver for the Beagle");
MODULE_VERSION("0.1");

static unsigned int gpioLED = 60;       // P9_12/P2.8 (GPIO60)
static unsigned int gpioButton = 46;    // P8_16/P2.22 (GPIO46)
static unsigned int irqNumber;          // share IRQ num within file
static unsigned int numberPresses = 0;  // store number of presses
static bool         ledOn = 0;          // used to invert state of LED

// prototype for the custom IRQ handler function, function below
static irq_handler_t  ebb_gpio_irq_handler(unsigned int irq, void
                                *dev_id, struct pt_regs *regs);

/** @brief The LKM initialization function */
static int __init ebb_gpio_init(void){
   int result = 0;
   printk(KERN_INFO "GPIO_TEST: Initializing the GPIO_TEST LKM\n");
   if (!gpio_is_valid(gpioLED)){
      printk(KERN_INFO "GPIO_TEST: invalid LED GPIO\n");
      return -ENODEV;
   }
   ledOn = true;
   gpio_request(gpioLED, "sysfs");          // request LED GPIO
   gpio_direction_output(gpioLED, ledOn);   // set in output mode and on
// gpio_set_value(gpioLED, ledOn);          // not required
   gpio_export(gpioLED, false);             // appears in /sys/class/gpio
                                            // false prevents direction change
   gpio_request(gpioButton, "sysfs");       // set up gpioButton
   gpio_direction_input(gpioButton);        // set up as input
// gpio_set_debounce(gpioButton, 200);      // debounce delay of 200ms
   gpio_export(gpioButton, false);          // appears in /sys/class/gpio
```

```
   printk(KERN_INFO "GPIO_TEST: button value is currently: %d\n",
          gpio_get_value(gpioButton));
   irqNumber = gpio_to_irq(gpioButton);      // map GPIO to IRQ number
   printk(KERN_INFO "GPIO_TEST: button mapped to IRQ: %d\n", irqNumber);

   // This next call requests an interrupt line
   result = request_irq(irqNumber,           // interrupt number requested
           (irq_handler_t) ebb_gpio_irq_handler, // handler function
           IRQF_TRIGGER_RISING,  // on rising edge (press, not release)
           "ebb_gpio_handler",   // used in /proc/interrupts
           NULL);                // *dev_id for shared interrupt lines
   printk(KERN_INFO "GPIO_TEST: IRQ request result is: %d\n", result);
   return result;
}


/** @brief The LKM cleanup function  */
static void __exit ebb_gpio_exit(void){
   printk(KERN_INFO "GPIO_TEST: button value is currently: %d\n",
          gpio_get_value(gpioButton));
   printk(KERN_INFO "GPIO_TEST: pressed %d times\n", numberPresses);
   gpio_set_value(gpioLED, 0);       // turn the LED off
   gpio_unexport(gpioLED);           // unexport the LED GPIO
   free_irq(irqNumber, NULL);        // free the IRQ number, no *dev_id
   gpio_unexport(gpioButton);        // unexport the Button GPIO
   gpio_free(gpioLED);               // free the LED GPIO
   gpio_free(gpioButton);            // free the Button GPIO
   printk(KERN_INFO "GPIO_TEST: Goodbye from the LKM!\n");
}


/** @brief The GPIO IRQ Handler function
 * A custom interrupt handler that is attached to the GPIO. The same
 * interrupt handler cannot be invoked concurrently as the line is
 * masked out until the function is complete. This function is static
 * as it should not be invoked directly from outside of this file.
 * @param irq    the IRQ number associated with the GPIO
 * @param dev_id the *dev_id that is provided - used to identify
 * which device caused the interrupt. Not used here.
 * @param regs   h/w specific register values -used for debugging.
 * return returns IRQ_HANDLED if successful - return IRQ_NONE otherwise.
 */
static irq_handler_t ebb_gpio_irq_handler(unsigned int irq,
                     void *dev_id, struct pt_regs *regs){
   ledOn = !ledOn;                          // invert the LED state
   gpio_set_value(gpioLED, ledOn);     // set LED accordingly
   printk(KERN_INFO "GPIO_TEST: Interrupt! (button is %d)\n",
          gpio_get_value(gpioButton));
   numberPresses++;                         // global counter
   return (irq_handler_t) IRQ_HANDLED; // announce IRQ handled
}
```

> **NOTE**   If you see the message in the kernel logs "no symbol version for module_ layout," you should perform a `make clean` in the project directory and then download the `Module.symvers` file again (step 4). Finally, perform a `make` in the project directory. This issue can occur if you should type `sudo make` instead of `make` in the example directories.

The LKM that is described in Listing 16-3 can be built and loaded using the same steps as for the first LKM example.

```
debian@ebb:~/exploringbb/chp16/gpio$ ls -l
-rw-r--r-- 1 debian debian 4608 Sep 14 01:58 gpio_test.c
-rw-r--r-- 1 debian debian  158 Sep 14 01:53 Makefile
debian@ebb:~/exploringbb/chp16/gpio$ make
make -C /lib/modules/4.14.67-ti-rt-r73/build/ ...
make[1]: Entering dir '/usr/src/linux-headers-4.14.67-ti-rt-r73'
  CC [M]  /home/debian/exploringbb/chp16/gpio/gpio_test.o
  Building modules, stage 2.
  MODPOST 1 modules
  CC      /home/debian/exploringbb/chp16/gpio/gpio_test.mod.o
  LD [M]  /home/debian/exploringbb/chp16/gpio/gpio_test.ko
make[1]: Leaving dir '/usr/src/linux-headers-4.14.67-ti-rt-r73'
debian@ebb:~/exploringbb/chp16/gpio$ ls
gpio_test.c   gpio_test.mod.c  gpio_test.o   modules.order
gpio_test.ko  gpio_test.mod.o  Makefile      Module.symvers
debian@ebb:~/exploringbb/chp16/gpio$ sudo insmod gpio_test.ko
```

Then when the physical momentary push button that is wired as in Figure 16-2(a) is pressed, the kernel log reacts as follows:

```
debian@ebb:~/exploringbb/chp16/gpio$ dmesg
[678135.343606] GPIO_TEST: Initializing the GPIO_TEST LKM
[678135.344229] GPIO_TEST: button value is currently: 0
[678135.344240] GPIO_TEST: button mapped to IRQ: 109
[678135.350039] GPIO_TEST: IRQ request result is: 0
[678150.761332] GPIO_TEST: Interrupt! (button is 1)
[678150.905016] GPIO_TEST: Interrupt! (button is 1)
```

At this point, you can view the `/proc/interrupts` entry, and you can see that the name of the interrupt handler is listed as `ebb_gpio_handler`, as configured in the code in Listing 16-3. You can also see that the interrupt associated with the GPIO has number 109, which aligns with the value that is outputted in the preceding kernel logs.

```
debian@ebb:/proc$ cat interrupts | grep 109:
109:           8 4804c000.gpio  14 Edge      ebb_gpio_handler
```

Again, it is important to note that the interrupt number 109 is not the GPIO number, which is GPIO46 ($PINS 14) for the button. When the module is unloaded, the log output becomes the following:

```
debian@ebb:~/exploringbb/chp16/gpio$ sudo rmmod gpio_test
debian@ebb:~/exploringbb/chp16/gpio$ dmesg | tail -n 5
```

```
[678151.485877] GPIO_TEST: Interrupt! (button is 1)
[678151.486047] GPIO_TEST: Interrupt! (button is 1)
[678597.926764] GPIO_TEST: button value is currently: 0
[678597.926784] GPIO_TEST: pressed 6 times
[678597.936407] GPIO_TEST: Goodbye from the LKM!
```

Performance

One useful feature of this LKM is that it allows you to evaluate the response time (interrupt latency time) of the system as a whole. A press of the momentary push button results in the inversion of the state of the LED; if the LED is on, it turns off when the button is pressed. To measure this delay, an oscilloscope is used, which is configured to trigger on the rising edge of the button signal. The oscilloscope provides an independent time measurement, and its output is displayed in Figure 16-2(b). The latency is approximately 90µs. On repeated testing this delay varies between a minimum of 80µs to a maximum of 100µs approximately.

Enhanced Button GPIO Driver LKM

The third example builds on the second example to create an enhanced GPIO driver, which permits a user to configure and interact with a GPIO button using sysfs. This module allows a GPIO button to be mapped to Linux user space where it can be utilized directly. The best way to explain the capability of this module is with a use case example. In this example, the button is attached to GPIO46, and once the LKM is loaded, it can be accessed and manipulated as follows:

```
debian@ebb:~/exploringbb/chp16/button$ sudo insmod button.ko
debian@ebb:~/exploringbb/chp16/button$ lsmod | grep button
button                 16384  0
debian@ebb:~/exploringbb/chp16/button$ cd /sys/ebb/gpio46/
debian@ebb:/sys/ebb/gpio46$ ls -l
total 0
-r--r--r-- 1 root root 4096 Sep 14 23:09 diffTime
-rw-rw-r-- 1 root root 4096 Sep 14 23:09 isDebounce
-r--r--r-- 1 root root 4096 Sep 14 23:09 lastTime
-r--r--r-- 1 root root 4096 Sep 14 23:09 ledOn
-rw-rw-r-- 1 root root 4096 Sep 14 23:09 numberPresses
debian@ebb:/sys/ebb/gpio46$ cat numberPresses
0
debian@ebb:/sys/ebb/gpio46$ cat numberPresses
2
debian@ebb:/sys/ebb/gpio46$ cat ledOn
1
debian@ebb:/sys/ebb/gpio46$ cat lastTime
22:09:46:727954425
```

```
debian@ebb:/sys/ebb/gpio46$ cat diffTime
0.226262367
debian@ebb:/sys/ebb/gpio46$ sudo sh -c "echo 0 > isDebounce"
debian@ebb:/sys/ebb/gpio46$ cat isDebounce
0
debian@ebb:/sys/ebb/gpio46$ sudo sh -c "echo 1 > isDebounce"
debian@ebb:/sys/ebb/gpio46$ cat isDebounce
1
```

Despite the complexity involved in creating this LKM, the user interface is straightforward and can be utilized by an executable program on your embedded system that can be written in any programming language. Sysfs is a memory-based file system that provides a mechanism to export kernel data structures, attributes, and linkages to Linux user space. The infrastructure that enables sysfs to function is heavily based on the kobject interface.

The kobject Interface

The driver model in Linux uses a kobject abstraction. To understand this model, you must first appreciate the following important concepts:[1]

- **kobject:** A kobject is a struct that consists of a name, a reference count, a type, a sysfs representation, and a pointer to a parent object (see Listing 16-4). Importantly, kobjects are not useful on their own; instead, they are embedded within other data structures and used to control access. This is similar to the object-oriented concept of generalized top-level parent classes (e.g., the Object class in Java, or the QObject class in Qt).

- **ktype:** A ktype is the type of the object that the kobject is embedded within. It controls what happens when the object is created and destroyed.

- **kset:** A kset is a group of kobjects that can be of different ktypes. A kset of kobjects can be thought of as a sysfs directory that contains a collection of subdirectories (kobjects).

Listing 16-4: The kobject Structure

```
#define KOBJ_NAME_LEN    20

struct kobject {
    char                *k_name;      // kobject name pointer (not NULL)
    char                name[KOBJ_NAME_LEN];  // short internal name
    struct kref         kref;         // the reference count
    struct list_head    entry;        // linked list to members of the kset
    struct kobject      *parent;      // the parent kobject
    struct kset         *kset;        // kobject can be a member of a set
```

---

[1]From "Everything you never wanted to know about kobjects, ksets, and ktypes", Greg Kroah-Hartman, www.kernel.org/doc/Documentation/kobject.txt

```
        struct kobj_type   *ktype;    // kobj_type describes object type
        struct dentry      *dentry;   // the sysfs directory entry
};
```

For this example LKM, a single kobject is required, which is mapped to /sys/ebb/ on the file system. This single kobject contains all the attributes required for the interaction that is demonstrated earlier (e.g., viewing the numberPresses entry). This is achieved in Listing 16-5 through the use of the kobject_create_and_add() function, as follows:

```
static struct kobject *ebb_kobj;
ebb_kobj = kobject_create_and_add("ebb", kernel_kobj->parent);
```

The kernel_kobj pointer provides a reference to /sys/kernel/. If you remove the call to ->parent, the ebb entry will be placed at /sys/kernel/ebb/, but for clarity, I have placed it at /sys/ebb/; this is not best practice! (Also, sysfs_create_dir() performs the same role.) For this example LKM, a set of subsystem-specific callback functions must be implemented to expose its attributes via sysfs using functions of the following form:

```
static ssize_t dev_attribute_show(struct kobject *kobj,
                  struct kobj_attribute *attr, char *buf);
static ssize_t dev_attribute_store(struct kobject *kobj,
                  struct kobj_attribute *attr, char *buf);
```

When a sysfs attribute is read from or written to, the _show and _store functions are called respectively. The sysfs.h header file defines the following helper macros that make defining the attributes more straightforward:

- __ATTR(_name,_mode,_show,_store): Long-hand version. You must pass the attribute variable name _name, the access mode _mode (e.g., 0664 for read/write access, except for *others*), the pointer to the show function _show, and the pointer to the store function _store.

- __ATTR_RO(_name): Short-hand read-only attribute macro. You must pass the attribute variable name _name, and the macro sets the _mode to be 0444 (read-only) and the _show function to be _name_show.

- __ATTR_WO(_name) and __ATTR_RW(_name): Write-only and read/write.

Listing 16-5 provides the full source code for the enhanced GPIO button LKM. It may appear to be quite lengthy, but you will see that this is because there is a lot of comment and additional printk() calls so that you can see exactly what is happening as the code is executing. This example builds on the work in Listing 16-3; it also includes an LED so that you can observe interaction at the circuit itself.

Listing 16-5: .../chp16/button/button.c

```c
#include <linux/init.h>
#include <linux/module.h>
#include <linux/kernel.h>
#include <linux/gpio.h>          // Required for the GPIO functions
#include <linux/interrupt.h>     // Required for the IRQ code
#include <linux/kobject.h>       // Using kobjects for the sysfs bindings
#include <linux/time.h>          // Using clock to measure button press times
#define  DEBOUNCE_TIME 200       // The default bounce time -- 200ms

MODULE_LICENSE("GPL");
MODULE_AUTHOR("Derek Molloy");
MODULE_DESCRIPTION("A simple Linux GPIO Button LKM for the Beagle");
MODULE_VERSION("0.1");

static bool isRising = 1;                   // rising edge default IRQ property
module_param(isRising, bool, S_IRUGO);      // S_IRUGO read/not changed
MODULE_PARM_DESC(isRising, " Rising edge = 1 (default), Falling edge = 0");

static unsigned int gpioButton = 46;        // default GPIO is 46
module_param(gpioButton, uint, S_IRUGO);    // S_IRUGO can be read/not changed
MODULE_PARM_DESC(gpioButton, " GPIO Button number (default=46)");

static unsigned int gpioLED = 60;           // default GPIO is 60
module_param(gpioLED, uint, S_IRUGO);       // S_IRUGO can be read/not changed
MODULE_PARM_DESC(gpioLED, " GPIO LED number (default=60)");

static char    gpioName[8] = "gpioXXX";     // null terminated default string
static int     irqNumber;                   // used to share the IRQ number
static int     numberPresses = 0;           // store number of button presses
static bool    ledOn = 0;                   // used to invert the LED state
static bool    isDebounce = 1;              // use to store debounce state
static struct timespec ts_last, ts_current, ts_diff;  // nano precision

// Function prototype for the custom IRQ handler function
static irq_handler_t  ebb_gpio_irq_handler(unsigned int irq,
                                void *dev_id, struct pt_regs *regs);

/** @brief A callback function to output the numberPresses variable
 *  @param kobj a kernel object device that appears in the sysfs filesystem
 *  @param attr the pointer to the kobj_attribute struct
 *  @param buf the buffer to which to write the number of presses
 *  @return return the total number of characters written to the buffer
 */
static ssize_t numberPresses_show(struct kobject *kobj,
                                struct kobj_attribute *attr, char *buf) {
   return sprintf(buf, "%d\n", numberPresses);
}

/** @brief A callback function to read in the numberPresses variable */
static ssize_t numberPresses_store(struct kobject *kobj, struct
                kobj_attribute *attr, const char *buf, size_t count) {
```

```c
    sscanf(buf, "%du", &numberPresses);
    return count;
}

/** @brief Displays if the LED is on or off */
static ssize_t ledOn_show(struct kobject *kobj, struct kobj_attribute *attr,
                          char *buf) {
    return sprintf(buf, "%d\n", ledOn);
}

/** @brief Displays the last time the button was pressed - manually output*/
static ssize_t lastTime_show(struct kobject *kobj,
                             struct kobj_attribute *attr, char *buf){
    return sprintf(buf, "%.2lu:%.2lu:%.2lu:%.9lu \n", (ts_last.tv_sec/3600)%24,
           (ts_last.tv_sec/60) % 60, ts_last.tv_sec % 60, ts_last.tv_nsec );
}

/** @brief Display the time diff in the form secs.nanosecs to 9 places */
static ssize_t diffTime_show(struct kobject *kobj,
                             struct kobj_attribute *attr, char *buf){
    return sprintf(buf, "%lu.%.9lu\n", ts_diff.tv_sec, ts_diff.tv_nsec);
}

/** @brief Displays if button debouncing is on or off */
static ssize_t isDebounce_show(struct kobject *kobj,
                               struct kobj_attribute *attr, char *buf){
    return sprintf(buf, "%d\n", isDebounce);
}

/** @brief Stores and sets the debounce state */
static ssize_t isDebounce_store(struct kobject *kobj, struct kobj_attribute
                                *attr, const char *buf, size_t count){
    unsigned int temp;
    sscanf(buf, "%du", &temp);        // use temp var for correct int->bool
    gpio_set_debounce(gpioButton,0);
    isDebounce = temp;
    if(isDebounce) { gpio_set_debounce(gpioButton, DEBOUNCE_TIME);
       printk(KERN_INFO "EBB Button: Debounce on\n");
    }
    else { gpio_set_debounce(gpioButton, 0);  // set the debounce time to 0
       printk(KERN_INFO "EBB Button: Debounce off\n");
    }
    return count;
}

/**  Use these helper macros to define the name and access levels of the
 * kobj_attributes. The kobj_attribute has an attribute attr (name and mode),
 * show and store function pointers. The count variable is associated with
 * the numberPresses variable and it is to be exposed with mode 0664 using
 * the numberPresses_show and numberPresses_store functions above
 */
static struct kobj_attribute count_attr = __ATTR(numberPresses, 0664, →
  numberPresses_show, numberPresses_store);
```

```
static struct kobj_attribute debounce_attr = __ATTR(isDebounce, 0664, →
  isDebounce_show, isDebounce_store);

/** The __ATTR_RO macro defines a read-only attribute. There is no need to
 * identify that the function is called _show, but it must be present.
 * __ATTR_WO can be used for a write-only attribute only Linux 3.11.x+
 */
static struct kobj_attribute ledon_attr = __ATTR_RO(ledOn);
static struct kobj_attribute time_attr  = __ATTR_RO(lastTime);
static struct kobj_attribute diff_attr  = __ATTR_RO(diffTime);

/** The ebb_attrs[] is an array of attributes that is used to create the
 * attribute group below. The attr property of the kobj_attribute is used
 * to extract the attribute struct
 */
static struct attribute *ebb_attrs[] = {
      &count_attr.attr,        // the number of button presses
      &ledon_attr.attr,        // is the LED on or off?
      &time_attr.attr,         // button press time in HH:MM:SS:NNNNNNNNN
      &diff_attr.attr,         // time difference between last two presses
      &debounce_attr.attr,     // is debounce state true or false
      NULL,
};

/** The attribute group uses the attribute array and a name, which is
 * exposed on sysfs -- in this case it is gpio46, which is automatically
 * defined in the ebb_button_init() function below using the custom kernel
 * parameter that can be passed when the module is loaded.
 */
static struct attribute_group attr_group = {
      .name  = gpioName,         // the name generated in ebb_button_init()
      .attrs = ebb_attrs,        // the attributes array defined just above
};

static struct kobject *ebb_kobj;

/** @brief The LKM initialization function */
static int __init ebb_button_init(void){
   int result = 0;
   unsigned long IRQflags = IRQF_TRIGGER_RISING;
   printk(KERN_INFO "EBB Button: Initializing the button LKM\n");
   sprintf(gpioName, "gpio%d", gpioButton);   // create /sys/ebb/gpio46

   // create the kobject sysfs entry at /sys/ebb
   ebb_kobj = kobject_create_and_add("ebb", kernel_kobj->parent);
   if(!ebb_kobj){
      printk(KERN_ALERT "EBB Button: failed to create kobject mapping\n");
      return -ENOMEM;
   }
   // add the attributes to /sys/ebb/ e.g., /sys/ebb/gpio46/numberPresses
   result = sysfs_create_group(ebb_kobj, &attr_group);
   if(result) {
```

```
        printk(KERN_ALERT "EBB Button: failed to create sysfs group\n");
        kobject_put(ebb_kobj);                  // clean up remove entry
        return result;
    }
    getnstimeofday(&ts_last);                    // set last time to current
    ts_diff = timespec_sub(ts_last, ts_last);  // set initial time diff=0

    // set up the LED. It is a GPIO in output mode and will be on by default
    ledOn = true;
    gpio_request(gpioLED, "sysfs");             // gpioLED is hardcoded to 60
    gpio_direction_output(gpioLED, ledOn);      // set in output mode
    gpio_export(gpioLED, false);                // appears in /sys/class/gpio/
    gpio_request(gpioButton, "sysfs");          // set up the gpioButton
    gpio_direction_input(gpioButton);           // set up as an input
    gpio_set_debounce(gpioButton, DEBOUNCE_TIME); // ddebounce the button
    gpio_export(gpioButton, false);             // appears in /sys/class/gpio/
    printk(KERN_INFO "EBB Button: button state: %d\n",
           gpio_get_value(gpioButton));
    irqNumber = gpio_to_irq(gpioButton);
    printk(KERN_INFO "EBB Button: button mapped to IRQ: %d\n", irqNumber);
    if(!isRising){                              // if kernel param isRising=0
        IRQflags = IRQF_TRIGGER_FALLING;        // set on falling edge
    }
    // This next call requests an interrupt line
    result = request_irq(irqNumber,             // the interrupt number
                         (irq_handler_t) ebb_gpio_irq_handler,
                         IRQflags,              // use custom kernel param
                         "ebb_button_handler", // used in /proc/interrupts
                         NULL);                 // the *dev_id for shared lines
    return result;
}

static void __exit ebb_button_exit(void){
    printk(KERN_INFO "EBB Button: The button was pressed %d times\n",
           numberPresses);
    kobject_put(ebb_kobj);          // clean up, remove kobject sysfs entry
    gpio_set_value(gpioLED, 0);     // turn the LED off, device was unloaded
    gpio_unexport(gpioLED);         // unexport the LED GPIO
    free_irq(irqNumber, NULL);      // free IRQ number, no *dev_id reqd here
    gpio_unexport(gpioButton);      // unexport the Button GPIO
    gpio_free(gpioLED);             // free the LED GPIO
    gpio_free(gpioButton);          // free the Button GPIO
    printk(KERN_INFO "EBB Button: Goodbye from the EBB Button LKM!\n");
}

/** @brief The GPIO IRQ Handler function
 *  This function is a custom interrupt handler that is attached to the GPIO
 *  above. The same interrupt handler cannot be invoked concurrently as the
 *  interrupt line is masked out until the function is complete. This function
 *  is static as it should not be invoked directly from outside of this file.
 *  @param irq   IRQ number associated with the GPIO -- useful for logging.
 *  @param dev_id the *dev_id that is provided -- can be used to identify
 *      which device caused the interrupt
```

```
 *   Not used in this example as NULL is passed.
 *   @param regs   h/w specific register values -- only used for debugging.
 *   return returns IRQ_HANDLED if successful -- return IRQ_NONE otherwise.
 */
static irq_handler_t ebb_gpio_irq_handler(unsigned int irq,
                                   void *dev_id, struct pt_regs *regs){
   ledOn = !ledOn;                         // invert LED on each button press
   gpio_set_value(gpioLED, ledOn);    // set the physical LED accordingly
   getnstimeofday(&ts_current);       // get the current time as ts_current
   ts_diff = timespec_sub(ts_current, ts_last);   // determine the time diff
   ts_last = ts_current;               // store current time as ts_last
   printk(KERN_INFO "EBB Button: The button state is currently: %d\n",
                gpio_get_value(gpioButton));
   numberPresses++;                    // count number of presses
   return (irq_handler_t) IRQ_HANDLED;  // announce IRQ was handled correctly
}


// This next calls are  mandatory -- they identify the initialization function
// and the cleanup function (as above).
module_init(ebb_button_init);
module_exit(ebb_button_exit);
```

The code in Listing 16-5 is described by the comments throughout; however, there are a few more points that are worth mentioning.

- Three module parameters are made available to be configured as the LKM is loaded (isRising, gpioButton, and gpioLED). The use of LKM parameters is described in the first LKM example. This allows you to define different GPIOs for the button input and LED output; their sysfs mount names are automatically adjusted. The code also allows for a falling-edge interrupt in place of the default rising-edge interrupt.

- There are five attributes associated with the kobject entry (ebb). These are diffTime, isDebounce, lastTime, ledOn, and numberPresses. They are all read-only, with the exception of isDebounce and numberPresses (i.e., can be set to any value, e.g., reset to 0).

- The ebb_gpio_irq_handler() function performs the majority of the timing. The clock time is stored, and the inter-press time is determined each time that the interrupt is handled.

The module can be loaded in falling-edge mode and tested using the following:

```
debian@ebb:~/exploringbb/chp16/button$ make
debian@ebb:~/exploringbb/chp16/button$ sudo insmod button.ko
debian@ebb:~/exploringbb/chp16/button$ lsmod | grep button
button                 16384  0
debian@ebb:~/exploringbb/chp16/button$ cd /sys/ebb
```

```
debian@ebb:/sys/ebb$ ls
gpio46
debian@ebb:/sys/ebb$ cd gpio46/
debian@ebb:/sys/ebb/gpio46$ ls -l
-r--r--r-- 1 root root 4096 Sep 14 23:03 diffTime
-rw-rw-r-- 1 root root 4096 Sep 14 23:03 isDebounce
-r--r--r-- 1 root root 4096 Sep 14 23:03 lastTime
-r--r--r-- 1 root root 4096 Sep 14 23:03 ledOn
-rw-rw-r-- 1 root root 4096 Sep 14 23:03 numberPresses
debian@ebb:/sys/ebb/gpio46$ cat numberPresses
0
debian@ebb:/sys/ebb/gpio46$ cat numberPresses
2
debian@ebb:/sys/ebb/gpio46$ cat diffTime
0.258064856
debian@ebb:/sys/ebb/gpio46$ cat lastTime
22:03:08:843581297
debian@ebb:/sys/ebb/gpio46$ sudo sh -c "echo 0 > numberPresses"
debian@ebb:/sys/ebb/gpio46$ cat numberPresses
0
debian@ebb:/sys/ebb/gpio46$ cat numberPresses
1
debian@ebb:/sys/ebb/gpio46$ cd ~/exploringbb/chp16/button/
debian@ebb:~/exploringbb/chp16/button$ sudo rmmod button
```

Note the permissions (0664) on the isDebounce and numberPresses entries, which correlate directly with the program code in Listing 16-5. Ensure that you exit the /sys/ebb/ directory before unloading the module; otherwise, you will cause a kernel panic if you perform an operation such as ls.

The simultaneous output in the kernel logs (/var/log/kern.log) is as follows:

```
debian@ebb:~/exploringbb/chp16/button$ dmesg
[752877.425661] EBB Button: Initializing the button LKM
[752877.426364] EBB Button: button state: 0
[752877.426376] EBB Button: button mapped to IRQ: 109
[752908.518265] EBB Button: The button state is currently: 1
[752908.776338] EBB Button: The button state is currently: 1
[752953.694400] EBB Button: The button state is currently: 1
[752972.465413] EBB Button: The button was pressed 1 times
[752972.473613] EBB Button: Goodbye from the EBB Button LKM!
```

Enhanced LED GPIO Driver LKM

The final example in this chapter is a driver for controlling an LED using an LKM. This example is designed to introduce the use of kernel threads, kthreads, which can be started in response to an event that occurs in our LKM. In this example, kthreads are used to flash the LED at a user-defined interval.

Kernel Threads

The general structure of the code in this example is provided in Listing 16-6. This is a reasonably unusual thread in the Linux kernel, as we require a specific sleep time to get a consistent flash period. The return of resources to the kthread scheduler is usually performed with a call to `schedule()`.

The call to `kthread_run()` is quite similar to the user space pthread function `pthread_create()`. (See the section on POSIX threads in Chapter 6.) The `kthread_run()` call expects a pointer to the thread function (`flash()` in this case), the data to be sent to the thread (NULL in this case), and the name of the thread, which is displayed in the output from a call to `top` or `ps`. The `kthread_run()` function returns a `task_struct`, which is shared between the various functions within this C file as `*task`.

Listing 16-6: An Outline of the kthread Implementation

```
#include <linux/kthread.h>
static struct task_struct *task;          // pointer to the thread task

static int flash(void *arg) {
   while(!kthread_should_stop()){          // kthread_stop() call returns true
      set_current_state(TASK_RUNNING);     // prevent sleeps temporarily
      ...                                  // state change instructions (flash)
      set_current_state(TASK_INTERRUPTIBLE);    // sleep but can be awoken
      msleep(...);                              // millisecond sleep
   }
}

static int __init ebb_LED_init(void) {
   task = kthread_run(flash, NULL, "LED_flash_thread");   // start kthread
   ...
}

static void __exit ebb_LED_exit(void) {
   kthread_stop(task);                      // Stop the LED flashing kthread
   ...
}
```

The final source code is not presented here because it is lengthy and similar to Listing 16-5, but with the addition of the thread code. It is available at `/chp16/LED/led.c`, and the comments therein provide a full description of the integration of all the tasks. However, there are a few additional points worth noting.

- An enumeration, called *modes*, is used to define the three possible running states. When you are passing commands to a LKM, you have to carefully parse the data to ensure it is valid and within range. In this example, the string command can be only one of three values ("on," "off," or "flash"), and the period value must be between 2 and 10000 (ms).

■ The kthread_should_stop() evaluates to a bool. When a function such as kthread_stop() is called on the kthread, this function will wake and return true. This causes the kthread to run to completion, after which the return value from the kthread will be returned by the kthread_stop() function.

This example can be built and executed as follows, where you can increase the frequency of the flash by reducing the sleep period to be 2ms so that you can observe the CPU loading, using the following call:

```
debian@ebb:~/exploringbb/chp16/LED$ make
debian@ebb:~/exploringbb/chp16/LED$ sudo insmod led.ko
debian@ebb:~/exploringbb/chp16/LED$ lsmod | grep led
led                    16384  0
debian@ebb:~/exploringbb/chp16/LED$ cd /sys/ebb/led60/
debian@ebb:/sys/ebb/led60$ ls -l
total 0
-rw-rw-r-- 1 root root 4096 Sep 14 23:29 blinkPeriod
-rw-rw-r-- 1 root root 4096 Sep 14 23:29 mode
debian@ebb:/sys/ebb/led60$ cat blinkPeriod
1000
debian@ebb:/sys/ebb/led60$ sudo sh -c "echo 100 > blinkPeriod"
debian@ebb:/sys/ebb/led60$ cat blinkPeriod
100
```

The CPU loading of this LKM is quite low at ~0.0 percent of CPU when it is flashing with a sleep duration of 2ms:

```
debian@ebb:/sys/ebb/led60$ sudo sh -c "echo 2 > blinkPeriod"
debian@ebb:/sys/ebb/led60$ ps aux | grep LED
root  6330 0.0 0.0 0   0 ? D  23:29 0:00 [LED_flash_thread]
debian@ebb:/sys/ebb/led60$ sudo sh -c "echo off > mode"
debian@ebb:/sys/ebb/led60$ sudo sh -c "echo on > mode"
debian@ebb:/sys/ebb/led60$ sudo sh -c "echo flash > mode"
debian@ebb:/sys/ebb/led60$ cd ~/exploringbb/chp16/LED/
debian@ebb:~/exploringbb/chp16/LED$ sudo rmmod led
```

The kernel logs give the following output:

```
[754476.056631] EBB LED: Initializing the EBB LED LKM
[754476.063535] EBB LED: Thread has started running
[754734.149136] EBB LED: Thread has run to completion
[754734.155086] EBB LED: Goodbye from the Beagle LED LKM!
```

The results for this approach are quite impressive when compared to similar tests in Linux user space. The results have a consistent ~50 percent duty cycle, and the range of frequency values is quite consistent.

Conclusions

Remember that the kernel is essentially a program—a big and complex program but a program nevertheless. It is possible to make changes to the kernel code, recompile, redeploy, and then reboot, which is quite a lengthy process. This chapter has exposed you to writing your own Linux loadable kernel modules, which allow you to create binary code that can be loaded and unloaded from the kernel at run time.

The examples that are presented in this chapter are for the purpose of learning. It is unlikely that you would ever need to write a LKM to control pushbuttons or LEDs directly. For example, there are GPIO-keys and GPIO-LEDs drivers available in Linux to provide sophisticated kernel support for such circuits. However, these examples should provide a strong basis for other embedded LKM development tasks.

For further information on GPIO kernel programming under Linux, see the following:

- The GPIO Sysfs Interface for User Space: `tiny.cc/beagle1602`
- GPIO Interfaces (in Kernel Space): `tiny.cc/beagle1603`
- *Linux Kernel Development*, Robert Love, Addison-Wesley Professional; third edition (July 2, 2010) 978-0672329463

Summary

After completing this chapter, you should be able to do the following:

- Write a basic Linux loadable kernel module (LKM) that can receive a kernel argument
- Build, load, and unload a custom LKM on a Beagle board
- Undertake the steps required to build a module for embedded devices that can control GPIOs
- Appreciate some of the concepts required to build LKMs on an embedded Linux device, such as interrupts, kobjects, and kernel threads

Index

>> Linux command, 113–114
> Linux command, 113–114

A

A2DP (Advanced Audio Distribution
    Profile) audio, 666–667
ABI (application binary interface), 310
accelerometers, ADXL345, 347
accessories, 19
    Ethernet cable, 22
    HDMI cable, 22–23
    micro-HDMI to VGA adapters, 25
    micro-SD cards, 20–21
    optional, 24–26
    PocketBeagle, headers, 20
    power supply, external, 5V, 22
    USB hub, 25
    USB keyboard and mouse, 26
    USB-to-serial UART TTL cable, 23–24
    USB webcam, 25–26
access specifier keyword, 231
actuators, 402
    linear, 402
    precision, 402
    relays
        EMRs (electromechanical relays),
            417–418
        SSRs (solid-state rays), 417–418
Adafruit IO service, MQTT and, 497
Adafruit Proto cape, 27
adapters

micro-HDMI to VGA, 25
support, 7
Wi-Fi, 25
ADC (analog-to-digital conversion), 139
    inputs
        diode clamping circuit, 421–422
        op-amp clamping, 422–426
    operational amplifiers
        ideal, 178–180
        negative feedback, 181
        positive feedback, 181
    quantization, 178
    sampling rate, 177–178
    sampling resolution, 177
    successive approximation, 280
ADXL335 conditioning, 436–437
ADXL345 SPI interface, 370–373
.a library, 452–453
Altoids tins, 11
AM335x ARM Technical Reference Manual
    (TRM), 84–85
AM335x (ZCZ) processor, 11
    PRU-ICSS
        remoteproc setup, 679–680
        remoteproc testing, 680–682
amps, 143
analog inputs
    enabling, 280–282
    light meter application, 282–284
    SAR (successive approximation register),
        280

virtual cape, 280
Vref, 283–285
analog outputs
  PWM (pulse-width modulation), 285–290
  servo motor application, 289–290
analog read, BoneScript and, 292–293
analog sensors
  acceleration, 419
  ADC inputs, 420
    diode clamping circuit, 421–422
    op-amp clamping, 422–426
  applications, 419
  digital, comparison, 420
  distance, 419
  instruments, 419
  interfacing examples
    ADXL335 conditioning, 436–437
    IR distance sensing, 431–436
  light level, 419
  magnetic fields, 419
  motion detection, 419
  sensors, 419
  signal conditioning, scaling
    signal offsetting and, 428–431
    voltage division and, 427–428
  sound, 419
  temperature, 419
  touch, 419
  transducers, 418–419
  types, 419
analog to digital converters, external,
  424–426
analog write, PWM (pulse width
  modulation), 293–294
Android app development, Bluetooth and,
  563–564
Ångström, 33
  Dropbear, 44
Apache Server, 86–87
applications
  PRU-ICSS
    GPIOs, 702–704
    performance tests, 698–701
    PWM generator, 704–707
    sine wave generator, 708–709
    ultrasonic sensor, 709–714
  real-time interfacing, 7
apt update, 313
Arch Linux, 33
Arduino microcontroller, 7, 471–474

I²C slave
  C/C++ slave communication, 488–490
  register echo example, 482–484
  temperature sensor example, 484–485
  temperature sensor with warning
    LED, 486–488
  test circuit, 481–482
  ultrasonic sensor, 490–493
serial slave, 474
  UART echo test, 475–478
UART command control, 478–481
arguments, functions, 211
armhf architecture emulation, 312–313
ARM NEON, 188
ASLA utilities, audio and, 661
assembly language, PRU program, 688–690
audio
  Bluetooth, 660
  HDMI, 660
  McASP (multichannel audio serial port),
    660
  software tools
    ASLA utilities, 661
    Libav, 661
    MPlayer, 661
  USB, 660
audio devices
  Bluetooth A2DP, 666–667, 666–669
  HDMI, 661–664
  Internet radio, 664
  network streaming, 666
  recording audio, 664–665
    WAV files, 665
  text-to-speech, 669–670
  USB, 661–664
AVR microcontroller, 7

B

background processes, 122–124
ball-grid array (BGA) package, 5
bash, 192, 193–197
bash terminal window, Cloud9, 67
BeagleBoard, 10
BeagleBoard Black System Reference
  Manual (SRM), 9
BeagleBoard.org, documentation, 8–9
BeagleBoard.org Foundation, 4
Beagle boards. *See* boards
BeagleBoard X15, 10
BeagleBoard xM, 10

BeagleBone, 10
  buttons, 15
  connectors, 15
  DC power, 15
  debug, 15
  Ethernet processor, 15
  expansion headers, 15
  graphics, 15
  LEDs, 15
  memory, 15
  network, 15
  on-board storage, 15
  power, 15
  power management, 15
  processor, 15
  SD card, 15
  serial debug, 15
    cabling and, 24
  subsystems, 15
  USB, 15
  versions, 10–12
  video out, 15
BeagleBone Black (BBB), 10, 16
  Ethernet, 11
  UI (user interface), 600
BeagleBone Black Wireless, 10
BeagleBone Blue Wireless, 10, 12
BeagleBone Enhanced, 10
BeagleBone Green, 10
BeagleBone White, 10
BGA (ball-grid array), 5
bidirectional data buses, 396–397
bidirectional transmission, 343
  SPI in C, 370–376
binaries, multicall, 228–229
binary numbers, 169–170
BJTs (bipolar junction transistors), 158
Black Wireless board, 5–6
Bluetooth, 557–558
  A2DP audio, 666–667
  adapter installation, 558–559
    configuration, 560–561
    discoverability, 561–563
    LKM (loadable kernel module),
      559–560
  Android app development, 563–564
  audio, 660
  GPIO (general-purpose input/output)
    and, 248
  input peripherals, connecting, 603–604

LE (low energy), 556
SIG (Special Interest Group), 557
SNK (sink device), 667
SPP (Serial Port Profile), 561
SRC (source device), 667
Boa, 501
boards, 3–4
  audio devices
    Bluetooth A2DP, 666–667, 666–669
    HDMI, 661–664
    Internet radio, 664
    network streaming, 666
    recording audio, 664–666
    text-to-speech, 669–670
    USB, 661–664
  Black Wireless, 5–6
  booting
    bootloaders, 74–83
    kernel space, 83–85
    system and service manager, 85–90
    user space, 83–85
  build-your-own, 5
  capes, 26–27
  cautions, 27–29
  comparison, 13–14
  drivers, installation, 34–35
  email, 524–526
  I²C (Inter-Integrated Circuit) and,
    344–346
  Octavo Systems System-in-Package (SiP),
    5
  open-hardware, 4
  open-software, 4
  PCB (printed circuit board), 4–5
  PHP, 506–507
  physical appearance, 4
  power use, 4
  SBC (single-board computing) boards, 4
  Texas Instruments Sitara AM 335x System
    on Chip (SOC), 5
  web clients, 498
  web servers, 498
    sensors, 501–512
  when not to use, 7–8
  when to use, 7
Bone101, 511–512
BoneScript, 64
  analog read, 292–293
  analog write, PWM (pulse width
    modulation), 293–294

digital read/write, 290–292
GPIO and, 294–295
bonescript module, 68
BoneScript Node.js library, 6, 67–69
   bonescript module, 68
Boost, 659–660
Boost.Python, 239–242
booting
   boot configuration files, 278–279
   bootloaders, 74–75
      /boot directory, 75
      boot sequence, 77
      building for boards, 77–78
      Das U-Boot, 75, 82–83
      device tree, 82
      DTB (device tree binary), 82
      dtc (device tree compiler), 82
      FAT partition, 81–82
      file deletion, 77
      first stage bootloader, 76
      getting started directory, 76
      kernel, 75
      kernel module, 84
      kernel space, 83–85
      memory mappings, 78–80
      MLO, 76
      primary program loader, 76
      second stage program loader, 76
      system and service manager, 85–90
      u-boot.img, 76
      user space, 83–85
breadboards
   circuits, implementation, 147–148
   digital multimeters, 149
   ICs, removing, 148
building boards, 5
bus communication, 342. *See also* I²C
      (Inter-Integrated Circuit); SPI (Serial
      Peripheral Interface)
   bidirectional transmission, 343
   capacitance effects, 344
   data transfer, 343
   logic-level translation, 396–398
   multi-master bus facilities, 343
buses, GPIO (general-purpose input/
      output), 248
BusyBox, 33
buttons, 166–168
   BeagleBone, 15
   PocketBeagle, 15

C
cabling
   Ethernet, 22
      crossover, 35
   HDMI, 22–23
   USB-to-serial UART TTL, 23–24
Cairo-Dock desktop, 134
cal Linux command, 51
CAN (Controller Area Network) Bus, 342,
      388–389
   Beagle boards, 389–390
   SocketCAN, 390–392
      Can-utils tools, 393–394
      C example, 394–396
   test circuit, 392–393
capacitance effects, 344
capacitors
   decoupling, 156–158
   smoothing, 156–158
capes, 26–27
cat Linux command, 117–118
C/C++, 187, 207–208. *See also* gcc
   advantages/disadvantages,
      209–210
   client/server, 545–548
   compiling, 211–213
      dynamic, 215
      static, 215
   constructors, 235
   cout, 226
   C-style strings, 221–222
   DC motors, 411–412
   destructors, 235
   directives, #include, 210
   functions
      arguments, 211
      callback functions, 295–296
      fopen( ), 224
      function pointers, 296
      main( ), 210–211
      output stream operator, 211
      parameters, 211
      passing values to, 226–227
      printf( ), 226
      writeLED( ), 224
   GPIO (general-purpose input/output)
      callback functions, 295–296
      Linux poll, 298–299
      POSIX threads (Pthreads),
         297–298

header files, 210, 236
    `iostream`, 210, 226
    `sstream`, 226
I²C (Inter-Integrated Circuit), 356–358
    classes, 358–360
implementation files, 236
keywords
    `typedef`, 218
    `virtual`, 236
LED flashing, 223–224, 227–228
`less helloworld.s`, 212
`less processed.cpp`, 212
libraries, 445–446
    CMake, 447–453
    makefiles, 446–447
linking, 211–213
methods
    `flash( )`, 235
    `outputState( )`, 235
    overriding, 232
    `powerOn( )`, 230
    `removeTrigger( )`, 235
    `turnOff( )`, 235
    `turnOn( )`, 235
    `writeLED( )`, 235
namespaces, 226
operators, 215–218
    `sizeof(c)`, 215–216
pointers, 219–221
PRU program, 686–688
shortest program, 213–214
SPI (Serial Peripheral Interface), 367–370
    bidirectional communication, 370–376
SPI devices, classes, 373–374
stepper motors, 415–417
string library, 225–226
variables, 215–218
    local variables, 215
cd Linux command, 50
CentOS, 32
CGI (Common Gateway Interface), 504
character LCD modules, 441–445
chown Linux command, 98
Chrome
    Secure Shell Extension, 46
    SSH client and, 45–46
CircuitCo, 6
circuits
    amps, 143
    breadboard implementation, 147–148

capacitors
    decoupling, 156–158
    smoothing, 156–158
current, 143
    division, 146–147
DC, interfacing to, 265–267
diodes, 151, 152–153
DMM (digital multimeter), 140–141
half-wave rectifier, 153
JK flip-flop circuit, 172
LEDs (light-emitting diodes), 153–156
ohms, 144
optocouplers/optoisolators, 164–165
oscilloscopes, 141–143
PTC (Positive Temperature Coefficient),
    151
resistance, 144
switches, 151
voltage, 143
    division, 145–146
    regulation, 150–151
volts, 143
classes
    C, I²C (Inter-Integrated Circuit), 358–360
    `fstream`, 227–228
    OOP
        behavior, 229
        data, 229
        methods, 229
        states, 229
    `QObject`, 617
client-server model, 513
clock phase, 362
clock polarity, 362
clock stretching, 345
Cloud9 IDE, 6, 64, 66–67
    `bash` terminal window, 67
    PocketBeagle, 68
CMake, 447–448
    .a library, 452–453
    C/C++ library, 449–452
    Hello World, 448–449
    .so library, 452–453
Coley, Gerald, 6
combinational logic, 169, 170
command-line debugging, 323–324
    remote, 324–325
commands
    data values, 442–443
    filter commands, 115–117

Git, 133
git add, 128–129, 133
git branch, 130–132
git branch -d, 132–133
git clone, 133
git commit, 129, 133
git diff, 133
git fetch, 133
git init, 133
git merge, 132
git pull, 133
git push, 129–130, 133
git status, 128, 133
Linux, 48
   Beagle-specific commands, 58–60
   cal, 51
   cat, 117–118
   cd, 50
   chown, 98
   cp, 50
   date, 54
   diff, 118–119
   echo, 117–118
   environment variables, 52–53
   extundelete, 52
   file system, 50–51
   filter commands, 115–117
   find, 109–110
   i2cdetect, 348–349
   i2cdump, 349–353
   i2cset, 354–355
   kill, 123
   ls, 50
   md5sum, 120–121
   mkdir, 50
   more, 49, 51, 110–111
   mv, 51
   output, 113–114
   package management, 56–58
   passwd, 49
   pipes (|), 113–114
   ps, 49
   pwd, 50
   redirection, 113–114
   rm, 50
   sudo shutdown, 63
   tar, 119–120
   top, 49
   touch, 51
   uptime, 49

   whereis, 109–110
   whoami, 49
man, 94
sudo apt install sshd, 7
sudo passwd root, 91
sudo visudo, 91
systemctl, 86–87
systemd, 87–88
common anode display, 366
common cathode display, 366
compiled languages, 204
   compilers, 204
compiling, C/C++, 211–213
   dynamic, 215
   static, 215
COM port number, serial connections, 42
computer-mode emulation, 312–313
config-pin tool, 252
connections
   serial
      over USB, 42–43
      speed, 42
      USB-to-TTL 3.3V cable, 43–44
   speed, serial connections, 42
   SSH (Secure Shell), 44
      PuTTY and, 45
   START.htm guide, 35
   wired, 35–36
      Ethernet
         crossover cable, 35, 40–41
         regular, 35, 39–40
      Internet-over-USB, 35, 36–39
connectors
   Beaglebone, 15
   PocketBeagle, 15
connect( ) system call, 514
console.log( ) method, 65
cout, 226
cp Linux command, 50
CPS (cyber-physical systems), 498–499
CPU, frequency, setting, 190–191
cron scheduler, crontab, 521–522
   system, 521–522
   user, 523–524
cross building, Linux, 330–331
   kernel, 331–335
   Poky, 335–340
cross compiling, 308–309
   ABI (application binary interface), 310
   EABI (embedded ABI), 310

Eclipse
    configuring, 316–318
    debugging, remote, 322–328
    desktop Linux installation, 315–316
    Doxygen, 328–330
    GitHub and, 322
    RSE (Remote System Explorer),
        318–322
third-party libraries, 314–315
toolchain
    armhf architecture emulation,
        312–313
    Debian, 309–311
    multiarch, 314–315
    testing, 311–312
    third-party libraries, 314–315
current
    circuits, 143
    DCA (DC current), 149
    division, 146–147
current-limiting resistors, 154
CVCS (centralized VCS), 125
Cython, 189, 239–242

D
DAC (digital-to-analog conversion), 285
Darlington pair arrangement, 266
Das U-Boot, 272
data transfer
    bidirectional, 343
    synchronous, 343
data values, commands, 442–443
date Linux command, 54
DCA (DC current), 149
DC circuits, powered, interfacing to,
        265–267
DC motors, 402–403, 403–406
    C++ and, 411–412
    large, driving, 409–410
    small, driving, 406–407
    sysfs, 407–409
DC power
    BeagleBone, 15
    PocketBeagle, 15
DCV (DC voltage), 149
Debian, 32
    cross compiling, 308–309
    debootstrap, 310
Debian Cross-Toolchains, 32
Debian Stretch IoT, 33

Debian Stretch LXQt, 32
debootstrap, 310–311
debugging
    BeagleBone, 15
    command line, 323–324
        remote, 324–325
    PocketBeagle, 15
    remote, Eclipse, 322–328
decoupling capacitors, 156–158
dereferencing, pointers, 219–220
desktop Linux, network sharing settings,
        38–39
desktop virtualization, 134–135
device drivers, 7
device tree
    boot configuration files, 278–279
    FDT (flattened device tree), 271, 272–276
        DTS (device tree source), 272
    IEEE Standard for Boot (Initialization
        Configuration) Firmware, 271–272
    modifying, 276–277
DHCP (Dynamic Host Configuration
    Protocol), 39, 551
    IP addresses, 40
    lease time, 40
diff Linux command, 118–119
Digilent Analog Discovery 2 with
    Waveforms oscilloscope, 141–143
DigiMesh protocol, 579–580
digital read/write in BoneScript, 290–292
digital sensors, analog comparison, 420
diode clamping, 421–422
diodes, 151
    forward biased, 152
    half-wave rectifier, 153
    reverse biased, 152
    Zener, 152
directories
    listings, 93
    root, 102–103
DMM (digital multimeter), 140–141
    breadboards, 149
documentation
    BeagleBoard Black System Reference
        Manual (SRM), 9
    BeagleBoard.org, 8–9
    for book, 135–136
    Doxygen, 328–330
    PocketBeagle System Reference Manual
        (SRM), 9

Sitara AM335x ARM Cortex-A8
Technical Reference Manual
(TRM), 9
websites, 9
Doxygen, 328–330
drivers, 4
installation, 34–35
Drivers folder, 34–35
Dropbear, 44
dtb-rebuilder script, 276
DTS (device tree source), 272
DVCS (distributed VCS), 125
dynamically compiled languages
functions
calling asynchronously, 202
instruction pointer, 202
program counter, 202
JavaScript, 201–203
Node.js, 201–203
dynamic compiling, C/C++, 215
dynamic translation, 201
dynamic types, OOP, 232
dynamic web content, 504

E
EABI (embedded ABI), 310
EasyDriver stepper motor driver, 413–414
driver circuit, 414
echo Linux command, 117–118
Eclipse
cross compilation and
configuring, 316–318
debugging, remote, 322–328
desktop Linux installation, 315–316
Doxygen, 328–330
GitHub and, 322
RSE (Remote System Explorer),
318–322
Oxygen, 317–318
electronic circuits. *See* circuits
Element14, 6
eLinux.org Wiki, 9
email, 524–526
embedded Linux, 72
advantages, 73
characteristics, 72
disadvantages, 73
examples, 72
Embedded Product design, 6
Embest, 6

emulation, armhf architecture, 312–313
encapsulation (OOP), 230–231
environment variables, Linux commands,
52–53
Ethernet
BeagleBone Black (BBB), 11
cable, 22
crossover cable, 35, 40–41
GPIO (general-purpose input/output)
and, 248
regular, 35, 39–40
Ethernet processor
BeagleBone, 15
PocketBeagle, 15
expansion headers
BeagleBone, 15
functionality available, 17–19
GPIO (general-purpose input/output),
248
interfacing to, 250
PocketBeagle, 15
extundelete Linux command, 52

F
fat-client applications, 608
Qt GUI, 626–629
fat-client as a server, 635–641
FDT (flattened device tree), 272–276
DTS (device tree source), 272
Fedora, 32
FETs (field effect transistors), 162–163
file editing, Linux, GNU nano editor,
53–54
file permissions, 93
files
hard links, 94–95
service files, 86
soft links, 94–95
file system, Linux
change ownership, 98
commands, 103–109
find, 109–110
more, 110–111
whereis, 109–110
directories, 93
groups, 95–98
hard links, 94–95
inodes, 92
inode tables, 92
man pages, 94

permissions, 93, 98–101
root directory, 102–103
SD card/eMMC, 111–113
soft links, 94–95
users, 95–98
file transfer
    psftp (PuTTY secure file transfer
        protocol), 46–48
    PuTTY, 46–48
filter commands, 115–117
find Linux command, 109–110
firewalls, Linux kernel, 39
flasher images, 60
flashing LED
    C/C++, 223–224, 227–228
    OOP and, 233–236
flash( ) method, 235
floating inputs, logic gates, 173
folders, Drivers, 34–35
fopen( ) function, 224
foreground processes, 122–124
forward-biased diodes, 152
FPGAs (field-programmable gate arrays),
    458
FPUs (floating-point units), 310
fstream file stream class, 227–228
function( ) method, 65
functions
    calling
        asynchronously, 202
        instruction pointer, 202
        program counter, 202
    C/C++
        arguments, 211
        fopen( ), 224
        main( ), 210–211
        output stream operator, 211
        parameters, 211
        passing values to, 226–227
        printf( ), 226
        writeLED( ), 224
    gethostbyname( ), 514

G
Gadget Serial device, 42
Gadget Serial driver COM port, 35
gcc, 208
gcc/g++ compilers, 215
gdb, 323–324
gdbserver, 324

gethostbyname( ) function, 514
Git, 124–126
    commands
        git add, 128–129, 133
        git branch, 130–132
        git branch -d, 132–133
        git clone, 133
        git commit, 129, 133
        git diff, 133
        git fetch, 133
        git init, 133
        git merge, 132
        git pull, 133
        git push, 129–130, 133
        git status, 128, 133
git add command, 128–129, 133
git branch command, 130–132
git branch -d command, 132–133
git clone command, 133
git commit command, 129, 133
git diff command, 133
git fetch command, 133
GitHub, 125
    Eclipse and, 322
    repositories, cloning, 126–127
git init command, 133
git merge command, 132
git pull command, 133
git push command, 129–130, 133
git status command, 128, 133
glibc (GNU C Library), 84
global memory, PRU-ICSS, 692–696
GNU debugger, 323–324
gnueabihf, 215
GNU GPL (General Public License),
    74
GNU nano editor, shortcut keys, 54
gnuplot, 434–435
GPIO (general-purpose input/output), 139,
    247, 456, 717
    Bluetooth and, 248
    BoneScript and, 294–295
    buses, 248
    C/C++
        callback functions, 295–296
        control, 267–271
        Linux poll, 298–299
        POSIX threads (Pthreads), 297–298
    configuration, 257
        internal pull-down resistors, 258

internal pull-up resistors, 258
pin configuration settings, 258–265
enhanced class, 299–302
Ethernet and, 248
expansion headers, 248
analog input, 250
analog output, 250
digital input, 250, 255–257
digital output, 250–255
extended availability, 458–468
MCP23S17, 464–465
MCP23x17 devices, C++ class, 465–468
MCP23017, 460–461
GPIO button state, 462
interrupt configuration, 463–464
LED circuit control, 461–462
mmode (multiplexer mode), 258–259
PRU-ICSS, 702–704
root permission, 304–305
sudo and, 302–304
switching, memory-based, 270
USB modules, 248
Wi-Fi and, 248
ZigBee and, 248
GPL (General Public License), 74
GPS application, UART, 386–388
graphics
BeagleBone, 15
PocketBeagle, 15
GTK+
event-driven programming model, 610–611
Hello World app, 609–610
temperature application, 611–612
GUI (graphical user interface), 608
fat-client application, 626–629

H

half-wave rectifier, 153
hard links, 94–95
hard real-time systems, 456
hardware
Altoids tins, 11
BeagleBoard, 10
BeagleBoard X15, 10
BeagleBoard xM, 10
BeagleBone, 10
BeagleBone Black, 10
BeagleBone Black (BBB), 16
BeagleBone Black Wireless, 10

BeagleBone Blue Wireless, 10
BeagleBone Enhanced, 10
BeagleBone Green, 10
JTAG connector, 12
open-hardware system, 5
PocketBeagle, 10
real-time, 458
Sitara AM335x Cortex A8 ARM, 12
SPI (Serial Peripheral Interface), 361–363
UI (user interface) architecture
comparisons, 601
general-purpose computing, 600, 601–604
LCD touchscreen display, 600, 604–605
remote fat-client applications, 600, 608
VNC (virtual network computing), 600, 605–608
HDLs (hardware description languages), 458
HDMI
audio, 660
audio playback devices, 661–664
cable, 22–23
header files
C/C++
iostream, 210, 226
sstream, 226
headers, PocketBeagle, 20
high-definition video, 8
hosted hypervisors, 135
HTTP (Hypertext Transfer Protocol), 498
HTTPS (secure HTTP), 498
hypervisors, 134
hosted hypervisors, 135
hysteresis, 168

I

I²C (Inter-Integrated Circuit), 342
ADXL345 accelerometer, 347–348
Beagle boards and, 344–346
bidirectional transmission, 343
C and, 356–358
classes, 358–360
capacitance effects, 344
clock stretching, 345
Debian Linux Image, 345
Fast-mode Plus devices, 344–345
hardware, 343–344
master devices, 343

MCP23017 and, 460–464
multi-master bus facilities, 343
NTP (Network Time Protocol), 346
SCL (Serial Clock) line, 343
SDA (Serial Data) line, 343
serial resistors (R$_s$), 345
slave, Arduino microcontroller
    C/C++ slave communication, 488–490
    register echo example, 482–484
    temperature sensor example, 484–485
    temperature sensor with warning
      LED, 486–488
    test circuit, 481–482
    ultrasonic sensor, 490–493
slave devices, 343
SPI comparison, 362
synchronous transfer, 343
termination resistors, 345
test circuit
    RTC (real-time clock), 346–347,
      350–353
    wiring, 348
i2cdetect Linux command, 348–349
i2cdump Linux command, 349–353
i2cset Linux command, 354–355
i2c-tools, 348
    i2cdetect, 348–349
    i2cdump, 349–353
    i2cget, 353–354
ICs
    numbers, 170
    open-collector outputs, 175
    package types, 171
    PMIC (Power Management IC), 150
    power, 147
    power supply line load, 158
    removing from breadboard, 148
    TTL (transistor-transistor logic), 171, 173
IEEE Standard for Boot (Initialization
    Configuration) Firmware, 271–272
ifconfig, 40
IFTTT (If This Then That), 526–528
image capture
    USB webcams, 644–645
    V4L2 (Video4Linux2), 646
      image capture utility, 647–648
      utilities, 648–650
      writing programs, 650–652
image processing
    Boost, 659–660

OpenCV and, 654–656
    computer vision and, 656–659
images
    flasher images, 60
    OpenCV (Open Source Computer
      Vision), 643
implementation files, C/C++, 236
#include directive, 210
inheritance, OOP, 231–233
inodes, 92
inode tables, 92
inputs/outputs. *See also* interface
    analog
      enabling, 280–282
      light meter application, 282–285
      PWM (pulse-width modulation),
        285–290
      SAR (successive approximation
        register), 280
      servo motor application, 289–290
      virtual cape, 280
    GPIO (general-purpose input/output),
      247
      Bluetooth and, 248
      buses, 248
      configuration, 257–265
      digital input, 255–257
      digital output, 250–255
      Ethernet and, 248
      expansion headers, 248, 250–255
      USB modules, 248
      Wi-Fi and, 248
      ZigBee and, 248
    PWM (pulse-width modulated) output,
      247
installation, drivers, 34–35
interface. *See also* inputs/outputs; rich UIs
    (user interfaces)
    expansion headers, 250
    Linux OS
      glibc, 238
      syscall( ), 238
    powered DC circuits, 265–267
Internet-over-USB connections, 35, 36–39
    time and, 55–56
Internet radio playback, 664
interpreted programming languages, 203
    advantages/disadvantages, 200
    bash, 192, 193–197
    Lua, 192

Perl, 192, 197–198
Python, 192, 198–200
`int` type, 217
`iostream` header, 210
IoT (Internet of Things), 497, 498–499, 528–529
  Adafruit IO, 539–540
    account configuration, 540–541
    connection, MQTT and, 542–543
    Node.js publish, 543–544
  devices
    PoE (Power over Ethernet), 551–554
    remote monitoring, 548–549
    static IP addresses, 551
    watchdog timers, 549–551
  MQTT (Message Queuing Telemetry Transport)
    brokers, 529
    code, writing, 535–539
    delta messaging, 530–531
    last will messaging, 531
    mqtt-spy debug tool, 534
    publisher clients, 529
    publisher/subscriber, 533–534
    retain messaging, 530
    server/broker, 531–533
    subscriber clients, 529
    topics, 529
  sensor, 499–501
IP addresses
  DHCP, 40
  finding, 40
  static, 40
`iptables`, Linux kernel firewalls, 39
IR (infrared) distance sensing, 431–436
ISRs (interrupt service routines), 717

J
Java, 187
  Beagle and, advantages/disadvantages, 206–207
  byte codes, 205
  installation, 204
  javac (Java compiler), 205
  JRE (Java Runtime Environment), 205
  Oracle Java SE, 207
  VM (virtual machine), 205
JavaScript, 201–203
JDK (Java Development Kit), 204
JIT (just-in-time) compiled languages, 189, 201

jitter, 456
JK flip-flop circuit, 172
JSP (Java Server Pages), 197
JTAG connector, 12

K
kernel
  LKM (loadable kernel module), 84
  real-time kernels, 456–457
    jitter, 456
  updating, 60
kernel modules, 84
  loadable
    clean up, 719
    execution, 719
    execution privilege level, 720
    floating-point support, 720
    interruptable, 720
    `printf( )`, 719
  writing, 718–719
kernel space, bootloaders, 83–85
keywords
  C/C++, `typedef`, 218
  OOP, access specifier, 231
  virtual, 236
`kill` command, 123
Kirchoff's voltage law, 145–147, 146–147
Kridner, Jason, 67
  BoneScript Node.js library, 6

L
languages. *See* programming language
latency, 457
layouts, 5
LCD capes, 26–27, 604–605
LCD modules, character LCD modules, 441–445
lease time, 40
LEDs (light-emitting diodes), 153
  BeagleBone, 15
  current-limiting resistors and, 154
  flashing
    C/C++, 227–228
    in C/C++, 223–224
    OOP and, 233–236
  on-board, interacting with, 61–63
  PocketBeagle, 15
Libav, audio and, 661
libraries
  .a, 452–453

C/C++
    CMake, 447–453
    makefiles, 446–447
    .so, 452–453
    string libraries in C/C++, 225–226
light meter application of analog input,
    282–284
linear actuators, 402
linking, C/C++, 211–213
Linux, 4. *See also* embedded Linux
    commands, 48
        <, 113–114
        >, 113–114
        >>, 113–114
        Beagle-specific, 58–60
        cal, 51
        cat, 117–118
        cd, 50
        chown, 98
        cp, 50
        date, 54
        diff, 118–119
        echo, 117–118
        environment variables, 52–53
        extundelete, 52
        filter commands, 115–117
        find, 109–110
        i2cdetect, 348–349
        i2cdump, 349–353
        i2cset, 354–355
        kill, 123
        ls, 50
        md5sum, 120–121
        mkdir, 50
        more, 49, 51, 110–111
        mv, 51
        output, 113–114
        package management, 56–58
        passwd, 49
        pipes (|), 114–115
        ps, 49
        pwd, 50
        redirection, 113–114
        rm, 50
        sudo shutdown, 63
        tar, 119–120
        top, 49
        touch, 51
        uptime, 49
        whereis, 109–110
        whoami, 49

cross-building, 330–331
    kernel source download, 331–332
    Poky, 335–340
desktop users, network sharing settings,
    38–39
device tree, 271–272
    boot configuration files, 278–279
    FDT (flattened device tree), 271,
        272–276
    IEEE Standard for Boot (Initialization
        Configuration) Firmware, 271–272
    modifying, 276–277
distributions, 32
    Ångström, 33
    Arch Linux, 33
    BusyBox, 33
    Debian Cross-Toolchains, 32
    Debian Stretch IoT, 33
    Debian Stretch LXQt, 32
    Ubuntu, 33
file editing, GNU nano editor, 53–54
file permissions, 93
i2c-tools, 348–349, 349–353, 353–354
images, flasher images, 60
kernel
    cross-building, 330–335
    firewalls, 39
    updating, 60
microcontrollers and, 7
micro-SD card images, 33–34
open source, 74
processes
    background, 122–124
    controlling, 121
    foreground, 122–124
shortcut keys, 51–52
udev rules, 303
< Linux command, 113–114
Linux Foundation, 9
Linux OS, interfacing to, 236–237
    glibc, 237–238
    syscall( ), 238
Linux systems
    root account, 90
    super user, 90
    system administration
        file system, 92–93
        file system commands, 103–111
        file system permissions, 98–101
        groups, 95–98
        hard links, 94–95

root directory, 102–103
SD card/eMMC file systems, 111–113
soft links, 94–95
users, 95–98
user privileges, 91
Linux USB Ethernet/RNDIS Gadget, 35
LKM (loadable kernel module), 84, 209, 717, 718
building on Beagle board, 723–724
enhanced GPIO driver, 733–734
kobject, 734–741
enhanced LED GPIO driver, 741
kernel threads, 742–743
example, 720–722
embedded example, 727–728
testing, 724–727
interrupt service, 729–733
Makefile, 722–723
performance, 733
local displays
character LCD modules, 441–445
MAX7219, 438–441
local memory, PRU-ICSS, 692–696
local variables
C/C++, 215
memory stack and, 215
logic gates, 169–173
binary numbers and, 169–170
combinational logic, 169, 170
inputs, floating, 173
interconnecting, 175–176
outputs
open-collector, 174–175
open-drain, 174–175
propagation delay and, 171
resistors, pull-up/pull-down, 173–174
sequential logic, 169
universal, 175
logic-level translation, 396–398
ls Linux command, 50
Lua, 192
LXQt (Lightweight Qt Desktop), 32, 90

M

main( ) function, 210–211
makefiles, 446–447
man command, 94
man pages, 94
McASP (multichannel audio serial port), audio, 660
MCP23S17, SPI bus, 464–465

MCP23017, I²C bus and, 460–464
md5sum Linux command, 120–121
memory, 216
BeagleBone, 15
PocketBeagle, 15
values, reading directly, 84–85
memory stack, local variables and, 215
methods
C/C++
flash( ), 235
outputState( ), 235
overriding, 232
powerOn( ), 230
removeTrigger( ), 235
turnOff( ), 235
turnOn( ), 235
writeLED( ), 235
console.log( ), 65
function( ), 65
OOP, 229
server.listen( ), 65
microcontrollers
Arduino, 7
AVR, 7
PIC, 7
PRUs (programmable real-time units), 7
real-time, 7–8
micro-HDMI to VGA adapters, 25
microprocessors, Sitara AM335x Cortex A8 ARM, 12
micro-SD cards, 20–21
file system expansion, 59
Linux distribution image, 33–34
Mint, 32
MISO (master in-slave out), 361
mkdir Linux command, 50
MMC (multimedia card), 111–113
Monkey, 501
more Linux command, 49, 51, 110–111
MOSI (master out-slave in), 361
motors
DC, 403–406
C++ and, 411–412
large, driving, 409–410
small, driving, 406–407
sysfs, 407–409
stepper motors, 412–413
C++ and, 415–417
EasyDriver, 413–414
pdriver circuit, 414
types, 402–403

Mozilla, 188
MPlayer, 661
multiarch, cross-compilation, 314–315
multicall binaries, 228–229
multiplexed pins, 248–249
mv Linux command, 51

N

namespaces, C/C++, 226
NAND-based flash memory, 111–113
n-body, 187
  numerical computation time, 188
Nelson, Robert C., 276
networks
  BeagleBone, 15
  connections, 514
  inter-process communication, 514
  IP addresses, 513
  OpenSSL, 516–517
  PocketBeagle, 15
  port numbers, 513
  sockets, 513
    datagram sockets, 513
    stream sockets, 513
    TCP, 513
    types, 513
  UDP (User Datagram Protocol), 514
  VNC (virtual network computing),
    599
  VoIP (voice over IP), 514
NFC (near field communication), 556,
  593–596
  RFID (radio frequency identification),
    593
Nginx, 501
nmap, 40
Node.js, 64, 67–69, 187, 201–203
  connections, web server, 65
  event-driven programming, 64
  http module, 65
  nonblocking I/O and, 64
NodeMCU slave processor, 568
  connecting, 570–571
  ESP32, 568–569
  firmware, 569
  JSON, 575–577
  MQTT and, 577–579
  programming, 571–573
  USB-to-UART conversion, 569
  web server interface, 574–575
NTP (Network Time Protocol), 346

O

Octavo Systems System-in-Package (SiP), 5
ohms, 144
OLED (organic LED), 441
on-board LEDs, 61
  flashing LEDs, 62
    timer, 62–63
  USR3 LED, 62
on-board storage
  BeagleBone, 15
  PocketBeagle, 15
OO (object-oriented) framework, 207
OOP (object-oriented programming), 185
  classes
    behavior, 229
    data, 229
    methods, 229
    states, 229
  encapsulated, 230–231
  inheritance, 231–233
  keywords, access specifier, 231
  LED flashing, 233–236
  Lua and, 192
  overloading, 232
  Perl and, 192
  polymorphism, 232
  Python and, 192
  types
    dynamic, 232
    static, 232
op-amp clamping, 422–426
OpenCV (Open Source Computer Vision),
  643
  computer vision, 656–659
  image processing, 654–656
open-hardware platform, 5
open-source software, drivers, 4
OpenSSL, 516–517
OpenSUSE, 32
operational amplifiers, ADC (analog-to-
  digital conversion)
  ideal, 178–181
  negative feedback, 181
  positive feedback, 181
operators, C/C++, 215–218
  sizeof(c), 215–216
optocouplers/optoisolators, 164–165
oscilloscopes, 141–143
  Digilent Analog Discovery 2 with
    Waveforms, 141–143
output commands, 113–114

outputState( ) method, 235
overriding methods, 232
Oxygen, 317–318

P

PaaS (Platform as a Service), 497
package management, commands, 56
parameters, functions, 211
passwd command, 49
PCB (printed circuit board), 4–5
performance tests, PRU-ICSS, 698–701
peripherals, support, 7
Perl, 187, 192, 197–198
permissions, root, setuid and, 304–305
PHP, 506–507
PIC microcontroller, 7
pinmux tool, 264
pins, multiplexed, 248–249
pipes (|), 113–114
platforms
    users, 6
    Xilinx Zynq platform, 8
PMIC (Power Management IC), 150
PocketBeagle, 10, 12
    accessories, headers, 20
    board, 5–6
    buttons, 15
    Cloud9 IDE, 68
    connectors, 15
    DC power, 15
    debug, 15
    Ethernet processor, 15
    expansion headers, 15
    graphics, 15
    LEDs, 15
    memory, 15
    network, 15
    on-board storage, 15
    power, 15
    power management, 15
    processor, 15
    SD card, 15
    serial debug, 15
        cabling and, 24
    subsystems, 15
    USB, 15
        ports, adding, 21
    USB On-the-Go (OTG), 12
    video out, 15
PocketBeagle System Reference Manual
    (SRM), 9

PoE (Power of Ethernet), 497
pointers
    C/C++, 219–221
    passing values to functions, 226–227
polymorphism, OOP, 232
    overloading, 232
port forwarding, 551
port mapping, 551
port-scanning, nmap, 40
POSIX threads (Pthreads), GPIO and,
    297–298
power
    BeagleBone, 15
    PocketBeagle, 15
powered DC circuits, interfacing to,
    265–267
power management
    BeagleBone, 15
    PocketBeagle, 15
powerOn( ) method, 230
power supply, external, 5V, 22
precision actuators, 402
preemption period, 457
preemptive scheduling, 457
printf( ) function, 226
processes
    background, 122–124
    controlling, 121
    foreground, 122–124
processor
    BeagleBone, 15
    PocketBeagle, 15
programming
    CPU frequency, 190–191
    overview, 186
programming languages, 186–190
    C, 207–208
    C++, 207–208
    compiled languages, compilers, 204
    Cython, 189
    dynamically compiled
        JavaScript, 201–203
        Node.js, 201–203
    functions
        calling asynchronously, 202
        instruction pointer, 202
        program counter, 202
    interpreted, 189
    interpreted languages
        advantages/disadvantages, 200
        bash, 192, 193–197

Lua, 192
Perl, 192, 197–198
Python, 192, 198–200
JIT (just-in-time), 189
OO (object-oriented) framework, 207
scripting languages
advantages/disadvantages, 200
bash, 192, 193–197
Lua, 192
Perl, 192, 197–198
Python, 192, 198–200
propagation delay, logic gates and, 171
PRU Debugger User Guide, 676
PRU-ICSS (Programmable Real-Time Unit
and Industrial Communication
Subsystem), 674
AM335x
remoteproc setup, 679–680
remoteproc testing, 680–682
applications
GPIOs, 702–704
performance tests, 698–701
PWM generator, 704–707
sine wave generator, 708–709
ultrasonic sensor, 709–714
architecture, 674–675
Enhanced GPIO, 675
INTC (interrupt controller), 675
Interface/OCP slave port, 675
MAC (multiplier w/ optional
accumulation), 675
OCP master port, 675
SCR (Switched Central Resource), 675
SPAD (scratch pad), 675
UART0, 675
assembly instruction set, 696–697
development tools, 676
CGT (Code Generation Tools), 677
PRU Debugger, 677–679
documentation, 676
enhanced GPIOs, 683–685
immediate value, 696
ISA (instruction set architecture), 696
memory
global, 692–696
local, 692–696
opcode (operation code), 696
PRU-ICSS Reference Guide, 696
PRU program
assembly language, 688–690
C, 686–688

registers, 691–692
remoteproc framework, 675–676
rpmsg (remote processor messaging
framework), 676
PRU-ICSS Getting Started Guide on
Linux, 676
PRU-ICSS Reference Guide, 676
PRUs (programmable real-time units), 7,
673
constants table, 695–696
psftp (PuTTY secure file transfer
protocol), file transfer, 46–48
ps Linux command, 49
PuTTY, 42, 606–607
secure shell connections, 45
Windows Device Manager, 42
pwd Linux command, 50
PWM generator, PRU-ICSS, 704–707
PWM (pulse-width modulated) output,
247
analog writes, 293–294
Python, 187, 192, 198–200
Boost.Python, 242–243
Cython, 239–242
dynamic typing, 198
statically typed, 198
strongly typed, 198

Q
QMetaObject object, 617
QNX Neutrino RTOS on OMAP and
Sitara, 457
QObject class, 617
Qt, 612–613
development tools, 618–619
development tools installation, 613
fat-client GUI application, 626–629
Hellow World application, 613–615
Meta-Object System, 617
modules
QtCore, 615
QtGui, 615
QtMultimedia, 615
QtNetwork, 616
QtOpenGL, 616
QtScript, 616
QtSql, 616
QtSvg, 616
QtTest, 616
QtWebKit, 616
QtXml, 616

QObject class, 617
Qt Creator, 618
  application example, 620–621
  forms, 619
  GUI temperature sensor, 621–625
  visual design editor, 619
Qt Designer, 618
signals and slots, 617–618
quantization, ADC (analog-to-digital
  conversion), 178

R
Raspberry Pi board, 8
read( ) system call, 514
read/write
  analog read, BoneScript and, 292–293
  analog write, PWM (pulse-width
    modulation), 293–294
  digital in BoneScript, 290–292
RealTerm, 42
real-time
  control tasks, 8
  hard real-time systems, 456
  hardware solutions, 458
  interfacing applications, 7
  kernels, 456–457
    jitter, 456
  latency, 457
  microcontrollers, 7–8
  preemption period, 457
  preemptive scheduling, 457
  sampling, 8
  soft real-time systems, 456
recording audio, 664–665
  WAV files, 665
Red Hat Enterprise, 32
redirect commands, 113–114
references, passing values to functions,
  226–227
regular Ethernet, 35, 39–40
relays
  EMRs (electromechanical relays),
    417–418
  SSRs (solid-state rays), 417–418
remote debugging
  command-line, 324–325
  Eclipse, 322–328
Remote Processor Framework, 676
remoteproc framework, 675–676
  rpmsg (remote processor messaging
    framework), 676

channels, 676
  destination rpmsg address, 676
  rpmsg core, 676
remote UI applications
  fat-client applications, 626–629
  multithreaded server applications,
    629–632
  multithreaded temperature service,
    632–635
removeTrigger( ) method, 235
Replicape, 27
repositories
  git add command, 128–129
  git commit command, 129
  git push command, 129–130
  git status command, 128
  version control, 125
resistance, 149
  circuits, 144
resistors, pull-up/pull-down, 173–174
reverse- biased diodes, 152
RFID (radio frequency identification), 557
rich UIs (user interfaces), 599
  application development, 608–609
    GTK+ and, 609–612
    Qt, 612–615
  board architecture, 600–608
Ritchie, Dennis, 207
rm Linux command, 50
RNDIS (Remote Network Driver Interface
  Specification), 35
root directory, 102–103
root permissions, setuid and, 304–305
RSE (Remote System Explorer), 318–322
rsync, 321
RTC (real-time clock), 350–353
  clock phase, 362
  clock polarity, 362
  I²C (Inter-Integrated Circuit), 346–347
RTOS (real-time operating systems), 73
Rust, 187, 188

S
sampling rate, ADC (analog-to-digital
  conversion), 177–178
sampling resolution, ADC (analog-to-
  digital conversion), 177
SBC (single-board computing) boards, 4
scheduling, preemptive scheduling, 457
schematics, 5
SCL (Serial Clock Line), 343

scp, 320–321
SCR (Switched Central Resource), 675
scripting languages
  advantages/disadvantages, 200
  bash, 192, 193–197
  Lua, 192
  Perl, 192, 197–198
  Python, 192, 198–200
scripts for book, 135–136
SDA (Serial Data) line, 343
SD card
  BeagleBone, 15
  file systems, reliability, 111–113
  micro, 20–21
  PocketBeagle, 15
SD card/eMMC file systems, 111–113
secure copy, 320–321
Secure Shell Extension (Chrome), 46
semiconductors, diodes, 151
sensor fusion, 347
sequential logic, 169
  JK flip-flop circuit, 172
serial connections
  over USB, 42–43
  USB-to-TTL 3.3V cable, 43–44
serial debug
  BeagleBone, 15
  PocketBeagle, 15
serial resistors (R_s), 345
server.listen( ) method, 65
service files, 86
servo motors, 402–403
setuid, root permissions and, 304–305
SFTP (SSH File Transfer Protocol), 44
shortcut keys
  GNU nano editor, 54
  Linux, 51–52
shutdown, 63
SimpleWebServer.js, 67
sine wave generator, PRU-ICSS, 708–709
SiP (System-in-Package), 5
Sitara AM335x ARM Cortex-A8 Technical
    Reference Manual (TRM), 9
Sitara AM335x Cortex A8 ARM, 12
Sitara AM335x System on Chip (SOC), 5
sizeof(c) operator, 215–216
slave devices, real-time kernels, 456–457
smoothing capacitors, 156–158
snapshots, 135
SOC (System on Chip), 5
SocketCAN, 390–392

Can-utils tools, 393–394
  C example, 394–396
SocketClient class, 545–546
SocketServer class, 546–547
socket( ) system call, 514
soft links, 94–95
soft real-time systems, 456
software, audio
  ASLA utilities, 661
  Libav, 661
  MPlayer, 661
.so library, 452–453
source code for book, 135–136
SPI (Serial Peripheral Interface), 342,
    360–361
  74HC5956, 365–366
    circuit wiring, 366–367
  application, 365–370
  bus testing, 363–365
  C and, 367–370
    bidirectional communication, 370–376
  C/C++ classes, 373–374
  communication modes, 362
  four-wire communications, 363
  full duplex, 361
  hardware, 361–363
  I²C comparison, 362
  master devices, 361–363
  slave devices, 361–363
    multiple, 376–377
  three-wire communications, 363, 375–376
SPP (Serial Port Profile), 561
SSH (secure shell) server, 7, 44
  Chrome apps, 45–46
  PuTTY and, 45
StarterWare for ARM-based TI Sitara
    processors, 457
START.htm guide, 35
states, OOP, 229
static compiling, C/C++, 215
static types, OOP, 232
stepper motors, 402–403, 412–413
  C++ and, 415–417
  EasyDriver, 413–414
    driver circuit, 414
streaming audio, 666
streaming video, 652–654
strings
  C/C++, 225–226
  C-style strings, 221–222
Stroustrup, Bjarne, 207

subsystems
  BeagleBone, 15
  PocketBeagle, 15
sudo, GPIOs and, 302–304
sudo apt install sshd command, 7
sudo passwd root command, 91
sudo shutdown Linux command, 63
sudo visudo command, 91
support, website resources, 9
switches, 166–168
  hysteresis, 168
synchronous data transfer, 343
syscall( ) function, 238
sysfs, 61–63
systemctl command, 86–87
systemd
  commands, 87–88
  service files, 86
  target units, 89
System V (SysV) init, 85
Sziklai pair, 266

T
target units, systemd, 89
tar Linux command, 119–120
TCP (Transmission Control Protocol), 497
  client/server, 498
termination resistors, 345
testing, cross compiling, 310–311
Texas Instruments Sitara AM 335x System
  on Chip (SOC), 5
text-to-speech, 669–670
The Processor Messaging Framework, 676
ThingSpeak, 497, 518–520
TI PinMux Tool, 264–265
top Linux command, 49
Torvalds, Linus, 32
touch Linux command, 51
transducers, 418–419
transferring files
  psftp (PuTTY secure file transfer
    protocol), 46–48
  PuTTY, 46–48
transistors
  BJTs (bipolar junction transistors), 158
    NPN, 158
    PNP, 158
  FETs (field effect transistors), 158,
    162–163
transmission line capacitance, 344

turnOff( ) method, 235
turnOn( ) method, 235
typedef, 218

U
UART (Universal Asynchronous Receiver/
  Transmitter) devices, 342, 377–378
  boards, 378–380
  C and, 380–381
    LED serial server, 383–385
    serial client, 381–382
  external, 468–471
  GPS application, 386–388
Ubuntu, 32, 33
udev rules, 303
  USB devices, 470–471
UI (user interface). *See* rich UIs (user
  interfaces)
  hardware architecture
    comparisons, 601
    general-purpose computing, 600,
      601–604
    LCD touchscreen display, 600,
      604–605
    remote fat-client applications, 600, 608
    VNC (virtual network computing),
      600, 605–608
  remote applications, 625–626
    fat-client applications, 626–629
    multithreaded server applications,
      629–632
    multithreaded temperature service,
      632–635
ultrasonic sensor, PRU-ICSS, 709–714
unidirectional data buses, 396–397
universal logic gates, 175
uptime Linux command, 49
USB
  audio, 660
    ALSA utilities, 663–664
  audio playback devices, 661–664
  BeagleBone, 15
  hub, 25
  keyboard, 26
  modules, GPIO (general-purpose input/
    output), 248
  mouse, 26
  PocketBeagle, 15
  ports, adding to PocketBeagle, 21
  serial connections, 42–43

support, 7
udev rules, 470–471
Velleman USB hub, 661–662
webcams, 25–26
image capture, 644–645
USB On-the-Go (OTG), PocketBeagle, 12
USB-to-serial UART TTL cable, 23–24
USB-to-TTL 3.3V cable, serial connections,
43–44
users, privileges, 91
user space, bootloaders, 83–85

V
V4L2 (Video4Linux2), image capture, 646
image capture utility, 647–648
utilities, 648–650
writing programs, 650–652
Valent F(x) LOGi-Bone-2 FPGA
development board, 458
values
memory, reading directly, 84–85
passing to a function, 226–227
variables
C/C++
local, 215–218
pointers, 219–221
environment variables, Linux
commands, 52–53
VCS (version control system), 125
Velleman USB hub, 661–662
Verilog, 458
version control
Git, 124–126
repository, 125
video, high-definition, 8
video out
BeagleBone, 15
PocketBeagle, 15
video streaming, 652–654
VirtualBox, 134
virtual cape, 280
virtualization
desktop, 134–135
snapshots, 135
virtual keyword, 236
visudo, 91
VMs (virtual machines), 134
Java virtual machine, 205
VMware Player, 134
VNC (virtual network computing), 599

UI architecture
desktop Linux, 607–608
PuTTY, 606–607
VNC viewer, 605–606
Xming, 606–607
void pointers, 221
voltage
circuits, 143
DCV (DC voltage), 149
division, 145–146
regulation, 150–151
volts, 143
Vref, 283–285

W
WAV files, 665
web clients, 498
C/C++, 512–518
localhost, 516
loopback virtual network interface, 516
web sensors, PaaS (Platform as a Service),
498
web servers, 498
Bone101, 511–512
dynamic web content, 504
GNU Cgicc, 508–510
installation, 502–507
sensors, 501–512
websites, support, 9
whereis Linux command, 109–110
whoami Linux command, 49
widgets, 600
Wi-Fi, 555
adapters, 25
GPIO (general-purpose input/output)
and, 248
NodeMCU slave processor, 568
connecting, 570–571
ESP32, 568–569
firmware, 569
JSON, 575–577
MQTT and, 577–579
programming, 571–573
USB-to-UART conversion, 569
web server interface, 574–575
Windows Device Manager, PuTTY serial
connection, 42
wired connections, 35–36
Ethernet, 35, 39–40
Internet-over-USB, 35, 36–39

wireless communications
  Bluetooth, 556, 557–558
    adapter installation, 558–563
    Android app development,
      563–564
    LE (low energy), 556
  NFC (near field communication), 556,
    593–596
  PANs (personal area networks), 556
  RFID (radio frequency identification),
    557
  Wi-Fi, 556
    adapter installation, 564–567
    NodeMCU slave processor, 568–579
  ZigBee, 556, 557
writeLED( ), 224, 235
write( ) system call, 514

X-Z
XBee ZigBee devices, 555, 579–582
  configuration, 582–584
Xenomai, 457
Xilinx Zyng platform, 8
Xming, 606–607

Zener diode, 152
Zenmap, 40
ZigBee, 555, 557
  GPIO (general-purpose input/output)
    and, 248
  XBee
    API mode, 589–593
    configuration, XCTU, 582–584
    devices, 579–582
    AT mode, 584–588